ORLANDO

& Walt Disney World

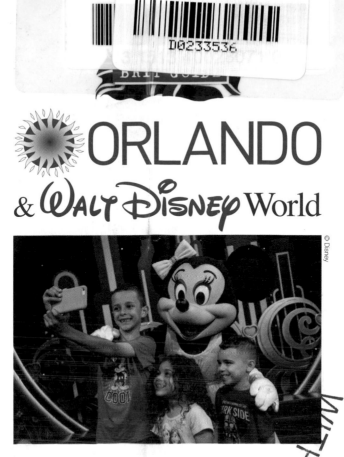

© Disney

2017

Simon & Susan Veness

foulsham

LONDON • NEW YORK • TORONTO • SYDNEY

W. Foulsham & Co. Ltd

for Foulsham Publishing Ltd
The Old Barrel Store, Drayman's Lane, Marlow, Bucks SL7 2FF

Foulsham books can be found in all good bookshops or direct
from www.foulsham.com

While every effort has been made to ensure the accuracy of all the information contained
within this book, neither the author nor the publisher can be liable for any errors. In
particular, since prices, times and any holiday or hotel details change on a regular basis, it is
vital that each individual checks relevant information for themselves.

ISBN: 978-0-572-04628-6

The moral rights

The Copyright A   iking of copies
of any copyright   aking of
copies by photoco   or copies must
therefore normal   o consult the
publisher if in an   taken.

Look out for the
Brit Guide to Las V
Brit Guide to Disne
Brit Guide to New !

Dedication: To o   ark – who help
make our work fun!

SPECIAL THANKS
Special thanks for this edition go to: Visit Orlando, Experience Kissimmee, Visit Florida, The
Walt Disney Company, Universal Orlando & SeaWorld Parks & Entertainment.

Our sincere thanks also go to Wendy Hobson, Jane Hotson and all the hard-working people at
Foulsham who help to bring our work to life every year.

Printed in Malta by Melita Press

CONTENTS

Foreword

Simon says… Welcome to the start of a wonderful holiday adventure. Orlando is, without doubt, an epic destination that just gets better every year, with an ever-increasing array of attractions. It has universal appeal and almost limitless potential, even given a month to try to 'do it all'. What you can't actually do is 'do it all', especially if you only have one or two weeks. That's where we come in. No-one knows this vast area of Central Florida as well as we do, and no other guidebook can steer you through the full range of fun and excitement as well as the *Brit Guide*. After more than 20 years and now being resident here, we have chapter and verse on all that's in store and, make no mistake, that's a lot to tackle! Even if you have been before, things change with dizzying regularity, hence you need a 'good companion' to help you hit the highs and avoid the lows (the latter of which lie in wait for the unprepared). You, of course, *will* be prepared because you have us at hand, ready to advise on the best preparation, the best rides, the best places to stay, eat and shop, and provide the very best overall experience you can possibly have. It's all waiting for you in the Sunshine State's theme park wonderland. Are you excited yet…?

Susan says… Orlando has a new watchword for 2017, and that watchword is 'thrills'! With the opening of SeaWorld's Mako hyper-coaster and Busch Gardens' spectacular Cobra's Curse coaster, plus Epcot's Frozen Ever After attraction in Norway, all-new night-time entertainment at Disney's Animal Kingdom, a galaxy of Star Wars fun at Hollywood Studios, and two new thrill rides and an entire themed water park coming to Universal Orlando, 2017 is truly a thrilling time to visit. Add new shopping and dining venues at Disney Springs' recently opened Town Center and there is a *lot* to look forward to in the Vacation Capital of the World.

And if you want to make sure you get the very best out of your holiday without wasting time or money, let us help with our unique Touring Plans (p39).

So if you're ready, let's get on with the planning…!

Simon and Susan Veness
(visit us at **www.venesstravelmedia.com**, or email **britsguide@yahoo.com**, and follow Veness Travel Media on Twitter and Facebook.

Introduction

Fun. Excitement. Thrills. Fantasy. Food (lots of food!). They are all waiting for you in this vast area of Central Florida we call Orlando. It is an amazing array of choice, temptation and all-out holiday appeal that has no equal anywhere else on earth. It is a fully-fledged assault on the senses and it draws families, couples and singles, young and old alike. It runs the gamut from astounding theme parks to world-class shopping, superb nature and fabulous nightlife.

Most of all, though, this is a BIG venture in every sense and it's vital you do some 'homework' first. Walt Disney World is the leading attraction and is the size of a small city, plus there is a strong supporting cast led by Universal Orlando and SeaWorld. There's something for all tastes and ages, but it exacts a high toll. You'll walk a lot, queue a lot and probably eat a lot. You WILL have a fabulous time, but you'll probably end up exhausted, too. But stick with us, and you'll have the best possible preparation for what's in store.

Eight theme parks

In simple terms, there are eight major theme parks, and several need two days to enjoy fully. Add a day at a water park, a trip to one of the wildlife or nature attractions and the lure of the Kennedy Space Center, and you already have two full weeks of pure adventure mania. Then mix in the night-time fun of Disney Springs, Universal's CityWalk and a host of dinner shows, plus superb shopping, and you start to understand the awesome scope of the place. Even with two weeks, something has to give – just make sure it isn't your patience, wallet – or sanity.

The key to all this is Planning. On pages 345–46 is a handy outline guide for a typical two-week stay. Be aware

Cinderella Castle

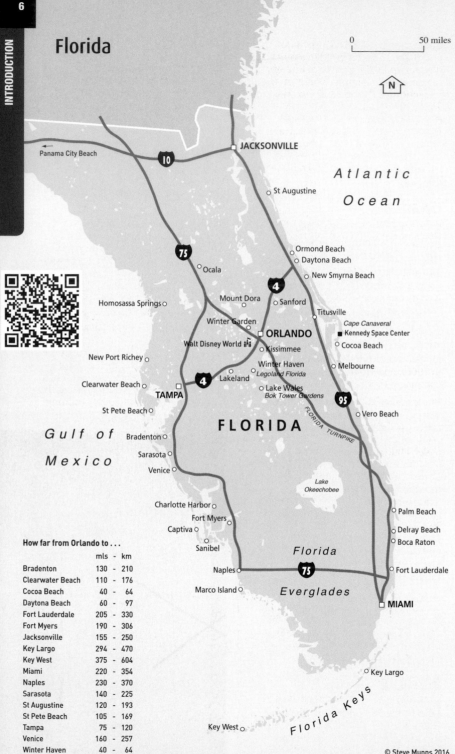

Florida

0   50 miles

N

Panama City Beach ←

JACKSONVILLE

Atlantic Ocean

St Augustine

10

75

Ormond Beach
Daytona Beach
New Smyrna Beach

Ocala

4

Mount Dora
Winter Garden
Sanford

Homosassa Springs

Titusville

ORLANDO
Cape Canaveral
■ Kennedy Space Center

Walt Disney World
Kissimmee
Cocoa Beach

New Port Richey

Winter Haven
Legoland Florida
Melbourne

4
Lakeland

Clearwater Beach

Lake Wales
Bok Tower Gardens

TAMPA

95

St Pete Beach

FLORIDA

FLORIDA TURNPIKE

Vero Beach

Gulf of
Bradenton

Sarasota

Mexico
Venice

Lake
Okeechobee

Charlotte Harbor
Fort Myers
Captiva

Palm Beach

Sanibel

Delray Beach
Boca Raton

Florida

Naples

Fort Lauderdale

Marco Island

Everglades

75

MIAMI

Key Largo

Florida Keys

Key West

© Steve Munns 2016

How far from Orlando to . . .

	mls	-	km
Bradenton	130	-	210
Clearwater Beach	110	-	176
Cocoa Beach	40	-	64
Daytona Beach	60	-	97
Fort Lauderdale	205	-	330
Fort Myers	190	-	306
Jacksonville	155	-	250
Key Largo	294	-	470
Key West	375	-	604
Miami	220	-	354
Naples	230	-	370
Sarasota	140	-	225
St Augustine	120	-	193
St Pete Beach	105	-	169
Tampa	75	-	120
Venice	160	-	257
Winter Haven	40	-	64

of the time demands of the parks and make sure you build in a quiet day or two by the pool or at one of the smaller attractions. Focus on the attractions that appeal to you most, try not to be too ambitious, and don't underestimate the vast scale involved – this is a huge area and it takes time even to get from park to park. But do stop to admire the imagination and detail of what's on offer as it is all world class.

Orlando

In tourist terms, 'Orlando' has grown to encompass much of Central Florida, an area almost twice the size of Yorkshire. Yes, that big. The city itself is north of the main tourist areas and many people won't even see it as they charge from park to park, which is a shame as it is a bright and happening place. When Walt Disney's dream of a vast resort opened in 1971 with the Magic Kingdom (sadly, he never saw it realised as he died in 1966), it led to a huge tourist expansion that continues to this day.

There are seven counties in Central Florida. **Orange County**, home to the city of Orlando, with Walt Disney World in the south-west corner, part of which is also in **Osceola County**, with Kissimmee its main town; **Seminole County**, home of Orlando Sanford International Airport, north-east of Orange; **Lake County** to the north-west, with Mount Dora its principal town; **Polk** to the south-west, home to many vacation villas and LEGOLAND Florida; and east to **Brevard** and **Volusia Counties,** home to the Kennedy Space Center and Daytona Beach.

Each year, some 60 million people holiday in Orlando, and the area boasts 116,000 hotel rooms, 26,000 vacation homes, more than 4,000 places to eat and 30 malls. Here's a taste of the main attractions.

Walt Disney World

This is where the magic really starts. This vast resort consists of four separate theme parks, 20 themed hotel resorts, a camping ground, two water parks, a sports complex, five golf courses, mini-golf and a huge shopping and entertainment district (Disney Springs). It covers 47ml^2/122km^2 and Alton Towers and Thorpe Park would comfortably fit into its car parks! At peak periods, it holds over 200,000 visitors. Disney does things with the most style and there are always new projects on the drawing board. It maintains a high level of customer service, where everyone who works for them is a Cast Member, not just staff, and they take that ethos to heart.

Magic Kingdom: The essential Disney, with the magic of its wonderful films, the adventures of the Wild West and Africa, the excitement of thrill rides like Space Mountain (an indoor roller-coaster), the eye-catching Fantasyland and splendid parades and fireworks.

Epcot: Disney's two-part park, with the technology-inspired Future World, plus a potted journey around the globe in World Showcase. More educational than adventurous, it has some memorable rides, including the superb Soarin', plus excellent dining.

Tree of Life at Animal Kingdom

Disney's Hollywood Studios:
Ride the movies in style, meet Star Wars™, the Muppets and Indiana Jones; visit the dreaded Tower of Terror; go inside films on The Great Movie Ride; and try the Toy Story Mania ride.

Disney's Animal Kingdom:
Realistic animal habitats, including a 100acre/40.5ha safari savannah, captivating shows and terrific rides, like the grand Expedition Everest. New 'land' Pandora: The World of Avatar is due to open in 2017.

Disney's Typhoon Lagoon Water Park: Splash down waterslides and learn to surf in the world's biggest man-made lagoon.

Disney's Blizzard Beach Water Park: The big brother of all the water parks, with a massive spread of rides in a 'snowy' environment.

Disney Springs: Almost a mile of themed restaurants, bars, shops, a cinema multiplex, bowling centre, House of Blues music venue and world-famous Cirque du Soleil®.

The world's most famous Mouse

Wedding Pavilion: A fairytale venue overlooking Seven Seas Lagoon for picture-perfect marriage ceremonies.

ESPN Wide World of Sports: A huge sporting venue to both play and watch top events.

The other parks
If you think Orlando is only about Disney, prepare to be amazed.

Universal Orlando: The other main resort has two theme parks, an entertainment district and five themed hotels. At Universal Studios you encounter The Simpsons, the Rip Ride Rockit roller-coaster, Woody Woodpecker's KidZone, TRANSFORMERS: The Ride – 3D and the Wizarding World of Harry Potter – Diagon Alley. Islands of Adventure (IoA) features another Wizarding World area, plus a superb blend of thrill rides, family attractions, shows, great design and high-tech features such as the Amazing Adventures of Spider-Man. The huge Volcano Bay water park is also due to open in 2017.

Wet 'n Wild: This long-standing attraction on International Drive closes at the end of 2016.

SeaWorld: THE place for creatures of the deep, with killer whales, dolphins and penguins, a refreshing atmosphere, the Blue Horizons and One Ocean shows, fabulous Antarctica attraction, thrill rides like Manta, Kraken and the new Mako, plus an area of rides and activities just for kids.

Discovery Cove: Its exclusive neighbour offers the chance to swim with dolphins, among other things.

Aquatica: A fab water park providing even more fun and animal encounters in a colourful South Seas setting.

BRITTIP
Be realistic about the tickets you need. You simply won't get full use out of, say, a 14-day Disney ticket and the Orlando FlexTicket Plus in a two-week holiday.

Busch Gardens: In nearby Tampa, SeaWorld's sister park offers creatures of the land, plus great rides and shows. Highlights are coasters Cheetah Hunt, SheiKra, Falcon's Fury drop-tower ride, the Edge of Africa 'safari' experience and ice-skating show Iceplorations and the new Cobra's Curse. A family treat and a must for coaster fans.

Other key attractions

These include: the dramatically upgraded **Kennedy Space Center**, with the new Heroes & Legends exhibit; the surprisingly fun and humorous **Gatorland**; **LEGOLAND Florida**, great for the 2–12 age group; **I-Drive 360**, featuring the 400ft/120m Orlando Eye; **Forever Florida**, a mix of local nature and high-energy zipline adventures; and **Boggy Creek Airboats** and **Wild Florida**, for a close-up with Kissimmee nature. Plus there is great mini-golf almost everywhere and other attractions along International Drive.

Disney tickets

This is where things get complicated and it's important to work out what tickets you need. Most people buy one of three multi-day passes specifically for the UK market that allow visits to more than one park a day. They are great value for a two or three-week visit and provide full flexibility. But they aren't cheap and, if you want only two or three of the Disney parks, you have to buy a Magic Your Way ticket in Orlando. Be aware you can't walk between the parks (they can be miles apart) and trying to do more than one a day is hard work, especially in summer.

◄█► BRITTIP

Buy your theme park tickets in advance, NOT at the park gates. You will save time AND money, as most outlets offer an advance purchase discount.

Disney's ticket system is called Magic Your Way and is horribly complicated (although there is a simplified choice for UK visitors; see below). Multi-day tickets offer savings against one-day tickets but unused days expire after 14 days of first use.

Magic Your Way: If you just turn up at the ticket booths (or buy in advance from a US broker), you must choose:

- The number of days you want (up to 10).

- If you want Park Hopping (the ability to move between parks on the same day) for $55–69/ticket.

- If you want the Water Park Fun & More Option (2–10 visits to the water parks and ESPN Wide World of Sports™) for $64/ticket. Disney also offers one free round at the nine-hole Oak Trail golf course (book in advance on 407 939 4653; club hire NOT included) and two free rounds of mini-golf.

- Or if you want both Park Hopping *and* Water Park Fun & More for $95/ticket.

Per-day ticket savings increase with the more days you buy: 1 day = $97–114 plus tax; 10 days = $400 plus tax, or $40/day. There is also seasonal pricing for one-day tickets, making it more expensive at peak periods.

UK tickets: In the UK, there are three tickets on offer: the 7, 14 and 21-day Ultimate Ticket (see chart p11), plus a new 2-day ticket with mini-golf

Other tickets

The choice is equally complicated for Universal Orlando, SeaWorld, Busch Gardens and Aquatica. Do check periodic special offers (see Orlando Ticket Deals, p10).

- **Orlando FlexTicket:** 14 days at Universal parks, SeaWorld and Aquatica. Add Busch Gardens with **FlexTicket Plus** (NB: not in 2017).

- **1, 2, 3 or 4-day Tickets:** For Universal alone, **one park per day** or **both parks each day**.

- **2 and 3-Park Bonus Ticket:** 14 days at Universal Studios and IoA or those two plus Volcano Bay (once open); buy in the UK.

- **1, 2, 3 or Unlimited Visits:** To SeaWorld, Busch Gardens and Aquatica (unlimited valid for 14 consecutive days and including free parking). **2** or **3-Park** Tickets for 14 days available in UK (with parking).

- **Discovery Cove:** A day ticket includes a 14-Day Pass for SeaWorld and Aquatica. The Ultimate Package adds Busch Gardens for 14 days for an extra $25 (plus free parking).
- **Party Pass:** For Universal's CityWalk ($11.99 plus tax) or a Party Pass with Movie ($15 plus tax) at the 20-screen cinema.
- **14-Day Combo Pass:** Offered by many UK brokers, for Disney & Universal, or various combinations of Disney, Universal, SeaWorld, LEGOLAND and the water parks, plus a Freedom Ticket, or similar, for all eight parks plus the water parks. This is NOT a single ticket but a bundle of two or three tickets.
- **Go Orlando Card:** Two, three or five days of visits within 14 days to 33 attractions and activities, including Kennedy Space Center, LEGOLAND Florida, Gatorland, WonderWorks, Fun Spot, airboat rides, mini-golf and more ($130–275 adults, $120–265 3–12s). There is also an **Explorer Pass** for three or five visits, and a **Build-Your-Own** choice which represents 20–55% savings and comes with a handy attractions guidebook. See **www.goorlandocard.com**.
- **Eat and Play Card:** A discount card for groups of up to four, valid for 90 days from first use. Save 10–20% off 50-plus restaurants, from McDonald's, Denny's, Pizza Hut and TGI Friday's to upmarket choices like Big Fin Seafood, Café Tu-Tu Tango and Bongos Cuban Café, all in the main tourist areas and including alcohol in some cases; 10–30% on attractions like golf, mini-golf, Gatorland, Ripley's Believe It Or Not and more; and 10–20% off in shops like Macy's and Reebok Outlet Stores, plus the Outta Control Magic Dinner Show and Golfsmith shops. It costs a bargain $25 and covers the entire bill for up to four people each time, so you can make significant savings. Available

from **www.eatandplaycard. com** (or call 001 613 680 7109) or select ticket brokers and tour operators.

With annual price hikes, try to buy your tickets as soon as you can, but be aware that some discounted tickets must be used for the first time in the year of purchase (e.g. 'first use by 31 Dec 2016'). Shop around, as many outlets have sales and special offers, but use a reputable agent and use your credit card for added security. The following companies all come well recommended.

Attraction Tickets Direct: Britain's top direct-sell Florida ticket broker, with a sharp bookings team, no credit card fees, free delivery in seven days and a promise to match any UK brochure price, plus a huge range of dinner shows, excursions, sports, theme park backstage tours and special offers, and a keen online Florida Forum and info centre to which we contribute (0800 188 4619, **www.attraction-tickets-direct.co.uk**).

FloridaTix: Independent ticket specialist featuring all the theme parks, plus the likes of Kennedy Space Center, Blue Man Group, dinner shows, many tours and excursions, no credit card fees and a £10 deposit ticket offer (0330 100 3130, **www.floridatix.co.uk**).

Ocean Florida: Independent Florida specialist also offers a well-priced ticket service, featuring all the theme parks, plus Kennedy Space Center and Miami Seaquarium (020 7939 7775, **www.ocean-florida.co.uk**).

Orlando Attractions: A UK-owned ticket service based in Orlando, it will post tickets to the UK and offers all the parks and the likes of airboat rides, fishing and other activities, plus some good combo tickets. Fully ABTA-bonded. Free shipping, price includes tax and no credit card fees (0800 294 9458, **www.orlandoattractions. com/tickets**).

Orlando Ticket Deals: A keenly priced and helpful broker that also issues real tickets (not vouchers), has a next-day delivery service and offers a significant Price Promise for all its attractions, including all the parks, dinner shows

Choosing a ticket

Ticket type	Park	Allowance
1-Day Ticket	Any Disney park, Universal Orlando parks, SeaWorld or Busch Gardens	Access to one park ONLY for one day; not available in advance
7, 14 and 21-Day Ultimate Ticket	All Disney parks	Unlimited access to all Disney attractions, including water parks, *ESPN Wide World of Sports™* and nine-hole Oak Trail golf course (clubs not included) for 14 days after first use; available only in advance in the UK
Disney Platinum Pass	*Magic Kingdom Park, Epcot, Disney's Hollywood Studios, Disney's Animal Kingdom;* plus discounts for shops, dining and tours	Unlimited admission and *free parking* for 365 days after purchase date. If ordered online, you get a voucher that must be activated at a park; the 365 days start on the first day you activate the pass. Now with free PhotoPass downloads.
Disney Platinum Plus Pass	All Disney parks; plus numerous discounts for shops, dining and tours	Unlimited admission and *free parking* for 365 days after purchase date; plus discounts on sports and recreation, and free PhotoPass downloads.
2, 3 or 4-Day 1 Park Ticket	Universal Studios, Islands of Adventure	Access to one of the Universal parks each day for 2–4 days, plus CityWalk; valid for 14 days
2, 3 or 4-Day 2-Park Ticket	Universal Studios, Islands of Adventure	Access to both Universal parks each day for 2–4 days, plus CityWalk; valid for 14 days
2-Park Bonus Ticket	Universal Studios, Islands of Adventure and CityWalk	14 consecutive days' access to both Universal parks, plus CityWalk clubs; sold in UK only
3-Park Explorer Ticket	Universal Studios, Islands of Adventure, Volcano Bay and CityWalk (from Jun 2017)	14 consecutive days' access to all three parks, plus CityWalk clubs; sold in UK only
Orlando FlexTicket	Universal Studios, Islands of Adventure, SeaWorld, Wet 'n Wild/Volcano Bay, Aquatica	Access to all five parks, with multiple parks on same day, for 14 days from first use, plus CityWalk clubs. NB: This ticket is unlikely to be on sale for 2017.
Orlando FlexTicket Plus	All the above, plus Busch Gardens	Access to all six parks, with multiple parks on same day, for 14 days from first use, plus CityWalk clubs
2-Park Ticket	SeaWorld and Busch Gardens	14 consecutive days' access to both parks
2-Park Ticket	SeaWorld and Aquatica	14 consecutive days' access to both parks
3-Park Ticket	SeaWorld, Busch Gardens and Aquatica	14 consecutive days' access to all three parks (all 3 available in UK only)

and many excursions (0800 188 4631, **www.orlando-ticket-deals.co.uk**).

There are others, including the main tour operators (p20), while you can also visit the Official Visitor Center on International Drive (**www.visitorlando.com**), but beware offers for 'free' tickets as these are purely timeshare lures. And NEVER buy resale tickets from a booth in Orlando – they are often unusable. Stick with the main brokers, who offer good products, service and local knowledge. And don't forget to plan with our sample Busy Day Guide (p346). You'll be exhausted if you try to do all the parks in one go!

BRITTIP

For all your theme park tickets, be sure to check out *Brit Guide* partner Orlando Ticket Deals first, as it features an exclusive money-saving offer for our readers (see inside back cover).

The climate

Sub-tropical Florida can be hot – *really* hot in May–Oct – so be ready for temperatures above 32°C/89°F, with high humidity which makes it feel like 38°C/100°F or more. Add fierce – but rarely long – thunderstorms, with lots of lightning (Florida is the lightning capital of the world!), and the weather can be a challenge, especially in the height of summer. Mar/Apr and Nov/Dec can be close to idyllic, while it is also possible for Dec–Feb to see occasional night-time temps drop to 0°C/32°F. Winter sees the biggest range of temperature, from as high as 30°C/86°F down to barely 7°C/45°F during the day. Rain rarely lasts for more than a day in winter but can still be extremely heavy (be careful when driving on the motorways). If you are governed by school holidays, the latter half of Aug is your best bet.

The mood

Orlando is big, brash and fun, but above all it's American and that means everything is well organised, but with some cultural differences such as tipping (see right). It's clean, well maintained and eager to please. Floridians generally are an affable bunch, but they take affability to new heights in the theme parks, where staff are almost painfully keen to make sure you 'have a nice day'.

Tipping

With the exception of fast-food restaurant servers, just about everyone who serves in hotels, bars, restaurants, buses, taxis, airports and public amenities will expect a tip, not least because all service industry workers are taxed on the basis of receiving 15% in tips, whether they're given or not.

- Bars, restaurants and taxis: 15%.
- Porters: $1/bag.
- Chambermaids: $1/day per adult.

◀🇬🇧▶ BRITTIP

Tipping guide

Bill	Suggested tip
$15	$2.25
$20	$3.00
$25	$3.75
$30	$4.50
$40	$6.00
$50	$7.50

ESTA and immigration

Anyone flying to the USA on the Visa Waiver Programme MUST register online via the Electronic System for Travel Authorization (ESTA) no later than three days before departure. For all flights to the US, this has now replaced the old green Visa Waiver form (I-94W).

ESTA: ESTA is a pre-authorisation process prior to arriving at US immigration. The fee is $14 per person and is valid for any visits in a two-year span (so you do NOT pay the $14 fee again in that time).

Apply at **https://esta.cbp.dhs.gov/esta/** and fill in your basic immigration info – passport, address in the USA, flight and employment details (where necessary), email address and a few security questions. Have your holiday address details available both for the ESTA and your Advance Passenger Information for your flight online.

Orlando Airboat ride

Ask your tour operator if you don't have a specific address (e.g. for a villa allocated on arrival) as it will have a formula for this. Your application should generate an immediate response of 'Authorization Approved' or 'Pending'. If the response 'Travel Not Authorized' is generated, the applicant is unable to travel under the Visa Waiver Programme and must apply for a visa in advance. Remember to record or print your Application Number during the process so you can amend it for future visits within two years.

BRITTIP
If you need to fill in the white I-94 immigration form for visa holders, do so carefully in block capitals. Mistakes are often sent to the back of the queue. Please be courteous to immigration officials – they do a difficult job in demanding circumstances, and jokes about terrorism are NOT appreciated.

The ESTA speeds up the immigration process and cuts out most form filling. An ESTA must be completed for each member of your group or family travelling under the Visa Waiver Programme. Those who have a US visa because they are not eligible to travel under the Visa Waiver Programme (i.e. because of a criminal record – see p15) still need to fill in a white I-94 form en route (fill in the front only) but they do NOT pay the $14 ESTA fee. However, anyone with a US work visa and who is travelling to America for a holiday, WILL need to fill in an ESTA and pay the fee.

BRITTIP
Beware unofficial websites that offer to fill in the ESTA form for you – for a fee. Stick with the official US government website and just pay the $14/person fee (or 'Travel Promotion Act fee').

Customs: You still need to complete a white customs form en route (it'll be given to you on the plane or at check-in and it's best to complete it in advance). Fill in one customs form per family, with some of the same basic info but also the value of any goods that will stay in the USA (put $0 unless you are arriving with gifts for friends). Hand the documents with your passports to the immigration official who checks you through and takes a fingerprint scan and photo. The customs form will be handed back to you to present to another official when you exit the baggage hall.

Visa requirements
Holiday visitors to America do not need a visa providing they hold a valid machine-readable British passport (MRP). Any passport issued from 26 October 2005 must include a digital photograph (not glued or laminated). All passports issued from 26 October 2006 must

Donald Duck at Animal Kingdom

© Hillary White

include the new biometric data. Each family member must have their own passport, valid for the FULL duration of the holiday. However, British subjects, those without an MRP or those who fail to meet the photo/biometric data criteria DO need a visa ($131), and should apply at least two months in advance to the US Embassy.

US immigration requires ALL visitors aged 14–79 to give fingerprint and photo ID on arrival. It is a simple process, though – first the four fingers and thumb of one hand, and then the same for the other hand, then stand still for the camera.

Some travellers may NOT be eligible under the Visa Waiver Programme and will have to apply for a special restricted visa or they may be refused entry. This applies to those who have been arrested in the past (even if it did not result in a conviction), have a criminal record (the Rehabilitation of Offenders Act does not apply to US visa law), have a serious communicable illness (but no longer including AIDS/HIV), or have previously been refused admission into, been deported from, or have overstayed in the US on the Visa Waiver Programme. Minor traffic offences do not count. Visa appointments can be arranged online at **https://ais.usvisa-info.com/en-gb/niv** or call 020 3608 6998.

Contacts

- **England, Scotland and Wales:** Visa Office, US Embassy, 24 Grosvenor Square, London W1A 2LQ (020 7499 9000). NB: for mailing address use postcode W1K 6AH.

- **Northern Ireland:** US Consulate General, Danesfort House, 223 Stranmillis Road, Belfast BT9 5GR (028 9038 6100).

- **More detailed advice:** https://uk.usembassy.gov/

Travel information

Luggage is liable to random searches in the US and you are advised NOT to lock your suitcases at check-in for the flight home as TSA officials have the

authority to break into them. Using zip-lock seals that can easily be snipped open is permissible and some airlines provide them free, while you can also buy TSA-approved reusable locks at some travel shops. It is best to leave any gifts you are taking home unwrapped, just in case screening requires them to be opened; and be sure to put scissors and other sharp items in checked bags, never in your hand luggage.

BRITTIP
Cabin baggage restrictions often change, so check with your airline in advance for up-to-date info.

What's new?

Walt Disney World: You should see the debut of **Pandora: The World of Avatar** in 2017 as this dramatic new part of the Animal Kingdom park finally comes to life after almost six years of planning and construction. It will feature two blockbuster main attractions and a fully themed environment from the planet Pandora in James Cameron's *Avatar* and forthcoming follow-up movies.

Universal: 2017 will see the opening of **Volcano Bay**, Orlando's latest water park and the first fully designed to sit alongside their two main theme parks. It follows the closure of their Wet 'n Wild park on International Drive and features a signature volcanic mountain as well as a host of innovative rides and slides. At **Universal Studios**, there will be two new rides: **Fast & Furious: Supercharged**, a high-energy whirl into the world of the *Fast & Furious* film franchise; and **Ride Through New York starring Jimmy Fallon**, which will be another ride experience with the host of the *Tonight* chat show in comic style around The Big Apple.

Take the train: Elsewhere in Florida the big news should be the arrival of **Brightline**, the state's first high-speed rail link – Orlando to Miami in under 3hrs, with the first stage opening in mid-2017 from West Palm Beach to Miami.

What's on?

Central Florida is home to some wonderful annual events that are well worth taking in:

February
Mardi Gras (to Apr), Universal Studios: **www.universalorlando.com**
Mount Dora Arts Festival, Mount Dora: **http://mountdoracenterforthearts.org/arts-festival**
Silver Spurs Rodeo, Kissimmee: **www.silverspursrodeo.com**

March
Flower & Garden Festival (to May), Epcot: **www.disneyworld.com**
Bands, Brew & BBQ, SeaWorld (to Apr): **http://seaworldparks.com/en/seaworld-orlando/events/bands-brew-and-bbq/**
Food & Wine Festival, Busch Gardens (to Apr): **http://seaworldparks.com/en/buschgardens-tampa/food-and-wine/**
Sidewalk Art Festival, Winter Park: **www.wpsaf.org**

April
Florida Film Festival, Orlando: **www.floridafilmfestival.com**

May
International Fringe Theatre Festival, Orlando: **http://orlandofringe.org/**

June
Sounds Like Summer concerts (to July), Epcot: **www.disneyworld.com**
Summer Nights (to July), SeaWorld and Busch Gardens: **www.seaworldparks.com**

September
Mickey's Not-So-Scary Halloween Party (to Oct), Magic Kingdom: **www.disneyworld.com**
Halloween Horror Nights (to Oct), Universal Studios: **www.universalorlando.com**
Howl-O-Scream, Busch Gardens (to Oct): **www.howloscream.com**
International Food & Wine Festival, Epcot (to Nov): **www.disneyworld.com**

October
Halloween Spooktacular, SeaWorld: **http://seaworldparks.com/en/seaworld-orlando/spooktacular/**
Silver Spurs Rodeo, Kissimmee: **www.silverspursrodeo.com**

November
Mickey's Very Merry Christmas Party (to Dec), Magic Kingdom: **www.disneyworld.com**
Snowing Nightly, Celebration (to Dec): **http://celebrationtowncenter.com/events/**
SeaWorld's Christmas Celebration (to Dec): **https://seaworldparks.com/en/seaworld-orlando/events/**
Christmas Town, Busch Gardens (to Dec): **https://seaworldparks.com/en/buschgardens-tampa/events/christmas-town/**

Santa Goofy

© Hilary White

💲 BRITBONUS

Don't forget to keep an eye out for the Brit Bonus, which features special offers and discounts with various hotels, attractions and restaurants. In addition, *Brit Guide* partners Gray Line Orlando now offer an exclusive 15% discount to our readers on a live booking option on our website, **www.britguideorlando.net**.

Plan your visit

The next few chapters will tell you all you need to know to plan the ideal holiday. Make a rough itinerary and then fine tune it with this book. You can also take advantage of our unique Touring Plans Service (p39).

2 Planning and Practicalities

or How to *Almost* Do It All and Live to Tell the Tale

Advance planning is vital to a memorable Orlando holiday, especially since Disney introduced My Magic+ in 2014. You simply have to do some homework in advance, or risk being frustrated and/or exhausted!

This huge and demanding place can pull you in a dozen directions at once, with a dazzling array of options for practically everything. Nowhere else in the world can be so complex to navigate, so it's vital to plan your visit in advance. Start with WHEN you want to go; WHERE you'd like to stay; WHAT sort of holiday you want; WHO to book with; and finally HOW MUCH to try to do. (Hint: you can't do it all!)

When to go

To avoid the worst of the crowds, the best times to go are Oct–Dec (but not Thanksgiving week in Nov or 20 Dec to New Year); early Jan–mid-Mar; and the week after Easter to the end of May.

Busiest times: Orlando is seldom quiet but is busiest at:

- Christmas/New Year period (about 17 Dec–7 Jan).
- Mid-Mar to week after Easter.
- From Memorial Day (the last Mon in May, the official start of the summer season) to mid-Aug, notably around 4 July
- Labor Day weekend in early Sept, the last holiday of summer.
- Thanksgiving week (Wed–Sun).

Daytona Beach marina

Hurricane alert?

June–Nov is officially hurricane season, but it is not anything to worry about. Even the unprecedented extremes of 2004, when three major storms hit Central Florida, caused no significant damage to the parks and the biggest inconvenience was losing electricity for a few days. In the unlikely event of a major storm, switch your TV to the Weather Channel or local news station WESH 2 and follow its advice.

The parks can close to new arrivals by mid-morning at these times – especially at Christmas.

BRITTIP

Thanksgiving is the 4th Thurs in Nov; George Washington's birthday, or President's Day, is the 3rd Mon in Feb, and both make for above-average long-weekend crowds.

Best times: The best combination of good weather and smaller crowds is in Apr (after Easter) and Oct. Rain isn't a big factor (although outdoor rides and the water parks will close if lightning threatens), but the crowds will noticeably thin out when it does rain and you can take advantage by bringing waterproofs or buying a cheap plastic poncho (all the parks sell them, but they are cheaper from local supermarkets). In the colder months, take a few warm layers for early morning queues. When it

heats up, leave them in the park lockers. When it gets really hot, seek out the air-conditioned attractions. The humidity alone will knock you sideways in summer and it's vital to rehydrate at regular intervals.

Simon & Susan's 10 Commandments

1 Drink water frequently

2 Use sunscreen regularly

3 Bring a lightweight rain jacket

4 Pre-book Disney dining

5 Use FastPass+

6 Slow down

7 Remember: you can't do it all

8 Wear comfortable walking shoes

9 Be sure to actually see some of Florida

10 Don't forget to tip

Where to stay

This is equally important and, again, there's a huge choice. As a rough guide, four main areas make up the great Orlando tourist conglomeration.

Walt Disney World: Some of the most sophisticated, convenient and fun places to stay are Disney's own hotels.

The same imagination that created the theme parks also worked on the likes of Disney's Polynesian Village and Animal Kingdom Lodge. They all feature free transport, MagicBand (see p98), free

Disney's Polynesian Village Resort

Virgin's V-Room

All Virgin Holidays guests have the option of the V-Room lounge at Gatwick and Manchester, a private hideaway with a kids' play area, video games, big-screen TV, internet access, adults-only area, free breakfast, snacks, fruit, soft drinks, tea and coffee, and fast-track security channel. It costs £24.50 adults and £14 2–11s in advance (£25 and £15 on day of travel), free with Platinum bookings. NB: The Gatwick V-Room was closed in 2016 but is due to re-open in a new space in the North Terminal in Jan 2017 as part of the Gatwick revamp.

parking and the BIG bonus of Extra Magic Hours. This allows Disney resort guests entry to one theme park each day, either one hour before official opening or for two hours after closing, so you can do many of the attractions with fewer crowds (though evenings can still be busy). Many also have kids' clubs and babysitting services. However, with the exception of Disney's All-Star, Pop Century and Art of Animation Resorts, its hotels are among the most expensive, especially to eat in, and are not close to the other attractions. They make a good one-week base, though.

BRITTIP ————
Beware holiday homes (and some hotels) that insist they are 'just minutes from Disney World' – which may actually mean 30mins or more from the parks. Check the exact address.

Lake Buena Vista: On the eastern edge of Walt Disney World and along Interstate 4, this features a good mix of hotels. It is handy for Disney (and slightly cheaper), with most hotels offering free transport to the parks, plus there is good dining and shopping.

International Drive: The ribbon development of I-Drive lies mid-way between Disney and downtown Orlando, running parallel to I-4, and is an excellent central location about 20mins drive from Disney and close

to Universal and SeaWorld. It is a well-developed tourist area, with great shops, restaurants and attractions like I-Drive 360, Ripley's Believe It Or Not, WonderWorks and iFLY Orlando, plus its own transport service, the I-Ride Trolley. The downside is it gets congested in peak times, but it is good value and one of the few areas with extensive pavement, making it easy to explore on foot. A sub-district off I-Drive is the Universal area of Kirkman Road and Major Boulevard.

BRITTIP ————
I-Drive south of Sand Lake Road offers some of the best hotels and restaurants. To the north, it is more budget hotels, fast food and gift shops.

Kissimmee: Budget holiday-makers can be found in their greatest numbers along the tourist sprawl of Highway 192 (the Irlo Bronson Memorial Highway), an almost unbroken 20ml/32km strip of hotels, motels, restaurants and shops. It offers some of the best economy accommodation and is handy for Disney, though further from Universal and SeaWorld. A car is advisable here, although there is extensive pavement, landscaping, bus shelters and benches. **Highway 27** is often referred to as 'Kissimmee' but is actually either in Lake County (north) or Polk County (south). This is prime holiday-home territory, with many developments.

Split holidays

Florida has so much to offer, many opt to spend a week in Orlando and a week somewhere else. The Atlantic coast has great beaches an hour to the east; the Everglades are 3–4 hours to the south; and there are more wonderful beaches to the west. There's great shopping almost everywhere, stunning golf courses and opportunities to play or watch tennis, soccer and basketball, go fishing, boating or kayaking. The tour operators all offer a huge variety of packages, plus cruise-and-stay options. The ideal option,

Dining Plan options

Most tour operators offer the Disney Dining Plan as an optional extra with Disney hotel packages and it can be good value if you spend ALL your time in Walt Disney World, where there are few cheap dining outlets. But, because ALL members of the family must be included for the FULL length of your stay, even the Quick Service plan adds £1,260 for a family of four (with children 3–9) staying for two weeks; the main Dining Plan would be £1,736; and the Deluxe Plan a huge £2,912. It is a LOT of food to contend with, especially when it's hot, and you often need to book the full-service restaurants well in advance. You can eat cheaper elsewhere, so don't book unless you are sure. However, tour operators occasionally offer the Dining Plan as a FREE perk at quieter times of the year – a BIG bonus. See more on Disney Dining Plan on p56.

budget permitting, is two weeks in Orlando then a week relaxing on a beach. A two-week, 50/50 split is popular, but can make it hectic in Orlando so the 60/40 splits can be better. Fly-drives are flexible, but there is a lot to tempt you and you may find it better to book a two-centre stay that includes a car and accommodation so you can still travel but avoid too much packing and unpacking (see also Chapter 9).

Booking your holiday

The big question these days is whether to book a package or do it yourself (booking the flight, accommodation, car hire, etc, all separately). The number of tour operators has dwindled of late and the DIY approach can pay dividends (although at peak periods a package may still be cheaper). Shop around, and use the Internet. Increasingly, it pays to book early, especially for the summer and Christmas holidays, but you can still pick up some late bargains at quieter times of the year. Always book with agents who are ABTA and ATOL-bonded. Start by looking at prices with the Big Boys (Virgin, Thomson and Co) and then compare with some of the online specialists like Expedia and Opodo. For the DIY approach, also look up the 'aggregator' websites like Skyscanner and Kayak that check flights/hotels/car hire from a number of sources.

The Big Boys: You'll find a good range of package holidays, featuring both Orlando and the Gulf Coast from

British Airways Holidays (0844 493 0787, **www.britishairways.com/en-gb/ destinations/florida/holidays-in-florida**); **Thomas Cook** (01733 224 808, **www.thomascook.com**); **Thomson** (0871 231 4691, **www.thomson. co.uk**); and US specialist **Travel City Direct** (0344 557 6969, **www. travelcitydirect.com**). Thomas Cook (from Belfast, Cardiff, Glasgow, Gatwick, Manchester and Stansted) and Thomson (from Birmingham, East Midlands, Edinburgh, Glasgow, Gatwick, Stansted, Manchester and Newcastle to Orlando Sanford Airport) also offer flights-only seasonally. **Virgin Holidays** remain Britain's leading tour operator for Florida, with the widest range of choice, variety and perks, including early entry to the Wizarding World of Harry Potter at Universal Orlando and to SeaWorld, plus return flight check-in at Disney Springs, wedding services, vow renewals and exclusive options on Singer Island, Marco Island and Key West (0844 557 4321, **www.virginholidays.co.uk**).

The Specialists: There is also a good variety of smaller operators who specialise in Florida and the US. Take your pick from:

- **James Villa Holidays** (0800 074 0122, **www.jamesvillas.co.uk**)

- **Jetsave** (0330 332 1837, **www.jetsave.com**)

- **Kuoni** (0800 140 0845, **www.kuoni.co.uk**)

- **My America Holiday** (020 3773 8827, **www.myamericaholiday.co.uk**)

Complete Orlando

The highly rated Attraction Tickets Direct company has a full ATOL-bonded travel operator called Complete Orlando, which is well worth trying for packages, flights, hotels, car hire and travel insurance. It offers a wide range of accommodation (usually with some great deals, especially on Disney hotels), plus handy online videos, and no credit card fees or hidden extras. Call 0800 294 8844, **www.completeorlando.co.uk**.

- **Trailfinders** (020 7368 1200, **www.trailfinders.com**)
- **Travelbag** (0871 402 1644, **www.travelbag.co.uk**)
- **USAirtours** (0800 0350 149, **www.usairtours.co.uk**)
- Perhaps the best of the bunch here, though, is **Ocean Florida** (020 7939 7775, **www.ocean-florida.co.uk**), who have built up a solid Florida reputation in recent years.

Online agents: in addition to the tour operators, you can also price-check with a variety of online agencies who provide packages, flights, hotels and car hire. Try any of:

- **Cheap Flights** (**www.cheapflights. co.uk**)
- **Dial A Flight** (**www.dialaflight.com**)
- **eBookers** (**www.ebookers.com**)
- **Expedia** (**www.expedia.co.uk**)
- **Flight Centre** (**www.flightcentre.co.uk**)
- **Kelkoo** (**http://travel.kelkoo.co.uk/**)
- **Kayak** (**www.kayak.co.uk**)
- **NetFlights** (**www.netflights.com**)
- **Opodo** (**www.opodo.co.uk**)
- **Sky Scanner** (**www.skyscanner.net**)
- **Travel Supermarket** (**www.travelsupermarket.com**).

Scheduled flights

When it comes to DIY bookings, the first item to look at is your flight. Here are the airlines that offer scheduled, year-round services to Orlando.

Aer Lingus: The main Irish airline offers direct flights from Dublin (0333 004 5000, **ww.aerlingus.com**).

British Airways: The big national carrier flies direct daily from Gatwick to Orlando and Tampa, as well as from Heathrow to Miami. 0844 493 0787, **www.britishairways.com**).

Icelandair: Fly via Reykjavik, Iceland, from any of Heathrow, Glasgow and Manchester (020 7874 1000, **www.icelandair.co.uk**).

Norwegian: The smart, low-cost carrier now flies direct to Orlando and Fort Lauderdale from Gatwick, with some tempting prices and all using the Boeing Dreamliner (0330 828 0854, **www.norwegian.com/uk/**).

Virgin Atlantic: With multiple direct flights each week from Gatwick, Manchester and Glasgow, plus summer peak from Belfast, as well as daily from Heathrow to Miami (0844 209 7777, **www.virgin-atlantic.co.uk**).

However, you can often save money on indirect flights with these carriers:

American Airlines: now incorporating US Airways, from Heathrow, Manchester, Glasgow or Dublin via Boston, Chicago, Charlotte, Dallas, New York, Philadelphia and Washington (0844 369 9899, **www.americanairlines.co.uk**).

Delta/KLM: Gatwick via Atlanta; Heathrow via Atlanta, Boston, Minneapolis, Detroit or New York; Manchester via New York or Atlanta; or Edinburgh and Glasgow via New York (020 7660 0293, **www.klm.com**).

Relaxing on the Gulf Coast

United: Heathrow via Washington, Houston, New York or Chicago, or Manchester, Birmingham, Belfast, Dublin, Glasgow or Edinburgh via New York or Washington; 0845 607 6760, **www.united.com**).

The obvious drawback is the extra journey time, and the connecting flight may land you in Orlando late in the evening. However, it does break the journey and places like Detroit and Dallas often process international passengers quicker than Orlando, meaning less hassle when you arrive in Florida.

What to see when

The best way to end up exhausted is to head for the nearest theme park, then the next and so on. You'll need rest days and to take advantage of quieter days at the parks.

Using the Planner on p345 as an example (or with the *Brit Guide* Touring Plans service, p39), list the attractions you want to see, planning around the eight 'must-see' parks. If you have only a week, drop Busch Gardens and focus on Disney, Universal and SeaWorld. Kennedy Space Center is also hard to overlook.

- **Magic Kingdom:** 2 days – the biggest hit with young children.

- **Epcot:** 2 days – one day is not really enough, but there are fewer rides to amuse children.

- **Animal Kingdom:** 1 day – a little short on appeal for the youngest but now with evening entertainment.

- **Disney's Hollywood Studios:** 1 day – plus two great evening shows.

- **SeaWorld:** 1–2 days.

- **Islands of Adventure:** 1–2 days.

- **Universal Studios:** 1–2 days.

- **Busch Gardens:** 1 day – popular with Brits, 75mins away in Tampa.

- **LEGOLAND Florida**, 45mins away in Winter Haven, is also a full day's outing, while the attractions of **I-Drive 360** can be fitted around the main parks. Look at the detail in Chapters 5–8 before you plan.

Our must-do experiences

- Soarin' and IllumiNations show (Epcot)
- Cirque du Soleil® (Disney Springs)
- Wizarding Worlds of Harry Potter at Universal Orlando
- Boggy Creek Airboats/Wild Florida (Kissimmee)
- Expedition Everest and Festival of The Lion King (Animal Kingdom)
- Wishes fireworks, Pirates of the Caribbean and Haunted Mansion rides (Magic Kingdom)
- Fantasmic! show and Star Tours ride (Disney's Hollywood Studios)
- The Orlando Eye at I-Drive 360
- Shopping!
- Antarctica: Empire of the Penguin and Blue Horizons show (SeaWorld)
- Cheetah Hunt and SheiKra coasters (Busch Gardens)
- Space Shuttle Atlantis (Kennedy Space Center)
- A Disney character meal
- A day at a water park

Smaller attractions

Of the other, smaller-scale attractions, **Forever Florida** is a full day out as it also involves an hour's drive to get there, but everything else can be fitted around your Big Eight itinerary. The **water parks** or the quieter **Bok Tower Gardens** make for a relaxing half-day, while **Gatorland** (at least half a day) is a unique look at some of Florida's oldest inhabitants and is a good combination with **Boggy Creek Airboats** or **Wild Florida**. Then there are the likes of **Ripley's Believe It Or Not** museum, the **WhirlyDome** and the **WonderWorks** house of fun, all offering several hours' entertainment, the thrills of **iFLY Orlando** (an indoor 'sky-diving' wind tunnel) and the lure of old-fashioned go-karts and other fairground-type rides at **Fun Spot** and **Magical Midway**. Many stay open after the parks close.

Each main area is also well served with creatively designed **mini-golf** courses.

Evenings

The evening entertainment features a similarly wide choice. By far the best, and worth at least one evening each, are **Disney Springs** and Universal's **CityWalk** – the latter will keep you busy until the early hours! Dinner shows provide a lot of fun: two-hour cabarets based on themes such as medieval knights, pirates, Al Capone and murder mysteries that all include a hearty meal. Downtown Orlando (the actual city centre) is also well worth a visit these days.

Shopping

Shopping in Orlando is world class (see Chapter 12) and your battle plan should include at least a day to visit the spectacular malls and discount centres, like the two excellent **Orlando Premium Outlets** centres, **Lake Buena Vista Factory Stores**, **Mall at Millenia** and the **Florida Mall**. Busy at weekends, they're handy if it rains.

What to do when

There are several guidelines for avoiding the worst of the tourist hordes, even in high season.

Avoid busy days: Most Americans arrive at weekends and head for the main theme parks first, so Sun and Mon are often bad times to visit the Magic Kingdom, while Tues is usually also busy at Epcot. New rides like Skull Island: Reign of Kong (at Islands of Adventure) also create longer queues, notably at weekends. The Animal Kingdom is the hardest to navigate when crowded, while Epcot handles the crowds best. Disney's Blizzard Beach and Typhoon Lagoon water parks hit high tide at weekends, and Thurs and Fri in summer. If Walt Disney World is humming early in the week, that makes it a good time to visit SeaWorld, Busch Gardens or the Kennedy Space Center. Try to avoid Volcano Bay and Aquatica at weekends, too.

Disney's Extra Magic Hours: Allowing Disney guests early and late access (see p57) creates bigger crowds, too. So, if you are NOT staying at a Disney hotel, avoid these EMH mornings. For much of the year, they run as follows: Magic Kingdom, Tues or Fri (morning EMH) and Weds (evening EMH); Epcot, Tues or Thurs (morning), Mon (evening); Disney's Hollywood Studios, Sun (morning), Fri (evening); Animal Kingdom, Mon and Sat (morning only). Be aware EMH days can change at short notice, and several parks can have multiple successive days at peak periods. See the Park Hours page at **https://disneyworld.disney.go.com/calendars/**

Universal Orlando: The picture is different here as only the two Wizarding Worlds of Harry Potter have daily early opening privileges (for guests at Universal hotels). This often means heavier crowds early in the week, while the parks also get busiest at weekends.

✚ BRITTIP

If your hotel is not far away, take a mid-afternoon break from the park and return for a siesta or a swim. Your car park ticket is valid all day, and the evening is often the best time to be in the parks.

Arrive early: Getting the most out of your days at the parks is another art form, and there are several options. The opening times seldom vary from 9am (Magic Kingdom and Animal Kingdom can be 8am at peak times), but arriving early is highly advisable. Apart from being near the head of the queues (and they are SERIOUS queues, or 'lines'), the parks

Hogwart's Express

© Universal Orlando Resort

Medical marvels

The **Medical Concierge®** is a great choice for local medical care with doctors and paediatricians throughout the tourist areas, making house calls to hotels and villas 24/7. They also have several key clinic locations, notably close to Universal Orlando, and I-Drive, Lake Buena Vista, Kissimmee and Haines City/Davenport, but you must call for an appointment. Their doctors have mobile pharmacies and even X-ray units and they specialise in providing healthcare to overseas visitors, hence their staff are familiar with dealing with Brits. They can often arrange same-day dental and other specialist appointments and take many UK travel insurance polices, meaning they deal directly with the insurance company. Their switchboard is manned around the clock with medically trained staff, ensuring you never deal with an answering machine. Call 1855 932 5252, or visit **www.themedicalconcierge.com**.

occasionally open early if the crowds build up. So you can be a step ahead by arriving at least 30mins before opening time (or an hour early during peak periods). You will also be better placed to park in the huge car parks and catch the tram to the main gates.

Prioritise: Once you are in pole position, don't waste time on the shops, scenery and other frippery that will lure the unprepared first-timer. Instead, head straight for some of the main rides and get a few big-time thrills under your belt before the main hordes arrive. You will quickly work out where the most popular attractions are as the majority of early birds will flock to them. Use Chapters 5 and 6 to plan your park strategies.

Pace yourself: Disney's parks, notably the Magic Kingdom, stay open late for the main holidays, until midnight at times, and that can be a l-o-n-g day for kids. It's vital to pace yourself, especially if you arrive early. There are plenty of options to take time off for a drink or a sit-down somewhere

air-conditioned, and these latter are vital in summer.

FastPass+: make *sure* you use this Disney system to your advantage in advance (see p99).

Meal breaks: Benefit from the American habit of dining en masse at lunchtime (midday–1.30pm) and dinner (5.30–7pm) by planning your meals outside those times. It pays to take an early lunch (before noon), snack in mid-afternoon and then enjoy a relative drop-off in crowds in late afternoon. But try not to have all your meals in the parks; eating here can be expensive (at least $13/person for a basic meal). A good breakfast before you arrive and a light lunch will save you $$$s!

BRITTIP
The water IS safe to drink in the US, but it might not taste great as it's heavily fluoridated. If you buy bottled water, do so at supermarkets, not at the parks, where it is exorbitantly expensive.

Comfort and clothing

You may feel jetlagged for the first day or so after your arrival, but avoiding alcohol and coffee on the plane and keeping hydrated by drinking plenty of water can reduce this.

Shoes: The most important part of your holiday wardrobe is your footwear – you'll be on your feet a LOT, even at off-peak periods. The smallest park is 'only' 100acres/40ha, but that is irrelevant to the time spent queuing. This is not the time to break in new sandals or trainers. Comfortable, well-worn shoes or trainers are essential (many rate Croc-type shoes as ideal park footwear).

BRITTIP
Look after your feet and avoid the onset of blisters by buying some moleskin footpads from a supermarket or 'drug-store' like Walgreens and CVS.

Casual clothes: Parks and nearly all restaurants accept casual dress. However, swimwear is not acceptable

Footy frenzy

You don't need a specialist sports bar to find British football on TV these days. The Premier League is extensively covered by NBC (up to three games on Sat and Sun, plus the Mon night games) while the Champions League and FA Cup is on Fox Sports. You should check if your villa/hotel has NBC Sports for some games, though, as it is a cable channel that not everyone gets. And don't forget to check out our own team – Orlando City – at **www.orlandocitysc.com**.

away from pool areas. If you want a change of clothes or a sweater for the evening, use the lockers in all the parks (unlimited use all day for a small fee).

BRITTIP

Don't be tempted to pack a lot of smart or formal clothing – you really won't need it in hot, informal Florida.

Baby services: All the parks are well equipped with pushchairs, or 'strollers', for hire (although it pays to have your own), and baby services are located at regular intervals. You can even hire pushchairs for your full holiday period from Orlando Stroller Rentals from $100 for two weeks (1800 281 0884, **www.orlandostrollerrentals.com**).

Sunscreen: It is VITAL to use high-factor sun creams (30-plus) at all times, even during the winter when the sun may not feel strong but can still burn. Orlando has a subtropical climate and you need higher factor creams than in the Mediterranean, and waterproof if you are swimming. Use sun block on sensitive areas like nose and ears, and splash on the after-sun liberally at the end of the day. Skincare products are widely available and usually inexpensive (at Wal-Mart, Publix or Target). Wear a hat during the day, and avoid alcohol, coffee and fizzy drinks until the evening as they are dehydrating and make you liable to heatstroke. You must increase your fluid intake SIGNIFICANTLY in the summer, but stick to sports drinks and lots of water.

BRITTIP

One of the best ways to keep cool in the sun is to buy a simple mist spray fan (about $7.99) from a supermarket.

Medical help

Should you need medical treatment consult your tour operator's info about local hospitals and surgeries. In the event of an emergency, dial 911 as you would 999 in Britain. It cannot be overstressed, however, you should take out comprehensive travel insurance (see p28) for any trip to America, as there is NO National Health Service

Drop Slide at Volcano Bay

Attractions with warnings for expectant mothers

Animal Kingdom: Dinosaur!, Expedition Everest, Kali River Rapids, Kilimanjaro Safari, Primeval Whirl.

Busch Gardens: Cheetah Hunt, Cobra's Curse, Congo River Rapids, Falcon's Fury, Kumba, Montu, Phoenix, Sand Serpent, Scorpion, SheiKra, Stanley Falls Log Flume, Ubanga-Banga Bumper Cars.

Epcot: Mission: SPACE, Soarin', Test Track.

Hollywood Studios: Rock 'n Roller Coaster, Star Tours, Twilight Zone Tower of Terror.

Islands of Adventure: Amazing Adventures of Spider-Man, Cat in the Hat, Dragon Challenge, Dr Doom's Fearfall, Dudley Do-Right's Ripsaw Falls, Flight of the Hippogriff, Harry Potter and the Forbidden Journey, Incredible Hulk Coaster, Jurassic Park River Adventure, Popeye & Bluto's Bilge Rat Barges, Reign of Kong, Storm Force Accelatron.

Magic Kingdom: Barnstormer, Big Thunder Mountain Railroad, Seven Dwarfs Mine Train, Space Mountain, Splash Mountain.

SeaWorld: Antarctica: Empire of the Penguin (Wild version of ride), Journey to Atlantis, Jazzie Jellies, Kraken, Manta, Mako, Rock Wall, Shamu Express, Swishy Fishies, Wild Arctic (ride portion).

Universal Studios: ET Adventure, Fast & Furious: Supercharged, Harry Potter and the Escape from Gringotts, Men in Black Alien Attack, Revenge of the Mummy, Shrek 4-D, Terminator 2: 3-D and Despicable Me: Minion Mayhem (stationary seats available), TRANSFORMERS: The Ride – 3D, Woody Woodpecker's Nuthouse Coaster.

Gator safety

Alligators are found in many bodies of water in Florida but are rarely a threat. However, they should NEVER be approached or fed (the latter of which is illegal). They usually avoid humans, but swimming in lakes in the evening is not advised and small children should never be allowed in open water on their own.

and any form of medical treatment is expensive. Keep all the receipts and put in a claim on your return home.

◀▚ BRITTIP
Look for local insect-repellent brands Cutter, Repel and Off! and use them away from the parks.

Emergency outpatients: These can be found with Centra Care at Florida Hospital Medical Center in more than 20 Central Florida locations (407 200 2273; **https://centracare.org/florida/**), as well as full family and paediatric care.

Open 8am–8pm (5pm at weekends), there are four locations open to

midnight Mon–Fri, including at 12500 S Apopka-Vineland Road near the Crossroads shopping centre and Disney Springs at Lake Buena Vista (8pm Sat and Sun; 407 934 2273). Other notable tourist area locations are: 8201 West Irlo Bronson Memorial Highway (192), by Orange Lake Resort (407 465 0846); on Sand Lake Road, between John Young Parkway and Orange Blossom Trail (9am–5pm Sat and Sun; 407 851 6478); and 4320 West Vine Street, near Medieval Times (407 390 1888).

If you need an emergency dentist, **Mobile Dental ER** has a mobile facility that can visit anywhere in the Orlando area, seven days a week (9am–5pm). Payment accepted with all major credit cards (but be sure to save receipts for your insurance company). Call 1888 707 4985 or visit **www.mobiledentaler.com**.

◀▚ BRITTIP
If you take regular prescription drugs, find out the different UK and US names from your doctor or pharmacist and carry the info with you (e.g. adrenaline is known as epinephrine, paracetamol is acetaminophen).

At-a-glance kids' height requirements

Height	Park	Rides
2ft 8in/82cm	Disney's Blizzard Beach	Chairlift
Must be with a child 3ft–4ft 8in/91–142cm	Islands of Adventure	Pteranodon Flyers
3ft/91cm	Disney's Magic Kingdom Universal Studios Islands of Adventure	The Barnstormer Woody Woodpecker's Nuthouse Coaster The Cat in the Hat, Skull Island: Reign of Kong (3–4 ft with adult)
3ft 4in/101cm	Disney's Animal Kingdom Disney's Hollywood Studios Disney's Magic Kingdom Epcot Islands of Adventure Universal Studios	DINOSAUR! Star Tours, The Twilight Zone Tower of Terror Splash Mountain, Big Thunder Mountain Railroad, Seven Dwarfs Mine Train Ride Test Track, Soarin' The Amazing Adventures of Spider-Man The Simpsons Ride, TRANSFORMERS: The Ride – 3D, Harry Potter and the Escape from Gringotts
3ft 6in/106cm	Aquatica Busch Gardens Disney's Animal Kingdom Islands of Adventure SeaWorld Universal Studios	Walhalla Wave, HooRoo Run, Taumata Racer The Wild Surge (3ft 2in/96cm with adult), Congo River Rapids, Ubanga-Banga Bumper Cars, Scorpion, Sand Serpent (age 6 minimum), Cobra's Curse Kali River Rapids Jurassic Park River Adventure Journey to Atlantis, Wild Arctic (Polar Express at Christmas) Men in Black: Alien Attack
3ft 8 in/111cm	Disney's Animal Kingdom Disney's Magic Kingdom Epcot Islands of Adventure	Expedition: Everest Space Mountain Mission: SPACE Dudley Do-Right's Ripsaw Falls
3ft 10in/116cm	Busch Gardens	Stanley Falls
Under 4ft/122cm only	Aquatica Disney's Blizzard Beach Disney's Typhoon Lagoon	Kata's Kookaburra Cove Tike's Peak Ketchakiddee Creek
4ft/122cm	Aquatica Busch Gardens Disney's Animal Kingdom Disney's Blizzard Beach Disney's Hollywood Studios Disney's Typhoon Lagoon Islands of Adventure Universal Studios	Dolphin Plunge, Ihu's Breakaway Falls, Omaka Rocka Jungle Flyers Primeval Whirl Summit Plummet, Slush Gusher, Downhill Double Dipper Rock 'n' Roller Coaster Starring Aerosmith Crush 'n' Gusher, Humunga Kowabunga Popeye And Bluto's Bilge-Rat Barges, Flight of the Hippogriff, Harry Potter and the Forbidden Journey Revenge of the Mummy, ET Adventure
4ft 3in/130cm	Universal Studios	Hollywood Rip Ride Rockit!
4ft 4in/132cm	Disney's Magic Kingdom Islands of Adventure	Tomorrowland Speedway (for child to drive alone) Dr Doom's Fearfall
4ft 6in/137cm	Busch Gardens Islands of Adventure SeaWorld	SheiKra, Kumba, Montu, Cheetah Hunt, Falcon's Fury The Incredible Hulk Coaster, Dragon Challenge Kraken, Manta, Mako

Measurements

US clothes sizes are smaller than ours, hence a US size 12 dress is a UK 14, or an American jacket sized 42 is a 44. Shoes are the opposite: a US 10 should fit a British size 9 foot. The measuring system is imperial, not metric.

The Dr P Phillips Hospital, 9400 Turkey Lake Road, also has an emergency outpatients (the Emergency Room, or ER in America) open 24hrs (407 351 8500).

Better still, call The Medical Concierge® (407 648 5252 or freephone at 1855 932 5252, or **www.themedicalconcierge.com**; see panel on p24) who make hotel and villa 'house calls' 24 hours a day.

Chemists: The largest chemists ('drug stores') are Walgreens (**www.walgreens. com**) and CVS (**www.cvs.com**), and the Walgreens at 12100 S Apopka-Vineland Road (near Disney Springs), 5935 W Irlo Bronson Memorial Highway (Highway 192 in Kissimmee), 6201, 8959 and 12650 International Drive (among others, plus the new one at the corner of I-Drive and Sand Lake Rd), are open 24 hours.

Travel insurance

You shouldn't travel without insurance, but you shouldn't pay more than you need to and you don't need to buy your travel agent's policy. Your policy should cover all these options.

- Medical cover of at least £2m.

- Personal liability up to £2m (this won't cover driving abroad; you still need Supplementary Liability Insurance with your car hire firm).

- Cancellation or curtailment cover up to £5,000.

- Personal property cover up to £1,500 (but check on expensive items, as most policies limit single articles to £250).

- Cash and document cover, including your passport and tickets.

- 24hr emergency helpline.

- If you want to go horse-riding, check your policy includes dangerous sports cover.

Shop around at reputable dealers such as:

- **Allianz Assistance** (0371 200 0428, **http://www.allianz-assistance.co.uk/**).

- **American Express** (0800 028 7573, **www.americanexpress.com/uk**).

- **Aviva** (0345 307 8586, **www.aviva.co.uk**).

- **AXA** (0330 024 1307, **www.axa.co.uk/insurance/personal/travel/**).

- **Club Direct** (0800 083 2455, **www.clubdirect.com**).

- **Columbus** (0800 068 0080, **www.columbusdirect.com**).

- **Direct Travel** (0330 880 3600, **www.direct-travel.co.uk**).

- **Money Supermarket** also compares travel insurers online at **www.moneysupermarket.com/travel-insurance/**.

Florida with children

We are often asked what we think is the right age to take children to Orlando, and there is no set answer. Some toddlers take to it instantly, while some 6–7-year-olds are overwhelmed. Very often, the best attractions for young children are the hotel swimming pool or the tram ride to a park's front gates! Some love the Disney characters instantly, while others find them frightening. There is no predicting how they'll react but, at 4½, Simon's oldest boy loved just about every second of his first experience (apart from the fireworks!) and still talks about it. A 3-year-old may not remember much, but will have fun and provide you with great memories, photos and videos. Here are some top tips for travelling with youngsters.

The flight: Pack a bag with lots of little things for them (comics, sweets, colouring books, small surprise toys, etc.) and keep vital extras like Calpol (in sachets, if possible), a change of clothes, a small first-aid kit, plasters, antiseptic cream, baby wipes, sunglasses, a hat and sunscreen in your hand luggage.

Once you're there: Take things slowly and let your children dictate the pace to a large extent. In hot, humid summer, only the most placid children (and few under-5s, in our experience) will happily queue for an hour or more at a ride, so use Disney's FastPass+ system (p99) judiciously. The heat, in particular, can result in grizzly kids in no time, so take breaks for drinks and splash zones or head for attractions with air-conditioning. Remember to carry your small first-aid kit. Baby wipes always come in handy, and it's a good idea to take spare clothes, which you can leave in park lockers. Going back to the hotel for an afternoon snooze is a good idea – you will also dodge the worst of the heat and crowds.

BRITTIP

The **Kids-eat free** and **Eat & Play** cards (see p10) are great ways for families to save money in many tourist-area restaurants. They feature more than 50 options, from the standard McDonald's and Dunkin Donuts to upmarket Cedar's and Big Fin Seafood.

In the sun: Carry sun cream and sun block at all times and use it often, in queues, on buses, etc. Use a children's after-sun lotion and make sure they drink a lot of water or non-fizzy drinks; tiredness and irritability are often the signs of mild dehydration.

Dining out: Look for Kids-eat-free deals as they can apply to children up to 12, and take advantage of the many buffet options (see Chapter 11, Dining Out) to fill up the family or for picky eaters. Many restaurants do Meals To Go if you want a quiet meal in your own accommodation without the worry of the kids playing up. And try to let your children get used to the characters (especially their size) before you go to one of the many wonderful character meals.

Having fun: Let your children do some of the decision-making and be prepared to go with the flow if they find something unexpected – the many squirt fountains and splash zones in the parks are an example (bring swimsuits and/or a change of clothes!). The Orlando rule of 'You Can't Do It All' applies especially with kids. Be aware some youngsters find the evening fireworks too loud, but the hotels around the Magic Kingdom offer a view from a distance.

Baby centres: All the parks have facilities for nursing mothers and can provide baby food and nappies on request (locations are on the park map). The centres can even provide spare children's underpants for those little accidents. All Disney hotel gift shops stock baby food and nappies. Expectant mothers are strongly advised not to ride some of the more dynamic attractions and coasters, and there will be clear warnings on park maps and at the rides.

Pushchairs: 'Strollers' are essential, even if your children are a year or so out of them. The walking wears kids out quickly and a pushchair can save a lot of discomfort. You can take your own, hire them at the parks or buy one for as little as $25 at a local supermarket. Babysitting is available through many Disney resorts and some of the bigger hotels elsewhere.

BRITTIP

Bringing your mobile phone to the US can be costly with overseas roaming charges. Either switch off the data roaming (and just use WiFi, which is free in many places, including the theme parks) or buy a pre-paid data Sim before you go. To call the US from the UK, dial 001, then the number; from the US to the UK, dial 011 44 and leave off the first 0 of the number.

Character dining at The Kitchen

Travellers with disabilities

The parks pay close attention to the needs of visitors with disabilities and Florida is extremely disabled-friendly (Americans use the word 'handicapped' as we use 'disabled').

Access: Wheelchair availability and access is usually good (though there are a few rides that cannot cater for them) and all hotels have disabled-accessible rooms. For hearing-impaired guests, there are assistive listening devices and reflective captioning where a commentary is part of a show. Braille guidebooks are available, plus rest areas for guide dogs, and there are Audio Descriptions for blind guests. Disney, Universal and SeaWorld offer Accessibility Guides for disabled guests in all their main parks (and online). Life-jackets are always on hand at water parks. For Disney disability assistance, call 407 824 4321 (TTY 407 827 5141); for Universal, call 407 224 4233.

Guest Assistance: If you need help with queuing or have children with special needs, visit any Disney theme park Guest Relations office, with the person in question, and request a Disability Access Service card (DAS), which has replaced the old Guest Assistance Card. It doesn't provide front-of-line access, but instead provides a return time based on the current queue at each attraction.

As soon as the Guest finishes one attraction, they can receive a return time for another. This can be used in addition to Disney's FastPass+ service. Universal, SeaWorld and Busch

Brewlando Tours

Gardens provide similar assistance through their Guest Services offices.

Parking permits: To use any of the plentiful designated disabled parking areas in all public areas (including the parks), UK drivers must obtain a **Temporary Disabled Parking Permit**, which costs $15. You can either go to a local tax collection office, with your UK blue badge and passport, when you arrive (most open 8.30am–4pm Mon–Fri only), OR apply by post, fax or email at least four weeks in advance (but no more than six). By mail, send a photocopy of your Blue Badge (both sides), a copy of your passport ID page, your home address and address while in Florida, arrival and departure date and a money order (in US dollars) for $15; do NOT send cash for safety reasons. The Osceola County tax office has a special service for UK visitors with a dedicated team to deal with all requests (8am–4.30pm Mon–Fri). By mail: Patsy Heffner Tax Collector, 1300 9th Street, Suite 101-B, St Cloud, Florida 34769, USA; by fax: 407 892 8076; and include an email address for return confirmation. By email: **TaxCollectorTPL@osceola.org** with a scanned copy of your details (as above, but NOT your credit card details) and they will email you back with a number to call to arrange payment (there is a 2.5% service charge for using a credit or debit card). If you cannot reach them for any reason or don't get a response within two working days, try **webinfo@osceola.org** or 407 742 4000.

For a list of tax offices in Orange County (for the Orlando area), call 407 836 4145 (**www.octaxcol.com**, and click Office Locations); in Osceola County (for Kissimmee), call 407 742 4000 (**www.osceolataxcollector.com**). The temporary permits are valid for 90 days from issue date so it's best to apply no sooner than 5–6 weeks before travelling to ensure it will be valid for your stay. However, you may renew a permit within 12 months for no fee.

- **Walker Mobility:** Specialises in electric scooters and wheelchair rentals, with free delivery and pick-up, even from holiday villas (407 518 6000, **www.walkermobility.com**).

Repeat visitors

Repeat visitors are a large part of the Orlando market and are usually on the lookout for something new. Chapters 8 and 9 (Off The Beaten Track and The Twin Centre Option) are largely designed with them in mind. Here are 10 things worth doing once you have Been There and Done That:

1   Behind the scenes tours at the Disney parks.

2   Dolphin watch cruise from Dolphin Landings at St Pete Beach.

3   Wildlife eco-tour with Island Boat Lines at Cocoa Beach.

4   The scenic boat ride and Morse Museum in Winter Park.

5   Bok Tower Gardens.

6   St John's River Eco Tour Cruise in Debary.

7   Boggy Creek Airboats or Wild Florida.

8   Eco-park at Forever Florida or Orlando Tree Trek.

9   Merritt Island National Wildlife Refuge at Titusville.

10 Kayaking at The Paddling Center in Kissimmee.

- **Wheelchair Vans of America:** Has specially-equipped vans for hire for wheelchair users (1800 910 8267 or 407 674 8769, **www.wheelchairvansofamerica.com**).

 **BRITTIP**

'We used CARE Medical Equipment to hire a charger for our electric wheelchair as the 110v currency in the US does not work with a chair's 220v charging needs. They delivered to our villa within an hour and even stayed to make sure it worked. Some UK battery chargers will work but not all, so please check before you leave.' – Reader Lisa Smith, County Durham

- **CARE Medical Equipment:** Another company highly recommended for sale, rent or repair of powered scooters and wheelchairs and other medical equipment (407 856 2273, **www.caremedicalequipment.com**).

The excellent AllEars website has a big section on advice for a whole range of concerns, from children with ADD to vegetarian and vegan food. Visit **http://allears.net/pl/special.htm**.

Orlando for grown-ups

You don't need to have kids in tow to enjoy Orlando. There is so much clever detail and imagination, adults usually get the most out of the experience.

In fact, as many couples and singles visit the parks as do families with children. Certainly, when you look at the entertainment at Disney Springs and CityWalk and the great range of bars and fine restaurants, it is easy to see the attraction for those 21 and over. As well as Florida being a key honeymoon destination, its friendly, sociable atmosphere is ideal for singles, while couples without children can also take advantage of late opening at the parks and clubs. Even better, the downtown area of the city of Orlando is coming back as a happening night-time venue, with a lot to recommend it for a lively evening out, and the Craft Beer scene is booming, with companies like Orlando Brewing Company offering great ways to sample it (see p304).

 **BRITTIP**

If you have a fridge in your hotel, put drink cartons in the freezer overnight and they will be cool for much of the next day in your back-pack. Better still, buy a cheap coolbag, freeze it with some water bottles in, and leave it in the car – great after a day in the parks.

Lombard's Seafood Grille at Universal

© Universal Orlando Resort

Orlando for seniors

Mature travellers can also benefit from a healthy dose of the Sunshine State, as they are likely to have just as much fun, just within slightly different parameters. Seniors can also take advantage of numerous discounts and special deals for their age group at many attractions, plus restaurants and hotels. The official Visitor Center on I-Drive (p40) publishes a brochure of all the deals.

Hotels: For the older person, staying in a Disney hotel is highly recommended as it removes the stress of driving. The extra cost is offset by the convenience and relaxation factor.

Parks: There is still plenty to do here, even if the thrill rides are not a draw – just watching can be entertainment enough! Both Epcot and Disney's Animal Kingdom have much to engage the older visitor, while the shows of Disney's Hollywood Studios make that a popular choice, too, and the Magic Kingdom, while a bit hectic, is still an essential experience.

Evenings: Disney Springs area can feel a bit frenetic for the senior crowd, but the Boardwalk Resort is popular and the whole Epcot resort area offers much in the way of fine dining and relaxation. It is often a prime area for seniors, notably the quieter Disney's Yacht and Beach Club Resorts, and Swan-Dolphin complex.

Attractions: We also highlight the following for the senior age group.

- **Animal Kingdom:** Kilimanjaro Safaris, the Maharajah Jungle Trek, Pangani Forest Trail, Finding Nemo show, Rivers of Light and Festival of the Lion King.

- **Disney's Hollywood Studios:** Jim Henson's Muppet Vision 3-D, Great Movie Ride, Indiana Jones Stunt Show, Beauty and the Beast, Launch Bay, Stars Wars: A Galactic Spectacular and Fantasmic!.

- **Epcot:** Spaceship Earth, Soarin', Universe of Energy, all of World Showcase and IllumiNations (plus the superb gardens and architecture).

- **Magic Kingdom:** The Haunted Mansion, Jungle Cruise, Pirates of the Caribbean, Mickey's PhilharMagic and Festival of Fantasy Parade.

- **Universal Studios and Islands of Adventure:** The amazing Wizarding Worlds of Harry Potter.

- **Others:** Watching the children at the many parades and character greetings; dinner at the California Grill in Disney's Contemporary Resort (and other fine dining locations); shopping at Orlando Premium Outlets.

- **More options:** SeaWorld remains hugely popular for seniors and even Busch Gardens, despite its many roller-coasters, has plenty to offer. The local Segway Tours (in Kissimmee, Mount Dora, St Petersburg, Port Canaveral and Clearwater Beach) are highly recommended, while Mount Dora and Winter Park (see also Chapter 8) are also perfect senior fare.

Weather: Mar and late Oct/Nov are ideal times to visit, but the summer months are hard going for older folks. Good coats (and gloves) may still be necessary at times in winter.

You've got mail

You won't find many post boxes and some post offices don't seem to know the fees for postage to the UK. All the parks have post boxes and you can get stamp books from most stamp machines and City Hall at the Magic Kingdom. A standard postcard or greetings card in an envelope to the UK both need a $1.15 stamp; standard postage within the US is 47c.

The main post offices are:

- **Disney area:** 10450 Turkey Lake Road (just north of the junction of Palm Parkway and Central Florida Parkway; 8am–7pm Mon–Fri, 9am–5pm Sat).

- **Kissimmee:** 1415 W Oak Street (8.30am–5pm Mon–Fri, 9am–2pm Sat).

There is also a small post office inside the **Mall at Millenia**, off the lower level of the Grand Court.

American-speak

Many words and phrases have a different meaning across the Atlantic. For instance, when Americans say the first floor, they mean the ground floor, the second floor is really the first, and so on. (NB: NEVER ask for a packet of fags; 'fag' is a crude, slang term for a homosexual.) Here are a few everyday words to help you:

American	English	American	English
ATM	Cash machine	Faucet	Tap
Appetizer	Starter	Fender	Car bumper
Band aid	Plaster	Freeway	Motorway
Bathroom	Private toilet	Fries	Chips
Biscuit	Savoury scone	Gas	Petrol
Broiled	Grilled	Graham cracker	Digestive biscuit
Cellphone	Mobile phone	Hood	Car bonnet
Check	Bill	Intersection	Junction
Chips	Crisps	Nickel	5 cents
Collect call	Reverse charge phone call	No standing	No parking OR stopping
Cookie	Biscuit	'Pound sign'	The # on a phone keypad
Cot/rollaway	Fold-up bed	Purse	Handbag
Crib	Cot	Quarter	25 cents
Diaper	Nappy	Ramp	Slip road
Dime	10 cents	Restroom	Public toilet
Divided highway	Dual carriageway	Seltzer	Soda water
Eggplant	Aubergine	Shrimp	King prawn
Eggs 'over easy'	Eggs fried on both sides but soft	Soda	Fizzy drink
		Stroller	Pushchair
Eggs 'sunny side up'	Eggs fried on just 1 side (soft)	Trunk	Car boot
		Turn-out	Lay-by
Entrée	Main course	Yield	Give way
Facecloth/washcloth	Flannel	Zucchini	Courgette

Wedding bells

Florida is a popular choice for couples wanting to tie the knot. Its almost guaranteed sunshine and lush, natural landscape make it a huge hit as a wedding backdrop. Orlando also has terrific services, co-ordinators and venues like Wild Florida, Cypress Grove Estate House, Winter Park wedding chapel, Casa Feliz, Leu Gardens, Ceviche in downtown Orlando and hotels like Rosen Shingle Creek, Walt Disney World Swan and Dolphin and the Omni Orlando Champions Gate. Even scenic golf courses such as Celebration Golf Club and Grand Cypress can stage grand occasions extremely well. More unusual ones include the Hard Rock Café, a hot-air balloon or helicopter, Danville B&B (p262), on the beach or a luxury yacht, or even on the new Orlando Eye ride. All the tour operators feature wedding options and services, or you can pick a local specialist like Get Married In Florida (see below). Prices vary from around £300/couple (for a basic civil ceremony) to more than £5,000.

BRITTIP

Looking for essential travel accessories and useful knick-knacks, like TSA-approved locks, plug adapters and waterproof accessories? Type in **essentials4travel** on Amazon. Asda supermarkets also sell a good travel range.

Walt Disney World's Wedding Pavilion: True fairytale romance, with the backdrop of Cinderella Castle, you can opt for traditional elegance in this Victorian setting with up to 260 guests or the full Disney experience, arriving in Cinderella's coach with Mickey and Minnie as guests. Disney's wedding planners can tailor-make the occasion for you (407 828 3400) but at a price – rates START at $5,000 for the basic ceremony and can top $60,000!

Licence: To obtain a marriage licence, visit a local courthouse: Osceola County Courthouse, Courthouse Square, Suite 2000, Kissimmee (just off Bryan Street in downtown Kissimmee) 8am–4pm Mon–Fri (407 343 3500); Orange County Courthouse, 425 N Orange Avenue (downtown Orlando) 7.30am–4pm Mon–Fri (407 836 2067); or Clermont Courthouse at Minneola City Hall, 800 North Highway 27, Minneola, 8.30am–4.30pm (closed noon–1pm; 352 394 2018). All are closed on US bank holidays. Both parties must be present to apply for a licence, which costs $93.50 (in cash, travellers' cheques or by credit card) and is valid for 60 days, while a ceremony (equivalent to a British register office) can be performed at the same time by the clerk for an extra $20. You'll need passports, birth certificates and, if you have been married before, your decree absolute. After acquiring a licence, a couple can marry anywhere in Florida. It is also possible to obtain a licence BEFORE arriving in Florida (see **www.floridamarriagelicencebypost. com**). For flowers and floral design, be

Top 10 romantic restaurants

1 Tchoup Chop, Universal's Royal Pacific Resort
2 California Grill, Disney's Contemporary Resort
3 Todd English's bluezoo, Walt Disney World Dolphin Resort
4 Jiko, Disney's Animal Kingdom Lodge
5 Capa, Four Seasons Orlando
6 Old Hickory Steakhouse, Gaylord Palms Resort
7 Bice, Universal's Portofino Bay Hotel
8 Cala Bella, Shingle Creek Resort
9 Narcoossee's, Disney's Grand Floridian Resort
10 Urbain 40, Sand Lake Road

We could actually list several dozen more, including Hillstone, Luma on Park and The Bistro on Park Avenue (Winter Park), Bull & Bear (Waldorf-Astoria), Norman's (Ritz-Carlton), The Venetian Room (Caribe Royale Resort), Seasons 52, Eddie V's and Roy's (Sand Lake Road), and Kres Chophouse, Ceviche and The Boheme (downtown Orlando).

sure to look up Flourish on 407 601 4948 or **www.flourishproductions.com**.

Get Married in Florida: This local business has been dedicated to organising weddings for UK couples since 2002. Ideally placed to deliver great personal service, it offers the complete package for the perfect wedding (321 945 1563, **www.getmarriedinflorida.com**).

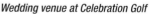

Wedding venue at Celebration Golf

Top things to do for FREE!

Disney's Boardwalk Resort: Free nightly entertainment includes jugglers, comedians and live music. Time your visit to coincide with the 9pm IllumiNations fireworks extravaganza at nearby Epcot.

Downtown Concert Series: Four times a year, local radio station WMMO stages free open-air concerts in front of City Hall with the likes of Peter Frampton and Blues Traveler. Great day out, with festival atmosphere (**www.wmmo.com/s/dcs/**).

Downtown Orlando Historic Tour: From the Visitor Center on Orange Avenue, local historian Richard Forbes leads a free tour of downtown at 9.30am on the first Fri of every month from Oct–May. Must call in advance to check availability on 407 246 3789 (**http://downtownorlando.com**).

Lake Eola Park: Take a walk on the mild side in downtown Orlando. The kids can play or feed the swans and summer sees live music at the Walt Disney Amphitheater; **www.cityoforlando.net/parks/lake-eola-park/**

Lake Tibet-Butler Preserve: Just 5mins from Disney but a world away from the theme park bustle (on local highway 535, Winter Garden-Vineland Road) is this local nature preserve, with quiet trails, lake overlook and interpretive centre. Open 9am–dusk (not public holidays), it is on the Great Florida Birding Trail and is a minor gem of native wildlife; **www.sfwmd.gov**.

Lakeridge Winery and Vineyards: Join one of its fun, free wine-tasting tours and you'll know why Lakeridge (in nearby Clermont) has won more than 700 awards. Designate a driver as sample sizes are generous! 10am–5pm Mon–Sat, 11am–5pm Sun (**www.lakeridgewinery.com**).

Morse Museum of American Art: This superb little museum in tranquil Winter Park, dedicated to American paintings, ceramics and representative arts from the 19th and 20th centuries, is free 4–8pm every Fri, Nov–Apr (**www.morsemuseum.org**).

Old Town, Kissimmee: The biggest vintage car parade in the US every Sat, with cars on display from 1pm and the Classic Car Cruise at 8.30pm, plus a Muscle Car Cruise 8.30pm each Fri and Show 'N Shine each Sun with trucks, jeeps and SUVs, and live music 5–9pm (**https://myoldtownusa.com/**).

Osceola County History Museum: Part of the new Welcome Center on Highway 192 in Kissimmee (by Marker 15), this offers a great insight into the region's back story and heritage (**www.osceolahistory.org**; see also p257; closed on public hols).

PLUS: Watching the participants at iFLY Orlando on I-Drive (p234); the Cornell Fine Arts Museum at Rollins College in Winter Park (p247); and the hiking trails of Ocala National Forest, north of Orlando (**www.stateparks.com/Ocala.html**).

BRITTIP

Looking for a good pay-as-you-go mobile option for the USA? Check out Three and their £15 add-on option: **www.three.co.uk/Discover/Phones/Feel_At_Home**.

Disney special occasions

Birthday badges: Get free badges from City Hall in the Magic Kingdom and Guest Services at Epcot, Disney's Hollywood Studios and Disney's Animal Kingdom. Cast Members make a fuss over children (and adults!) wearing a birthday badge.

Birthday cakes: Contact room service at your resort or Guest Services at one of the parks. All Disney restaurants can offer ready-made 15cm/6in cakes ($25 at each restaurant) or something larger ($55–380) if ordered 48 hours in advance on 407 827 2253. If someone in your group has a birthday, tell the Cast Member at check-in (or when you make your reservation), as well as hostesses and/or servers in restaurants. While not guaranteed, Disney staff often go out of their way to make the day special. If characters know it's a birthday when they sign a child's autograph book, they may add a special birthday wish.

Birthday cruise: The IllumiNations Celebration Cruise (to Epcot) provides snacks, drinks, streamers and balloons for a 90min tour, for up to 10, from Disney's Yacht and Beach Club Resort marina for $375 (407 939 7529).

Disney's Pirate Adventure: This two-hour activity for kids 4–12 sails (on pontoon boats) from four of the resorts (Grand Floridian, Yacht/Beach Club, Port Orleans and Caribbean Beach at 9.30am) to find pirate 'booty' at different ports of call, with a final stop for lunch; $37 per child (407 939 7529, up to 180 days in advance).

Money matters

You'll need to carry ID for both cheques and some credit card purchases (take your UK driving licence card).

Cash: It is worth separating larger notes from smaller ones in your wallet to avoid flashing all your money in view. Losing £300 of travellers' cheques shouldn't ruin your holiday – but losing $600 in cash might. All the theme parks have ATMs (cash machines).

Credit cards: Having a credit card is almost essential (especially for car hire) as they are accepted everywhere and provide extra buying security. Visa,

The Grinch at Universal

© Universal Orlando Resort

Mastercard and American Express are all widely accepted.

FairFX card: Perhaps the best option is this convenient card, which you preload to a chosen amount (**www.fairfx.com**). The exchange rate is fixed at loading and you can save 5–10% on High Street currency rates.

Travellers' cheques: Dollar travellers' cheques can be used as cash almost everywhere (though a few places, like Golden Corral restaurants, no longer accept them) and can be replaced if lost or stolen, so it is not necessary (or advisable) to carry lots of cash. Sterling travellers' cheques can be cashed only in major banks.

Safety and security

While crime is not a serious issue in Florida, this is still big-city America. Tourism is such a vital part of the economy, the authorities have a highly safety-conscious attitude. Just don't ignore the usual safety guidelines for travelling abroad.

BRITTIP

For your journey to the US, use a business rather than your home address on your luggage. It is less conspicuous and safer should any item be lost or stolen.

Common-sense tips: A bumbag (Americans say 'fanny pack'!) is better than a handbag or shoulder bag in the parks, and make sure bags are always firmly zipped up when not in use. Don't leave camera equipment on view in the car (especially as the heat could damage it anyway).

The VERY strong police advice in the unlikely event of being confronted by

Christmas cheer

We're often asked our favourite time of year here and it has to be the festive season, from late Nov–1 Jan. Every park adds a fab Christmas overlay and there is more to enjoy everywhere, even at the smaller attractions and places like Disney Springs and the town of Celebration. It can get seriously crowded 20 Dec–4 Jan, but visit in early Dec and you get all the festivities with fewer crowds.

Walt Disney World: Every park has its own extensive decorations and magnificent Christmas tree, with a daily lighting ceremony at the **Magic Kingdom**, plus Mickey's Once Upon A Christmastime Parade, the Castle Dream Lights (a stunning effect on Cinderella Castle) and the chance to meet Santa, as well as the extra-ticket event of Mickey's Very Merry Christmas Party (p116). At **Epcot**, the standout feature is the Candlelight Processional, a choral retelling of the Christmas story with a guest narrator, as well as Holidays Around The World, with traditional storytellers at each World Showcase pavilion. Mrs and Mrs Claus visit at the American Adventure pavilion, where vocal group Voices of Liberty become carollers for the season. The nightly IllumiNations show also has a special Yule finale. **Disney Springs** features the Spirit of the Season, with Santa's chalet, school choirs and more lavish decorations. Each resort also boasts plenty of Christmas cheer, with the best being Disney's Grand Floridian, offering a life-size Gingerbread House.

Universal Orlando: Miles more garland, lights and tinsel are on offer here, plus two daily features. At **Universal Studios**, Macy's Holiday Parade is the highlight, a fabulous cavalcade of floats, giant balloons, Father Christmas (and his Rockette-style dancers!) and a tree-lighting ceremony at dusk each day, as well as strolling carollers, hot cocoa kiosks and a Christmas Village of traditional fare and gifts. **Islands of Adventure** offers Christmas Dr Seuss style, with Grinchmas all around Seuss Landing, including the epic, family-friendly stage show of *The Grinch Who Stole Christmas*, and a Grinch & Friends character breakfast.

SeaWorld: Arguably the biggest Christmas celebration is here, with magnificent shows, special effects and extravagant theming. It starts with a Polar Express makeover for the Wild Arctic ride and continues with the Sea of Trees, an eye-catching sequence of well-lit 'trees' spread over the main lagoon. A Christmas Marketplace highlights one end of the park, while 2 unmissable seasonal shows are Winter Wonderland On Ice and O Wondrous Night, a nativity tale with a difference. Both the Shamu and Sea-Lion shows have their own festive additions, and nightly 'snowfalls', dancers, musicians and the Christmas Celebration fireworks round out a glittering seasonal occasion.

Busch Gardens: The highlight here is Christmas Town, another after-dark spectacular throughout the park, with themed areas, shows and decorations (each Fri, Sat and Sun from late Nov/early Dec, and nightly from mid-Dec). Highlights include the Carol of the Bells, an Ice Show, the Three Kings Journey and a lavish array of seasonal dining and shopping, plus Santa's 'North Pole' home and some more superb lighting effects.

Gaylord Palms Resort: equally astounding is their annual ICE! exhibition, a mind-boggling presentation of 2 MILLION pounds of ice in marvellous tableaux, hand-carved by 40 Chinese artisans in the special 'Florida Freezer,' including 4 huge ice slides. There are festive presentations, shows, musicians, trees, kids' activities, character meet-and-greets from Dreamworks and the chance to meet Santa, making for an amazing Christmas offering. Book in advance, though, at **www.marriott.com/hotels/travel/mcogp-gaylord-palms/**

Celebration: This pretty Disney-inspired town offers nightly 'snow-falls' 6–9pm on Market Street in Dec and also features ice-skating for kids, horse-drawn carriage rides, carollers and other festive touches.

And more: downtown Orlando is well worth a visit for its many festive touches, notably around **Lake Eola**, which has Christmas trees, ice-skating and the nightly Holiday Lights show. The child-sized fun of **LEGOLAND Florida** boasts a superb array of decorations and the daily Tree Lighting, while all the dinner shows add in suitably festive theming and extra Christmas elements. One final amazing event is staged at the huge First Baptist Church on John Young Parkway just off I-4, where The Singing Christmas Trees is a stunning choral show presentation of music, stage and lighting each Fri, Sat and Sun for the first two weeks in Dec. Find out more at **www.firstorlando.com/worship/singing_trees**.

an assailant is: DO NOT resist or 'have a go', because this can often make a bad situation worse. However, it is comforting to know Orlando does not have any no-go areas in the main tourist parts. The nearest is the portion of the Orange Blossom Trail south of downtown Orlando (a selection of strip clubs and 'adult bars' that can be downright seedy) and the Parramore area south-west of downtown.

Hotel security: While in your hotel, always use door peepholes and security chains when someone knocks at the door. DON'T open the door to strangers without asking for identification, and check with the hotel desk if you are still not sure. It is stating the obvious, but keep doors and windows locked and always use deadlocks and security chains. Take cash, credit cards, valuables and car keys when you go out (or put them in the room safe), and don't leave the door open, even if you just pop down the corridor to the ice machine.

Most hotels now have electronic card-locks for extra security and can offer deposit boxes in addition to the standard in-room mini-safes. Don't be afraid to ask reception staff for safety advice for surrounding areas or if you are travelling somewhere you are not sure about. Safety is a major issue for the Central Florida Hotel & Lodging Association (**www.cfhla.org**) and hotel staff are well briefed to be helpful.

◀▚ BRITTIP

If your room has already been cleaned before you go out for the day, hang the 'Do Not Disturb' sign on the door. Always keep your valuables out of sight, whether in the hotel or the car.

Portofino Bay Hotel

Car safety: Make the basic safety checks of your hire car straight away and familiarise yourself with the car's controls BEFORE driving away. Try to memorise your route in advance, even if it's only a case of knowing the road numbers. Most hire firms now give good directions to all the hotels, so check them before you set off (or, better still, hire a GPS system). Make sure the fuel tank is well filled and never let it get near empty so you risk running out of 'gas' in an unfamiliar area. If you do stray off your pre-determined route, stick to well-lit areas and ask for directions only from official businesses like hotels and petrol stations, or the police. Try to park close to your destination where there are plenty of lights and DO NOT get out if there are suspicious characters around. Don't forget to lock the car when you leave it – and note that not all rental cars have central locking.

More info: For more info on safety, contact the Orange County Police (407 254 7000 or **www.ocso.com**) or the I-Drive police team office (407 351 9368). If you are the victim of theft in Orange County, call 407 836 4357.

Emergencies

Emergency services: For police, fire department or ambulance, dial 911 (9-911 from your hotel room). Make sure your children know this number.

General: For smaller-scale crises (e.g. mislaid tickets, lost passports or rescheduled flights), your holiday company should have an emergency contact number in the hotel reception.

Independent travellers: If you run into passport or other problems that need help from the British Consulate, its main office is now at 1001 Brickell Bay Drive, Miami, Florida 33131 on 305 300 6400, but there is still a small office in downtown Orlando offering consular services, such as lost documents and aid for those hospitalised or arrested and detained, on 407 254 3300 (**www.gov.uk/ government/world/usa**).

You'll find masses of info on all things Orlando on the discussion forums

Let us take the stress out of your holiday ...

...with our unique Touring Plans

The *Brit Guide* Touring Plans will ensure you get the most out of your time in central Florida. This is a service no one else can offer, as we provide you with daily touring plans for the parks, attractions and shopping in central Florida.

Your full Touring Plan (which usually runs to 40 pages for a 2-week holiday) will: walk you through your day so you make the most of your time and your tickets; highlight any rides that may be closed for refurbishment; include shopping guides if you plan to take advantage of all the savings to be had at the malls and outlets; provide key advice right from the source of the fun, as well as a host of Brit Tip Extras and Brit Picks (our special favourites) we can't fit into the book, plus a special Busy Day Guide for your visit. Just go to **www.britguideorlando.net** and click Touring Plans.

Fill out the online form with your travel dates, choose the type of Plan you need (be sure to see our FAQ to help you decide which Plan is right for you), and indicate which parks/shopping/etc you want to fit into your visit. Submit the form, with your payment, and you'll receive, by email, your unique Touring Plan, which will consist of:

1   An official *Brit Guide* welcome from Susan and Simon Veness.

2   A daily plan for each of the parks, water parks and shopping centres you will visit.

3   Touring strategies in each day's plan to help you avoid the longest queues and take advantage of the latest developments.

4   Alternative suggestions in case of bad weather.

5   A note of any rides/shows that are closed during your visit (please see our FAQ for further info).

6   A special selection of Brit Tip Extras and local advice.

7   Our Brit Picks – a guide to a range of personal favourites, from restaurants to shops.

8   The ultimate insider knowledge, as Susan and Simon are based in the heart of the Orlando magic and are fully up to date on all developments.

9   Our special bonus: an EXCLUSIVE Platinum VIP Passport for Orlando Premium Outlets (not available to the public), with extra savings at select stores at this great shopping venue.

10 Best of all, you will receive a Busy Day Guide especially for your holiday dates so that you can assemble the best possible day-by-day plan.

All in all, it adds up to the most comprehensive package of specialised holiday info anywhere, and it represents the secret to the most fun, in the most hassle-free way, in the most exciting place on earth. What more could you ask for? Just check out our website and we'll do the rest.

Please note: There is a minimum order period, so check online and apply in good time before your holiday (*at least* 10 days). Book owners receive a discount on the price of the Touring Plans, so have it with you when you register as you'll need a password from the book.

The password is random and expires on 31 Dec of the edition's year, NO EXCEPTIONS. We are not a travel agency or ticket service and you MUST know your park and shopping requirements in advance.

We urge you to read our FAQ before ordering, as it will assist you in choosing the right plan for your holiday, answer the most common questions we receive, and ensure you order with confidence.

at **www.attraction-tickets-direct.co.uk** and, as we are both Moderators on the site, you can come and 'talk' to us and pass on your own ideas and experiences. It's a fun, friendly community and we're always happy to see new faces.

Know before you go

Here are the best sources for additional info before you go.

* **Kissimmee:** More useful online info and an e-guide to download on this link, **http://bit.ly/ExpKissMag**, plus the UK website **www. experiencekissimmee.com/uk/**.

* **Fan websites:** An ever-growing choice, try any of the **www.thedibb. co.uk** ('Disney with a British accent'), the fully comprehensive **www.allears. net** (notably for its Disney dining section) and **www.wdwinfo.com**.

* **Orlando Attractions mag:** (which we also write for) offers a superb website full of features and videos at **www. attractionsmagazine.com**, plus a weekly magazine-style programme called *The Show*.

* **Orlando Sentinel:** The online local paper (**www.orlandosentinel.com**) is packed with info, especially for shopping, dining and nightlife, while the **Orlando Weekly** is also handy (**www.orlandoweekly.com**).

* **Orlando Visitor Center:** It's worth checking Orlando's ONLY official Visitor Center, 8.30am– 6.30pm daily at 8723 International Drive (407 363 5872 or email **info@ visitorlando. com**) for discounted attraction tickets, and free brochures, accommodation advice, info pamphlets and maps.

* **Visit Florida:** Offers a free info pack, as well as many online e-brochures (01737 644 882, **www.visitflorida.com/en-uk.html**).

* **Visit Orlando:** has a 24hr info line, plus a website where you order its free Holiday Planning kit (0800 018 6760, **www.visitorlando.com/en-gl/uk/**).

Don't Visit Florida Without Seeing Florida

Central Florida is an amazing place (it's one of the reasons we live here) but it's not all about the theme parks. Venture beyond the main tourist areas and you'll discover the *real* Florida, which is bursting with great scenery and wildlife. It's not hard to see alligators, deer, raccoons, armadillos and even bobcats in the wild. There are also panthers, bears, wild pigs and foxes. The exotic birdlife includes eagles, ospreys, herons, cranes and egrets, and the waterways boast manatees, dolphins, rays and dozens of types of fish. Chapters 8 and 9 highlight all the ways to discover these great opportunities and we urge readers to seek out at least one to experience what truly makes Florida special. There are dozens of state parks and wildlife preserves and, increasingly, nature tours and trails to enjoy them. There is also more history – dating back to the 16th century – than you'd imagine, plus fabulous museums and other cultural aspects. Florida had cowboys (or 'crackers') before the Wild West and is still a huge cattle-producing state. Cute towns and suburbs like Gulfport, Mount Dora, Winter Park and Tarpon Springs abound, while the beaches are simply superb – everywhere. The varied tropical terrain boasts lakes, marshes, cypress forests, sandhills, flatwoods and prairies, and is about as different to most European landscapes as it's possible to get. It all adds up to way more than you thought when you decided Orlando was the place for you – just make sure you see some of it!

Now, on to the next step of the holiday, your transport….

Gulf Coast beach

3 Getting Around

or The Secret of Driving on the Wrong Side of the Road!

Arriving and driving in Orlando are among the biggest concerns for visitors, especially first-timers, but there's no need to worry. Although most people begin their holiday by leaving the airport in a newly acquired, automatic, left-hand-drive hire car on roads that can appear bewildering, driving here is a lot easier and more enjoyable than in the UK. Anyone familiar with the M25 should find Florida FAR less stressful.

Before you get to your hire car, though, you need to be aware of the arrival process at the two airports.

BRITTIP
Don't forget you must have filled in your ESTA form and immigration details online before you travel (see p12). For country of residence put UNITED KINGDOM; for Passport Issuing Country, put UK – BRITISH CITIZEN. You must give a valid US address for your accommodation.

Orlando International
This is one of the most modern and enjoyable airports in the world, but anywhere new can be confusing. All flights arrive at one of four satellite terminals and you then take a shuttle tram to the main terminal. Allow at least an hour from landing to ground transportation.

International arrivals: If you arrive with British Airways, Virgin Atlantic or Thomas Cook, you disembark at the satellite for Gates 70–99. With Aer Lingus or Norwegian, it is 1–29. Join one of the two main queues that feed into the immigration kiosks. Once through Immigration, collect your baggage from the carousel and go through the Customs check. The airport now has a series of self-service kiosks where you input your flight info and passport details, fingerprints and photo before reaching the Immigration officer, which can save considerable time. Just follow the instructions and take your receipt, with your passports and customs form, to the officer.

BRITTIP
Visit www.orlandoairports.net for a photo preview of the arrival process at Orlando International Airport (click *Getting Around MCO*, then *Airport Guide*, followed by *Arrival & Departure Guides*, and *International Arrival Guide*) and other info.

Option 1: Deposit your checked luggage on a second conveyor belt to take it to the main terminal while you go upstairs to the shuttle with your hand luggage. Once in the main terminal you are on Level 3 and you follow signs down to Baggage Claim B on Level 2 (BA and Thomas Cook), Baggage Claim A on Level 2 (Aer Lingus and Norwegian) or Baggage Claim A Level 1 (Virgin).

Option 2: If you can manage your luggage without a trolley, take it on the escalator up to the shuttle and go straight to pick up your transport on Level 1 (or, if a specific driver is meeting you, Level 2).

Domestic arrivals: For anyone arriving on a US domestic flight (from another US gateway), you disembark at the satellite terminal and proceed straight to the main terminal on the shuttle to collect your baggage on Level 2 (either A or B side, depending on arrival gate). Once at the main baggage claim, porters can help you to Level 1 (tip $1/bag) for car hire, shuttles and buses. Trolleys need $3 in change (or a credit card).

BRITTIP

The biggest change in Orlando International is the automated arrivals process (p41) and the number of car hire firms on site instead of needing a shuttle bus. There will be more changes as construction is under way on a South Terminal.

Transfers: Kerbside pick-up is outside the doors on Level 2, either at the bottom of the escalators or by your baggage reclaim. Several tour operators have help desks here, too, while Virgin has a reception desk on Level 1.

The public bus system, Lynx (p44), operates ONLY from the A side of Level 1 (6am–10.30pm; 9.30pm on Suns and public holidays), in spaces 38–41. Links 11 and 51 depart every 30mins (less often on Sun or bank holidays) for Orlando city centre (45mins), while Link 42 serves

Atlas V rocket launch at Kennedy Space Center

© Kennedy Space Center

I-Drive (1hr) and Link 111 goes to the SeaWorld via the Florida Mall.

Car hire: All the main hire companies are on site (with 19 off-airport). The main 10 to choose from include *Brit Guide* partner **Alamo** (with new automated self-service kiosks), **Dollar**, **National**, **Thrifty**, **Hertz** and **Avis**, and all offer a full service. Complete your paperwork, then walk out of Level 1 across the road to the multi-storey car park.

If you arrive late, consider staying overnight at the Hyatt Regency hotel at the airport rather than driving tired. You will be fresher and ready to drive next day (and the car hire queues will be shorter). Several tour operators also offer an arrival-day transfer, with car hire pick-up the next day.

BRITTIP

If you are hiring a car from one of the on-airport companies, save time by sending the driver to complete the paperwork BEFORE collecting your luggage on Level 2.

Leaving the airport: When you drive out of the airport, DON'T follow signs to 'Orlando'. The main tourist areas are south and west of the city, so follow the signs for your accommodation.

The Martin Andersen Beachline Expressway (528) and Greeneway (417) are both toll roads, so make sure you have some US currency before leaving the airport. Toll booths hate to change notes above $20, while some auto-tolls take ONLY coins.

- **For International Drive:** (I-Drive), take the north exit and the Beachline Expressway (Route 528) west until it crosses I-Drive just north of SeaWorld at exit 1 (it costs $2.25 in toll fees). Most hotels on I-Drive are to the north, so keep right at the exit. NB: there is now only one toll kiosk on this route but the fee is still $2.25.

- **For Kissimmee, Disney and villas in Clermont/Davenport:** Take the south exit for 3ml/5km and pick up the Central Florida Greeneway (Highway 417) west.

Florida Rail

Considering Florida was originally opened up by railways in the late 1800s by railroad baron Henry Flagler, travelling by rail hasn't been a modern option, until recently. Central Florida's commuter rail system **Sunrail** arrived in 2014 and, while it is mainly for locals, it offers a few possibilities as it runs over a 32ml/50km, 12-station stretch from east Sand Lake Rd (at S Orange Ave) north to DeBary. A 17ml/27km southern extension, to Poinciana via Kissimmee, is due for completion in early 2018. From Sand Lake Rd station, it runs north to downtown Orlando (three stations, including Church St Station) and up to Winter Park. However, it ONLY operates Mon–Fri, every 30mins in peak periods and every 2hrs otherwise, 5.30am–10pm. Fares are modest ($3.75/adult for a round-trip from Sand Lake Rd to Winter Park while an unlimited seven-day weekly SunCard is $34) and tickets can be bought in machines at each station using cash or credit card. Just tap your ticket on the validator machine on the platform before you board and at your destination. There are also Lynx bus connections at every Sunrail station, including Link 111 from SeaWorld and Link 42 from I-Drive to the Sand Lake Rd station. (**www.sunrail.com**).

Starting in late 2017, **Brightline** will be Florida's first high-speed rail link from Orlando to Miami (but initially just Miami to West Palm Beach). Orlando International Airport to downtown Miami will take just under 3hrs and feature the latest trains, two classes of travel and on-board comforts (including dining and free WiFi). Once complete, it will make the journey to Miami far more enticing, with day-trips from 16 departures each way every day. Check out **www.gobrightline.com** for the latest info.

- **For most Disney resorts:** Take exit 6 and follow the signs ($3 in tolls).
- **For Animal Kingdom resorts:** Use exit 3 and take Osceola Parkway west ($3.75).

BRITTIP
For traffic news and reports, tune to 96.5FM (WDBO) or **www.news965. com**. Call 511 on a mobile phone for motorway traffic info or **www.II511.com**.

- **For eastern Kissimmee:** Come off Highway 417 at exit 11, the Orange Blossom Trail (Highway 17/92), and go south ($2.25 in tolls).
- **For west Kissimmee and Clermont/ Davenport (Highway 27):** Take exit 2, turn right on Celebration Avenue and left (west) on Highway 192 all the way to Highway 27 (you will need $3.75 in toll fees).

Orlando Sanford International Airport

Arriving at Sanford (in Seminole County) couldn't be easier. The list of airlines visiting this easy-to-use airport includes Thomson Airways, TUI (to Amsterdam) and Jetairfly (Brussels). It generally takes only 30–40mins from arrival to leaving the baggage hall, but there may be delays in peak season. It's a short walk from the plane to the immigration hall (where two queues feed through to the kiosks); you then collect your baggage, pass through Customs and walk straight out to car hire, shuttle or taxi pick-up.

Car hire: As you exit the Customs Hall, the Thomson welcome desks are across the road in front of you, next to the Car Rental centre. The one exception is for *Brit Guide* partner Alamo, which has its own centre via a covered walkway and boardwalk behind this building, and its British-dedicated operation is very smooth. Look up more on **www.orlandosanfordairport.com**.

Leaving the airport: It may be 35ml/56km to the north and involve more driving (and taxis and shuttles are much more expensive – a town car service would be around $140

BRITTIP
Don't want to drive? Consider a multi-centre stay within Orlando itself, staying first at, say, I-Drive or Universal Orlando and then a Disney resort, to get the best of the free or cheap transport options.

one-way to Walt Disney World and a taxi $100, while one-way shuttle services are around $60/person), but you usually save time by your quicker exit. There is one main road out, on to Lake Mary Boulevard, and you then take Seminole Expressway (Highway 417, which becomes Central Florida Greeneway in Orange County) south. The slip road to this toll motorway is just under the flyover on your LEFT, and you need $8 to reach Disney or Kissimmee or $6.50 for I-Drive (via the Beachline Expressway). You can avoid the tolls by staying on Lake Mary Blvd for 6ml/10km until you get to I-4, but you're likely to hit traffic through the city. The Expressway/Greeneway is an easy-driving introduction to Orlando, even if it does cost a few dollars.

BRITTIP
If you suspect you may need more boot space, upgrade when you book at home as it is usually more expensive to upgrade when you arrive.

WITHOUT A CAR

Although being mobile is advisable, you can survive without a car. However, few attractions are within walking distance of hotels, and taxis can be expensive. You also need to plan in extra travelling time (and with children, taking buses can be tiring). For non-drivers, your best base is either Walt Disney World itself (free transport throughout, but harder to get to the rest of Orlando) or I-Drive for its location, 'walkability' and the great I-Ride Trolley. Many hotels have free shuttles to some of the parks or a cheap, regular mini-bus service. The main options are: public transport; shuttle services; town cars and limousines; and taxis.

BRITTIP
Although Disney has free and extensive transport services, it can be slow. Bus rides from many hotels to the parks can take a good 30mins while getting from Disney Springs to Animal Kingdom Lodge – the longest journey from one side to the other – takes more than 45mins.

Public transport

Lynx bus system: Reliable and cheap but slightly plodding, it covers much of metro Orlando. Its online system map shows all its routes (or 'links') and main attractions (407 841 5969, **www.golynx.com**).

- **Link 18:** Kissimmee to downtown Orlando (from Osceola Square Mall, east on Highway 192 north on Boggy Creek Road, Buenaventura and Orange Ave).
- **Link 38:** I-Drive to downtown Orlando (from the Convention Center via Kirkman Road and I-4).
- **Link 42:** Orlando International Airport to I-Drive.
- **Link 50:** Disney's Transportation & Ticket Center (TTC) to downtown Orlando (via SeaWorld and I-4).
- **Link 55:** Kissimmee to Four Corners (from Osceola Square Mall west via Highway 192 and Summer Bay Resort).
- **Link 56:** Kissimmee to Disney's Magic Kingdom (from Osceola Square Mall, along Highway 192 via Old Town and Celebration to TTC.
- **Link 300:** Disney Springs to downtown Orlando (via I-4).
- **Link 304:** Top of I-Drive to Disney Springs (from Oak Ridge Road via Sand Lake Drive).

BRITTIP
Lynx buses use the Disney Springs West Side Transfer Center as their Disney hub, with Links 301, 302, 303, 305 and 306 going to the parks and resorts.

Lynx fares are $2/ride (free transfers) or $16 for a weekly pass (children six and under free with a full-fare passenger). The service is every 30mins in the main areas, every 15mins 6–9am and 3.30–6.30pm, but you must have the right change. All buses are wheelchair accessible and stop at the pink paw-print Lynx stops.

There can be *long* bus queues at park closing. Taking a taxi can save a lot of hassle to return to I-Drive – about

Park Maps

Each of the park maps contains a QR code that you can scan with your smartphone or tablet to take you to a high-res online map. Download a QR reader from iTunes or Play Store.

$35 from Epcot and the Studios park; about $40 from Magic Kingdom and Animal Kingdom.

I-Ride Trolley: Great-value, two-route service along a 14ml/23km stretch of this tourist corridor.

- **The Main/Red Line:** 77 stops from Orlando Premium Outlets at the top of I-Drive to SeaWorld and Aquatica via Westwood Boulevard and Sea Harbor Drive, then Premium Outlets (Vineland Ave).

- **The Green Line:** 33 stops from the Universal resort (Windhover Drive and Major Boulevard) south to Orlando Premium Outlets via Universal Boulevard, the Convention Center and SeaWorld.

Every day, 8am–10.30pm roughly every 20mins (30mins on the Green Line), it costs $2/trip ($1/kids 3–9, 25c/seniors) – have the right change – or you can buy Unlimited Ride Passes for 1, 3, 5, 7 or 14 days at $5, $7, $9, $12, $18. If you need to transfer between routes, ask for a transfer coupon when you board (not needed with Unlimited Ride Passes). All trolleys have hydraulic wheelchair lifts. Buy a pass at 100+ locations in the I-Drive area, including the Official Visitor Center and most hotel desks, plus online, but NOT on the trolleys themselves (407 248 9590 or US freephone 1866 243 7483, **www.iridetrolley.com**).

Busch Shuttle Express: Seven departure points in this regular daily service, 8.15–9.40am, from SeaWorld to Busch Gardens.

It costs $10/person but is FREE if you have Busch tickets in advance (included in the FlexTicket Plus or 3-Park Ticket with SeaWorld and Aquatica). For more info, call 1800 221 1339 in Orlando toll-free.

BRITTIP

The cheapest way to get from I-Drive to Disney is the $2 Lynx bus Link 50 from SeaWorld – 6600 Sea Harbor Drive – to the TTC next to the Magic Kingdom. All Disney transport then operates from there. Use the I-Ride Trolley to get to SeaWorld.

Shuttle services

Alternatives to public transport are more than a dozen firms offering set-fee shuttles – from Hummers to buses – from hotels to attractions.

Florida Fun Shuttle: A range of attraction options, plus tours to St Augustine, Daytona and Cocoa Beach, and even winery, craft beer, kayaking, and sports trips. Also one-way visits to the beaches, with pick-ups a few days later, and Port Canaveral transfers (321 231 0005, **www.floridafunshuttle.com**).

Lake Buena Vista Factory Stores: Shuttle collects guests free each day from 60 hotels in the Orlando and Kissimmee areas (407 363 1093, or **www.lbvfs.com**).

Magic Shuttle: Services to and from both airports, all the main attractions, dinner shows, restaurants and even shopping services (407 402 4283, **www.magicshuttle.net**).

Maingate Transportation: From the Highway 192 area ($15 round-trip to Universal, $12 to SeaWorld and $11 to Disney parks; 407 390 0000, **www.maingatetaxi.com**).

Disney's monorail to the Magic Kingdom

© Hilary White

Mears: The most comprehensive service, with a 1,000-vehicle fleet from limousines to town cars and coaches. Typical round-trip shuttle fares: Airport to Walt Disney World, $37 adults, $28 under-12s, under-4s free ($23 and $18 one way); Airport to I-Drive, $33 and $25 ($21 and $16 one way); Airport to Highway 192 in Kissimmee, $49 and $38 ($29 and $23 one way); Walt Disney World to Universal Orlando, $21 round trip; I-Drive to Walt Disney World, $21; I-Drive or Walt Disney World to Kennedy Space Center, $37.

You can book a shuttle on arrival at the Mears' desks in the luggage halls, but it can be a longish trip if it has a full van stopping at several hotels before yours (407 423 5566, **www.mearstransportation.com**).

Excursions: There are also excursion services offered by *Brit Guide* partners Gray Line Orlando (407 522 5911, **http://graylineorlando.com**) and Florida Dolphin Tours (p266).

Town cars and limos
There's a huge choice (more than 150 at the last count), but the following all earn a *Brit Guide* recommendation:

◀🇬🇧 **BRITTIP**

With the abolition in 2015 of the old paper part of the UK driving licence, drivers are technically required to obtain an on-line code (from the DVLA website **www.gov.uk/view-driving-licence**) to show the rental company, if requested. It is highly unlikely any car hire company will ask for the code, or even the old paper part of the licence (*Brit Guide* partners Alamo say they will not require it for US rentals) but it is best to have it just in case.

FL Tours: This well-established and popular company specialises in both airport–Disney routes and Port Canaveral transfers. One-way trips start from $75 and round trips from $130 ($135 and $245 from Orlando Sanford), plus tip; it also offers a free 30min grocery stop, free kids' booster and car seats, 24-hour online reservation access, and no extra charge for late pick-ups (407 857 9606, **www.fltours.com**).

Quick Transportation: A good bet for airport transfers and tailor-made transport packages, its town cars comfortably cope with a family of four, while luxury vans cater for larger parties and all offer a 30min grocery stop for an extra $20. Up to 11 can use a van for a small additional fee per person. Larger parties may need a luggage trailer for $25 extra each way. It serves all the parks and attractions and offers online quotes for all services, while it can also supply vehicles for the disabled (407 354 2456 or 1888 784 2522, **www.quicktransportation.com**).

Sky Limousine: This company has one of the largest selections of vehicles, from Hummers and Lincolns to executive vans, offering airport transfers, group services and limo transport to parks and attractions. Other options cover much of central Florida, including cruise transfers, a night out, all-day services, beach trips, concerts and tailor-made excursions (407 352 4644, **www.skyorlando.com**).

Taxis

For groups of four or five, taxis can be more cost-effective than shuttles. Orlando International Airport to I-Drive would be around $45 (plus tip); $50–60 for the Kissimmee area; $65 to Magic Kingdom resorts and $60 for the Epcot resort area; $15–20 from I-Drive to Universal Orlando; and $30–40 from I-Drive to Disney Springs. You'll find plenty of taxis in ranks at the parks, hotels and shopping centres, but they do not cruise for fares. Outside those areas, you should pre-book. Reliable companies will clearly show the driver's ID, insurance and rates. It's illegal for drivers to look for fares in the baggage hall at Orlando Airport; all taxis will be on the rank on Level 1.

Most taxis are metered but you can ask in advance what the fare will be. Some hotels have town cars at their ranks and these won't have meters, so either ask for the fare or call one of the following reliable companies. **Mears**, who operate Checker Cabs Yellow Cabs and City Cabs (407 422 2222), are also the main taxi company for Orlando Sanford Airport (pre-book cabs for around $110 to I-Drive, $120 to Lake Buena Vista and $130 to Disney hotels); **Ace Metro Cab** (407 855 1111); **Star Taxis** (407 857 9999); or **Diamond Cab** (407 523 3333).

App-based ride-sharing services **Uber** and **Lyft** are both available in Orlando, with the usual caveat about prices varying with demand and drivers who are not licensed in the same way as taxi drivers. Look them up at **www.uber.com/cities/orlando/** and **www.lyft.com/cities/orlando**.

THE CAR

Ultimately, having a car is the key to being in charge of your holiday and, on a weekly basis, car hire tends to be reasonable: weekly rates can be as low as $120 for the smallest car. The scale of the car hire operation is huge, with as many as 1,000 visitors arriving at a time.

BRITTIP
Your first call for car hire should be to *Brit Guide* partner Alamo. See inside the front cover for our special offer.

The cars will be mainly American – Chevrolet, Dodge, Buick, plus international makes like Kia, Hyundai, Honda and Nissan.

- **Economy or Subcompact:** Usually a Vauxhall Corsa-sized hatchback.
- **Compact:** Small family saloon like a Nissan Versa.
- **Midsize or Intermediate:** 4-door, 5-seater like a Toyota Corolla.
- **Fullsize:** Larger-style executive car like a Ford Mondeo.
- **Premium, Luxury, Convertible, SUV and Minivan:** Upmarket options, while the Minivan is a Ford Galaxy or Renault Espace type.

Most holiday companies offer 'free car hire', but that doesn't mean it won't cost you anything. Only the rental cost is free and you must still pay the insurances and taxes (which makes the all-inclusive packages more attractive).

BRITTIP
Be firm with the car hire company check-in clerk, if they push you for extras, like car upgrades you won't need.

Also beware low starting rates – there are essential insurances, taxes and surcharges that can take the weekly rate above $300. However, all the big rental companies now offer all-inclusive rates, which can work out cheaper if booked in advance in the UK.

BRITTIP
Be sure to pick the right car for your group size – and luggage. You simply won't get seven people AND all their cases in a seven-seater van!

Car rental companies: Alamo is our *Brit Guide* partner and offers excellent rates and service (see inside back cover). You also benefit with Alamo from being able to choose your own car from the different ranges, where most other companies assign you a specific car. For alternatives, try Dollar (**www.dollar.co.uk**), Avis (**www. avis.co.uk**; 0808 284 0014), Budget (**www.budget.co.uk**, 0808 284 4444), or Thrifty (**www.thrifty.co.uk**), or try the comparison website **www.carrentals.co.uk**.

Insurance: Having a credit card is essential, and there are two main kinds of insurance, the most important being the Loss or Collision Damage Waiver (LDW or CDW). This costs $25–27/day and covers you for any damage to your hire car. You can do without it, but the hire company will insist on a deposit around $1,500 on your credit card (and you are liable for ANY damage). You will also be offered Liability Insurance Supplement (LIS) or Extended Protection at $12–15 a day, which is not essential but does cover you for most damage you might cause.

Another option is Underinsured Motorists Protection (in case someone with minimal cover runs into you) at around $8 a day.

Specialist insurance: You can cut costs by taking insurance through specialists like Insurance4CarHire (0844 892 1770, **www.insurance4carhire.com**), whose US and Canada cover offers up to 60 days' continuous rental, including CDW/LDW and LIS, for £109. **iCarHire Insurance** also features independent insurance, including CDW/LDW from £5.99/day (**www.icarhireinsurance.com**).

Other costs: Drivers must be at least 21, and those under 25 have to pay an extra $25 a day. Other costs include local and state taxes, plus Airport Access and 'Facility' fees, which can add more than $40 a week. Many companies also offer a Roadside Plus (around $5/day), which covers flat tyres, running out of fuel or locking your keys in the car, but again this is optional.

Fuel: 'Gas' is still cheaper than in the UK. You can either pre-pay for a full tank (so you bring it back empty; the charge is usually slightly under the local rate/gallon for this); fill it up yourself so you have a full tank on return; or pay a fuel surcharge at the end for the company to refill the tank (the most expensive option).

Pre-pay tolls: You can also opt for the SunPass auto-pay system for toll roads, so you just drive through without stopping; all your tolls are auto-recorded for payment when you return the car. It is called PlatePass and there is a flat-rate fee ($5–11/day, depending on the company, up to a maximum of $15–53/month). This is great for peace of mind but can be expensive unless you are using the toll roads *a lot*.

◀▓▶ BRITTIP

You must stop at the toll booths marked 'Change Given' (in green) or 'Exact Change Only' (in blue) unless you have accepted the SunPass pre-pay auto-toll option from the car rental firm, in which case, use 'Sunpass' or 'E-Pass'.

Enter Mapman

By far the best and most up-to-date area map is a British production, created by Disney fan and cartographer Steve 'Mapman' Munns, who is also our *Brit Guide* mapman. It is superbly detailed for the I-4 corridor, Highway 192, Highway 27 and Walt Disney World, with sections on I-Drive and villa locations. All the main attractions, hotels and restaurants are marked, with text and photos, with more detail on the website. A new edition was due in autumn 2016 and it's great value at £8 (plus p & p): **www.orlandomaps.co.uk**.

Getting used to your car

Most people soon find driving in America is a pleasure, mainly because nearly all hire cars are automatics and nearly all new. And, because speed limits are lower (and rigidly enforced), you won't often be rushed into taking a wrong turn.

- All cars have air-conditioning, which is essential for most of the year. Turn on the fan as well as the A/C button or it won't work! A small pool of liquid will form under the car from condensation.

- Power steering is universal.

- Larger cars have cruise control, so you can set the desired speed and take your foot off the accelerator. There will be two buttons on the steering wheel, one to switch on cruise control, the other to set the speed. To cancel, either press the first button or touch the brake.

- Some cars have an extra pedal to the left of the brake, which you need to push to engage the handbrake. To release it, pull the tab just above it, if there is one, or give a second push on the pedal.

- Keep your foot on the brake when you are stationary as automatics tend to creep forward. Always put the gear lever in 'P' (Park) when switching off.

- To start, put the gear in 'P' and depress the brake, then put in 'D' to

The satnav solution

The best way to navigate is by a GPS. All car hire companies offer this as an extra (at around $90/week) or you can bring your own. If your system has only the base-level (i.e. UK) maps loaded, download the maps for south-east USA for around £35. If you are thinking of buying a GPS system, the likes of Wal-Mart offer new systems, fully loaded for the US, for around $150.

The three Speedway stations in Walt Disney World are, surprisingly, among the cheapest, while the Wal-Mart on Vineland Road is also a cheaper option. Petrol stations just outside Disney and the airport are the most expensive.

Finding your way

Your car hire company should provide you with a basic map of Orlando, plus directions to your hotel.

BRITTIP

Be organised – get your directions in advance off the internet at sites like **www.mapquest.com** or use Google Earth to source maps, directions and even check out the lie of the land in advance. Download it free from its website at **http://earth.google.com**.

drive. D1 and D2 are extra gears for hills (none in Florida)!

- Not all cars have central locking, so make sure you lock ALL the doors before leaving it. With an automatic, you won't be able to take the keys out of the ignition unless you put the gear lever in 'Park'.

Fuel: All local gas stations are self-service and you usually pay before filling up. However, the pumps should allow you to pay by credit card without having to visit the cashier (some stations ask for a local zip code with a credit card swipe, which means you DO need to go inside). To activate the petrol pump, you may need first to lift the lever underneath the pump nozzle. RaceTrac and Speedway petrol stations are often the cheapest.

Signposting: You'll easily find the main attractions, but retracing your steps can be tricky as the exit road may be different from the way in. Familiarise yourself with the main roads in advance and learn to navigate by road numbers (given on the signposts), exit numbers off the main roads, and directions around the attractions (i.e. if you want I-4 east or west or 192 as you exit Walt Disney World).

Daytona Speedway

Lanes and exits: Exits off motorways can be on EITHER side of the carriageway, not just on the right, and you don't get much notice. You can overtake in ANY lane on multi-lane highways, so sit in the middle lane until you see your exit.

Road names: Around town, road names are displayed at every junction suspended ABOVE the road underneath the traffic lights. This road name is NOT the road you are on, but the one you are CROSSING. Again there is little advance notice of each junction and the road names can be hard to read as you approach, especially at night, so keep your speed down if you think you are close to your turn-off to allow time to get into the correct lane. If you do miss a turning, most roads are on a grid system, so it's easy to work back.

Occasionally you will meet a crossroads where no right of way is obvious. This is a Four-Way Stop, and the priority goes in order of arrival. So, when it's your turn, just indicate and pull out slowly (America doesn't have many roundabouts, so this may be the closest you get to one).

Local maps: Those supplied by the rental companies and the free tourist maps are pretty basic. AA members have their own map options (p52), but we recommend getting the Orlando Map by Steve Munns (p48).

Rules and regulations

As well as the obvious difference of driving on the opposite side of the road, there are several differences in procedure.

Tolls: For toll roads, have some change handy in amounts from 25c to $3. Most give change (in the GREEN lanes), but you will get through quicker if you have the correct money (in the BLUE lanes). On minor exits of Osceola Parkway and the Greeneway, there are auto-toll machines *only*, so keep some loose change to hand. Several exits of the Florida Turnpike will now take SunPass *only*, not cash, hence PlatePass is valuable if you plan to travel widely (p48).

BRITTIP

On nearly all toll roads, for the manned toll booths you have to pull in to a slip road on the right to pay. It is SunPass/E-Pass only on the main carriageway. This can catch you out when you have just left the airport.

Traffic lights: The most frequent British errors occur at traffic lights (which are hung above the road). At a red light, you can still turn RIGHT providing there is no traffic coming from the left. Stop, check there are no pedestrians crossing and make your turn – unless there is a sign indicating

An aerial view of Orlando

© Gray Line Tours

'No turn on red'. Turning left at the lights, you have the right of way with a green ARROW but must give way to traffic from the other direction on a SOLID green. A YELLOW flashing arrow means it is OK to turn left providing the way is clear.

Left turns: The majority of accidents involving overseas visitors take place on left turns, so take extra care. There is also no amber light from red to green, but there IS from green to red. A flashing amber light at a junction means proceed but watch for traffic joining the carriageway, while a flashing red light indicates it is okay to turn if the carriageway is clear.

🇬🇧 BRITTIP

The Osceola Parkway toll road (522) that runs parallel to Highway 192 is a better route in to Walt Disney World from eastern Kissimmee and costs only $1.75. Use Sherberth Road for Disney access from west 192 or the new Western Beltway (Highway 429).

Speed limits: Speed limits are always well marked with black numbering on white signs and the police are pretty hot on speeding, with steep fines. There are varying limits of 55–70mph/88–113kph on the Interstates, where there is also a 40mph/64kph minimum speed limit. It can also be just 15–25mph/24–40kph in built-up areas.

🇬🇧 BRITTIP

There are no fixed speed cameras in Florida (although many traffic lights DO have cameras to catch red-light offences), but the police often use hand-held radar guns.

Seat belts: These are compulsory for all passengers, while child seats must be used for under-4s and can be hired from the car companies at $10–15 a day (so bring your own or buy one locally for $70–80). Also 4 and 5-year-olds *must* use either a car seat or booster seat, depending on the child's size.

Parking: It is illegal to park within 10ft/3m of a fire hydrant or a lowered kerb, and never park in front of a yellow-painted kerb – they are stopping points for emergency vehicles and you will be towed away. Never park ON a kerb, either. Park bonnet first – reverse parking is frowned upon because number plates are only on the rear of cars and police then can't see them. If you park parallel to the kerb, you must point in the direction of traffic.

Other traffic laws: Flashing orange lights over the road indicate a school zone, and school buses must NOT be overtaken in either direction when they are unloading and have their hazard lights on. U-turns are forbidden in built-up areas and where there is a solid line down the middle of the road. You must pull to the side of the road to allow emergency vehicles to pass, in either direction, when they have lights and/or sirens going. Also, on multi-lane highways in Florida, the Move Over law means you must pull into an adjacent lane if you see a police car on the hard shoulder, or slow to a stop if you can't move over. And you must put on your lights in the rain.

Finally, DON'T drink and drive. Florida has strict laws, with penalties of up to 6 months in prison for first-time offenders. The blood-alcohol limit is lower than in Britain, so it is safer not to drink at all if you are driving. It is also illegal to carry open containers of alcohol in the car.

Bonus for AA members: Your membership is recognised by the equivalent AAA in the US and you benefit from various special offers.

Scenic Boat Tour, Winter Park

© Gray Line Tours

Take your AA card and produce it where you see the AAA 'Show & Save' signs to enjoy some handy discounts. Visit **http://autoclubsouth.aaa.com** and click Discounts & Rewards for the full range, which includes shopping and dining, like 10% off at Hard Rock Café and Dennys restaurants (use the zip code 32819 if required). You can also get maps and books from their office in Lake Mary in Seminole County (near Sanford).

Accidents

In the unlikely event of an accident, no matter how minor, you must contact the police before the cars can be moved (except on the busy I-4). Car hire firms will insist on a full police report for the insurance. If you break down, there should be an emergency number for the hire company in its literature or, if you are on a main highway, raise the bonnet and wait for one of the frequent police patrol cars to stop (or dial *FHP on your mobile). *Always* carry your driving licence and car hire forms when driving, in case you are stopped by the police.

Key routes

All main motorways are prefixed I, the even numbers going east–west and odd numbers north–south. Federal Highways are the next grade down,

Renaissance Orlando Resort

with black numerals on white shields, while state roads are prefixed SR (black numbers on white circular or rectangular signs).

All American motorways have their junctions numbered in mileage terms, which makes it easy to calculate journey distances. I-4 starts at exit 1 in Tampa and goes to exit 132 at Daytona, 132ml/211km away. In Orlando, the main junctions run from exit 55, at Highway 27, to exit 87 (Winter Park) and exit 101 for the Seminole Expressway (417) and Orlando Sanford International Airport. Downtown Orlando can be found off exits 82B to 85.

Interstate 4: I-4 is the main route through Orlando, a four, six or eight-lane motorway linking the coasts. Interstates are always indicated on blue shield-shaped signs. For most of its length, I-4 travels east–west but, around Orlando, it swings north–south, though directions are still given east (for north) or west (for south). All the attractions of Walt Disney World, plus SeaWorld and Universal Orlando are well signposted from I-4. LEGOLAND Florida in Winter Haven, Lake Wales and Bok Tower Gardens are a 45min drive from Orlando west on I-4 and then south on Highway 27, while Busch Gardens is 75–90mins down I-4 to Tampa. Be aware I-4 can be packed with traffic for long sections in the morning and evening rush hours. You can check for major roadworks on **www.cflroads.com**.

International Drive: I-Drive is the second key local roadway, linking a 14½ml/24km ribbon of hotels, shops, restaurants and attractions like I-Drive 360, Pointe Orlando and Orlando Premium Outlets (I-Drive South, from Highway 192 in Kissimmee north to Route 535 is NOT the main stretch and the two sections are linked via Route 535 and World Center Drive). From I-4, take exits 71, 72, 74A or 75A going east, or 75A, 74A or 72 going west. To the north, I-Drive runs into Oak Ridge Road and the South Orange Blossom Trail, which leads to downtown Orlando (junctions 82B, 83A and 85 off I-4). I-Drive is also bisected by Sand Lake Road and runs into World Center Drive (536) to the south, also convenient for Disney.

🇬🇧 BRITTIP

Be ready for MAJOR roadworks on I-4 north of Universal (at Kirkman Rd) all the way to north of downtown. It is a road widening project that will add toll lanes for the first time. Completion date 2021! See **http://i4ultimate.com/**.

I-Drive is a major tourist centre and makes an excellent base, especially around the Sand Lake Road junction, as it is fully pedestrian-friendly. It's a 20min drive to Disney and 10mins from Universal. However, at peak times, heavy traffic means it's best to avoid the stretch from the Convention Center north. Use Universal Boulevard instead.

Also, try to avoid I-4 eastbound from exits 65–68 in the morning and evening rush-hours as traffic can be severe here. Equally, I-4 westbound from 78–74B will be really congested through 2017 as the Kirkman Rd junction undergoes major reconstruction.

Kissimmee: The other main tourist area, south of Orlando and south-east of Disney, its features are grouped along a 20ml/32km stretch of the Irlo Bronson Memorial Highway (192), which intersects I-4 at junction 64B, and is close to Walt Disney World (though a good 25mins from SeaWorld and Universal). Downtown Kissimmee is off Main Street, Broadway and Emmett Street, and is ideal for walking.

Highway 192: A handy visual along here is the Marker Series from Formosa Gardens (number 4) to just past Medieval Times (number 15). These highly visible signs are good locators for hotels, restaurants and attractions, and much of this stretch is also walkable (though few places are close together). Try to avoid the area of the 192 east

of Marker 15, though; it is rather run-down and unappealing. For downtown Kissimmee (which we DO recommend) use the Osceola Parkway and S Orange Blossom Trail (441).

The unique Disney-inspired town of Celebration is also here (just south of Walt Disney World).

Highway 27: This is at the west end of Highway 192, running north to Clermont and south to Davenport (and Haines City). A major area of holiday villa developments, these are generally quite convenient for Disney. Many home owners claim they are 'only 5mins from Disney' but it is at least 10mins from Highway 27 to the edge of Disney property; often more. The area is also starting to add shops and restaurants, notably in the Cagan Crossings junction (just north of where 192 meets 27), where there is also a large Wal-Mart, and Berry Town Center (to the south).

Western Beltway: Highway 429 provides a western Orlando bypass, avoiding the often-crowded I-4 to link with the Florida Turnpike and Apopka to the north. It also offers a western gateway to Walt Disney World at exit 8 (Western Way), which is handy for the Davenport/Clermont areas. This junction is also being developed as a new area called Flamingo Crossings at the junction of the 429 and Western Way, with the first two hotels now open and more to follow.

Now, let's go on to the next vital step – your holiday accommodation….

I-Drive from the top of the Orlando Eye

Metro Orlando has the second highest concentration of hotels in the world (after Las Vegas) and more are being built all the time. There are almost 120,000 rooms, not to mention 26,000 villas for rent. Therefore, what follows is only a general guide to the various types, plus our recommendations and favourites.

The main choice is between a traditional hotel and one of the many self-catering options, which can be villas/vacation homes, town homes or condos.

HOTELS
Orlando is very heavily chain-hotel territory. You will find all the big brand names here, plus a handful of independents and local groups, like the Rosen hotels. The general standard is consistently good, with rooms often much larger than their

Disney's All-Star Music Resort

European counterparts. Many feature two queen-sized beds but couples without children can request a king room for extra space. All US hotels charge per room, and not per person, and a family of four (with younger children) can usually fit in one room. Most hotels are sold on a room-only basis, not bed-and-breakfast. A lot of the budget-priced hotels will *not* have a restaurant or bar, but you usually can't go 100 yards here without finding one.

Most hotels are big, clean, efficient and great value. You'll find plenty of soft-drink and ice machines (though it's cheaper to buy drinks from a supermarket), with ice buckets in all rooms. Rooms are all air-conditioned, hence you'll need to get used to the drone of the A/C unit. If you need a more spacious room, look for one of the many suite hotels, which provide sitting rooms and mini-kitchens, as well as 1–3 bedrooms.

Deals and bookings: If you've just arrived and need a hotel, visit the official Visitor Center at 8723 I-Drive, just north of Pointe Orlando (on the corner of Austrian Court; 8.30am–6.30pm daily; 407 363 5872), where they have brochures on all current deals. There are also many online hotel specialist agents like Priceline **www.priceline.com**, Expedia (**www.expedia.co.uk**), Hotels.com (**www.hotels.com**), Orbitz (**www.orbitz.com**), Trivago (**www.trivago.com**) and Hotwire (**www.hotwire.com**).

BRITTIP

Buy soft drinks at the supermarket, and (if your hotel room doesn't have a fridge) buy a polystyrene cooler for about $5 that you can fill from your hotel ice machine to keep drinks cold.

Prices: Hotel rates will be cheaper out of the main holiday periods, with special deals at times. Always ask for rates if you book directly and check if special rates apply during your visit (don't be afraid to ask for their 'best rate' at off-peak times, which can be lower than published or 'rack' rates). There may be an additional charge

for more than two adults sharing a room ($5–15 per person), plus there is state tax and, sometimes, a sneaky resort fee that can add $15–25/day.

A key pricing factor is location (the closer to Disney and other parks, the higher the price), so you can save if you don't mind a longer journey.

Suite things
Suites hotels provide a combination of hotel and apartment, with extra value for large families or groups. Typically, a suites room gives you a living room and kitchenette, including microwave, coffee-maker, fridge, cutlery and crockery, while many offer a complimentary continental breakfast (or better).

All have pools and grocery stores or snack bars and several have restaurants. They vary only in the number of bedrooms and can usually sleep 6–10.

Disney hotels
Our review of Orlando's hotels starts with Walt Disney World. Situated conveniently for all its attractions – and linked by an excellent free transport system of monorail, buses and boats – Disney's hotels, villas and campsites are all magnificently appointed and maintained.

- **Value:** Pop Century, All Star and Art of Animation Resorts.
- **Moderate:** Port Orleans, Caribbean Beach and Coronado Springs Resorts.
- **Deluxe:** Contemporary, Polynesian Village, Boardwalk Inn, Wilderness Lodge, Grand Floridian, Yacht and Beach Club, Swan and Dolphin, and Animal Kingdom Lodge resorts.
- **Deluxe Villas:** (Disney's timeshare properties, or Disney Vacation Club) – Old Key West, Saratoga Springs, Bay Lake Tower, Animal Kingdom Villas, Beach Club Villas, Boardwalk Villas, Polynesian Village Villas, Grand Floridian Villas and Wilderness Lodge Villas.
- **Campground:** Fort Wilderness (cabins, campsites and RV sites).

Disney Dining Plan

This is another perk of staying onsite with Disney. Hotel guests can pre-pay most meals at a set fee per day. However, it is an EXPENSIVE option if you are staying for a week or more. There are 3 different Plans to choose from (prices as of summer 2016):

Quick Service Dining Plan: Provides two counter-service meals and one snack a day, plus one refillable resort mug/person. Counter-service meals are an entrée or combo meal, plus a dessert and a (non-alcoholic) drink for lunch or dinner; and an entrée or combo meal and a drink for breakfast.

Snacks can be any item such as an ice-cream, popcorn, pastry, a piece of fruit, a bag of crisps, a bottled drink, a medium soda or tea/coffee. Cost: $44.13/day for adults, $19.04 for 3–9s (children must order off the Children's Menu).

Disney Dining Plan: Provides one table service meal, one counter-service and one snack per person per day. Table-service meals are an entrée, a dessert and a (non-alcoholic) drink. Cost: $63.70 and $22.85/day (slightly more in peak season).

Deluxe Dining Plan: Provides three meals (table or counter-service) and two snacks per person per day, plus one refillable resort mug per person. Cost: $115.08 and $35.49/day (more in peak season).

All meals do NOT have to be used per day and can be spread over the duration of your stay, so you can miss a table-service meal one day, then use two credits another day for a signature restaurant or dinner show. Gratuities are NOT included. When you check in at a Disney hotel, your MagicBand is loaded with all your Dining Plan meals and that monitors your daily usage. The Dining Plans CAN be used for Character Meals, when one table-service meal is required per person (two at ultra-popular Cinderella's Royal Table in Magic Kingdom), and for the 14 signature restaurants in Walt Disney World (like Jiko at Animal Kingdom Lodge, California Grill at the Contemporary Resort and Citricos at the Grand Floridian Resort), which all require two table-service meals. They can even be used at Disney's Dinner Shows (p295), subject to availability, at two table-service credits per person.

However, ALL members of the group must book the Plan for the full duration of the stay and inclusive of park tickets. It is also advisable to pre-book (on 407 939 1947 or 0800 16 60 748 in the UK) full-service meals well in advance as the sit-down restaurants usually book up early. Not all restaurants are on the Plan but you still have more than 100 options. More info at **www.disneyworld.co.uk,** where you can book all table service restaurants online.

They range from $98/night (All Star Sports resort) to over $2,000 (Grand Floridian), while dining at Disney resorts is not cheap as there are few fast-food options. However, staying with the world-famous Mouse is one of the great thrills, for the style, service and extras.

The 20 resorts, with 22,000 rooms, offer superb facilities that children especially love. The benefits are:

- **MagicBand:** Every guest receives this wristband, which is the room key, theme park entry, FastPass+ reservations and PhotoPass collector, as well as a 'charge card' for almost all on-site purchases. Disney hotel guests can also book FastPass+ 60 days in advance instead of 30.

- **Package delivery:** Park purchases can be sent back to your hotel.

- **Free parking:** At all the parks.

- **Refillable mugs:** All Disney resorts sell drinking mugs, which are well worth buying (at a fixed price of $17.99 for your stay) as you then get free refills at their self-service cafés.

- **Dining priority:** Many Disney restaurants hold tables for guests, and you can book 180 days in advance, *plus* the length of your stay if you're staying in a Disney resort. Call 407 939 1947 or 0800 16 90 748 in the UK.

- **Children's services:** All resorts have in-room or group babysitting (subject to availability) and eight

Kidsuites = happy families

Orlando has pioneered a great family accommodation style, worth seeking out if you have kids who enjoy bunk beds. Basically, a kidsuite is a separate area within the hotel room that gives the kids their own 'bedroom' (with bunks), usually also with their own TV and games consoles.

of the nine Deluxe resorts have supervised activity centres and dinner clubs (at $15/child/hr or $55/child), usually open till midnight.

- **Mickey on call:** An alarm call from the Mouse (or other Disney characters) himself.

- **Extra Magic Hours:** The BIG bonus is getting into one of the parks each day either 1hr early or for 2hrs after regular park closing to enjoy rides with reduced crowds.

- **Disney's Magical Express:** The free airport transfer service for guests at Disney hotels. Book at least 10 days before arrival through **www. disneyworld.co.uk** or a travel agent.

BRITTIP

All Disney's deluxe resorts offer valet parking. If you use it, the average tip is $3–5, handed to the valet when he or she returns with your car.

Value resorts

Disney's All-Star Resorts: Here you can stay in one of five Sports-themed blocks centred on a massive food court, two swimming pools, a games arcade and shops; the Music-themed version; or the Movies complex – possibly the most imaginative, with its Fantasia pool and kids' play areas. Standard rooms are bright and compact (read 'tight' for families with older children), but well designed for those who want the Disney convenience but not the price. The All Star Music Resort (Jazz and Calypso buildings) also has 192 impressive

two-room Family Suites (combining two standard rooms) that sleep up to six. Each suite has two bathrooms, a well-stocked kitchenette, lounge and master bedroom, making the space more flexible. All three centres, with 5,794 rooms, have pool bars, shops, laundries, video games rooms and pizza delivery. Close to the entrance is a large McDonald's. All resort transport is provided by an efficient bus service.

BRITTIP

To make a reservation at any Walt Disney World hotel call 407 939 1936, 0800 16 90 730 from the UK, or see **www.disneyworld.co.uk.**

Disney's Pop Century Resort: In a similar vein, themed round the decades of the 2nd half of the 20th century, here are five blocks with giant icons – yo-yos, Rubik's cubes and juke-boxes – and a riot of period sayings and visual gags. It features a pool like a 10-pin bowling lane (others shaped like a computer and a flower), a huge table football set-up and open-air Twister mats. Blocks are grouped around a main building housing the check-in area (with a large-screen TV showing Disney films), an imaginative food court, a lounge (with quick-breakfast bar), a Disney store and a games arcade. The 177acre/72ha complex also features a central lake and lots of bright landscaping, plus a well-organised bus service to the parks. The drawbacks: long queues to check in and a rather hectic feel. You need to request a hairdryer from reception and rooms are rather small.

Disney's Art of Animation Resort: This suites-style hotel builds on the popularity of the Family Suites at the All Star Music Resort and is a four-part, 1,984-room complex (1,120 suites, 864 standard rooms) based around *The Lion King, The Little Mermaid, Finding Nemo* and *Cars.*

It has an elaborate main pool and children's play areas themed with *Finding Nemo* characters, two 'quiet' pools, the excellent animation-themed Landscape of Flavors food court with four sections, huge games arcade and the Ink and Paint gift shop. The four courtyards are heavily themed, with larger-than-life icons, interactive sculptures, fountains, extensive photo ops, and other play features, and theming in all the rooms (look for fun 'character reveals'), with the suites offering a master bedroom, two bathrooms and three separate sleeping areas in the living space, including the Inovabed, which converts from a table or work-desk into a bed, plus a small kitchenette with mini fridge, microwave and coffee maker. The pool area is vivid and colourful with plenty of kid-appeal as it even features an underwater sound system! All park transport is by bus.

Moderate resorts

Disney's Caribbean Beach Resort: This 2,112-room complex is spread over five Caribbean 'islands' (with an inter-island bus service). The resort's basic rooms are quite plain, but comfortably sleep four, while the Pirate Rooms (request at booking) take the swashbuckling theme to a new level, with ship-shaped beds and other decor. The Market Street food court, main restaurant Shutters and outdoor activities (with a lakeside recreation area with themed waterfalls, slides, games arcade and bike rentals) are a big hit with kids. The six food court outlets at the Old Port Royale resort hub can get busy in the morning, and the Trinidad South and Barbados 'islands' are a fair walk from the centre. Trinidad South

rooms feature the pirate theming (for a supplement) and there are other imaginative touches, like Parrot Cay Island with its tropical birds and play area. Transport to all parks is by bus.

Disney's Coronado Springs Resort: Possibly the best value of this trio, it has slightly more facilities for its 1,921 rooms spread over 125acres/50ha: four pools (including the massive Lost City of Cibola activity pool with waterslide), two games arcades, restaurant, food court, café/ convenience store, lounge bar, gift shop, beauty salon, health club, business centre and two launderettes. There's also the chic Rix Lounge – a bar/nightclub serving cocktails and appetisers.

Constructed on a scenic Mexican/ Spanish theme in three 'villages' (Casitas, Ranchos and Cabañas), Coronado is an often-overlooked treasure. Check out the Maya Grill and its New Latino cuisine; sample the recently revamped food court dining style of the Pepper Market or a snack or drink from Café Rix to enjoy with the splendid lake views from the outdoor terrace. Coronado Springs is 5mins from Animal Kingdom and well served by the bus network.

BRITTIP

Disney resort restaurants can (and, we think, should) be visited even if you aren't staying there. Advance book at any of the parks, call 407 939 1947 or 0800 16 60 748 in the UK, or visit **www.disneyworld.co.uk.**

Disney's Port Orleans Riverside

Disney's Port Orleans Resort: This is a two-part complex. The 2,048-room Riverside has a steamboat reception area, a great Riverside Mill food court, Boatwright's full-service restaurant, the River Roost lounge (with live entertainment on certain nights) and an old-fashioned General Store (gift shop). It also features Royal Guest Rooms, themed for Princes and Princesses right down to headboards that perform fibre-optic fireworks! Also here is the 1,008-room French Quarter, with the Sassagoula Floatworks and Food Factory court, two bars, games room and shopping arcade.

The Riverside includes the great Ol' Man Island, a 3½acre/1.5ha playground with swimming pool, kids' area and a fishing hole, while the French Quarter has Doubloon Lagoon, with Mardi Gras dragon slide, alligator fountains and a play area. The design varies from rustic Bayou backwoods to turn-of-the-century New Orleans. Transport for both is by bus to the parks and bus or boat to Disney Springs.

Deluxe resorts

More than anything, Disney specialises in high-quality deluxe hotels with grand design features, amenities and restaurants. All nine offer a concierge level, which adds an exclusive service, and a private lounge with meals and snacks.

Disney's Animal Kingdom Lodge: This stunning 'private game lodge' is set on a 33acre/13ha animal-filled savannah, which many rooms overlook. The pervasive African theme and the effect of opening your curtains to a vista of giraffes and zebras is immense. The lavishness and detail are superb, right down to the guides who can tell guests about the animals and their habitats, the African folklore around the outdoor fire pit and the chance for children to become junior safari researchers while Mum and Dad do some wine-tasting (from a huge collection of South African wines).

All this creativity comes before you consider the amenities: two restaurants, café, bar, elaborately themed 'watering-hole' main pool (with waterslide) and kids' pool, massage and fitness centre, large gift shop, children's play area and an awesome four-storey atrium. The main restaurant, Jiko, is spectacular, but there is also the superb buffet-style Boma, a 'marketplace' restaurant featuring African-tinged dishes from a wood-burning grill and rotisserie for breakfast and dinner.

BRITTIP

Wine aficionados take note: Jiko at Disney's Animal Kingdom Lodge offers a fabulous array of South African wines in a wonderfully romantic setting. A superb choice for date night.

Rooms range from standard doubles to one and two-bedroom suites, some of which have bunk beds. Part of the main building, Jambo House, has been converted into studios and one and two-bed villas (the latter with full kitchens) for Disney Vacation Club guests, sleeping 4–12, but these are also available to regular guests when not in use by DVC. The newer Kidani Village wing adds still more (p65). Simba's Cubhouse is for 3–12s (4.30pm–midnight), and all transport is by bus (with the Animal Kingdom barely 5mins away).

Disney's Boardwalk Inn and Villas: One of the Crescent Lake resorts next to Epcot is this 45acre/18ha extravagant inn and entertainment 'district'. It features a 512-room hotel, 383 villas, four themed restaurants, a TV sports club and two nightclubs,

Disney's Animal Kingdom Lodge

plus shops, sports facilities and a huge, freeform pool with a waterslide, all on a semi-circular boardwalk around the lake. The effect is stunning, and the in-room attention to detail excellent, notably in the 'summer cottage' Villas (also part of the Disney Vacation Club).

For dining, the Big River Grille is a great bar/restaurant with its own micro-brewery while the remodelled Flying Fish is an upmarket seafood option with a creative (if a bit pricey) menu and new lounge-bar, the magic-themed AbracadaBar. Trattoria al Forno offers creative Italian 'comfort food', wood-oven pizza and risottos. There's also the Boardwalk Bakery for a snack and new Ample Hills Creamery for ice cream treats. It's a delightful place to visit for a meal, the nightlife (especially Jellyrolls piano bar and ESPN Club) or just to wander along the boardwalk. Transport is by boat to Epcot and Disney's Hollywood Studios and bus to the other parks.

Disney's Contemporary Resort: On the monorail next to the Magic Kingdom, this 15-storey resort boasts 655 rooms, a cavernous foyer, five shops, four restaurants, four lounges, a sandy beach, a marina, two pools (one with waterslide), two tennis courts, a video games centre and health club – and fab views, especially from the superb, hotel-top California

Disney's Contemporary Resort

Grill (one of the most romantic settings in Orlando; aim to go to coincide with the park's fireworks).

Don't miss Chef Mickey's for a breakfast or dinner buffet with your favourite characters, while the monorail runs through the hotel – great for kids. Rooms are some of Disney's largest, with elegant décor, dark-wood furniture and comfy duvets. Chic restaurant/lounge The Wave features a modern bar and dining area with a varied menu and is well worth trying for dinner or just a cocktail, while the Contempo Café adds a light meal option 6am–midnight. Within walking distance of the Magic Kingdom, transport to other parks is by bus.

Disney's Grand Floridian Resort & Spa: This true five-star hotel is like an elaborate Victorian mansion, with 867 rooms, an impressive domed foyer, and staff in period costume.

One stop on the monorail from the Magic Kingdom, the rooms and facilities are truly luxurious – hence the mega prices, though it's worth a look even if you're not staying. Its six restaurants include the top-of-the-range Victoria and Albert's (where the set six-course dinner with wine costs $215, or you could sample the Chef's Table at $315 – with wine – per person), the chic seafood-based Narcoossee's (one of our favourites), with its excellent view over Seven Seas Lagoon, and Mediterranean-styled Citricos. There are also four bars and impressive sports and relaxation facilities, notably the fabulous Senses Spa. There's a main pool and a great second pool area with zero-depth entry and waterslide. The Mouseketeer Club caters for 4–12s (4.30pm–midnight) and the 1900 Park Fare restaurant is very popular for character breakfasts and dinners, plus children's activities.

The Garden View Lounge serves a variety of traditional afternoon teas 2–5pm daily, $30–48/person. Transport to the Magic Kingdom is by boat and monorail; by bus to the other parks.

BRITTIP

Watch out for the free nightly
Electrical Water Pageant on Bay Lake
and Seven Seas Lagoon, on view from all
the Magic Kingdom resorts.

Disney's Polynesian Village Resort:
This is a South Seas tropical fantasy,
with modern sophistication and
comfort. Beautiful beaches, lush
vegetation and architecture are home
to 853 rooms built in wooden long-
house style, all with balconies and
superb views. Also on the monorail
opposite the Magic Kingdom, it
boasts a lovely three-storey atrium,
with landscaped seating areas and
an iconic Tiki god. The large rooms
have been extensively refurbished to
revive the Pacific isles theme, with
custom-made furniture, tapestries
and warm colours. The dining
is excellent: 'Ohana is a stylish
dinner venue with lively character
breakfasts. Kona Café is less formal
but still with an extensive menu.
Captain Cook's Snack Company has
more basic counter-service fare.
New in 2015 was interactive tropical
lounge Trader Sam's Grog Grotto
(4pm–midnight) with appetisers
and exotic cocktails. Then there is
a beautiful 'Volcano' pool area with
waterslide, a games room, shops
and children's playground. Lilo's
Playhouse caters for 3–12s (4pm–
midnight). Catch the monorail or
boat to the Magic Kingdom and
buses to the other parks. The Poly
is also home to the Spirit of Aloha
dinner show (p296), which is open to
non-resort guests and makes a great
evening among the torch-lit gardens.
The Resort's beach is a great area
from which to view the nightly Magic
Kingdom fireworks.

A major renovation in 2015 added
360 Disney Vacation Club deluxe
studios with private balcony or porch,
and room for five. Then there are 20
gorgeous lakefront two-bed, two-
bath bungalows (on stilts over Seven
Seas Lagoon), to sleep eight, with full
kitchens, living and dining rooms,
outdoor deck with individual plunge
pool, and a grandstand view of the
fireworks. But beware the price – from
$2,270 a night!

Disney's Wilderness Lodge: One of
the most picturesque and romantic
resorts, this is a re-creation of
a National Park lodge, from the
stream running through the massive
wooden balcony-lined atrium into
the gardens, past the swimming pool
(with hot and cold spas) to a geyser
that erupts each hour. Offering
backwoods charm with luxury, the
resort is connected to the Magic
Kingdom by boat and bus (and buses
to the other parks). Rooms are all
spacious and well furnished, while
the Courtyard View rooms are the
best of the regular rooms (though
at a slight premium). Deluxe rooms

Disney's Polynesian Village Resort

© Hilary White

sleep up to six and the suites (at up
to $1,025/night) are sumptuous. It
also has two restaurants: the brilliant
Artist's Point (lunch and dinner)
and the Whispering Canyon Café
(lively breakfast and huge all-you-
can-eat family meals) – plus a snack
bar and pool bar. The Cubs' Den
is for 4–12s (4.30pm–midnight).
The Villas at Wilderness Lodge is a
Disney Vacation Club development
of 136 studios and one and two-bed
villas. Facilities include living areas,
kitchens, private balconies and
whirlpool baths. There is a quiet pool
area, a spa and health club.

**Disney's Yacht and Beach Club
Resorts:** There is more refined quality
with this duo, featuring 630 and 580
nautical-themed rooms respectively.
Set around Crescent Lake next to the

Epcot park, they help to form a massive resort area that is a delight to walk around at any time but especially at night. For dinner, the Yachtsman Steakhouse offers friendly, elegant dining at the Yacht Club, while the sister hotel features Cape May Café for lovely character breakfasts and a nightly New England-style clambake buffet. Beaches & Cream can also be found here, a classic 1950s-style diner for burgers, shakes and sundaes. Both resorts are set along a white-sand beach like a tropical island paradise and share water fun at Stormalong Bay, a superb 2½acre/1ha recreation area with waterslides and a sandy lagoon. You can go boating or catch a water-shuttle to Epcot or Disney's Hollywood Studios; other park transport is by bus. The Sand Castle Club here caters for youngsters aged 3–12 (4.30pm–midnight).

BRITTIP

The Crew's Cup Lounge in the Yacht Club Resort is a true hidden gem, ideal for a cocktail before dinner, or to unwind after a day in the parks.

Walt Disney World Swan and Dolphin Resort: These unmistakable twin hotels are not owned by Disney but conform to the same high standards, with some of the best facilities, location, restaurants and a night-time view second to none, while usually slightly cheaper than most Deluxe resorts. They're within walking distance of Epcot and Disney's Hollywood Studios, Disney's Boardwalk Resort and the Fantasia Gardens Miniature Golf Courses, but also have a boat service to both parks (and bus to the others). The unique architecture is extensive, with the Swan topped by a 45ft/14m statue, as well as 758 large rooms (including 55 suites), while the Dolphin (1,509 rooms, 112 suites) is crowned by two even bigger statues. Both have been extensively refurbished to include the Westin Heavenly Bed® and high-speed wi-fi, while adding a sumptuous Grand Deluxe room category with enhanced bathrooms,

personalised in-room fridge, new furniture and contemporary décor. The Dolphin also boasts the Balinese-inspired Mandara Spa, with a relaxing tea garden and Meru Temple. This resort has 17 restaurants and lounges, four tennis courts, five pools (one an amazing grotto pool with hidden alcoves and waterslide), a kids' pool and white-sand beach, two health clubs, a great range of shops, a video arcade and the Camp Dolphin centre for 4–12s (5.30pm–12am, $10/hour per child).

Disney's Yacht and Beach Club Resort

Even for non-guests, Dolphin's Shula's Steak House and celebrity chef Todd English's Bluezoo are worth seeking out. Fresh, a Mediterranean-style market, serves breakfast and lunch, featuring all made-to-order menu items and both à la carte and tableside dining. Picabu is open 24 hours with all-American favourites, while The Fountain is a great choice for ice creams, sundaes, milkshakes and other speciality desserts, as well as classic diner fare.

Walt Disney World and Lake Buena Vista Accommodation

Toll road

Lake Buena Vista Resort & Spa

Parc Soleil by Hilton Grand Vacations

Homewood Suites by Hilton

Residence Inn

Home 2 Suites Orlando

Embassy Suites

Hilton Grand Vacation Suites

Hampton Inn

Quality Suites Lake Buena Vista

Floridays

Extended Stay America

Clarion Inn

Hilton Grand Vacation Suites

Crossroads Center

Hawthorn Suites

Comfort Inn

Caribe Royale

Hyatt Place LBV

Grand Beach Resort

Radisson Lake Buena Vista

Bryan's Spanish Cove

Staybridge Suites

Courtyard Orlando

Courtyard by Marriott, Fairfield Inn, SpringHill Suites

Marriott Village

Blue Heron Beach Resort

Buena Vista Suites

Fairfield Inn & Suites

Resort Lake Buena Vista

Holiday Inn LBV Resort

Worldquest Resort

Sheraton LBV Resort

Delta Orlando Resort

Holiday Inn

Marriott Vacation Club

Holiday Inn Orlando Suites

Cypress Pointe Resort

Hyatt Regency Grand Cypress

Doubletree Guest Suites

Wyndham LBV Resort

Vistana Resort

LBV

Best Western LBV

Hilton Orlando Resort

Orlando World Center Marriott Resort

Buena Vista Palace

Saratoga Springs Resort & Spa, & Treehouse Villas

DISNEY SPRINGS

Old Key West Resort

Typhoon Lagoon

Four Seasons Hotel and Disney's Golden Oak Villas

Port Orleans Riverside Resort

Port Orleans French Quarter Resort

Waldorf-Astoria, Hilton Orlando and Wyndham Grand Resort at Bonnet Creek

Pop Century Resort

Caribbean Beach Resort

Epcot

Disney's Art of Animation Resort

Walt Disney World

Beach Club

Boardwalk

Yacht Club

Swan

Dolphin

Disney's Hollywood Studios

Victory Way

Fort Wilderness Resort & Campground

Wilderness Lodge

Blizzard Beach

Contemporary Resort, & Bay Lake Tower

Seven Seas

Transportation & Ticket Center

Coronado Springs Resort

Bay Lake

Car Park

All-Star Resorts

Magic Kingdom

Grand Floridian Resort & Spa

Polynesian Village Resort

BAY LAKE

Animal Kingdom

Animal Kingdom Lodge Resort & Kidani Village

© Steve Munns 2016

N

In the Swan, you'll find Il Mulino Trattoria, New York's top Italian restaurant, and the Garden Grove Café, with decor and atmosphere inspired by the gardens of New York's Central Park, serving à la carte or buffet breakfasts, with Disney characters each evening and breakfasts at the weekend. The intimate Kimonos offers sushi and a karaoke bar. With its ideal location and amenities, this is possibly the perfect resort (407 934 1609, **www.swandolphin.com**).

Four Seasons Resort: (see Golden Oak, p66).

BRITTIP

Most Disney hotel rooms will sleep four, except Port Orleans Riverside (which can take an extra child on a truckle bed). For larger groups, consider Old Key West, Saratoga Springs, the Boardwalk Villas, the villas at Animal Kingdom Lodge, Wilderness Lodge Villas, Fort Wilderness cabins or two-room suites at the All Star Music and Art of Animation Resorts.

Campground and cabins

Disney's Fort Wilderness Resort & Campground: Possibly the best value of all the Disney properties, situated on Bay Lake opposite the Magic Kingdom, it offers impressive camping facilities and chalet-style cabins housing up to six in a 750acre/304ha spread of countryside. Two 'trading posts' supply fresh groceries and there is a lounge/bar and full-service restaurant. The on-site activities include two swimming pools, the thrice-nightly Hoop-Dee-Doo Musical Revue, Mickey's Backyard Barbecue (a seasonal character buffet dinner), campfire programme, open-air films, sports, games and a prime position to view the nightly Electrical Water Pageant. You can rent bikes or boats or take horse rides around the country trails, while the Tri-Circle D ranch has a small petting zoo. There is even a Segway Tour (the great two-wheeled personal transports), the Wilderness Back Trail Adventure, providing a two-hour trundle around the many trails ($96/person, over-15s only; 8.30 and 11.30am Tues, Fri, Sat; call 407 939 8687 to book).

The Trail's End restaurant (sit-down and takeaway) offers a great value buffet breakfast, à la carte lunch and buffet dinner, while Crockett's Tavern serves pizza and appetisers (dinner only). Buses and boats link the resort with other areas (and the short boat ride to the Magic Kingdom is a great start to the day). If you need a break from the Magic Kingdom, hop on the

Disney's Art of Animation Resort

© Disney

boat here and try the family-friendly Trail's End for lunch or the dinner buffet ($27/ adult, $16/3–9s).

◀▶ BRITTIP

If you're interested in a new dining experience, try the fab **Weekend Brunch** (7.30am–2pm) every Sat and Sun at the Trail's End restaurant at Fort Wilderness. It is buffet-style at $23 adults, $13 3–9s.

Disney Vacation Club resorts

Disney's Old Key West Resort: Disney's first Vacation Club resort, this is primarily a five-star holiday ownership scheme (one of nine resorts), but the one, two or three-bed studios in a Key West setting can be rented nightly when not in use by members. Facilities include four pools, tennis courts, a games room, shops and a fitness centre, plus the lovely Olivia's restaurant. Transport to all parks is by bus, plus boat to Disney Springs.

◀▶ BRITTIP

Looking for a handy diversion from Disney Springs? Take the boat from the West Side (not Marketplace) to Old Key West and try a meal at Olivia's for a lovely, laid-back holiday vibe.

Disney's Saratoga Springs Resort & Spa: The most extensive DVC resort, this 65acre/26ha apartment complex is opposite Disney Springs, has some wonderful views over the lake and is next to scenic Lake Buena Vista Golf Course. It boasts 828 units, from standard two-bed hotel-style studio rooms to massive two-storey, three-bed apartments sleeping 12.

Disney's Boardwalk Resort

© Hilary White

The theme is the 1880s' New York resort of the same name, with a gracious look and great facilities, from the freeform, zero-depth entry main pool (with waterslide and squirt-fountains), a smaller quiet pool, varied dining (the Artist's Palette for counter-service breakfast, lunch and dinner, the Paddock Grill for more quick-service fare and the upscale Turf Club Bar & Grill, with a cocktail lounge and pool table, plus food shop), a large video arcade, tennis courts and a wonderful full-service spa and gym. All but the hotel-style studios have a kitchen (with dishwasher and microwave), washer-dryer, whirlpool bath and DVD player, with TVs in each living room and bedroom.

The resort includes room service, babysitting and childminding, plus a ferry to Disney Springs.

Rates for the three-bed villas top $1,000 a night, but the one-bed units are more modestly priced and, although it is a Vacation Club property, rooms are usually available to the public.

Also here are 60 three-bed Treehouse Villas, beautiful chalets raised 10ft/3m off the ground among a heavily wooded area next to Sassagoula River. Sleeping up to nine, they feature sumptuous furnishings, including granite counter-tops and flatscreen TVs, two full bathrooms and outdoor barbecue grills. They also have their own leisure pool and whirlpool spa. Transport to all parks is by bus.

Bay Lake Tower at Disney's Contemporary Resort: Linked to the Contemporary Resort by a 5th-floor bridge, this features its own pool, waterslide and whirlpool spa, kids' water-play area, shuffleboard and bocce courts. The 14-storey, 295-room Tower, studio rooms and spacious one, two and three-bed villas have modern decor. The studios (sleeping up to four) have small fridges, microwaves and coffee-makers, while the villas (up to 12) have full kitchens and laundry facilities. The Tower affords wonderful views over the Magic Kingdom and nightly fireworks from its exclusive rooftop lounge and viewing deck (DVC members only).

B Resort at Walt Disney World

Looking for something different, hotel-wise? **B Resort at Walt Disney World** offers 394 rooms in five categories, with suites accommodating up to five and family rooms with kids' bunks. It features fresh, contemporary decor and excellent personal amenities in the upscale-but-relaxed style of the new B brand. There is a high-quality restaurant called American Kitchen (serving classic comfort food with a modern twist), a Grab 'n Go deli-café, landscaped pool (with interactive water elements) and pool bar, four tennis courts, stylish Aveda Spa, fitness centre, coin-op laundry and kid zone with films and games.

Standard rooms have a sitting area while the magnificent two-room suites boast a huge lounge and all feature clean, crisp design, Blissful beds, 47in/120cm flatscreen TVs, mini-fridge and superb bathrooms. Other elements include free high-speed Internet access throughout the resort, courtesy iPads, game consoles and Monscierge®, a digital touchscreen concierge and destination guide. The attention to detail and that 'something different' style is highly noticeable here but be aware there is a $20 resort fee and self-parking is $16/day (407 828 2828, **www.bresortlbv.com**).

There is also a pool bar and grill, and easy access to the restaurants of the Contemporary Resort. Transport by monorail or bus (or on foot to Magic Kingdom).

Disney's Animal Kingdom Lodge–Kidani Village: An addition to the Animal Kingdom Lodge, this is divided into hotel-room studios (sleeping up to four) and one, two and three-bed villas (sleeping five, nine or 12), offering full kitchens and laundry facilities. The low-rise architecture and decor continue the African theme and the three-bed villas are spacious. There is a separate wildlife preserve in four animal savannah areas, a fabulous pool and kids' play area, and another restaurant, Sanaa, which continues the Lodge's reputation for fine dining. The stunning Samawati Springs – a huge zero-depth entry pool – is open to all Animal Kingdom Lodge guests, while children will make a beeline for Uwanja Camp, a three-part interactive water playground (for ages 4 and under, 5–7s, and 8+). Other amenities include a video arcade, basketball

court, fitness centre, gift shop and animal programmes, from flamingo-feeding to campfire story-telling. Transport to all parks is by bus.

Grand Floridian Villas: These sumptuous additions to the DVC inventory provide 147 stylish one and two-bed villas sleeping 5–9, plus 'grand villas' that sleep 12 and include a media room with home theatre system. The elegant building, with subtle Mary Poppins theming, has a reception, children's water-play area and private beach.

Golden Oak: In an ultra-exclusive corner of Walt Disney World is this small-scale community of holiday homes for private sale. Like most villa developments, it has its own luxurious Clubhouse, but homes are NOT rented out and feature VIP perks such as concierge service, private transport to the parks and special events. The price is equally exclusive – they START at $2m!

Four Seasons Resort: Within the gates of Golden Oak but a separate entity (and also open to non-guests for its spectacular dining), is the first Central Florida hotel of this fabulous five-star brand, featuring 444 capacious rooms and even larger suites, with marbled bathrooms, and in an oasis of tranquillity within the Disney confines. Built in luxurious Spanish Revival style, it has an amazing array of amenities, including five restaurants, three pools, a lazy river and water-play

B Resort at Walt Disney World

area, tennis courts, extensive spa, state-of-the-art gym and its own golf course. The huge kids club (for 4–12s, open 10am–6pm) is free to guests and offers a superb spread of activities and there is a good choice of inter-connecting family rooms, as well as adults-only rooms with luxurious king beds and great views to both sides. Rooms with views of the parks – and the Magic Kingdom fireworks – come at a premium while the rooftop Spanish steakhouse restaurant Capa is one of Orlando's most spectacular. Authentic Italian restaurant Ravello, with its show kitchen, is a show-stopper and the golf clubhouse diner, Plancha, features Cuban-American cuisine in a lakeside setting. It offers a full Disney Planning Centre, grab-and-go café, teen hangout and deluxe 'extras' – a shoe-shine service, twice-daily housekeeping, refrigerated private bar and unobtrusive service – that go with the brand. Regular room rates start at $549/night and reach $12,000/night (!) for the nine bedroom Royal Suite (1800 267 3046, **www.fourseasons.com/orlando/**).

 **BRITTIP**

Book dinner at Capa at the Four Seasons to coincide with the nightly Wishes show at the Magic Kingdom and you will have a superb high-level view of the fireworks.

Disney Hotel Plaza

If Disney's hotel prices are out of your range, consider the seven on-site 'guest' hotels that come with a less hefty price-tag, on Hotel Plaza Boulevard on the doorstep of Disney Springs. There's a free bus service to the parks, guaranteed admission (even on the busiest days), and you can make reservations for shows and restaurants before the general public. It's also handy to be able to walk to Disney Springs and the Crossroads shopping plaza. For more info on these, go to **www.disneyspringshotels.com**.

- **Best Western Lake Buena Vista:** Budget-priced choice.

- **B Resort:** (see p66).

- **Buena Vista Palace Hotel & Spa:** Extensive and recently refurbished resort.

- **DoubleTree Suites by Hilton:** Well-priced and versatile option.

- **Hilton Orlando Resort:** Ultra-smart executive-style resort with many mod cons.

- **Holiday Inn:** A surprisingly fresh and modern style, with great dining.

- **Wyndham Garden:** Right opposite Disney Springs and with a great array of amenities.

 **BRITTIP**

Look out for a 'Free Breakfast' and special Advance Purchase offers at the **Holiday Inn Walt Disney World**. Book seven nights or more and qualify for free breakfast for two adults. Look them up on **www.hiorlando.com/specials.htm**.

Beyond Disney

Once you move away from Walt Disney World, your hotel choice becomes more diverse. Budget types are most common, and *where* you stay tends to affect the price: the further away from Disney on Kissimmee's Highway 192, the

Disney's Grand Floridian Resort and Spa

Our Budget recommendations

Budget hotels we rate as above average include:

In Kissimmee/Highway 192:

Champions World Resort: Converted Howard Johnson on west Highway 192, a sound choice with three pools, free theme park transport and wi-fi (1800 638 7829, www.championsworldresort.com).

Destiny Palms Hotel Maingate East: Well situated for Disney, this pleasant motel also offers free wi-fi and a continental breakfast (407 396 1600, http://destinypalmsmaingate.com/web/).

Golden Link Resort Motel: On Highway 192, this quaint little retro motel with free continental breakfast and wi-fi consistently gets rave reviews (407 396 0555, www.goldenlinkmotel.com).

Super 8 Kissimmee/Maingate: Above average for this low-cost chain, with good customer feedback (407 396 8883, www.super8maingate.com).

Travelodge Suites East Gate Orange: Higher quality from a basic chain motel, with wi-fi, microwave and fridge in all rooms, a good pool and kiddie pool (407 396 7666, www.travelodge.com).

International Drive area:

Econo Lodge International Drive: Basic, clean and reliable, with free wi-fi, continental breakfast, and a nice picnic area (407 313 1090, www.choicehotels.com/florida/orlando/econo-lodge-hotels/fl894).

Sunsol International Drive: Fresh, low-cost choice in a great location close to Universal, with free shuttle service, wi-fi and continental breakfast (407 345 8880, www.sunsolhotels.net).

Motel 6 International Drive: Consistently gets above-average reviews (407 351 6500, www.motel6.com/en/motels.fl.orlando.1079.html).

cheaper (and more basic) the hotel/motel, while I-Drive south of Sand Lake Road is more expensive than the northern stretch. All the chain brands can be found here, with rates as low as $35/room off-peak (but remember the local sales tax). Some rooms feature a kitchenette or 'efficiency'. Be prepared to shop around, especially on Highway 192, where many hotels advertise their rates, and feel free to ask to see a room before you book.

◀╋▶BRITTIP
Coffee-makers are standard in most hotel rooms, but tea-making facilities are rare. Bring your own teabags or look for PG Tips and Yorkshire Tea in the International aisles at Publix and Wal-Mart.

Budget hotels

Chain hotels can be found at their most numerous at the cheaper end of the spectrum, and you'll find few frills. All have pools, but not many have restaurants, bars or lounges (though some provide a free continental breakfast and many offer fridges, microwaves and free wi-fi). The main ones are:

- **America's Best Value Inn** (1888 315 2378, www.americasbestvalueinn.com).
- **Days Inn** (1800 225 3297, www.daysinn.com).
- **Econo Lodge** (1877 424 6423, www.choicehotels.com/econo-lodge);.
- **Howard Johnson** (1800 221 5801, www.hojo.com).
- **Knights Inn** (1800 477 0629, www.knightsinn.com).
- **Motel 6** (1800 899 9841, www.motel6.com).
- **Red Roof Inn** (1800 733 7663, www.redroof.com).
- **Rodeway Inn** (1877 424 6423, www.choicehotels.com/rodeway-inn).
- **Super 8 Motel,** with above average 'Pride' hotels (1800 454 3213, www.super8.com).
- **Travelodge** (1800 525 4055, www.travelodge.com).

There are dozens of smaller independent outfits that offer special rates periodically, especially a battery of cheap and cheerful motels along Highway 192 in Kissimmee (but try to stay west of Marker 14).

> **BRITTIP**
> Hotels designated Maingate East or Maingate West should be close to Disney's main entrance on Highway 192, though it is wise to check.

Moderate choices

As you go up the scale of the bigger chains, you find more modern facilities and a better array of amenities. Most still don't have their own restaurant, but do provide a breakfast option. Choose from:

Baymont Inn & Suites: Smart group, boasting several new hotels, all with free breakfast and wi-fi (1800 337 0550, **www.baymontinns.com**).

Best Western: Good, family-style brand with more amenities (1800 780 7234 in US, **www.bestwestern.com**).

Choice Hotels: Group comprising Comfort Inn, Comfort Suites, Clarion Inn and Quality Inn, some with an exercise room and free continental breakfast (1877 424 6423, **www.choicehotels.com**).

Country Inn & Suites: A smart choice, with spacious rooms and a pleasant country-house lobby, and an extensive free breakfast (1800 830 5222, **www.countryinns.com**).

Doubletree by Hilton: A contemporary, upscale choice with fewer frills but spacious, ultra-comfy rooms featuring their Sweet Dreams sleep experience and welcome cookies (1800 560 7753, **http://doubletree3.hilton.com/en/index.html**).

Extended Stay America: Clean and consistent chain with more space than many in this group, a free grab-and-go breakfast and wi-fi, plus full kitchens (1800 804 3724, **www.extendedstayamerica.com**).

Fairfield Inn: Budget version of the Marriott chain, usually with newer hotels, with gyms, free wi-fi and hot breakfast (1888 236 2427, **http://fairfield.marriott.com/**).

Hampton Inn and Suites: A lot included with this brand, including free wi-fi, breakfast and tea/coffee in the lobby 24hrs (1800 560 7809, **http://hamptoninn3.hilton.com/en/index.html**).

Hawthorn Suites by Wyndham: A smart suites hotel featuring spacious studios and two-room suites with full kitchens, plus free breakfast daily (1800 337 0202, **www.hawthorn.com**).

Holiday Inn and Holiday Inn Express: More upmarket these days but still offering good value in moderate-priced territory (1877 536 2509, **www.ihg.com/holidayinn/hotels/us/en/reservation**).

Homewood Suites: With über-spacious rooms and a sleek, modern touch, also a free hot breakfast and wi-fi, plus full kitchens in every room (1800 445 8667, **http://homewoodsuites3.hilton.com/en/index.html**).

La Quinta Inn and Suites: Some notably smart hotels in Orlando (1800 753 3757, **www.lq.com**).

Radisson: Possibly the best overall value here, with some excellently priced hotels, all with above-average amenities and services (1800 976 9033, **www.radisson.com**).

Ramada: Good value at this level, usually with free wi-fi and breakfast (1800 854 9517, **www.ramada.com**).

Residence Inns: Identikit but consistent, with free breakfast and exercise rooms, plus microwave, fridge and tea/coffee-making facilities (1888 236 2427, **www.residenceinn.marriott.com**).

Springhill Suites: Also part of the Marriott group, they offer reliable, comfortable value (1888 236 2427, **http://springhillsuites.marriott.com/**).

Country Inn & Suites

More recommendations

Our reliable choices in the Moderate group include:

In Kissimmee/Highway 192:

Galleria Palms Hotel: At Maingate West, just off Highway 192, this has a smart, contemporary look, ultra-comfy rooms, a great location close to Disney, free shuttle to the parks, free breakfast and wi-fi (407 396 6300, **www.gphkissimmee.com/**).

Holiday Inn Maingate East: Between Markers 8 and 9, with well-maintained rooms (including kidsuites) in two high-rise towers, and a great range of amenities, plus a Kids-eat-free programme (407 396 4222, **www.holidayinnmge.com**).

Palms Hotel & Villas: Just off Highway 192 and close to I-4, with spacious one and two-room suites with full kitchens, two large pools and kiddie pool, sports court, free breakfast and shuttle to Disney parks (407 396 2229, **www.thepalmshotelandvillas.com**).

International Drive area:

Avanti Resort: A fab resort pool (including kids' water fun section), fitness centre, coffee shop and poolside bar and grill. Free daily shuttles to Universal, SeaWorld, Epcot and Aquatica (407 313 0100, **www.avantiresort.com**).

Drury Inn & Suites: A smart choice with a lot included for your money (free wi-fi, parking, hot breakfast, phone calls, snacks and drinks daily and popcorn and soft drinks in the lobby 3–10pm; 407 354 1101, **https://druryhotels.com/**).

Extended Stay America Orlando Convention Center Studios: A high-quality choice in this chain, in a great location for Universal and I-Drive (407 903 1500, **www.extendedstayamerica.com**).

Ramada Plaza Resort & Suites: Great value choice in a good I-Drive location with free wi-fi,continental breakfast and Disney transport, plus over-sized rooms (407 345 5340, **www.michotel.com**).

Rosen Inn at Pointe Orlando: One of I-Drive's 'old faithfuls', this continues to be a reliable and sound value-for-money choice, with plenty of amenities and the bonus of a good bar and restaurant (407 996 8585, **www.roseninn9000.com**).

Rosen Inn International: Another long-serving Rosen hotel still providing great value in budget territory but with more facilities and comfort than you would expect for the price (407 996 1600; **www.roseninn7600.com**).

Wyndham Orlando Resort: In the heart of I-Drive and with great facilities, this boasts two pools, a fab poolside bar and restaurant, ice-cream shop, and fitness centre, all set in landscaped grounds but without a hefty price tag. The $18/day resort fee includes parking and wi-fi (407 351 2420; **www.wyndham.com**).

In Lake Buena Vista:

Extended Stay America Lake Buena Vista: Another good choice in a quieter area but still convenient for Disney that usually delivers good value for money (407 239 4300, **www.extendedstayamerica. com**).

Holiday Inn at Walt Disney World: Among the seven resorts along Hotel Boulevard next to Disney Springs, this is a fresh and quality-conscious hotel in a great area. Excellent amenities, dining and an overall South Beach vibe that would not be out of place in chic Miami (407 828 8888, **www.hiorlando.com/**).

Radisson Lake Buena Vista: Convenient for Disney and the Crossroads area, with sleek decor and furnishings, it boasts a stylish bar and grill, small gym and free wi-fi, plus extra-spacious rooms (407 597 3400, **www.radisson.com**).

Wingate Inn: Modern chain, with gyms, free breakfast and wi-fi (1800 337 0077, **www.wingatehotels.com**).

◀▣▶ **BRITTIP**

Not all hotels provide hairdryers, though they can often be ordered from the front desk. For your own, you will need a US plug adaptor (with two flat pins). The voltage is 110–120AC (ours is 220) so UK appliances will be sluggish.

More upmarket
If you're looking for more amenities, including the guarantee of a restaurant and bar, this range of big-brand hotels is worth considering. All provide a good pool (often with extras like a waterslide, kids' pool and/or playground) and at least one restaurant, bar and café, plus extra in-room comforts.

Courtyard Marriott: A recently revamped brand with an eye for business travellers, it features stylish rooms, free wi-fi, bistro restaurant, gym and pool in each case (1888 236 2427, **http://courtyard.marriott.com/**).

Crowne Plaza Hotels: Some eye-catching properties featuring great pool areas, smart restaurants, fitness centres and ultra-comfy rooms (1877 536 2509, **www.ihg.com/crowneplaza/**).

Delta Hotels: A brand new Marriott brand, this offers a fresh, inviting style but without the price tag you might expect (1888 236 2427, **www.marriott.com/delta-hotels/travel.mi**).

◀▣▶ **BRITTIP**

It is usual to tip hotel chambermaids by leaving $1/adult each day before your room is made up.

Embassy Suites: A popular and highly quality-conscious choice, with a great range of facilities, plus a free cooked breakfast and evening receptions with free snacks and drinks (1800 445 8667, **http://embassysuites3.hilton.com/en/index.html**).

Hilton Garden Inn: This chain has really struck the right note with a modern, comfortable and family-friendly style, featuring attractive new hotels (1800 445 8667, **http://hiltongardeninn3.hilton.com/en/index.html**).

Hyatt Place: A chic, contemporary choice with stylish rooms, free breakfast and wi-fi, a 24hr café and evening bar service (1800 233 1234, **http://place.hyatt.com/en/hyattplace.html**).

Hyatt Regency: The Hyatt brand's more upmarket choice, with all mod cons, great array of facilities and excellent dining (1888 591 1234, **www.regency.hyatt.com**).

Marriott: Another well-represented group, with some of the smartest hotels in this category, often providing extra facilities, multiple restaurants and some of the largest standard rooms. Features include its signature Revive beds (1888 236 2427, **www.marriott.com**).

Sheraton Hotels: These boast a smart look. Several are themed and feature extra facilities and above-average dining (1800 325 35353, **www.starwoodhotels.com/sheraton**).

Wyndham Hotels: Another brand that has raised its game in recent years, with a sleek, modern look in most places (1877 999 3223; **www.wyndham.com**).

The stand-out individuals
Looking at the three key areas of I-Drive/Universal Orlando, Highway 192, and Lake Buena Vista, there are a number of hotels that stand out, many for the dining options or great pool areas that make them feel special. None comes cheap, but they

Springhill Suites Orlando Airport

© Marriott Group

all deliver great value for money and a resort experience that is in keeping with the creativity in the parks.

In Kissimmee/Highway 192: This area remains more budget focused, but the following trio are well above average:

Bohemian Hotel: In the Disney-inspired town of Celebration just off Highway 192, this boutique hotel offers refreshing small-town America style that is a long way from the usual tourist hurly-burly. With just 115 rooms in its 1920s' wood-frame design, it has a classy ambience and a wealth of high-quality touches, notably in the ultra-comfy rooms and highly-regarded Lakeside Bar & Grill. It is just a short stroll to the town's shops, restaurants and lakeside walks and makes a great romantic choice (407 566 6000, **www.celebrationhotel.com**).

Gaylord Palms Resort: One of the most dramatic hotels, with 1,406 rooms, it is a cross between a spaceship and a vast turn-of-the-century Florida mansion, featuring 4½acres/2ha of indoor themed gardens, fountains and landscaped waters under a glass dome, with live entertainment nightly. The array of restaurants and bars includes the spectacular 2-level Wreckers sports bar, fine steakhouse dining of Old Hickory, MOOR (featuring fine seafood), Mediterranean buffet-style Villa de Flora and SORA Sushi Bar. The Cypress Springs Family Fun Water Park is a huge zero-entry pool featuring 4 water slides, a massive water play structure, lagoon and toddler splash area. Grown-ups appreciate the relaxed ambience of the South Beach Pool (with private cabañas). Standard rooms are some of the smartest and most spacious, while

Ice slide at the Gaylord Palms Resort

© Gray Line Tours

the suites are enormous. One area is themed like the Everglades (with alligator feeding!); another copies St Augustine's old-world charm, with a replica Spanish fort; and the third is eclectic Key West, with a marina and sailboat. Then there is the signature Relâche Spa, one of the area's largest, with 25 treatment rooms, fitness centre and beauty salon. Find unique shopping along the indoor 'retail street', plus the Cocoa Bean coffee shop and Honeybells Frozen Yoghurt. The hotel stages regular special events and is a great wedding venue (407 586 0000, **www.gaylordpalms.com**).

BRITTIP

The Gaylord Palms features the stunning Christmas celebration ICE!, a wonderland of ice sculptures, snow scenery and ice slides, plus other festive touches. Early Nov–3 Jan, tickets $30 adults, $29 over-55s and $17 4–12s, extra for snow tubing.

Meliã Orlando Hotel: One of the finest condo-hotels, on Highway 192 at the entrance to Celebration, this is a luxury 5-storey, 240-unit property set around a spectacular 'vanishing edge' swimming pool and boasting upmarket dining at the Gastrobar and Fuego Restaurant. The beautifully furnished 1 and 2-bed suites feature full kitchens and ultra-comfy bedrooms, with designer toiletries. Balconies overlook the infinity pool or lush landscaping. There is also privileged use of the Celebration Spa and Golf Club (407 964 7000; **www.meliaorlando.com**).

Others worth considering: Radisson Resort Orlando Celebration (**www.radissonorlandoresort.com**);

Champions World Resort (**www.championsworldresort.com**); and the Park Inn by Radisson (**www.parkinn.com/orlando**).

International Drive area

This long stretch of 'tourist central' has the widest variety of hotels in the area, and is possibly the most convenient for its overall location and great array of dining, shops and other attractions.

Kissimmee Accommodation

Walt Disney World

LBV

DISNEY SPRINGS

Epcot

Boardwalk

Disney's Hollywood Studios

Animal Kingdom

Animal Kingdom Lodge Resort

Kidani Village

Continental Plaza

Clarion Suites Maingate

Formosa Gardens Village

Grand Lake Resort

Galleria Palms

Quality Inn & Suites Maingate

Westgate Towers

Magic Tree Resort

Ramada Gateway

Knights Inn Maingate

Maingate Lakeside Resort

Silver Lake

All-Star Sports Resort

All-Star Music Resort

All-Star Movies Resort

Coronado Springs Resort

Pop Century Resort

Disney's Art of Animation Resort

Baymont Inn & Suites Celebration

Park Inn by Radisson

Vistana Resort

Orlando World Center Marriott Resort

Worldquest Resort

Gaylord Palms

Parkway International

Rodeway Inn Maingate

The Palms Hotel, Vacation Village at Parkway

Radisson Resort Orlando Celebration

Fairfield Inn & Suites

Meliá Orlando Suite Hotel

Celebration Suites, Royale Parc Suites

Seralago Hotel

Comfort Suites Maingate East

OLD TOWN KISSIMMEE

Regal Oaks

Bohemian Hotel

CELEBRATION

Blue Heron Beach Resort

Grand Beach Resort

Caribe Royale

Lake Bryan

Marriott VC

Buena Vista Suites

Holiday Inn Resort Orlando Suites

Lake Buena Vista Resort & Spa

Lake Buena Vista Factory Stores

Holiday Inn Express LBV East

Hampton Inn & Suites Orlando South

Calypso Cay

Embassy Suites

Magic Castle Inn, Fantasy World

EconoLodge Kissimmee

Days Inn Kissimmee

Knights Inn

Comfort Inn

Red Roof Inn & HoJo Enchanted Land

Palm Lakefront Hostel

Golden Link Resort

Quality Inn & Suites Eastgate

Holiday Inn Orlando SW

Super 8, Mote. 6

Travelodge East Gate

Publix

Sam's Club

Super Target

Best Western Premier Saratoga Resort Villas

Villas at Seven Dwarfs Resort

Club Cortile

Econo Lodge

Knights Inn Kissimmee

Sevilla Inn

Magnuson Hotel Kissimmee Maingate

Rodeway Inn Country Hearth Inn

HoJo Tropical Palms (further east)

Medieval Times

Wal-Mart

© Steve Munns 2016

Highway 27

Town Center at Orange Lakes

Publix

Oakwater

Windsor Hills

Mystic Dunes

Indian Ridge

Rolling Hills

Formosa Gardens

Oak Island

Indian Creek

Windsor Palms

Tempus Palms

WESTERN BELTWAY (TOLL)

OSCEOLA PARKWAY

POINCIANA BOULEVARD

Upmarket choices

From our third group, we highlight the following:

International Drive area:

Crowne Plaza Orlando – Universal: With a spectacular atrium, two restaurants, cocktail lounge, fitness centre and huge heated pool, this provides plenty of value in an ideal location on Universal Boulevard (407 355 0550, **www.cporlando.com**).

Doubletree by Hilton Orlando at SeaWorld: A recently remodelled hotel just off I-Drive set in 28acres/11ha. It offers three pools, two kids' pools, a playground, mini golf and extra-large suites for a luxury feel (407 352 1100, **www.doubletreeorlandoidrive.com).**

Embassy Suites International Drive Convention Center: A consistent 'old faithful' in the heart of I-Drive that was extensively refurbished in 2016, with spacious rooms, great outdoor pool deck, kids' splash pool and indoor pool, plus sauna, gym and good dining options, with a free breakfast (407 352 1400, **www.embassysuitesorlando.com**).

Four Points By Sheraton Orlando Studio City: A 21-storey icon near Universal Orlando, this features a heated tropical pool and paddling pool, games room, mini-golf and fitness room, while the Tropical Palms restaurant is a minor gem, with an inviting ambience for breakfast, lunch or dinner (407 351 2100, **www.fourpointsorlandostudiocity.com**).

Home2 Suites: A new brand with a creative style, featuring excellent rooms with a lot of self-catering facilities and plenty of space (ideal for stays of two weeks or more). A free breakfast and wi-fi, plus a neat gym and laundry, provide lots of built-in value, while its location right next to Orlando Premium Outlets (and several restaurants) is another bonus (407 944 1705, **http://home2suites3.hilton.com/**).

Sonesta ES Suites: This refreshing, spacious and Brit-friendly choice features one and two-bed suites sleeping 4–8 in thee versatile layouts, including full kitchens. Includes hot and cold breakfast buffet, and the pool area and hot tub provide a great retreat at the end of the day. The inviting bar area extends to an outdoor patio that guarantees a good social gathering and there is also a fitness centre, snack shop and coin-op laundry, plus free wi-fi and a daily shuttle to the parks (407 352 2400, **www.sonesta.com/ orlando**).

In Lake Buena Vista:

Embassy Suites Lake Buena Vista South: This recent example of the brand is an oasis of calm and modernity, close to Disney yet a wonderful retreat, and with the latest features (407 597 4000, **http:// embassysuites3.hilton.com/**).

Hyatt Place Lake Buena Vista: In an ideal location, close to the Disney hustle-bustle but just out of the way, this drastically modernised hotel is a great example of the contemporary brand, as everything looks and feels like new (407 778 5500, **http://orlandolakebuenavista.place.hyatt.com/en/hotel/home. html**).

Sheraton Lake Buena Vista Resort: A popular choice with Brits, with spacious, well-furnished rooms, spectacular pool complex and fitness centre, and impressive restaurant and lounge (407 239 0444, **www.sheratonlakebuenavistaresort.com**).

Melia Orlando Hotel

Castle Hotel: A unique one-off boutique hotel in the heart of I-Drive, with a luxury touch from a recent renovation that gives it a distinctive Bavarian feel. Plush rooms, sophisticated amenities – including a gorgeous spa – and creative dining combine for an unusually individual style in mass market territory. Check out the Garden Bistro & Bar for chic décor and cuisine, and the heated outdoor pool for a bijou chill-out zone (407 345 1511, **www.castlehotelorlando.com**).

CoCo Key Water Resort: This ultra-family-friendly option offers excellent amenities, notably its extensive water park. Formerly a Ramada, it now boasts a chic lobby and 391 rooms, all with flatscreen TVs, smart bedding and furniture, coffee-maker and free wi-fi. There is a quiet adults' pool, with fountain and Jacuzzi, buffet breakfast room (Tradewinds), food court, indoor sports bar and outdoor Tiki Bar overlooking the Key West-themed water park, with a canopy roof to protect from the sun (but also an uncovered play area and terrace). There is a fitness centre, games arcade, gift shop and kids' club. The water park is a marvel: Parrot's Perch, an interactive jungle-gym; Minnow Lagoon, for pre-school kids, with a zero-depth entry pool, water cannons with mini-slides and other small-scale fun; Coral Reef Cove, the teen activity pool, with the Cyclone

body-slide; and the outdoor Water-Park, with 9 slides, including the Over The Falls and Surfer Splash body-slides and Boomerango double-rider tube slide. There is a 'resort fee' for using the water park, but at $24/room/day, it isn't unreasonable (and it includes wi-fi and parking). Day guests are also allowed when the resort is not full, at $25–27/person (kids under 3ft are free; 407 351 2626, **www.cocokeyorlando.com**).

> ✚ **BRITTIP**
> Need a moderate hotel that is truly family friendly? Consider the CoCo Key Hotel and Water Resort, one of the most thoughtful and feature-packed hotels we've seen in ages.

Hilton Orlando: This impressive 1,400-room hotel on I-Drive next to the big Convention Center boasts superb leisure facilities. It features fabulous dining, including upscale steakhouse, Spencer's, a full-service spa, a large state-of-the-art fitness centre, 2 pools, lazy river (in a wonderful 'tropical island' setting), tennis, volleyball and basketball

Castle Hotel

Coming up Rosen

One notable local operator in Orlando is the Rosen Hotels & Resorts group, with a good variety of 7 well-run, value-conscious properties. Four are budget-minded, the Brit-popular Rosen Inn at Pointe Orlando, Rosen Inn International and Rosen Inn on I-Drive, and the Clarion Inn Lake Buena Vista. All have been impressively refurbished and offer standard amenities but thoughtful touches, like family-style buffet restaurants, kids facilities, plenty of pool choice and free wi-fi. The other hotels are the upscale pair of Rosen Center Hotel and Rosen Plaza Hotel (see below) and the deluxe Rosen Shingle Creek Hotel (p78) (1866 337 6736, **www.rosenhotels.com**).

courts, and a neat 9-hole putting golf course. The Resort pool boasts a waterslide and kids' fountain, while the Quiet pool has several Jacuzzis. Rooms feature Hilton 'Serenity' bedding, HD TVs and high-quality toiletries, while an executive level includes a private lounge and extra services (407 313 4300, **www.thehiltonorlando.com**).

Hyatt Regency Orlando: This huge I-Drive resort appeals largely to convention business but is also well-stocked for holiday fun. Between its 2 towers, it boasts an Olympic-size rooftop pool and a lushly landscaped 3acre/1.2ha recreation area with 3 pools, tropical pool bar and cabañas; tennis courts; a huge fitness centre and spa; and no fewer than 7 restaurants, bars and lounges, including the eclectic, 24hr B-Line Diner and gourmet Italian of Fiorenza. Rooms are gorgeous and wonderfully spacious, but conference business can make the hotel a bit hectic at times (407 284 1234, **www.orlando.regency.hyatt.com**).

Renaissance Orlando Resort: This superb resort next to SeaWorld features a wonderful children's water-park, complete with water-jets, rain-tree and more. It has a massive 10-storey atrium lobby and huge rooms and suites, a lavish spa and fitness centre and a video arcade. All rooms feature extra bathroom amenities, flatscreen TVs and Marriott's Revive bedding. The impressive dining line-up consists of Mist Sushi & Spirits (cocktails and full-service dining), Boardwalk Sports Bar, the upscale but casual Tradewinds for breakfast, lunch and

dinner, Palms Pool Bar & Grill, a smart Starbucks café and ice-cream parlour. The hotel offers great packages in conjunction with SeaWorld, which is a 2min walk across the car park, and its rates are often the best in upmarket territory (407 351 5555, **www.marriott.com/hotels/travel/mcosr-renaissance-orlando-at-seaworld**).

Rosen Center Hotel: This spectacular 24-storey property, one of the area's largest, caters heavily to the Convention Center next door but also offers excellent facilities. It has a huge swimming grotto, tennis courts, an exercise centre, high-quality restaurants (the excellent steak-and-seafood Everglades and casual 24-hour deli, Café Gauguin), the chic Banshoo Sushi bar and 98Forty Tapas & Tequila bar. The style is luxurious, yet prices aren't (1800 204 7234, **www.rosencenter.com**).

Rosen Plaza Hotel: Another trademark I-Drive hotel that has served well over the years but continues to be well looked after and gracious. It offers an excellent pool and Jacuzzi, state-of-the-art gym, business centre and a great array of dining and evening entertainment, including the swish Jack's Place (great steaks and seafood) and its own nightclub, Club 39. It is especially good for Kosher guests (407 996 9700, **www.rosenplaza.com**).

Rosen Shingle Creek Hotel: This 230acre/93ha resort ranks among the grandest for its location, quality and style. In the middle of the Shingle Creek Golf Club on lower Universal Boulevard, it boasts 1,500 rooms and suites, all with sumptuous decor and comfort, as well as a full-service spa

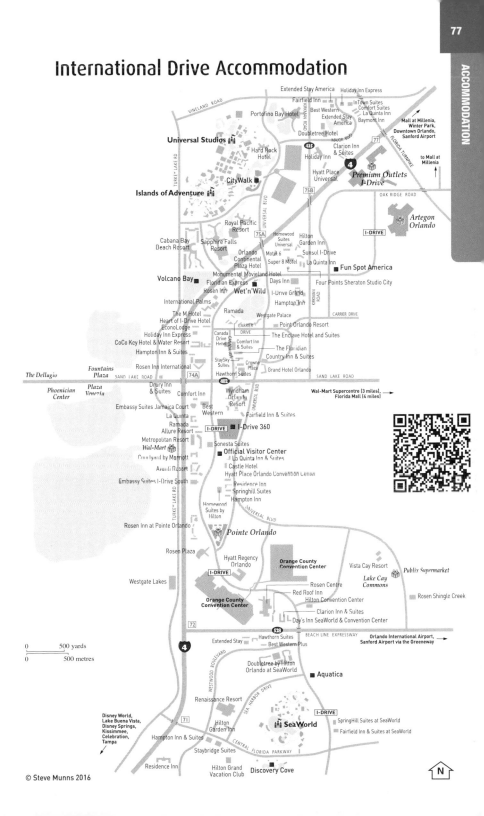

International Drive Accommodation

Extended Stay America · Holiday Inn Express
Fairfield Inn
InTown Suites
VINELAND ROAD
Comfort Suites · La Quinta Inn
Portofino Bay Hotel · Best Western · Baymont Inn
Extended Stay America
Mall at Millenia,
Winter Park,
Downtown Orlando,
Sanford Airport
Doubletree Hotel
Universal Studios
Clarion Inn & Suites
Hard Rock Hotel
Holiday Inn
to Mall at Millenia
Hyatt Place Universal
CityWalk
Premium Outlets I-Drive
75B
Islands of Adventure
OAK RIDGE ROAD
I-DRIVE
Artegon Orlando
Royal Pacific Resort
75A
Homewood Suites Universal · Hilton Garden Inn
I-DRIVE
Cabana Bay Beach Resort · Sapphire Falls Resort
Orlando Continental Plaza Hotel
Motel 6 · Sunsol I-Drive
Super 8 Motel · La Quinta Inn
Fun Spot America
Monumental Movieland Hotel
Volcano Bay
Floridian Express · Days Inn
Four Points Sheraton Studio City
Rosen Inn · Wet'n'Wild
I-Drive Grand
International Palms
Hampton Inn
Ramada
The M Hotel · Westgate Palace
Heart of I-Drive Hotel
CARRIER DRIVE
EconoLodge
Point Orlando Resort
CARRIER DRIVE
Holiday Inn Express
Canada Drive Hotel · The Enclave Hotel and Suites
CoCo Key Hotel & Water Resort
Comfort Inn & Suites
Hampton Inn & Suites
The Floridian
StaySky Suites · Country Inn & Suites
Rosen Inn International · Crowne Plaza
Fountains Plaza · Grand Hotel Orlando
The Dellagio
Hawthorn Suites
SAND LAKE ROAD
Phoenician Center · Plaza Venezia
Drury Inn & Suites
Comfort Inn
Wal-Mart Supercentre (3 miles),
Florida Mall (4 miles)
Wyndham Orlando Resort
Embassy Suites Jamaica Court · Best Western
La Quinta · Fairfield Inn & Suites
Ramada Allure Resort
I-DRIVE · I-Drive 360
Metropolitan Resort
Wal-Mart · Sonesta Suites
Courtyard by Marriott · Official Visitor Center
La Quinta Inn & Suites
Avanti Resort · Castle Hotel
Hyatt Place Orlando Convention Center
Embassy Suites I-Drive South
Residence Inn
Springhill Suites
Hampton Inn
Homewood Suites by Hilton
Rosen Inn at Pointe Orlando
Pointe Orlando
Rosen Plaza
Hyatt Regency Orlando
Orange County Convention Center · Vista Cay Resort · Publix Supermarket
I-DRIVE
Lake Cay Commons
Westgate Lakes
Rosen Centre
Red Roof Inn · Rosen Shingle Creek
Orange County Convention Center
Hilton Convention Center
Clarion Inn & Suites
Day's Inn SeaWorld & Convention Center
72
BEACH LINE EXPRESSWAY
Orlando International Airport,
Sanford Airport via the Greeneway
Extended Stay · Hawthorn Suites
Best Western Plus
Doubletree by Hilton Orlando at SeaWorld
Aquatica
Renaissance Resort
Disney World,
Lake Buena Vista,
Disney Springs,
Kissimmee,
Celebration,
Tampa
71
Hilton Garden Inn · SeaWorld
I-DRIVE
SpringHill Suites at SeaWorld
Hampton Inn & Suites
Fairfield Inn & Suites at SeaWorld
Staybridge Suites
Residence Inn
Hilton Grand Vacation Club · Discovery Cove

0 500 yards
0 500 metres

© Steve Munns 2016

N

and fitness centre. Amenities include 5 restaurants, 4 bars, a lounge, coffee house, deli and ice-creamery, plus 3 outdoor pools, tennis, basketball and volleyball courts and nature trails. There is also a shopping gallery and babysitting service. The resort is built in a 1900s Spanish revival style and offers flawless service. Don't miss A Land Remembered, one of the best steakhouses in the state, in the Golf Clubhouse, and Cala Bella, a fine-dining Italian restaurant, with heavenly desserts from its renowned pastry chef (407 996 6338, **www.rosenshinglecreek.com**).

Others worth considering: Embassy Suites by Hilton International Drive Jamaican Court (**http://embassysuites3. hilton.com/**); Wyndham Orlando Resort (**www.wyndhamorlandoresort.com**); and the stylish The Point Orlando Resort (**www.thepointorlando.com**).

Universal Orlando

The five Universal hotels form their own sub-area just off I-Drive and provide special park benefits for guests.

- Free transportation to the Universal parks, SeaWorld and Aquatica.
- Early entry to the Wizarding Worlds of Harry Potter 1hr before park opening.
- Resort-wide charging privileges with room key.
- In-park merchandise delivered to hotel room.
- Character appearances.
- Special golf privileges at 4 nearby courses.
- FREE Universal Express unlimited ride access (for Portofino Bay, Royal Pacific and Hard Rock hotels only).

There's also a lot of variety.

Cabana Bay Beach Resort: Opened in 2014, Universal's first moderate hotel is split into two parts either side of a central reception with classic 1950s styling. There are 1,800 standard rooms and family suites with kitchenettes, sleeping up to six, set around an efficient 600-seat Food Court, with food stations including burgers and milk shakes, salads, pizza

Hard Rock Hotel

The SeaWorld bonus

For anyone planning on a lot of SeaWorld and Aquatica visits, consider a **SeaWorld Official Partner Hotel** for a range of benefits and money-saving offers. All 8 feature free Quick Queue at SeaWorld, a free behind-the-scenes Rescue Tour, free shuttle service to SeaWorld and Aquatica, early park entry on select days, free signature show seating, 10% off dining and 10% off merchandise purchases of $50 or more. Alternatively, there are another 8 hotels that offer the early entry, show seating, and 10% discounts. See **https://seaworldparks.com/en/seaworld-orlando/vacations/hotels/benefits/**.

and pasta, a bakery, sandwiches and Grab & Go section. Other options include a retro Starbucks coffee shop, lobby bar and two elaborate pool bars offering signature frozen drinks and smoothies. The Lazy River Courtyard also offers the Hideaway Bar & Grille for lunch and dinner. Guests can even have pizza delivered to rooms that feature all mod cons, with flatscreen TVs, mini fridge, wi-fi and a clever bathroom that features two wash-basins and separate bathtub/shower. Amenities include a 10-lane bowling alley with its own bar/restaurant, and two feature-packed resort pool areas, with zero-depth entry, sandy beaches, waterslide and Universal's first lazy river, all with extensive period theming. Extras include a large video games room and themed fitness centre with lockers and showers (handy if your room isn't ready and you want to change for the parks). It has its own shuttle bus to CityWalk, or a 15min walk (407 503 4000, **www.loewshotels.com/cabana-bay-hotel**).

Hard Rock Hotel: Possibly the coolest hotel in Orlando, this icon of rock chic is themed as a former rock star's home, with 650 rooms and suites in California mission style: high ceilings, wooden beams, marble floors and eclectic artwork. The rock-star theme is in most public areas, with music memorabilia, black-suited staff and fairly constant music. The hotel features three bars (including the ultra-cool Velvet Bar), two restaurants (the full-service The Kitchen and five-star, dinner-only Palm Restaurant), plus a takeaway café, fitness centre, gift shop and games room. The Kitchen features a character breakfast every

Tues. The lido area features a huge, freeform pool with underwater sound system and 240ft/73m waterslide, two Jacuzzis, beach volleyball, shuffleboard and life-size chess and draughts. The 650 big rooms (with 12 kidsuites and 10 king suites) are beautifully furnished and comfortable (407 503 2000, **www.loewshotels.com/hard-rock-hotel**).

Portofino Bay Hotel: The stunning jewel in Universal's crown is a splendid re-creation of the famous Italian port. Elaborate porticos, *trompe l'oeil* painting, harbourside piazza and waterfront ornamentation make it one of Florida's most memorable settings. With 750 rooms, even standard rooms are sumptuous, with huge beds, spacious bathrooms, mini-bar and coffee facilities, ironing board and hairdryer. The 94 Club Rooms offer concierge service with private lounge, extra room amenities and free entry to the Mandara Spa fitness centre. There are 18 *Despicable Me* themed kidsuites with separate bedrooms (complete with missile beds!). Resort facilities are equally smart – a Roman aqueduct-style pool with waterslide, an enclosed kids' play area and wading pool, a separate quiet pool, Jacuzzis, the Mandara Spa, business centre, an array of gift shops and a video games room. The Portofino also has an amazing eight restaurants and lounges, including the five-star Bice Ristorante (p311), the boisterous Trattoria del Porto, Mama Della's, an Italian family dining experience (watch out for Mama herself!), an aromatic deli, a pizzeria, gelateria and swanky Bar American. It is only a short distance from the parks, but is light-years away

The Sky's the limit

For a good cross-section, from budget hotels to villas and community resorts, **Sky Hotels & Resorts** offers great value and some prime locations in Orlando and Daytona Beach. The **Enclave Suites** make for great family value in an ideal location just off I-Drive while nearby the **staySky Suites I-Drive Orlando** feature one-bedroom suites and full kitchens with a newly designed lobby and Marketplace Bar serving cocktails and bar food. There is free breakfast, shuttle transport to the parks and wi-fi, as well as a fitness centre, heated pool and hot tub, games room and free parking. Closer to Disney, the **Hawthorn Suites Lake Buena Vista** have 1-bed suites and a shuttle to the Disney parks, while staySky also feature the excellent **Lake Buena Vista Resort Village & Spa** (p87). **Coral Cay Resort** in Kissimmee is a well-designed gated development of three and four-bed town-homes (terraced villas). For a fab beach break, the three-star **Hawaiian Inn** is a great option on the oceanfront at Daytona Beach (1866 455 4062, **www.staysky.com**).

in terms of its tranquil ambience (407 503 1000, **www.loewshotels.com/ portofino-bay-hotel**).

◀▶ BRITTIP

For a romantic dinner, book a table at the Portofino Bay's Bice for early evening, when the restaurant is serenaded at sunset by opera singers Musica della Notte from the piazza below.

Royal Pacific Resort: This 1,000-room resort has an exotic 1930s South Seas style, and you feel as if you have stepped into another world as you cross the bamboo bridge into the elegant lobby. Extensive use of rich, dark woods, stone floors and masses of greenery give it an opulent, colonial feel. Standard rooms feature hand-carved Balinese furniture among many refined touches, and there is also a Club level, with separate lounge and extended facilities, and 51 superlative suites – including eight Jurassic Park-themed kidsuites (dinosaurs not included!). The Islands Dining Room offers breakfast, lunch and dinner in an oriental setting (children have their own buffet area with TV screen, plus a Sunday character breakfast), while fine dining is taken to new heights by celebrity chef Emeril Lagasse in Tchoup Chop (p312). There's a pool snack bar and luau garden area, with the Wantilan Luau Saturday nights, featuring a

Polynesian feast and dinner show ($69–76 adults, $35–40 under-13s; 407 503 3463 to book). The huge freeform pool is ideal for kids, with zero-depth entry and a boat-shaped interactive play area of squirting fountains. Add a health club (with Jacuzzi, sauna and gym), kids' club (with computer games, TVs and activities), video arcade and two shops and you have excellent value, even at this end of the scale (407 503 3000, **www.loewshotels.com/ royal-pacific-resort**).

Sapphire Falls Resort: New in summer 2016 was this Caribbean-themed tropical oasis, with 1,000 rooms (including 77 ultra-spacious suites and kidsuites) and a glittering array of amenities. A resort-style pool features a waterslide, children's play area, sand beach, Jacuzzi, private cabañas and fire pit, forming a central courtyard surrounded by guest rooms. A full-service Caribbean restaurant, Amatista, offers scenic views and outdoor dining, while there's also a quick-service marketplace, a lobby lounge and fancy poolside bar, Drhum Club Kantine, plus state-of-the-art fitness centre with saunas. Like the three deluxe resorts, there is water taxi and shuttle access to CityWalk and it is one of Universal's most picturesque hotels, with flowing rivers and waterfalls in addition to the main pool and elegant outdoor terraces (1888 430 4999, **www.loewshotels.com/ sapphire-falls-resort**).

BRITTIP

Don't miss the superb Strong Water Tavern at Sapphire Falls. It features a unique array of vintage rums, plus a fabulous Caribbean small-plate menu.

Lake Buena Vista

Moving to the other major resort area, there is a growing range of distinctive choice here, too.

Caribe Royale Resort: A huge, quality-conscious suites hotel boasting a great array of amenities (including a tropical pool with waterslide, tennis courts, basketball and modern fitness centre), plus great dining, notably at the award-winning Venetian Chop House, which offers some of the best contemporary cuisine in town (1800 823 8300, **www.cariberoyale.com**).

Delta Orlando: The 'new kid on the block,' ideally located by the Crossroads area at the entrance to Disney Springs, this extensive conversion of the old Orlando Vista Hotel is now a US trail-blazer for the Delta brand, with chic dining, excellent family pool and super-comfy rooms (the beds are superb).

The style is bright and welcoming and the lobby features an excellent bar/lounge, as well as D Flats, their combo coffee bar and café, featuring pizzas, flatbreads and paninis. Organic breakfast choices, low-energy features throughout the hotel, an imaginative kids play-room and an outdoor patio with fire-fountain feature highlight this as well above average (407 387 9999, **www.marriott.com**).

BRITTIP

Most villas and resorts do not have electric kettles, but you can find them at stores such as Wal-Mart and Super Target. Small versions are reasonably priced.

Holiday Inn Resort Orlando Suites: Formerly the high-energy Nickelodeon Suites, now refurbished as a smart family resort with masses of amenities. The choice includes two huge water-play areas (with 13 slides and flumes), video arcade, mini-golf and laser tag. The resort's Marketplace hub is home to an array of shops and dining, with a smart bar, plus Antonio's Pizzeria, Stackers Deli and Lakeside Café. Rooms come in one-bed kitchen suites and two and three-bed kidsuites, with living room and bathroom, microwave and fridge

Delta Orlando Resort

(and full kitchen with some). Close to Disney and with free transport, it is a mini theme park in its own right (407 387 5437; **www.ihg.com/ holidayinnresorts/hotels/us/en/orlando/ disfs/hoteldetail**).

Hilton at Bonnet Creek Resort: Extensive and unique development inside Walt Disney World but privately owned (the one piece of land Walt was unable to buy in 1966), it's part of a 482acre/194ha resort with the Waldorf-Astoria (below) and shares some of the facilities. The Hilton features 1,000 rooms, four restaurants, a lagoon pool complex with lazy river and waterslide, 18-hole golf course, tennis courts and the adjoining full-service European spa and fitness centre. The chic modern Italian-themed La Luce restaurant provides fine dining, while the Harvest Bistro offers the main alternative (kids 12 and under eat free with a full-paying adult), along with the Muse grab-and-go deli and coffee bar, Zeta Bar and Sushi Lounge and Beech Pool Bar and Grill. Just minutes from the Disney parks, it benefits from the full Hilton package of stylish accommodation and excellent kids' activities, as well as blissfully comfy rooms (407 597 3600, **www.hiltonbonnetcreek.com**).

Hyatt Regency Grand Cypress: The area's first genuine deluxe hotel in 1984, this is still one of the best. A mature 1,500acre/608ha resort with a unique mix of facilities, it has a rare nine-hole pitch-and-putt golf course, 27 holes of regular golf (designed by Jack Nicklaus), a golf academy, boating lake and superb pool complex with a kids' water park, rock-climbing wall and snack bar. Recent extensive enhancements were made to every guest room, fitness centre and restaurants. The elegant lobby boasts Zen-inspired décor with some highly relaxing touches, while all 750 rooms have a bright, contemporary finish, with large, flatscreen TVs, large shower units and elaborate lighting. The dining choice is among the best of any Orlando resort, and the location remains ideal, almost on the doorstep of

Disney yet blissfully reclusive (on Winter Garden-Vineland Road, around the corner from the Crossroads area). The huge freeform swimming pool boasts Jacuzzis, waterfalls and slide, while the white sand beach and restaurants make for a sumptuous stay, especially Hemingway's, its Key West-styled dinner spot with a Cuban twist, and Lake House, the all-day option with its two-storey atrium and beautiful lake views. There's also the On the Rocks pool bar, Perks coffee bar, an inviting lobby lounge and Hurricanes Lounge for some excellent cocktails (try their Papa Doble). Boating, kayaking, fishing, tennis and bike rentals are all covered by the one-off resort fee. And, once among its richly landscaped grounds, you could be light years from the theme-park bustle (407 239 1234, **http:// grandcypress.hyatt.com**).

◀▶ BRITTIP

The Hyatt regency Grand Cypress features the fun Marilyn Monroe Spa, a great option for a chillout break, whether you are staying at the hotel or not. It offers hairstyling, manicures, pedicures, a make-up bar, facials and massages, all with a suitably glamorous touch (321 558 7818 for appointments).

Orlando World Center Marriott: We love this impressive landmark on Disney's outskirts, set in 200 landscaped acres and surrounded by a beautiful golf course. With 2,000 rooms and suites (most with great views), six restaurants, food court and a series of pools, including a huge freeform tropical pool and three water slides, it is a monumental prospect. Its facilities include a Bill Madonna Golf Academy, tennis courts, volleyball, basketball, spa and state-of-the-art gym. Highlights are the Mikado Japanese Steakhouse, Hawk's Landing Steakhouse, Siro Urban Italian Kitchen and High Velocity Sports Bar, while there are excellent children's amenities and programmes. It gets busy with convention business, but the picturesque pool complex offers true relaxation and the spacious rooms are equally impressive (407 239 4200, **www.marriottworldcenter.com**).

Waldorf-Astoria: The second part of the Bonnet Creek development, this 497-room hotel was the first US Waldorf outside New York in 2009. Stately and serene, the famous-name hotel features 313 standard rooms with Italian marble bathrooms and HD flat-screen TVs, plus 185 grand suites with butler service. The zero-entry pool has cabañas and waiter service, while the dining choice is superb, from the poolside grille and classic Bull & Bear Steakhouse to the small-plate cuisine of Peacock Alley, gourmet style of Oscar's brasserie and private club atmosphere of Sir Harry's Lounge. The spa is equally classy, and other amenities include basketball, tennis, jogging trails, bike rentals, state-of-the-art fitness centre (with personal trainers), yoga and aerobics classes and boutique shops to match the Waldorf's luxury cachet. The WA Kids Club provides active, creative fun for 5–12s, with Day Escape (10.30am–2.30pm) and After Dark (6–10pm) programmes with a meal and games at $75/child and $25 each additional child (407 597 5500, **www.waldorfastoriaorlando.com**).

Wyndham Grand: Another high-quality resort nestled inside the Bonnet Creek area, with more sumptuous style in a Mediterranean character. Beautifully fitted rooms are matched by excellent dining choices, notably the Deep Blu Seafood Grille, flexible Tesoro Cove (buffet breakfast and Italian-style bistro) and Back Bay Bar and Grill overlooking the 10acre/4ha lake. An excellent fitness centre, lagoon-style pool and blissful spa complete a superbly appointed resort (407 390 2300, **www.wyndhamgrandorlando.com**).

Others worth considering: Buena Vista Suites (**www.buenavistasuites. com**); Embassy Suites Lake Buena Vista (**http://embassysuites3.hilton.com/**);

and the Holiday Inn Resort Lake Buena Vista (**www.hiresortlbv.com**).

◀▎▶ BRITTIP

If you're like many travellers who have trouble falling asleep with a whirring air conditioner in your room, drop by Wal-Mart, Walgreens, or CVS and pick up a packet of soft foam earplugs. Effective enough to filter out the drone without making you deaf to 'important' noises.

Further afield

There are also a handful of hotels worth pointing out that are not in the main tourist areas but still have great appeal.

Alfond Inn: In an ideal quiet part of Winter Park, but handy for the shops, restaurants and museums, this gorgeous boutique hotel is owned by nearby Rollins College and run with great style. The rooms are opulent, the service is gracious and the dining is some of the best in the area. There is also a fabulous roof-top pool, gym and outdoor patio, plus a popular cocktail bar and library lounge (407 998 8090, **www.alfondinn.com**).

◀▎▶ BRITTIP

Even if you don't stay at the Alfond Inn, it is worth a visit if you are in Winter Park, especially for **Hamilton's Kitchen**, an award-winning restaurant that serves modern Southern cuisine with panache for lunch and dinner (p326).

Grande Lakes Orlando: You'll find extensive luxury at this 500acre/200ha combination of a 584-room, Ritz-Carlton Hotel, a 1,000-room JW Marriott Hotel, grand spa, 18-hole Greg Norman golf course, tennis centre and upscale range of shops and restaurants, like the outstanding Norman's, featuring the 'new world' cuisine of celebrity

Alfond Inn

chef Norman Van Aken. On the edge of a forestry preserve, it feels secluded and remote – quite a feat in this area. It is slightly off the beaten track – at the junction of John Young and Central Florida Parkway – yet is only 10ml/16km from Disney and Orlando Airport.

JW Marriott: This flagship hotel of the Marriott group has Spanish-Moorish design and fabulous dining, including the fresh organic produce of Whisper Creek Farm: The Kitchen (with its own craft brewery), classic Italian at Primo, Starbucks, sushi bar and a pool bar and grill. It has a great lazy river mini-water park, plus a kids' pool and splash fountain. Rooms are plush and ultra-comfortable; 70% with balconies, and there are 64 grand suites.

Ritz-Carlton: This offers wonderful scale and detail, with lush gardens, abundant lakes and streams, Venetian-inspired architecture and a wealth of antiques. It has a large, sloped-entry pool, kids' pool, three floodlit tennis courts, a shop and five dining choices, plus a separate children's check-in and the excellent Ritz Kids Club (5–12s; also for JW Marriott guests). As well as the highly rated Norman's, the restaurants include Southern-inspired Highball and Harvest (one of our faves; p327), Fairways Pub and Bleu pool bar and grill. The rooms are beautifully furnished, with high-quality products, marbled bathrooms, plasma-screen TVs, radio/CD, mini-bar, slippers and robes. There are 66 spacious suites and 92 Club rooms on the top two floors, with concierge and butler service. The immaculate golf course offers the ultimate Caddie Concierge programme. The beautiful citrus-tinged spa boasts a huge fitness centre and aerobics studio, lap pool (all free to guests at both hotels), lovely restaurant and a huge range of treatments. The pricing is suitably upmarket, but it is a rare treat.

Barefoot'n Resort

© Diamond Resorts and Hotels

Note the $30 daily resort fee (407 206 2300/2400, **www.grandelakes.com**).

Omni Orlando Resort at Champions Gate: This imposing hotel offers 720 rooms overlooking a superb golf set-up, with two Greg Norman-designed courses. The impressive facilities include the HQ of the renowned David Leadbetter golf academy, a main swimming pool and activity pool (including a lazy river, fountains and waterslide), four restaurants (notably the superb Asian cuisine of Zen and chic David's Club bar-grill), coffee bar, deli, three lounge bars, state-of-the-art health club and full-service spa. Just 15mins south of Disney off I-4, this is well situated yet off the beaten track for those (especially golfers) looking for something different. Set in 1,500 landscaped acres/607ha and with a magnificent vista as you walk in, it suits both business travellers and leisure-seekers. It also has 59 superb 2 and 3-bed villas, affording a more private stay, with full kitchens and opulent furnishings (407 390 6664, **www.omnihotels.com/hotels/orlando-championsgate**).

Airport convenience

If you need to stay near the airport, either if you have a late arrival or you prefer to collect your hire car in the morning rather than straight after a long flight, consider this duo.

Hyatt Regency: It doesn't get more convenient than a hotel inside the airport, and this one also benefits from excellent restaurants, pool deck, fitness room, lounge and business centre. Rooms are ultra- spacious, particularly the corner rooms, and many feature internal balconies overlooking the airport atrium. We especially enjoy dining or drinks at McCoy's (breakfast, lunch and dinner) Restaurant, with its appealing menu and sushi bar, while Hemisphere has award-winning steaks and seafood (breakfast and dinner only) as well as great views. There is no noticeable aircraft noise and none of the bustle you expect at an airport hotel and staying here is a real boon if you're looking for a stress-free arrival (407 825 1234, **http://orlandoairport.hyatt.com**).

Doubletree by Hilton at Orlando Airport: Just 5mins north of the airport, this is another good choice for relaxation. A pool area provides plenty of chill-out potential while the spacious rooms feature flatscreen TVs, wi-fi, coffee-makers and either a king bed or two doubles. The junior suites add a living area, larger TV, kitchenette and dining table. The lobby features welcome cookies (a Doubletree speciality) and a lounge-bar and restaurant that is especially inviting at night. There is a modern fitness centre and business centre with computers. Bistro 436 features the trademark Wake-up Doubletree breakfast buffet, plus lunch and dinner. Extremely disabled-friendly, it used to be the Crowne Plaza but benefits from the Hilton brand (407 856 0100, **www.OrlandoAirport. DoubleTree.com**).

SELF-CATERING

This is now a big choice for British visitors, many of whom prefer the extra space and convenience of the villa communities, town homes, studios and condo resorts, all of which are essentially self-catering (although some still offer restaurants and other hotel-type amenities). They tend to be further away from the parks but represent a flexible option, especially for larger groups. They usually have fewer amenities than a hotel but can be more comfortable for a two-week (or longer) stay, and you can save money on not having to dine out all the time and doing your own laundry.

Bahama Bay Resort: A wonderful lakeside location in Davenport (south of Highway 192), this is spread over 70acres/28ha, with 498 condos in 38 two and three-storey buildings. It is woven with tropical landscaping that includes water features, a recreation centre and clubhouse, Tradewinds Restaurant & Bar, Mambo's Poolside Bar & Grille, Cenote Day Spa, fitness centre, tennis, basketball and volleyball, four heated pools

and kiddie pools. You can fish in the lake, plus there are nature trails and billiard tables. You can arrange shuttle transport to the parks for a small charge. The four types of condo offer two-bed, two-bath (sleeping six, with a sofa-bed in the lounge) and three-bed, two-bath (sleeping eight, again with sofa-bed), with fitted kitchen, laundry room, living room and dining area. The Grand Bahama three-bed condo has 1,739ft^2/162m^2 of space and is one of the most elegant (1877 299 4481 or **www.wyndhamvacationrentals.com**).

Barefoot'n Resort: This boutique timeshare of 82 one- and two-bed condos is tucked away next to Old Town in Kissimmee. There's a main pool, kids' pool, whirlpool, children's play area, volleyball and barbecue stations (407 856 7190, **www.barefootn.com**).

 BRITTIP

If you prefer a tranquil Lake View room at the Blue Heron Beach Resort, you can still get a view of Disney's fireworks at night from the outdoor corridor/terrace on each floor.

Blue Heron Beach Resort: A superb complex of two high-rise towers on Apopka-Vineland Rd (Highway 535) in Lake Buena Vista, this features 283 beautifully furnished one and two-bed condos, with two bathrooms, a balcony and fully equipped kitchen, including washer-dryer. There are bunk beds in the spacious one and two-bed units,

Encore Club

© Encore Resort Homes

ACCOMMODATION

which comfortably sleep 6–8. All master bedrooms include a whirlpool tub. All have balconies overlooking Lake Bryan while the two-bed Deluxe suites have a second balcony with a Disney fireworks view. There is a superb lido deck, with a large pool, kids' pool and hot tub, plus a boardwalk fronting the lake and watersports (jet-skis and water-skiing, for an extra charge), with the Hawaiian Rumble mini-golf course next door. There is a smart Tiki Bar as well as two fitness centres, but no restaurant (although there are plenty nearby, including a CiCi's Pizza, Starbucks, Dunkin' Donuts, Subway and Hurricane Grill). As a self-catering resort, housekeeping is available for a charge, but there's a free daily shuttle to Disney and SeaWorld and, for $12/person, to Universal (407 387 2200, **www.blueheronbeachresort.com**).

BRITBONUS

Get seven nights for the price of five or 14 for the price of 10 at the Blue Heron Beach Resort. Call 407 387 2900 or 1888 258 3684 and mention booking code 'BRIT75'. Valid until 18 Dec 2017; not valid with any other discount or coupon. Based on average Bar Rate and availability; blackout dates apply.

Encantada Resort: A lovely development of two and three-bed town-homes, this offers a lot of facilities at the central clubhouse and a great location south of west Highway 192 but still close to Disney. Each home has two bathrooms and a separate W/C, kitchen, dining area and living room with big-screen LCD TV and home cinema, a private terrace, fitted with mosquito nets,

Floridays Resort

Self-catering definitions

To avoid confusion, here's the correct terminology for self-catering accommodation (but check with the operator for the exact type if it's not clear):

Villa: Detached vacation home, usually with its own screened-in pool, in self-contained residential communities.

Town-home: Two-storey terraced-style house, rarely with its own pool; found in many Resorts.

Condo: One, two or three-bed apartment-style unit, usually in a low-rise block but sometimes 10 or more storeys.

Studio: One-room accommodation unit with kitchen facilities.

Resort: Collection of condos (or town-homes) built around central features like pools, recreation facilities and, sometimes, a restaurant/bar or two.

sunbeds, table, chairs and Jacuzzi. The bedrooms are on the first floor with the master bed featuring a 30in/50cm TV and en-suite bathroom. The clubhouse has a heated zero-entry pool, a swimming pool with a Jacuzzi, a children's play area and a private lake surrounded by a walking/jogging trail. It also has a 24hr reception, a bar with a pool table, cyber café, games arcade and a well-equipped gym, as well as the Team Marina kids' club (407 997 9478, **www.encantadaflorida.com**).

Encore Club: Adjacent to the huge Reunion Resort (p90), this is the latest community of high-quality villas surrounding an ultra-impressive, well-appointed clubhouse. The homes vary from five bedrooms (all with en suite bathrooms) to massive 10-bed mansions, all with private pools, designer kitchens and the smartest mod cons, many including Jacuzzis, games rooms and home theatres. Some even come with themed bedrooms. The wonderful clubhouse includes a whole Aquapark with an array of slides, flumes and water features, as well as a resort pool, large

Lake Buena Vista Resort

fitness centre, the Hang Ten Hideaway for kids, Grab & Go market, full-service restaurant (the excellent Finns) and bar/lounge. There is a fully staffed reception desk and a concierge that can arrange tickets and transportation to the parks, plus services like baby-sitting, personal chefs and grocery deliveries (407 396 9000, **www.encoreresorthomes.com**).

BRITTIP

If the designer homes of the Encore Club sound good, check out the rental options with British-owned Jeeves Management (p96) for a great selection.

Floridays Resort: One of the smartest of the area's condo-hotels, this is situated in a quieter part of I-Drive, but close to Orlando Premium Outlets and with a free shuttle to the parks. The 18 tropical acres feature six towers (each with 72 rooms), two pools (including the elaborate main zero-depth entry pool and water-play area), a pool bar and grill, fitness centre, stylish Welcome Center, kids' activity centre and games room, a small grocery store, plus concierge services, business centre and meeting facilities. The spacious two and three-bed suites are beautifully furnished, sleep 6–10, and have either a balcony or patio. Living rooms include flatscreen TV, high-speed wi-fi, games console and stereos, while there are two bathrooms, one with a Jacuzzi. There's also a delivery service (8am–10pm) from the Café & Marketplace,

which serves Starbucks coffee. All rooms are wheelchair-accessible and some are adapted for the disabled with roll-in showers (1866 994 6321, **www.floridaysresortorlando.com**).

Fountains Resort: This high-quality timeshare, available to the public when not fully booked, is on the quieter stretch of I-Drive (south of SeaWorld). It has superb two-bed, two-bath condos, with full kitchens, plus a huge pool area with waterslides and poolside bar, all in a beautiful tropical environment, with the large Clubhouse boasting a games room, kids' activity centre, bar, coffee lounge and spa services (1800 456 0009, **www.bluegreenrentals.com**).

Hapimag Orlando Resort: An unusual mix of vacation home and resort, this is the Swiss timeshare operator's only US property (but with NO timeshare solicitation) inside the mature Lake Berkley villa community (almost behind Medieval Times). It comprises a self-contained circle of two and three-bed town-homes, around a busy clubhouse with pool, volleyball court, small fitness centre and gift shop.

There are also a handful of fully furnished four-bed villas elsewhere in the community, which has its own clubhouse and smart pool area with kids' pool, plus another gym, games room and internet room. There is a scenic walkway around the lake, with two white-sand beaches (407 390 9083, **www.orlando-hapimag.com**).

BRITBONUS

Stay six nights in a row at Hapimag Orlando Resort and the 7th is free. Special rates for one, two and three-bed units of $97, $108 & $129/night low season and $120, $130 & $151/night high season; and $140, $151 & $172 at Christmas (plus tax). All offers valid to end 2017; subject to availability; some blackout dates apply. Quote code 'Brit Guide 2017' when booking on 407 390 9083 or email **www.orlando@hapimag.com**.

Lake Buena Vista Resort Village & Spa: This stylish condo-hotel features five tower blocks of two, three and four-bed condos, next to Lake Buena Vista Factory Stores on Highway 535. The impressive facilities include a superb freeform swimming pool, with pirate play-ship, a quiet pool, a state-of-the-art fitness centre, video games room and Kids' Club. There is a convenience store and gift shop, a Pizza Hut Express, Frankie Farrell's Irish Pub & Grille and Lani's Luau, a pool-side bar and grill, as well as a shuttle to the main theme parks (as part of the resort fee). The rooms (all with full kitchens, Jacuzzi bathtubs, digital TVs and wi-fi) are comfortable and stylish, with the four-bed condos super-spacious. Housekeeping is available either daily or weekly for a charge, while the resort fee covers a grocery delivery and dry-cleaning service, although all rooms come with a washer and dryer. The Reflections Spa & Salon offers some wonderfully relaxing treatments (407 597 0214, **www.lbvorlandoresort.com**).

BRITTIP

Visiting Lake Buena Vista Factory Stores? Relieve aching limbs by popping next door to the Reflections Spa in the Resort Village for a soothing pedicure, massage or other treatment (407 597 1695).

Liki Tiki Village: On the western fringe of Highway 192, this timeshare set-up often has good-value condos to rent on a weekly basis. It features spacious one, two and three-bed condos, all with well-equipped kitchens (including coffee and ice-makers), while the 64acre/26ha complex has two pools, a mini water park, tennis courts, paddle boats, mini-golf, pool-bar and grill, free wi-fi and kids activity programmes Mon–Fri (407 239 5000, **www.likitiki.com**).

Magic Village Resort: Beautiful new community of three and four-bed town-homes, close to Disney but in a quiet location, and with a Brazilian/ Mediterranean design quality. The central clubhouse features a gorgeous main pool, kids' play-room, gym and an excellent restaurant, Villaggio, which features gourmet pizza in a creative menu. The bar offers beer, wine and sake, which can all be served poolside, with a view of the Disney fireworks at night. There is a free shuttle to Disney's Animal Kingdom, 24hr reception and a concierge desk that can arrange in-home private parties, private chefs and grocery delivery. The homes are equally stylish, with the latest kitchen appliances, high-speed wi-fi, bathrooms with every bedroom and a

Magic Village Resort

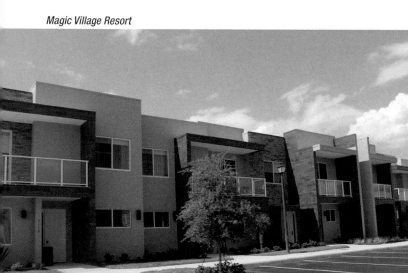

first-floor balcony with sun-loungers. Some have outdoor barbecue grills or Jacuzzis, and all have washers and dryers and HD flatscreen TVs (407 507 5900, **www.magicvillagevacationhomes. com**).

MargaritaVillage: Due to begin opening in late 2017 is this immense resort on Highway 192 in Kissimmee (by Formosa Gardens). Based on the 'Floribbean' style of musician Jimmy Buffett, it will feature a 174-room Margaritaville Hotel, plus 500 vacation homes, a timeshare element *and* condos, making this the most multi-use resort in the area. The array of features – including a 3acre/1 1/2ha freshwater swimming lagoon, water park, wedding pavilion, spa, fishing school and multiple pools – is dazzling, along with waterfalls and other water features that will bring a Key West feel to the resort. More details on the website **www.margaritavilleorlandoresort.com**.

Mystic Dunes Resort & Golf Club: This holiday ownership property is tucked away in a quiet corner of Kissimmee and offers hotel-type rentals, often at terrific rates.

It features just about every facility, including four pools, waterslide and water-play area, plus one, two and three-bed condos that sleep up to 12, a championship-quality golf course, mini-golf and great dining (1877 747 4747, **www.mystic-dunes-resort.com**).

Orange Lake Resort: This vast resort on west Highway 192 offers a mixture of well-furnished one, two and three-bed condos (Orange Lake refers to them as 'villas' but they are apartment-type) and studios that sleep 4–12, plus golf, watersports and cinema. Then there are kids' activities, exercise classes, tennis, racquetball, mini-golf and a Marketplace of general store, pizzeria and golf shop. The River Island water park has a lazy river, two zero-depth entry pools, mini-golf, whirlpool tubs, waterfalls and a clubhouse, arcade and fitness centre, while the Water's Edge Beach Club adds a restaurant, pool bar, cabañas, stage and gift shop, plus an Olympic-size pool with beach-style entry. There is also a Publix supermarket, and this resort gets consistently good feedback, if occasionally a bit strong on the timeshare sales (407 239 0000, **http://experienceorangelake.com/**).

Palisades Resort: A real find out at the rural western end of Highway 192 in Kissimmee, this smart condo-hotel features spacious one, two and three-bed condos that sleep 4–8, with

An artist's impression of the Kissimmee MargaritaVillage

fully equipped kitchens, including washer-dryers, and private balconies. Each unit offers generous living and dining areas, two bathrooms (master bed with oversized bath) and flatscreen TVs. The tropical lido deck has a large outdoor pool in lush surroundings, plus there is a sauna, fitness centre, small shop for sundries and free wi-fi. It is close enough to benefit from the shops and restaurants along Highway 192 (and be 10mins from Disney), but still be tranquil. There is no bar or restaurant, but a Publix supermarket is only 5mins away (321 250 3030, **www.palisadesvacations.com**).

$ BRITBONUS

Holiday Inn Club Vacations @ Orange Lake Resort are offering a Resort Credit package for use in the resort for things like pizza, lazy-river tube rentals, play passes or a family dinner. Enjoy villa-style accommodation and receive a $50 resort credit when you stay two nights, plus an extra $25 credit for each extra night. Call 1866 892 5890 and mention IKREC or book online at **www.hiclubvacations.com**.

Regal Oaks at Old Town: This mix of stylish two, three and four-bed town-homes (with two or three baths), follows the successful blueprint of accommodations set around an elaborate clubhouse, with fabulous water features (zero-entry pool, waterslide, whirlpool and lazy river), Tiki Bar and other facilities. All the homes feature an enclosed patio with Jacuzzi, there is a full-service restaurant, market, tennis courts, bike rentals and fitness centre. Next to all

Sheraton Vistana Resort

© Sheraton Vistana

the fun and shopping of Old Town in Kissimmee, it offers terrific value (407 997 1000, **www.regaloaks. com**).

Regal Palms Resort & Spa: Next door to the serene Highlands Reserve villa community on Highway 27 is this mix of three and four-bed town-homes and four and five-bed villas set around a beautiful clubhouse that includes a mini water park (with lazy river and waterslides), pools, Jacuzzis, extensive sun terraces and free wi-fi. The sister resort to Regal Oaks, it has a pub that shows live UK sports, a business centre, gym and gift shop/ grocery store, plus an indulgent Spa & Health Club (407 965 3887, **www.regalpalmsorlando.com**).

Reunion Resort & Club: One of the most extensive resorts, this will interest golfers who appreciate the chance to stay where they play and lovers of the high life. On Highway 532 in Kissimmee (just off exit 58 of I-4 south of Disney), this 'community' boasts a vast line-up of condos, town-homes and luxury villas set around three superb golf courses (designed by Arnold Palmer, Tom Watson and Jack Nicklaus). The choice is deluxe, featuring one and two-bed condos (many with stunning golf-course views); a range of private homes, from modest three-beds to mansion-style 15-beds; a stylish golf clubhouse with excellent bar and restaurant; a full-service spa; 11 pools, including the scenic Seven Eagles pool, complete with The Cove bar and grill, Jacuzzis, fitness room and kids' play centre; floodlit tennis courts; an amazing water park consisting of lazy river, slides, pools, waterfalls and interactive kids' area; and miles of biking and hiking trails.

High-rise condo, the Reunion Grande, features 82 luxurious one and two-bed suites, brilliant Italian cuisine restaurant Forte, a modern gym and chic rooftop pool-bar, Eleven, offering American fare, cocktails and panoramic views. It all comes with concierge service and private in-room dining that marks this out as one of Florida's most upmarket resorts. Only those staying here or members can play on the courses, but the scale of the resort is superb (407 662 1000, **www.reunionresort.com**). Reunion is also home to the state-of-the-art ANNIKA Academy, created under the direction of top golfer Annika Sorenstam.

⚡ BRITTIP

At both Sheraton Vistana properties, for a nominal fee, you can arrange to have your condo pre-stocked with food and laundry products.

Sheraton Vistana Resort: This sprawling family-friendly resort set-up in Lake Buena Vista, close to Walt Disney World, is a mature development of modern, roomy one and two-bed/two-bath condos (sleeping 4–8; again, they are called 'villas' but are definitely apartment-type) with fully equipped kitchens and magnificent resort facilities. Multiple TVs, DVD player and a screened-in private patio or balcony, plus large washer-dryers, which all serves to underline the great self-catering value of this type of accommodation. There are seven giant pools, 13 floodlit tennis courts, smart Marketplace deli (with Starbucks coffee), casual café/restaurant and three pool bars, plus massage treatments. There is complimentary scheduled transport to select Disney parks and lots of family-orientated activities, including poolside parties, crafts and more (407 239 3100, **www.sheratonvistanaresortvillas.com**).

💲 BRITBONUS

Reserve a one or two-bed villa at the Sheraton Vistana Resort or Sheraton Vistana Villages and receive $50 in resort credit. You must reserve directly by calling toll free: 0203 564 6335 ask for Rate Code BGRC50 and stay a minimum of five consecutive nights. You must also show your *Brit Guide* on check-in to receive the credit; no cash value/no refund on unused portion. Not available through third party reservations.

Sheraton Vistana Villages: The sister property, located on I-Drive south of SeaWorld, this upmarket family resort offers spacious one and two-bed/two-bath condos with fully equipped kitchen or kitchenette, dining area, washer-dryer and more, in five and six-storey blocks set around scenic landscaping or pool areas. The beautiful lobby opens on to a stunning pool with waterfalls, Jacuzzis and children's play areas, while there's the smart Flagler Station Bar & Grill for breakfast, lunch and dinner and a mini-market/deli. Less than 6ml/10km from Disney, guests enjoy extensive amenities like complimentary scheduled transport to select Disney parks, daily activities, three pool areas (some with slides and water-play areas), a state-of-the-art fitness centre, games rooms, basketball and tennis courts and a grocery store, plus there is a big Publix supermarket and the Premium Outlets shops nearby (407 238 5000, **www.sheratonvistanavillages.com**).

Tuscana: This Mediterranean-inspired condo-resort bordering the Champions Gate golf courses offers 288 large, elegant two and three-bed condos, each with two baths, balcony, fully equipped kitchen, washer and dryer. The excellent clubhouse boasts the Tuscana Tavern bar and grill, poolside sports bar, kiddie pool, cabañas, fitness centre, 30-seat cinema and spa treatments (407 787 4800, **www.tuscanaresort.com**).

Villas at Grand Cypress: Arguably Orlando's top golf resort, this is also an upmarket option in a beautiful setting behind Walt Disney World, making it among the most convenient

Villas at Grand Cypress

villa options. It offers 146 single-room club suites and one, two, three and four-bed condo-style villas furnished in luxury style, with fully equipped kitchens and patios or balconies. There is a pool with saunas and bar, bike rentals and two restaurants (The Club sports bar and fine-dining Nine18 overlooking the North-South golf course), the Golf Academy for personal lessons, plus 24hr room service. Villa guests also get full use of all the amenities of the nearby Hyatt Regency Grand Cypress (p82), a 5min ride on the free on-demand shuttle service. Literally just minutes from Disney, the villas' relaxed ambiance and lush surroundings make you feel light years away (407 239 4700, **www.grandcypress.com**).

Vista Cay: This timeshare resort offers some of the most extensive facilities in the I-Drive/Universal Boulevard area (behind the Convention Center North). Convenient for the attractions but away from the main bustle, it has beautiful two and three-bed executive suites and three-bed town-homes, plus a large clubhouse and pool set in tropical grounds; whirlpool spa, kids' pool and basketball court; games room, cinema, business centre and fitness centre. The spacious suites offer full kitchens, large HD TVs with DVD players, dining rooms, master bedrooms with separate Roman tubs and showers, private balconies and free wi-fi (407 996 4647, **www.vistacayholidays.com**).

Windsor Palms Resort: Just off west Highway 192 in Kissimmee, this popular gated community has a mix of two-bed condos, two and three-bed town-homes, and three to six-bed private pool villas. Amenities include a large clubhouse and fitness centre, tennis courts, an Olympic-sized pool, a kiddie pool and spa, basketball, billiard room, volleyball court, video arcade, playground and a 58-seat cinema. The sister resort of **Windsor Hills** on Old Lake Wilson Road offers the same accommodation choice and impressive amenities, like its huge lagoon-style pool with waterslide and state-of-the-art fitness centre and is even closer to the Disney parks. New in 2016 was **Windsor at Westside** in Davenport, with four and five-bed town-homes and gorgeous six to nine-bed private pool villas. The clubhouse facilities are equally impressive, with huge resort pool, lazy river, waterslide, tiki bar, fitness centre, video arcade and sports courts (407 396 0642, **www.globalresorthomes.com**).

HOLIDAY HOMES

This is in many ways the biggest area of accommodation for UK visitors as it has become hugely popular, as well as being a cost-effective way for large families and groups to stay together. The homes – individual or in communities – are sometimes gated, and most have a private pool, while some have access to communal facilities like pools and recreation areas. They are always equipped with full kitchen, laundry facilities and multiple TVs. Some are classed as 'executive', which means more facilities (games rooms, barbecues, Jacuzzis, etc.) rather than an increase in size. A hire car is usually essential, but the savings can be significant. Prices can be as low as $450/week off-peak, but expect to pay at least $1,600/week for a five or six-bed villa in high season. A word of warning: once you've experienced pool-at-home life, you may never go back to a hotel!

If you book independently, there are several key questions. Do you need to go to an office to pick up the keys or is there a combination lockbox at the house? Is there a local contact if anything goes wrong, and is the property maintained by a local

Windsor Palms Resort

Pool heat

To heat or not to heat is a common question for those renting a villa in Florida. Typically, pools will NOT need heating from mid-May to mid-Oct, when the sun is usually enough to heat them to at least 80°F/26.6°C. But, at other times of the year, and especially Nov–Apr, you will almost certainly need pool heating. Systems can be electric or (propane) gas, with the latter usually more expensive. Expect to pay anywhere from $25–30/day for electric heating and $30–40/day for gas. It can also take up to 48hrs to heat a pool to 85°F/28°C during the colder months and, if the air temperature drops below 55°F/13°C, the heating may not function fully to more than 15°F above air temperature. Pool heat will also be in addition to the villa rental costs.

Proper Pie Company

company? Does it offer a secure bonding for your booking, and is it a member of a reputable organisation, such as the Better Business Bureau of Central Florida? In winter, is the pool heated, and what is the charge for heating? Is it as close to Disney as it says (some can be half an hour away, but still insist they are 'just minutes from Disney')?

There are more than 26,000 villas on offer across Osceola, Polk and Lake Counties to the west and south-west of Disney, most in well-established developments. Be aware homes within a particular community can still vary in quality depending on the care and attention of owners and/or property managers, hence just being in, say, Cumbrian Lakes, is not a guarantee of executive quality. You can rent direct from the owners or a property management company that will look after multiple villas. For direct rentals, check sites like **www.vrbo.com, www.lastminutevillas. net** and **www.thedibb.co.uk/forums/ villa-search.php. Owner Direct** also have a well-vetted Orlando selection of more than 500 properties and are often good for late deals at **www.ownerdirect.com/ accommodation/ disney-world-central-florida**.

BRITTIP

For home comforts, the British owned **The Proper Pie Company** on Ridge Center Drive (off Highway 27 in Davenport, just south of I-4) offers a fabulous range of home-made pies, pasties and British groceries, plus fresh-made fish and chips. See more at **www.properpiecompany.com** or call 863 438 2705.

There are increasing numbers of terrace-style town-homes, so, for a 'detached' house, ask for a 'single family home'. The bottom line is you must do your homework, shop around, and check with bodies like the Florida Vacation Rental Managers Association (**https://fvrma.wildapricot. org/**). This is the only acknowledged umbrella organisation for the holiday home business and helps to provide a level of credibility.

The following companies all pass the *Brit Guide* credibility test.

Advantage Vacation Homes: In the villa business for more than 20 years and one of the largest companies, it keeps its 2–6-bed homes (the majority on west Highway 192 and Highway 27 in Clermont and Davenport) fresh while also managing a range of condos (notably in the Bahama Bay Resort) and town-homes. It offers 24hr management, with courteous and efficient staff at its office just off Highway 192 (9am–10pm daily). Its holiday homes are rated Silver,

Rental Accommodation

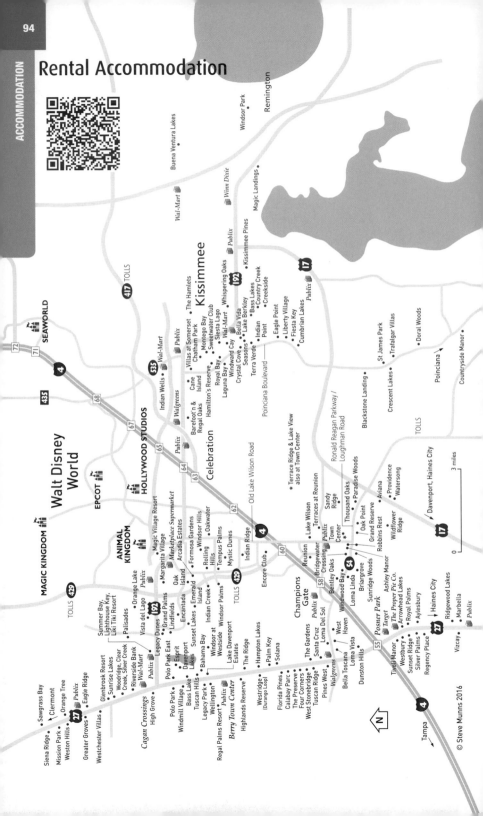

© Steve Munns 2016

Gold or Platinum, with the difference measured in extras rather than size (flatscreen TVs, tiled floors rather than carpeting, a Jacuzzi or games room, etc.), though some of the more exclusive villas might be in a golf community or have tennis courts (407 396 2262 in the US, **www.advantagevacationhomes.com**).

Alexander Holiday Homes: Family-owned Alexander manages more than 200 properties in Kissimmee, from standard two, three and four-bed condos to luxury seven-bed executive homes sleeping 14, all with pools and immaculately furnished, within 15–20mins of Disney, including some of the closest to the parks. This company was the first of its kind in Orlando (in 1981) and still offers a personable, efficient service. It was only the third management company to earn the distinguished AAA (American Automobile Association) Three Diamond rating, as well as being fully accredited with the official Walt Disney World Vacation Rental Home Connection (where homes are inspected quarterly) and definitely gets our approval. It shows prices in UK and US currency and offers a free guest services concierge (using the latest mobile technology) to ensure you get to your home, as well as arrival grocery packages, barbecue rentals, scooter and wheelchair hire. Its informative website provides photo tours of all its homes, useful blogs and other features (0871 711 5371 in the UK, 1800 621 7888 in the US, **www.floridasunshine.com**).

All Star Vacation Homes: Offering a growing collection of villa rentals, from two-bed condos to massive 14-bed homes, all located within 6mls/10km of Disney (plus homes in the Gulf Coast resorts of Sanibel and Captiva), All Star features luxurious amenities, including pools with spas, multiple master suites, games rooms and home theatres (321 281 4966, **www.AllStarVacationHomes.com**).

Florida Leisure Vacation Homes: Another British-owned company we know and recommend, it pays great attention to detail, with an upscale, almost boutique approach that sets it apart from the more mass-market operators. With 100 homes (3–7 beds) in the Kissimmee area, most just a few years old and many in the highly regarded Cumbrian Lakes community, it prides itself on a personal touch (even down to providing personal chef, massage and concierge services) and offers some of the biggest and newest properties, as well as an online booking system. Many are in the Executive range, with the fullest array of amenities as well as private, screened pools, and often in gated communities. All villas have lockboxes, so you don't need to visit the office to check in. You can see all

Reunion Resort and Club

© Reunion Resort

its homes online (in extended photo and video) plus lots of local info, while its new testimonial sections provide first-hand feedback. Also accredited to the Walt Disney World Vacation Rental Home Connection, its office is well placed on east Highway 192 in Kissimmee, just past Osceola Square Mall (407 870 1600; www.floridaleisurevacationhomes.com).

Jeeves Holiday Homes: For the deluxe villa touch and immaculate style, British-owned Jeeves is one of the best in the business. They specialise in high-end properties – including some of the largest and most sumptuous mansions in Reunion Resort, with 10, 13 and even 16 bedrooms – and have a boutique approach, offering bespoke services and concierge luxury. Need an in-villa private chef, spa treatment or butler? Ask Jeeves! They have also selected some of the most eye-catching properties in Central Florida, notably several with fully themed bedrooms that wouldn't be out of place in the theme parks. They offer welcome packs, special-occasion services and a 'Car on the Drive' option for those who don't want to pick up their hire car straight away. Their knowledge of the area is first class and they feature villas in the gorgeous new Encore Club community (407 704 8986, www.jeevesfloridarentals.com).

BRITBONUS
Receive 5% off regular rates PLUS a welcome grocery pack with stays of 10 nights or more with **Jeeves Management**. Use the code BRITS5% when booking online or by phone.

Jeeves Management

Loyalty Homes: For a luxury touch, all these homes (2–7 bedrooms) are no more than 4ml/6.5km from Disney and all offer true 'executive' style, with the likes of digital door locks (so no key collection required), cable TV and many with games rooms. The website offers video tours, too (call 0121 468 0016 in the UK or 863 420 1010 in the US, www.loyaltyusa.com).

Premier Home Management: A good range of properties with 3–7 bedrooms, sleeping up to 12, in secure residential communities within a 15–20min drive of Disney. All are privately owned and have been furnished as holiday homes, with screened pools, two TVs, fully equipped kitchens, at least one king or queen bed and free local phone calls. Maid service can be added for a fee. In addition to the villas, there are town-home and condo options (863 421 6115, www.premiervacationhomesorlando.com).

BRITTIP
You'll find Marmite, Ribena, McVities and a handful of other British groceries at Publix and Winn-Dixie supermarkets, and most Wal-Marts (International aisle).

Villa Direct: Another major Orlando specialist, and one of the biggest, with an extensive range of properties in the area, from two-bed condos to luxury seven-bed villas, and a good user-friendly website, plus an excellent range of guest services, including arrival groceries, a personalised concierge service, car hire and mobility equipment rental. Also on the Walt Disney World Vacation Rental Home Connection, their welcome centre is easily found on west Highway 192 in Kissimmee (407 397 1210, www.villadirect.com).

OK, that's enough accommodation advice. Now it's on to the parks….

5 The Theme Parks: Disney's Fab Four

or Spending the Day with Mickey and the Gang

Now let's prepare you for the main business of any visit to Orlando: Walt Disney World. This is the heart of all the excitement and fun in store (along with the other big theme parks of Universal Orlando, SeaWorld and Busch Gardens).

In our opinion, two weeks are barely enough to see all of Disney on its own, let alone the other theme parks and smaller scale attractions, so you start to realise the awesome scope of an Orlando holiday!

◀🇬🇧▶ **BRITTIP**
Before you leave home, photocopy the back of your park passes and your passport, then you'll have the info you need should you lose them.

Buying your tickets in advance is highly advisable (it saves time and is often better value), but work out your requirements first – you won't get full value for the 14-day Disney, Universal AND SeaWorld tickets in just a fortnight. Try to use your credit card for all purchases – there is built-in additional security (for our list of recommended ticket outlets; p10).

Discount options: You will find a welter of discount coupons for many of the smaller attractions in tourist publications distributed in Orlando (or from your hotel Guest Services desk – it's often worth asking), while the tour operators' welcome meetings usually have special offers and tickets for the latest excursions. What you won't find is discounted Disney tickets (unless it is a timeshare lure). Disney never discount,

Chip at Rivers of America

apart from occasional '5ᵗʰ Day Free' offers through the official outlets.

BRITTIP
I-Drive has the only genuine Official Visitor Center. Offers of 'free' Disney tickets usually mean timeshare firms, which also claim to have 'official' visitor centres.

Official Visitor Center: Check this out for discounts at 8723 International Drive in the Gala Center on the corner of Austrian Row (407 363 5872). It IS possible to bag free tickets by attending timeshare presentations but they can easily take half a day of hard-sell out of your precious holiday.

Timeshare: If you DO want to look at timeshare options, look first at Disney Vacation Club for the guarantee of memorable holidays. A tour (for which you will be picked up) will take about 3hrs and you'll receive a small parting gift (dining coupon, etc). Call 0800 783 2893 or visit **http://disneyvacationclub.disney.go.com.**

BRITTIP
Smoking is not permitted in the restaurants or in the parks, apart from in a handful of designated areas. Check park maps for their exact locations.

Ratings
Our unique rating system splits attractions into thrill rides and scenic rides, earning **T** or **A** ratings out of 5.

- **TTTTT** is as exciting as they get and, along with **AAAAA** is unmissable. These will have the longest queues, so you should plan your visit around them.
- **TTTT** or **AAAA** should be high on your 'must do' list.

Character dining at Chef Mickey's

© Gray Line Tours

- **TTT** or **AAA** should be seen if you have time.
- **TT** is worth seeing only if there is no queue, **AA** is likely to be twee and missable.
- **T** or **A** is not worth your time.

Some rides have height restrictions and are not advisable for people with back, neck or heart problems or for expectant mothers. Where this is the case we say, for example, '**R**: 3ft 6in/106cm'. Height restrictions (strictly enforced) are based on the average five-year-old being 3ft 6in/106cm tall, those aged six being 3ft 9in/114cm and nines being 4ft 4in/132cm. You can also refer to our Height Restriction Guide, p27.

My Magic+
This high-tech system of guest interaction is designed to personalise and enhance many aspects of park visits. Free for Disney resort guests, but available for offsite guests to buy, the MagicBand wristband acts as an all-purpose ticket, optional payment card, FastPass+ and PhotoPass card, and allows various special features, like pre-booking FastPass+ and cataloguing your dining reservations. It works in conjunction with My Disney Experience (see below), where you fill in your trip details (as much or as little as you prefer) and use the mobile app for all the latest info, such as queuing wait times and dining reservations. MagicBands come in different colours and styles and are designed to be collectible. Intended to be 'transformational' in the way we enjoy the parks, it can be difficult to navigate, somewhat glitchy, and the need to pre-book 60 days in advance for onsite guests or 30 days in advance for offsite guests makes people feel they need to plan to the nth degree (thus, actually taking some of the fun out of the whole experience), so check out the website carefully before you sign up. All Disney parks have free Wi-Fi, too. You do not have to sign up for My Magic+, but you will not be able to access all the perks available if you choose not to participate in the programme.

Character dining

Having a meal with Mickey and Co is one of the great Disney experiences – even without children – and is often the best way to meet your favourite characters without a wait. Make reservations up to 180 days in advance (180 plus your length of stay if you are booked at a Disney hotel) by phoning 407 WDW DINE (939 3463), calling at any Guest Services desk in a hotel, or on the **www.disneyworld.com** site.

Some meals are difficult to get. Breakfast at Cinderella's Royal Table or Be Our Guest at the Magic Kingdom usually sell out within minutes of the 180-day window being open. Chef Mickey's and the Princess meals also go quickly. If you cannot book in advance, try calling the day you'd like to dine or, as a last resort, show up to see if there have been any cancellations. You must check in at the podium 10mins before your time and you will be given the next available table. Some characters don't enter the restaurant so, if they are in the lobby, meet them before you are seated. Dining is all-you-can-eat, served buffet, pre-plated or family-style. Inside the restaurant, characters circulate among the tables giving attention to each group (particularly when children are holding the camera!).

Character interaction is top-notch, especially if you dine off-hours when the restaurant is quieter. Bring your autograph book, a fat pen or marker (easier for the characters to hold) and an extra digital card. Some characters are huge, and children may be put off by them. If you aren't sure how they'll react, see how they are with the characters in the park before booking. Price range: breakfast $22–60 adults, $14 35 children; lunch $27–67 and $15–40; dinner $31–75 and $17–45 (NB: beware the peak season price rises – Disney has resorted to raising its rates in high season and even at weekends, and some of those children's meal prices are outrageously high, in our opinion.).

Disney has an App for that

Get all the latest park updates on your mobile phone or tablet, including park hours, wait times, menus, reservations, attraction info and FastPass+ reminders, plus games and more. Available free for iPhone and Android, from **https://disneyworld. disney.go.com/plan/mobile-apps/**

My Disney Experience

This is the online platform that allows guests to make dining reservations, schedule FastPass+ times, add Photopass, and link their Disney resort reservations and theme park admission. You must have a My Disney Experience account and valid theme park admission to schedule FastPass+ selections in advance. Using the online system, guests are also able to connect Friends and Family in-park experiences. To create an account, visit **https://disneyworld. disney.go.com/plan/my-disney-experience.**

Disney's FastPass+

Most of the attractions have this essential aid to queuing (free with admission), which allows you to roam while you wait for your scheduled ride time. Onsite guests can schedule three FP+ times in one park per day, up to 60 days in advance (30 days for offsite guests; starting at 7am US Eastern Standard Time, or noon UK time) using the online My Disney Experience system or Disney's free mobile app. Guests may also schedule FP+ times at in-park kiosks or by using the mobile app. Buy your park passes, create a My Disney Experience account, and follow instructions for scheduling FP+, booking dining reservations, and adding 'reminders'. You can then link your experiences to others in your party, make changes as needed, and customise your account with additional options. However, each guest can choose their own FP+ selections if they would like to experience attractions separately.

Character Dining: the meals

MAGIC KINGDOM: Crystal Palace for breakfast, lunch or dinner with Winnie the Pooh and Co – especially good for smaller children; and **Cinderella's Royal Table** for the (expensive) Once Upon A Breakfast, with Cinderella and her Princess Friends; Fairytale Lunch (Cinderella and Friends); and Dreams Come True Dinner (Fairy Godmother only). Breakfast (off-peak) is $60 adults, $35 children; lunch $67 and $40; dinner $75 and $45. Credit card payment in full is required to book and you WILL be charged the full price if you cancel less than 24hrs in advance (photo package and gratuity included, additional photos for a fee).

EPCOT: Garden Grill for lunch or dinner with Farmer Mickey, Pluto, Chip and Dale; Princess Storybook Dining at **Restaurant Akershus** (Norway) for breakfast, lunch and dinner; an alternative to Cinderella's, with some of Belle, Jasmine, Snow White, Mulan, Aurora (Sleeping Beauty) and Mary Poppins. Breakfast $42 adults, $25 children; lunch $43 and $26; dinner $48 and $26. Credit card needed to book; full charge applied for cancelling less than 24hrs in advance.

DISNEY'S HOLLYWOOD STUDIOS: Hollywood & Vine for breakfast or lunch with the Play 'n Dine pals, including Doc McStuffins, Sophia the First, Handy Manny, and Jake and the Neverland Pirates.

DISNEY'S ANIMAL KINGDOM: Donald's Dining Safari Breakfast and Lunch at **Tusker House** with Donald, Goofy, Pluto and sometimes Daisy and Mickey.

DISNEY RESORTS

Beach Club Resort: At **Cape May Café**, breakfast with Goofy, Minnie and Donald.

Contemporary Resort: At **Chef Mickey's**, breakfast or dinner with Mickey, Minnie, Goofy, Pluto, Donald Duck – peak times book up quickly.

Fort Wilderness: At **Mickey's Backyard Barbecue**, $57 adults and $33 3–9s, games, storytelling, live entertainment, music and dancing with Mickey, Minnie and Co; chicken, hot dogs, burgers, ribs, beer, wine, iced tea and lemonade (select nights only, 6.30pm, Mar–Dec).

Four Seasons Hotel: At **Ravello**, Thurs and Sat (plus Tues during peak seasons) breakfast with Goofy and pals.

Grand Floridian: At **1900 Park Fare**, breakfast with Alice, Mary Poppins and Mad Hatter; dinner with Cinderella, Anastasia, Drizella, Lady Tremaine and, sometimes, Prince Charming – book early. Wonderland Tea Party 2–3pm Mon–Fri, 4–12s only, $52.19, meal, activities and storytelling with Alice and friends ($10 no-show). Perfectly Princess Tea Party with Princess Aurora, 10.30am–12pm (not Tues and Sat), 3–11 with an adult, $290 for 1 adult with 1 child age 3–11. Meal (tea, cake, finger sandwiches), singalong, story time, Disney Girl doll, bracelet, necklace, rose, tiara, and scrapbook page.

Polynesian Resort: At **'Ohana**, breakfast with Lilo, Stitch, Pluto and Mickey.

Walt Disney World Swan: At **Garden Grove Café**, Mon–Fri, Timon and Rafiki; Sat and Sun breakfast with Goofy and Pluto.

◀▙▶ BRITTIP

Disney's FastPass+ system makes it essential to schedule your ride times well in advance using MyMagic+. It is likely FP+ times for the major attractions will be gone if you leave it until the day, especially in peak seasons.

Epcot and Disney's Hollywood Studios both use a tiered system for FastPass+.

Tier 1 indicates attractions from which you must choose only one; Tier 2 allows you to schedule two attractions. Watch for FP+ (choose two) and FP+1 (choose one) indications in our attraction descriptions. Guests who opt out of My Disney Experience can still use their regular ticket for park admission.

Onsite guests will each receive a MagicBand (waterproof wrist band with RFID chip) in place of an admission ticket, which can also be used to open their room door, charge purchases (if desired), allow FP+ access, and more. MagicBands will not be shipped overseas, but will be presented on check-in. However, you can still book FP+ in advance with a confirmation code. Offsite guests can buy MagicBands to replace their admission tickets, if they like.

◀◢▣▶ **BRITTIP**

You can schedule additional FP+ using the My Disney Experience app on your phone rather than queuing up at the FastPass kiosks, once you have used your initial three FP+.

All Disney's parks offer pushchair ('stroller') hire, and you can save money by buying a multi-day rental at your first park. Children of ALL ages seem to get a big thrill from collecting autographs from the various Disney characters, and most shops sell autograph books ($7.95). Parents wanting healthier dining options for kids in Disney parks and resorts should look on the menu for Mickey Check, a standard for more nutritious meals. You should find at least one choice at every counter-service and full-service restaurant (**www.disneymickeycheck.com**). The Power Pack lunch at some counter-service options serves healthier snacks in boxes, containing things like juice, yoghurt, string cheese, crackers, carrots and apple sauce.

PhotoPass

This worthwhile scheme is available in all Disney's parks and (occasionally) in Disney Springs. Disney photographers take photos of guests that are linked to an online account via a card you receive with your first photo or via Memory Maker (see below). There is no charge for a card or for viewing them online, but there is if you want to download and print them. Photos can be enhanced with Disney characters and special effects, while there are 'magical' photos where photographers ask guests to pose in a fun way and Tinker

Bell (or Stitch, or Simba or Mickey) will appear in the frame.

Guests have 30 days after the photos are taken to decide if they want to buy at **www.mydisneyphotopass.com.**

Memory Maker: This is a digital package linked to a My Disney Experience account (p99), that collects every PhotoPass photo, on-ride photo and character dining photo for $169. Images can be put on to mugs, mouse pads and more. Just swipe your card, or Magic Band, with every photo. Ride photos are added automatically with a Band. Some tickets, notably Annual Passes, now include Memory Maker.

Cast Members

Disney employees are called Cast Members or CMs (never 'staff' as they all play a role in the entertainment) and they're renowned for their helpful, cheerful style, always willing to assist, advise or chat. If you've had exceptional service or a CM has gone out of their way to help, let Disney know (at Guest Relations or City Hall) as it values feedback and CMs get credit for it.

Child Swap

If you have children under a height restriction, you needn't queue twice. At the entrance, tell the operator you want to do a Child Swap. Then Mum can ride while Dad looks after the youngster in a quiet area and, then they swap. At some attractions you may get a Child Swap ticket while you wait.

Park security

Visitors with bags must go through a security check before the turnstiles. There is a separate lane for those without bags, but all visitors can be asked to go through additional metal detector screening. When you put your ticket or MagicBand across the electronic terminal, you must give a finger scan (which stops others from using your ticket). **Selfie sticks** are banned from all Disney parks and must be left in your car.

Magic Kingdom Park

The starting point for any visit, the Magic Kingdom – the original development that sparked the Orlando tourist boom in 1971 – best embodies the genuine enchantment Disney bestows on its visitors. A few rides are the same as those in Disneyland Paris or Disneyland in LA, but there are key differences, notably on Pirates of the Caribbean, Big Thunder Mountain Railroad, Haunted Mansion and especially Space Mountain. And, even if a couple of attractions are closed for refurbishment, you won't be short of things to do! Here's our guide to a typical day, including the rides, shows and places to eat; how to park, how to avoid the worst of the crowds – and how much you should expect to pay.

The Magic Kingdom takes up just 107acres/43ha of Disney's near 31,000acres/12,555ha but attracts almost as many as the rest put together. It has six 'lands', like slices of a cake, centred on Florida's most famous landmark, Cinderella Castle. More than 40 attractions are packed into the park, plus shops and restaurants. It's easy to get overwhelmed, especially as it gets so busy (even the fast-food restaurants have long queues in high season), so plan around what most takes your fancy, but do look out for the interactive queues at some rides, including Big Thunder Mountain Railroad, Haunted Mansion, Peter Pan's Flight, Space Mountain, Little Mermaid, Winnie the Pooh and Seven Dwarfs Mine Train.

Magic Kingdom Park at a glance

Location	Off World Drive, Walt Disney World
Size	107 acres/43ha in 6 'lands'
Hours	9am–7pm off peak; 9am–10pm President's Day (see Brit Tip, p18); spring school holidays; 8am–11pm or midnight high season (Easter, summer holidays, Thanksgiving and Christmas)
Admission	Under-3s free; 3–9 $99–118 (1–day base ticket, priced seasonally), $320 (5–day Magic Your Way), £309 (14–day Ultimate); adult (10+) $105–124, $340, £329. Prices do not include tax.
Parking	$20
Lockers	To the right of the main entrance $12 ($5 deposit)
Pushchairs	$15 and $31 (underneath Main Street Train Station; $13 and $27 per day for multiple days)
Wheelchairs	$12 or $70 ($20 deposit refunded) underneath Main Street Train Station
Top attractions	Splash Mountain, Space Mountain, Seven Dwarfs' Mine Train, Big Thunder Mountain Railroad, Pirates of the Caribbean, Haunted Mansion, most rides in Fantasyland
Don't miss	Festival of Fantasy Parade, Main Street Electrical Parade and Wishes fireworks (most nights)
Hidden costs	**Meals** Burger, chips and coke $14.58 3-course dinner (Tony's Town Square) $34–$58 Kids' counter service meal $5.99–6.49 **T-shirts** $24.95–36.95 Kids $18.95–27.95 **Souvenirs** $1.05–4,300 **Sundries** Chalk colour portraits $17.95, or Silhouettes $8, with oval frame $15.95

Location

The Magic Kingdom is situated at the innermost end of Walt Disney World, with its entrance Toll Plaza three-quarters of the way along World Drive, the main entrance off Highway 192. World Drive runs north–south, while the Interstate 4 (I-4) entrance, Epcot Drive, runs east–west. Unless you are staying at a Disney resort or are an Annual Pass holder, you must pay the $20 parking fee at the Toll Plaza to bring you into the massive car park.

◀▦▶ BRITTIP

For the smoothest entry by road from Highway 192, take Seralago Boulevard (opposite the Seralago Hotel & Suites next to Old Town), turn left on to a non-toll stretch of Osceola Parkway and follow the signs to your chosen park. On West 192, turn off on Sherberth Road, go north to the first traffic lights and turn right, then pick up the Disney signs.

The majority arrive from 9.30–11.30am, so the car parks are busiest then – another good reason to get here EARLY. If you can't make it by 9am during peak periods, you might want to wait until after 1pm, or even later when the park is open as late as midnight. Remember to note exactly where you park: there are two sides to the 'parking lot', Heroes and Villains, with subsections for Woody, Simba, Rapunzel, Aladdin, Peter Pan and Mulan, then Ursula, Jafar, Zurg, Hook, Scar and Cruella. Be sure to note which side, section and number you're in – Ursula row 94, Hook 77, etc – as many hire cars look the same!

◀▦▶ BRITTIP

Take a photo of the Section and Row number on your camera or phone so you know where you've parked.

A motorised tram takes you from the car park to the Transportation and Ticket Center. Unless you already have your ticket (which will save valuable time), you visit the ticket booths here. Then, to get to the Magic Kingdom itself, the monorail (straight ahead) is quicker if there isn't a queue, otherwise bear left and take a slower ferryboat. If you're staying at a Disney hotel, the resort buses deliver you almost to the front door (or the monorail or boat will if you are staying at one of the Magic Kingdom resorts). Finally, the Magic Kingdom is the only 'dry' park – that is, there's NO alcohol on sale (except at the Be Our Guest restaurant at dinner).

Main Street USA

Right, we've finally reached the park itself… but not quite. Hopefully, you've arrived early and are among the leading hordes aiming to swarm through the entrance. The published opening time may say 9am, but the gates can open up to 45mins earlier.

Main Street is the first of the six 'lands' and, at opening time, there is a Welcome Parade, with singers, dancers and the Character Train arriving at Main Street Station with characters for a meet-and-greet in Town Square (get those autograph books ready!). A family is chosen at random to sprinkle some 'pixie dust' to open the park officially for the day. On your right is **Town Square Theater**, the place to meet Magician Mickey and Tinker Bell.

◀▦▶ BRITTIP

Meet Mickey without the long wait by scheduling your time in advance using the FastPass+ system.

On your left is **City Hall**, where you can pick up a park map and daily schedule (if you haven't already got

Daily flag retreat ceremony in Main Street USA

one en route) and book restaurants (highly advisable at peak periods). You can also find out where and when the characters will appear. Ahead is **Town Square**, where you can take a one-way ride on a horse-drawn bus or fire engine. The Street itself houses the park's best shopping (check out the massive **Emporium**), and the **Walt Disney World Railroad** AAA, a Western-themed steam train that circles the park and is one of the better attractions when queues are long elsewhere (though Town Square station is often the busiest).

Sorcerers of the Magic Kingdom: This interactive game takes place throughout the park (except Tomorrowland) but has its HQ at The Firehouse in Town Square (with a second station at Ye Olde Christmas Shoppe in Liberty Square), where guests sign up for a role in saving the Magic Kingdom from various Disney villains. With the help of role-playing cards, players visit special 'portals' (cleverly disguised video screens) to discover their task and use their cards to help Merlin defeat the villains.

It is designed for all ages and can get quite complex for serious role-playing gamers, using cards to cast 'spells' that ward off evil-doers and save the day in each land. Like an interactive scavenger hunt, it is aimed at children but adults will enjoy it, too. AAA

Dining: The Italian-style **Tony's Town Square Restaurant** serves lunch and dinner; **The Plaza Restaurant** offers salads and sandwiches (lunch and dinner); and **The Crystal Palace** (breakfast $27 adult, $15 ages 3–9; lunch $32 & $18; dinner $42 & $20)

Magic Kingdom parade

is buffet-style food with Winnie the Pooh and Co. Quick bites can be bought from **Casey's Corner** (hot dogs, chips and soft drinks), **Main Street Bakery** (a Starbucks coffee shop, also serving wonderful pastries), **Main Street Confectionery** (chocolate and sweets) and the **Plaza Ice Cream Parlor**. Disney characters also appear periodically throughout the Square.

Info: Check the **Guest Information Board** at the top of Main Street (on the left) as it gives waiting times for all the attractions. The **Baby Center** (for nursing mothers) is also at the top of Main Street, to the left next to Crystal Palace, along with the **First Aid** station.

◀🇬🇧▶ BRITTIP

Can't find Mickey and Co? This is often one of the main laments of those who arrive unprepared. At City Hall they can tell you where to find the characters. In fact, City Hall is your best friend for many queries, from baby facilities to meal bookings (but there are NO baby facilities at City Hall itself). Character meet-and-greets are also shown on all park maps with a 'Mickey glove' icon.

Beating the queues: Unless you are late, skip Main Street and head for the end of the street to the real entrance to the park, where you await official opening hour. Adopt one of three tactics, each aimed at doing some of the most popular rides before the queues build up (wait times of 2hrs for Splash Mountain are not unknown). 1: If you fancy the five-star, log-flume Splash Mountain, keep left in front of the Crystal Palace with the majority, who will head the same way. 2: If you have young children who can't wait to try the Fantasyland rides, stay in the middle and pass around the Castle. 3: If the thrills of indoor roller-coaster Space Mountain appeal, move right by The Plaza Restaurant for Tomorrowland. Now you're in pole position for the initial rush (and it will be a rush; take care with children).

MAGIC KINGDOM PARK

ADVENTURELAND
1 Swiss Family Treehouse
2 Jungle Cruise
3 Magic Carpets of Aladdin
4 The Enchanted Tiki Room
5 Pirates of the Caribbean

FRONTIERLAND
6 Splash Mountain
7 Big Thunder Mountain Railroad
8 County Bear Jamboree
9 Raft to Tom Sawyer Island

LIBERTY SQUARE
10 Liberty Tree Tavern
11 Liberty Square Riverboat
12 The Haunted Mansion
13 The Hall of Presidents

FANTASYLAND
14 'It's a Small World'
15 Prince Charming Regal Carrousel
16 Mad Tea Party
17 The Many Adventures of Winnie The Pooh
18 Princess Fairytale Hall
19 Dumbo The Flying Elephant
20 Mickey's PhilharMagic
21 The Barnstormer starring The Great Goofini
22 Casey Jr Splash 'n' Soak Station

23 Peter Pan's Flight
24 Castle Forecourt Stage
25 Cinderella's Royal Table
26 Brave – Meet Merida
27 Enchanted Tales with Belle
28 Be Our Guest Restaurant
29 Under The Sea – Journey of the Little Mermaid
30 Ariel's Grotto
31 Seven Dwarfs Mine Train

TOMORROWLAND
32 Space Mountain
33 Tomorrowland Indy Speedway
34 Walt Disney's Carousel of Progress
35 Astro Orbiter
36 Tomorrowland Transit Authority
37 Stitch's Great Escape!
38 Buzz Lightyear's Space Ranger Spin
39 Monsters Inc. Laugh Floor
40 Club 626 Dance Party

TRANSPORT
41 Walt Disney World Railroad Stations
42 Boat Dock
43 Monorail Station
44 Bus Station

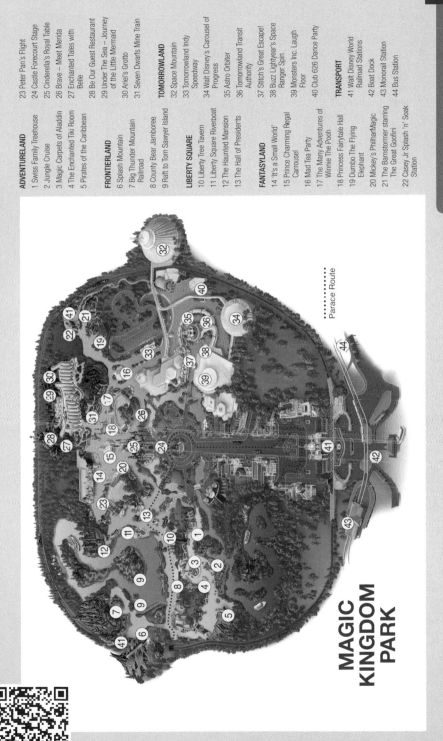

············ Parace Route

MAGIC KINGDOM PARK

BRITTIP

The Move It! Shake It! Dance & Play It! Street Party begins in Town Square, but the real action takes place around the Castle Hub. Stake out a spot in advance if you want an up-front view.

Other entertainment: Watch out for the **Move It! Shake It! Dance & Play It! Street Party** up to three times daily, from Town Square, along Main Street, ending up in the Hub area as Disney characters, stilt walkers and dancers lead guests in a high-energy street party. The **Main Street Trolley Show** happens 3–4 times a day, with the horse-drawn trolley arriving on Main Street for a 6min song-and-dance interlude. The fun barbershop quartet the **Dapper Dans** and brass band **Main Street Philharmonic** (who also play in Storybook Circus) add lively regular musical interludes, as does **Casey's Corner Pianist**, and don't miss the **Glass Blowing Demonstrations** at Crystal Arts Shop. There is also a daily **Flag Retreat** at 5pm each day, with a military veteran helping the Security Colour Guard to bring down the national flag.

Adventureland

Head left (going round clockwise) to enter Adventureland. If you're going to Splash Mountain first, pass the Swiss Family Treehouse on your left and bear right through an archway (with toilets) into Frontierland, where you turn left and Splash Mountain is ahead. Stopping in Adventureland, these are the attractions.

Swiss Family Treehouse: This imitation banyan tree is a clever

Adventureland

replica of the treehouse from Disney's 1960 film *Swiss Family Robinson*. It's a walk-through attraction where the queues (rarely long) move steadily if not quickly, providing a neat glimpse of the ultimate tree house. AA

BRITTIP

The special deal on autograph book and fat pen combo can be cheaper than buying them separately.

Jungle Cruise: It's not so much the scenic, geographically suspect boat ride (where the Nile suddenly becomes the Amazon) that is so amusing as the non-stop yarn about your adventure from the boat's captain. Long queues, so visit early morning (opens 10am) or late afternoon (evening queues are shortest, but you'll miss some of the detail in the dark). AAAA FP+

Pirates of the Caribbean: One of Disney's most impressive attractions that involves Walt's pioneering work in audio-animatronics, life-size figures that move, talk and, in this instance, lay siege to a Caribbean island! Your 8min underground boat ride visits a typical pirate adventure and the world of Captain Jack Sparrow and nemesis Captain Barbossa as they search for buried treasure. It's terrific family fun (though perhaps a bit spooky for young children, with one small drop in the dark). Queues are longest from late morning to mid-afternoon. ΛΛΛΛ (**TTTT** under-10s) FP+

The Enchanted Tiki Room: A classic bird-laden, South Seas audio-animatronic show starring various parrots, macaws and other tropical feathered friends – plus the angry Tiki Gods! Queues are rare and it is air-conditioned. AA

Magic Carpets of Aladdin: In an Agrabah-themed area, this ride spins you up, down and around as you try to dodge the spitting camel! Your 'flying carpet' tilts as well as levitates, simple stuff geared for younger children (like the Magic Carpets of Agrabah ride in Disneyland Paris). TT (**TTTT** under-5s), FP+.

A Pirate's Adventure: Treasure of the Seven Seas: A variation on the Sorcerers of the Magic Kingdom interactive card game (p104), with the chance to help Captain Jack Sparrow fight off his foes and locate different treasures around Adventureland, using a pirate map and magic talisman. Visit the special kiosk through the archway past the Pirates ride to get started. AAA

Other entertainment: Outside the Pirates of the Caribbean ride (and a must for young swashbucklers), **Captain Jack Sparrow's Pirate Tutorial** runs several times daily. Captain Jack and sidekick Mack invite youngsters to join them in sword fights and treasure hunting, ending with the Pirate Oath to become honorary buccaneers.

Disney characters also turn up at the Adventureland entrance (Peter Pan) and next to the Magic Carpets ride (characters from Aladdin).

Shopping: The best shopping is in **Pirates Bazaar**, where **Pirates League** (9am–4pm) offers a chance for young swashbucklers to transform into fully-fledged pirates, with various packages ($39.95) that include accessories like earrings, eye patches, swords, coin necklaces and temporary tattoos (photos sold separately).

Dining: Skipper Canteen is casual full service 'adventure dining' themed like the Jungle Cruise and in three different dining rooms. It features 'World Famous Jungle Cuisine', served by Jungle Cruise skippers, and is an excellent choice for lunch or dinner, offering surprisingly upscale food for a theme park. **Aloha Isle** adds signature Dole Whips and **Sunshine Tree Terrace** has ice cream and drinks, and **Tortuga Tavern** (open seasonally) features tacos, empanadas and salads.

Frontierland

This Western-themed area is one of the busiest and is best avoided from late morning to late afternoon.

Splash Mountain: Based on the 1946 classic Disney cartoon *Song of the South*, this is a watery journey into the world of Brer Rabbit, Brer Fox and Brer Bear. The first part is all jolly cartoon scenery and fun with the main characters and a couple of minor swoops in your eight-passenger log boat. The conclusion, a five-storey plummet at 45° into a mist-shrouded pool, seems like you are falling off the edge of the world! A huge adrenalin rush, but busy almost all day (try it first thing or during one of the parades to avoid the longest queues).

Splash Mountain

© Hilary White

Some riders also get VERY wet! **R:** 3ft 4in/101cm. **TTTT** FP+

Big Thunder Mountain Railroad: When Disney does a roller-coaster it will be one of the classiest, and here it is – a runaway mine train that swoops, tilts and plunges through a mock mine filled with clever scenery. You have to ride it at least twice to appreciate all the detail, but again queues are heavy, so go early (after Splash Mountain) or late in the day. **R:** 3ft 4in/101cm. **TTTT** FP+

Country Bear Jamboree: Here's a novelty: a 16min musical revue by audio-animatronic bears! It's great family fun with plenty of novel touches (watch for the talking moose head). Crowds are rare, so it's a good one when it's busy elsewhere. AAA

Frontierland Shootin' Arcade: The park's single attraction that costs extra ($1 for 35 shots), as you take aim at a series of animated targets. **T**

Tom Sawyer Island: Take a raft over to an overgrown playground of mysterious caves, grottos and mazes, rope bridges and Fort Sam Clemens, where you can fire air guns at passing boats (opens 9am). A good choice in early afternoon when the queues are long elsewhere. Aunt Polly's Dockside Inn allows time off your feet, but the only drinks are from a vending machine. **TT**

Other entertainment: The comic trio of The Notorious Banjo Brothers and Bob, and Hoedown Happening with the Country Bears provide musical interludes. *Toy Story* characters can be found next to Splash Mountain.

Big Thunder Mountain Railroad

Shopping: Frontierland shops sell cowboy hats and badges, as well as Native American and Mexican crafts. Look out for the nicely themed **Briar Patch** and **Prairie Outpost** for interesting gifts.

Dining: Try **Pecos Bill Tall Tale Inn & Café** (burgers, Tex-Mex, Fajitas), **Golden Oak Outpost** (chicken nuggets, BLT or BBQ pork, waffle fries and drinks) or **Turkey Leg Cart** (massive, smoke-grilled turkey legs).

Liberty Square

The clockwise tour brings you to a homage to post-independence America. A lot of the historical content will go over the heads of British visitors, but it still has some great attractions.

Liberty Square Riverboat: Cruise America's 'rivers' on an authentic paddle steamer, be menaced by river pirates and thrill to the stories of How the West Was Won (10am–8pm). This is also good at busier times of the day, especially early afternoon. AAA

The Haunted Mansion: A clever delve into the world of Master Gracey's ghostly bride that is neither too scary for most kids nor too twee for adults. Not so much a thrill ride as a scenic adventure. Watch out at the end when the 'hitch-hiking ghosts' might drop in! Longish queues for much of the day, however, so try to visit late on. AAAA (**TTTT** under-6s), FP+

The Hall of Presidents: The attraction likely to mean least to us, a two-part show that is a film about the US Constitution and an audio-animatronic parade of all 45 US presidents (opens 9am). Technically impressive, it may bore young 'uns (though it is air-conditioned). AAA

Shopping: Look for **Ye Olde Christmas Shoppe** and the fabulous Haunted Mansion-themed **Memento Mori**.

Dining: Eating options are the full-service **Liberty Tree Tavern** (hearty soups, salads, and traditional dishes like roast turkey, carved beef and

Meet Buzz Lightyear and Woody

© Hilary White

BRITTIP

Watch for enhanced allergy-friendly menus in the parks. If you're still not sure, a chef is always happy to speak to you directly. Just ask!

Peter Pan's Flight: This may seem a rather tame ride but is another Walt classic and a big hit with kids. Its novel effect of flying with Peter Pan is good fun and there's a lot of clever detail as your ship sails to Neverland. The addition of an interactive queue in 2015 helps pass the time in air-conditioned comfort. AAA (AAAAA under-6s) FP+

Mickey's PhilharMagic: This fun-tastic 10min 3-D film show has a host of special effects as Donald tries to conduct the Enchanted Orchestra – to comic effect. It features a 150ft/46m wide screen to immerse guests in the 3D world of *Beauty and the Beast*, *The Little Mermaid*, *The Lion King*, *Peter Pan* and *Aladdin*, with hapless Donald surviving a string of adventures before Mickey brings him back to earth. The lavish theatre, artistic animation, special effects (you can 'smell' the food!) and all-round family entertainment make for a hugely enjoyable attraction. There is no scare factor (though the sudden plunge into dark at one point and noise of the 'orchestra' can spook young children), while you'll be enchanted when Tinker Bell seems to fly out of the screen in front of you. AAAAA FP+

It's a Small World

smoked ham), **Columbia Harbor House** (counter-service platters, good soups, salads and sandwiches, notably for vegetarians) and **Sleepy Hollow** (a picnic area serving desserts and drinks).

Fantasyland

Leaving Liberty Square, you come to the park's spiritual heart, the area that most enchants young children. The attractions, in three areas, are designed with kids in mind, but the shops are sophisticated and the Tangled 'village' (basically a courtyard with restrooms) is wonderfully scenic.

'It's a Small World': This could almost be Disney's theme ride, a family boat trip around the world, each continent represented by hundreds of dancing, singing audio-animatronic dolls in delightful set-piece pageants. If it sounds twee, it actually creates a surprisingly striking effect, accompanied by an annoyingly catchy theme song that young children adore. Crowds peak in early afternoon. AAAA FP+

Prince Charming Regal Carrousel: The Fantasyland centrepiece shouldn't need any more explanation other than it is a vintage carousel that kids love. Long queues for much of the day, though. **T** (**TTT** under-5s)

The Many Adventures of Winnie the Pooh: Building on the timeless popularity of Pooh, Piglet and Co, this family ride offers a musical jaunt through Hundred Acre Wood with some clever effects (get ready to 'bounce' with Tigger!) and an original soundtrack. Wait times are made easier by hands-on elements throughout the queue. **AAA** (**AAAAA** under-5s) **FP+**

Mad Tea Party: The kids will insist you take them in these spinning, oversized tea cups that have their own 'steering wheel' to add to the whirling effect. Actually, they're just a heavily disguised fairground ride. Again, go early or expect crowds. Characters from *Alice in Wonderland* also visit periodically. **TT** (**TTTT** under-5s) **FP+**

Princess Fairytale Hall: This elaborate 'royal' residence features a dramatic castle gallery area where visitors gather before being summoned for an audience with some of the Disney princesses (choose from Cinderella or Rapunzel, who then have another princess friend with them; (characters alternate) **AAA** (**AAAAA** under 13 girls!) **FP+**

Enchanted Tales with Belle: A wonderfully clever Beauty and the Beast character show, here you visit Maurice's Workshop, nestled in the shadow of the Beast's Castle, and guests are transported via a magic mirror to the Castle Library for a memorable interactive story-time with Belle and Lumière. **AAAA FP+**

Under the Sea – Journey of the Little Mermaid: Be a part of her world as you journey under the sea with Ariel in this gentle ride aboard stylised clamshells, past colourful scenes from the movie. Ariel, Prince Eric, Flounder, Scuttle, Sebastian, King Triton and evil sea witch Ursula all make appearances, while favourite songs add to this charming adventure (with some surprising special effects!) that is sure to have a happy ending. **AAAA. FP+**

Ariel's Grotto: Next door is the elaborate setting for a meeting with the Little Mermaid. **FP+**

The Seven Dwarfs Mine Train: It's 'off to work we go' in this charming dark ride through a gem-laden mine. Your trip begins as a family-friendly outdoor coaster, enters the mine for a gentle (and slightly dark) journey past

Under the Sea – Journey of the Little Mermaid

The Barnstormer

the Dwarfs as they dig, dig, dig, then plunges back outside as a coaster again for the grand finale. The mine cars have the swaying motion of a real mine train (though you actually feel very little sway, as the banked turns overpower it), all the charm of the fairytale from which it originates, and the sense of being 'in the film' is convincing. Watch for the surprise visitor at the end! **TTT** (**TTTTT** under 10s) FP+

Storybook Circus

The former Toontown area of Fantasyland is now themed for the classic film *Dumbo* and features more family-friendly fun.

Dumbo the Flying Elephant: Young children cannot pass this one by and, thankfully, with all-new dual Dumbos (doubling the capacity of the old ride) and a clever interactive, air-conditioned queue, parents should be less put off by the prospect of a long wait. It's a 2min ride on the back of a swooping, circling, flying elephant, and its charm is undeniable. **TT** (**TTTT** under-5s) FP+

The Barnstormer: Get ready for a junior-sized coaster in the company of classic stunt pilot The Great Goofini as this surprisingly whizzy (but very short) ride takes some sharp twists and turns in best circus style. **R:** 2ft 11in/89cm. **TTT** (**TTTTT** 4–8s) FP+

Casey Jr Splash 'n' Soak Station: The Circus Train has pulled into a siding – and sprung a leak! In fact, it is a cleverly disguised water-play area,

with all manner of squirting fountains, pop-jets and dumping buckets guaranteed to get the kids good and wet – so don't forget swimsuits OR a change of clothes. AAAA (under 10s)

Pete's Silly Sideshow: More themed fun under the Big Top as Minnie, Goofy, Donald and Daisy (in circus-style character) line up for a clever meet-and-greet. AAA

Other entertainment:

Mickey's Royal Friendship Faire: This stage show on the Castle Forecourt Stage (up to six times daily) features Mickey, Goofy, Donald and Daisy as they invite their friends Princess Tiana and Prince Naveen, Rapunzel and Flynn Rider, and Olaf, Anna and Elsa to a grand festival of music, dancing, and the celebration of friendship. (AAA)

In Storybook Circus, look out for **The Royal Majesty Makers** group of strolling performers in the Castle Courtyard, with a variety of regal routines (including the revived Sword in the Stone ceremony), while the **Fairy Godmother** meets children periodically at Cinderella's Fountain. Other **character experiences** include Meet Merida from the 2012 film *Brave* in the Fairytale Garden, Pooh and friends next to the Winnie the Pooh ride, Gaston outside Gaston's Tavern and *Alice in Wonderland* characters next to the Mad Tea Party.

Shopping: Shop at **Castle Couture**, the excellent **Sir Mickey's**, **Fantasy Faire**, **Pooh's Thotful Shop**, **Big Top Souvenirs** and **Bonjour! Village Gifts**. There is also an outlet of the **Bibbidi Bobbidi Boutique** here (the other is in Disney Springs), where 'little princesses' three and older can choose from three makeover styles ($64–207), the Crown, Courtyard and Castle packages, with three different hairstyles, Disney Diva, Color Star and Fairytale Princess, from 8:45am–7:30pm (reservations highly recommended on 407 939 7895).

Dining: Eating opportunities are at **Pinocchio Village Haus** (flatbreads, salad, chicken nuggets, and sandwiches), **Storybook Treats** (ice-cream), the **Cheshire Cafe** (cupcakes, muffins, fruit) and **Friar's Nook** (mac and cheese, hot dogs, desserts and drinks). **Cinderella's Royal Table** is a fine setting for the popular character breakfast, lunch and dinner with various Disney princesses (Cinderella greets guests in the foyer only). The majestic hall, waitresses in costume and well-presented food – salads, beef, fish, shrimp, pork tenderloin and chicken – provide a memorable experience. Be aware you pay in FULL by credit card when you book, there is a $10/person fee if you cancel more than 24hrs in advance, and, if you cancel less than 24hrs in advance, there is NO refund. More fun (and better value) is the spectacular **Be Our Guest** restaurant inside the Beast's Castle, a unique 550-seat counter service breakfast and lunch option by day and a full-service restaurant by night, with beer and wine (the only Magic Kingdom venue serving alcohol). Set in three themed sections – the Ballroom (complete with snow on the outdoor terrace!), Rose Gallery and the dark and moody West Wing – it is one of Disney's most ornate dining options. Breakfast includes pastries, breakfast sandwiches and quiche ($24 adults, $14 kids; 8–10am); lunch ($7–17

adults, $7–9 kids meal; 10.30am–2.30pm) offers soups, salads, quiche, sandwiches and braised pork; and dinner ($34–55/$14–16; 4pm–10pm or park closing during low season) offers a richer range of French-influenced dishes like Ratatouille and Thyme-scented Pork Rack Chop. Dinner books up FAST, so try to get a reservation at the 180-day mark (407 939 3463 or online at **www.disneyworld.com**; credit card deposit required, $10/person charge if you don't turn up). Lunch is also by reservation, though walk-ins may find availability before 11am. **Gaston's Tavern** is a counter-service cafe featuring an eclectic menu of snacks, drinks, pastries and a Tavern Beef Stew, again with some great *Beauty and the Beast* theming.

BRITTIP

The unique Le Fou's Brew (frozen apple juice with marshmallow) is a must-try drink! Try Le Fou's Winter Brew (hot cocoa) when temperatures drop.

Tomorrowland

This area's cartoon-like space-age styling, novel shops and varied rides provide guaranteed all-round appeal.

Space Mountain

© Disney

Space Mountain: One of the three most popular attractions, its reputation is deserved. Launching from Starport 75, this is a high-thrills, tight-turning roller-coaster, completely in the dark save for occasional flashes as you whiz through the galaxy. Don't do this on a full stomach! The only way to beat the crowds is to go either first thing, late in the day or during one of the parades (or get a FastPass+). Ride photos are available for $20.95–24.95 or $14.95 for digital delivery. **R:** 3ft 8in/111cm. **TTTTT FP+**

Tomorrowland Speedway: Despite the long queues, this is a rather tame ride on supposed race tracks that just putt-putts along on rails with little real steering required (children must be 4ft 4in/132cm to drive alone). **T** (**TTTT** under-6s) **FP+**

Astro Orbiter: A jazzed-up version of Dumbo in Fantasyland, this ride is a bit faster and higher and features rockets. Long, slow-moving queues are a reason to give this a miss unless you have young children. **TT** (**TTTT** under-10s).

Walt Disney's Carousel of Progress: This overlooked gem will surprise, entertain and amuse. It is a journey through 20th-century technology with audio-animatronics in a revolving theatre that reveals different periods in history. Its 22min duration is rarely threatened by crowds. **AAA**

Tomorrowland Transit Authority: A neat 'future transport system', this offers an elevated view of the area, including a glimpse inside Space Mountain, in electro-magnetic cars. Short queues. **AAA** (**TTT** under-8s)

Stitch's Great Escape: This 15min experience receives mixed reviews – some like it for the audio-animatronic prequel to Disney's *Lilo & Stitch*, with visitors being recruited into the madcap Galactic Federation prison service (where Stitch's arrival causes havoc), while others find it puzzling and rather lame. Young children can also be scared by the complete darkness at times. There are two pre-show areas before recruits are

ushered into the sit-down chamber (with shoulder restraints) where Stitch is let loose to bounce, dribble and even belch over the unwary audience. **R:** 3ft 2in/101cm. **AA**

Buzz Lightyear's Space Ranger Spin: Ride into action against evil Emperor Zurg and the robot army – and shoot them with laser cannons! A sure-fire family winner, especially as you keep score. **TTT** (**TTTT** under-8s) **FP+**

Monsters Inc Laugh Floor: With 'live' animation, special effects and high-tech voice links, guests can meet and match wits with the likes of Mike, Sulley and Roz from *Monsters Inc* and be entertained by their patter and antics. Billy Boil opens the show, introducing comedians (including two-headed jokester Sam-n-Ella), with the aim of capturing the audience's laughter. Guest interaction is essential! Watch the screen – you may be featured! **AAA FP+**

Other entertainment: *Incredibles* fans should enjoy the **INCREDIBLES Super Dance Party** (daily 5–10pm) with the chance to bop along with a live DJ and various *Incredibles* characters, led by Mr & Mrs Incredible, while **Disney characters** are often on hand by the **Carousel of Progress**, notably Buzz Lightyear.

Shopping: Highlights are provided by **Mickey's Star Traders** and **Merchant of Venus**.

Dining: For food, try **Cosmic Ray's Starlight Café** (good burgers, chicken, sandwiches, soups, salads and flavoured iced coffees), **Auntie Gravity's Galactic Goodies** (ice-cream, smoothies and juices), the **Lunching Pad** (speciality

Monsters Inc. Laugh Floor

hot-dogs, pretzels and frozen drinks) or **Tomorrowland Terrace** (burgers, hot dogs sandwiches and salads; open seasonally).

Having come full circle you're now back at Main Street USA and it's best to return here in the afternoon to avoid the crowds and enjoy the impressive shops.

Disney parades

Disney really knows how to do a parade. Coupled with its range of special seasonal events, there is always much more to look forward to than just the rides.

BRITTIP

To watch a parade, sit on the left side of Main Street USA (facing the Castle) to stay in the shade if it's hot, or grab a spot in the Hub or Frontierland. People start staking out the best places an HOUR in advance.

Festival of Fantasy Parade: A dazzling and unmissable pageant of creative floats, costumes, dancers and music. The seven featured floats

Festival of Fantasy Parade

include The Little Mermaid, Disney Princes and Princesses (including *Frozen*'s Anna and Elsa), Maleficent (with a magnificent fire-breathing steam-punk style dragon!), Tangled and Peter Pan and friends, plus a special balloon-like vehicle for Mickey and Minnie. The energetic dancers, stilt-walkers and rather menacing outfits of the 'Raven' men combine for dramatic effect. AAAAA FP+ for special viewing area.

Sadly, Walt Disney World said goodbye to the fabulous spectacle of the **Main Street Electrical Parade** in October 2016, as it heads for a 2017 curtain-call over at Disneyland in California. The MSEP had been a park favourite since 1977 and was a technological marvel of its age. There was no immediate word on what would take its place at the Magic Kingdom, but rumours from Disney's California home suggested that their special evening parade, **Paint The Night**, might be making the return journey across the country to light up the Orlando park in 2017.

Main Street USA closes 30mins after the rest of the park, so you can avoid the inevitable mad rush for the car parks by lingering here to shop or enjoy an ice-cream.

Celebrate The Magic!: This stunning nightly state-of-the-art projection show uses the Cinderella Castle as its backdrop, incorporating animated special effects and video that make the castle seem to come alive, transforming again and again with a sequence of Disney characters and films in dynamic colour. Watch as a magical paintbrush brings to life favourite characters and scenes from classic Disney films, as the imagery weaves visual trick after trick in a kaleidoscopic pattern that will leave your eyeballs breathless! AAAA

Wishes: Most nights also finish with this spectacular fireworks show over the Castle. With a clever soundtrack narrated by Jiminy Cricket and featuring memorable moments from various Disney classics, it is magnificently choreographed and culminates in a sequence of dazzling pyrotechnic explosions

MAGIC KINGDOM PARK with children

Here is a rough guide to the attractions that appeal to different age groups (height restrictions have been taken into account):

Under-5s

Buzz Lightyear's Space Ranger Spin, Country Bear Jamboree, Mickey's Royal Friendship Faire, Dumbo the Flying Elephant, Enchanted Tales With Belle, The Enchanted Tiki Room, Festival of Fantasy Parade, 'It's a Small World', Journey of the Little Mermaid, Jungle Cruise, Liberty Square Riverboat, Main Street Vehicles, Many Adventures of Winnie the Pooh, Mickey's PhilharMagic, Monsters Inc Laugh Floor, Move It! Shake It! Dance & Play It! Street Party, Peter Pan's Flight, Prince Charming Regal Carousel, Tomorrowland Speedway (with a parent), Tomorrowland Transit Authority, Walt Disney World Railroad.

5–8s

Astro Orbiter, The Barnstormer, Big Thunder Mountain Railroad, Buzz Lightyear's Space Ranger Spin, Country Bear Jamboree, Enchanted Tales With Belle, The Enchanted Tiki Room, Festival of Fantasy Parade, Haunted Mansion, Journey of the Little Mermaid, Jungle Cruise, Liberty Square Riverboat, Mad Tea Party, Magic Carpets of Aladdin, Many Adventures of Winnie the Pooh, Mickey's PhilharMagic, Mickey's Royal Friendship Faire, Monsters Inc Laugh Floor, Move It! Shake It! Dance & Play It! Street Party, Pirates of the Caribbean, Seven Dwarfs Mine Train Ride, Space Mountain (with parental discretion), Splash Mountain, Stitch's Great Escape!, Swiss Family Treehouse, Tom Sawyer Island, Tomorrowland Speedway (with a parent), Tomorrowland Transit Authority, Walt Disney's Carousel of Progress, Walt Disney World Railroad.

9–12s

Astro Orbiter, Big Thunder Mountain Railroad, Buzz Lightyear's Space Ranger Spin, Country Bear Jamboree, Festival of Fantasy Parade, The Haunted Mansion, Journey of the Little Mermaid, Mad Tea Party, Mickey's PhilharMagic, Monsters Inc. Laugh Floor, Move It! Shake It! Dance & Play It! Street Party, Pirates of the Caribbean, Seven Dwarfs Mine Train Ride, Space Mountain, Splash Mountain, Stitch's Great Escape!, Tomorrowland Indy Speedway (without a parent), Wishes fireworks.

Over-12s

Astro Orbiter, Big Thunder Mountain Railroad, Buzz Lightyear's Space Ranger Spin, Festival of Fantasy parade, Haunted Mansion, Mad Tea Party, Mickey's PhilharMagic, Move It! Shake It! Dance & Play It! Street Party, Pirates of the Caribbean, Seven Dwarfs Mine Train, Space Mountain, Splash Mountain, Stitch's Great Escape!, Wishes fireworks.

(many designed especially for this show). Starting with an appearance by Tinker Bell (from the Castle's top turret), it continues for 12mins of typical Disney emotional appeal; the perfect pixie-dust farewell to a memorable day. AAAAA FP+

🇬🇧 BRITTIP

After the fireworks crowd exits, you are allowed to take the Resort Only monorail back to the Transportation & Ticket Center, rather than queue for the main Express monorail.

Wishes Cruises: If you prefer not to fight the crowds for a fab view of Wishes, book one of three speciality cruises to view the fireworks from Seven Seas Lagoon. The Basic Cruise holds up to eight guests onboard a 21ft/6m pontoon boat and costs $318; the Premium Cruise holds up to 10 on a 25ft/7.6m pontoon boat (for $372). Both include water, soft drinks, snacks and an audio feed to the Wishes music; or splash out for the Celebration Cruise, which adds special occasion decorations to the Basic and Premium Cruises for an added fee, depending on decorations. All can be booked 90 days in advance.

Pirate and Pals Fireworks Voyage: This kid-friendly Wishes cruise includes meeting Mr Smee and

Captain Hook before cruising the Seven Seas Lagoon to view the Electrical Water Pageant and Wishes. Snacks and drinks are provided while you enjoy a retelling of the PeterPan story, then meet Pan himself at the end of your voyage ($69 adults, $41 3–9; can be booked 180 days in advance).

BRITTIP
For a final bit of typical Disney entertainment, head outside the Magic Kingdom at 10.25pm and catch the Electrical Water Pageant passing by on Seven Seas Lagoon in front of the park.

Leaving the park

When it comes to leaving, the monorail is quicker than the ferry but it can still take up to an hour to get back to your car. Also, if the crowds get too heavy during the day, you can escape by leaving in the early afternoon (your car park ticket is valid all day) and returning to your hotel for a few hours' rest or a dip in the pool. Alternatively, catch a boat to one of the Disney resorts. Fort Wilderness is especially fun for kids and boasts the good value Trails End restaurant for lunch or dinner.

Halloween and Christmas

Two additional annual events in the Magic Kingdom provide a separate, party-style ticketed event 7pm–midnight, with most of the rides open and extra themed fun and games.

Mickey's Not So Scary Halloween Party: Sept–Oct sees many visitors

Halloween at the Magic Kingdom

dress up for the American trick-or-treat fun, with plenty of treats for all. With special features, shows, Mickey's Boo To You Halloween Parade and the splendid HalloWishes fireworks (with lighting effects), tickets ($72–105 adults, $67–100 for children 3–9), go on sale about five months in advance and sell quickly.

Mickey's Very Merry Christmas Party: The Christmas party (Nov–Dec; variously from $86–99 adults, $81–94 children 3–9) sees 'snow' on Main Street and magnificent festive decorations and theming. There is free hot chocolate and cookies, a parade and more fireworks. The atmosphere is enchanting, though the evening can be prone to unfriendly weather.

BRITTIP
Although the special evening parties don't start officially until 7pm, you can use the ticket to gain entry to the park from 4pm, which gives you 8 full hours to enjoy all the attractions.

Park tours

Keys to the Kingdom: One of the park's little-known secrets is this 4–5hr guided tour of many backstage areas, including the service tunnel under the park, and entertainment production buildings. It's an extra $79 (including lunch; not available for under-16s) but is a superb journey into the park's creation.

Disney's Family Magic: This is a 2hr guided adventure that takes you on a search for clues throughout the park at $39/person.

Magic Behind Our Steam Trains Tour: A 3hr tour ($54/person; no under-10s) that joins the crew that prepares the park's trains each day.

Walt Disney: Marceline to Magic Kingdom: A 3hr tour on how the inspiration of Walt's early years in Marceline, Missouri, culminated in the creation of the Magic Kingdom ($35/person; no under-12s).

Epcot

Epcot originally stood for 'Experimental Prototype Community of Tomorrow', but it might be more accurate to say Every Person Comes Out Tired. For this is a BIG park, with a lot to see and do, and much legwork required to cover its 300acre/122ha extent. Actually, it is not so much a vision of the future as a look at the world and technology of today, with a strong educational and environmental message. At almost three times the size of the Magic Kingdom Park, it is more likely to require a two-day visit (though under-5s might find it less entertaining) and your feet in particular will notice the difference! Remember FP+1 means you can pick only ONE of these FastPass attractions, while FP+ indicates where you can select two.

Location

Epcot opened in October 1982 and its giant car park can hold 9,000 vehicles, so a tram takes you to the main entrance (though if you are staying at a Disney hotel you can catch the monorail, boat or bus service to the gates; International Gateway is a separate entrance for guests at the Epcot resort hotels). Don't forget to note where you have parked (e.g. Create, row 49). If you have your ticket or MagicBand, you pass through the gate area and wait in the immediate entrance plaza for Rope Drop, which is signalled by Mickey and Co arriving to greet guests.

Beating the queues: Epcot is divided into two distinct parts arranged in a figure of eight and there are two tactics to avoid the worst of the

Epcot at a glance

Location	Off Epcot Drive, Walt Disney World
Size	300 acres/122ha in Future World and World Showcase
Hours	9am–9pm Future World (except Universe of Energy, Imagination, 9am–7pm), 11am–9pm (World Showcase)
Admission	Under-3s free; 3–9 $91–108 (1–day base ticket, priced seasonally), $320 (5–day Magic Your Way), £309 (14–day Ultimate); adult (10+) $97–114, $340, £329 Prices do not include tax.
Parking	$20
Lockers	Through the main entrance to the right hand side and at International Gateway $12 small, $14 large ($5 deposit each)
Pushchairs	$15 and $31 to the left after the main entrance and at International Gateway; $13 and $27 per day for multiple days
Wheelchairs	$12 or $70 ($20 deposit refunded) with pushchairs
Top attractions	Mission: SPACE, Test Track, Spaceship Earth, Soarin' Around The World, Universe of Energy, American Adventure
Don't miss	IllumiNations: Reflections of Earth, Disney Character Spot, Turtle Talk With Crush, live entertainment (including American Music Machine, JAMMitors and Voices of Liberty in America), and dinner at any of the World Showcase pavilions
Hidden costs	Meals	Burger, chips and coke $14.28 3-course dinner $40–53 (La Hacienda, Mexico) Kids' meal $8.50–15
	T-shirts	$24.95–39.95 Kids' T-shirts $12.95–29.95
	Souvenirs	$1.05–6,900
	Sundries	Epcot 'Passport' $9.95

Future World

1 Universe of Energy
2 Mission: SPACE
3 Test Track
4 Odyssey Center
5 Imagination!
6 The Land (including Soarin' Around the World)
7 The Seas with Nemo and Friends
8 Spaceship Earth
9 Character Spot
10 Innoventions East
11 Innoventions West

World Showcase

12 Mexico
13 Norway
14 China
15 The Outpost
16 Germany
17 Italy
18 The American Adventure
19 Japan
20 Morocco
21 France
22 International Gateway (to Epcot resort hotels)
23 United Kingdom
24 Canada
25 Friendship Boats to Italy and Morocco
26 America Gardens Theater
27 Showcase Plaza
28 Monorail Station

K Kidcot Fun Stops

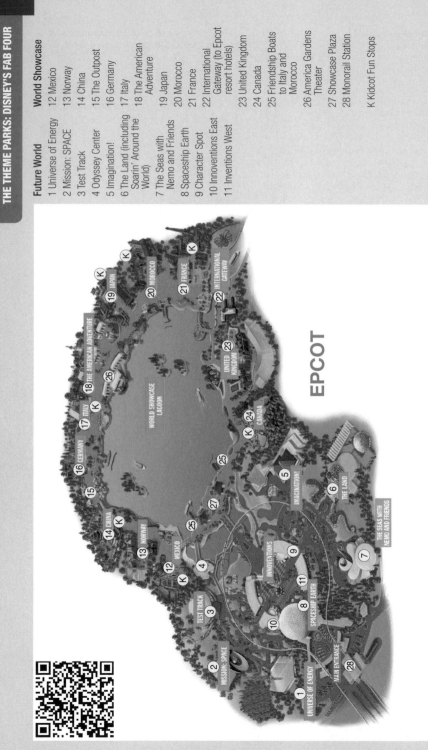

EPCOT

crowds. The first or upper half of the park is Future World, with six pavilions arranged around Spaceship Earth (which dominates the skyline) and the two Innoventions centres.

The second part is World Showcase, a potted journey round the world via 11 international pavilions featuring each country's culture, shopping, entertainment and cuisine. Once through the entrance plaza, aim to try the three big-time rides – Test Track, Mission: Space and Soarin' Around the World™ – first, then move into World Showcase, which opens at 11am. Continue in World Showcase until 4–5pm, then return to Future World for the other attractions there, as the majority will have moved on (apart from at the three main rides).

As a general tactic, head first for the magnificent Soarin' Around the World, then head to the other side of Future World for Test Track, if you haven't got an FP in advance (and you can book only one with the two-tiered FP+ system). While you wait for your ride time, you can queue for Mission: SPACE and perhaps even take in Universe of Energy. Alternatively, if the rides don't appeal quite so much

as a visit to such diverse cultures as Japan and Morocco, have a lie-in or enjoy your pool, then head into World Showcase at 11am and you'll be ahead of the crowds for the first hour. Also early on, book lunch or dinner at one of the fine restaurants around World Showcase (Mexico, Italy, France and Morocco are all highly recommended). The best reservations go fast, but check in at Guest Relations (on the left after Spaceship Earth) for advice and bookings.

Planning your visit
If you plan a two-day visit, try to get an early FastPass+ for either Test Track or Soarin' Around the World, then, after riding it, head straight to World Showcase for its 11am opening as the majority will stay in Future World for a while. Book an evening meal for around 5.30pm, then linger around the lagoon for the evening entertainment.

For your second visit, look to get a FP+ for whichever of Test Track or Soarin' you didn't do first time. If you can add Mission: Space, even better (or just head there first). If you linger in Future World, you should find queues for Spaceship Earth, Universe

Mission: Space

© Disney

of Energy, Mission: Space and Journey into Imagination much shorter in mid-afternoon. You CAN do Epcot in a day – if you arrive early, put in some speedy legwork and give most of the detail a miss. But, of all the parks, it is a shame to hurry this one. Browse in the 60-plus shops when the rides are busiest.

Kidcot Fun Stops: At 11 activity centres around Epcot (each country in World Showcase), children can decorate a cardboard character and get a stamp from each country on the handle attached to the character.

Future World

Here's what you'll find in the first part of your Epcot adventure.

Universe of Energy: The one attraction here is a stunner. Ellen's Energy Adventure is a 35min show-and-ride with comedienne Ellen DeGeneres and Bill Nye the Science Guy exploring the creation of fuels from the age of dinosaurs to the modern day. You think you are in a conventional theatre until your seats rearrange themselves into 96-person solar-powered cars and you are off on a journey through the prehistoric era, with some realistic dinosaurs! Queues are steady but not overwhelming from mid-morning. AAAAA

Mission: SPACE: This is more high-tech Disney imagination, a journey into the future at the International Space Training Center. The space-age building prepares you for a major adventure as you enter through Planetary Plaza, with its giant replica planets (check out the model showing the moon landings). At the entry there's a choice of two queues – Standby and FastPass+ Return, and

the clever organisation keeps things moving. As you enter the facility, there are some superb models and graphics (like the giant Gravity Wheel) to look at while you queue to reach Team Dispatch. For the ride, you form into teams of four in the ready rooms – Pilot, Navigator, Engineer or Commander – each with different functions. You also have the choice of the full, dynamic version of the ride (the 'orange' version) or a toned-down alternative that avoids the 'spinning' effect (the 'green' version). Once briefed, by actor Gary Sinise, you enter the Preparation Room to learn your mission: a flight to Mars. Then it's into the ride vehicle, capsules that close down tightly with outer doors, shoulder restraints and screens that move forward to just in front of your face (this is not ideal for those with claustrophobia, prone to motion sickness, or expectant mothers). The sense of realism, with the consoles, individual speakers and countdown is magnificent, though.

For those on the full version, a very real blast-off simulates some of the genuine forces of a rocket launch (thanks to its huge centrifuge, which is part-ride and part-simulator). Each team member has to perform their duties on cue and you experience a simulated sling-shot around the moon and on to Mars, where the landing is an adventure in itself. It's a truly original, aggressive ride, but you should heed the advice to keep your head still and look straight into the screen or you WILL feel sick (unless you are on the tamer version, where the capsules just tilt and turn). We think the full-on experience is too intense for young children, and there is no backing out once you blast off (parents could try it first). **R**: 3ft 8in/112cm. TTTTT FP+

Elaborate post-show and activities include **Space Base** – an excellent play area for children who can't ride (and those who just like to climb, slide and crawl); **Space Race** – a great game for two teams of 60 players to propel a rocket back to Earth via a series of on-screen challenges; **Expedition Mars** – a computer

Test Track

© Disney

game to rescue stranded astronauts; and **Postcards from Space** – where you can email a 'space video' to friends and family. There is then the inevitable (and well-stocked) gift shop. All in all, it's a terrific experience.

Test Track: This equally big-scale production – a 5½min whirl along Disney's longest, fastest track – offers a journey into the world of Chevrolet car design and technology. It starts with an interactive queue that invites riders to digitally design their own car according to Capability, Efficiency, Responsiveness and Power, which they then carry on to their prototype vehicle. Once aboard, it is off through an elaborate digital computer world of performance tests, with the car put through its paces on hair-pin bends, rough surfaces, temperature extremes and a final high-speed section outside the building at up to 67mph/108kph. Each guest's car design is computer tested alongside the vehicle and scored according to how it fares. The final post-ride area shows more about the testing process and its four key design elements. The vivid lighting, which makes you feel as if you're inside a computer (like the film *Tron*), sharp twists and turns and other special effects add up to a unique whirl through this high-tech world (complete with Chevy gift shop), but it does draw BIG queues and the FP+ option can run out well in advance during busy seasons. If you're on your own or don't mind your family being split up, the Single Rider option is handy here. **R**: 3ft 4in/101cm. **TTTT** (**TTT** teens) **FP+1**

The Odyssey Center: Baby-care, first-aid, telephones and restrooms.

Imagination!: This two-part attraction starts with **Journey into Imagination with Figment**, an uneven but quirky ride into experiments with imagination with Eric Idle (as Dr Nigel Channing of the Imagination Institute) and the cartoon dragon Figment. The sight laboratory sees Figment having fun with a vision chart, the sound lab is a symphony of imaginative melodies

and Figment's house is a truly topsy-turvy world (watch out for the skunk in the smell lab!). It's gentle fun and rarely draws a crowd. AAA FP+ You exit into **Image Works – The 'What If' Labs**, an interactive playground of sight and sound, which usually amuses kids more than adults (though you might be tempted to buy cartoon images and select-your-own CDs).

The Land: A three-element entertaining and educational experience on food and nutrition plus the spectacular thrill-ride of Soarin'. **Living with the Land** is an informative 14min boat ride well worth the sometimes long queue. A journey through food production may sound dull, but it is informative and enjoyable, with plenty to make children sit up and take notice of its three ecological communities, especially the greenhouse finale. AAAA FP

The Circle of Life: This 15min animated tale features characters from *The Lion King* explaining ecological concerns that are easily digestible for kids. Queues are rare. AA

Soarin' Around the World™: One of Disney's most imaginative attractions, this 'flight simulator' offers an exhilarating ride for all ages, a breathtaking global journey that swoops over the Great Wall of China, Sydney Harbour Bridge, the Matterhorn in Switzerland and other world icons. An interactive game for mobile devices leads to the 'departure lounge', with passengers embarking on rows of seats that are hoisted into the air over a giant screen. The feeling is like taking a hang-glider ride as the special film,

Soarin' Around the World

© Disney

sounds and scents become all-encompassing. Feet dangling, you soar up, over and around the great sights that also include the Pyramids and Eiffel Tower, with the ride's newly enhanced projection system, special effects, magnificent music and superb technology ensuring a five-star experience. The ride capacity was boosted in 2016 but queues still build up, so use FastPass+ or visit either early or in the last two hours of the day. R: 3ft 4in/101cm. AAAAA FP+1

Dining: The **Sunshine Seasons Food Court** offers the chance to eat some of Disney's home-grown produce, while the **Garden Grill** restaurant is a slowly revolving platform that offers more traditional food, including beef, turkey, sausages and salad, all in the company of Mickey, Goofy, Pluto and Chip 'n' Dale.

◄► **BRITTIP**

Queues for Soarin' and Test Track are notably shorter in the last hour of the day, and you're guaranteed to get on provided you are in the queue before 9pm.

The Seas with Nemo & Friends: This pavilion does for the oceans what The Land does for terra firma, in the company of the characters from *Finding Nemo*. You start with the signature ride, **The Seas With Nemo and Friends**, which takes riders on an underwater journey in 'clam-mobiles' to meet Nemo and Co (brilliantly interwoven into the huge aquarium, apparently

The Seas with Nemo and Friends

© Disney

swimming with the real fish!). Nemo has gone missing (again), hence the ride becomes a quest to reunite him with teacher Mr Ray and the rest of the class in a rousing musical finale. AAAA FP+ You then exit into **Sea Base**, a two-level development offering six modules featuring stories of undersea exploration and marine life, including a research centre that provides a close encounter with the endangered manatee. Plenty of interactive elements and educational touch-screens are on offer, plus additional tanks displaying Caribbean reef fish, jellyfish and cuttlefish, while there is an excellent demonstration of a diving chamber. Crowds are steady, but queues rarely get too long – with one exception. **Turtle Talk with Crush** is a brilliantly interactive meet-and-greet with the surfer dude turtle, plus Dory and other characters from the films *Finding Nemo* and *Finding Dory*. Crush is the star, though, as he swims up and engages children in the audience with some fun live banter. AAAA FP+ Next door, **Bruce's Sub House** is a kids' play area including photo opportunities with more of the Nemo characters (**TTT** under-6s). **Nemo and Friends** is more hands-on fun for kids, while **Mr Ray's Lagoon** showcases some real stingrays.

Dining: The pavilion includes the highly recommended **Coral Reef Restaurant** that serves great seafood with a grandstand view of the massive aquarium. Dinner will be $28–47 (starter and main), depending on your choices, which isn't cheap, but the food is first class (kids' menu $10–13).

Spaceship Earth: Spiralling up 18 storeys, this attraction is a convincing time-travel story into various technologies narrated by Dame Judi Dench. From cave paintings to the internet (with a superb depiction of Michelangelo's Sistine Chapel), the gentle ride unfolds in imaginative historical stages, culminating in an interactive finale that invites riders to 'predict' the future. Sponsor Siemens (the electronics giant) has added a post-show interactive demonstration area (including predictive surgery and a driving challenge), which makes for an entertaining diversion after the 15min ride. Queues are heavy all morning, but almost non-existent late in the day. AAAA FP+

Innoventions: These two centres of hands-on exhibits were undergoing a complete re-think in content and purpose as we went to press, hence it is unclear what will be on offer here in 2017. The few existing attractions remaining at **Innoventions East** were **Storm Struck**, where visitors experience a violent storm from a special viewing theatre, and **Colortopia**, with interactive ways to experience colour via The Power of Color Theater, Color Lab and Color Our World, using 'magic paintbrush' technology to teach guests about the art of colour. **Innoventions West** had been completely emptied in summer 2016, with strong rumours that this will become a new meet-and-greet area for more Disney characters, expanding the popular Character Spot next door. Expect more news on this in early 2017, so visit **www.disneyworld.com**.

BRITTIP

If Innoventions East and West are open, they are quiet places in which to spend time if you need to cool down, escape the crowds, or if it's raining.

Other entertainment: Live fun is also provided periodically around Future World by the unique JAMMitors percussion group, while the **Epcot Character Spot** (across from Innoventions West, 9am–9pm at peak times, 10am–6pm off-peak, FP+1) offers a fabulous themed meet-and-greet with many Disney characters. Daisy Duck and Goofy can often be found just inside the main entrance. The majestic **Plaza Fountain** choreographs to musical performances every 15min.

Shopping: Mouse Gear next to Innoventions East features a massive variety of Epcot and Disney merchandise (and don't miss the wacky ceiling architecture!), while the **Art of Disney** features superb signature art and animator drawings.

Dining: Food outlets include the counter-service **Electric Umbrella**

Spaceship Earth

Restaurant for lunch and dinner (sandwiches, burgers and flatbread) and the **Fountainview Café** for Starbucks coffees, cold drinks, pastries and sandwiches. Look out also for **Club Cool** presented by Coca-Cola®, where you can enjoy international Coke products and souvenirs, along with various free tastes from around the world (beware the Beverly!).

World Showcase

If you found Future World amazing, prepare to be astounded by the imaginative pavilions around the World Showcase Lagoon, each featuring a glimpse of a different country in dramatic settings. Several have rides or films to showcase their main features, while the restaurants offer some outstanding fare and many character greeting spots can be found here (check the daily Times Guide for locations and timings).

Agent P's World Showcase Adventure: As in all of the sign-up station for this interactive and family-friendly challenge game, based on the *Phineas & Ferb* TV series, on the bridge over to World Showcase (and with other stations at International Gateway, Norway and Italy), or download the app at **www. agentpwsa.com**, then activate it at the Agent P kiosks. With the aid of the Field Operative Notification Equipment (or FONE), guest 'agents'

follow the clues around each World Showcase pavilion to help the boys' pet platypus Perry (Agent P) in his bid to foil his nemesis Dr Doofenschmirtz. Complete all the tasks on your FONE and you foil the evil Dr and free Perry from his predicament.

 BRITTIP

Don't waste your three precious FastPasses on attractions such is Imagination, Spaceship Earth, or IllumiNations. Queues for the two rides are generally non-existent in late afternoon, and it usually isn't difficult to find a good spot to view IllumiNations.

Mexico: Starting at the bottom left of the circular tour of the lagoon and moving clockwise, your first encounter is inside the spectacular pyramid. Here you have the amusing boat ride **Gran Fiesta Tour Starring The Three Caballeros**, a 9min journey through the people and history of the country guided by Donald, Panchito and José Carioca. Queues build up in mid-afternoon but are usually light otherwise. AAA

Other entertainment: As in all of the World Showcase pavilions, there is live entertainment, with periodic 25min music shows from **Mariachi Cobre**, while Donald Duck puts in character appearances.

Shopping: Much of the pavilion comprises market-style gift shops.

Frozen Ever After

© Disney

Dining: The San Angel Inn is a romantic Mexican restaurant (lunch from 11:30am–4pm, dinner 4.30–9pm), and **La Cava del Tequila** has tempting cocktails, light bites and tequilas. Outside, choose from the revamped counter service **Cantina de San Angel** (open-air, serving tacos, nachos and tortillas) and full-service **La Hacienda de San Angel** (dinner from 4pm) serving authentic Mexican fare with a superb lagoon view and grandstand seat for the IllumiNations show. This gets our thumbs-up as a stand-out choice.

Norway: A reproduction of Oslo's splendid Akershus Fortress is the exterior façade, while the interior is given over to the new headline attraction, **Frozen Ever After**. This boat ride through the realm of Arendelle features a 'Winter in Summer' celebration that visits Queen Elsa in her Ice Palace, as well as Troll Valley and the Bay of Arendelle to share in some of *Frozen*'s iconic moments. Clever animatronics, projection screens and extra animated scenes bring the journey to life in classic Disney story-telling style, while *Frozen* fans can then visit Elsa and Princess Anna in their all new **Sommerhus**, a special highly themed location for character meet-and-greets. FP+ (for ride AAA) and FP+1 (for meet-n-greet AAAAA).

Dining: The **Akershus Royal Banquet Hall** offers the Princess Storybook dining for breakfast, lunch and dinner, complete with a host of Disney Princesses, while the counter-service café serves sandwiches, pastries and drinks.

BRITTIP

If you can't get a booking for Cinderella's Royal Table in the Magic Kingdom, the Akershus Royal Banquet (8.30am–8.30pm; $35–59 for adults, and $25–27 kids 3–9) is the next best thing and should keep most young 'princesses' happy! Call 407 939 3463 up to 180 days in advance or book online at **www.disneyworld.com.**

Shopping: New gift shop **Wandering Reindeer** features all things *Frozen*, while **Puffins Roost** stocks Norwegian clothes, toys, perfume, food and spirits.

China: The spectacular landscapes of China are well served by the main attraction of this pavilion, the stunning **Reflections of China**, a 360° film in the circular Temple of Heaven, where you are surrounded by the sights and sounds of one of the world's most enigmatic countries. Queues build up to 30mins during the main part of the day (but it is fully air-conditioned). AAAA

Other entertainment: Don't miss the periodic shows from the spectacular **Jeweled Dragon Acrobats** on the plaza in front of the temple, while Disney characters from *Mulan* also appear throughout the day.

Shopping: Yong Feng Shangdian Dept Store is a warehouse of Chinese gifts and artefacts.

Dining: Two restaurants, the **Nine Dragons** and the counter-service **Lotus Blossom Café** offer tastes of the Orient.

The Outpost: Between China and Germany features hut-style shops and snacks, with crafts from Africa and the Caribbean.

Germany: There is more in the way of shopping and eating than entertainment, though you still find a magnificent re-creation of a **Bavarian Biergarten**, with lively Oktoberfest shows featuring the resident Musikanten brass band at regular intervals. It also offers hearty portions of German sausage, sauerkraut and rotisserie chicken. The Sommerfest is fast food German-style (bratwurst and strudel), while there are eight shops, more than anywhere else in

Les Halles Boulangérie-Patisserie

© Disney

Epcot, including chocolates, wines, crystal, porcelain, toys and cuckoo clocks.

BRITTIP

With seating for 400, Biergarten often takes walk-ups even when Disney's reservations system indicates the restaurant is full.

Other entertainment: An elaborate outdoor **model railway** is popular with children, and look out for character appearances from Snow White.

Italy: Similarly, Italy has pretty, authentic architecture, including a superb reproduction of Venice's St Mark's Square, three gift shops with wine, chocolates, Armani gifts, fine crystal, porcelain and Venetian masks, and two full-service restaurants. **Tutto Italia** is the fine-dining option, designed like the Medici Palace, complete with a gluten-free menu and a splendid cellar-style wine bar, **Tutto Gusto**, that offers small plates and light bites (reservations not needed), while the superb **Via Napoli** is a delightful pizzeria, featuring wood-burning ovens and genuine Neapolitan style, as well as an outdoor terrace.

Other entertainment: Watch out for the fun entertainment of **Sergio**, a madcap juggler who loves to involve his audience, and the eye-catching **Sbandieratori Di Sansepolcro** flag-waving team.

The American Adventure: At the top of the lagoon and dominating World Showcase is this huge edifice, not so much a pavilion as a celebration of the country's history and Constitution. Two wonderful singing groups add authentic sounds to the 18th-century setting, overlooked by a reproduction of Philadelphia's Liberty Hall. Inside, you have the **American Adventure** show, a magnificent half-hour film and audio-animatronic production that details the country's founding, its struggles and triumphs, presidents, statesmen and heroes. It's a glossy, patriotic display, featuring some outstanding technology and, while some of it will be unfamiliar to foreign visitors, it's difficult not to be impressed. A good choice at most times of the day – and it's all in the cool! AAAA If you have time to spare, check out the special exhibitions in the American Heritage Gallery.

Other entertainment: American Music Machine is an outstanding *à capella* group that should not be

The American Adventure

© Disney

missed. It's one of the most talented and creative groups we've seen in a long time, featuring close-harmony vocals from the 1960s to present day. Another superb à *capella* group, **Voices of Liberty**, appear in the pavilion's rotunda several times a day, while the **America Gardens Theater**, next to the lagoon, presents concerts from international artists during the Flower & Garden Festival, Sounds Like Summer series and Food & Wine Festival.

Shopping: Antiques and handcarts provide touches of nostalgia, along with the **Heritage Manor Gifts** store.

Dining: Liberty Inn offers fast-food lunch and dinner and the **Block & Hans** kiosk has craft beers, wine and pretzels.

Japan: Next up on the clockwise tour, you are introduced to typical Japanese style and architecture, including a five-storey 8th-century **Pagoda**, some magnificent art exhibits, notably in the **Bijutsu-kan Gallery**, featuring art and insights into Japanese history and culture, a tranquil **Bonsai garden** (complete with carp pond) and landmark Torii gate.

Other entertainment: Live shows are key here, with periodic presentations from the superb **Matsuriza** taiko drummers.

Shopping: The huge **Mitsukoshi** store adds fascinating shopping, from traditional calligraphy, tea kettles and wind chimes to Hello Kitty souvenirs.

Dining: Great food is a real highlight, and the restaurant line-up consists of the wonderful fine dining of **Teppan Edo** (with its traditional chefs at each table) and **Tokyo Dining**, featuring Japanese cuisine and ingredients, showcasing sushi and innovative presentation. **Katsura Grill** is its fast-food equivalent, with great soups, teriyaki and sushi dishes while the **Kabuki Café** serves sake, beer, plum wine, tea and soft drinks.

Morocco: As you would expect, this is another shopping experience, with bazaars, alleyways and stalls selling a well-priced array of carpets, leather

goods, clothing, brass ornaments, pottery and antiques.

All the building materials were imported for the pavilion, which was hand-built to give Morocco a greater degree of authenticity, even by World Showcase's high standards. The **Gallery of Arts and History** offers more historical and cultural insights, while the **Fez House** depicts a typical Moroccan home.

Other entertainment: Characters from Disney's *Aladdin* appear from time to time.

Dining: Restaurant Marrakesh provides a full dining experience, complete with traditional musicians and their own belly dancer. It's rather pricey but the lively atmosphere is entertaining. Better value can be had at **Tangierine Café**, with its roast lamb, hummus, tabbouleh, couscous, lentil salad and Moroccan breads ($8.99–14.99; kids' meals $7.99). **Spice Road Table**, a clever indoor/outdoor café and bar, offers superb small-plate, Mediterranean-style meals and snacks plus signature cocktails and other drinks, all with a great Lagoon

Morocco

© Hilary White

view (select tables are ideal for the nightly IllumiNations show).

BRITTIP

The **Tangierine Café** in Morocco is a peaceful haven in which to enjoy a quiet, healthy lunch, especially if you are vegetarian, plus there is a tempting coffee and pastry counter. **Spice Road Table** can often accommodate late-comers for a good table-service lunch or dinner.

France: Predictably overlooked by a replica Eiffel Tower, this is a clean and cheerful pre-World War I Paris, with comedy street theatre adding to the rather dreamy atmosphere and pleasant gardens, plus stylish shopping and dining. Don't miss **Impressions de France**, a big-film production that serves up all the grandest sights of the country to the music of Offenbach, Debussy, Saint-Saëns and Satie. Crowds are rarely heavy, and it's air-conditioned. AAAA

Other entertainment: Look out for the visual comedy and amazing balancing act of **Serveur Amusant** (not when it's too windy), while **Princess Aurora** (Sleeping Beauty) makes regular appearances, along with *Beauty and the Beast* characters.

Shopping: Suitably chic, there's an authentic **Wine Shop** and elegant **Guerlain** and **Givenchy** perfumeries (ask about the free perfume tour during the Flower and Garden Festival).

Dining: This is THE pavilion for a gastronomic experience provided by three restaurants, of which **Les Chefs de France** and **Monsieur Paul** are

major discoveries. The former is a classic, full-service establishment featuring top-quality French cuisine for lunch and dinner, while the latter, upstairs, is named (and themed) for famous chef Paul Bocuse, with his well-trained team in charge of both. Monsieur Paul is a touch more formal and upscale, with a 4-course prix fixe menu ($89/person), and, while an expensive meal (dinner only; appetisers from $15–29 and main courses $39–44), it is a fabulous choice. Also here is the **Les Halles Boulangerie Patisserie**, a genuine French patisserie featuring freshly made baguettes, croissants, salads, quiches and fab pastries, and **L'Artisan des Glaces**, an artisan ice-cream and sorbet shop, with everything made fresh in-house every day (and with liqueur treats for grown-ups!).

BRITTIP

The special dining events in the France pavilion are often the highlight of the annual Food & Wine Festival and are worth signing up for.

United Kingdom: The least inspiring of all the pavilions, and certainly with little to entertain those who have ever visited a pub or shopped for Royal Doulton or Burberry goods, it is partly offset by some good live entertainment and pleasant gardens, but that is about it.

Other entertainment: Live music is provided by **British Revolution**, offering the sounds of the 60s, 70s and 80s up to five times a day, while the **Pub Musician** performs several times daily and folk group **Quickstep** features traditional British and Irish

Epcot Flower & Garden Festival

© Hilary White

EPCOT with children

Here is our rough guide to the attractions that appeal to different age groups:

Under-5s

Circle of Life, Frozen Ever After, Gran Fiesta Tour Starring The Three Caballeros, Journey into Imagination with Figment, Kidcot stops, Living with the Land, The Seas with Nemo and Friends, Soarin Around the World'™ (if tall enough), Spaceship Earth, Turtle Talk with Crush, Universe of Energy.

5–8s

All the above, plus The American Adventure, Image Works, JAMMitors, Test Track, Agent P's World Showcase Adventure.

9–12s

All the above, plus American Music Machine, Impressions de France, Matsuriza Drummers, Mission: SPACE, O Canada!, Reflections of China, Sergio, Le Serveur Amusant.

Over-12s

The American Adventure, American Music Machine, Bijutsu-kan Gallery, JAMMitors, Impressions de France, Living with the Land, Matsuriza Drummers, Mission: SPACE, The Seas with Nemo and Friends, O Canada!, Reflections of China, Soarin' Over the World™, Spaceship Earth, Test Track, Universe of Energy.

music. Mary Poppins, Winnie the Pooh, Tigger and Alice can also be found here.

Shopping: The best shops are the **Tea Caddy**, the **Queen's Table**, **Crown and Crest** (perfumes and heraldry), **Sportsman Shoppe** (sweaters, kilts, football shirts) and **Toy Soldier** (traditional games and toys), but prices are WAY above what you'd pay at home.

Dining: The Rose and Crown Pub is antiseptically authentic but you can get better elsewhere at these prices (New York strip steak $32, bangers and mash $19 or fish and chips $21, and a pint of Bass for a whopping $9). There's also a takeaway **Yorkshire County** fish and chippie.

Canada: Completing the World Showcase circle, the main features here are **Victoria Gardens**, based on the world-famous Butchart Gardens on Vancouver Island, some spectacular Rocky Mountain scenery, a replica French gothic mansion, the Hôtel de Canada, and another stunning 360° film, *O Canada!*

As with China and France, this showcases the country's sights and scenery in a terrific, 17min advert for the Canadian Tourist Board led

by comedian Martin Short. It's at its busiest in late afternoon. AAA

Other entertainment: Canada has been through several live entertainment shows recently and it isn't clear what will be on offer in 2017. Check your park show guide for current acts.

Shopping: The Trading Post and **Northwest Mercantile** provide a range of Canadian clothing and souvenirs, notably wonderful glass ornaments and Deauville perfume.

BRITTIP
Best way to tour World Showcase? Start in Canada and continue anticlockwise or jump on Friendship Boats and go straight to Italy or Morocco.

Dining and shopping: Le Cellier Steakhouse is an excellent dining room, offering great steaks, prime

Journey into Imagination

© Disney

rib, seafood, chicken and several vegetarian dishes for lunch and dinner.

IllumiNations: Reflections of Earth

The day's big finale and an absolute show-stopper, this firework and special-effects extravaganza is awesome even by Disney standards. British composer Gavin Greenaway provided the original music for a 15min performance of vivid brilliance. Some 2,800 firework shells are launched as a celestial backdrop to a series of fire-and-water effects on the World Showcase lagoon. The central icon is a 28ft/9m video globe of Earth that opens in a spectacular climax of choreographed pyrotechnics. However, people start staking out the best lagoon-side spots up to 2 HOURS in advance.

FP+1 for special viewing area. The ultimate way to view IllumiNations is by private boat on one of two cruises from Disney's Boardwalk or Yacht & Beach Club Resorts (for non-residents, too). The price range is $318–372/boat (holding 4–10) and can be used for special celebrations. Both include water, soft drinks and snacks (call 407 939 7529 up to 90 days in advance to book).

Behind-the-scenes tours

Epcot also has a big range of tours. Book all tours on 407 939 8687.

Dolphins in Depth: This is a 3hr dip into the research areas of The Seas pavilion, including a chance to meet the dolphins ($199, with refreshments, photo and T-shirt; 13–17s must be accompanied by an adult; swimming costume required).

Undiscovered Future World: A 4½hr journey into the creation of Epcot, Walt's vision and backstage areas like IllumiNations ($69).

Behind the Seeds: This 1hr tour, every 45mins from 9.45am–4.30pm at The Land pavilion, looks at Disney's innovative gardening practices ($20 adults, $16 3–9s).

Dive Quest: A 3hr experience, with a 40min dive into The Seas aquarium, plus a backstage look at the facility at 4.30 and 5.30pm daily, Must have scuba certification; park admission not required ($175/person, 10 and over, includes T-shirt and certificate).

Seas Aqua Tour: A similar tour without the scuba diving, daily at 12.30pm ($145/person, 8 and over; under-18s accompanied by an adult).

Backstage Magic: The most comprehensive tour goes behind the scenes of Epcot, Magic Kingdom and Disney's Hollywood Studios on a 7hr foray into little-seen aspects, like the backstage areas of the Studios and tunnels below Magic Kingdom ($255, 16 and over).

DestiNations Discovered: This 5hr walking tour highlights the history, culture and cuisine of each World Showcase country, including a cultural demonstration, peek behind the scenes and lunch. Two tours daily, at 9.30 and 10am ($109/person, 16 and over, no photography backstage).

Annual festivals

There are two main annual Epcot events to watch out for.

International Flower and Garden Festival: This puts the whole park in full bloom with an amazing series of set-pieces, topiaries, seminars and mini-exhibitions from early Mar to late May. All exhibits and some lectures are free, and they add a beautiful aspect to an already scenic park, along with new food kiosks around World Showcase that offer regional tastes and drinks.

Food and Wine Festival: From late Sept to mid-Nov, this showcases national and regional cuisines, wines and beers, with the chance to attend grand Winemakers' Dinners and Tasting Events, or just sample the offerings of more than 20 food booths dotted around World Showcase.

Both festivals also offer free concerts several times a day at the America Gardens Theater (weekends only for Flower & Garden).

Disney's Hollywood Studios

Welcome to a journey into the world of film and TV, an epic voyage of adventure, creation – and fun. Here you will learn plenty of tricks of the trade; movie-making secrets and behind-the-scenes glimpses that have been cleverly turned into rides, shows and other attractions with guaranteed entertainment appeal. Be aware, this is a park undergoing a huge transition as many attractions have closed to make way for new Star Wars and Pixar lands, and extensive hoardings disrupt the flow as you move from one area to another. You can easily see it all in a day, even if you arrive mid-day and stay for the evening entertainment. There are already a lot of extra Star Wars elements, so fans of Luke and Co should be in their element.

Bigger than the Magic Kingdom at 154acres/62ha but smaller than Epcot, this is a different experience again with its rather chaotic combination of attractions, street entertainment, film sets and smart gift shops. Like the Magic Kingdom, the food may not win awards, but some of the restaurants (notably the Sci-Fi Dine-in Theater and 50s Prime Time Café) have imaginative settings.

Location

The entrance arrangements will be familiar if you have already visited the other parks. Disney's Hollywood Studios is located on Buena Vista Drive (between World Drive and Epcot Drive) and you should make

Disney's Hollywood Studios at a glance

Location	Off Buena Vista Drive or World Drive, Walt Disney World		
Size	154 acres/62ha		
Hours	9am–7pm off peak; 9am–10pm high season (Easter, summer holidays, Thanksgiving and Christmas)		
Admission	Under-3s free; 3–9 $91–108 (1-day base ticket, priced seasonally), $320 (5-day Magic Your Way), £309 (14-day Ultimate); adult (10+) $97–114, $340, £329. Prices do not include tax.		
Parking	$20		
Lockers	From the Crossroads kiosk through the main entrance; $12 small, $14 large ($5 deposit each)		
Pushchairs	$15 and $31 Oscar's Super Service Station; $13 and $27 per day for multiple days		
Wheelchairs	$12 or $70 ($20 deposit refunded), from Oscar's		
Top attractions	Toy Story Mania, Twilight Zone™ Tower of Terror, Rock 'n' Roller Coaster Starring Aerosmith, Star Tours, The Great Movie Ride, Voyage of the Little Mermaid, Muppet*Vision 3-D		
Don't miss	Indiana Jones™ Epic Stunt Spectacular, Beauty and the Beast – Live on Stage, Fantasmic!, Stars Wars: A Galactic Spectacular		
Hidden costs	Meals	Burger, chips and coke $13.58 3-course dinner $38–71, child's $15–21 (Brown Derby) Beer $6.75–8 Kids' meal $5.49–6.49	
	T-shirts	$24.95–36.95 Kids' T-shirts $19.95–29.95	
	Souvenirs	$1.05–4,000	
	Sundries	Special effects make-up $12–$18	

1 The Great Movie Ride
2 For the First Time in Forever
3 Indiana Jones™ Epic Stunt Spectacular
4 Star Tours
5 Jim Henson's Muppet*Vision 3-D
6 ABC Sound Studio
7 Toy Story Mania
8 Walt Disney: One Man's Dream
9 Voyage of the Little Mermaid
10 Star Wars Launch Bay
11 Disney Junior – Live on Stage!
12 Rock 'n' Roller Coaster Starring Aerosmith
13 The Twilight Zone™ Tower of Terror
14 Beauty and the Beast – Live on Stage
15 Fantasmic!
16 Guest Information Board
17 PizzeRizzo
18 Centre Stage
19 Premier Theater
20 '50s Prime Time Café
21 Hollywood and Vine
22 Hollywood Brown Derby
23 Mama Melrose's
24 Sunset Ranch Market
25 Sci-Fi Dine-in Theater Restaurant

Under development as Star Wars and Toy Story Playland

DISNEY'S HOLLYWOOD STUDIOS

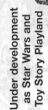

a note of where you park before you catch the tram to the main gates, where you wait for the official opening time. If queues build up quickly, the gates will open early, so be ready for a running start.

Once through the gates, you are into Hollywood Boulevard, a street of gift shops, then you have to decide which of the main attractions to head for first, as these are the ones where the queues will be heaviest most of the day. Try to ignore the lure of the shops as it is better to browse in the early afternoon when the attractions are at their busiest.

BRITTIP

It is crucial to schedule your Hollywood Studios FastPass+ times 60 days in advance if you are staying onsite, or 30 days in advance if you are staying offsite. Main attraction Toy Story Mania books up well in advance.

Incidentally, if you thought Disney had elevated queuing to an art form in its other parks, wait until you see how clever they are here. Just when you think you have reached the ride itself, there is another twist to the queue you hadn't seen or an extra element to the ride that holds you up.

The latter are 'holding pens', which are an ingenious way of making it seem you are being entertained instead of queuing. Look out for them in particular at the Great Movie Ride, Twilight Zone™ Tower of Terror and Muppet*Vision 3-D.

The main attractions

The park is laid out in a more confusing fashion than its counterparts, with their neatly packaged 'lands', so have your map handy to keep your bearings. This is especially important now that a large area of the park is behind hoardings, notably near Toy Story Midway Mania.

Beating the queues: The opening-gate crowds will all surge in one of three directions. By far the biggest attraction is **Toy Story Mania**, so head here first if you don't have a FastPass+ time scheduled. The other crowd-pullers are **Twilight Zone™ Tower of Terror**, a magnificent haunted hotel ride that ends in a 13-storey drop in a lift, where queues hit 2hrs at peak periods, and **Rock 'n' Roller Coaster Starring Aerosmith**. Head straight up Hollywood Boulevard, turn right into Sunset Boulevard and you'll see them at the end of the street. They are both FP+ rides (p99).

Toy Story Mania

© Disney/

Star Tours, the remodelled Star Wars™ simulator ride is another of the park's serious queue-builders (and also a FP+ attraction). If you are not up for the really big thrills, schedule a FP+ for Toy Story Mania if there are any available, then head for Star Tours (across the main square past the Indiana Jones™ show). After Star Tours and Toy Story Mania, another gentler experience (and also worth doing early on) is the hilarious Muppet*Vision 3-D show, which is another big draw later in the day. It has the benefit of being air-conditioned, too, for when you need a rest.

Hollywood Boulevard

Move around the park in a (roughly) clockwise direction, starting along this street of shops and services that are best visited in early afternoon when it's busier elsewhere.

Immediately to the left through the turnstiles are the Guest Relations and First Aid offices, plus the Baby Care centre. An up-to-the-minute check on queue times at the attractions is kept on a Guest Information Board on Hollywood Boulevard, just past its junction with Sunset Boulevard, where you can also book restaurants. To the right is Oscar's Station for

Sunset Boulevard

© Hilary White

pushchair and wheelchair hire, while locker hire is obtained at the Crossroads kiosk in front of you.

Indiana Jones Epic Stunt Spectacular

© Hilary White

The Great Movie Ride: This faces you as you walk in along Hollywood Boulevard and is a good place to start if the crowds are not too serious.

An all-star audio-animatronics cast re-creates a number of box office smashes, including Jimmy Cagney's *Public Enemy*, Julie Andrews in *Mary Poppins*, Gene Kelly in *Singin' in the Rain* and many more masterful set-pieces. Young children may find the menace of *The Alien* too strong, but otherwise the ride has universal appeal and features some clever live twists (there are two variations on this ride, a cowboy and a gangster version – ask a Cast Member if there's one you especially want to do). AAAA FP+

Other entertainment: A series of **Citizens of Hollywood** acts enliven Hollywood Boulevard throughout the day, staging impromptu movie shoots, casting calls or even detective investigations. Have fun with them you just might end up the star of the show! Also, look out for **Disney characters** during the morning. New in 2016 was the **Star Wars: A Galaxy Far, Far Away** stage show, featuring film clips and live appearances by Darth Vader, Darth Maul, Chewbacca, R2-D2, C-3PO, Boba Fett, Stormtroopers, BB-8 and more in an epic showdown between good and evil

Shopping: Hollywood Boulevard has the best of the park's shopping (nine of the 21 stores), including **Sid Caheunga's One-of-a-Kind** (rare movie and TV items, including celebrity autographs), **Keystone Clothiers** (some of the best apparel), **Mickey's of Hollywood** (souvenirs and gift items) and **The Darkroom** (for camera items).

Dining: The Brown Derby is the park's signature restaurant, offering fine dining in best vintage Hollywood style (reservations usually necessary) while the **Brown Derby Lounge** offers outdoor dining with a full bar and terrific people-watching (noon-park closing). **Trolley Car Café** quick-service offers breakfast-all-day, plus cakes and Starbucks coffee.

Echo Lake

Turn left out of Hollywood Boulevard to find another area that pays homage to the movies of the 1930s and 40s.

For The First Time in Forever: Join Anna and Elsa and the Royal Arendelle Historians for a *Frozen* Sing-Along Celebration, with music and clips from the movie. AAA (AAAAA+ under 8s). FP+

Indiana Jones™ Epic Stunt Spectacular: Consult your park Times Guide for show times as a special movie set creates three different backdrops for Indiana Jones'™ stunt people to put on a dazzling demonstration of scenes and special effects from the films. Audience participation is an element and there are some amusing sub-plots. Queues for the 30min show begin up to 30mins beforehand, but the auditorium holds more than 2,000 so everyone usually gets in. TTTT FP+

Star Tours – the Adventure Continues: The popular Star Wars™ simulator ride has had a complete revamp. Climb into your

Jedi Training – Trials Of The Temple

Prime Time Café

StarSpeeder 1000 for a stunning high-speed journey through the worlds created by George Lucas, including Coruscant, Naboo, Kashyyyk (the Wookiee planet) Jakku from *The Force Awakens*, and Tatooine, where riders blast into the Boonta Eve Classic Podrace with dramatic results. New robots AC-38 ('Ace') and Aly San San prepare you for your flight, but predictably it all goes wrong, and droids R2-D2 and C-3PO must save your Speeder from disaster as they evade the Imperial Forces and a determined bounty hunter. Master Yoda, Boba Fett, Darth Vader and a

Meet Olaf

new branch of stormtroopers, called 'Skytroopers', join the pursuit. With the option to change the story at four points, making for 96 ride options, you never know how it will turn out! The realism of the Star Wars™ world, from the queue to the post-ride gift shop, is immersive and lots of fun. **R:** 3ft 4in/101cm, no under-3s. **TTTT AAAAA FP+**

Other entertainment: Kids should make a beeline for **Jedi Training: Trials of the Temple**, on stage outside Star Tours up to eight times a day. Here, young Jedi hopefuls try their light-sabre technique under the eyes of a Jedi master, before taking on Darth Vader, Kylo Ren or the Seventh Sister Inquisitor. Great fun just to watch. New in 2016 was **Celebrity Spotlight**, a chance to meet cuddlesome snowman Olaf from *Frozen* (**TTTT** for under-12s).

BRITTIP

Youngsters (ages 4–12) keen to try Jedi Training should sign up at the Indiana Jones Adventure Outpost first thing in the morning, as it is popular and availability is limited.

Shopping: Shop for Star Wars™ goods at **Tatooine Traders** (at the exit to Star Tours) and Indiana Jones souvenirs at the **Indy Truck and Adventure Outpost**.

Dining: There are also two good dining choices: the **'50s Prime Time Café** is fun as you sit in mock stage sets from 1950s American TV sitcoms and eat meals 'just like Mom used to make' (the waiters all claim to be your aunt, uncle or cousin and warn you to take your elbows off the table – good fun) while a varied buffet dinner is served at **Hollywood & Vine** as well as

Sci-fi Dine-in Theatre

the Play 'n Dine character breakfast and lunch with the Disney Junior Pals, available 8.30am–3pm ($30 adults, $18 3–9s breakfast; $42/25 lunch).

Muppet Courtyard

The former Streets of America area of the park has been renamed around the only remaining attraction. The full Star Wars Land will eventually take shape here, but it's still worth visiting for the comedy-rich fun of 'the lone survivor'!

Muppet*Vision 3-D: The 3-D is crossed out here and 4-D substituted, so be warned strange things are about to happen! A wonderful 10min holding-pen pre-show takes you into the Muppet Theater for a 20min experience with all the Muppets, 3-D special effects and more – when Fozzie Bear points his squirty flower at you, prepare to get wet! It's a gem, and the kids love it. Queues build up through the main parts of the day, but Disney's queuing expertise makes them seem shorter. AAAAA FP+

Dining: For full-service dining try **Mama Melrose's Ristorante Italiano,** a wonderful table-service Italian option (one of our faves). Early in 2017 will see the debut of Muppet-themed PizzeRizzo (pizza, salad and drinks) in the old home of the Toy Story Pizza Planet counter-service diner.

Commissary Lane

This is just a one-way street at the moment from the central plaza, with two dining options, plus one big draw – the chance to meet Mickey and Minnie Mouse. The **Sci-Fi Dine-In Theater Restaurant** is a big hit with kids as you dine in a mock drive-in cinema, with cars as tables, car-hop waitresses and a big film screen showing old science-fiction movie clips. It features gourmet burgers, ribs, steak, pasta and sandwiches, as well as signature milkshakes and sodas ($35 for three-course lunch, $13–15 kids' meal). The counter-service **ABC Commissary** serves standard fare that includes burgers, sandwiches and salads.

Mickey and Minnie Starring in Red Carpet Dreams: Meet the main Mouse and his best girl at this themed meet-and-greet, with Mickey dressed for his role in The Sorcerer's Apprentice and Minnie in a dazzling show-stopper gown.

Pixar Place

This area is styled after the real-life Pixar film studios in California, and houses one of the most popular rides.

Toy Story Midway Mania: A real family fun fiesta, a 3-D ride into a fantasy fairground of games with the *Toy Story* characters. To start with

Disney Junior – Live on Stage!

© Disney

Muppet*Vision 3D

you are 'shrunk' to toy-size and board carnival vehicles (each equipped with individual spring-action shooters) to go through Andy's Bedroom, where the toys have set up a Midway Games Play Set with five challenges, plus a practice round. Thanks to a pair of 3D glasses, riders can 'see' everything their shooter fires at the sequence of targets (while, with the magic of Disney's special effects, they might also 'feel' objects whirring past as they burst out of the screens; and, if you hit a water balloon, watch out!). Throw virtual eggs at barnyard targets, launch darts at prehistoric balloon targets, break plates with baseballs, land rings on Buzz Lightyear's alien friends and finish up in Woody's Rootin' Tootin' Shootin' Gallery (with a bonus roundup) before totting up your scores. The *Toy Story* characters cheer you on, pass on hints to boost your score and give an amusing commentary. At times it is a touch raucous and chaotic, but kids are sure to love the shooting game element and the whole family can enjoy the amusing ride through the toys' world. Even the queuing area is fun, with a huge animatronic Mr Potato Head acting as a fairground barker to entertain while you wait (AAA TTTT FP+). A 2016 makeover added extra capacity but this is still

the place to use your FastPass+, or get here *early*.

Other entertainment: Look out for the *Toy Story* characters meet-and-greet here.

Shopping: Toy Story Dept. carries clothes and toys.

Dining: Hey Howdy Hey Take Away offers counter-service ice-cream, snacks and drinks.

Animation Courtyard
Get ready for a series of wonderful family-friendly shows in this area of the park. And Star Wars fans take notice!

Voyage of the Little Mermaid: A 17min live performance that is primarily for children who have seen the Disney animated film. It brings together a mix of actors, animation and puppetry to re-create the film's highlights. Parents will still enjoy the special effects, but queues tend to be long, so go early or late. You may also get a little wet. AAA (AAAAA under-9s; FP+)

BRITTIP
Try to sit at least halfway back in the Mermaid Theatre, especially if you are with young children, as the stage front is a bit high.

Disney Junior – Live on Stage!:
Mickey, Goofy, Donald and Daisy are
throwing a surprise birthday party for
Minnie, but need the help of friends
like Jake and the Neverland Pirates,
Doc McStuffins and Sofia the First to
make this the best celebration ever.
It's colourful and entertaining and
pre-schoolers love it. AA (AAAAA
under-5s) FP+

Other entertainment: Youngsters
can meet all their favourite Disney
Junior characters in **Animation
Courtyard**, several times daily.
In advance of Star Wars land, the
fabulous **Launch Bay** features meet-
and-greets with Chewbacca and
Kylo Ren, and a fan-friendly 10min
film in the **Launch Bay Theater**,
giving a behind-the-scenes look at
the making of the Star Wars movies.
There are dozens of prop replicas and
exhibits, plus a Disney Infinity 3.0
gaming centre.

Shopping: The enormous **Launch
Bay Cargo** shop has everything a Star
Wars fan could possibly desire.

BRITTIP
Bring along a small, inexpensive
token to trade with the Jawa in
Launch Bay. You'll be rewarded with a small
'gift' in return!

Sunset Boulevard

The final area contains the two high-
thrill rides, and the night-time finale,
but it's also the busiest from midday
on, so go here first or use FastPass+.

**Rock 'n' Roller Coaster Starring
Aerosmith:** Disney's first big-thrill
inverted coaster is a sure-fire draw for
the adrenalin ride addicts, with a
great indoor setting and nerve-
jangling ride. It features a clever
holographic-style film show starring
rock group Aerosmith in their
recording studio. That leads to the
real fun, set to specially recorded
tracks and with outrageous speaker
systems, as riders aboard Cadillac
cars for a memorable whiz through
'Los Angeles' (watch out for a close
encounter with the Hollywood sign!).
The high-speed launch and
inversions ensure a dynamic coaster
experience. Go first thing or expect
serious queues, and do check out
your ride photo ($20.95–24.95, or
$14.95 delivered digitally).
R: 4ft/124cm. TTTTT FP+1

BRITTIP
If only one or two in your group want
to ride Rock 'n' Roller Coaster, or you
want to save significant time waiting, opt for
the Single Rider queue. You will be split up,
but the wait will be much shorter.

Twilight Zone Tower of Terror

© Hilary White

DISNEY'S HOLLYWOOD STUDIOS with children

Here is our guide to the attractions that appeal to the different age groups in this park:

Under-5s
Beauty and the Beast – Live on Stage, Disney Junior–Live On Stage!, Fantasmic!, For The First Time In Forever, Voyage of the Little Mermaid.

5–8s
Beauty and the Beast – Live On Stage, Fantasmic!, For the First Time In Forever, Indiana Jones™ Epic Stunt Spectacular, Jedi Training: Trials of the Temple, Muppet*Vision 3-D, Toy Story Midway Mania, Voyage of the Little Mermaid.

9–12s
Beauty and the Beast – Live On Stage, Fantasmic!, Indiana Jones™ Epic Stunt Spectacular, Jedi Training: Trials of the Temple, Muppet*Vision 3-D, Rock 'n' Roller Coaster Starring Aerosmith, Star Tours, The Great Movie Ride, Twilight Zone™ Tower of Terror, Toy Story Midway Mania.

Over-12s
Fantasmic!, The Great Movie Ride, Indiana Jones™ Epic Stunt Spectacular, Muppet*Vision 3-D, Rock 'n' Roller Coaster Starring Aerosmith, Star Tours, Toy Story Midway Mania, Twilight Zone™ Tower of Terror.

The Twilight Zone™ Tower of Terror: This 199ft/60m landmark invites you to experience another dimension in the strange Hollywood Tower Hotel that time forgot. The exterior is intriguing, the interior fascinating, the ride scintillating and the queues huge! Just when you think you are through to the ride, there's another queue, so spend your time inspecting the superb detail. There's a lot more to this than just the big 13-storey drop, however, as the 'Twilight Zone' theme adds an inventive element. Your elevator car twists and turns unexpectedly before it is time to 'drop in', and the random drop sequence provides

Rock 'n' Roller Coaster Starring Aerosmith

hair-raising thrills before you exit!
R: 3ft 4in/101cm. **TTTTT** FP+

Beauty and the Beast – Live on Stage:
An enchanting live musical song and
dance performance of the highlights
of this Disney classic will entertain
the whole family for 30min up to five
times a day in the Theater of the Stars.
Check the daily schedule for show
times, usually starting at 11.45am.
AAA FP+1

Fantasmic!: A not-to-be-missed
special-effects spectacular. Staged
nightly (twice nightly in peak periods)
in a 6,900-seat amphitheatre, it
features the dreams of Mickey,
portrayed as the Sorcerer's
Apprentice, through films such as
Pocahontas, *The Lion King* and *Snow
White*, but hijacked by the Disney
villains, leading to an epic battle,
with Our Hero emerging triumphant.
Dancing waters, shooting comets,
animated fountains, swirling stars
and balls of fire combine in a
breathtaking presentation, especially
the giant, fire-breathing dragon! The
25min show begins seating up to 2hrs
in advance and it's best to head there
at least 30min before (watch out for
the splash zones!). AAAAA FP+1

Star Wars: A Galactic Spectacular:
Nightly fireworks (and some stunning
new pyrotechnics and special effects)
take on a whole new meaning in
this dramatic battle between good
and evil, where bursts look like TIE
Fighters, battle scenes, the twin suns
of Tatooine and more, all set to John
Williams' original Star Wars scores.
Watch for the 'wow' moment as
columns of flames and giant light-
sabres rise into the night sky. AAAAA

Other entertainment: Sunset
Boulevard is also home to more of the
park's **Citizens of Hollywood**
characters.

◀▶ BRITTIP
While the Galactic Spectacular
fireworks show is genuinely
breathtaking, the full effects can only be
viewed from the Center Stage hub area in
front of the Great Movie Ride.

**Shopping: Legends of Hollywood,
Planet Hollywood Super Store** and
the **Sunset Boulevard** shops (for
limited edition watches, clothing and
other collectibles) are the best.

Dining: Rosie's All-American Café
(chicken, burgers and salads) and
Catalina Eddie's (pizza) are the best
of Sunset Boulevard's five market-
style eateries.

Star Wars: a Galactic Spectacular

© Disney

Disney's Animal Kingdom Theme Park

Disney's newest and smartest theme park opened in 1998 representing a completely different experience. With an emphasis on conservation and nature, it largely eschews non-stop thrills and attractions for more relaxing pace, although still in Disney's usual seamless entertainment style and with some excellent rides, including one of its best. The attractions are relatively few, with just six out-and-out rides, but there are then two elaborate wildlife trails, four shows (including two that are almost worth the entry fee alone), an extravagant adventure playground, conservation station and a petting zoo, and two magnificent evening shows. In 2017, Pandora: The World of Avatar will open, adding even more to the park's appeal.

It is also outrageously scenic, notably with the 145ft/44m Tree of Life, the Kilimanjaro Safaris and the Asian village of Serka Zong (home to the gigantic Expedition: Everest™ ride), but it won't overwhelm you with Disney's usual grand fantasy. Rather, it is a chance to explore and experience; to learn and understand; and to soak up the gentler more natural ambience. It is not a zoo in the conventional sense, but it is home to 200-plus species of birds and animals (in some wonderfully naturalistic settings). The educational tone is fairly strong, but children in particular may pick up easily on the essential conservation undertones of things like Kilimanjaro Safaris and Maharajah Jungle Trek. However, the park does get crowded, the walkways can be congested and there are fewer places to cool down. It is definitely a good idea to be here on time and use FastPass+ (p99) to minimise queuing.

Disney's Animal Kingdom Theme Park at a glance

Location	Directly off Osceola Parkway, also via World Drive and Buena Vista Drive		
Size	500 acres/203ha divided into 6 'lands'		
Hours	8 or 9am–6, 8, 9 or 11pm seasonally		
Admission	Under 3s free; 3–9 $91–108 (1–day base ticket, priced seasonally), $320 (5–day Magic Your Way), £309 (14–day Ultimate); adult (10+) $97–114, $340, £329. Prices do not include tax.		
Parking	$20		
Lockers	Either side of Entrance Plaza; $12 small, $14 large ($5 deposit each)		
Pushchairs	$15 and $31 at Garden Gate Gifts, through entrance on right, $13 and $27 per day for multiple days		
Wheelchairs	$12 or $70 ($20 deposit refunded) with pushchairs		
Top attractions	DINOSAUR!, Kilimanjaro Safaris, It's Tough to Be a Bug!, Kali River Rapids, Festival of the Lion King, Finding Nemo – The Musical, Expedition: Everest™		
Don't miss	Pangani Forest Exploration Trail, Maharajah Jungle Trek, Rafiki's Planet Watch, dining at Rainforest Café, Rivers of Light night-time show.		
Hidden costs	Meals	Burger, chips and coke $15.58 3-course meal at Yak & Yeti $36.50–49 (kid's entrée and dessert $11.48) Beer $7–9.50 Kids' meal $6.99–$8.49	
	T-shirts	$24.95–36.95 Kids' T-shirts $12.99–24.99	
	Souvenirs	$1.35–398	
	Sundries	Magic Band accessories: $8–28	

The Oasis

1 The Oasis Tropical Garden

Discovery Island

2 The Tree of Life
3 It's Tough To Be A Bug
4 Discovery Island Trails
5 Flame Tree Barbecue
6 Pizzafari
7 Adventurers' Outpost
8 Tiffins

Dinoland USA

9 DINOSAUR!
10 The Boneyard
11 Finding Nemo – The Musical
12 Chester And Hester's Dino-Rama!
13 TriceraTOP Spin
14 Primeval Whirl
15 Restaurantosaurus

Africa

16 Harambe
17 Kilimanjaro Safaris
18 Rafiki's Planet Watch
19 Pangani Forest Trail
20 Tusker House Restaurant
21 Festival Of The Lion King
22 Harambe Market

Asia

23 Flights Of Wonder
24 Kali River Rapids
25 Maharajah Jungle Trek
26 Expedition: Everest™
27 Yak 'n Yeti Restaurant
28 Rainforest Café
29 Rivers of Light

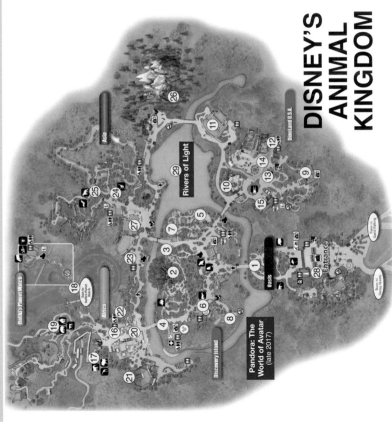

DISNEY'S ANIMAL KINGDOM

Rivers of Light

Dinoland U.S.A.

Asia

Africa

Rafiki's Planet Watch

Oasis

Entrance

Pandora: The World of Avatar (late 2017)

Discovery Island

Location

If you are staying in the Kissimmee area, Disney's Animal Kingdom is the easiest of the parks to find. Just get on the (toll) Osceola Parkway and follow it all the way to the toll booths. Alternatively, coming down I-4, take exit 65 on to Osceola Parkway. From West Highway 192, come in on Sherberth Road and turn right at the first traffic lights. If you arrive early (which is advisable), you can walk to the Entrance Plaza. Otherwise, the usual tram system takes you in, so make a note of the row you park in (e.g. Unicorn, 67). The entrance plaza is overlooked by the Rainforest Café, with its 65ft/20m waterfall, which is open for breakfast, lunch and dinner (but is busy 12.30–3.30pm and an hour before closing). With Orlando so hot in summer, you need to be here as early as possible to see the animals before they hide in the shade.

An early start is especially advised for Kilimanjaro Safaris in summer. If you don't arrive early, plan this attraction for its latest daytime excursion.

Beating the queues: For the early birds, here is your best plan of campaign. Once through the gates, animal lovers should head first for **Kilimanjaro Safaris**, through the Oasis, Discovery Island and Africa. After the Safari, go straight to **Pangani Forest Exploration Trail** and you will have experienced two of the park's best animal encounters before it gets too hot. Alternatively, thrill-seekers should walk straight through Discovery Island for Asia, where the **Expedition: Everest™** ride is the big draw. Then head to Kilimanjaro Safaris or the nearby **Kali River Rapids** raft ride, followed by the scenic **Maharajah Jungle Trek**. The best combination for the first arrivals is to get a FastPass+ for Expedition: Everest™ (if you don't already have one), then ride Kilimanjaro Safaris and, once you have done that (and depending on your FP+ time), either do your Everest ride or go straight to Kali River Rapids. Check your show schedule for **Festival of the Lion King** and try to catch one of the first two performances, as the later ones draw sizeable queues. The wait time board at the entrance to Discovery Island is helpful. Those are your main tactics – here is the full rundown.

The Oasis

Tropical Garden: A gentle, walk-through introduction to the park, this is a rocky, tree-covered area featuring animal habitats, streams, waterfalls and lush plant life. Here you meet miniature deer, a giant anteater,

Kilimanjaro Safaris

© Disney

© Disney

Creature Comforts

exotic boars, macaws, waterfowl, a Patagonian cavy and wallabies in an understated environment that leads you across a stone bridge to the main park area. Visit in early afternoon when many of the rides are busy. AAA

Shopping: Stop at **Garden Gate Gifts** (on the right) for pushchair, wheelchair and locker hire, while Guest Relations is on the left.

Dining: The fun **Rainforest Café** also has an entrance inside the park here. If you haven't seen the one at Disney Springs, you should call in to view the amazing jungle interior with its audio-animatronic animals, waterfalls, thunderstorms and aquariums. A 3-course meal costs $35–$62, but the setting alone is worth it and the food is above average. Try breakfast or an early dinner to avoid the crowds.

Discovery Island

This colourful village is the park hub, themed as a tropical artists' colony, with animal-inspired artwork, nature trails, four main shops and four eateries. You will also find the Baby Center and First Aid station here (look for the 'ladybird' lights).

The Tree of Life: This arboreal edifice is the park centrepiece, an awesome creation that seems to have a different perspective from wherever you view it. The trunk and roots are covered in 325 carvings representing the Circle of Life, from the dolphin to the lion. Trails lead round the tree, interspersed with habitats for flamingos, otters, ring-tailed lemurs, macaws, axis deer, cranes, storks, ducks, porcupines, kangaroos and tortoises. The tree canopy spreads 160ft/49m, the trunk is 50ft/15m wide and the diameter of the roots is 170ft/52m. It has 103,000 leaves (all attached by hand) on more than 8,000 branches! AAAA

Tree Trails: These pretty trails at the foot of the Tree of Life feature habitats for the cotton-top tamarin, African crested porcupine, Galapagos tortoise, shark catfish and more.

It's Tough To Be A Bug!: Winding down among the Tree's roots brings you 'underground' to a 430-seat theatre and another example of Disney's artistry in 3-D films and special effects. This hysterical 10min show, in the company of Flick from the Pixar film *A Bug's Life*, is a homage to 80 per cent of the animal world, featuring grasshoppers, beetles, spiders, stink bugs and termites (beware the 'acid' spray!) as well as several tricks we couldn't possibly reveal. Sit towards the back in the middle (allow a good number of people in first as the rows are filled up from the far side) to get the best of the 3-D effects. Queues build up from midday, but they do move quite steadily. Don't miss the 'forthcoming attractions' posters in the foyer for some excruciating bug puns on famous films. AAAAA FP+

◀╋▶ BRITTIP

The dark, special effects and mock creepy-crawlies in It's Tough To Be A Bug! can be extremely scary for young 'uns. Use caution.

Other entertainment: The Island is home to the lively **Viva Gaia Street Band** and various **Disney characters**, notably Pocahontas at Character Landing (opposite Flame Tree Barbecue), Tarzan near Discovery Island Trail, and two of the characters from *UP!* near Disney Outfitters. **Adventurers Outpost** is the setting to meet Mickey and Minnie. FP+ Children can also sign up for the novel **Wilderness Explorers** programme here (also based on *UP!*), with the chance to visit 30 locations around the park for interactive lessons and animal experiences, earning sticker badges along the way that act as a gentle educational story. **Winged Encounters – The Kingdom Takes Flight** free-flight macaw show takes place over Discovery Island several times daily.

Shopping: You will find a huge range of merchandise, souvenirs and gifts here, notably in **Disney Outfitters** (artwork and collectables) and **Island Mercantile**.

Dining: Counter-service restaurants **Pizzafari** (pizza, salads, sandwiches) and **Flame Tree Barbecue** (barbecued ribs, beef and pork, chicken sandwiches and salads) are both good choices. If it's not too hot, the Flame Tree is a picturesque option, set among pretty gardens and fountains on the Discovery River; the air-conditioned Pizzafari is better in summer months. New full-service restaurant **Tiffins** features an imaginative lunch and dinner menu in a creative, art-gallery style setting. Dishes promise a 'global culinary expedition' with the likes of Thai Curry Soup, Berbere-spiced Lamb, South American Chocolate Ganache, and many more internationally-flavoured creations (main courses from $29–53). Situated along the river, it includes the laid-back **Nomad Lounge**, with a waters-edge view. **Creature Comforts** carries Starbucks coffee, pastries and sandwiches, while **Isle of Java** has pastries, bagels, coffees and soft drinks.

Pandora: The World of Avatar

Due to open late in 2017 is the park's newest 'land' and it should be a real headline-maker. This delve into the world of film-maker James Cameron's *Avatar* series is a full-on recreation of a section of the planet Pandora, with masses of scenery, special effects and two blockbuster rides. Guests arrive on Pandora via Alpha Centauri Expeditions and will be able to marvel at the mystical 'Floating Mountains' and plants that light up at a touch among a host of visually creative set-pieces and immersive landscaping.

Pandora - World of Avatar

© Disney

Some of the detail had still to be revealed, but look for the following experiences:

Na'vi River Journey: Get ready for an eye-popping ride into the heart of the mysteries and wonders of Pandora's bioluminescent forests in this large-scale diorama that gives visitors a close-up view, using new-generation animatronics, high-definition film projections and all-new lighting effects. AAAAA (expected).

Avatar: Flight of Passage: This simulator ride promises to deliver the latest in motion-based technology as visitors get to travel on the back of a Banshee and take flight over Pandora and its many scenic wonders. Be prepared for sudden swoops and drops in the company of these dragon-like creatures that can soar to great heights and also dive and zip through the treetops. TTTTT (expected)

There will also be some imaginative food, as well as a huge Pandora-themed gift shop, plus previews of Cameron's new trio of films that extend the *Avatar* story to 2020.

Africa

The largest land in the park recreates the forests, grasslands and rocky homelands of East Africa's most fascinating residents in a richly landscaped setting that is part vintage port town and part savannah. The central area, Harambe Village, is a

superb Imagineer's eye-view of a Kenyan port town, with white coral walls and thatched roofs, and is the starting point for your adventure. The Arab-influenced Swahili culture is also depicted in the native tribal costumes and architecture.

BRITTIP

It is difficult to take photographs during the Sunset Kilimanjaro Safari, so ride during the day when the animals are most visible.

Festival of the Lion King: This not-to-be-missed, high-powered 25min production (seven to 10 times a day) brings the film to life in spectacular fashion, with giant moving stages, huge animated figures, singers, dancers, acrobats and stilt-walkers, plus some fun audience participation. All the well-known songs are given an airing in a fiesta of colour and sound, with the usual Disney quality. Queuing often begins an hour in advance for the 1,000-seat (air-conditioned) theatre, so use FastPass+ or take in one of the early shows. AAAAA FP+ Sign language shows are performed at 4pm each Tues and Sat; arrive at least 25mins early and ask a Cast Member if you can sit in the Warthog section.

Kilimanjaro Safaris: The queuing area alone earns high marks for authenticity, preparing you for the sights and sounds of the

Festival of the Lion King

© Disney

© Disney

Harambe

110acre/45ha savannah beyond. You board a 32-passenger truck, with your driver relaying information about the flora and fauna on view and a bush ranger-pilot overhead relaying facts and figures on the wildlife, including the dangers threatening them in the outside world. Scores of animals are spread out in various habitats, with no fences in sight (ditches and barriers are all concealed) as you splash through fords and cross rickety bridges, and you should get good close-ups of lions, rhinos, elephants, giraffes, antelope, hippos and ostriches. Once again, the whole thing looks really authentic (okay, some of the tyre 'ruts' and termite mounds are concrete and the baobab trees are fake). The animals roam over a wide area, though, and can disappear from view. Not recommended for expectant mothers or anyone with back or neck problems. AAAAA FP+

Kilimanjaro Safaris – Nocturnal Encounters: The route may be the same, but that's where the similarity to the daytime safari ends. Most of Harambe Reserve is lit only by natural moonlight once the sun goes down, giving guests the experience of seeing the animals in a 'whole new light', and with a whole new level of activity. Other areas are softly illuminated as if lit by the rising moon, while a stand-out 'sunset' section creates stunning silhouettes as the animals roam past. It is a must-see experience, but with the same cautions as the daytime safari. AAAAA FP+

Pangani Forest Exploration Trail: As you leave the Safari, you turn on to a serious nature trail that showcases gorillas, hippos, okapi, zebras, meerkats and rare tropical birds. You wander the trail at your own pace and visit 'research' stations to learn more about the animals, including the underwater view of the hippos (check out the size of a hippo skull and those teeth!) and the savannah overlook, where giraffes and antelope graze and the meerkats frolic. The walk-through aviary introduces you to the carmine bee-eater, pygmy goose, African green pigeon, ibis and brimstone canary, among others, but the real centre-piece is the silverback gorilla habitat (in fact, two of them). The family group is often just inches away from the plate-glass window, while the bachelor group further along can prove more elusive. Again, the natural aspect of the trail is fabulous and it provides a host of photo opportunities. Do this early or save it for late in the day when it is less busy. AAAAA

Rafiki's Planet Watch: This subsection of Africa involves a (rather dull) rustic train ride, with a peek into some of the backstage areas, as a preamble to the park's interactive and educational exhibits (especially for children). The three-part journey starts with Habitat Habit!, where you can see cotton-top tamarins and learn how conservation begins in your own garden. Conservation Station offers a series of exhibits, shows and information stations about the environment and threats to its ecology. Look out for Sounds of the Rain Forest (in listening booths) and the Live Animal Cams that show many of the park's inhabitants in their backstage areas. Then observe the park's Veterinary Treatment Center (including a hatchery and neo-natal care) and Training Exhibits. You can easily spend an hour here, inspired by Disney's Worldwide Conservation Fund.

Finally, the Affection Section petting zoo consists of a collection of goats, sheep and a miniature donkey. AAA

Other entertainment: There's plenty more to enjoy here, with the splendid African sounds of **The Burudika Band** and the pageantry and rhythms of **Tam Tam Drummers of Harambe**. With luck you'll also spot the wonderful **DiVine**, a 'moving' part of the foliage (also in The Oasis at times).

Shopping: Harambe is home to the **Mombasa Marketplace/Ziwani Traders**, where you can suit up safari-style, while Rafiki's Planet Watch has **Out of the Wild** for more gifts and souvenirs. Harambe Marketplace

Kali River Rapids

© Disney

offers more African-inspired shopping at **Mariya's Souvenirs** (apparel, Vinylmation colectibles, camera accessories, housewares, toys) and **Duka La Filimu** (toys, Vinylmation, pins).

Dining: Tusker House Restaurant (featuring Donald's Dining Safari for breakfast at $30 adults, $18 children, and lunch at $42 and $25) is one of the best diners in the park, with a mouth-watering array of salads, a hot carvery, rotisserie chicken, stews and vegetarian dishes ($42 and $25 for dinner, without characters). There are also 4 snack and drink bars, most notably the **Kusafiri Coffee Shop** (muffins, pastries, coffee), while **Tamu Tamu Refreshments** offers some ice cream and soft drinks, and the **Dawa Bar** is a great place to sit with a beer or cocktail and soak up the scenery. The Harambe Market has **Kitamu Grill** (chicken skewers and kebab flatbread), **Famous Sausages** (South African-style corn dogs), **Wanjohi Refreshments** (beer, wine, speciality drinks) and **Chef Mwanga's** (ribs).

Asia

The next 'land' is elaborately themed as the gateway to the imaginary south-east Asian region of Anandapur, with temples, ruined forts, landscape and wildlife. The element of reality is startling and the architecture is full of faithful representations of genuine locations. The elaborate ruined temple showcases for the gibbons and siamangs are worth looking out for – and you may well hear them wherever you are in the park!

Flights of Wonder: Another wildlife show, this portrays the talents and traits of the park's avian inhabitants. A trainer showcases the behaviours of various birds, including macaws and hawks, before being interrupted by a bumbling tour guide, who needs to be reminded of key conservation issues. This is the cue for some frolics with our feathered friends, including vultures, eagles, toucans and a singing parrot. The Caravan Stage is open-air, though, and can be hot in summer. AAA

Kali River Rapids: Part thrill-ride, part scenic journey, this bouncy raft ride will get you pretty wet (not great for early morning in winter). It starts out in tropical forest territory before launching into a scene of logging devastation, warning of the dangers of clear-cut burning. Your raft then plunges down a waterfall (and one unlucky soul – usually the one with their back to the drop – gets seriously damp) before you finish more sedately. Queues can be long through the main part of the day, so use FastPass+ here. **R:** 3ft 6in/106cm (a few rafts have adult-and-child seats allowing smaller children to ride). **TTT AAAA FP+**

Maharajah Jungle Trek: Asia's version of the wildlife trail is another picturesque walk past decaying temple ruins and animal encounters. The first few exhibits – the Malayan tapir, Komodo dragon and a bat enclosure (including the flying fox bat, the world's largest) – lead to the main viewing area, the 5acre/2ha Tiger Range, whose pool and fountains are a popular playground early in the day for these magnificent big cats. An antelope enclosure and walk-through aviary complete this breathtaking trek (which rarely draws heavy crowds). **AAAAA**

Expedition: Everest™: A major attraction, this clever roller-coaster takes you deep into the Himalayas for an encounter with the mythical Yeti. The queuing area alone will convince you of its authentic location (try to do the main queue at least once rather than FastPass to appreciate all the fine detail) as it delivers you to an old abandoned tea plantation railway station. Here you undertake the ride to the foothills of Mount Everest, but you must first brave the perils of the Forbidden Mountain – lair of the Yeti. Will the beast be in evidence? You bet! The ride becomes a typically fast-paced whiz (but no inversions), forwards AND backwards, as you attempt to escape the creature's domain. The final encounter with a massive audio-animatronic Yeti is jaw-dropping and underlines the splendidly creative nature of this ride. It is a fabulous attraction but draws equally impressive crowds all day, so make it one of the first things you do. You can also take advantage of a Single Rider queue here (at the FP entrance) if you don't mind your group being split up. You can get ride photos here, too ($20.95–24.95, or $14.95 delivered digitally). **R:** 3ft 8in/115cm. **TTTTT FP+**

🇬🇧 **BRITTIP**
Although Expedition: Everest™ is a FastPass+ ride, its popularity means FP+s often run out, so schedule in advance, if possible. Don't leave it too late.

Expedition Everest

© Disney

Other entertainment: Have fun with **DJ Anaan and his Bangra Dance Party** next to the Local Foods Café, along with the **Chakranadi** duo, sitar and tabla musicians, and find *Jungle Book* characters at Upcountry Landing.

Shopping and dining: The retail options are limited in Asia (just two minor kiosks), but it is home to the fab **Yak and Yeti** combination diner. Outside is the counter-service **Local Foods Café** (honey chicken, Teriyaki beef bowl, roasted vegetable couscous wrap, chicken salad and Korean stir-fry), while inside the two-storey structure is the full restaurant. Yak and Yeti offers some imaginative cuisine, from a Dim Sum basket to Chicken Tikka Masala and a Malaysian Seafood Curry, as well as more standard Asian-fusion dishes, like Kalbi Steak and Coconut Shrimp, and Pork Pot Stickers. A good range of drinks and cocktails complement this superior eatery. Extra incentive to visit: a full range of bar drinks to go, while you can just sit at the bar for a drink or a full meal. The **Anandapur Ice Cream Truck** is also popular and the **Royal Anandapur Tea Company** features a great range of speciality teas, coffees and soft drinks. **Thirsty River Bar and Trek Snacks** offers pastries, fruit, hummus, ice cream, beer, wine and cocktails.

DinoLand USA

The final area of the park is somewhat at odds with the natural theme of the rest, a full-scale palaeontology exercise, with the accent on a 'university fossil dig'. Energetically tongue-in-cheek (the students who work the area have the motto 'Been there, dug that', while you enter under a mock brachiosaurus skeleton, the 'Oldengate Bridge' – groan!), it still features some glimpses into genuine research and artefacts.

DINOSAUR!: Renamed after Disney's big animated film (it was initially called *Countdown to Extinction*), this is a herky-jerky ride experience, rather dark and intense (and often too scary for young children). It is also a wonderfully realistic journey back to the end of the Cretaceous period, when a giant meteor put paid to dinosaur life. You enter the high-tech Dino Institute for a multimedia history show that leads to a briefing room for your 'mission' 65 million years in the past. However, one of the Institute's scientists hijacks your trip to capture a dinosaur, and you career back to a prehistoric jungle in a 12-passenger Time Rover. The threat of a carnotaurus (quite frightening for children; try to sit them on the inside of the car) and the impending doom of the meteor add up to a whirl through a menacing environment. You will need to ride at least twice to appreciate all the detail, but queues build up quickly, so go either first thing or late in the day. **R:** 3ft 4in/101cm. **TTTT** AAAA FP+

DINOSAUR!

© Disney

DISNEY'S ANIMAL KINGDOM THEME PARK with children

Here is our guide to the attractions that appeal to the different age groups in this park:

Under-5s
Affection Section, The Boneyard, Discovery Island Trails, Festival of the Lion King, Finding Nemo – The Musical, Kilimanjaro Safaris, Maharajah Jungle Trek, Na'vi River Journey, Pangani Forest Exploration Trail, Rivers of Light, TriceraTOP Spin.

5–8s
All the above, plus Conservation Station, DINOSAUR! (with parental discretion), Flights of Wonder, Habitat Habit!, It's Tough To Be A Bug (with parental discretion), Kali River Rapids, Primeval Whirl.

9–12s
All the above, plus Avatar: Flight of Passage, Expedition: Everest™.

Over-12s
Avatar: Flight of Passage, DINOSAUR!, Expedition: Everest™, Festival of the Lion King, Flights of Wonder, It's Tough To Be A Bug!, Kali River Rapids, Kilimanjaro Safaris, Maharajah Jungle Trek, Na'vi River Journey, Pangani Forest Exploration Trail, Primeval Whirl, Rivers of Light.

The Boneyard: An imaginative adventure playground, offering kids the chance to slip, slide and climb through the 'fossilised' remains of triceratops and brontosaurs, explore caves, dig for bones and splash through a mini waterfall. The amusing signage will be wasted on most kids, but it's ideal for parents to let their young 'uns loose for up to an hour (though not just after the neighbouring Finding Nemo show has finished). **TTTT** (kids only).

Finding Nemo – The Musical: This lovely show is a first for Disney, taking a regular animated feature and turning it into a full musical. The show combines colourful puppets, dancers, acrobats and animated backdrops with innovative lighting, sound and special effects.

The basic idea remains faithful to the story of Nemo, his dad Marlin and friends Dory and Crush and features larger-than-life puppetry, plus rod, bunraku and shadow puppets, all designed by Michael Curry, who created the award-winning Broadway version of Disney's *The Lion King* show. It's a spectacular combination of music and grand staging, and the 30min show performs up to five times a day. **AAAA FP+**

BRITTIP
Finding Nemo – The Musical is popular, but although it draws long queues, the theatre seats 1,500, so most people usually get in.

Chester & Hester's Dino-Rama!: This mini-land of rides, fairground games and stalls adds a rather garish element to the park. Its main icon is a towering concretosaurus (!), and it is designed to have a quirky, tongue-in-cheek style reminiscent of 1950s' American roadside attractions. There are two rides.

TriceraTOP Spin: Another version of the Dumbo/Aladdin rides in the Magic Kingdom, where a flying, twirling, spinning top bounces you up and down with a surprise at the top. **AA** (**TTTT** under-5s).

Primeval Whirl

© Disney

Primeval Whirl: Coaster fans will get a laugh out of this wacky offering that sends its riders through a maze of curves, hills and (quite sharp) drops that make it seem faster than it actually is. It's basically a lampoon of the DINOSAUR! ride, a mock journey 'way back in time', with plenty of cartoon frippery. Extra fun is provided by the fact the cars spin, giving each ride an unpredictable element. The queuing area is a riot of visual gags, but the ride isn't recommended for anyone with back or neck problems. R: 4ft/122cm. **TTTT** FP+

Other entertainment: Dino-Rama also features the **Fossil Fun Games**, six fairground-type stalls (costing $5 for a single ticket, $10/3 tickets, $15/5, $20/7, $30/10) designed to tempt you to try to win a cuddly dinosaur. **Disney characters** Goofy and Pluto meet guests across from TriceraTop Spin, with Donald Duck nearby.

Shopping: Chester and Hester's Dinosaur Treasures (the 'Fossiliferous Gift Store' – groan!) offers a wide range of dino-related souvenirs.

Dining: Buy a counter-service meal at the **Restaurantosaurus** (burgers, hot dogs, sandwiches, chicken nuggets and salad) or ice-cream and pastries at **Dino Bite Snacks**.

Other entertainment

Rivers of Light: This new nightly spectacular is a stunning special effects extravaganza in front of a new amphitheatre area, staged on the lake between Discovery Island and Expedition Everest. It tells the mythical story of animal spirits transitioning into the sky to become the Aurora Borealis, through the live artistry of puppetry, song and dance,

a sea of glowing lanterns, 'water lily' fountains with immense water-screen effects, and sensational floats bearing animal imagery. Combined with a superb original soundtrack, dazzling lighting effects and staging, it is a Disney triumph. AAAAA FP+

The Tree of Life: Night-time Awakenings: Projected onto the Tree of Life each night, this series of short shows tells stories as the carvings on the tree's trunk 'magically' awaken, and its branches glow with the light of thousands of fireflies. Through colour and imagery, the animals 'come to life' in 3min vignettes, transitioning into a procession of clips from classic Disney nature-inspired films. Viewing is from the entry to Discovery Island and is standing-room only. AAA

Other night-time fun (when the park stays open as late as 11pm) includes the **Harambe Wildlife Parti**, with local street musicians and other entertainers roaming the Africa area, as well as the **Discovery Island Carnevale**, with more live music, dancing, costumes, stilt-walkers and special food and beverage carts. It all builds up to the nightly Rivers of Light show and ensures the Animal Kingdom is a true all-day option.

Tours: Finally, for a behind-the-scenes look at the park, **Backstage Tales** is a wonderful almost four-hour journey into the handling and care of all the animals (7.30am daily; $90, no under-12s, under 18s with adult). For something really different, try the **Wild Africa Trek**, a three-hour ride- and-trek into the African savannah. From a precarious rope bridge crossing high above Harambe Reserve to a VIP safari in special open-air vehicles and a visit to Harambe's private camp, this exclusive experience, in groups of no more than 12, is open to ages 8+ (minimum 4ft/122cm tall; under 18s with adult), six times daily. Closed-toe shoes required, dresses/skirts not advised; weight limit 310lb/141kg. Seasonal pricing $189–249. Book tours on 407 939 8687.

That's the full Disney theme park story, but there is still PLENTY more in store…!

Rivers of Light

6 Five More of the Best

or Wizards, Wildlife and Wonders

I t's time to leave the wonderful world of Disney and explore the rest of Central Florida's attractions. And there's still a terrific amount in store, including some of the most thrilling rides and dazzling creativity. Yes, Universal Orlando and the SeaWorld parks are that good.

Universal has developed astronomically in recent years, with new hotels, entertainment, restaurants and, above all, headline attractions. In 2014, it opened the massive Cabana Bay Beach Resort, extensively revamped its CityWalk district and introduced the most eye catching themed area in 15 years with the Wizarding World of Harry Potter – Diagon Alley. In 2016, it unveiled the Sapphire Falls Resort, a new King Kong attraction and more CityWalk enhancements, with a whole new water park, Volcano Bay, due in 2017. SeaWorld added another major thrill with its Mako roller coaster in 2016, while Busch Gardens brought us its own new coaster, Cobra's Curse.

With five hotels, all connected by boat, bus or path to the CityWalk hub, from where the two parks radiate, Universal is an increasingly dynamic proposition, and more centralised than Disney. For UK visitors, the 2 and 3-Park Bonus Tickets are extremely well priced. It does not offer a free FastPass+ system like Disney but you can buy the Universal Express pass that covers a one-time front-of-queue access to nearly all the rides (but not the three headline Harry Potter attractions or King Kong). It is not cheap – from $40–109 depending upon time of year and $65–119 for both parks,

The new Cobra's Curse at Busch Gardens

Universal Dining Plan

Visitors can choose to add a daily meal allowance to their hotel bookings, or a daily Quick Service meal plan if they are just visiting the parks. The full Dining Plan can only be booked via Universal's own reservation system as part of a vacation package – **www.universalorlandovacations.com** – and offers one table-service meal (entrée, dessert and soft drink), one counter-service meal (entrée and soft drink), one snack (popcorn, ice-cream, etc) from food carts or counter service restaurants, and one additional soft drink per day for about $59/day per adult and $20/day per child. It can be used at most dining venues in the parks and seven in CityWalk (but, strangely, none in the hotels). The Quick Service option costs $22/adult and $14/child per day and offers one counter service meal (entrée and soft drink), one snack and one soft drink per day. The Quick Service option can be purchased on the day or in advance online. There is also the Coca-Cola Freestyle cup at $13/person (plus $10 for additional days) with unlimited free refills all day at the special Coca-Cola Freestyle outlets (five in each park), offering more than 100 different drinks.

but can save a lot of queuing at peak periods. A limited number go on sale after park opening and are snapped up, but they can also be bought online for a specific day at **www.universalorlando.com** or in the parks themselves for another day. The Park-to-Park Unlimited Express provides unlimited Express access to both parks for 1–4 days, $85–150.

Universal hotel guests (except those at Cabana Bay Beach Resort and Sapphire Falls) benefit from Express ride priority all day by showing their room key and all five enjoy the major perk of early access to The Wizarding Worlds of Harry Potter each day. In addition, some rides have Single Rider queues, which save time if you want to go by yourself or don't mind splitting up your group. Once again, height/health restrictions (R) are noted in ride descriptions. Universal is also home to some of the best (and most grisly!) Halloween celebrations on earth, with their Halloween Horror Nights programme (p165).

Hollywood Rip Ride Rocket

© Universal Orlando Resort

Universal Studios Florida®

Universal opened its first Florida park in June 1990 and quickly became a serious rival to Disney. For the visitor, it means a consistently high standard and good value (though the choice can be bewildering), but there are few similarities to their Los Angeles park. Universal is also a different proposition to Disney, with a more edgy style that appeals especially to teens. Younger children are still well catered for, though. Universal parks can also need more than a full day in high season. Strategies are the same: arrive EARLY (up to 30mins before opening), do the big rides first, avoid main meal times and take time out for an afternoon break (try shopping, dining or visiting the cinemas at CityWalk) if it gets too crowded.

Location

Universal Studios Florida® is divided into seven main areas, set around a lagoon, but there are no great distinguishing features. The main resort entrance is just off Interstate 4 (I-4 eastbound take exit 75A; westbound take exit 74B) or via Universal Boulevard from I-Drive. Parking is in its massive multi-storey car park and there is quite a walk (with moving walkways) to the front gates.

Photo connect

Universal's photo sharing system allows guests to collect all their ride photos in one source and is cheaper than buying them individually. Just ask for a Photo Connect card when you buy your first ride photo and all subsequent ones will end up on the same account for that day. You can then download your pics, add fancy borders and other features, share or have them put on posters, keychains, mugs and more at the Photo Connect kiosk when you leave. Or look for the Star Card, which allows you to

Universal Studios Florida® at a glance

Location	Off exits 75A and 74B from I-4; Universal Boulevard and Kirkman Road		
Size	110 acres/45ha in 7 themed areas		
Hours	9am–6 or 7pm off peak; 9am–10pm high season (Washington's birthday, Easter, summer holidays, Thanksgiving, Christmas)		
Admission	Under 3s free; 3–9 $112 (1-day ticket), $210 (2-day Park-to-Park ticket), adult (10+) $119, $220. Prices do not include tax.		
Parking	$20 (preferred parking $30; valet parking $40)		
Lockers	Immediately to left in Front Lot $10–12		
Pushchairs	$15 and $25		
Wheelchairs	$12 and $50 (with photo ID as deposit), with pushchairs		
Top attractions	Harry Potter and The Escape From Gringotts, Hogwarts Express, Revenge of the Mummy, Men in Black, Despicable Me: Minion Mayhem, TRANSFORMERS: The Ride – 3-D, The Simpsons, Hollywood Rip, Ride Rockit!		
Don't miss	Universal's Cinematic Spectacular, Universal's Superstar Parade, Curious George Playground (for kids), The Blues Brothers, Tales of Beedle the Bard		
Hidden costs	Meals	Burger, chips and coke $13 3-course dinner $26–36 (Lombard's) Kids meals $8 ($7–10 in Finnegan's)	
	T-shirts	$21.95–34.95	
	Souvenirs	95c–$2,999	
	Sundries	Temporary tattoos $7–10, Henna $12–25	

Production Central

1 Main Entrance
2 Shrek – 4-D
3 Despicable Me
4 Hollywood Rip, Ride, Rockit!
5 Meet Shrek & Donkey
6 Monsters Café
7 Transformers: The Ride – 3-D

New York

8 Race Through New York Starring Jimmy Fallon
9 Revenge of the Mummy
10 The Blues Brothers
11 Finnegan's Bar and Grill
12 Louie's Italian Restaurant

San Francisco

13 Fast and Furious – Supercharged
14 Richter's Burger Co.
15 Lombard's Seafood Grill

The Wizarding World of Harry Potter – Diagon Alley

16 Hogwarts Express

17 The Leaky Cauldron
18 Diagon Alley
19 Harry Potter and the Escape from Gringotts
20 Carkitt Market

World Expo

21 Men in Black – Alien Attack
22 Fear Factor Live!
23 The Simpsons Ride
24 Kang amd Kodos' Twirl 'n Hurl
25 Duff Brewery & Shop

KidZone

26 Animal Actors on Location!
27 Fievel's Playland
28 A Day in The Park with Barney
29 ET Adventure
30 Woody Woodpecker's Nuthouse Coaster
31 Curious George Goes To Town

Hollywood

32 Universal's Horror Make-Up Show
33 Terminator 2: 3-D Battle Across Time
34 Hello Kitty

compile ALL your Universal photos (including ride ones) on the 1 card account for either 1 day ($50), 3 days ($99), or a 14-day Digital Package ($149). You can pre-order it with a discount at **https://photoconnect. amazingpictures.com/** and share it on social media with their Amazing Pictures app.

Beating the queues: With the opening of The Wizarding World of Harry Potter – Diagon Alley, this has become THE place to visit first, with heavy queues building up quickly and lasting all day. It is at the back of the park, so try to avoid all the other attractions if this is your top target. Turn right on Rodeo Drive, continue through Sunset Boulevard and the Springfield area of The Simpsons, and go left across the bridge straight to the Wizarding World. If you are not a Potter fan (although you should still give Diagon Alley a look at some stage) and want some of the big-time thrills, stop first at Hollywood Rip Ride Rockit (on your left in Production Central) and then take in TRANSFORMERS: The Ride – 3-D and the nearby Revenge of the Mummy in New York. For interactive fun, take in Despicable Me first, then head back to the Springfield area and do The Simpsons and Men In Black. Many of the other attractions are now easy to do with the crowds flocking to Diagon Alley.

Here's a full guide to the Studios (for CityWalk, see Chapter 10).

Production Central

Coming straight through the gates brings you into the administrative centre, with a couple of large gift stores plus Studio Sweets. Call at **Guest Services** for guides for disabled visitors, TDD and assisted listening devices, and to make restaurant bookings, which can also be made at a kiosk to the right after the turnstiles, next to the **Beverly Hills Boulangerie**. **First aid** is available here (and on Canal Street between New York and San Francisco), while there are facilities for nursing mothers at **Family Services** by the bank through the gates on the right. Coming to the top of the Plaza of the Stars brings you to the business end of the park.

Shrek 4-D: This adds a fun dimension to 3-D films as the original cast (Mike Myers, Eddie Murphy, Cameron Diaz and John Lithgow) reprise their Oscar-winning roles. The amusing 7min pre-show leads into the 500-seat main theatre, where you don your Ogre Vision 3-D glasses and prepare to enter a new world. The film is funny enough as Shrek and Donkey save the Princess, but the special effects (watch out for the spiders!) and moving seats add a startling extra element that is hugely entertaining. State-of-the-art digital projection and audio systems, lighting effects and smoke (plus a hilarious finale featuring an out-of-control Tinker Bell) ensure a real laugh-fest. Queues stay long for much of the day. AAAAA+

Despicable Me – Minion Mayhem: This outrageously funny 3-D simulator ride is based on the

Shrek 4-D

© Universal Orlando Resort

© Universal Orlando Resort

Despicable Me – Minion Mayhem

animated films starring Steve Carell. You enter the home of super-villain Gru and visit his lab where you are 'shrunk' to undergo Minion training. In the company of Gru's daughters, Margo, Edith and Agnes, the zany scheme goes awry and his 'recruits' suffer some hair-raising adventures that need Gru's intervention to save the day. It ends happily, of course, with a fun Minion dance party (and gift shop). With dynamic, motion-based seats, things can get bumpy, so those with heart, neck, or back problems should ask for the stationary seats. **TTT+ AAAA (TTTTT under-10s)**

Hollywood Rip Ride Rockit!: This iconic ride is a high-tech colossus, with an onboard system that allows you to select your own ride music – then take home the DVD. You can't miss this vivid red steel beast as it loops right through park. It starts with a video intro while you queue that reveals five music choices (Rap/Hip Hop, Country, Classic Rock/Metal, Pop/ Disco and Club Electronica), each with six tracks. You're then strapped into an open-sided car that goes straight up a 17-storey vertical lift-hill, then into a steep dive followed by the signature Double Take, the world's first non-inverted loop (you don't actually go upside-down but it feels like it!). You will soar over the heads of people in the queue, dive below ground level and fly around a 150° banked turn, all in the course of the 1min 40sec ride. The innovative open cars make the whole experience feel even faster and more dynamic, while the mix of pounding music (from your headrest and speakers along the track) and concert-style lighting (flashy during the day, stunning at night) ensures this is a ride that really rocks. You can buy the ride video, complete with your musical selection, captured by multiple cameras (for $35; ride photos $20–70). It looks more frightening than it actually is, but it is truly exhilarating. Leave this for later in the day when queues tend to drop off. **R: 4ft 3in/130cm. TTTTT+**

Revenge of the Mummy

© Universal Orlando Resort

BRITTIP
Universal Orlando now has metal detectors at the bag check area that all guests must walk through. To help move crowds through faster, be sure to have your bags open and coins, cell phones and keys removed from pockets.

TRANSFORMERS: The Ride – 3-D: The latest generation of Universal's dramatic 3-D technology allied with a dynamic ride vehicle, this puts guests at the heart of an explosive battle between the Autobots, led by Optimus Prime and the evil Decepticons of Megatron. It feels like walking into a movie as the long, elaborate queuing area prepares riders for joining the planet-defending forces of NEST, and then a larger-than-life whirl through a Decepticon attack in a bid to defend the AllSpark – and the earth's existence! The combination of ultra-HD film, real scenery and dramatic special effects is breathtaking (if loud). Even those who have never seen one of the films will not feel left out as the whole scenario is explained while you queue. Crowds build up quickly, hence you need to ride early on or late in the day. **R:** 3ft 4in/101cm. **TTTT**

Character appearances: Optimus Prime, Bumblebee and Megatron have a brilliant set-piece **Transformers photo spot** next to the ride, or meet Shrek, Fiona and Donkey at **Meet Shrek & Donkey**, well worth catching for the amusing patter. You'll find **Minion photo ops** in the Super Silly Stuff shop.

Shopping: Great shops here, including **Supply Vault** for all things Transformers, **On Location** (film, clothes, sundries and 2-way radio rentals), **Super Silly Stuff** (Despicable Me merchandise), the massive **Universal Studios Store** (with everything) and **It's A Wrap** (discounted items).

Dining: The main eating outlet is the wonderful **Monsters Café** (peak season only) offering salads, lasagne, meatloaf, burgers, hotdogs and pizza. The counter-service area is themed like Frankenstein's lab, with the dining areas showing black-and-white horror film clips.

New York

Now head to New York with its impressive architecture, street scenes and park.

Race Through New York Starring Jimmy Fallon: New for summer 2017, comedian and Tonight Show host Jimmy Fallon stars in this 3-D ride experience (similar to Harry Potter and the Forbidden Journey) through the streets of New York City. Enter through 'Studio 6B' in the city's famous NBC Studios at 30 Rockefeller Plaza, where Jimmy challenges his audience (you) to a 'race through New York.' Dive through subway tunnels, 'fly' around skyscrapers, and encounter Jimmy's celebrity friends in a special-effects filled, high-adrenalin laugh-fest. **TTTT** (expected)

Revenge of the Mummy: This superb offering is a high-thrill, high-fun journey into the Ancient Egypt of *The Mummy* film series, fusing coaster technology with space-age robotics and special effects. It starts out as a slow, dark ride through curse-ridden Hamunaptra, but soon takes an ingenious launch into something more dynamic, using the novel idea of the film studio becoming a full archaeological discovery, with a host of special effects and audio animatronics as you brave the Mummy's realm. The high-speed whiz in the dark (backwards to start with) doesn't involve inversions but is still a thrill with its tight turns and dips, while there are several clever twists (the front row may get slightly damp!). It is a hugely immersive experience and rates five-stars with the elaborate queuing area, but may be too scary for under-8s. Preview your ride photos ($30–35) as you enter the gift shop. **R:** 4ft/122cm. **TTTT½**

BRITTIP
For the best ride experience on Revenge of the Mummy, try to get a back row seat. You are not allowed to carry anything on the ride – loose items must be left in the (free) lockers provided.

Chez Alcatraz

The Blues Brothers: Fans of the film will not want to miss this live show as Jake and Elwood Blues (or pretty good doubles anyway) put on a stormin' performance on New York's Delancey Street several times a day. They cruise up in their Bluesmobile and go through a series of the film's hits before heading off into the sunset, stopping only for autographs. AAAA

Other entertainment: The energetic can try the **42nd Street Wall Climb** (rock wall) on 5th Avenue ($5). New York also boasts the inevitable **amusement arcade**. Or just grab a drink at **Finnegan's bar** and listen to the live music from their fun singer-guitarist.

Shopping: Check out **Sahara Traders** for Mummy souvenirs, as well as jewellery and toys, and **Rosie's Irish Imports** for all things Irish.

Dining: You have two main restaurants: **Finnegan's Bar and Grill** offers shepherd's pie, fish and chips, corned beef and cabbage, along with steak, burgers, fries and a good range of beers, plus Irish-tinged entertainment, while **Louie's Italian Restaurant** has counter-service pizza and pasta, ice-cream and tiramisu. There's also a **Ben and Jerry's** store for ice-cream and smoothies, and a **Starbucks** for coffee and pastries.

San Francisco

Cross Canal Street to get to an area of the park undergoing a major refit.

Fast And Furious – Supercharged: This fabulous ride-and-show experience (due in late 2017) is based on the underground street racing world made famous in the films starring Vin Diesel and Paul Walker. It takes visitors on an all-new adventure with the high-speed stars, using the latest ride technology and giving it an immersive twist thanks to digital film and sound-surround effects. In addition, there will be a chance to get up close with some of the super-charged cars from the films, including *The Fast 8*, which is due for release in April 2017. AAAA/ TTTT (expected)

Other entertainment: Although the **Jaws** ride is gone, you can still get a photo with the 'Great White' next to the **Chez Alcatraz** dockside bar, or try the **Amazing Pictures** kiosk and have your face added to a famous view or magazine ($29–127).

Shopping: Look for a new **Fast and Furious** gift shop here in 2017.

Dining: Try the park's best dining choice, **Lombard's Seafood Grille** (high season only; reservations accepted) for great seafood, steak, pasta and sandwiches, accompanied by a wonderful view over the Central Lagoon. **San Francisco Pastry Co** offers desserts and coffee and **Richter's Burger Co** has some tempting burgers.

Transformers – the Ride, Optimus Prime

© Universal Orlando Resort

The Wizarding World of Harry Potter – Diagon Alley

This is the most amazing theme park experience in the world today. The second part of Universal's hugely impressive Potter-verse not only repeats the immersive, film-like setting of Hogsmeade in Islands of Adventure (with a unique link between the two), it goes even deeper into JK Rowling's creation and leaves you in awe of the design and innovation. And that's before you get to the two rides, the live entertainment and the food!

Diagon Alley: Hidden behind a realistic setting of The Embankment lies the secret wizarding street and a full array of complex theming, with the entrance next to a façade of Leicester Square tube station. The external design is modern London, right down to the ¼-scale King's Cross Station and a working version of Piccadilly's Eros Statue, where you will also find the iconic Knight Bus. Other elements include Grimmauld Place and the Wyndham Theatre but then visitors walk through the jumbled red-brick barrier next to the tube station and emerge in the jaw-dropping recreation of Diagon Alley, where the towering shop-fronts and mysterious businesses envelop visitors with the full visual effect of the films. Also here is the brooding Knockturn Alley, where the dark arts rule and every nook and cranny is sinister as it is always night. Another area, Carkitt Market was created by JK Rowling purely for Universal. It is all new yet it LOOKS like it has been here for 150 years. Its mix of shops and dining are all jumbled together in a seamless way, making this as much of an attraction as the rides themselves. AAAAA+

Harry Potter and The Escape From Gringotts: Prepare to be mesmerised as you enter the vaults – and dangers – of the wizarding world's bank. A fire-breathing dragon sits high atop the building and, if that doesn't take your breath away, the stunning entry hall will as realistic goblins – the bank staff – lift the animatronic art to new heights, including an ultra-realistic head clerk who talks to visitors while you wait. The queue twists and turns through the filing office and backrooms before reaching Bill Weasley's office, where you learn you have arrived during the famous episode when Harry, Ron and Hermione break into the vaults. Then you take the elevator deep underground and climb a flight of steel stairs into a vast cavern that only feels like it's miles below the bank. Here you board the ride to share in the perils of Harry and Co as they search for a crucial Horcrux. Half coaster and half 3-D simulator ride, it changes pace as riders brave the various guardians of the vaults, including the dangerous Bellatrix Lestrange, a fire-breathing dragon, an enchanted waterfall, goblin guards and, finally, a close encounter with Lord Voldemort himself (which may be too intense for young children). Riders do escape, of course, and the sense of realism will have you coming back for more – just be aware this draws the longest queues in the park from first thing, so head here straight away or expect a l-o n g wait. R. 3ft6in/106cm. TTTTT+

Hogwarts Express: This neat, realistic ride operates between the two parks, as guests journey to Hogsmeade from King's Cross Station. Again, the sense of realism is superb as you arrive at Platform 9¾ to board a replica of the famous Hogwarts train, complete with separate compartments and pulled by a Hull-class locomotive. While it runs on a special track backstage, the enclosed carriage 'windows' show highlights of the journey north to Scotland, including a close encounter with Hagrid on his flying motorcycle, the flying Ford Anglia – and some dangerous Dementors. Oh, and look out for Harry, Hermione and Ron on the train! As this ride goes from park to park, you will need a 2-park ticket to ride, hence there is a real ticket office to check you through, or sell you a ticket to complete the journey. The queue area here is vast but waits rarely top 30mins. AAAAA+

Other entertainment: Look out for two original shows in Carkitt Market, where **Celestina Warbeck & The Banshees** take the stage several times a day to deliver a rollicking four-song performance. The 'Singing Sorceress' is not dissimilar to Shirley Bassey in a 1940s big-band jazz style, and the songs are all originals, including the classics 'You Stole My Cauldron But You Can't Have My Heart' and 'Beat Back Those Bludgers, Boys' and 'Chuck That Quaffle Here'! AAAA. Also on the Market stage is the elaborate story-telling of **Tales of Beedle the Bard**, a combination of live actor and puppetry show, with the intricate puppets created by award-winning designer Michael Curry. It's especially engaging for children, and Potter fans. AAA. Other live entertainment is provided by the essential wizard's shop of **Ollivander's**, where 'the wand chooses the wizard' and all manner of strange goings-on highlight this fun actor-staged show. AAA. Look out also for the **Knight Bus Conductor**, who will engage visitors as they enter the Wizarding World, and don't miss the bus's Talking Shrunken Head, as his wisecracks might be aimed at YOU!

Shopping: Another key experience, with eight immersive stores to please the eye and tease the wallet. **Weasley's Wizard Wheezes** is a multi-storey joke shop with all manner of gags, then there is **Wiseacre's Wizarding Equipment** (for all your essential school gear), **Quality Quidditch Supplies**, **Madam Malkin's Robes** (school uniforms and accessories), **Borgin & Burkes** (the Dark Arts

store in Knockturn Alley), **Magical Menagerie** (a soft toy emporium – listen for the animals scurrying about in the upper levels!) and **Scribbulus**, for other Hogwarts mementos. The shops also feature interactive windows that work with the special wands on sale at **Ollivander's** and **Wands By Gregorovitch** at $40–48 each. Look for the markers in the pavement, say the magic command and wave your wand for a host of surprises. You can even change dollars into wizarding notes at the **Money Exchange**, complete with a Goblin host. Be ready to spend a fair bit of time here, as well as money!

Dining: The essential reality of the Wizarding World is continued into the main dining outlet of **The Leaky Cauldron**, a superb recreation of Diagon Alley's hallmark pub. The food may seem standard pub fare, but the Cottage Pie is excellent, as is the Beef, Lamb and Guinness Stew, while their Ploughman's Platter is positively indulgent with its array of three cheeses, pickle, salad, scotch egg and fresh bread (priced variously from $9–20). There is also Toad in the Hole (which Simon may just have helped with!), Fish 'n Chips, two types of sandwich (sausage and chicken) and a Fisherman's Pie. Kids can choose from a mini-pie, mac and cheese and their own fish 'n chips ($6.99). There are then three tempting desserts, of which the Sticky Toffee Pudding is to die for. All this can be washed down with drinks such as Fishy Green Ale (a variation on bubble tea, and non-alcoholic), Otter's Fizzy Orange Juice, Tongue-Tying Lemon Squash and Gilly Water, as well as two outstanding beers – the IPA-like Dragon Scale Ale and porter-style Wizards Brew. You order at the counter and are then given a 'magical' candle and shown to a table, where the food will find you thanks to a clever GPS device in the candle! There is a separate menu for breakfast. Still hungry? Head for **Florean Fortescue's Ice Cream Parlour** where Universal's culinary wizards have come up with a superb array of flavours that are all worth trying, including Earl Grey &

Diagon Alley

© Universal Orlando Resort

Halloween Horror Nights

Universal's massively popular Halloween celebration occurs through late Sept and all of Oct each year and is a wonderfully bloodthirsty – and thoroughly entertaining! – series of evening events. The Horror Nights have become a real trademark and add a suitably grisly touch to park proceedings. The park is transformed with imaginative set pieces from various horror movies, plus live shows and character interaction. The general mix is eight indoor Scare Houses, each with its own macabre theme (such as Texas Chainsaw Massacre and The Exorcist in 2016), plus open-air Scare Zones, with atmospheric dry ice and characters (zombies, chainsaw guys and various beasts!) lurking in dark corners, and two or three live presentations, including the signature Bill & Ted's Excellent Halloween Adventure (an annual comedy special that heavily satirises pop culture icons). All horror genres are well represented, and the Scare Houses feature some superb 'scare actors' and special effects. The rides are all open (and often with fairly short queues), adding more novelty to the park experience, but this over-the-top (and occasionally downright gruesome) extravaganza is definitely not for kids, especially as the atmosphere can get a bit raucous late in the evening as alcohol is widely available. It goes down a treat with adults with the right sense of humour, though, and begins every evening at 6.30pm until 1 or 2am. It is a separate event costing $102/person (but there are savings of up to $52 if you add it on to a daytime ticket of any kind). There is even a Frequent Fear Pass for multiple visits on selected evenings (not Sat, when crowds are heaviest and queues for the Scare Houses can reach 2 hours) and a HHN Universal Express pass for $70–120 (depending on dates), plus a Frequent Fear Plus Express Pass (including Friday) for $280. No costumes are allowed on any evening, though. Look up more at **www.halloweenhorrornights.com**.

Lavender, Apple Crumble, Chocolate Chilli and Clotted Cream. You can also grab a drink – alcoholic and otherwise – at the **Hopping Pot** and **Fountain of Fair Fortune**.

World Expo

Continuing around the park brings you to an extensive area that is home to Fear, Aliens and The Simpsons.

Men in Black – Alien Attack: This combination thrill/dark ride takes up where the hit films, starring Will Smith, left off. Visitors are introduced to the MIB Institute in an inventive mock-futuristic setting and enrolled as trainees for a battle around the streets of New York with a horde of escaped aliens. Your six-person car is equipped with laser zappers for an interactive shoot-out that is like a real-life arcade game, as the aliens can also shoot back to send your car spinning. The finale features a close encounter with a giant bug that is all mouth. Only your collective shooting skills can save the day, and there are numerous ride variations according to your accuracy. Fast, frantic and a bit confusing, you'll want to come

back until you can top 250,000 (for Defender status). R: 3ft 6in/106cm.

BRITTIP

For a big score in Men In Black, when you meet the Big Bug – push the big red button!

Fear Factor Live: (high season only) This live-action version of the reality TV show asks audience volunteers to take part in some hair-raising (and stomach-churning!) challenges, with a head-to-head competition to find the biggest daredevil. Auditions take place 70mins before each show, and the audience then gets to see the chosen few battle it out, with clips from the TV show interspersed with live action. Some of the stunts are distinctly off-colour (anyone for a maggot milkshake?) and may not be good for young children (or anyone of a weak disposition!). TTT

The Simpsons Ride: The headline attraction in the Springfield sub-area of World Expo, this brings the TV characters to vibrant life in a colourful and amusing production, even if you're not a fan of The Simpsons. It is themed as Krustyland amusement park, brainchild of irascible Krusty the Clown, a bizarre funfair that is the setting for a hectic, breathtaking ride in the company of the Simpson clan. A wicked sound system and state-of-the-art motion simulator technology ensure a frantic race through outlandish attractions (watch out for the Tooth Chipper!). The feel of the 'ride' is amazing and the huge domed screen ensures an outrageously comical sensory experience. However, this can also be a big draw, hence you should visit early or expect a serious wait. **R**: 3ft 4in/101cm. **TTTTT**

Kang and Kodos' Twirl 'n' Hurl: A standard fairground whirligig with some clever touches as the alien duo take 'foolish humans' into 'orbit' and provide a challenge as you twirl. **TT** (**TTTTT** under 6s).

Other entertainment: In Springfield, chance your hand at a series of fairground-type games that require $6 to play ($25 for five games), like the groan-inducing Sledge-Homer. Look out for Simpsons **character meet-and-greets** at regular intervals, and **photo ops** with Springfield icons like the Lard Lad Donuts statue, Founders statue and The Seven Little Duffs.

Shopping: Visit **MIB Gear** (at the exit to the ride) for Men In Black-themed clothing and souvenirs (plus photo opportunities with the MIB themselves). To complete the immersive Springfield effect, visit the **Kwik-E-Mart** for Simpsons souvenirs (plus more gags).

Kang and Kodos' Twirl 'n' Hurl

Dining: Expo Eats offers drinks and snacks, then there's the clever counter-service offerings of the **Fast Food Boulevard** food-court, where you can dine in true Homer fashion (albeit with better quality) at **Krusty Burger**, **Luigi's Pizza**, **Frying Dutchmen**, **Cletus' Chicken Shack** and **Moe's Tavern** (complete with the non-alcoholic Flaming Moe cocktail). For a specially-made brew, you can visit the **Duff Brewery & Shop** with a fab view of the Lagoon. **Bumblebee Man's Taco Truck** completes the picture here.

◀▶ BRITTIP

Along the lagoon in the Springfield/KidZone area is East Green, a quiet spot where you can stop to take a break for a while.

KidZone

This is a great place to let the kids loose on their own, but it does also feature several great family attractions. It is rumoured to be the likely site for a Nintendo-themed land in future.

Animal Actors On Location!: An amusing mix of video, animal performance and audience interaction, several children are invited to help present some unlikely feats and stunts featuring a range of wildlife, from parakeets and pigs to cats, dogs and an orang-utan. Many have been rescued from animal shelters and gone on to feature in films before finding a home at Universal. The theatre also provides an escape from the queues. AAAA

Fievel's Playland: Strictly for kids, this playground, based on the enlarged world of the cartoon mouse, offers the chance to bounce under a 1,000-gallon hat, crawl through a giant boot, climb a giant spider's web and shoot the rapids (a 200ft/61m waterslide) in Fievel's sardine can. **TTTT** (young 'uns only!)

A Day in the Park with Barney: Again strictly for the younger set (2–5), the purple dinosaur from kids' TV is brought to super-dee-duper life in a large arena that features a pre-show before the 15min main event, plus an interactive post-show area. **AA** (**AAAAA** under-5s)

ET Adventure: This is as glorious as scenic rides come, with a picturesque queuing area from the film and then a spectacular leap on the trademark flying bicycles to save ET's home planet. Steven Spielberg has added some special effects and characters, and you have an individual ET greeting at the end. The masses often overlook this corner of the park, The ride reaches only 28ft/8m high and 22mph, but it seems the real deal to young 'uns. However, the height restriction is still 3ft/91cm. **TTTT** (juniors only)

> ◀🇬🇧▶ **BRITTIP**
>
> If you want to let your youngsters loose in the Curious George playground, it is advisable to bring swimsuits or a change of clothing.

Curious George Goes To Town: Kids of all ages love this adventure playground with plenty of ways to get wet. It combines toddler play, water-based play stations and a huge interactive ball pool, and is a real bonus for harassed parents. The town theme includes buildings to climb, pumps and hoses to spray water, a ball factory in which to shoot, dump and blast thousands of foam balls and – the tour de force – two huge buckets of water that flood the street below at regular intervals. **TTTTT** (under-12s) Curious George roams the KidZone from time to time, while other characters make regular appearances.

Other entertainment: Young 'uns should head for **Barney's Backyard**, a neat indoor play area for those under 36in/91cm tall, including a **photo opportunity** with Barney himself (in addition to the one at the end of each show). It also has the parental benefit of being in the air-conditioned cool!

Shopping and dining: Shop at the fun **Spongebob Storepants** for everything to do with Spongebob and friends in an immersive environment, complete with character photo opportunity, plus the **Barney Store** and **ET's Toy Closet** and **Photo Spot**. For a quick bite, **Kidzone Pizza Company** offers pizza and chicken fingers.

Hollywood

Finally, your circular tour of Universal returns you to the main entrance via Hollywood (where else?).

Universal's Horror Make-Up Show: Not recommended for under-12s, this demonstrates some of the ways in which films have terrorised us, from classic black-and-white examples to modern horror movies. Using film clips and special effects 'experts', the audience is treated to a slapstick approach to horror make-up. It's a 20min show, queues are rarely long and the special effects are amusing. **AAA**

Terminator 2: 3-D Battle Across Time: Another first-of-its-kind attraction, this is part film, part show, part experience but all action, and usually leaves its audience in awe. The 'Wow!' factor works overtime as you go through a 10min pre-show representing a trip to the Cyberdyne Systems company from the Terminator films and then into a 700-seat theatre for a 'presentation' on its latest robot creations. The show is interrupted, though, by John and Sarah Connor and mayhem ensues, with the audience subjected to an array of (loud) special effects, including real actors interacting with the screen and the audience, indoor pyrotechnics and a climactic

Terminator 2: 3-D Battle Across Time

© Universal Orlando Resort

3-D film finale that takes the Terminator story a step further. **TTTTT**

Hello Kitty: Fans of the popular Sanrio character Hello Kitty (and others like Chococat and My Melody) should be thrilled to discover this extensive new retail and character meet-and-greet opportunity, replacing the old Lucille Ball tribute exhibit.

Other entertainment: The **Hollywood Character Zone** provides numerous character appearances throughout the day along Hollywood Boulevard, from Scooby Doo and Shaggy to Dudley Do-Right and The Flintstones, along with music from the **Studio Brass Band**. The **Character Party Zone** features various members of the Superstar Parade periodically next to Mel's Drive-In.

> **BRITTIP**
> Ever wanted to take home a truly unique souvenir from the Universal parks? **Williams of Hollywood** is the place to find original props and artifacts for sale.

Shopping: Look for Terminator gifts and clothing in **Cyber Image**, all manner of headgear in **The Brown Derby**, Hollywood legends' jewellery in **Studio Styles** and movie memorabilia in **Silver Screen Collectibles**.

Dining: There are four contrasting eateries: **Mel's Drive-In**, a re-creation from the film *American Graffiti*, serving burgers and hot dogs (though Richter's has better burgers); **Café La**

Universal's Cinematic Spectacular

© Universal Orlando Resort

Bamba for the daily Parade Character Breakfast (see right); **Schwab's Pharmacy**, with traditional ice-cream, milkshakes and sundaes; and **Beverly Hills Boulangerie** for a range of sandwiches, cheesecake, pastries, juices and coffee.

Parade time!

Universal's Superstar Parade: The daily performance takes place at 3 or 5pm in a vibrant and lively style, with dozens of performers and interactive characters. The four main sets of 'superstars' are led by Gru and his Minions from *Despicable Me* and followed by Spongebob Squarepants and his Bikini Bottom pals, including skaters and stilt walkers – and with the world's biggest pineapple! EB and the bunnies from the 2011 film *Hop* take over, including some snazzy live drumming, while Nickelodeon stars Dora and Diego from *Dora The Explorer* and *Go, Diego, Go!* complete the line-up, with aerialists and other high-energy performers. The huge floats – especially for the Minions – are feature-packed, and the parade has two dance stops to allow characters to meet guests. It is just 15mins but there are up to four other meet-and-greet performances during the day when characters come into the park for their own Street Parties. **AAAA**

> **BRITTIP**
> The two best viewing spots for the Parade are halfway along the main New York street (opposite the Palace Arcade) or on Hollywood Boulevard, outside the Cyber Image shop.

The Parade also has a **Character Breakfast** 9–11am (Thurs–Sun), with the chance to meet the Minions, pose with Spongebob, get autographs from Dora and Diego and enjoy a full breakfast at **Café La Bamba** ($26 adults, $13 3–9s). Those booking the breakfast also receive VIP viewing for the Parade and early access to selected rides.

Universal's Cinematic Spectacular: The nightly finale is this 20min film, firework, fountain and special

UNIVERSAL STUDIOS with children

Our guide to the attractions that generally appeal to the different age groups:

Under-5s
Animal Actors On Location!, Curious George Goes To Town, A Day in the Park With Barney, ET Adventure, Fievel's Playland, Kang & Kodos' Twirl 'n' Hurl, Universal's Superstar Parade.

5–8s
All the above (minus Barney), plus Despicable Me, Hogwarts Express, Men In Black, Shrek 4-D, The Simpsons, TRANSFORMERS: The Ride – 3-D (with parental discretion), Universal's Cinematic Spectacular, Woody Woodpecker's Nuthouse Coaster.

9–12s
All the above, plus Hollywood Rip Ride Rockit, Fear Factor Live!, Fast & Furious, Harry Potter and The Escape From Gringotts, Revenge of the Mummy, Terminator 2: 3-D Battle Across Time, TRANSFORMERS: The Ride – 3-D, Race Through New York Starring Jimmy Fallon.

Over-12s
The Blues Brothers, Despicable Me, ET Adventure, Fast & Furious, Race Through New York Starring Jimmy Fallon, Fear Factor Live, Hollywood Rip Ride Rockit, Men In Black – Alien Attack, Revenge of the Mummy, Shrek 4-D, The Simpsons, Terminator 2: 3-D, TRANSFORMERS: The Ride – 3-D, Universal's Cinematic Spectacular, Universal's Horror Make-Up Show.

effect-laden performance on the Main Lagoon. With three 'stages' and numerous water effects, it celebrates 100 years of Universal movies with clips choreographed to some spectacular fountains and pyrotechnics. See how many movies you can spot, as well-known moments from the likes of *E.T.*, *Apollo 13*, *Jurassic Park*, *The Mummy* and *The Fast & The Furious* are projected on to the fountains, all with narration by Morgan Freeman. The show culminates in a firework frenzy, underscored by dramatic music (on 300 outdoor speakers) and superb digital projection for a truly original presentation. There is a seasonal version for Christmas, too. **TTTT**

For VIP viewing of the Spectacular, book the **Cinematic Dining Experience** with dinner at Lombard's Seafood Grille and an exclusive spectator area for the show with dessert buffet ($45 for adults, $13 3–9s). Book on 407 224 7554 or at **www.universalorlando.com**.

Special programmes
Universal Studios features some brilliant extra seasonal entertainment for **Mardi Gras**, with a hectic, head-throwing parade, plus music, street entertainment and authentic New Orleans food each Sat at 6pm mid-Feb–mid-Apr (and free with park admission). The spectacular Parade alone is worth coming to see, along with authentic Zydeco bands in the French Quarter Courtyard The day culminates in a live concert with well-known acts (including Diana Ross, Kool & The Gang and REO Speedwagon in 2016), but it does draw HUGE crowds. Universal also throws a party for **Fourth of July**, when the park presents a major firework spectacular. And don't miss the Studios at Christmas (p37).

Mardi Gras at UOR

© Universal Orlando Resort

Islands of Adventure

With the arrival of Diagon Alley at Universal Studios, you'd think there might be slightly less focus on the original Harry Potter development here, but not a bit of it. In fact, with the Hogwarts Express ride now connecting the two areas, it was as busy as ever in 2016 and hit the attendance jackpot again with the grand opening of the new King Kong attraction.

The Islands of Adventure opened in 1999 under the supervision of creative consultant Steven Spielberg, and it provided one of the most complete and thrilling theme parks you could imagine, containing an upbeat collection of high-adrenalin rides, shows and entertainment, plus some fine dining. Then JK Rowling's boy wizard arrived and added a whole new 'world' of excitement.

The park has a full range of attractions, from out-and-out thrills to pure family entertainment. OK, so they aren't really islands (the areas form a chain around the central lagoon), but that's the only illusion. And you get a lot for your money here, unless you have extremely timid children or under-5s. Seuss Landing will usually keep preschoolers amused for several hours, while Camp Jurassic is a clever adventure playground for 5–12s, but the rest of the park, with its nine 5-star thrill rides and other attractions, is primarily geared to kids of 10 and over, their parents and especially teenagers. There are six elements that look alarming, but don't be put off – they all deliver immense fun as well as terrific spectator value! If any one ride sums up IoA, it is Harry Potter and the Forbidden Journey, which

Islands of Adventure at a glance

Location	Off exits 75A and 74B from I-4; Universal Boulevard and Kirkman Road
Size	110 acres/45ha in 6 'islands'
Hours	9am–6, 7 or 8pm off peak; 8 or 9am–9 or 10pm high season (Washington's birthday, Easter, summer holidays, Thanksgiving, Christmas)
Admission	Under-3s free; 3–9 $112 (1-day ticket), $210 (2-day Park-to-Park ticket), adult (10+) $119, $220. Prices do not include tax.
Parking	$20 (preferred parking $30; valet parking $40)
Lockers	Immediately to left through main gates; $10–12
Pushchairs	$15 and $25
Wheelchairs	$12 and $50 (with photo ID as deposit)
Top attractions	Harry Potter and the Forbidden Journey, Hogwarts Express, Amazing Adventures Of Spider-Man, Dragon Challenge, Incredible Hulk Coaster, Jurassic Park River Adventure, Skull Island: Reign of Kong
Don't miss	Eighth Voyage Of Sindbad, Jurassic Park Discovery Centre, If I Ran The Zoo playground (for toddlers), Three Broomsticks restaurant and Ollivander's Wand Shop
Hidden costs	**Meals** — Burger, chips and soda $13.19 / 3-course lunch $20–36 (Confisco Grill) / Kids' meal $6.99
	T-shirts — $21.95–37.95, Kids $17.95–27.95
	Souvenirs — 95c—$6,500
	Sundries — Butterbeer $6 regular, $7 frozen

took theme park ride technology to a whole new level.

Private nursing facilities, an open area for feeding and resting (with high chairs) and nappy-changing stations, can be found at the **Family Service Facility** at Guest Services (to the right inside the main gates), while ALL restrooms throughout the park are equipped with nappy-changing facilities. First aid is provided in Sindbad's Village in the Lost Continent, just across from Oasis Coolers, and in Port of Entry.

Port of Entry

You arrive for IoA as you do for Universal Studios, in the big multi-storey car parks off I-4 and Universal Boulevard and pass right through the CityWalk area, where you come to the main entrance plaza (head for the huge Pharos Lighthouse). As with Universal Studios, you can purchase the Universal Express pass for Islands of Adventure ($40–109, depending on time of year) at various locations throughout the park and at Guest Services. Once through the gates, the lockers, pushchair and wheelchair hire are on your left as the Port of Entry opens up before you. This elaborate 'village' consists of shops and eateries, so push straight on until you hit the main lagoon. Above all, be sure to take in the wonderful architecture throughout Port of Entry, which borrows from Middle East, Far East and African themes and uses bric-a-brac from all over the world.

Shopping: Later in the day, return to check out the extensive retail experience at places like **IoA Trading Company** and **Ocean Trader Market** for a full range of Islands of Adventure merchandise.

Dining: You can enjoy a coffee and pastry at the inevitable **Starbucks** or the **Croissant Moon Bakery** (also with croissants and sandwiches), or sample the huge cinnamon rolls and pastries of **Cinnabon**. Alternatively, try lunch or dinner at **Confisco Grille** with tastes from around the world including Italian, Mexican and Asian as well as American, and a range of

dishes from sandwiches and burgers to salads, Fajitas, ribs, pizza and pasta. Or just grab a beverage and a snack at the **Backwater Bar** (Happy Hour 4–7pm).

Beating the queues: At the end of the street, you will need to decide which way to head first as there are nine attractions where the queues build up quickly and remain that way. If you are among the majority lured by Harry Potter, turn right (through Seuss Landing and The Lost Continent. If you're after the big thrill rides, turn left into Marvel Super-Hero Island and head straight to Spider-Man, then do Dr Doom's Fearfall and the Incredible Hulk Coaster. The new King Kong attraction (between Toon Lagoon and Jurassic Park) is a big draw, too, so you may want to head here first, and then visit Hogsmeade.

BRITTIP
There are two entrances to the Wizarding World of Harry Potter from Jurassic Park and The Lost Continent. The latter is much more dramatic and offers the full Hogsmeade Village panorama.

Dinosaur fans should go left around the lagoon to Jurassic Park for the River Adventure before the majority arrive. Once you are nice and wet, go back to Toon Lagoon for Ripsaw Falls and the Bilge-Rat Barges. Or, if you have younger children, turn right into the multicoloured world of Seuss Landing and enjoy The Cat in the Hat and High In The Sky Seuss Trolley Train Ride prior to the main crowd build-up.

Turning right, in an anti-clockwise direction, here's what you find.

Seuss Landing

There is not a straight line to be seen in this vivid 3-D working of the books of Dr Seuss. The characters may not mean much to those unfamiliar with the children's stories, but everyone can relate to the fun here (though queues build up quickly). Take your time and try not to miss the clever detail,

Port of Entry
1 Ocean Trader Market
2 Confisco Grille

Marvel Super-Hero Island
3 Incredible Hulk Coaster
4 Dr Doom's Fearfall
5 Café 4
6 Captain America Diner
7 The Amazing Adventures of Spider-Man
8 Storm Force Accelatron

Toon Lagoon
9 Popeye And Bluto's Bilge-Rat Barges
10 Dudley Do-Right's Ripsaw Falls
11 Me Ship, The Olive
12 Comic Strip Café
13 Toon Lagoon Amphitheater

Jurassic Park
14 Jurassic Park River Adventure
15 Pteranodon Flyers
16 Camp Jurassic
17 Discovery Center
18 Skull Kingdom: Reign of Kong
19 Raptor Encounter

The Wizarding World of Harry Potter
20 Harry Potter and the Forbidden Journey
21 Filch's Emporium
22 Flight of the Hippogriff
23 Olivander's
24 Dervish and Banges
25 Three Broomsticks
26 Zonko's
27 Dragon Challenge
28 Hogwart's Express

The Lost Continent
29 Mythos Restaurant
30 Mystic Fountain
31 The Eighth Volage of Sindbad
32 Poseidon's Fury

Seuss Landing
33 Circus McGurkus Café Stoo-pendous
34 High In The Sky Seuss Trolley Train Ride
35 Caro-Seuss-el
36 If I Ran The Zoo
37 The Cat in the Hat
38 One Fish, Two Fish, Red Fish, Blue Fish

© Universal Orlando Resort

The High in the Sky Seuss Trolley Train Ride

from squirt ponds to beach scenes, while the lagoon-front area provides a quieter corner to escape the crowds.

Caro-Seuss-el: This intricate carousel ride on some of the Seuss characters – cowfish, elephant-birds and dog-a-lopes, for example – has rider-activated features that are a big hit with children. **AA** (**AAAA** under-5s).

One Fish, Two Fish, Red Fish, Blue Fish: A fairground ride with a twist as you pilot these Scussian fish up and down according to the rhyme that plays while you ride. Get it wrong and you get squirted! More fun for the younger set. **TTT** (**TTTTT** under-5s)

The Cat in the Hat: Prepare for a ride with a difference as you board these crazy 6-passenger 'couches' to meet the world's most adventurous cat and friends Thing One and Thing Two. You literally go for a spin through this storybook world, and it may be a bit much for very young children. The slow-moving queues are a bit of a drag, so try to get here early or leave it until later in the day. **AAAA**/**TTT**

If I Ran the Zoo: Interactive playgrounds don't get much better for the pre-school brigade than with these Seuss character scenarios, some of which can be pretty wet! Hugely imaginative and great fun to watch. **TTTTT** (under-5s)

The High in the Sky Seuss Trolley Train Ride: This fun family adventure high above Seuss Landing has terrific appeal to youngsters as you board a trolley to journey into the world of the Sneetches, visiting the Inking and Stamping Room, the Star Wash Room and a tour inside the Circus McGurkus Café Stoo-pendous. It is slow-paced and scenic, but it does draw slow-moving queues, so head here early with under-9s. **AAAA**

Character appearances: Look out for The Cat in the Hat, Thing One and Thing Two and The Grinch outside the Circus McGurkus, and the character-filled celebration of the Oh! The Stories You'll Hear street show.

Shopping: If the land has captivated you, you can buy the books at **Dr Seuss' All The Books You Can Read Store**, or a full variety of character merchandise at the **Mulberry Street Store**. **Snookers and Snookers Sweet Candy Cookers** is a super sweet shop.

Dining: Snacks and drinks can be had at **Hop On Pop Ice Cream Shop**, **Moose Juice Goose Juice** and **Green Eggs and Ham Café** (sandwiches and burgers). The **Circus McGurkus Café Stoo-pendous** is a mind-boggling eatery for fried chicken, lasagne, spaghetti, burgers and pizza – with clowns and pipe organs.

The Lost Continent

This land underwent a rather drastic reduction to accommodate Harry Potter, but it still offers some eye-catching locations.

The Eighth Voyage of Sindbad: This stunt and special effects show is fun for both elaborate staging and performance. Mythical adventurer

Seuss Landing

© Universal Orlando Resort

Sindbad and side-kick Kabob tackle evil witch Miseria in a bid to rescue Princess Amoura, and the action springs up in surprising places. There are several loud bangs that could scare young children but otherwise it's good family fun. The cast appear for photos and autographs post-show. **TT** AAAA

Poseidon's Fury: A walk-through show that puts its audience at the heart of the action as a journey in the company of a hapless young archaeologist takes a turn for the worse in the lost temple of Poseidon. You pass through an amazing water vortex before your expedition awakens an ancient demon. There is an element of suspense, but the special effects showdown between Poseidon and the demon is amazing. Queuing is tedious, but it is inside. **TTT**

Other entertainment: Try a bit of mystic manipulation with the **Psychic Readers**. But beware **The Mystic Fountain**; it can strike up a conversation – and then soak you!

Shopping: Find some original souvenirs at **The Coin Mint** (watch coins forged and struck) and **Coat Of Arms** (explore the history of your family name and coat of arms), **Treasures of Poseidon** (jewellery, clothing), and **The Pearl Factory** (pick an oyster).

Dining: Food options include **The Fire-Eater's Grill** (chicken fingers, hotdogs, salads, fries and drinks) and **Frozen Desert** (sundaes and sodas). The ornate **Mythos Restaurant** provides the best dining in IoA; the food (seafood, salads, grills, pizza and

Dragon Challenge

© Universal Orlando Resort

pasta) is first class, but the setting (inside a dormant volcano with fountains and clever lighting) is a real attraction (3-course meal $19–36, kids' meals $6.99–10.99).

Wizarding World of Harry Potter – Hogsmeade

This 'Island' has significantly boosted the park's attendance since it opened in 2010 and draws BIG crowds. The magnificent edifice of Hogwarts Castle looms large over the 20acre/8ha spread of the famous Wizarding World but the whole area is completely immersive as it uses the design genius behind the films. Entering from The Lost Continent area provides the grand view, through Hogsmeade and with Hogwarts seemingly towering above (the use of architectural perspective is masterful), and you are drawn into an all-encompassing realm where chimneys smoke, icicles glitter, owls roost, visitors are warned to 'Observe the spell limits' and Butterbeer is real!

Hogsmeade Village: Walk through the grand archway into the Wizarding World and a powerful sense of realism envelops you. This is a shimmering, snow-covered version of the magical settlement Harry, Ron and Hermione inhabit. It is the shopping and dining heart of the Wizarding World, but is an attraction in itself. Here you will find a wonderful photo opportunity with the **Hogwarts Express**, while nearly all the shop windows feature 'wizardly' animatronic touches. The Owl Clock comes to life every 15mins; the wooden-raftered Owlery is a work of art; and you may just encounter Moaning Myrtle in the loos! Numerous other clever effects and design touches all help to transform this corner of Florida into JK Rowling's authentic creation (see also Shopping and Dining). AAAAA+

Dragon Challenge: This towering coaster delves into the Goblet of Fire story involving the big contest between the wizarding schools of Hogwarts, Durmstrang and Beauxbatons, represented by the billowing banners at the entrance. The long, elaborate

Hagrid's Hut

queuing area (we LOVE the Corridor of Candles!) sets the scene for your 'flight' on either a Chinese Fireball or Hungarian Horntail dragon, with perils aplenty. You choose which dragon to ride (the tracks differ slightly) and this is a suspended coaster, so your legs dangle free – the initial drop is therefore like going into free-fall! Coaster aficionados reckon the best ride is in the back of the Hungarian (blue) dragon, but both offer an awesome experience. The coaster features a 100ft/30m drop, 5 rapid-fire inversions among the intertwined tracks and hits a top speed of 60mph/96kph. R: 4ft 6in/137cm; all loose items must be left in the lockers by the entrance. TTTTT+

🇬🇧 **BRITTIP**
The lockers for Dragon Challenge are in the Hogsmeade train station, but are free only for the duration of your ride. You MUST remove all metal objects from your pockets before riding.

The Flight of The Hippogriff:
This junior-sized coaster is aimed primarily at youngsters and features a journey into Hagrid's realm, where his love of outlandish creatures gives rise to this swooping ride. Hagrid offers instructions and warnings as you wind through the queue, and you may even hear Fang barking from inside his hut. There are no big

drops, but it delivers a surprisingly fast-paced whirl. Be sure to bow to the Hippogriff at the start of the ride. **R:** 3ft 4in/92cm. **TTT (TTTT for 6–12s)**

Harry Potter and the Forbidden Journey: This is the Big One: a trip inside the legendary halls of Hogwarts, and a breathtaking plunge on a state-of-the-art ride, Quidditch and all. The basic premise is that 'muggles' (non-wizarding types, i.e. you!) have been invited to tour the school for the first time and see much of the castle's interior. The queuing area is part discovery, part storytelling and part entertainment as it winds through, out, around and back in again for some 1,500ft/400m before you even get to the ride. Be ready for a LONG time on your feet as you traverse the corridors, traipse through the greenhouse, tiptoe along the Portrait Hall (where the paintings of the four founders of Hogwarts come to life in magical fashion) and tread the stone floors of the Gryffindor common room. Along the way, you'll be greeted by Professor Dumbledore in his study (complete with more talking portraits), be accosted by the Fat Lady (another painting-come-to-life) and enter the Defence Against the Dark Arts classroom, where Harry, Ron and Hermione urge visitors to abandon their 'boring' tour and come to the Quidditch match (with the aid of a magic spell).

Finally, you reach the Room of Requirement (past the Sorting Hat), where your mode of transport to the match is revealed – magical flying benches. With some pre-ride warnings, you are then strapped in to your 'bench' and are up, up and away. Only things don't go as planned and, before you can say 'Expecto Patronum' you're on a crazy dash through some of the young wizard's most dangerous adventures. Your unique ride vehicle – which moves on a giant robotic arm – sweeps you through dramatic settings that combine clever film technology with full-scale, all-encompassing scenery, creating a totally convincing effect as you move up, down, backwards, forwards and even sideways.

There is a close encounter with a fire-breathing dragon, an army of giant spiders, a Death Eater and a narrow escape from the clutches of the Whomping Willow before the big finale in a spooky underground cavern where it's up to Harry, naturally, to try to save the day. The 4min whirl will seem a LOT longer as the ride's breathtaking sequence of special effects make this an eye-popping extravaganza of sound, movement and high-tech dynamics. It is an astounding theme park experience, but it WILL scare small children (and those with arachnophobia!), and it draws HUGE queues – in excess of 2hrs at peak times – so you are strongly advised to do this early in the day. **R**: 4ft/122cm. **TTTTT+** NB: Universal's Express Pass does NOT cover this ride. You exit through **Filch's Emporium of Confiscated Goods**, where you'll find plush Hedwig owls, Crookshank cats, Scabbers rats and three-headed dogs (watch out, he growls!), plus a range of tempting Azkaban and House-related clothing and gifts. You also pick up your ride photos here ($30–35).

Harry Potter and the Forbidden Journey

© Universal Orlando Resort

© Universal Orlando Resort

Hogwart's Castle

Hogwart's Express: This is the new element in Hogsmeade, the 'northern' end of the famous train ride from King's Cross Station. With its own station (and queue area), it provides the full effect of arriving at or departing from this mythical Scottish village. The station is almost completely enclosed to allow the designers to build up the illusion, and then you pass through a small section of the Forbidden Forest to reach Hogsmeade itself and enjoy your first full view of the village with Hogwarts towering behind it. The ride from Hogsmeade to King's Cross is also different, screen-wise, from the one that brings you here, with more scenes of London and some of Harry's other exploits from the films. Don't forget, you need a 2-park ticket to ride the Express, or you can pay the extra fee at the ticket office. AAAAA+

BRITTIP

Butterbeer is non-alcoholic and comes in three sweet varieties, 'regular', frozen (slushie style) and hot. Try them all as they taste quite different! It's also usually easier to get served in the Hog's Head rather than at the busy street carts.

Other entertainment: The **TriWizard Spirit Rally** celebrates the upcoming tournament, with the Beauxbatons Academy ribbon dancers and staff-fighting wizards from Durmstrang Institute. Hogwarts is represented by the **Frog Choir** (four students and two enormous frogs!), an ensemble whose vocal talents result in an entertaining show.

Shopping: As with all things here, the level of detail given to shopping and dining locations is so intricate they are attractions in their own right. Whether you pull your wallet out or not, be sure to have a wander through each to soak up the atmosphere. When shopping, be sure to visit the famous sweetshop **Honeydukes**, the place to buy Cauldron Cakes, Bertie Bott's Every Flavour Beans, Chocolate Frogs and more. Find 136 varieties of sweets, many from the Harry Potter films or well-known British favourites (including jelly babies, humbugs and sherbet lemons). **Dervish and Banges** supplies 'students' with Quidditch gear and school related clothing, Luna Lovegood's 3-D Quibbler, and even the Nimbus 2001 broomsticks. At **Owl Post**, you can buy your wand, and don't miss sending a letter by owl! Your mail will receive one of four different Hogsmeade postmarks, a detail friends and family back home can enjoy. Also here are stationery and owl-related gifts. Every wizard needs a wand, and **Ollivander's** has 13 varieties to choose from. Here, 'the wand also chooses the wizard,' with surprising special effects similar to those Harry experienced when choosing his wand. Because the environment is interactive and the shop is small, a limited number are allowed inside for each 'show' and wait times are long all day. AAAAA

Dining: There is only one sit-down dining location here, but it's a corker. A 'Cathedral to Butterbeer', the **Three Broomsticks** menu features British favourites such as shepherd's pie, fish and chips and Cornish pasties, along with the Great Feast, a family-style meal of salad, ribs, chicken, roast potatoes and corn on the cob ($50 party of 4; $12.99 per extra person). Entrées $10–16.49, with desserts $3.49–5.29, including strawberry and peanut-butter ice cream, found only in the Wizarding World. They also serve a different menu for breakfast. Next door is the **Hog's Head Pub**, complete with animatronic boar's

© Universal Orlando Resort

Jurassic Park River Adventure

head, where you'll find Hog's Head Brew ($7.50–8.50 a pint).

> **BRITTIP**
>
> Of all the buildings, the Three Broomsticks is a must-see experience of dramatic interior design and special effects. Look up in the rafters for arriving owls, magical maids and the roaming House Elf!

All in all, it's an immense collection of dramatic and charming elements (witness the animated Prisoner of Azkaban poster in Hogsmeade) that add up to a vivid portrayal of JK Rowling's work. You don't need to be

Three Broomsticks

© Universal Orlando Resort

a fan to enjoy the Wizarding World and, like the Diagon Alley area in Universal Studios, the only snag is the huge crowd it draws for much of the day, as most of the shops are quite small and quickly feel congested. Arriving early is highly advisable (hence the early entry perk with Universal hotels is so valuable here), but you should also try to see it after dark, when the lighting effects make it even more dramatic.

Jurassic Park

Now travel back to the Cretaceous age and the make-believe dinosaur film world where extravagant scenery will have you looking over your shoulder for stray dinos.

Jurassic Park River Adventure: From scenic splendour, the mood changes to hidden menace as your journey into this waterborne realm brings you up close and personal with some realistic dinosaurs. Inevitably, your passage is diverted to the hazardous, and the danger increases as the 16-person raft travels through the main building – with raptors loose everywhere. You are aware of something large lurking in the shadows – will you fall prey to the T-Rex, or will your boat take the 85ft/26m plunge to safety (plus a good soaking)? Queues usually move briskly but will top an hour in mid-afternoon. **R**: 3ft 6in/106cm. The ride photo comes in various packages ($30–35). **TTTT**

BRITTIP

Keep your valuables dry on the River Adventure by leaving them in the lockers at the start of the queue.

Pteranodon Flyers: The slow-moving queues are a major turn-off, especially for a fairly average ride, which glides gently over much of Jurassic Park (though it reaches a height of almost 30ft/9m). **R**: It is designed mainly for kids, and anyone OVER the height range of 3ft–4ft 8in/91–142cm (usually 11+) must be accompanied by a child of the right height. **TT** (**TTTT** under-9s). The Universal Express pass is not valid here, either.

Camp Jurassic: More excellent kids' fare with the mountainous jungle giving way to an 'active' volcano for youngsters to explore, climb and slide down. Squirt guns and spitter dinosaurs add to the fun (for kids, but parents can explore!). **TTTT**

Discovery Center: This indoor centre offers various interactive games, like creating a dinosaur via DNA sequencing, mixing your own DNA with a dino on a touch screen, seeing through the eyes of various large reptiles and handling 'dino eggs', plus other hands-on exhibits. It's ideal in summer as it's fully air-conditioned (10am–4pm; 5pm peak season). **AAA**

Other entertainment: The more adventurous can try the **Rock Climbing Wall** (just outside River Adventure) for an extra $5, while there are also fairground games at an extra $6 a time, or $25 for five games.

Shopping: Visit **Dinostore** and **Jurassic Outfitters** for the best shopping.

Dining: Try **Burger Digs** (huge burger platters), **Pizza Predatoria**, **Thunder Falls Terrace** (counter service rotisserie chicken, ribs, burgers, turkey legs and salads, plus a great view of River Adventure) or the **Watering Hole** (hot dogs, snacks and drinks).

Skull Island

This new 'land' opened in June 2016, featuring a chance to see the great ape himself.

Skull Island: Reign of Kong: Get ready to be at the centre of a battle between the mighty gorilla and marauding dinosaurs in a world created by Peter Jackson's 2005 remake of *King Kong* (and the new *Skull Island* movie in 2017). It is themed around a 1930s expedition to the mysterious isle, where, predictably, it all goes seriously wrong, and prehistoric predators are determined to eat your crew. Part

Skull Island: Reign of Kong

ride, part 3-D film spectacular, this large-scale truck journey encounters all manner of scary beasts, culminating in a big finale with a giant animatronic version of Kong that leaves riders convinced they face a terrible fate! The use of new high-def projection equipment, wrap-around film screens, superb sound systems and other effects make for a realistic environment, and the immense nature of the queue area, with warnings of weird Skull Island creatures (think extra-large bugs!), is worth seeing on its own. **R:** 36in/92cm, 36in–48in/123cm with adult. Parental discretion advised, no expectant mothers. But, although there are no ride restrictions, this may be too intense for most youngsters. **TTTT/AAAAA**.

Toon Lagoon

The thrills continue here with a watery theme and more comic-book elements from (US) newspaper cartoon characters. Children will also love the fountains, squirt pools and overflowing fire hydrants!

Popeye and Bluto's Bilge-Rat Barges: Every park seems to have a variation on the white-water raft ride, but this is one of the wettest! Fast, bouncy and unpredictable, it has water coming at you from every direction, a couple of sizeable drops and a whirl through the Octo-plus Grotto that adds to the fun. If you don't want to get wet, don't ride, because there is no escaping the deluge here. This is also one of the top five for long queues (at least when it's hot), but it's worth the wait. **R:** 4ft/ 122cm. Look for the Water Blasters (for 50c) on the bridge to give riders a wet start. **TTTTT**

Popeye and Bluto's Bilge-Rat Barges

© Universal Orlando Resort

Dudley Do-Right's Ripsaw Falls: A flume ride that sends its passengers on a wild (and steep!) journey in the company of guileless Mountie Dudley Do-Right, bidding to save girlfriend Nell from the evil Snidely Whiplash. The action builds to an explosive finale at the top of a 75ft/27m abyss that drops you through the roof of a ramshackle dynamite shack to the lagoon below. Wet? You bet! **R:** 3ft 8in/111cm. **TTTTT** More Water Blasters on the bridge overlooking the final drop get riders even wetter.

Me Ship, The Olive: A kids' playland designed as a three-storey boat full of interactive fun, including water cannons, bells and slides (ideal for squirting riders on the Bilge-Rat Barges below), in best Popeye style. **TTTT** (for youngsters).

Other entertainment: Comic Strip Lane is the place to meet the Classic Comic Book Characters like Beetle Bailey, Hagar the Horrible, Betty Boop, Popeye, and Dudley Do-Right. Plus various **fairground stall games** for $6, $25 for five games.

Shopping: There is the usual array of character shops, like **Gasoline Alley**, **Boop Oop A Doop** and **Toon Extra**.

Dining: Grab a humongous sandwich at **Blondie's** (home of the Dagwood), a trademark burger at **Wimpy's**, sample the food court of **Comic Strip Café** (burgers, fish, chicken, Chinese dishes, pizza and pasta), something cool at **Cathy's Ice Cream** or a cold beverage at **Ale To The Chief**.

Marvel Super-Hero Island

Finally, you arrive at total immersion in super-hero comic-book pages, with some of the best rides in the park.

The Incredible Hulk Coaster: Roller-coasters don't come much

ISLANDS OF ADVENTURE with children

Our guide to the attractions that generally appeal to the different age groups:

Under-5s
Caro-Seuss-el, The Cat in the Hat, High In The Sky Seuss Trolley Train Ride, If I Ran The Zoo, Jurassic Park Discovery Center, Me Ship, The Olive, One Fish, Two Fish, Red Fish, Blue Fish.

5–8s
All the above, plus Amazing Adventures Of Spider-Man, Camp Jurassic, Eighth Voyage of Sindbad, Flight of the Hippogriff, Harry Potter and the Forbidden Journey (if tall enough), Hogwarts Express, Jurassic Park River Adventure (with parental discretion), Pteranodon Flyers, Storm Force Accelatron.

9–12s
Amazing Adventures Of Spider-Man, Camp Jurassic, The Cat in the Hat, Dr Doom's Fearfall, Dudley Do-Right's Ripsaw Falls, Dragon Challenge, Eighth Voyage Of Sindbad, Flight of the Hippogriff, Harry Potter and the Forbidden Journey, Hogwarts Express, Incredible Hulk Coaster, Jurassic Park Discovery Center, Jurassic Park River Adventure, Popeye and Bluto's Bilge-Rat Barges, Pteranodon Flyers, Skull Island: Reign of Kong (with parental discretion),Storm Force Accelatron.

Over-12s
Amazing Adventures Of Spider-Man, Dr Doom's Fearfall, Dudley Do-Right's Ripsaw Falls, Dragon Challenge, Eighth Voyage Of Sindbad, Harry Potter and the Forbidden Journey, Hogwarts Express, Incredible Hulk Coaster, Jurassic Park Discovery Center, Jurassic Park River Adventure, Popeye and Bluto's Bilge-Rat Barges, Skull Island: Reign of Kong, Storm Force Accelatron.

more dramatic than this giant green edifice (completely rebuilt in 2016) that soars over the lagoon, blasting 0–40mph/64kph in 2secs, and reaching a top speed of 65mph/105kph. It looks awesome, sounds stunning and rides like a demon as you enter the gamma-ray world of Dr David Banner, aka the Incredible Hulk, and zoom into a weightless inversion 100ft/30m up.

 BRITTIP

At the Hulk Coaster, keep left where the queue splits up and you will be in line for the front car for an even more extreme Hulk experience.

Just watching is mind-boggling, and the effects are brain scrambling! Deposit ANY loose articles in the lockers at the front of the building

The Incredible Hulk Coaster loading platform

as the ride is guaranteed to shake anything out of your pockets. Crowds build up rapidly but queues move reasonably quickly. **R:** 4ft 6in/137cm. While DVDs of your ride are no longer available, you can purchase various photo packages from $20–65.

Dr Doom's Fearfall: Dr Doom's latest creation, Fearfall is a device for sucking fear out of his victims, and YOU are about to test it as 16 riders at a time are strapped into chairs at the bottom of a 200ft/60m tower. The dry ice rolls, and whoosh! Up you go at breakneck speed, only to plummet back seemingly even faster, with a split second when you feel suspended in mid-air. Summon up the courage to do this and we promise an astonishing (if brief!) experience. Substantial queues from mid-day. **R:** 4ft 4in/132cm. **TTTTT+**

The Amazing Adventures Of Spider- Man: A visit to the Daily Bugle, home of ace reporter Peter Parker (aka Spider-Man) turns into a mission in a 'Scoop' vehicle – and an audio-visual extravaganza. This roving 3-D motion simulator takes you into a battle with super-villains that includes a convincing 'drop' off a skyscraper. There are special effects aplenty and the whole ride is loaded with the 'wow' factor. Go early on or wait until late in the day – queues often top an hour by mid-morning. **R:** 3ft 4in/101cm. **TTTTT+** PS: If this seems similar to the TRANSFORMERS ride at Universal Studios, it's because they use the same ride platform.

BRITTIP

You can beat some of the queues on the Spider-Man ride at busy times by opting for the Single Rider queue.

Storm Force Accelatron: This ride, primarily for kids, puts you in the middle of a battle between X-Men heroine Storm and arch-nemesis Magneto. It's basically an updated spinning-cup ride but with some neat twists (like a 3-way rotation where the cars look set to collide). **TTT (TTTTT under-12s)**

BRITTIP

For some of the park's best shopping bargains, visit Port Provisions right by the exit gates (to the left as you come through) where all the merchandise is 30–50% off.

Other entertainment: The **Marvel Super-Heroes** appear here periodically for photos and autographs, while **Spider-Man** has his own meet-and-greet booth at The Marvel Alterniverse Store. A high energy **video arcade** can be found at the exit to Dr Doom's Fearfall.

Shopping: Each ride has its own character merchandise, while the **Comic Book Shop** and **Marvel Alterniverse Shop** sell other souvenirs.

Dining: For a bite to eat, try the Italian buffeteria **Café 4** (pizza, pasta, sandwiches and salads) or a burger, chicken fingers or salad at the **Captain America Diner**. And that, folks, is the full low-down on arguably the world's most thrilling and complete theme park. Not to be missed!

Springfield at Universal Orlando

SeaWorld

SeaWorld is firmly established as one of the most popular parks for its more peaceful and naturalistic aspect, the change of pace it offers and lack of substantial queues. It is large enough to handle big crowds well (though it still gets busy in peak season) and is a big hit with families in particular, but it has some fabulous rides and imaginative attractions too, including Antarctica: Empire of the Penguin, and a major new roller-coaster with the huge Mako.

Part of the SeaWorld Parks & Entertainment group, along with sister parks Busch Gardens in Tampa, with its animal encounters and roller-coasters (p200); Discovery Cove, an exotic tropical 'island' with dolphin, coral reef and snorkelling adventures (p196); and water-park Aquatica (p245), this makes for excellent multi-day tickets, notably Discovery Cove's Ultimate Ticket, which includes all four parks. SeaWorld's recent additions and brilliant Christmas overlay (p37) mean this remains a fresh and invigorating place to visit.

Happily, this is still a park where you can proceed at a relatively leisurely pace, see what you want without too much jostling and yet feel you have been well entertained (even if the restaurants get crowded at mealtimes). SeaWorld is a good starting point if this is your first Orlando visit as it gives you the hang of negotiating the vast areas, navigating by maps and learning to plan around the show times. There are special offers for booking online at **www.seaworld.com**, where you can print your tickets to save waiting in the queue, plus a website for UK visitors – **www.seaworldparks.co.uk**.

SeaWorld at a glance

Location	7007 SeaWorld Drive, off Central Florida Parkway (Junctions 71 and 72 off I-4)
Size	More than 200 acres/81ha, incorporating 26 attractions
Hours	9am–6pm off peak; 9am–7, 8 or 9pm some weekends; 9am–9pm high season (Easter, summer holidays, Thanksgiving, Christmas)
Admission	Under-3s free; 3–9 $94 (1-day ticket), $139 (2-Visit ticket, with 2nd day at SeaWorld, Aquatica or Busch Gardens, ages 3 and up), adult (10+) $99.
Parking	$18, $23 preferred parking
Lockers	Inside Entrance Plaza (next to Sweet Sailin' Candy), $10 and $13 and $15 (rent from Pushchair and Wheelchair location)
Pushchairs	$15 and $25, to right of Guest Services inside park
Wheelchairs	$12 manual, $50 electric, $65 ECV with canopy; with pushchairs
Top attractions	TurtleTrek, Antarctica: Empire Of The Penguin, One Ocean, Shark Encounter, Journey To Atlantis, Kraken, Manta, Wild Arctic, Blue Horizons, Mako
Don't miss	Manatee Rehabilitation, behind-the-scenes tours, Dolphin Nursery, dining at Sharks Underwater Grill

Hidden costs	**Meals**	Burger, chips and coke $13.28 3-course lunch $42–59 (Sharks Underwater Grill) Kids' meal $6.69 $13 at Sharks Underwater Gril
	T-shirts	$20–28
	Souvenirs	$1.99–1,500
	Sundries	Glitter Tattoo $10; Henna $17–27

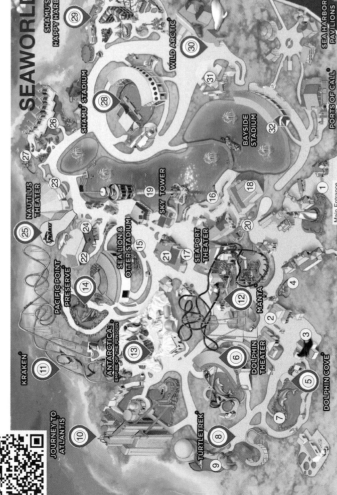

Tours

Private VIP Tour: 7hr tour with individual guide and reserved seats for the 3 main shows, just for your family or group, including preferred parking, animal interactions and lunch at Sharks Underwater Grill ($249/person).

Dolphin Encounter: Learn how SeaWorld cares for its resident dolphins with this opportunity to see the park's animal team in action at Dolphin Cove, learning about their behaviour and having a 5min interaction when you can touch a dolphin ($15/person).

BRITTIP

The great variety of behind-the-scenes tours provide great insight into the park's conservation and research programmes, as well as its entertainment resources. Book in advance: online, call 1 888 800 5447 or visit the Guided Tours counter.

Dolphins Up-Close Tour: Meet the park's resident dolphins during this 1hr hands-on tour, and learn the hand signals trainers use to communicate with the dolphins ($49 and $19)

Sharks Up-Close Tour: A chance to go backstage at the 700,000-gallon aquarium and learn how SeaWorld cares for its sharks. Visitors will also touch a small shark and hear about vital conservation issues ($15).

Sea Lions Up-Close Tour: A 1hr walking tour focusing on the care and training of the stars of the Clyde & Seamore show, including a photo with them and a chance to feed the Pacific Point Preserve sea lions ($44–59 and $24–39).

Penguins Up-Close Tour: This 45min family walk goes behind the scenes at Antarctica: Empire of the Penguin to learn the proper care for these cute birds and gives visitors the chance to interact with and touch a penguin ($59–79 and $39–59).

Wild Arctic Up-Close Experience: An interactive 60min tour into the care and animal interactions with the walrus, seals and beluga whales at this in-depth exhibit ($59 79/person, ages eight and up only).

Family Fun at Christmas Tour: A 3hr guided tour of the top children's attractions, with a penguin meet-and-greet, reserved seats at Elmo's Christmas Wish show, a meal at Santa's Fireside Feast and front-of-line access to the Polar Express Experience, finishing with an exclusive meet 'n' greet with Santa Claus ($59–79).

Marine Mammal Keeper Experience: An interactive programme, this takes two visitors daily to discover the care needed to rehabilitate injured manatees, plus bottle-feed some of them, meet the seals and walruses and prepare meals for the beluga whales (starts at 6.30am; lasts around 8hrs; $399/person including lunch, T-shirt, special book, souvenir photo and 7-day SeaWorld pass; must be 13 or older).

Behind The Scenes Tour: Join a knowledgeable tour guide for a 75min look backstage at the park's rescue

Sealion pup born at SeaWorld

and rehab facilities, including rescued manatees and sea turtles, as well as touch a shark and interact with a penguin ($29–39 and $9–19).

Expedition SeaWorld: Gain insight into the park and its inhabitants during this 6hr walking tour, which includes premium show seating, stingray and dolphin food, All Day Dining Deal and Quick Queue Unlimited. ($79–99 and $59–79)

Location

SeaWorld is located off Central Florida Parkway, between I-4 (exit 71 going east or 72 heading west) and I-Drive. It is still best to arrive before the opening time so you're in good position to book a backstage tour, dash to one of the attractions that draws a crowd, like Mako, Manta and Antarctica, or buy QuickQueue, the park's limited number of paid-for passes that provide front-of-the-line access to each of the main rides (priced seasonally at $20–35). There is also a Signature Show Seating option at $14–29/person.

The park covers more than 200acres/81ha, with five shows, six major rides, 10 large-scale continuous viewing attractions and seven smaller ones, plus a smart range of shops and restaurants. Try to eat before midday or after 2.30pm for a crowd-free lunch, and before 5.30pm if you want a leisurely dinner (better still, book Sharks Underwater Grill).

SeaWorld is arranged in various 'seas' on the park map but they are hard to follow, hence you will need to keep the map close to hand to navigate, as there is also a fair bit of to-ing and fro-ing to catch the various shows, with the show schedule listed on the back of the map. Going in a clockwise direction, here's what you find.

Port of Entry

Coming through the turnstiles brings you to the park's main business area, including the Information & Reservations kiosk, Lost & Found, and lockers, pushchair and wheelchair hire. You will also find some good shopping and snack options here. Look for **Shamu Emporium** for the full range of SeaWorld souvenirs, and **Sea World Rescue Store** for gifts and clothing, while **Adventure Photos** provides all your park pictures taken by the SeaWorld photographers. You can grab a quick breakfast (tasty pastries and coffee) at **Cypress Bakery** or

Returning sea turtles to the wild

Stingray Lagoon

something colder from the **Polar Parlor Ice Cream**. This is also the place for a photo opportunity with Shamu and friends.

All Day Dining Deal: Also worth considering, a wristband gives unlimited visits to seven restaurants (Spice Mill, Voyager's – excluding their baby-back ribs and sampler/ combo/ brisket platters – Mango Joe's, Seaport Pizza, Seafire Inn and Terrace BBQ, and Expedition Cafe), claiming an entrée, side dish or dessert and standard non-alcoholic drink each time ($34.99 and $19.99). It's good value if you eat at least twice in the park and can be booked at the Information & Reservations desk.

Photokey: If you'd like to collect all your SeaWorld photos digitally, including ride photos and character meet-and-greets (but not backstage tours), then sign up for this new service – either online in advance or when you arrive at the park – for a one-off $75 (**www.seaworld.com/ photokey**).

Sea of Shallows

A whole collection of exhibits is grouped together here, as well as the eye-catching Dolphin Theater and one of the signature rides.

There is also a clever Key West theme, starting with **Stingray Lagoon**, where you can feed (for $5) and touch fully grown rays, and there's a nursery for newborn rays. The centrepiece, though, is the 2.1acre/0.8ha **Dolphin**

Cove, a spectacular, naturalistic development that is home to a frisky community of Atlantic bottlenose dolphins, who make for great viewing, including from a special underwater window.

The whole Key West area is designed in the eclectic, tropical flavour of America's most southerly city, but it also underlines the environmental message through interactive graphics and video displays, and children will find it a fun, educational experience. AAA

Blue Horizons: This wonderful production serves up a big helping of dramatic animal behaviour in best Broadway style. It features dolphins, exotic birds (including an Andean condor), and a lot more besides as the general (and rather abstract) theme of a girl's dream about maritime wildlife is brought to life. The elaborate set design has a 40ft/12m sea-meets-sky backdrop that also conceals

Blue Horizons

the setting for a host of additional performers, from high divers to bungee jumpers and trapeze-like aerialists. There is subtle interaction between trainers and animals as the show moves from one scene to the next, both above and below the water, but there is plenty to admire as the stage is filled with graceful and daring action. A stirring score by the Seattle Symphony Orchestra underpins the complex staging and Broadway-style costumes and it makes for a magnificent 25mins that often draws a huge ovation. **AAAAA**

Manta: This ride turns a high-tech coaster into a unique mixture of ride and animal encounter. The elaborate queuing area winds through cool, rocky caverns, passing waterfalls and floor-to-ceiling windows showcasing some 300 rays and thousands of fish, which lead through to the 'undersea world' of the manta ray. Themed like a giant ray, riders are swung into a face-down position before being launched into an exhilarating series of four inversions along 3,359ft/1,024m of track, reaching nearly 60mph/96kph and 140ft/43m high as well as skimming the surface of the lagoon. The 'flying' nature of the coaster and smooth ride vehicles make this an original. It has great spectator appeal

and there is a separate walk-though aquarium with its own entry. Lockers located near the queue entry are available for use during your ride ($1/hour, $2/additional hours). **R:** 54in/137cm. **TTTTT**. For the most powerful effects of the Manta G-forces, opt for the back rows.

TurtleTrek: Right behind the Dolphin Theater is this thrilling experience that is part exhibit and part show. You enter down a ramp that introduces you to the undersea world of the sea turtle and marine conservation, passing by two huge man-made lagoons, the first for the endangered manatee and then some of SeaWorld's rescued turtles. A marine life host introduces the next part of the Trek and the doors open to reveal a domed cinema where you don 3-D glasses. Suddenly, you are in the world of the sea turtle, sharing the life-cycle journey from the dangers of leaving the egg to life in the open ocean and then the final return to the same beach where it was born. It all takes place in an immersive 3-D environment (you have to remember not to hold your breath!) with graphic encounters with a marauding crab, sharks and dolphins. You exit back up another ramp to two open-air pools (the top view of the lagoons you see

Manta

below) where you can learn more about sea turtle life and see them and the manatees being fed. There is also a TurtleTrek video game for kids, and another open-air exhibit showcasing some Florida alligators. AAAAA NB: The menace of the crab in the early scene may be a bit scary for very young children.

Other entertainment: The **Dolphin Nursery** provides wonderful close-up views with some of the park's younger dolphins. A new **Manatee Rehabilitation** area provides an up-close view of recovering manatees, with information boards and animal keepers on hand. Well worth making time for.

Shopping: There are three main gift shops here, the best being **Coconut Bay Traders** and **Trek Treasures** (apparel and soft toys), as well as **Manta Photo & Gifts**.

Dining: You can grab a turkey leg, cheese nachos or chicken tenders at **Captain Pete's Hot Dogs** or ice cream at **Dippin' Dots**, plus drinks, snacks and refills and several cart-style kiosks.

◀▌▶ **BRITTIP**
For a great soft drink deal, buy any souvenir cup at one of the restaurants for $11.99 and get free refills all day (or for $1.29 all season).

Sea of Legends
Continue past Dolphin Theater and you come to the park's serious thrill quotient.

Journey to Atlantis: This terrific water-coaster is a combination of special effects and water-ride that becomes a runaway roller-coaster. The discovery of Atlantis in your eight-passenger 'fishing boat' starts gently through the lost city. But evil spirit Allura takes over and riders plunge into a dash through Atlantis, dodging gushing fountains and water cannons, with hundreds of holographic and laser-generated illusions before the 60ft/18m drop and the entry to the roller-coaster finale back in the candle-filled catacombs. Be ready to get soaked,

which is great in summer but not so clever first thing on a winter morning. R: 3ft 6in/106cm. **TTTTT**

Kraken: One of Florida's most breathtaking roller-coasters, based on the mythical sea monster, it is an innovative pedestal ride (you are effectively sitting in a chair without a floor) that plunges an initial 144ft/44m, hits 65mph/105kph, dives underground three times, adds seven inversions (including a vertical loop, a diving loop, a zero-gravity roll and a cobra roll) and a flat spin before riders escape the beast's lair. The ride from the front row, especially down an opening drop at an angle best described as ludicrous, is blood-curdling, and sitting in the rear is thrilling, too. R: 4ft 6in/137cm. **TTTTT+**

Shopping: Don't miss the **Golden Seahorse** and **Jewel of the Sea** as you exit Journey to Atlantis, a combination gift shop and aquarium full of tropical fish (remember to look upwards), while there are coaster-orientated souvenirs in **Kraken Gifts** and **Manta Gifts**.

Dining: High Seas Market offers convenient grab-and-go snacks and drinks, and there is a **Dippin' Dots** for ice cream.

Sea of Ice
Getting back to the animal side of the park brings you to one of the most eye-catching sections of any park. It is both an extensive, themed area in its own right – and an amazing ride. It is the biggest expansion in SeaWorld history and their most immersive environment to date, an epic journey

Kraken

Antarctica: Empire of the Penguins

into the snow and ice-covered realm of the South Pole and its inhabitants.

Antarctica: Empire of the Penguin: Once you walk between the towering ice-and-snow-capped 'mountains,' the (indoor) ride awaits. It begins with a dramatic presentation about penguin life and then takes visitors on a unique expedition into the heart of the continent, following the story and guidance of Puck, a young Gentoo penguin. Guests board special vehicles in groups of eight and choose their own level of ride experience, either 'Mild' or 'Wild', and then set off through a mix of simulation and film elements that offer a realistic taste of the polar region, above and below the penguins' icy world, moving seemingly at random and with no obvious track. The dangers – including a typical Antarctic storm – and beauty of life in this extreme realm are graphically depicted as you track Puck's own life journey through the world's most extreme landscape before you then step out through a real penguin colony (cleverly but minimally screened off) to experience more of their 'empire.' And guess what? It is cold; like, *really* cold (the temperature drops during the ride, reaching -1C by the end) and you may want to visit the gift shop for a scarf or gloves before you set off! The Wild version of the ride is more fast-paced, with various bumps, slides, spins and rolls, but 'Mild' is still designed for all the family, with no height restriction. AAAAA+ This can also draw long queues throughout the afternoon.

BRITTIP

Take a look at the main 'mountain' in Antarctica. Does the shape look familiar? Yes, that's right – the whole edifice has been shaped like a towering mother penguin on the left, with her baby to the right.

Other entertainment: After the ride, there is a spectacular two-storey **underwater viewing area** where you can see the different species of penguin – Rockhopper, King, Adelie and Gentoo – at play. Then, back out in Antarctica, you can marvel at this realistic environment, which includes a special **Penguin Wall** for photo opportunities, and flatscreen TVs that offer more info about the region's main inhabitants. It even has its own original musical score that evokes images of the windswept frozen continent.

Shopping: Lone gift shop **Glacial Collections** has a huge selection of all things penguin-orientated and cuddly.

Dining: Expedition Café provides Italian, Asian and American food choices from their show kitchen which you can then enjoy in one of two clever 'Quonset Huts' that provide a South Pole setting.

BRITTIP

Be sure to come back to Antarctica at night to see how the brilliant blue lighting makes the whole setting even more impressive.

Sea of Delight

This extensive area features two more live shows plus some of the park's best dining and shopping.

Sea Lion and Otter Theater: The venue for another live show, this features the resident pinnipeds in *Clyde and Seamore's Sea Lion High,*

and offers 25mins of slapstick and watery stunts, with guest appearances by Opie Otter and Sir Winston Walrus. The basic premise is that Clyde and Seamore are in danger of flunking their high school exams and need help to get the necessary grades, which is the cue for all manner of school-type jokes and amazing antics from the animals (often at the expense of their human assistants!). The educational pre-show celebrates teachers the world over. AAAA

Pacific Point Preserve: A natural rocky habitat for the park's seals and sea lions with a hidden wave machine and lively talks from park attendants. You can also buy smelt ($5 per tray or five trays for $20) to feed the animals. AAA

Pets Ahoy!: Just inside the Waterfront is the air-conditioned haven of the Seaport Theater, which hosts this cute 25min giggle featuring an unlikely menagerie of dogs, cats, birds, rats, pot-bellied pigs and others, most from local animal rescue shelters. AAA. The Theater is also home to the seasonal show *Elmo's Christmas Wish,* when the Sesame Street characters help Elmo discover his Christmas wish.

Pacific Point Preserve

Sky Tower: This 400ft/122m landmark offers slowly rotating rides for a bird's-eye view of the park and surrounding areas. It used to cost extra but is now open to all-comers. NB: It will close if windy. AAA

Other entertainment: Look out for the zany antics of **The Longshoremen** periodically, as the hapless trio try their hand at various maintenance tasks.

Shopping: The **Waterfront** shops offer an extensive shopping plaza with a stylish range of souvenirs and other gift items (notably at **Allura's Treasure Trove** and **Artisans Hall**) while **Oyster's Secret** features the chance to see pearl divers in action (and buy a pearl afterwards).

Dining: The excellent eateries are: **Seafire Grille** (Fajitas, sandwiches, Tex-Mex); **Voyagers Smokehouse** BBQ (smoked chicken, barbecue ribs, salads, turkey sandwich and a children's menu with chicken nuggets, hot dog, macaroni and cheese, turkey sandwich or junior portion of ribs); and **Spice Mill Burgers** (flame-grilled burgers, salads, sandwiches, a low-fat vegetarian chilli), plus **Seaport Pizza** for cheese and pepperoni pizza. There are also three snack bars: **Café de Mar** for pastries, coffees, smoothies and soft drinks; and **Turkey Legs** for huge smoked turkey legs. The **SandBar** is a water's edge hideaway, serving beer, wine and snacks – THE place to watch the sun go down, or for Happy Hour from 3–5pm.

Rockhopper Penguins

🇬🇧 BRITTIP

Grab an evening meal at The Spice Mill, then head out on to its open-air terrace for one of the best seats in the house for the view over the central Lagoon – idyllic in summer.

Shark Wreck Reef

Continuing the clockwise tour brings you towards the back of the park and this newly re-themed 'underwater' area with the showpiece Mako ride.

Shark Encounter: Top of the bill, the world's largest collection of dangerous sea creatures can be found here, brought dramatically to life by the walk-through tubes that surround you with more than 50 prowling sharks (including sand tigers, black tips, nurse sharks and sandbars), sawfish, tropical fish and gigantic groupers. It's an eerie experience, but brilliantly presented and highly informative. Queues build up here at peak times. AAAA TTTT

The **Nautilus Theater** is home to weekend events throughout the year, notably Jack Hanna's Animal Adventure.

Mako: SeaWorld's dramatic new steel rollercoaster – the tallest and fastest in Orlando – rises up between the Shark Encounter and Nautilus Theater, giving the park another iconic ride for its growing collection. It reaches 200ft high and 73mph and is named and themed for the world's fastest shark, hence it's sure to give adrenalin junkies a real blast. Although there are no inversions, its big initial drop, tight twists and turns, fast pace and multiple 'air time' moments provide plenty of thrills, including a breathtaking U-shaped 'Hammerhead' turn and several camelbacks. TTTTT R: 54in/137cm.

🇬🇧 BRITTIP

Looking for a quiet spot for a break? Seek out the terrace along the lagoon (with tables and chairs) directly behind Fins gift shop and across from Sharks Underwater Grill.

Other entertainment: The flamingo pedal-boats on the lagoon rent for $5 per 20min (for two). You can also feed the sharks and stingrays outside **Shark Encounter** ($5 per tray). Also nearby is the revamped **Sea Garden**, a lovely spot for some time off your feet. As well as several clever sea-creature sculptures made completely out of reclaimed rubbish washed up on America's beaches by http://WashedAshore.org, the **Animal Connections** meet-and-greets here allow for encounters several times daily with various rescued and rehabilitated animals, including two small ponies, a possum, various hawks, a Kookaburra, a great horned owl, a Crested Caracara, a groundhog and others. Bring your camera, as photos are encouraged.

Shopping: There are 2 small-scale shops, **Fins Gifts**, for toys, apparel and jewellery, and the **Mako** store for all things shark-like.

Dining: At the entrance to Shark Encounter is the top dining choice, **Sharks Underwater Grill**, with an amazing backdrop for your meal in a subterranean environment (check out the mini-aquarium bar), and an upmarket menu of 'Floribbean' cuisine, blending local and spicy Caribbean fare. The emphasis is on seafood – with various wonderful creations – plus pasta, steaks and chicken, as well as fab desserts, cocktails (including non-alcoholic) and menus for under-10s. Open from 11.30am to an hour before park closing, it's busy at lunch but quieter in late afternoon, so we advise booking (at the restaurant) as soon as you arrive. The **Lakeside Panini Bistro** (high season only) offers fresh-grilled panini sandwiches, salads and drinks while the **Terrace BBQ** features delicious barbecue platters ($11.49–16.99) and the **Terrace Bar** serves craft beers.

Sea of Fun

This section is primarily for kids, with a fabulous children's play area, eight junior-sized rides, various snack kiosks and a delicious new pretzel café.

Shamu's Happy Harbor: 4acres/1.6ha of brilliantly designed adventure playground and rides await youngsters of all ages here. Activities include a 4-storey net climb, two tented ball rooms to wade through, a giant trampoline tent, a mock pirate ship and a water play area, **Water Works** (great on a hot day). The signature junior-sized coaster **Shamu Express** offers mild thrills over more than 800ft/245m of track (and a framed ride photo for $19.99). The **Jazzy Jellies** is a jellyfish-themed samba tower ride that lifts and spins, while **Swishy Fishes** features oversized seats that spin round a giant waterspout. **Flying Fiddler** (a 20ft/6.1m tower ride on a jumping giant crab), **Ocean Commotion** (a rocking tug ride), junior-sized **Seven Seas Railway** and **Sea Carousel** (a traditional carousel featuring 65 sea creatures) complete the line-up. The area gets busy from midday, but the kids seem to love it at any time. Next door is the arcade and **Games Area**, a series of fairground stalls for $5, or a Games Pass at $25 for 20 games, as you head toward the Nautilus Theater. **TTTT**. At the back of the Harbor is a well-equipped, comfortable **Baby Care Center** and the park's **First Aid** station.

Shopping: More cuddlies and other souvenirs at **Happy Harbor Gifts**.

Dining: Grab a drink and an ice cream treat at **Soft Serve & Starbucks Coffee**, while you should try **Mama's Pretzel Kitchen** for freshly baked pretzels with a variety of dipping sauces.

Shamu Express

BRITTIP
Busch Gardens' Twisted Tails Pretzels has proved so popular in that park that SeaWorld has copied the formula here, including the must-sample Bacon Pretzel Twist!

Sea of Power

The final main area of the park features the iconic Shamu Stadium, plus another engaging ride/animal attraction, and the high-season fireworks finale.

BRITTIP
The first 14 rows at Shamu Stadium get VERY wet (watch out for your cameras) – when a killer whale leaps into the air in front of you, it displaces a LOT of water on landing. In fact, the Splash Zones should be renamed Soak Zones!

Shamu Stadium: 'What can one person do?' That is the message One Ocean brings to SeaWorld in a spectacular show filled with brilliant splashes of colour – especially of the black and white variety! In the past, the whales' relationship with their trainers was the main focus, and while that bond remains strong, the heart of One Ocean lies with the relationship between the whales themselves. Behaviours common to whales in the wild combine with learned behaviours in a celebration of joyful play, reminding us we are all connected and, when we pull together, we can do amazing things. And if the biggest thrills in past

Turtle Trek

Shamu shows came from seeing these magnificent animals jump, spin, and cover the Soak Zone in a wall of water, you're in for a real treat! Even better, the charming Side By Side scene features the connection between mother and baby, so have those cameras ready. Shamu Stadium is extremely popular, so try to take in an early show. And, if you think it looks good during the day, return in the evening (in high season) for an even more dramatic, music-orientated presentation under the lights, **Shamu's Celebration: Light Up The Night**. AAAAA+

BRITTIP
Be sure to arrive early for One Ocean, especially if you have a smart-phone. You may get a sneak peek behind the scenes during the pre-show!

All guests can then enjoy the **Shamu Underwater Viewing area**.

Wild Arctic: This interactive ride-and-view is an exciting simulator jet helicopter journey into the white wilderness, where passengers see seals, beluga whales and walruses. This one is not to be missed (but avoid just after One Ocean when the hordes descend). **R**: 3ft 6in/106cm. **TTTT** AAAAA. Those who don't want to do the (dynamic) ride can just walk to the Base Station.

Bayside Stadium: The final element is this large outdoor arena facing the central Lagoon. It's home to various seasonal entertainments, including the Bands, Brew & BBQ concerts and an ice-skating show at Christmas.

BRITTIP
Any purchases can be sent to Package Pick-up in Shamu's Emporium to collect on your way out, if you give at least an hour's notice.

Shopping: Wild Arctic Gifts is the best of the three stores here.

SEAWORLD with children

The following gives a general idea of the appeal of the attractions to the different age groups:

Under-5s
Antarctica: Empire of the Penguin, Blue Horizons, Clyde and Seamore's Sea Lion High, Dolphin Cove, Elmo Show, One Ocean, Pacific Point Preserve, Pets Ahoy!, Shamu's Happy Harbor, Wild Arctic (without the ride).

5–8s
All the above, plus Turtle Trek, Shark Encounter, Wild Arctic (with the ride).

9–12s
All the above, plus Journey to Atlantis, Manta, Kraken and Mako.

Over-12s
Antarctica: Empire of the Penguin, One Ocean, Blue Horizons, Clyde And Seamore's Sea Lion High, Journey To Atlantis, Turtle Trek, Manta, Kraken, Shark Encounter, Wild Arctic, Mako.

Dining: Mango Joe's Burgers offers grilled burgers, speciality salads and sandwiches, while **Dippin' Dots** features more ice cream treats and there are two snack and drinks counters at Shamu Stadium. Killer whale fans may also want to splash out (!) on the **Dine With Shamu** experience, backstage at Shamu Stadium, where a buffet lunch or dinner featuring seasonal, organic and sustainable menu items is served while some of the trainers meet with guests and show off more of the whale behaviours in spectacular, close-up fashion (times changes seasonally, with prices from $36 adults and $25 children; book in advance on 1888 800 5447, online at **www.seaworldparks.com** or at the Information Kiosk when you arrive).

🇬🇧 **BRITTIP**
Learn more about SeaWorld's conservation and environmental efforts at **www.seaworld.org**.

Summer extras
During the official summer season (mid-June–early-Aug), SeaWorld has extended hours to 9pm and offers extra live entertainment as part of its **Summer Nights** programme. The 'rock 'n' roll' party atmosphere

is generated by live DJs and other entertainers and features extra shows, notably **Shamu's Celebration: Light up The Night**, which adds a more high-energy version of the main show, including new, original music and production elements, as well as new killer whale behaviours and dramatic lighting. **Summer Nights Central**, on the Bayside Stadium pathway, features live DJs (and bands at weekends) to add a family-friendly dance party from 6pm.

For SeaWorld's amazing **Christmas Celebration** (late Nov–31 Dec each year), see our Christmas section (p37).

And there's more
Other seasonal events (all FREE with park admission) include **Bands, Brew & BBQ**, weekends in Feb and Mar that provide a festival atmosphere with live music, barbecue kiosks and craft beer stalls, as well as a special guest concert (beer and barbecue extra, including a 'Sampler' package for $22/person); the Apr–May weekends of **Viva La Musica** Latin festival (with more live bands and food); and the ultra child-friendly **Halloween Spooktacular**, when there are fun activities for kids of all ages, including trick-or-treating, Penelope's Party Zone, sweet treat decorating and strolling entertainers.

Discovery Cove

Fancy a day in your own tropical paradise, with the chance to swim with dolphins, encounter sharks, snorkel in a coral reef and dive through a waterfall into a tropical aviary? Well, Discovery Cove is all that and more. The only drawback is the price. This mini theme park comes at a premium because it is restricted to just 1,300 guests a day, creating an exclusive experience that is reflected in the admission fee.

The weather can get distinctly cool in the winter, but the water is always heated (apart from the dolphin lagoon, which remains at 72ºF/22ºC) and full wetsuits are available to keep out the chill. The attention to detail is superb, guest ratings are extremely high and it is hugely popular with British visitors. However, if any element falls below expectations, it's worth bringing it to the attention of a manager as they are always keen to rectify any oversights.

The costs

In 2016, the Dolphin Swim package was $259–359/person, or you could choose the Day Resort package, without dolphin swim, for $169–219, all depending on day and season (under 3s free; 3–5s cannot do the dolphin swim but must pay the Day Resort price). So, just what do you get

for your money? Well, as you would expect, it's a supremely personal park. You check in at the beautiful entrance lobby as you would for a hotel rather than a theme park, and you have a guide to take you in and get you set. All your basic requirements – towel, mask, snorkel, wet-jacket, lockers, beach umbrellas, animal-safe suncream, food and drink – are included, and the level of service is excellent. A pass for SeaWorld AND Aquatica is also included (valid for 14 consecutive days before or after your Discovery Cove visit), or you can upgrade to the Ultimate Package, which provides 14 days at SeaWorld, Aquatica AND Busch Gardens for just $25 extra (superb value). A full breakfast, snacks, beverages (including beer and cocktails) and an excellent lunch at the Laguna Grill are all included. But gift shop and photo prices reflect the entry fee – expensive. It is also an extra $199 to hire one of their swanky cabañas for the day (which include tables, chairs, loungers, towels and a fridge stocked with soft drinks) depending on position and view (must be booked in advance).

Therefore, for all its style and dolphin appeal, Discovery Cove will take a BIG bite out of your holiday budget. A family of 4, with children old enough

The Grand Reef

to do the Dolphin Swim, would pay $1,436 in peak season. Even with a free SeaWorld and Aquatica pass, it's a big outlay. The charge for ages 3–5 is also pretty steep, in our opinion. Your sundries can add up, too. A 6x8in/15x20cm photo is $20; then there are photo packages at $70 and $159, while the DVD of your experience (which includes 30mins of park highlights) costs $60 and the Discovery Package (7 6x8 photos, 1 4x6 photo, 2 key chains, digital photo CD, Interaction video, photo album, 16x24 poster) is $229. Poster-size photos (16x24 and 24x36) are $30 and $40, while a marble photo-tile is $45. However, despite the fees, the feedback we get is almost unfailingly positive and most people are captivated by the experience. One handy free perk, though, is the Horticulture Tour, twice a day, which takes guests through the care and maintenance of the park's tropical plant and tree life (sign up at Guest Relations).

◀🇬🇧▶ **BRITTIP**

Try to pick up your Discovery Cove photos before 4pm or you might find everyone else trying to do the same!

Trainer for a Day: This programme is an exciting opportunity to go behind the scenes into the park's training, feeding and welfare. You get to work with the experts as they interact with dolphins, birds, sharks, stingrays and tropical fish, including a behavioural training class, the chance to experience a double-foot push (ride on the front of two dolphins), a private photo session and enhanced deep-water interaction with the dolphins, and a behind-the-scenes tour. Participants must be at least six and in good health, and it costs $428–558 (seasonally). For all Discovery Cove bookings, call 1 877 577 7404(freephone 00800 3344 1818 in the UK) or visit **www.discoverycove. com**.

Location

Situated on Central Florida Parkway, almost opposite the SeaWorld entrance (open year-round 9am–5.30pm; parking free), the whole 30acre/12ha park is magnificently landscaped, with thatched buildings, palm trees, lush vegetation, white-sand beaches, gurgling streams – even hammocks to chill out in. The overall effect is of being transported to a relaxing tropical paradise away from the hurly-burly. The 5-star resort feel is enhanced by a high staff-to-guest ratio, there are no queues (though the restaurant may get busy at lunchtime), and the highlight Dolphin Encounter is world class. Visitors with disabilities are well catered for, with special wheelchairs that can move in sand and shallow water, and an area of the Dolphin Lagoon that allows those who can't enter the water to touch a dolphin.

The main attractions

Freshwater Oasis: This combination of animal environment, walking trails and pools offers the chance to get a close-up of the park's otters and marmosets in realistic, natural habitats. Children especially love watching the otters, and the way the animals are incorporated into the lush tropical scenery is a real gem of clever design. AAAA

Wind-away River: This 800yd/732m circuit of gently flowing bath-warm water is a variation on the lazy river feature of many of the water parks, though with a far more naturalistic aspect and none of the inner tubes. It is primarily designed

Freshwater Oasis

for snorkellers and features rocky lagoons, caves, a beach section, a tropical forest segment and sunken ruins. The lack of fish makes it a bit bland after the Grand Reef, but it is as much about relaxing as having fun. It is up to 8ft/2.4m deep at points, so non-swimmers are advised to use a flotation vest. It finishes in the freeform Serenity Bay pool, which provides more idyllic relaxation. AAA

Explorer's Aviary: This three-part adventure is both an area in its own right and a 120ft/37m section of the Tropical River. You can walk in off the beach or swim in through the waterfall from Wind-away River, fun for snorkellers. Some 250 tropical birds fill the main enclosure and, if you stand still, they are likely to use you as a perch. There is a small-bird sanctuary – full of finches, honeycreepers and hummingbirds – and a large-bird enclosure, featuring toucans and the red-legged seriema. Guides will introduce you to specific birds (which you can hand-feed) and tell you about their habitats and conservation issues. AAAA

Dolphin Swim: The big headline attraction is the encounter with the park's Atlantic bottlenose dolphin community. A 20min orientation programme in one of the beach cabañas, with a film and instruction from two trainers, sets you up for this thrilling experience. Groups of 6–8 go into the lagoon with the trainers and, starting off standing in the waist-deep (slightly chilly) water as one of the dolphins comes over, you gradually become more adventurous until you are swimming with them. Timid swimmers are well catered for and there are flotation vests for those who need them. The lagoon is up to 12ft/3.6m deep so there is a real feeling of being in the dolphins' environment. You learn how trainers use hand signals and positive reinforcement to communicate, and get the chance to stroke, feed and even kiss your dolphin. The encounter concludes dramatically as you are towed ashore by one of these awesome animals (which weigh up to 600lb/272kg), though activities vary according to their attention span. You spend around 30mins in the water and it is unforgettable. Under-6s are not allowed in the lagoon. TTTTT+

The Grand Reef: This area features a massive 2.5acre/1ha artificial reef with 125 species of sea creatures, including fish, rays, eels, sharks, urchins, and lionfish (the dangerous ones are behind glass!). White sand

The Grand Reef

beaches, meandering pathways and scenic bridges lead to shallow wading areas, waist-deep paddling pools and deep-water snorkelling, while underwater canyons and inviting grottos combine with brightly coloured artificial coral reefs for a convincing and exhilarating experience. It's like paradise, only better!

For an extra element of relaxation, stake out a hammock on the central island or consider hiring one of eight private waterside cabañas (with table, chairs, loungers and towels). There is a drinks kiosk here but no food outlets. AAAAA

🇬🇧 **BRITTIP**

The Sea Venture area is not accessible to snorkellers during tours, but you can swim there when a tour is not running.

Sea Venture: One of the most innovative features of the Grand Reef is this underwater walking tour. Equipped with special dive helmets, guests make a 20min trek along the bottom of the reef, passing sharks and lionfish and interacting with schools of fish and gentle rays. This is a totally immersive experience and a sensation like no other (how often can you explore underwater while standing up straight?). There are handrails throughout the journey, which takes groups of 4–9 at a time. Total tour time is 1hr, including preparation and underwater trek (for an extra $49–69 per person). Ages 10 and up only. **TTTT**

Discovery Cove 'extras'

This isn't a cheap day out, but the extra quality is everywhere. The Laguna Grill lunch is excellent and you can visit as often as you want, while a Calypso band adds to the tropical paradise feel. Conservation Cabaña allows guests to meet a neat selection of the park's small mammals (like an anteater and tree sloth); parking is free and you also receive an 8x6in/15x20cm welcome photo. While official opening time is 9am, they will check you in as early as 8am for the free breakfast.

Special occasions

Discovery Cove has a range of options that involve dolphin interaction and private beach cabañas.

The Celebration Package ($179) includes 6x8in/15x20cm photo, photo frame, plush toy, bag, T-shirt, souvenir buoy delivered by a dolphin and 20% off Ultimate photo package.

The Elite Package ($429) includes a buoy with personalised message delivered by a dolphin, signature tote bag, choice of deluxe photo frame, plush toy, a private cabaña with locker, snack and beverage service, Discovery Photo Package.

VIP Package ($799) offers the ultimate Discovery Cove experience as it includes a buoy with a personalised message, tote bag, photo frame, plush toy, cabana for the day, Discovery Photo Package, reserved seating at Laguna grill, a dedicated host/hostess and itinerary planner, and an additional up close animal encounter.

Park admission and dolphin swim package are required with all special occasion packages. You are advised to book at least three months in advance as they do sell out in peak periods and, in winter, the park is closed on some midweek days. There is also a 10% advance discount periodically for online bookings. See **www.discoverycove.com**.

SeaVenture

Busch Gardens

While the Orlando parks may get more publicity, the 335acre/136ha Busch Gardens in Tampa offers just as much in terms of attractions and – especially – Brit appeal. In fact, the sister park to SeaWorld, which started as a mini-menagerie for the wildlife collection of the brewery-owning Busch family in 1959, is often one of the most popular of all Florida attractions with UK visitors for its nature appeal – and superb roller-coasters. It is a major, multi-faceted family park, the biggest outside Orlando and just an hour from International Drive. It is rated among the top four zoos in America, with more than 2,700 animals representing over 320 species of mammals, birds, reptiles, amphibians and spiders. But that's just the start. It boasts a safari-like section of Africa spread over 65acres/26ha of grassy veldt, with special tours to hand-feed some of the animals. Interspersed among the animals are more than 20 bona fide theme park rides, including the mind-numbing coasters Kumba, SheiKra, Montu, Cheetah Hunt, and the new Cobra's Curse, plus the dramatic drop-tower ride, Falcon's Fury, with guaranteed fun for coaster addicts, plus plenty of scaled-down rides for children. Then there are animal shows, musicians and big-stage show productions.

The overall theme is Africa, hence the park is divided into areas like Nairobi and Morocco, and dining and shopping are just as good as the other parks. It doesn't quite have the pizzazz of Epcot or Universal, and the staff are a bit more laid back, but it has guaranteed 5-star family appeal, especially with its rides just for kids. It's a bit like the big brother of Chessington World of Adventures

Busch Gardens at a glance

Location	Busch Blvd, Tampa; 75–90mins' drive from Orlando		
Size	335 acres/136ha in 11 themed areas		
Hours	9 or 10am–6 or 7pm off peak; 9am–8pm Easter, Thanksgiving, Christmas; 9 or 9.30am–10.30pm summer		
Admission	Under-3s free; 3–9 $94 (1-day ticket), $139 (2-Visit ticket, with 2nd day at SeaWorld, Aquatica or Busch Gardens, ages 3 and up), adult (10+) $99.		
Parking	$18, $23 preferred parking, $29 valet		
Lockers	$10, $15, $20, in Morocco, Congo, Egypt and Stanleyville		
Pushchairs	$15 and $20		
Wheelchairs	$20, $50 and $62, with pushchairs		
Top attractions	Congo River Rapids, Kumba, Montu, Cheetah Hunt, SheiKra, Iceploration show, Falcon's Fury, Cobra's Curse		
Don't miss	Jungala, Edge of Africa, Animal Care Center, Myombe Reserve, Meet The Keepers talks		
Hidden costs	Meals	Burger, chips and coke $11 3-course meal $19-28 (Zambia Smokehouse) Kids meals: $6.99	
	T-shirts	$19.95–31.95, Kids $12–21.95	
	Souvenirs	99c–$250	
	Sundries	Face Painting $10–19	

Morocco
1 Marrakesh Theater
2 Moroccan Palace Theater
3 Myombe Reserve
4 Gwazi Gliders

Cheetah Hunt
5 Cheetah Run
6 Cheetah Hunt and Skyride Station

Bird Gardens
7 Gwazi Pavilion
8 Lory Landing
9 Walkabout Way

Sesame Street Safari of Fun
10 Air Grover
11 Sunny Day Theater
12 Big Bird's 123-Smile With Me

Stanleyville
13 SheiKra
14 Stanley Falls Flume
15 Stanleyville Train Station
16 Stanleyville Theater
17 Skyride Station
18 Zambia Smokehouse

Jungala
19 Jungle Flyers, The Wild Surge and Treetop Trails
20 Tiger Habitat
21 Orang Outpost

Congo
22 Kumba
23 Congo River Rapids
24 Ubanga-Banga Bumper Cars

Pantopia
25 Falcon's Fury
26 Sand Serpent
27 The Phoenix
28 Grand Caravan Carousel
29 Pantopia Theater

Nairobi
30 Curiosity Caverns
31 Serengeti Plain
32 Jambo Junction
33 Edge of Africa
34 Elephant Habitat
35 Animal Care Center

Egypt
36 Montu
37 Cobra's Curse

BUSCH GARDENS

in Surrey, though on a grander scale (and in a better climate). Busch Gardens is the only park to offer 1-day Tickets with a rain guarantee, which means if you get rained out on your visit, you can return FREE within seven days. Look for self-serve machines to the right of the park entrance to save time at ticket booths.

BRITTIP

Like SeaWorld, Busch Gardens offers QuickQueue, the limited number front-of-the-line pass for all the park's main rides. Price varies (seasonally), $19.99–44.99 for One-Time use, $39.99–69.99 for Unlimited use.

All Day Dining Deal: For just $33.99 ($16.99 3–9s) you can enjoy all-you-care-to-eat-and-drink privileges at five restaurants throughout the park. With your special wristband, choose one entrée, one side or dessert and a soft drink each time you pass through the dining queue (child's price valid for kids' meal only; baby back ribs excluded).

Photokey: If you'd like to collect all your park photos digitally, including ride photos and character meet-and-greets (but not backstage tours), sign up for this new service, either online in advance or when you arrive at the park, for $69 (**https://photokeyonline.com/**).

Meet the Keeper: Look out also for sessions around the park where the animal handlers explain various features of animal husbandry, notably with the gorillas, elephants and hippos. You will find them at the

Cheetah Run

Alligator Habitat, Myombe Reserve, Edge of Africa, Jungala, Elephant and Rhinoceros Habitats and Jambo Junction (where they feature various small-animal encounters).

Location

Busch Gardens can be hard to locate on the sketchy local maps as the sign-posting is not as sharp as it could be, but from Orlando the directions are simple. Head west on I-4 for almost an hour (it is 55ml/88km from I-4's junction with Highway 192) until you hit intersecting motorway I-75. Take I-75 north for 3½ml/5.5km to the exit for Fowler Avenue (Highway 582). Go west on Fowler for another 3½ml/5.5km, then, just past the University of South Florida on your right, turn LEFT into McKinley Drive. A mile/1.6km down McKinley Drive, the car park is on your left, where it costs $18 to park (those with disabled badges should continue on then turn right).

Those without a car can use the **Busch Gardens Shuttle Express** bus, which makes several $10 round trips a day from Orlando (FREE if you have park admission). You board at SeaWorld, Orlando Premium Outlets, Universal Studios, Ramada Maingate West, Best Western Lakeside or Old Town in Kissimmee and pick-up times range from 8.30 to 9.40am, returning at 6 or 7pm. Book at Guest Services at SeaWorld or call 1800 221 1339.

Beating the queues: Don't think you've left the high-season Orlando crowds behind. It's still advisable to be here at opening time, if only to be first in line to ride the dazzling roller-coasters, which all draw big queues (especially SheiKra and Cheetah Hunt). The Congo River Rapids and Stanley Falls Log Flume ride (both opportunities to get wet) are also prime draws in peak season. But queues take longer to build here, so for the first few hours you can enjoy a relatively crowd-free experience.

Adventure Tour Centre: On your left through the main gates, go here first (better still, book in advance on 1888 800 5447 or online at **www.buschgardens. com**) if you'd like to do the wonderful

Serengeti Safari or other Adventure Tours (p210–11). Busch Gardens is divided into 10 main sections, with the major rides all a bit of a hike from the main entrance. Check your park map for times and locations of various small-animal encounters throughout the park – then watch for passing flamingos as they take the first of their twice-daily promenades in the main courtyard!

Coaster fans flock to SheiKra, the world's second highest and fastest dive coaster, and peak-season queues can top an hour by mid-afternoon. So, if you want to ride this first, bear left through Morocco past the Zagora Café, through the Bird Gardens and up into Stanleyville. Then continue through Stanleyville to Congo for Kumba, and retrace your steps to do Congo River Rapids and the other two water rides. To start with the superb Cheetah Hunt coaster, veer right into Morocco and go past the Moroccan Palace Theater, opposite Crown Colony. After riding the Cheetah, try the Cobra's Curse coaster in nearby Egypt, then return to take the SkyRide to Stanleyville and take on the other big rides there. Here is the full layout of the park in a clockwise direction.

Morocco

Come through the main gates to the home of all the guest services and a lot of shops. Epcot's Moroccan pavilion sets the scene better, but the architecture is still impressive and this version won't tax your wallet as much as Disney's! Turning the corner brings you to the first animal encounter, the alligator pen. Morocco is also home to one of the park's biggest shows.

Moroccan Palace Theater: The setting for the lavish production **Iceploration**, a 25min stage show featuring ice skating, elaborate puppetry, trampoline artists and 20 live animals (including a Siberian lynx), plus in-theatre special effects. It tells the story of a technology-overdosed teen who gets to travel the world with his grandfather and learn the real-life mysteries of the African Serengeti, the Great Barrier Reef, the Arctic and the Amazon rainforest. With vivid

costuming, scintillating music and eye-catching performers – plus some wonderfully cute huskies! – it offers yet another dimension to the park's live entertainment 3–4 times a day. AAAAA Stay around to meet some of the performers; you can also buy a CD of the original music.

Myombe Reserve: One of the largest and most realistic habitats for the threatened highland gorillas and chimpanzees of Central Africa, this 3acre/1.2ha walk-through has a convincing tropical setting with high temperatures, lush forest landscaping and water mist sprays. Take your time, especially as there are good, seated vantage points, and catch these magnificent creatures on their daily routine. It is also highly informative, with attendants on hand to answer any questions. AAAAA

Gwazi Gliders: This gentle circling 'hang-gliding' ride is purely for the pre-school crowd. T (TTT under-6s)

Other entertainment: Basketball fans can try the **Hoops Challenge** (for $7, $10 for 2 plays) next to Gwazi Gliders, the **Gwazi Soccer** challenge ($7 and $10) or **Gwazi Climb** ($3 and $5).

SheiKra

Shopping: The Emporium and **Marrakesh Market** are the best of three shops.

Dining: For a quick meal, try **Zagora Café**, especially at breakfast, or the enticing **Sultan's Sweets** serves coffee and pastries.

Cheetah Hunt

This sub-area next to Morocco features the park's wonderful cheetah habitat – and signature ride.

Cheetah Hunt: This beast of a coaster re-creates the thrill of a cheetah in pursuit of its prey. Launching from the loading station out across the savannah, the hunt is on. A second launch spirals you 10 storeys up the ride's signature figure-of-eight tower (with an astonishing view) before taking an exhilarating 130ft/40m plunge into a subterranean gorge. Then you're off again, low and fast along the Serengeti. A final launch zips back across the grasslands (leaping over the heads of onlookers below and above the SkyRide!) and, just before you're completely out of breath, the hunt comes to an end. It's a sensational 2mins. The smooth ride, extensive theming and superb eye-appeal mark this out as possibly Florida's finest but it draws BIG queues, so try to do it early on. **R:** 4ft/120cm; **TTTTT**

Skyride: Take to the air with this one-way cable car trip to Stanleyville, getting a fabulous aerial view of the park, including part of the Serengeti Plain. **TT**

Cheetah Run: Here you have the chance to see these magnificent cats up close in a 250ft/7m sprint (chasing their favourite toy alongside Cheetah Hunt!), or just lounging around the splendid habitat designed especially for them. Sprints occur up to four times daily (check park map for times). Then, take time to learn more about cheetahs and the park's conservation efforts through nearby touch-screen technology.

Shopping and dining: Grab a souvenir at **Cheetah Gifts** or quick bite or drink from **Cheetah Snacks**.

Bird Gardens

The most peaceful area and the original starting point of the park in 1959, you can unwind here from the usual theme-park hurly-burly. The exhibits and shows are all family-orientated, too, with live shows, an elaborate kids' playground and more animal exhibits.

◀🇬🇧▶ **BRITTIP**
The Bird Gardens area is a good place to visit in mid-afternoon when most of the rides are busy.

Cheetah Hunt

Lory Landing: Walk through this tropical aviary featuring lorikeets, hornbills, parrots and more, with the chance to become a human perch and feed the friendly lorikeets. A cup of nectar costs $7, but makes for a great photo opportunity. **AAA**

Walkabout Way: This charming Australia-themed attraction offers the chance to feed the free-roaming kangaroos and wallabies ($6, or 2 for $10, ages 5 and up only) and meet other Down Under denizens like the emu. It is a surprisingly captivating area, perfect for a relaxed stroll. **AAA** Other encounters include the lush, walk-through Aviary, Flamingo Island and the Backyard Wildlife Habitat.

Other entertainment: Gwazi Park is home to the seasonal live musical entertainment during summer and other special events, like the new **Food & Wine Festival** (Mar/Apr).

Air Grover

Shopping: A real novelty here is the eye-catching **Xcursions** eco-friendly gift shop. Its live frog and gecko displays and conservation info on interactive touch-screens make it worth visiting whether you buy or not (but all proceeds contribute to the Busch Gardens Conservation Fund). **Garden Gate** is another imaginative shop.

Dining: Garden Gate Café offers excellent sandwiches, pizza, calzones, pretzels and craft beers, with pleasant outdoor seating.

Sesame Street Safari of Fun

This impressive children's interactive play area is the cheerful 'home away from home' for much-loved Sesame Street characters, dressed in best African Safari finery. You will be hard pressed to get pre-schoolers away when they catch sight of this land's seven rides (including a junior-sized coaster, a gentle flume ride and character-themed fairground style rides), entertaining stage show and the wonderfully extensive water play and climb-and-slide areas. The huge treehouse climb, ball pools and adventure play structures alone will keep most kids busy for hours! But there's more:

Air Grover: A whizzy little dip-and-turn coaster packing plenty of junior-sized thrills, piloted by everyone's favourite blue guy, Grover. **R:** 2ft 9in/97cm accompanied; 3ft 5in/104cm unaccompanied.

Sunny Day Theater: Elmo, Abby, Zoe, Grover and Cookie Monster star in *A is for Africa*, a delightfully zany stage show that brings tales of adventure to life, with a gently uplifting message. Children (and adults!) can't help but sing and clap along, and it is a great photo opportunity as the characters arrive and then come out for a meet-and-greet afterwards.

> **BRITTIP**
> Arrive early and find a seat in the first five rows for an unobstructed view at the Sunny Day Theater. Seat children on the ends for the best character interaction.

Big Bird's 1-2-3 Smile with Me: Big Bird and friends have their own meet-and-greet area, near Air Grover. The big bonus here is 1-on-1 time with the characters in a quiet, air conditioned room (photo packages $20–37).

Bert and Ernie's Watering Hole: Thoughtfully designed with even the smallest guests in mind, this gentle water-play area is filled with bubblers, water jets, dump buckets, geysers and splash tubs. Swimwear and sun block are available at Cookie Monster's trading Post if you forgot yours. Convenient seating surrounds the area. **TTTTT** (young 'uns only!)

Shopping: Look for **Abby Cadabby's Treasure Hut** and **Cookie Monster's Trading Post** for Sesame Street gifts and souvenirs.

Dining: For a quick bite, try **Snack-n-Getti Tribal Treats**. But the big opportunity is **Lunch with Elmo & Friends**, where visitors can enjoy lunch with Elmo and his chums in an outdoor covered dining area. A kid-friendly buffet along with a character song-and-dance show make this a delight for the younger set, with loads of time to meet their favourite characters ($22 for adults, $15 3–9s, including a 6x8in/15x20cm photo per family; every Saturday; Wed–Sat peak season).

Stanleyville

This brings you back into true ride territory, with the park's biggest coaster, a water ride and a seasonal show. You'll also find one of the three Train Stations here (next to SheiKra), for a gentle 35min journey round the park.

SheiKra: The park's outstanding big-thrill attraction is the giant steel structure of this monstrous coaster. At 200ft/62m tall and hitting 70mph/112kph, it puts Alton Towers' fearsome Oblivion in the shade. Higher, longer and faster, it features an initial drop at an angle as near

SheiKra

vertical as makes no difference (with a delicious moment of stop-go balance as you teeter on the edge!), a second drop of 138ft/42m into an underground tunnel, an Immelman loop (an exhilarating rolling manoeuvre) and a water splashdown over 0.6ml/1km of smooth-as-silk track. As if all that isn't enough, a 2007 modification removed the coaster's floor, so there is nothing between you and the track but air! The whole ride lasts less than 3min and is almost as much fun to watch as to ride. It also draws big queues, so get here early or expect a long wait (or use the paid-for QuickQueue system). You can buy the video of your ride for $30, a 6x8in/15x20cm photo for $20. **R**: 4ft 6in/137cm. **TTTTT+**

Stanley Falls: Almost identical to Log Flume rides at Chessington, LEGOLAND, Thorpe Park and Alton Towers, this guarantees a good soaking at the final 40ft/12m drop. **R**: 3ft 10in/116cm. **TTT**

> **BRITTIP**
> **Stanleyville Theater:** This air-conditioned venue hosts various live shows seasonally, with the Motown song and dance act **Motor City Groove** during summer 2016. **AAA**

Skyride: The other end of the park's cable-car ride (from Cheetah Hunt), it offers spectacular views over the Serengeti Plain (with a thrilling moment as Cheetah Hunt races above!). However, it closes when it's windy and queues can build up here in late afternoon. **AA**

Other entertainment: Try **Bahati Hoops** and other fairground games (next to SheiKra) for a small fee.

Shopping: The **Kariba Marketplace** has the best of the shopping.

Dining: For a hearty meal (and a great view of SheiKra), try **Zambia Smokehouse**, where its wood-smoked ribs platter is a delight among a heavily barbecue-orientated menu (also with salads, sandwiches and kids' meals).

Jungala

This 4acre/1.6ha land opened in 2008 adding a couple of small-scale rides, some superb animal habitats and a hugely elaborate children's play area, designed with older children in mind. It gets busy in the afternoon, so visit either early on or late in the day.

Jungle Flyers: This kids' ride (6–13s) is a junior-sized zipline journey over part of the Jungala area, a 1-seat there-and-back trip from the upper level of Treetop Trails. Great fun for kids, but a rather short ride, and queues build up quickly and move slowly most of the day. **R:** Maximum height 4ft 8in/145cm. **TTT**

The Wild Surge: Get ready to 'surge' 4 storeys into the air on this tower ride from inside a giant waterfall, with a (brief!) glimpse over Jungala before bouncing back down again. Be aware queues are long and slow-moving as the ride takes just 14 at a time. **R:** 3ft 6in/106cm to ride solo (3ft 2in/96cm with a parent). **TTT (TTTTT** under- 12s)

Treetop Trails: Climbing nets, elaborate bridges, crawl tubes and a multi-level maze are the basis of this fab 3-storey children's playground, with smaller-scale adventures at ground level, including squirt fountains and other watery fun (swimsuits or a change of clothes are advisable). It cleverly mixes in two different animal habitats, for the fun-loving gibbons, flying fox-bats and the rare tomistoma (an Asian crocodile). **TTTT** (young 'uns only)

◀🇬🇧▶ **BRITTIP**
The toddler play area in Treetop Trails is very thoughtfully in the shade.

Tiger Habitat: One of the park's most creative animal environments is this multi-level tiger exhibit (including its rare white tigers). Tiger Lodge is an air-conditioned overlook including conservation info and issues, and Tiger Trail is a walkthrough section with close-up opportunities, including a unique pop-up turret (with a separate queue) in the main enclosure and a rope-pull for guests to 'test their strength' (periodically) against the big cats. Huge windows provide maximum viewing of the animals at play, especially in their plunge pool. **AAAA**

Orang Outpost: Another brilliant animal habitat, the orang-utans love to look in on guests, viewing them as much as vice versa. A series of close-up windows, including a glass floor over a hammock play area and a kids' tunnel, provide superb observation of the specially designed forest environment. **AAAA**

Other entertainment: Look out for **Kareebu Jungala**, colourful stilt-walkers around the village area periodically (see map for times).

Shopping: Shop for gifts at **Tiger Treasures** (organic cotton T-shirts and conservation-related items) and **Cubs Closet** (kids' clothing).

Dining: Stop to eat at **Bengal Bistro** (fish, burgers, veggie wraps, salads and sandwiches) or the more snack-orientated **Orang Café** (chicken strips, hot dogs, fries, and funnel cakes).

Congo

As you continue into the Congo, this is primarily about just three rides, plus a stop on the Serengeti Railway.

Kumba: Another of the park's signature coasters, this unmistakable giant turquoise structure looms over the area. It's one of the largest and fastest in south-east USA and, at 60mph/97kph, features three

Falcon's Fury

high-thrill elements: a diving loop plunging a full 110ft/33m; a camel-back, with a 360° spiral; and a vertical loop. For good measure, it dives underground! It looks terrifying close up but is absolutely exhilarating, even for non-coaster fans. **R:** 4ft 6in/137cm. **TTTTT**

Congo River Rapids: These look pretty tame after Kumba, but don't be fooled. The giant rubber rafts will bounce you down some of the most convincing rapids outside of the Rockies, and you will end up with a fair soaking. **R:** 3ft 6in/106cm. **TTTT**

Ubanga-Banga Bumper Cars: Fairly typical fairground dodgems, you won't miss anything if you pass them by. **R:** 3ft 6in/106cm. **TT**

Shopping and dining: There is just the **Congo River Outfitters** gift shop here, plus three refreshment kiosks.

Pantopia

This redeveloped land opened in summer 2014 with a dramatic new look, name (formerly Timbuktu) and the park's most eye-catching ride. There is also a full back-story, as Pantopia was created by a mystical Key-Master who arrived by hot air balloon to create a place where travellers could meet. The doors of Pantopia tell a tale of the original owners and travellers who passed this way and the land includes clever kinetic sculptures and re-purposed vehicles, like an Asian tuk-tuk and various bikes and wagons. Another highlight is The Sitting Place, a modern-day watering hole where visitors can sit, relax and enjoy the views, as well as the signature food and drink offerings.

Falcon's Fury: The land's signature ride, this awe-inspiring tower lifts 32 riders at a time (slowly) up to its 300ft/91m height, tilts them forward so they are face down – then drops in best free-fall style. Yes, it's the world's highest drop-tower ride and it's for adrenalin addicts only as it really has that sky-dive feeling for several seconds before the brakes kick in and bring you more gently

back to earth. It is aptly named for the vertical dive of a falcon (which can hunt its prey at up to 160mph) and provides an amazing view from the top – if you can keep your eyes open. We think it's as much a spectator opportunity as something you'll actually want to ride but it does provide an iconic look to the park. It's a relatively brief experience and queues move slowly, so you may want to try this early on – or chicken out completely! **R:** 3ft 6in/106cm. **TTTTT**

Sand Serpent: This family-orientated 'Crazy Mouse' style coaster is surprisingly energetic, rising as it does some 46ft/14m and adding tight turns and swift drops. Top speed is only 22mph/35kph, but it seems faster and thrills younger kids. **TTT** (**TTTTT** under-10s)

The Phoenix: A positively evil invention that involves sitting in a gigantic, boat-shaped swing that eventually performs a 360° rotation in dramatic, slow-motion style. Don't eat just before this one! **R:** 4ft/122cm. **TTTT**

Scorpion: A 50mph/80kph roller-coaster, this features a 62ft/19m drop and a 360° loop that is guaranteed to dial D for dizzy for a while. It lasts just 120secs, but seems longer. Queues build here from late morning. **R:** 3ft 6in/106cm. **TTTT**

Grand Caravan Carousel: Join this 'Bedouin caravan' in its layers of tapestries and tenting for a genuine kiddie carousel ride. **TT** (**TTTT** under 5s)

Pantopia Theater: This indoor arena features terrific animal show *Opening Night Critters*. It follows the exploits of two wannabe stage presenters and their host of critter side-kicks, including dogs, cats, birds, pigs, a skunk and kangaroo, and is sure to raise laughs with all the family, while you can meet some of the stars of the show afterwards. **AAAA**

Other entertainment: The **Games Area** offers fairground-style games that require a few extra dollars, while the **Dragonfire Grill** – a Moroccan-influenced nightclub that is Pantopia's gathering place for artists from around the world – offers a show while you dine (or just sit and watch). In 2016 it was **Treasures of the Mirage**, an Arabian-inspired music and dance concoction, featuring belly dancers and a quick-change costume performer, with a chance to meet the cast after the show.

Shopping: This has been heavily redesigned for the Pantopia theme, with the **Painted Camel Bazaar** offering a wide range of creative merchandise, some of it made from recycled materials from around the world, as well as Falcon's Fury and other souvenir items.

Dining: Headline restaurant the **Dragonfire Grill** is a new food court-style offering featuring several innovative elements and including Italian, American, Asian and Southwestern cuisine, as well as a grab-and-go Starbucks coffee station and an extended selection of craft beers. Look out for rotisserie chicken, flatbread pizza, chicken teriyaki and Southwest Tortilla Bowls. **Twisted Tails Pretzels** is a delightful offering of fresh-rolled pretzels (don't miss the signature Bacon Pretzel Fury, along with the beer mustard sauce!), artisan sandwiches, pizza and pretzel dogs, as well as craft beers. **Lynx Frozen Treats** adds snowcones, smoothies and other icy delights and **Kettle Corn** is a haven for popcorn-lovers as well as serving turkey legs, potato twisters, chicken strips and drinks.

Nairobi

It's back to the animals as we enter this area, with five different habitats.

Serengeti Plain: A 49acre/20ha spread of African savannah, this is home to buffalo, antelope, zebras, giraffes, wildebeest, ostriches, hippos, rhinos and many exotic birds, and can be viewed for much of the journey on the Serengeti Express, a full-size, open-car steam train that chugs slowly from its main station in

Nairobi to the Congo, Stanleyville and back. **AAA**

BRITTIP

Take the Serengeti Railway from Nairobi (or Congo or Stanleyville) in mid-afternoon to give your feet a rest when it's busy elsewhere.

Jambo Junction: The park's nursery is an interesting animal encounter, with some friendly flamingos, small critters (lemurs, sloths, possums and babies needing extra care) on view through the large windows. This is the place to meet the park's Animal Ambassadors for education and conservation issues. **AA**

Animal Care Center: This is a peek into the way Busch Gardens cares for its residents, even down to performing live surgical procedures. The state-of-the-art facility is in three parts, for the Treatment Room, Nutrition Center and Pathology Lab, with live audio links to the vets and technicians working behind the big glass windows and keepers on hand to answer questions, whether it's a snake getting an ultrasound check-up or the daily preparation of mealworms for the possums! **AAAA**

Other entertainment: Look out for the **Elephant Interaction Wall** and periodic sessions with animal staff (notably the afternoon Elephant Wash), while you can see more park inhabitants at the **Reptile House**, **Curiosity Caverns** (nocturnal animals) and **Tortoise Habitat**. The meeting area for the Serengeti Safari is also here, next to Kenya Kanteen.

Shopping and dining: Caravan Crossing (safari apparel and hats) has the best shopping here while **Kenya Kanteen** offers drinks and snacks.

Egypt

The final area of Busch Gardens is somewhat tucked away, so it's best visited either first thing or late in the day. It sits in the park's bottom right corner and much of it is re-created pharaoh country, dominated by suspended coaster Montu, named after an ancient Egyptian warrior god. New coaster Cobra's Curse can also be found here.

Montu: You cannot miss the area's main attraction, another breathtaking inverted coaster, covering nearly 4,000ft/1,219m of track at up to 60mph/97kph and peaking with a G-force of 3.85! Like Kumba, it looks terrifying but really is a 5-star thrill as it leaves your legs dangling and twists and dives (underground at two points) for almost 3min of brain-scrambling fun. **R:** 4ft 6in/137cm. **TTTTT**

Cobra's Curse: This all-new coaster experience in summer 2016 added several new elements to the park's thrill rides, including an impressive vertical lift hill that brings riders face to fangs with a 70ft snake (well, an 'ancient cobra statue', at least!). From a height of 70ft/21.3m, it zips out into the African plain with multiple swoops and dips, twisting and turning as it snakes along more than 2,100ft/640m of track. It is a high-speed ride with a difference, as the cars will *reverse* and then spin at various points to provide a first-of-its-kind coaster experience. The clever theming, like an archaeological dig, plus live snake exhibits through the queuing area and use of the old

Tut's Tomb Egypt exhibit ensure this is good family fun. **TTTTT, R.** 3ft 6/106cm.

Edge of Africa: This is a 15acre/6ha 'safari experience', which can also be accessed through Egypt, guarantees a close-up almost like the real thing. The walk-through puts you in an authentic setting of native wilds and villages from which you can view giraffes, lions, baboons, meerkats, crocodiles, hyenas and vultures, and even an underwater hippo habitat. Wandering naturalists offer informal talks, and the attention to detail is superb.

BRITTIP

Edge of Africa offers some fantastic photo opportunities but, in the hot months, come here early in the day as many animals seek refuge from the heat later.

Shopping: Montu Gifts sells clothes, handbags and other merchandise, while the **Cobra's Curse** shop offers clothes, plush toys and gifts.

Dining: Victorian-style **Serengeti Overlook** looks out at Serengeti Plain and offers counter-service salads, sandwiches and pizzas, with an adjoining pub bar for a selection of craft beers, including selections from

Cobra's Curse

various local breweries ($7.99 or $11 for a flight of four samples).

◀︎🇬🇧 BRITTIP
We find the upstairs restaurant at **Serengeti Overlook** a blissful lunch stop in the hotter months when its cool interior and elegant ambience offer a welcome change of pace after all the rides.

Special tours

Busch Gardens features a wide range of behind-the-scenes tours and adventure expeditions that add an extra dimension to the park. For all tours, book at the Up Close Adventure Center in Morocco or, better still, book in advance on 1888 800 5447 or at **www.seaworldparks.com**.

Serengeti Safari: A 30min excursion (five times a day, up to 20 at a time) aboard flat-bed trucks, takes you to meet some of the Serengeti Plain's residents and feed the beautiful giraffes while learning about the park's environmental efforts. It fills up quickly and costs $29–39/person seasonally (ages 5+, 5-15s must be accompanied by an adult).

Serengeti Night Safari: (park admission not required) is a 2hr after-dark excursion into the Serengeti, with appetisers and hot and cold drinks (Nov–May, $69/person, ages 21+).

Guided Adventure Tour: This takes just 15 at a time on a 5hr VIP trek, with your own guide, reserved seating at the Moroccan Palace Theater, front-of-line access for major rides, counter-service lunch and close encounters with many of the animals, including the Serengeti Safari ($99/person).

Elite Adventure Tour: The ultimate personal park tour, a 7hr journey with front-of-line access to all rides, the Serengeti Safari, reserved seating at shows, free bottled water throughout and lunch at Crown Colony ($199/person, ages 5+).

Keeper for a Day: An exclusive 6½hr behind-the-scenes tour where you join the keepers as they feed, train and care for giraffes and antelope, then move on to assist the avian team on the Serengeti ($250/person, including park admission and lunch; ages 13+, book at least two weeks in advance).

Tiger Insider: A fascinating 45min group visit behind the scenes in Jungala to meet the keepers, see how they care for the magnificent tigers (you might even help to weigh one!) and learn some zoo husbandry secrets ($29/person, ages 5+).

Animal Care Center Behind The Scenes: A 75min tour with the park's vet and zoological staff, with hands-on opportunities, as they showcase medical check-ups and other treatments ($29/person, ages 8+).

Heart of Africa Tour: A 90min behind-the-scenes walking tour to get close to hippos, cheetahs and lions with their keepers ($39/person, ages 10+).

Special programmes

Food & Wine Festival: This imaginative event series is held weekends from Mar–Apr and is well worth sampling. Based in the Gwazi Pavilion area, it consists of a series of themed food and beverage kiosks offering dozens of fresh dishes, with new menus created especially by the park's culinary team. The festival runs from noon–9pm and starter-size samples range from $4–7, with wine and beers from $7–10, plus live entertainment and an evening concert at 6pm from the likes of Kenny Rogers, Commodores and Meatloaf, all as part of regular park admission. There are food and wine sampler packages from $25–45 while a series of giant topiaries and food sculptors add extra colour to the scene.

Summer Nights: Busch Gardens is open until 10pm (June–Aug) for this programme featuring outdoor food and drink, live entertainment (notably at the Dragonfire Grill and Gwazi Pavilion), music and DJs, plus clever lighting effects on coasters like SheiKra. A superb nightly high-energy finale, **Kinetix**, brings together live musicians, singers, dancers and acrobats for a 30min contemporary rock show enhanced by innovative lighting and with an all-new fireworks spectacular at the end.

Howl-O-Scream: Don't miss the park's special Halloween presentation each Sept–Oct. A separately ticketed event ($55–85/ person; see online for early-booking discounts) offering grisly goings-on and themed houses, it also offers the chance to ride all the big coasters at night (7.30pm–midnight or 1am). It features some imaginative shows with all the shock-horror effects, plus a dance party, but it is definitely not advised for young children. It is similar to Universal's Halloween Horror Nights programme (p165), with eight elaborately themed haunted houses – like Blood Asylum and Zombie Mortuary – plus a series of scare zones that change annually. The Busch Gardens version is more spread out and less frenetic than Universal's, but you may well want to try both. See more at **www. howloscream.com**.

Christmas: See p37.

Adventure Island: For a really full family day out, you can combine Busch Gardens with sister water park Adventure Island (on McKinley Drive), which is blissful when it's hot. The 25acres/10ha of watery fun, in a Key West theme, offer a full range of slides and rides, such as the **Colossal Curl**, a massive family raft ride, **Wahoo Run** raft ride, the exciting four-lane mat slide **Riptide**, leisurely **Rambling Bayou** lazy river and spiralling tube ride **Calypso Coaster**. Open mid-Mar to late Oct (weekends only Sept and Oct) 10am–5pm (9pm in summer). Tickets are $44 (ages 3 and up), while a Busch Gardens–Adventure Island combo is $148.

Well, that's the low-down on all the main theme parks, but there is still MUCH more to discover…

Serengeti Overlook at Busch Gardens

7 The Other Attractions

or One Giant Leap for Tourist Kind

If you think you can 'do' Orlando just by sticking to the main theme parks, think again! There is still a LOT more to discover, starting with Kennedy Space Center, which we rate as an essential place to spend a day.

Then there's LEGOLAND Florida – ideal for the 3–12 brigade – and Gatorland, another great-value experience. There are unique venues like WonderWorks, I-Drive 360 and Ripley's Believe It Or Not and, for more individual tastes, the amazing 'skydive' experience of iFLY Orlando and WhirlyDome fun centre, plus some great water parks. The choice is yours, but it's an immense selection. Let's start with One Giant Leap for Mankind.

Kennedy Space Center

Welcome to the past, present and future of NASA's space programme, and one of the most fascinating places in Florida. The KSC has undergone huge redevelopment in recent years, including the 2013 opening of their Space Shuttle Atlantis exhibit to showcase the last orbiter in the Shuttle programme, and a 2016 refresh that added the Heroes and Legends centre and helped to give the whole Visitor Complex an exciting, new look. This underlines its place among the first rank of local attractions and provides even more reason to justify an all-day visit. Apart from the Space Shuttle, there are a series of exhibits and shows (including two splendid

IMAX films), a children's play area, Cosmic Quest Adventure interactive game, the daily Astronaut Encounter, the poignant Astronaut Memorial, and the essential Space Center bus tours, which all add up to great value. There is also the brilliant Astronaut Training Experience, an extra programme into real-life astronaut missions and simulation. However, there is now a $10 parking fee, when it used to be free.

Getting there: Take the Beachline Expressway out of Orlando (Route 528, and a toll road, see map p214) for about 45mins, bear left on SR 407 (don't follow signs to Cape Canaveral or Cocoa Beach at this point) and turn right at the T-junction onto SR405. The Visitor Center is located 9ml/14km along on the right. Tours and IMAX presentations start at 10am (**www.KennedySpaceCenter.com** – check the website for periodic online ticket discounts).

✚ BRITTIP
Don't miss the original countdown clock and the clever water show at the Space Center's entry plaza, the latter of which runs every 15 minutes.

Once inside the Visitor Complex, the attractions are as follows. Start with the new Space Shuttle *Atlantis*, as this has proved THE big draw since it opened in June 2013. Late arrivals should do the Bus Tour first, though, then visit the Shuttle complex.

Atlantis: This dramatic $100m, 65,000ft²/6,000m² exhibit is the core experience of the new-look KSC, offering the 30-year history of the Shuttle programme through a mix of interactive media. Both hands-on and immersive, it features one of the three surviving orbiters (*Discovery* is on show at The Smithsonian in Washington and *Endeavour* at the California Science Center in Los Angeles). The six-storey building is clad in orange and gold, to symbolise the fiery glow of atmosphere re-entry, and is dominated outside by full-size replicas of the external fuel tank and solid rocket boosters, with their 184ft/56m height illustrating the power needed to put the Space Transport System (STS) in orbit. Visitors wind up a gently sloped ramp to a film pre-show into how and why the Shuttle programme was devised, and then doors open into the main theatre, offering a vivid sense surround presentation into the life and missions of *Atlantis* (stand about two-thirds of the way back to get the full effect of the wrap-around screens). The specially written musical score reaches an emotional crescendo that is accompanied by a real 'wow' moment as…no, we won't reveal it! It is a breathtaking show that leads into the main exhibit hall, with the orbiter displayed with its payload bay doors open and robotic arm extended alongside an elevated viewing platform. The hall is subdivided into areas for the International Space Station, Hubble Space Telescope and Astronaut Training Simulation Gallery (complete with the chance to land a Shuttle and dock with the Space Station). In all, there are more than 60 interactive touch-screen experiences and simulators, new Cosmic Quest Adventure game (see pg 218) and the climb-through Space Station, with its clear plastic tube suspended two storeys up, is quite a challenge. There are also parts of the launch platform and other support elements on show, while kids can try the Shuttle 'landing slide' and a jump-around hydrogen 'energy' game. You can easily spend a couple of hours in here and we strongly advise heading here first as queues build up quickly on the entry ramp. AAAAA+ The gift shop offers a great variety of souvenirs.

Kennedy Space Center at a glance

Location	Off State Road 405 in Titusville	
Size	Visitor Complex 70 acres/28.3ha	
Hours	9am–5 or 6pm) year-round (except Christmas Day)	
Admission	Under-3s free; 3–11 $40; adult (12+) $50; Atlantis annual pass $89/$71; Explorer annual pass $139/$109. Prices do not include tax	
Parking	$10	
Lockers	$5 and $8, just inside turnstiles to left.	
Pushchairs	$6 and $8 at Information Central (through entrance on left)	
Wheelchairs	$10 and $25 (electric scooter) at Information Central	
Top attractions	Space Shuttle Atlantis; Shuttle Launch Experience; IMAX films; Astronaut Encounter; KSC Bus Tours	
Don't miss	Apollo-Saturn V Center on Bus Tours; Astronaut Memorial; Rocket Garden	
Hidden costs	Meals	Burger, chips and coke $10.88 Kids' meal $5.49–7.59
	T-shirts	$15.99–39.99, Kids $9.99–19.99
	Souvenirs	99c–$1,500
	Sundries	Bus tour photos – $20 and $25

BRITTIP

Not sure what to do first at KSC? Visit the **Information Center** just to the left before the main turnstiles and they can provide a schedule for the day, working on your arrival time and what you'd like to see.

Shuttle Launch Experience: After seeing *Atlantis*, visitors should also walk up the long gantry for this well-made presentation into a real-life launch – with you on board! A clever pre-show, with dry ice, moody lighting and sound and vibration effects pave the way to the 'ready room' to prepare for your own blast-off. The capsules look like crew cabins in the cargo hold of the Shuttle, and you go through the launch procedure as the vehicle moves into a near vertical position for take-off. On the command 'Go for engine start', you are at the heart of a 5min simulation providing the features of a realistic launch, with vibration generators, sound effects, cabin movements and screen visuals. You get a taste of the G-forces involved, the Rocket Booster and External Tank separations, and a moment of 'weightlessness' as you enter Earth's orbit. Finally, the cargo doors open to reveal an awe-inspiring view. There is then a 'space walk' back to Earth via a spiral walkway surrounded by the stars and more satellite views of the planet. Don't miss the plaques to mark every Shuttle flight – and the memorials to the *Challenger* and *Columbia* tragedies. **R: 3ft 8in/112cm. TTT AAAAA**

Forever Remembered: Space Shuttle Memorial: Also inside the Atlantis exhibit is this moving two-part tribute to the astronauts who lost their lives in the *Challenger* and *Columbia* disasters. A short hallway features display cases dedicated to each astronaut, with artefacts, personal belongings and insights. A second hallway shows news footage of the physical recovery of shuttle parts, and the emotional recovery of the families. **AAAA.**

Heroes and Legends: This new exhibit was the former US Astronaut Hall of Fame (on Highway 405)

Apollo Saturn V Center

© Kennedy Space Center

and now is proudly incorporated in its own centre inside the Visitor Complex. Part interactive 3-D adventure, part memorial, it takes guests along on the earliest space missions and tells the astronauts' stories, for a real you-are-there experience using liberal touches of virtual reality. Then, you can interact (virtually) with the inductees into the Astronaut Hall of Fame. AAAA.

◀🇬🇧 BRITTIP

All of the Shuttle Launch Experience is fully wheelchair accessible, and there is a seat outside for potential riders to test their comfort level. For anyone wary of the full ride (although there is no need to be, unless you are pregnant or have neck or back problems), there is a bypass room where you can experience the attraction without the motion.

Bus tours: The KSC's signature coaches depart every 15mins from 10am and are narrated to provide a full overview of the Space Center. Each tour makes a main stop in addition to driving around much of the working area, including past the massive Vehicle Assembly Building and the former shuttle launch pads. The main stop is the Apollo/Saturn V Center, one of the KSC's great exhibits, where you can easily spend 90mins. It highlights the Apollo missions and first Moon landing with two impressive theatrical presentations on the risks and triumphs, a full-size 363ft/111m Saturn V rocket and a hands-on gallery of space exploration. Allow a couple of hours to do the tour justice but be aware the last bus leaves the Visitor Center at 3pm. AAAAA

IMAX films: Back at the Visitor Complex are the IMAX cinemas, twin 55ft/17m screens that give the impression of sitting on top of the action.

Journey To Space 3D is a 42min look at the story of the space shuttle programme and what comes next – a mission to Mars. The detailed and exciting film traces some amazing new developments in NASA's future.

New in 2016 was **A Beautiful Planet,** a documentary style film which follows a group of astronauts as they experience six months aboard the International Space Station, with astounding views of Earth, and insights into life in space. Narrated by actress Jennifer Lawrence, it highlights climate changes and human impact, with a particularly stunning view of the planet at night. Both films dazzle with the spirit of human achievement. AAAA Also in the IMAX building, you'll find **Science on a Sphere,** making use of projections on a 6ft/2m globe, teaching complex lessons about the Earth and the planets in an easy-to-understand way. Experts are on hand to narrate and answer questions.

Astronaut Encounter: This engaging feature is a daily talk and Q&A session, with personal observations and stories from various veterans of the space programmes, including Shuttle astronauts. It is held up to three times a day at the Astronaut Encounter Theater. AAAA

Eyes on the Universe: NASA's Space Telescopes: This fascinating 20min live presentation with 3-D photography explores star formation and distant galaxies, looking back 13.4 billion years via the Hubble Space Telescope, and anticipating the future of visual 'space travel' through the eyes of the James Webb Telescope, due to launch in 2018. AAAA

Journey To Mars: Explorers Wanted: What will it take to explore deep space? This interactive exhibit inspires thinking through live presentations, interactive games, simulators and a mock-up of NASA's Orion crew capsule. AAAA

Other exhibits: Nature and Technology showcases the unique

Heroes and Legends

© Kennedy Space Center

balance the Center maintains with the local environment, while youngsters have their own playground, the covered **Children's Play Dome**, which has a range of climbing/crawling/sliding elements. Also primarily for young 'uns is the splash fountain in the **Rocket Garden**, which showcases the full variety of spacecraft that have journeyed beyond the Earth's atmosphere since the 1950s. The Garden also features an Apollo capsule gantry, to give the feel of astronauts boarding the Saturn V rocket, and the chance to sit inside replicas of the tiny capsules of the Mercury, Gemini and Apollo astronauts. Free tours are given up to four times a day (times vary) and are well presented for all ages. Don't forget to stop at the moving **Astronaut Memorial**. AAAA

Cosmic Quest Adventure: This new interactive computer game challenges trainees (i.e. you) to test their space knowledge with various Lab Station missions, culminating in a final Adventure Challenge that decides if they're ready for promotion, or need a bit more training. Four Adventures are located around the Space Center, from building a Martian colony (Journey to Mars building), capturing a rogue asteroid (IMAX), launching a rocket (Apollo/Saturn V Center) or performing experiments on the International Space Station (Atlantis). Doing them all can take several hours, so this is best for a second or third visit. ($24.95 for game-activating badge, lanyard, and Training Manual; admission required; best for ages 8–16)

Shopping: The Visitor Complex has an excellent **Space Shop** (the world's largest store for space memorabilia

Rocket Garden

and gifts – enter at your peril!), **Shuttle Express** in the Atlantis building and **The Right Stuff Shop** at the Apollo/Saturn V Center.

Dining: Stop for lunch at **Orbit Café**, a modern counter-service diner where you order your food – a tempting array of salads, sandwiches, pizza, burgers and kids meals – at touchscreen kiosks (and can see some of the lettuce and herbs being grown in hydroponic towers), or the excellent **Rocket Garden Café**, for tasty sandwiches, salads, flatbreads and fish and chips, plus hot and cold breakfast 9–11am. Quick bites and drinks, including speciality coffees, can be found at several kiosks throughout the Visitor Center. You'll also find the **Rocket Fuel Food Truck** in the entry plaza and **Moon Rock Café** at the Apollo/Saturn V Center on the bus tour.

The Center then has five optional extra tours and three other features.

KSC Up-Close: Explore Tour: Travel nearly a ¼mile/800m within the perimeter security fence of Launch Pad 39-A and get a close view of the complex, including the flame trench and emergency escape system – with a photo opp during a stop near the pad. Other sites on the tour include drive-by views of Launch Pad 39-B, the Vehicle Assembly Building, mobile launch platforms and a stop at the Apollo/Saturn V Center ($25 adults, $19 for 3–11s).

KSC Up-Close: The Launch Control Center Tour: Go inside Firing Room 4, from which all 21 shuttle launches since 2006 were controlled. See the engineers' working computerised launch control systems, main launch countdown clock and large video monitors on the walls, then enter the 'bubble room' with its wall of interior windows through which the management team viewed the proceedings ($25 and $19).

Cape Canaveral: Then and Now: If you want to learn more about NASA history, try this 3hr+ guided tour (Thurs–Sun only) into the early days of space exploration around the older part of the facility. Highlights

include the Air Force Space & Missile Museum, Mercury launch sites and Memorial, original astronaut training facility and several active launch pads, all of which are otherwise off-limits. For this tour, international guests (including children) must present a valid passport to participate. You must check in at the Information Counter at least 30min prior to your tour ($25 and $19). Reserve online or call 1866 737 5235.

Astronaut Training Experience (ATX): Away from the main attractions, you have the choice of a thrilling half-day programme into Shuttle training, using a sequence of simulated hands-on preparations, with the input of various NASA veterans. The training provides activities from the multi-axis trainer and one-sixth gravity chair, to operating a Shuttle mock-up and taking the helm in Mission Control. You must be at least 14 (under-18s accompanied by a parent). Hardwearing clothes and athletic shoes are advised, and 'recruits' should be free of neck and back injuries. It costs $175 (including ATX gear) but guarantees a memorable day for 'space cadets'.

ATX Family: A chance for children as young as seven, with a parent, to participate in a half-day course. The session includes building and launching rockets, riding realistic simulators, meeting a veteran NASA Astronaut and working on a shuttle mission to the International Space Station in 'Mission Control'. It's $175/adults and $165/child (7–11) and you can book in advance on 1866 737 5235 or online (see below).

BRITTIP

The Space Center still has an extremely active rocket launch programme and you can see full details at **www.nasa.gov** and **www.visitspacecoast.com/launch-schedule/**.

Lunch with an Astronaut: For another fully engrossing feature at the Kennedy Space Center, a small group gets to dine with the star of the daily Astronaut Encounter. The featured person gives their own special briefing, adding extra insight into their space missions, plus answers individual questions, gives autographs and poses for photos. $30 adults, $16 children, at noon daily. Buy tickets online or call 1866 737 5235. We recommend this – the buffet-style lunch is pretty good, too!

Get a great astronaut photo opportunity at the Kennedy Space Center!

© Kennedy Space Center

LEGOLAND Florida

Children aged 2–12 – plus their parents and even grand parents – will all enjoy this bright and expansive park, which opened in 2011. In a beautiful lakeside setting on the site of the former Cypress Gardens – and including the old tropical gardens – it offers 150acres/60ha of guaranteed fun with its extensive main park and water park. In fact, while the typical LEGOLAND age range is 2–12, the Floridian version probably appeals to kids as old as 14 with its bigger rides and water flumes. There is plenty to do, with no fewer than 26 rides, three main shows, an extensive adventure play area, the amazing Miniland, LEGO Friends area and the new Ninjago World (for 2017). It has its own LEGO-themed hotel, with another due to open later in 2017. There is also great shopping, and their two-day ticket is great value. Even the dining options are fresh, healthy and appealing, and there are plenty of quiet corners and gardens in which to chill out.

Getting there: take I-4 west to Exit 55, then Highway 27 south for 18 miles to State Road 540. Turn right and the park is 4mls/6.4km along, on the left.

It does require a lot of legwork to see it all, though, as it sprawls round the southern shore of Lake Eloise and, when it's hot, there aren't so many places in the air-conditioned cool. But there is definitely something for all but older teens and we enjoy the clever landscaping and fun use of LEGO characters and features.

Location and tactics

LEGOLAND Florida is in Winter Haven, about 45mins south-east of the Disney/Kissimmee area. Shuttle service is available from the I-Drive 360 complex on International Drive at 9am next to the multi-storey car park, for $5/person round trip, reservations required on 1877 350 5346 or the Legoland website.

LEGOLAND Florida at a glance

Location	Off State Road 540 in Winter Haven	
Size	150acres	
Hours	10am–6 or 7pm in high season (Easter, summer, Thanksgiving and Christmas), 10am–5pm off peak; closed Tues and Wed off peak; Water Park 10.30am–5 or 6pm in summer; 10.30am–5pm Apr–May (closed some weekdays); 10.30am–5pm Sept– Oct (Sat–Sun only).	
Admission	Under-3s free; $89 (1-day ticket); $109 (1-day plus water park; $104 (2-day ticket) $144 (2-day plus water park)	
Parking	$17 ($15 if prepaid online); Preferred parking $22	
Lockers	$10	
Pushchairs	$14 and $24	
Wheelchairs	$12 and $45 ($55 with canopy)	
Top attractions	The Dragon, Coastersaurus, Technic Coaster, Driving School, Boating School, Wave Racers, Island in the Sky, The Quest for CHI, Royal Joust, Ninjago The Ride (2017)	
Don't miss	Miniland, Heartlake City, Fun Town 4-D Theater, Pirates Cove Water Ski Show, Cypress Gardens	
Hidden costs	Meals	Burger, chips and coke $13.25 Kids' meal $6.99
	Kids' T-shirts	$16.99–24.99
	Souvenirs	$0.99–370
	Sundries	Face painting $11–20; Photopass $49.99, $16 second day

You arrive into the large car park where the parking fee is $17 and walk to the entrance. The Preferred Parking area (closer to the entrance) features new solar panel technology that provides power to local homes. The park's 150acres/60ha spreads people out well but still draws queues at peak periods, hence your best bet is to head for LEGO Kingdoms, Land of Adventure, World of Chima and DUPLO Valley (girls may also want to check out Heartlake City), returning to Fun Town and Miniland later in the day. If your kids love the Ninjago characters, the new Ninjago World will be the area to go first. For a second day, start with your favourite rides then cool down in the water park (which closes an hour before the main park). Once through the gates, here's what you'll find, moving in an anti-clockwise direction (advisable). NB: All ratings are indicated for younger children rather than adults!

BRITTIP
LEGOLAND employees are called Model Citizens, and each wears at least one Mini-Figure on their name badge. Bring along (or purchase) your own mini-figure and they'll trade with you!

The Beginning: This offers the ticket centre, Guest Relations and functional elements like the lockers, pushchair and wheelchair hire.

There are no shows but the one ride, **Island in the Sky**, is a 150ft/46m lift into the air on a gently revolving platform that affords a magnificent view over the park, lake and surrounding areas. Under 4ft/122cm must be accompanied by adult. AAAA

Shopping and dining: Immediately to the left of the entrance is **The Big Shop** (one of the largest LEGO merchandise stores in the world). Dining is at **The Market Restaurant** (soups, salads, sandwiches; gluten free, fresh chicken and Asian stir-fry selections) with a quick-bite counter and coffee bar.

Fun Town: Here is where the squeals of delight really begin! In true

LEGOLAND style, you have entered a charming village complete with a working factory, 4-D cinema and carousel. Take a **Factory Tour** and watch working machinery as it goes through the process of making LEGO bricks, from moulding to packaging, then let the kids ride **The Grand Carousel** (**TT**; under 4ft/122cm must be accompanied by adult). Just beyond is **Wells Fargo Fun Town Theater**, featuring two 12min 4-D movies daily, both new in 2016.

The LEGO Movie 4D: The Next Adventure features the further madcap exploits of Emmet, Wyldstyle, Unikitty and Metalbeard as they encounter new villain Risky Business; **LEGO Nexo Knights: The Book of Creativity** offers kids the chance to join the Nexo Knights in a battle against the evil Jestro and the Book of Monsters. Both are fun and provide some clever special effects, and Nexo Knights takes it a step further with an interactive download that allows kids to search for six exclusive shields throughout the park that unlock exclusive NEXO Powers in the free LEGO NEXO KNIGHTS Merlok 2.0 mobile app (for iOS and Android devices). **TTT.** NEXO hero Lance Richmond will be available for meet-and-greets outside the theatre after the show.

BRITTIP
Fun Town Theater is a blissful air-conditioned haven in summer and ideal for visiting during the hottest parts of the day.

Duplo Valley

Shopping: All your favourite themed merchandise can be found at **LEGO Studios**, including Star Wars, SpongeBob, Indiana Jones, and Batman, the **Minifigure Market** and **Pick A Brick**.

Dining: Granny's Apple Fries serves up the park's signature dessert (apples, cinnamon and a creamy sauce), and **Fun Town Slushies** offers great cold treats. **Fun Town Pizza & Pasta Buffet** is a value-conscious choice ($15.99/$9.99).

DUPLO® Valley: Turn right out of Fun Town to the perfect place for toddlers to let their imaginations run wild as they explore a village sized just for them. Completely re-themed in 2014, this area features a junior-sized train that winds through the 'countryside', passing farms, campgrounds and fishing holes. Toddlers will love helping the 'farmer' find missing animals and plough the fields, and then cool down in the water play area. **TTTT** under-6s

World of Chima: This begins the large-scale fun for the six-plus brigade, themed for the LEGO Legends of Chima toy range, as brought to life by the Cartoon Network. Here, visitors enter the Lion Temple on **The Quest for CHI**, a challenging water ride where they battle Cragger the Crocodile King with water cannons as he bids to steal the CHI energy orbs. The journey travels through the full mystical animal world, including imaginative habitats for **Gorilla Forest** and **Raven's Roost**. **TTTT** Also here is the **Speedorz™** Arena, where players can build LEGO Speedorz and compete to win the precious supply of CHI in group challenges. For watery fun, check out **Cragger's Swamp**,

World of Chima

a children's play area featuring interactive water spouts and fountains. Kids can then meet Laval the Lion Prince and Cragger at a special **character meet-and-greet** station.

Shopping: Having ridden the ride, of course, you can then buy the LEGO at **Razar's Bazaar**.

LEGO Kingdoms: The next large-scale land features three major rides and a cool play area. Climb aboard **The Dragon** for a backstage view of life in an enchanted castle, then take off on a thrilling flight as this scenic dark ride becomes a dynamic outdoor coaster! **R:** 4ft/122cm or 3ft 4in/102cm with adult. Child Swap and ride photo available. **TTTT** Then, saddle up on LEGO-themed horses for **The Royal Joust**, where youngsters gallop through an enchanted forest, jousting with LEGO knights along the way. **R:** 3ft/91cm; max 12 yrs and 170lb/76kg. **TT** Also here is **Merlin's Challenge**, a fairly standard but quite whizzy fairground circular ride (4ft/122cm or 3ft 4in/102cm with adult). **TTT** Kids will also want to spend time in **The Forestmen's Hideout**, a multi-level climb, scramble and crawl treehouse adventure with ropes and slides. **AAAA** There are also the **Jester's Games** ($3–10).

Shopping: The Kings Market carries suitably themed gifts.

Dining: Castle Burger serves tasty burgers and chicken sandwiches.

Land of Adventure: Next is another BIG land, with two major rides and three other great kiddie attractions. The excitement continues at **Lost Kingdom Adventure** as you hunt for treasure while fighting off baddies with laser blasters. Youngsters will want to ride several times to better their score. **R:** 4ft 6in/137cm or 2ft 10in/86cm with adult. **TTT** Child Swap, ride photos available.

Next is another top thrill in the form of **Coastersaurus**, a classic wooden coaster that zips through a prehistoric jungle and past animated LEGO dinosaurs. **R:** 3ft/91cm or 4ft/122cm with adult. **TTTTT** Then you can just let young 'uns loose at **Pharaoh's Revenge**

© Legoland

multi-level climbing structure, with the added fun of being able to shoot soft foam balls at each other. **Beetle Bounce** shoots riders 15ft/4.5m high on this kid-friendly tower ride (**R**: 3ft/91cm; **TTTT**) while **Safari Trek** is the classic children's car ride, through a clever LEGO-themed African savannah full of lurking animals. **R**: 2ft 10in/86cm, or 4ft/122cm with adult, max age 12; **TTT** The **Adventure Games** are more fairground side-stalls for an extra few dollars.

Dining: Adventure Snacks is a good choice for hot dogs, nachos and cheese, and drinks and **Dino Treats** offers tasty desserts.

Ninjago World: This extensive new area is set up around the characters and exploits of the Ninjago warriors from the TV series, which spun off the LEGO sets. It features four outdoor experiences, designed to test visitors' balance and agility before they venture to the main event. **Ninjago – The Ride** is an indoor interactive 4-D adventure that sets up a battle to test your ninja skills in a series of 13 animated Dojo challenges. Using only hand and arm gestures, you fire lightning bolts, fireballs, shockwaves and ice at various targets, building up to a battle with the Great Devourer and the chance to earn full Spinjitsu Ninja status. **TTTT** (expected). **R**. Riders under 4ft/122cm must be accompanied by a responsible rider 4ft or taller.

Shopping: Check out the 22 Ninjago building sets – and more – at **Wu's Warehouse**.

Dining: Sample Asian cuisine at **Ninja Kitchen**, including Banh Mi sandwiches and steamed Bao Buns.

LEGO City: This popular area features some of the most classic attractions, themed like a real working town, starting with **Rescue Academy**, where families race each other to 'put out the fire'. But these fire trucks only move when you pump the levers! **R**: 4ft/122cm or 2ft 10in/86cm with adult; guests in wheelchairs must transfer. **TTT** LEGOLAND's ultra-popular **Driving School** (ages 6–13) and **Junior Driving School** (3–5s)

and **Boating School** (4ft/122cm or 2ft 10in/86cm with adult) are all here too, giving kids the chance to navigate electric cars and small boats to earn official LEGOLAND driving licences. **TT–TTTT** For something more dynamic, try **Flight School's** suspended steel coaster, one of the biggest thrills in the park and a major hit with coaster fans. **R**: 3ft 8in/111cm or 4ft 4in/130cm with adult. **TTTTT**

Shopping: Pick up some souvenirs at the **Driving School Store**.

Dining: Grab a tempting chicken lunch or dinner at the indoor **Fried Chicken Co**, a tasty burger at the new **LEGO City Burger Kitchen** or a light bite and drink at **City Slush**.

BRITTIP

See LEGOLAND's website for periodic discounts. They sometimes offer $15 off ALL tickets if booked in advance for a specific day.

LEGO Technic: This area is packed with fun and thrills for older children as it offers three super rides. **Project X** is the stand-out offering, a tall, fast-turning steel coaster where riders race, brake and bank in life-size LEGO Technic cars. **R**: 4ft/122cm or 3ft 6in/99cm with adult; **TTTTT** Ride the waves and dodge soaking blasts of water on the airboat-style **Aquazone Wave Racers**, a ride so cool you'll want to queue up straight away for another go! **R**: 4ft 4in/132cm or 3ft 4in/102cm with adult; **TTTT**). Kids can also try the more sedate **Technicyle** (**TT**) and have a go at the **Extreme Games** (for a few extra dollars), while toddlers will gravitate to **Technic Tot Spot** soft play area.

Star Wars in the Miniland section

© Legoland

Shopping: With a great view overlooking Lake Eloise, the **Extreme Brick Bargains Shop** offers end-of-range LEGO sets, clearance deals and last-chance items.

Dining: Neighbouring **Lakeside Sandwich Co** is a fab choice for fresh sandwiches, wraps, salads and drinks. **Robot Pit Stop** features hot dogs, nachos, novelty ice creams, and drinks.

> **◄📖 BRITTIP**
>
> Have kids who are nervous about coasters (even the junior kind)? LEGOLAND has a unique programme to help parents with 'Roller Coaster Readiness' tips, available online at **http://florida.legoland. com/PageFiles/1107/LLFBrochureWeb. pdf** and at the front gate.

Imagination Zone: Next up is the creative heart of the park, where kids put their imagination to work at seven all-new hands-on indoor play areas. They include the chance to try out touch-screen technology in the **Water Zone**; invent crazy aerial creations in **Flight Zone**; build and test race cars in the **Wheels Zone**; and build on the walls of the **Creation Zone**. Then there are the latest LEGO video games in the **Warner Bros. Games Zone** and computer-controlled robots in the

LEGO Mindstorms area. Outside, the **Kid Power Towers** then burn off excess energy as kids (and adults!) use ropes and pulleys to ascend colourful towers – and let go for a 'free fall' back down. **R:** 4ft/122cm or 3ft 4in/100cm with adult; **TTT** Child swap available, guests in wheelchairs must transfer.

Dining: Grab a tasty toasted sandwich, salad and drink at **Imagination Panini Grill**.

Cypress Gardens: Just behind and to the right of the Imagination Zone are the beautiful gardens this park was originally known for, now lovingly restored and a peaceful haven for strolling, complete with beautiful gazebo and tropical displays (and yes, that banyan tree is real, unlike the Disney version!). **AAAA**

Pirates Cove: Come back out of the Gardens and you'll find the place where swashbuckling meets water in an exciting battle on the 'high seas' in The Battle for Brickbeard's Bounty. LEGO characters and a life-sized pirate ship add to the fun of this water stunt show, with water-skiers, ski-jumping and other stunts that young children will not want to miss. **AAA**

Dining: Grab a take-away at one of the nearby quick-serves and have

Imagination Zone

© Legoland

Haven dining

If you stay in Winter Haven for dinner, there are two great choices on Highway 17 (3rd Street SW; turn left on Cypress Gardens Boulevard out of Legoland, go 3mls/5km then turn right on to 3rd St SW). **Fred's Southern Kitchen** features a true southern-style buffet with the likes of skillet cornbread, chicken and biscuits, collard greens, ribs and fried catfish as well as salads, soups and homemade desserts ($15 adults, $6 kids; soft drinks only; **www.fredssouthernkitchen.com**). Then there is the Winter Haven outlet of popular local chain **Manny's Chophouse**, with its signature steaks, chops and ribs, plus lively style and eclectic decor. With a good kids' menu and full bar service, it is easily the equal of its Brit-friendly Highway 27 counterpart and, while they don't take reservations, waits rarely top 20–30 mins (p314; **www.mannyschophouse.com**).

an al fresco lunch at the lakeside Imagination Pavilion picnic area.

Heartlake City: This area is dedicated to the LEGO Friends, with a high-energy character show, a whizzy ride and some fun additional elements. **Friends to the Rescue** is a neat show featuring the five main characters, with plenty of audience involvement, while **Mia's Riding Adventure** offers junior-sized horse-themed fun on a back-and-forth disk coaster. **The Heartlake Stepping Tones Fountain** is another interactive feature with LEGO instruments that play music.

Shopping: Pick up all the latest LEGO Friends collections and accessories at the **Heartlake Mall**.

Miniland USA: Completing the big LEGOLAND tour brings you to the park's other crown jewel, an iconic area featuring eight themed US locations in miniature – and the big bonus of a Star Wars-themed area. **Florida** shows off some of the state's gems, with separate areas devoted to a magnificent replica of the Kennedy Space Center (complete with Shuttle countdown!) and the huge Daytona International Speedway, where youngsters can race LEGO dragsters.

Las Vegas boasts the glittering resorts and other icons of Nevada's most famous city while **Washington DC** re-creates the White House, US Capitol, Smithsonian museum and the Washington and Jefferson monuments. Look closely and you'll see an animated parade and the cherry trees that bloom each spring. No mini-land would be complete without **New York City**, and this representation includes Rockefeller Plaza (complete with squirt fountains!), Times Square, Lady Liberty, the Empire State building, Bronx Zoo and Grand Central Station. Finally, there is a section devoted to the ever-popular subject of **Pirates**, and another miniland that highlights the state of **California**, plus the **Star Wars** zone, complete with scenes from six films, as well as one from animated series the Clone Wars.

Miniland's detail is amazing, with a riot of visual gags and fun touches (try to spot the surprised gent in the loos at Grand Central Station!), and you can easily spend an hour or more browsing here.

Water Park: This fabulous extra (for $20/person) is an opportunity to have fun in best LEGO style. Not as large as the likes of Blizzard Beach and Aquatica, but designed completely with young children in mind and easier to negotiate, it offers the full array of lockers, changing rooms, towel rental and gift shop (with swimming costumes for sale if you make a late decision to try it), plus **Beach-n-Brick Grill**, complete with shaded Tiki Bar for tired parents! Cabaña hire starts at $89. There are six main areas and it will require at least half a day of your time.

Creative Cove at LEGOLAND Water Park

© Legoland

As ever, have plenty of high-factor, waterproof suncream.

DUPLO Splash Safari: This is Toddler Central, featuring small-scale slides and interactive DUPLO creatures, all in just 6in/15cm of water (and within view of the Tiki bar!). AAAA

Joker Soaker: Older children will love this huge water-feature adventure playground and its slides, fountains, climbs, squirt guns and more, including a 300-gallon bucket that fills and tips periodically! **R:** 3ft/91cm on 3 lower slides, 3ft 6in/ 99cm on upper 4; under 3ft 6in/99cm must be accompanied by an adult. AAAAA

Build a Raft River: An imaginative variation on the lazy-river idea, with riders able to build their own floating raft with special LEGO bricks and then complete the 1,000ft/330m-long 3ft/91cm deep circuit. AAA

LEGO Wave Pool: Enjoy some gentle surf fun in this wide, walk-in pool that allows young children to splash happily while their older siblings can brave the 3ft 4in/100cm-plus depths. AAA

BRITTIP

There is no shade in the Miniland area, so be SURE to apply lots of high factor suncream before spending time here.

Twin Chasers: Older children will love the chance to ride these double flumes – one open, one enclosed – on individual rafts that sloosh down the 375ft/114m tubes, with a grand splash-down at the end. **R:** 4ft/122cm; TTTT

Splash Out: The ultimate thrill-ride for kids, a selection of 3 intertwined body-slides with a drop of 60ft/18m that afford a great view of the surrounding area – before you 'drop in'! **R:** 4ft/122cm; TTTTT

Creative Cove: New in summer 2016, this added the fun, hands-on Build-a-Boat attraction, where kids can create and race LEGO watercraft through fast-flowing rivers in a setting inspired by the popular LEGO City Coast Guard sets.

Seasonal fun: LEGOLAND adds more entertainment at different times of the year, notably **Night Lights** (mid-Jun to late Jul), with extended hours, more character appearances, Master Builder sessions and a big fireworks finale over Lake Eloise; **Brick-or-Treat** for the Halloween season (Oct) with trick or treating, scavenger hunts and a fireworks show; the **Christmas Bricktacular**, with festive decorations, a LEGO Santa and sleigh, Master Builder sessions, character appearances and more nightly fireworks; and even a **Kids New Year's Eve**, with the chance to party and celebrate at a more kid-friendly time.

If that's the park, here are some add-ons that may be worth including in your visit.

Bricks-n-Breakfast Character Breakfast: Meet all your favourite LEGO characters at this breakfast buffet. Each child receives a mini-figure and each group gets an Awesome Awaits pass to skip the queue at one attraction ($30, Sun only, park admission not required).

Red Brick Carpet VIP Experience: Tour the park with a VIP host who shares fascinating facts about the park and the models. It also offers priority access to rides, shows and attractions; a tour of the model shop; VIP gift bag; family photo and digital photo package, as well as park admission, valet parking, lunch, snacks and drinks ($495/adult, $445/child). **Red Brick Carpet & Water Park** adds water park admission, private cabana, locker, beach towels and photo ($595 and $545). Book VIP experiences on 1855 753 7777 or **www.legoland.com/florida/buy-tickets/vip-experiences/book-vip-experiences**.

Inside the LEGOLAND Hotel

Opening times: LEGOLAND closes on Tues and Wed at quiet times of the year and the water park is only open in the hotter months (and closes weekdays in the spring and autumn). Check in advance on 1877 350 5346 or **http://florida.legoland.com**.

LEGOLAND Hotel: This is a great way to stay right in the heart of the fun and take full advantage of those 2-day tickets. With 152 brightly coloured and themed rooms, there is bags of LEGO style throughout, from the giant dragon at the entrance to dozens of individual pieces in the rooms, where there is a special Treasure Hunt for kids to solve (and find a prize). Chose from Kingdom, Adventure, Pirates and LEGO Friends for the individual room themes, which all feature bunk beds and an entertainment unit for kids, while the two-room suites add a living room, pullout sofa and play area. The VIP Suites sleep up to six. There are king-sized beds for adults, two flatscreen TVs, a mini-fridge and coffee maker in every room. Premium rooms add more LEGO décor and models for kids to play with. The hotel includes a fabulous heated outdoor pool and its own buffet-style diner, Bricks Family Restaurant. A full breakfast is included in the daily rate, with exclusive Master Model Builder sessions (a major hit with children), early park admission, nightly LEGO building competitions and live entertainment, and there is also a lovely boardwalk on the edge of Lake Eloise. There are interactive play areas for kids throughout the hotel, and it doesn't get much better than walking straight out of the hotel – and straight INTO the park!

BRITTIP
Don't miss the 'Disco Elevators' at the LEGOLAND Hotel – you might not want to get out when it's your floor!

New later in 2017 will be the 2nd hotel, the **LEGOLAND Beach Retreat**, a lakefront resort with 83 village-style bungalows for a total of 166 rooms. Along with a cool Lego beach/surfer theme, the hotel will have a themed pool, sandy play area and buffet-style restaurant.

Gatorland

For a taste of Florida wildlife, this is as authentic as it gets and is popular with children of all ages. The 'Alligator Capital of the World' was founded in 1949 and is still family owned, so it has a natural, homespun charm few of its big-name rivals can match. And, when the wildlife consists of several thousand menacing alligators and crocodiles in various natural habitats and three fascinating shows – plus a fabulous Zip Line attraction that is disabled accessible – you know you're in for a different experience (although there is a LOT more to Gatorland than just gators – including their Bobcat Bayou). Overall, Gatorland is something you're unlikely to get anywhere else, and the sense of being in the 'real' Florida is terrific.

Getting there: Gatorland is on the South Orange Blossom Trail, 2ml/3km south of the Central Florida Greeneway and 3ml/5km north of Highway 192 (see map p14). Admission: $26.99 adults, $18.99 3–12s, 10am–5pm, parking free. Annual passes are only $45.99 and $31.99 if you plan more than one visit (407 855 5496, **www.gatorland.com**). Check website for current coupons.

BRITTIP
If you have an evening flight home from Orlando International, visit Gatorland for half a day on your final day as it is just 20mins' drive from the airport.

LEGOLAND Hotel

© Legoland

Gatorland Express tours: Start by taking the 15min train ride around the park to get an idea of its 110acre/45ha expanse. This has an added fee but is good for multiple rides, is amusingly narrated and is especially fun for kids. You also get a good look at the native animal habitat, which features whitetail deer, wild turkey and quail. Wander the natural beauty of the 2,000ft/610m Swamp Walk, as well as the Alligator Breeding Marsh Walkway, where a three-storey observation tower gives a neat overview. Ask yourself: are they hanging around in the hope someone might 'drop in' for lunch?

BRITTIP

If you are at Gatorland first thing in the morning, take the Swamp Walk straight away. There will be far more wildlife activity then and the peaceful ambience is quite invigorating.

Attractions: Breeding pens, baby alligator nurseries and rearing ponds are also situated throughout the park to provide an idea of the growth cycle of the gator and enhance the overall feeling that it is the visitor behind bars here, not the animals.

Simon tries gator wrestling at Gatorland!

Jungle Crocs features some of the deadliest animals of Egypt, Australia and Cuba, with authentic lairs and brilliant presentation (look out for Sultan and his 'harem' of lady crocs from the Nile). Many of the small-scale attractions have been designed with kids in mind and there is plenty to keep everyone amused. **Allie's Barnyard** is a petting zoo, while you can feed some friendly lorikeets at the **Very Merry Aviary**, and view the pink inhabitants of **Flamingo Island**.

White Gator Swamp: Don't miss this remarkable showcase for four rare and completely white alligators, which are totally leucistic (without pigment), with startling blue eyes, not pink like albinos. Other animals include owls, turtles, flamingos, tortoises, snakes, spiders, emus and deer; also hundreds of wading birds, providing a fascinating close-up of the nests during Mar–Aug.

Bobcat Bayou: This is the place to find Gatorland's two bobcats, while the park also showcases two rare Florida panthers in the **Panther Springs** exhibit.

BRITTIP

Lucy and Neiko, brother and sister panthers who live at Gatorland, are at their most lively first thing in the morning when they have been let out of their night quarters – just like any domestic cat!

Shows: The 800-seat **Wrestling Stadium** sets the scene for some real cracker-style feats (a 'cracker' is a Florida cowboy) as Gatorland's resident 'wranglers' catch a medium-sized gator and proceed to point out the animal's features, with the aid of some daredevil stunts that will have you questioning their sanity. The **Gator Jumparoo** is another eye-opening spectacle as some of the park's biggest creatures use their tails to 'jump' out of the water and be hand-fed tasty morsels, like whole chickens! **Up-Close Encounters** is another amusing showcase of creatures, from the expected snakes to less obvious cockroaches and scorpions. Great photo opportunities for brave children!

Gator Gully: This superb little water park features numerous ways for kids to cool down, get wet and generally have fun. The ½acre/0.2ha park features five elements, including a giant jalopy with water jets for spokes and a fountain radiator, an old shack that 'explodes' with water, and giant gators with squirt guns. The neighbouring dry play area and chairs and tables allow parents to sit and watch the kids expend some energy, perhaps with a drink from one of the kiosks.

But wait… that's not all!

Screamin' Gator Zip Line: Gatorland has fixed its eyes firmly on the brave of heart, introducing a first-of-its-kind zipline experience, with four zips soaring high above the park's most notorious residents. At 1,200ft/366m long and up to 56ft/17m high, the lines afford spectacular views of jumping Cuban Crocodiles and the scenic Alligator Breeding Marsh. Start at Tower One, where the 'bunny hill' builds up your courage (and your excitement). Tower Two soars over croc pools (look down – the view is outrageous!); Tower Three is the tallest launch point at 75ft/23m, and its 600ft/182m run zips straight over the breeding marsh at up to 35mph/56kph. Take the walking bridge over to Tower Four where you're met by a thrilling double zipline for a final race to the finish.

BRITTIP
Book the Screamin' Gator in advance to avoid disappointment. Capacity is limited to groups of 12 4–7 times a day and demand is high. Reserve by phone or online.

The experience includes orientation, full equipment check, the zipline and a trek across a swinging bridge. There is a separate fee, but at $69.99/person, it includes all-day admission to the park. A photographer will also chart your journey for purchase back on terra firma! **R:** Min weight 75lb/34kg, max 250lb/113kg. Must be able to climb stairs. Wear closed-toe shoes and trousers or long shorts. New in 2014, Gatorland installed a brilliant wheelchair-accessible,

one-segment zip line for guests with lower-body disabilities (must transfer to specially designed harness), providing a thrilling 350ft/106m glide over the gator marsh.

Shopping: In addition to three gift stores and the **Gator & Snake** photo opportunity, you should visit the **Gift Shop** complex at the entrance, which incorporates the trademark Gator Mouth entryway.

Dining: Grab a bite or drink at three snack bars: try **Gator Jake's Fudge Kitchen** or dine on smoked gator ribs and fried gator nuggets (as well as burgers and hotdogs) at **Pearl's Smokehouse**, with excellent kids' meals at $6.59.

Special events: Some unique options if you really want to get to know your gators are: **Trainer for a Day**, with the chance to work behind the scenes at the park 8am–10am, finding out what it takes to handle such dangerous animals, behavioural training and novice gator wrangling ($125 12s and over, max five people; includes park admission); **Gator Night Shine**, which takes guests into the Breeding Marsh after dark for a one-hour tour with a senior gator expert, with torches and gator food to lure the 'locals'. You can then marvel at how gator eyes shine like red beacons in the torchlight and learn more about the habits of these amazing animals – a real family treat, which kids seem to love (dusk, around 8.15pm summer, 6.30pm autumn and winter; $20 all ages; bug spray provided; reservations required); and **Adventure Hour**, a chance to go truly 'behind-the-scenes' in the Breeding Marsh to feed and pose for photos with the gators here ($10/person). Rookie Wrestling is every kid's chance to show

Screamin' Gator Zip Line

© Gatorland

his or her bravery and have the picture to prove it ($10 to kneel over a gator's back; extra for the photo).

International Drive

The 14½ml/23km tourist corridor of I-Drive (see maps p14 and 214) continues to be an ever-changing source of hotels, restaurants, shopping and fun. There are more than 42,000 hotel rooms, 150+ restaurants and almost 500 shops, as well as 15 attractions, including six mini-golf courses. The I-Ride Trolley links it all in transport terms and the website **www.internationaldriveorlando.com** highlights all the options. Its Official Visitors Guide has an I-Ride map and valuable money-off coupons, which you can download to get you started, plus a hotel booking facility. The I-Ride Trolley section provides 'NextTrolley' info as well as maps and listings of what is near each trolley stop.

Here's a look at the area's attractions (see also Chapter 10, Orlando By Night, and Chapter 12, Shopping, to get the full picture).

BRITTIP

I-Drive 360, Ripley's, Titanic, iFly Orlando, WonderWorks and WhirlyDome are all handy retreats to keep in mind for a rainy day or if you need time out of the sun.

I-Drive 360

Now the biggest attraction on International Drive is this multi-level entertainment, restaurant and shopping complex (on the site of the old Mercado Center).

It boasts five headline attractions, notably the 400ft/121m Orlando Eye, plus 2 restaurants, eight shops and two bars/nightclubs, and features free multi-storey car parking.

The landscaped centre also boasts an elaborate fountain and lighting, and is worth visiting both by day and night. Most iconic is the **Coca-Cola Orlando Eye** observation wheel (like the London Eye), a 20min journey that lifts visitors up in air-conditioned 15-passenger capsules for a panoramic view of this part of Central Florida (all the way to the Kennedy Space Center on a clear day). The experience starts with a green-screen photo and a fabulous pre-flight 4-D multi-sensory film of Florida's highlights, then passengers are loaded on the slow-moving Wheel for their flight, which is especially impressive in early evening. There is narration of the major sights, plus information pads on each side, and the vista is fabulous from the top, including the vast spread of Walt Disney World. The Eye costs $25 adults and $20 4–12s and is open 10am–10pm (midnight Fri and Sat). There is also a VIP Experience with priority boarding, fast-track access and a glass of champagne or soft drink for $39 and $34 (available 4.45–8.45pm).

On to **Madame Tussauds**, an extensive range of celebrity waxworks that allow you to rub shoulders (and take as many selfies as you want) with some of the most famous people on the planet, both past and present. The experience starts, suitably, with a Floridian entrance (and a neat photo opportunity) and a meeting with Spanish explorer Juan Ponce de Leon in 1513 as he discovers Florida.

There is a quick history tour of the US featuring the likes of President Lincoln, Uncle Sam, President Obama (in the Oval office, no less) and Martin Luther King, and then the journey continues with famous inventors and innovators (look out for a chance to visit with the man who brought Mickey to Orlando in the first place!). The Madame Tussaud story is well illustrated at the half-way point – along with the chance to have your hand cast in wax – and then the centre really turns on the style with a dazzling range of modern celebrities from the world of sports (including a certain David Beckham), music (the likes of Elvis, Madonna and Beyoncé), TV (with Oprah, Jim Parsons, Neil Patrick Harris and more) and Hollywood (with classic stars like Marilyn Monroe and modern icons Jennifer Lawrence and Taylor Lautner). Your tour concludes in the A-list Party, with an amazing selection of the biggest film stars of today, from Samuel L Jackson to Brad Pitt and Angelina Jolie. Look out for some engaging interactive features along the way, notably with Edison's Challenge. You'll need at least an hour to see everything, and taking photos with the 'stars' is actively encouraged ($25 and $20; 10am–10pm, 11pm Fri, Sat).

> **BRITTIP**
> If you are worried by heights on the Eye, there is a seat in the middle of the capsule with a central pole that provides a secure vantage point to enjoy the view with an extra feeling of reassurance.

The third part of the attraction is **SeaLife Orlando**, a huge indoor aquarium that features some fabulous exhibits and hands-on displays, ideal for children of all ages. The highlight is the 360-degree immersive tunnel through the main aquarium, with fish – including giant rays and sharks – floating all around you, but there are then a variety of smaller tanks and other underwater scenes, including a Rockpool experience, Stingray Cove and Everglades tableau. In all there are more than 5,000 animals to see and investigate, along with some clever 'Talking Aquarium' interactive talks and animal feedings throughout the day, as well as the chance to see the centre's divers feeding and cleaning at regular intervals. There is a Scavenger Hunt for children to follow along the way, and the different vantage points are geared towards smaller visitors, with a strong eco-friendly message throughout. There is even a multi-level play structure for young 'uns to climb and slide over. Your ticket is valid all day, so you can come and go as you please, but you will need a couple of hours for all the exhibits ($25 & $20, under 3 free; 10am–9pm). There are two Behind The Scenes tours, 25mins or 60mins, for an extra $5 and $15/person. Combo tickets for 2, 3 or 4 of these adventures (including LEGOLAND Florida) are really well priced at $31 and $26; $39 and $34; and $99 and $94 (advance discounts available online). There is also a Gift Shop for each attraction and

a central Food Court, making it a well-rounded and enjoyable half-day option, while the additional dining (p319) around the complex is excellent (10am–10pm Sun–Thurs, midnight Fri–Sat; **http://i-drive360.com**).

> **BRITTIP**
> Didn't bring a camera to Madame Tussauds? Not to worry – there are photographers at regular intervals to make sure you have great memories of the visit.

Separate to the three Merlin attractions is **Skeletons: Animals Unveiled**, a fascinating museum-with-a-difference boasting a look at some 400 animals of all types (including a great Africa section and a rare Sumatran rhino) in amazing anatomical detail, with full-size skeletons displayed in active poses and cool but educational dioramas that provide great photo opportunities. We especially like the Africa section, with the bull elephant, while the python exhibit shows off its staggering 900-plus bones, and you'll also learn the art form of turning animal carcases into these skeletons ($19.99 adults, $12.99 3–11s; 10am–11pm; **http://skeletonmuseum.com/**). There's also **Arcade City**, high-energy games arcade with all the latest video challenges and activities, including some high-tech variations on familiar games (with prizes to match; 10am–10pm; **www.arcadecityfun.com**).

Kings Bowl: This is a neighbouring part of the complex, a bowling centre with restaurant and bar. With a plush 1950s vibe but modern styling – notably with 22 high-tech bowling

Orlando Eye

lanes – it offers a grown-up atmosphere that is also family-friendly. Its elegant multi-bar and dining room set-up features 60 big-screen HDTVs, billiard tables, shuffleboard, bocce ball, serve-yourself beer booths and great cocktails. The food – from standard diner fare like burgers, pizza and fish and chips, to succulent steaks and scallops – is worth coming in for on its own, while the beer list is impressive and the desserts and sundaes decadent. Bowling is 11–2am daily, at $6/person Tues–Thurs, $7 Fri– Mon before 6pm and $7 after 6pm ($8 after 6pm on Fri and Sat). Shoe hire $4; 21 and over after 8pm (407 363 0200; **http://kingsbowlamerica. com/orlando/**). Kings Bowl can also be booked for private parties. Look up more at **www.i-drive360.com**

BRITTIP

Call ahead for a Priority Lane Reservation when you dine at Kings Bowl and your group will be bumped up to the next available lane once you have finished eating.

Ripley's Believe It Or not

You can't miss this particular attraction and its extraordinary tilted appearance as it's designed to seem as if it's falling into a Florida 'sinkhole'. However, once inside you soon get back on the level and, for an hour or so, you can wander through this quirky museum dedicated to the weird and wonderful. Robert L Ripley was an eccentric explorer and collector (a real-life Indiana Jones) who for 40 years travelled the world to assemble a collection of the greatest

Ripley's Believe It or Not

known oddities. The Orlando branch of this chain features 8,900ft2/830m2 of displays in 16 galleries, including authentic artefacts, interactive exhibits, illusions, video presentations and music. The elaborate re-creation of an Egyptian tomb showcases a mummy and three rare mummified animals, while the Primitive Gallery contains artefacts (some quite gruesome) from tribal societies around the world. There are then Human and Animal Oddities, Big and Little galleries, Illusions and Dinosaurs, plus extra interactive elements. The collection of miniatures includes the world's smallest violin and a single grain of rice hand-painted with a tropical sunset. Larger-scale exhibits include a balloon-powered chair that flew over the Rocky Mountains, a 2/3-scale 1907 Rolls-Royce built in matchsticks and a 26ft/8m tall 'painting' of Van Gogh made out of postcards! You can also attempt various puzzles and brain teasers, and try the shooting gallery with its odd array of targets.

Admission: $19.99 adult, $12.99 4–12s; 9am–12am (last entry 11pm; 407 345 0501, **www.ripleys.com/orlando**). AAA Ripleys is also included with Go Orlando Card.

BRITTIP

Receive a $3 discount/adult, $2/child (4–12s) on the regular admission price at Ripley's Believe It Or Not by visiting their website.

Titanic – The artefact exhibit

Go back in time at this fascinating attraction just north of Sand Lake Road. Guided tours start on the hour and weave through full-scale re-creations of the Titanic's famous rooms, including her grand staircase, first-class parlour suite, Verandah Café, Marconi Room, third class cabin and bridge. Costumed actors portray characters such as Captain Smith and Molly Brown, sharing stories of passengers and crew during the one-hour journey of the famous ship.

The 17-gallery attraction features an interactive Underwater Room, including a 15ft/4.5m 'iceberg' and a detailed replica of the vessel as she appears on the bottom of the Atlantic today. More than 400 artefacts and treasures, including memorabilia from James Cameron's blockbuster movie Titanic are also on display here, notably some ultra-rare pieces, including the 2nd-largest piece recovered from the wreck site. Both engaging and moving, it consistently gets good reviews from locals and tourists alike. PS: Make sure you keep your entry ticket – you'll need it at the end!

Admission: $21.95 adults, $15.95 5–11s ($2 off online; under-3 free); tours 10am–6pm (8 or 9pm peak seasons; **www.premierexhibitions.com**). AAAA Titanic is also included with Go Orlando Card.

Titanic Gala Dinner: For something special, try this 3hr theatre/dining occasion with the cast of the Exhibit. Starring Molly Brown, Captain Smith, Thomas Andrews and other high-society luminaries, it offers each table a front row seat for the whole Titanic story, setting the scene and delivering a dinner party with a difference, all in period style. Enjoy a sumptuous three-course meal, featuring fillet of beef and chicken, with tea, coffee and soft drinks (extra for unlimited beer and wine) in a splendid atmosphere. The Gala Dinner recreates Titanic's first-night sailing each Fri and Sat from 6.30pm ($69 for adults, $42 for 6–11s; not recommended for under-6s; book in advance on 407 248 1166).

Fun Spot America
Just off I-Drive on Fun Spot Way (look for the 250ft/76m SkyCoaster past the junction with Kirkman Road) is this extensive amusement park that offers a whole raft of family fun with coasters, go-karting, kiddie rides and arcade action. The go-kart thrills come from four challenging tracks, including the enlarged Quad Helix, the triple level corkscrew track of Conquest, the fiendish Thrasher and multi-level Commander. Then there are bumper cars and boats, five daring fairground-type rides (including the Space Invader swing ride and the whizzy Scrambler), one of the largest and most up-to-date video arcades in Florida, a Big Wheel, nine Kiddie Rides – including a classic two-storey carousel – and a Cadet track for the little ones. Fun Spot also boasts the world's second-largest SkyCoaster (a massive, free-fall swing) and three coasters – the impressive long steel-wooden hybrid of White Lightning, which races along at up to 48mph/76kph with a max drop of 75ft/23m; the tight-turning suspended ride of Freedom Flyer; and the child-friendly Sea Serpent. Another fun option is the high-spinning Enterprise, while the large Food Court serves hotdogs, burgers, salads, pizza, nachos, popcorn and ice-cream. Also check out **Gator Spot**, a separate area featuring almost 120 residents of Gatorland, including an albino gator, gift shop and some great photo opportunities (photos for a fee). Parking and admission are free, with a series of ride Passes geared around children's height (above and below 4ft 4in/1.32m), with younger children getting free run of all the rides (and as a passenger on the 2-seater go-karts with an adult).

Admission: Free; Single Day ticket (all day on all 4 tracks, plus all rides and unlimited Free Play arcade; Skycoaster not included) $46, kids 10 and under receive $10 in-park Fun-E-Card; SkyCoaster $45 single rider, $35ea double, $30ea triple, $25ea with Single Day pass. Open daily 10am–midnight (2pm-midnight off-peak; 407 363 3867, **http://fun-spot.com/orlando**). TTTT Also with Go Orlando card.

Magical Midway
Magical Midway back on I-Drive(just north of Sand Lake Road) offers more go-karts, games and thrill rides, including the Sling Shot (400ft/120m straight up!), the unique StarFlyer, a 230ft/70m tower with chair swings that lift and rotate for a dizzying view at 54mph/87kph, and Space Blast, another vertical-launch monster! The two elevated kart tracks, the double uphill corkscrew of The Avalanche and sharply banked Alpine are its

signature rides (you must be at least 12 and 4ft 8in/147cm tall to drive, at least 16 to drive a passenger, and at least five and 3ft/91cm to be a passenger). Fast Track, a flat concrete track with a 25° bank turn (riders must be 12 and 4ft 8in/147cm to drive; single cars only) completes the line-up. There are also bumper cars, boats, a merry-go-round, trampolines, a large arcade, a pizza parlour and ice-cream counter.

Admission: Free, then 3hr Armband (unlimited go-karts and midway rides for 3hrs, not Sling Shot) $25; All-Day Unlimited Armband (not Sling Shot) $32. Or $25 Sling Shot, $7 Starflyer (ride DVD $15), $8 go-karts, $3 all other rides. Must be 4ft/121cm for Bumper Cars, 3ft 6in/106cm for Bumper Boats and Kiddie Track; noon–midnight Mon–Fri, (407 370 5353, **www.magicalmidway.com**). TTTT See website for $2.50 off Go-Karts.

◀▶ BRITTIP
I-Drive 360, WonderWorks, Fun Spot, Magical Midway and WhirlyDome are all open until at least midnight in high season, long after most theme parks are shut, so you can have a day at the park, then let the kids loose here to tire them out completely!

WonderWorks

This interactive entertainment centre is I-Drive's most unmistakable landmark, a three-storey chamber of family fun with a host of novel elements. Unmistakable? The 82ft/25m building is upside-down – the result of a 'tornado experiment that went wrong.' You have to give full marks for imagination and, with various enhancements since it opened in 1998, there's a lot here, especially for 6–12s.

You enter through an 'inversion tunnel' that orientates you the same way round as the building (look out of the window to check!) and then progress to various chambers of entertaining and mildly educational hands-on experiences that demand several hours to explore fully. Without ever using the words 'science' or 'museum', WonderWorks steers you through six WonderZones of interactive activities, including natural disasters (earthquakes, hurricanes, famous disasters) and Google Earth virtual globe and map; physical challenges (Bubble Lab, Bed of Nails and the chance to make an impression of your entire body in 40,000 plastic nails at Wonderwall!); Light & Sound (challenges to beat the clock, shape the music and strike a pose); the Imagination Lab (with physical and mental challenges to create and have fun); and Space Discovery, where you have Jet Fighters (virtual reality F18 fighter jet), Shuttle Landers (your chance to pilot the Discovery Space Shuttle), a Mercury capsule mock-up, an astronaut spacesuit and Wonder Coaster (a pair of enclosed 'pods' that let you design and ride your own coaster), and Far Out Art Gallery with optical illusions. There is also a three-storey glow-in-the-dark ropes course with 20 obstacles, and the 4D XD Motion Theater with three simulator rides, plus the WonderWorks Gift Shop and Café. A Lazer Tag game on the top floor adds even more appeal for kids.

Also here is the fun of The Outta Control Magic Comedy Dinner Show (p298), with a good-value combo ticket.

Admission: $26.99 adults, $20.99 seniors (55+) and 4–12s (includes 1 4-D Motion Ride and Ropes Course); $29.99 for general admission and Lazer Tag; $29.99 and $19.99 for The Outta Control Dinner Show; $48.99 and $37.99 for WonderWorks/ dinner show; 9am–midnight (407 351 8800, **www.wonderworksonline.com/orlando**). TTT WonderWorks is also included with Go Orlando Card.

iFly Orlando

At the junction with I-Drive and Kirkman Road is this unmistakable blue and yellow funnel that houses one of the most fun 'rides' in town. It is billed as a 'free-fall skydiving adventure' but is much more than that – a fun, addictive, difficult but exhilarating 'flying' experience, with the bonus of a great spectator sport! It's basically a huge vertical wind tunnel, which provides the feeling of a freefall. The standard 1hr programme provides a full briefing with an instructor, then you're given helmet, pads, goggles, earplugs and flight suit, and your group of 8–12 returns to the flight deck, where you get two 1min supervised 'flights' (which seem a lot longer!). Just watching makes it seem all too easy but, as soon as you hit the tunnel, you discover how fiendishly tough it is to just 'hang' in this 125mph/200kph column of air. However, before long it becomes a fun and absorbing experience and it's almost guaranteed to make you want to try again. There is no fee for non-participating members of your group to watch from the observation deck, and you can also just turn up to see for yourself at any time (you might even see sky-dive groups practising).

Admission: Standard flight, which includes a certificate, is $59.95; add a photo USB for $39.95. Discount coupons (for return visitors) and gift certificates can be found on its website. Try a Spread Your Wings Package (double your flight time) for $99.95, Spread Your Wings for Two at $130.86 (including DVD), or a Family Package for up to five at $271.89, (including DVD).

For real addicts, a Take Flight package offers 10 1min flights or five double-flights for $219.95. Open 10am–10.30pm daily, reservations recommended (407 903 1150, **http://orlando.iflyworld.com**). **TTTT**.

Whirlydome

This indoor fun centre boasts a unique game, full-service restaurant, arcade and other novel elements.

Their stock in trade is the hilarious **WhirlyBall** game, a cross between bumper cars, basketball and lacrosse (!) as two teams of five battle for possession of a whiffle ball and try to hit a target at either end. There are two courts of $4,000ft^2/370m^2$ and the centre provides a ref. It is open to all-comers or groups and games are timed in periods of 10min. Guests must be at least 12 and 4ft 6in/137cm to play but it is easy to pick up and the

Whirlybugs, like fancy bumper-cars, are easy to drive. It is free just to turn up and watch (and is great spectator fun). Playing time is $8/player for 10min, or you can hire the court at $250/hr. In addition, the Dome also offers America's only genuine **F1 race simulator**, the SYM 026 from Italy ($8/3min), a huge **Laser Tag** venue ($8/10min) and a novel **Laser Frenzy** room, where players try to navigate a maze of laser beams, haze and mirrors ($3). More arcade games, and billiards and pool in the upstairs Bar fill out the entertainment, while the **Bloodhound Brew Pub & Eatery** is a surprisingly smart restaurant, with great local microbrews and a tempting menu (Happy Hour 4–7pm). The Dome is open 4–10pm Tues–Thurs, 4pm–midnight Fri, 11am–midnight Sat, 11am–10pm Sun. See more, including Monthly Specials, at **www.whirlydome.com** (407 212 3030).

Helicopter rides

These are another local staple, and you can try any one of nine tours with **Air Florida Helicopters** at 8990 International Drive. Each flight requires at least two passengers, and the choice includes a basic 8ml/13km flight around SeaWorld and I-Drive, tours of Disney, Universal and Downtown Orlando, plus a grand 30ml/48km journey that covers the homes of the rich and famous in Windermere. Just $20 for the short flight to $355 for the longest, plus a $4/person fuel surcharge ($20–325 for children; see website for discounts). No need to book; just turn up and go. They fly 9.30am–7pm daily (407 354 1400, **www.airfloridahelicopter.com**).

Air Florida Helicopters

© Air Florida Helicopters

Escape games

These have become all the rage in Orlando recently, with two major opportunities on I-Drive to test your wits in a Crystal Maze-type challenge.

America's Escape Game: Choose from Pandemic, Crisis At 1600, Face Off, The Caretaker and Lost Tomb Of Monthu to test your ability to solve puzzles and unscramble clues in teams at this venue next to the Official Visitor Center on Austrian Court. In groups of 8–10, visitors undergo an explanatory briefing about their 'mission' and then have an hour to work through the Game Room, under the supervision of a game minder, who can offer three clues if you get stuck. The countdown effect is very real and some of the puzzles are fiendishly difficult, which adds to the fun. Players ideally need to be 13 or older and the rooms include props, special effects and strobe lighting – be prepared for the unexpected! Single players are welcome to make up the number with other groups. You don't have to book in advance but it is advisable (1–10pm Tues–Thurs, 10am-1am Fri and Sat, 11.30am–9.30pm Sun, $35–39/person; 407 412 5585, **http://americasescapegame.com/**).

Escapology: This venue on southern I-Drive (in a shopping/office plaza just north of Sheraton Vistana Villages resort) offers a sophisticated style with a 'living room' to encourage visitors to relax before their briefing for 1 of 6 games (which change periodically), and enjoy a complimentary soft drink and debrief afterwards. Designed for families and friends in private groups of 2–6, the game rooms can even be used for side-by-side games to test each group. Visitors should book online and then turn up at the allotted time, get locked into their chosen game for 60mins and have to find the clues to escape from situations like Shanghaied, Cuban Crisis, Lost City, Budapest Express, Th3 Cod3, and Arizona Shootout. Again it's a real test of initiative, teamwork and lateral thinking, and each room has a Game Master to monitor progress and provide a few clues if needed

(9am-midnight Mon–Thurs, 8.30am-1am Fri–Sat, Sun 8.30–; $30/person; 407 278 1515, **www.escapology.com/orlando**).

◀▶ **BRITTIP**
Players are advised to arrive 15mins early for escape games to allow time for paperwork and briefing. No entry once the clock has started. It's important to select a leader and work as a team. Oh, and visit the loo first!

Also on I-Drive (on Hawaiian Court next to the Rosen Center hotel) is a new outlet of the **Chocolate Kingdom** (see p237).

Mini-golf

For those in need of more holiday fun, don't miss the six mini-golf outlets along International Drive (see p268).

Kissimmee

Old Town: This shopping and entertainment attraction in the heart of tourist Highway 192 in Kissimmee has recently undergone a major overhaul. As well as the shopping (p333), it's worth trying the live events, rides and attractions. Look for the high-energy **Games Arcade** and **Rootin and Tootan's Shooting Alley**, which is great fun for kids (and dads with a competitive streak). There are four new **kiddie rides**, including a classic carousel and Tilt-A-Whirl (on loan from Fun Spot) to keep young'uns happy. More family entertainment is provided by **The Great Magic Hall,** with live magic shows at 3, 7 and 9pm daily ($14/person). Rides are open 2–11pm Mon–Fri, noon–midnight Sat and noon–11pm Sun (407 396 4888, **www.myoldtownusa. com**). Old Town also features the **Saturday Classic Car Cruise**, the **Friday All-American Muscle Car Cruise** and **Little Darlin's Street Party & Cruise-In** each Wed. Also, Sun night features jeeps, trucks and SUVs.

Fun Spot America: Next door to Old Town is Kissimmee's version of this outlet of the Fun Spot theme parks collection, with a good selection of rides, including the high adrenalin SkyCoaster and four go-kart tracks.

The big daddy of them all is the amazing **SkyCoaster**, a 300ft/90m tower that sends up to three riders at a time on a free-fall plunge (for the first 120ft/37m) that turns into a giant swing – at 85mph/136kph! The more down-to-earth rides consist of two flat go-kart tracks, **Slick** and **Road Course**, and two multi-level tracks, the labyrinthine **Chaos** and **Vortex**, with its challenging banked bowl section. The other nine rides are almost as much fun, like the fairground style of **Flying Bobs**, **Fun Slide** and **Surf's Up,** the giant swing of the **Hot Seat** and a bigger version, **Headrush 360**. More swinging fun is provided by the **Screaming Eagles** and **YoYo**, while standard **Bumper Kars** complete the line-up. There's a well-stocked indoor **Snack Bar** when you need to cool down, as well as an **Ice Cream Kiosk**, while kids might gravitate to the **Arcade**, with 60 games (perfect for a wet or super-hot day).

Admission: Free, then ride prices are Single Day Pass ($45.95 per person (not including SkyCoaster, Bull Ride and Arcade), Combo Ticket $55.95 (adding a meal, souvenir cup and $10 Fun-E Card per child under 54in). SkyCoaster is $40 for one rider ($35ea double rider, $30ea triple, $25ea with Single Day pass). Open 10am–midnight (407 397 2509, **http://fun-spot.com/kissimmee**).

Chocolate Kingdom: Sandwiched between Old Town and Fun Spot is this cute and ultra child-friendly opportunity to see how chocolate is made – and get some tasty samples! Sign up for their 1hr tour (on the hour) and you join a quest to help a handsome prince woo the hand of a chocolate-loving princess, while getting a history lesson in the process. Select the pre-tour Chocolate Bar option and you can have a custom-made bar of your own created before your eyes at the end of the tour (10.30am–6pm daily, $16.95 adults, $12.95 4-12s; 407 705 3475, **www.chocolatekingdom.com**).

BRITTIP
Visiting the Orlando Information Center? Take exit 82B off I-4 and there are four multi-storey car parks nearby, including the Library park (take 4th right on Central Boulevard). Alternatively, take 2nd right, Church St, go across Orange Ave and turn left into the Plaza multi-storey garage, where it's slightly more expensive but more central.

DOWNTOWN ORLANDO

The last few years have seen a major revitalisation of Orlando's city centre ('downtown'), with new offices, apartments, shops and restaurants. This makes it a tourist attraction in its own right and it is well served by the Information Center on Orange Avenue (10am–5pm, Mon–Fri; 407 254 4636, **www.downtownorlando.com** – click 'Visit Downtown'). Start here to get a full overview, with a 3-D city model and ultra-helpful staff (plus free wi-fi). They can provide free maps of the area, a Historic Walking Tour guide and info on riding the free LYMMO bus service around downtown. There is also a free guided tour at 9.30am on the first Fri of each month with local historian Richard Forbes (Oct–May). Much of the former Church Street Station area is also vibrant again, **www.churchstreetdistrict.com**.

Orange County History Center

Getting there: On E Central Boulevard (exit 82B off I-4, go across South St and take 3rd right; see also map p214), park at the Public Library multi-storey

Old Town, Kissimmee

© Gray Line Tours

car park on Central Blvd. Admission: $8 adults, $7 seniors (60+), $6 5–12s; 10am–5pm Mon–Sat, noon–5pm Sun (407 836 8500, **www.thehistorycenter.org**).

This smart part of the downtown scene offers an imaginative journey into central Florida history, from the wildlife and Native Americans to today's tourist issues and space programme. The accent is on the interactive, with hands-on exhibits and audiovisual presentations, and it is very much a journey through time, starting with the Natural Environment and First Peoples exhibits and moving on to the 1800s, with an authentic pioneer 'cracker' home, tales of Florida's ranching days, a Seminole settlement, and tourism pre-Disney to modern times. Aviation explores World War II bombers to the outer reaches of space. The Theme-Park Era explores the opening of Walt Disney World and beyond, while an exhibit on African American history and a series of travelling exhibits round things off.

Getting around: Everywhere is walkable downtown, but the free Lymmo bus service connects the central area along Magnolia Avenue, from South Street and City Hall up to the Centroplex area. Or you could try the **Orlando Juice Bike Share** service, a bike-sharing scheme that allows bike rentals from specific hubs around the city centre, for as little as $8/hr (**https://orlando.socialbicycles.com/**).

Theatre and more

Orlando loves its theatre, and those wishing to take in a performance should look for the lavish new **Dr Phillips Center for the Performing Arts**, which features touring Broadway shows, ballet, concerts and more (407 839 0119; **www.drphillipscenter.org**); the amazing

Lake Eola

Amway Center, home to the Orlando Magic basketball team, Orlando Predators Arena League outfit and Orlando Solar Bears minor-league ice-hockey team, plus major concerts (407 440 7000; **www.amwaycenter.com**); the improv of **SAK Comedy Lab** at Eola Capital Loft on S Orange Avenue (407 648 0001, **www.sakcomedylab.com**); and **CityArts Factory** featuring local and national artists (407 648 7060, **www.orlandoslice.com**). Downtown also has a thriving public arts scheme, **See Art Orlando** (**http://seeartorlando.com/**).

Dining: The restaurant/bar choice is also pretty good here, too. Take your pick from **Frank & Steins** (with 300 craft beers, 40 on tap), **Wall Street Plaza** (a lively collection of bars and lounges that are the heart of downtown nightlife), the upscale **Kres Chophouse**, and Church Street Station, the remains of the old entertainment district, which still includes a cluster of fine restaurants and bars, notably the stylish Spanish cuisine of **Ceviche**, the fun **Harry Buffalo** and outrageous **Hamburger Mary's Bar & Grille**. The first US outlet of the famous **Ace Café** was also due to open here in late 2016. See more in Orlando By Night.

Lake Eola: Once you have sampled the hustle-bustle of downtown, head out to this gem, with more restaurants and shops, plus a beautiful lakeside walk, children's play area, swan paddle-boats, new artwork and a peaceful ambience. There are regular open-air concerts at the **Disney Amphitheater** and the **Sunday Farmers Market** (around Lake Eola, 10am–4pm) is another focal point, with vendors including local artists as well as wonderful fresh produce.

Dining: Stop for a great meal, with a view, at **310 Lakeside** (407 373 0310, **www.310parksouth.net**) or **Spice Modern Steakhouse** (407 481 9533, **http://spicesteakhouse.com**). Continue on to Thornton Park Central (at the junction of Summerlin Avenue and Central Boulevard, just south-east of Lake Eola), offering a mix of unique boutiques and trendy restaurants. **Soco** is a fabulous choice for Southern

© Gray Line Tours

contemporary cuisine (traditional southern comfort food given an all-new twist) and is a real locals' favourite (407 849 1800, **www. socothorntonpark.com**) while neighbouring sister restaurant **Baoery** is an Asian gastropub (407 849 9779, **www.baoery.com**). **Anthony's Pizzeria** is a great upmarket pizza restaurant (407 648 0009, **http://anthonyspizza.com**) and **Dexter's** is a smart café/wine bar with a fab Sunday brunch (407 648 2777, **http://thorntonpark.dexwine.com**).

BRITTIP

Don't miss the annual Spring and Fall Fiestas around Lake Eola, with hundreds of vendors, live entertainment and special fun for kids, the first weekend in April and Nov (**www.fiestainthepark.com**).

Loch Haven park

Continue north and you travel the 'Cultural Corridor' to Loch Haven Park and the area's fine collection of theatres, museums and the Orlando Science Center.

Getting there: On Princeton Street in downtown Orlando, just off exit 85 of I-4 (go east on Princeton; the Science Center is on the left but the multi-storey car park is on the RIGHT, see map p214).

Orlando Science Center: The Orlando Science Center is more than a mere museum and far more fun than the average science centre. Here you are given a series of hands-on experiences and habitats that entertain as well as inform, and school-age children in particular will benefit greatly from it. It has seven main permanent exhibits, plus periodic travelling ones (in 2016 it was the puzzles and brain-teasers of *Mindbender Mansion*), a night sky observatory, an inviting café, Science Store and a giant screen cinema.

NatureWorks gets you up close and personal with some of Florida's most fascinating reptiles (including gators and turtles) while you step back into the prehistoric age at **DinoDigs**.

Visitors discover the dynamic forces and systems that shape Earth, and other planets, in **Our Planet** (be sure to experience the Category One hurricane, and take on the challenges of **Kinetic Zone**. And there is more to explore with electricity, magnetism, lasers, soundwaves and nature's forces in **Science Park**. **Engineer It** is a chance to build using all manner of structures, boats and bridges. Pre-schoolers will appreciate **KidsTown**, an interactive playground dedicated to smaller explorers. Each Jan also sees the fun **Otronicon**, a four-day event celebrating the best in video game technology. If you like the game Rock Band, you'll LOVE Otronicon! In addition, the centre has several programmes in **Dr Phillips CineDome**, a 310-seat cinema that surrounds its audience with large-format films and digital planetarium shows. The **Digital Adventure Theater** adds educational films and Science Live! real-life experiments and interactive programmes in partnership with National Geographic.

Admission: $20 adults, $18 seniors (55+) and students with ID, $14 3–11s; parking $5, includes a mainscreen film (Fri, Sat and Sun). 10am–5pm daily (closed Wed, Easter Sunday, Thanksgiving, Christmas Eve and Christmas Day; **www.osc.org**) AAA

The extensive **Orlando Museum of Art** (407 896 4231, **www.omart.org**) is here, and, the diverse **Mennello Museum of American Art**, with a permanent collection by painter Earl Cunningham (407 246 4278, **www. mennellomuseum.com**), the **Orlando Philharmonic Orchestra** (407 770 0071, **www.orlandophil.org**) and **Orlando Shakespeare Theater** (407 447 1700, **www.orlandoshakes. org**). Parents should also note the superb **Orlando Rep**, a company specialising in family theatre, with youth academies and summer camps for kids. Their 2016 season included *Disney's The Little Mermaid, Junie B. Jones The Musical,*

Orlando Science Center

and Tales of a Fourth Grade Nothing
(407 896 7365, **www.orlandorep.com**).
Highly recommended.

The Water parks

Florida specialises in elaborate
water parks, and Orlando boasts the
very best. Predictably, Disney has
the two most sophisticated ones,
but SeaWorld's Aquatica adds real
competition and Universal's Volcano
Bay should be a brilliant addition to
the options in 2017. They adopt a
variety of styles that owe much to the
flair of the theme park creators, and
are imaginative for both the rides and
imagery around them. All require at
least half a day of splashing, sliding and
riding to get full value from their rather
high prices. Lockers are provided for
valuables and you can hire towels.

BRITTIP

Want a day of watery fun but don't
want to purchase an extra pass for
a water park? Consider CocoKey Water
Resort on I-Drive. You can buy a day pass
for $24.95–26.95; it's great for the pre-
school to 10-year-old crowd, and it's partly
covered, to protect kids from the harsh
Florida sun (**https://cocokeyorlando.com/
orlando-water-park**).

Disney's Typhoon Lagoon

© Disney

Disney's Typhoon Lagoon Water park

When Typhoon Lagoon opened
in 1989, it was the biggest and
finest of Florida's water parks.
And, although it has since been
superceded, in high season it is
still the busiest, so be prepared for
queues. Arrive half an hour early
if possible as entry often begins
before the official opening hour.
The park's 56acres/23ha are spread
out around the 2½acre/1ha lagoon
fringed with palm trees and white-
sand beaches. It is extravagantly
landscaped and the walk up Mount
Mayday provides a terrific overview
as well as adding scenic touches
like rope bridges and tropical
flowers. Sun loungers, chairs,
picnic tables and even hammocks
are provided to add to the comfort
and convenience of restful areas
like Getaway Glen. However, you
need to arrive early to bag a decent
spot. Or, for $60 extra (!) you can
reserve two beach loungers, two
towels, an umbrella and a small
table by stopping in at High 'n Dry
Rentals (or calling in advance).
Really want to splash out? Opt for
a Beachcomber Shack (cabaña),
which includes a locker, drinks
mug, cooler with ice, bottled water,
towels, loungers and table, and
waiter service. Full day rental for up
to six guests will set you back $350
(admission not included). Reserve in
advance on 407 939 7529 (we're fans
of arriving early and getting your
loungers for free!).

Getting there: On Buena Vista Drive,
½ml/800m from Disney Springs (see
map, p214). Admission: $60 adults,
$54 3–9s (under-3s free); included
with Ultimate tickets; parking free;
9am (10am off season) to dusk daily.
TTTT AAAAA

BRITTIP

Water parks provide both a great
way of cooling down and an easy
way of getting sunburn. So don't forget
the high-factor *waterproof* suncream, and
reapply often.

Beating the crowds: To avoid the worst of the summer crowds (when the park often reaches its 7,200 capacity), Monday morning is best (steer clear of weekends at all costs) and, on other days, arrive either before opening or in mid-afternoon, when many decide to dodge the daily rainstorm. Early evening is also pleasant when the park lights up.

> ◢◣▶ **BRITTIP**
> Want to learn to surf? Typhoon Lagoon offers Surfing School 2hrs before park opening every day. Call 407 939 7529 in advance to book at $165/person.

Slides and rides: The park is overlooked by **Mount Mayday**, on top of which is perched the luckless Miss Tilly, a shrimp boat that legend has it landed here during the typhoon that gave the park its name. Watch out for the water fountains that shoot from Miss Tilly's funnel at regular intervals, accompanied by a blast from the ship's siren, signalling another round of BIG waves in the **Surf Pool** (and they are big; take care with toddlers). Circling the lagoon is **Castaway Creek**, a 3ft/1m deep, lazy flowing river offering the chance to float along on rubber rings.

The slides and rides are all clustered around Mt Mayday and vary from the breathtaking body slides of **Humunga Kowabunga** that drop you 214ft/65m at up to 40mph/48kph down some steep inclines (make sure swimming costumes are securely fastened!) to **Ketchakiddee Creek**, which offers a selection of slides and pools for youngsters under 4ft/122cm. In between, you have the **Storm Slides**, body slides that twist and turn through caves, tunnels and waterfalls, **Mayday Falls**, a wild 460ft/140m single-rider inner-tube flume down a series of banked drops, **Keelhaul Falls**, a more sedate tube ride, and **Gangplank Falls**, a family ride inside rafts that take up to four people down 300ft/90m of mock rapids. **Crush 'n' Gusher** is a fabulous trio of 'water-coaster' tube rides, plus a large heated pool with zero-depth

entry (great for toddlers). It also has an extensive sandy beach, ideal for sunbathing. The three different slides feature tubes for one or two riders at a time that whoosh you down and UP several inclines before dropping you into the pool with a significant splash. This is busy from midday.

New in spring 2017 should be **Miss Fortune Falls**, the park's latest – and longest – attraction. Another family raft ride to rival Crush and Gusher, it will feature a long lift hill and then a wild white-water adventure over the 'Falls' in a bid to spot some of the treasures acquired by the ocean-going Captain Mary Oceaneer. At fully two minutes long, it will be longer than any other Disney water park ride.

> ◢◣▶ **BRITTIP**
> 'Buy a disposable waterproof camera to tie around your wrist when you visit the water parks. We bought one cheap at Wal-Mart and have some lovely photos from Typhoon Lagoon,' says reader Judith Bingham.

Keeping out of the sun can also be a problem as there's not much shade. A quick plunge into Castaway Creek

Disney's Crush 'n' Gusher

usually prevents overheating but do remember your sunscreen. There are height restrictions (4ft/122cm) on Humunga Kowabunga and Crush 'n' Gusher and they're not suitable for anyone with a bad back or neck, or expectant mothers.

Shopping: You can buy anything you have forgotten – even a swimsuit – at **Singapore Sal's**. You CAN'T bring your own snorkels, inner tubes or rafts, but snorkels are provided on Castaway Creek.

Dining: Lowtide Lou's and **Let's Go Slurpin'** both offer snacks and drinks, while **Typhoon Tilly's** and **Leaning Palms** serve a decent mix of sandwiches, burgers, salads and ice-cream. Avoid main mealtimes if you want to eat in relative comfort. You can bring your own picnic (unlike the main parks), although no alcohol or glass.

BRITTIP
As the busiest of the water parks, Typhoon Lagoon can hit capacity quite early in the day in summer. Call 407 560 4120 in advance to check on the crowds.

Disney's Blizzard Beach Water Park

Ever imagined a skiing resort in the middle of Florida? Well, here

it is. This park opened in 1995 and is still the largest, with all 66acres/27ha arranged as if it were in the Rocky Mountains rather than the subtropics! That means snow-effect scenery, Christmas trees and waterslides cunningly converted to look like skiing pistes and toboggan runs. The same 'premium' offer at Typhoon Lagoon applies here for two beach loungers, two towels, an umbrella and a small table for $60. Or, if the price doesn't scare you off completely, you can hire a Polar Patio (cabaña), which includes a locker, drinks mug, cooler with ice, bottled water, towels, loungers and table, and waiter service. Full day rental, accommodating up to six, is $350 (admission not included). Reserve in advance on 407 939 7529.24

Getting there: Just north of Disney's All-Star Resorts off Buena Vista Drive (see map p14). Admission: $60 adults, $54 3–9s (under-3s free); included with Premium and Ultimate tickets; parking free; 9am (10am off-season) to dusk daily. **TTTTT AAAAA**

BRITTIP
Adjacent to Blizzard Beach are the amazing Winter Summerland Miniature Golf Courses (where Santa's elves hang out!), with two elaborate courses that are a great diversion for children (p268).

Snow Stormers at Blizzard Beach

© Disney

Slides and rides: Main features are **Mount Gushmore**, a 90ft/27m mountain down which all the main slides run. A ski chair-lift operates to the top, providing a magnificent view. Don't miss the outstanding rides, including the world's tallest free-fall speed slide, the terrifying 120ft/37m **Summit Plummet**, which rockets you down a 'ski jump' at up to 60mph/97kph. For those not quite up to the big drop, the brilliantly named **Slush Gusher** is a slightly less terrifying body slide. Then there is **Teamboat Springs**, a wild family inner-tube adventure and arguably the best of all the water rides; **Runoff Rapids**, a choice of three tube plunges; **Snow Stormers**, a daring head-first 'toboggan' run; and **Toboggan Racers**, the chance to speed down the 'slopes' against seven other head-first riders. All four provide good-sized thrills without overdoing the scare factor. The side-by-side **Downhill Double Dipper** tubes send you down 230ft/70m tubes in a timed race, with a real jolt half-way down! **Tike's Peak** is a kiddie-sized version of the park's slides and a mock snow-beach, and **Ski-Patrol Training Camp** is a series of challenges and slides for pre-teens.

Melt-Away Bay is a 1acre/0.4ha pool fed by 'melting snow' (actually blissfully warm), and **Cross Country Creek** is a lazy-flowing 1½ml/800m river round the whole park that also floats guests through a chilly 'ice cave' (look out for the ice-water waterfalls!).

Shopping and dining: There is a 'village' area with a **Beach Haus** shop and **Lottawatta Lodge** fast-food restaurant (pizzas, burgers, salads and sandwiches), offering a grandstand view of Mount Gushmore. Snacks are also available at **Avalunch** (ouch!), the **Warming Hut**, **Polar Pub** and **Frostbite Freddie's Frozen Refreshments**.

Wet'n Wild

This Universal-owned I-Drive landmark was due to close at the end of 2016 to make way for their all-new on-site water park Volcano Bay in June 2017 (p244). If it dodges the axe for a while, here's the run-down of what it features.

There are five high-thrill experiences, starting with **Der Stuka**, a near six-storey body-slide that draws serious queues, plus its more evil twin, **The Bomb Bay**, which drops riders free-fall style on to the top of the slide. The competitive **Aqua Drag Racer** is a four-lane head-first plunge with mats down more than 360ft/11m of twisting track while **The Storm** is a swirling 'body coaster' down a tube and into a large bowl that then drops riders into the pool below. **Mach 5** is another twisting mat ride, again going head-first down one of three flumes.

There are six excellent family rides, from the two-person **The Black Hole: The Next Generation** (a quick turning flume largely in the dark) and **The Blast** (a tube ride along an open pipeline) to the four-rider hilarity of **Disco H2O**, which sends passengers along a steep tube into a 1970s swirling 'disco bowl' and then out through a waterfall. **Brain Wash** is another four-person slosh-and-roll ride into a giant tunnel, while **The Flyer** is a fun in-line toboggan ride down a long flume. The group rides are completed by **The Surge**, a five-storey, four-person tube ride down 600ft/18m of banked turns.

More gentle fun can be found at the **Lazy River**, the huge **Surf Lagoon**, and the children's area of **Blastaway Beach**, complete with a giant sandcastle, two pools, 15 junior-sized slides and over 100 interactive water elements.

Shopping and dining: Beach gear can be found at the **Beach Shop**. For food, **Bubba's Fried Chicken** serves chicken, fries and drinks, the **Surf Grill** features burgers, hotdogs, salads, chicken and sandwiches, and **Manny's Pizza** has pizza and subs. The **Wild Tiki Lounge** is a covered Polynesian-style restaurant and bar, **Carnival Treats** features sweet, and cakes and 6 more snack bars offer ice-cream, beer and more. You can also bring your own picnic, but not alcohol or glass containers.

With its future unclear, check **www.wetnwildorlando.com** for the latest details.

Volcano Bay

Universal's brand new water park with a South Seas theme is set to be 'the next generation of water theme parks', promising a whole new range of attractions and experiences when it opens in June 2017. Crowned by the iconic Krakatau, it features four main areas, with a huge central lagoon and an outstanding mix of rides and slides.

Just to start with, the 53acre/21ha park's centrepiece is an erupting 200ft/60m volcano, but, instead of spewing lava, a massive waterfall tumbles into the wave pool below. The volcano erupts throughout the day, with jets of water reaching 100ft.

The Volcano area features the 70-degree trap-door drop of **Ko'okiri Body Plunge**, the **Kola and Ta Nui Serpentine Body Slides** which drop riders two at a time down a pair of intertwined tubes; and **Punga Racers**, a four-lane mat plunge through mystical underwater sea caves.

As well as the tube slides that emerge from the volcano – including the duo with break-away floors – there are more than a dozen slides throughout the park. Fortunately, automatic lifts whisk inner-tubes to the top of each slide so riders don't have to carry them up the stairs!

BRITTIP

There are a lot of stairs to climb to reach the entry to most slides, and much of the queuing is not covered, so apply high factor waterproof sun cream often.

No water park would be complete without a lazy river, and Volcano Bay boasts two. One provides a lush, tropical float past pretty scenery and partially hidden lounge areas, while the other is a faster-moving river that winds through the volcano itself, with rapids and waterfalls to navigate.

The Rainforest Village is the biggest area of the park, with four main attractions, including the fast-flowing **TeAwa**, or Fearless River, and the Taniwha Tubes, a series of four flumes with crazily twisted tracks and mischievions statues that spray water at riders. The main attraction is the six-person **Maku Puihi Raft Ride**, while the **Ohyah** and **Ohno Drop Slides** each end with a significant drop into the pool below, hence their names!

The setting is heavily landscaped in South Pacific tropical splendour, with Easter Island-style heads, elaborate fountains and Polynesian-print coverings over the loading area at each attraction. A spectacular kiddie water-play area with child-size slides and pop-jets will keep young'uns happy, and Tiki-hut style cabanas with towels, locker, loungers and mini-fridge will be available for hire at around $300/day. Sundries are on sale at a large gift shop, with counter service dining and snack and beverage kiosks at various points throughout the park.

The four main areas are completed by the Wave Village, with the **Waturi Beach** lagoon, and River Village, boasting the two children's areas and some relaxing features for their parents. Parking and price details were still to be released, so

Universal's Volcano Bay

be sure to visit **www.universalorlando.com** for the latest info. UK ticket outlets will offer Volcano Bay as a 3-park ticket with the two theme parks.

Aquatica by SeaWorld

This eye-catching water park has a wonderful range of children's attractions and facilities, innovative rides and an all-you-can-eat-meal option, spread over 59acres/24ha of South Seas-inspired landscaping.

Getting there: Just across the road from SeaWorld on International Drive, exit 71 or 72 off I-4.

Admission: $58 adults, $53 3–9s; 2-Visit Ticket (with SeaWorld) $139 and $134; (save $10 by booking online; included with UK 2- and 3-Park tickets); parking $13, locker rental $20 and $35 (plus refundable $5); towels $4; 9am–6, 7 or 8pm (late May–Aug) or 10am–5pm (winter, spring and autumn; **www. aquaticabyseaworld.com**) TTTT AAAAA

Slides and rides: Aquatica's signature attraction is the **Dolphin Plunge** (4ft/122cm), a twin body slide that sends riders down 300ft/91.5m of tubes and through a lagoon of playful, black-and-white Commerson's dolphins (it's a touch gimmicky as you catch only the briefest glimpse of them on the way down, but it is an exhilarating slide). You can then view the Dolphins at the end of the ride through the huge lagoon window, where the inhabitants often hang out to look at their human visitors! The other standout attraction is **Ihu's Breakaway Falls**, with three enclosed tubes featuring break-away floors (complete with heartbeat effect while you're waiting for the drop!) and one outrageous non-breakaway tube that is every bit as scary. Each offers a completely different ride. **Whanau Way** is a quadruple raft ride with two distinct variations that twist and turn before landing with a resounding splash, while **Tassie's Twisters** are double bowl rides

that send riders down single or double tubes into giant bowls before splashing back into the **Loggerhead Lane** lazy river (which also has a coral reef viewing section). **Taumata Racer** (3ft 6in/107cm) is a fast-paced mat slide set up like an eight-lane racing toboggan run, partly enclosed and then with a double drop into daylight (queues can look long here but they usually move quickly). Family raft ride **Walhalla Wave** features a winding, enclosed section before a big splash finale; while **HooRoo Run** is a shorter, and straighter ride – with two distinct drops on the way (4ft/122cm must wear a life vest)!

Omaka Rocka features two high-speed single-rider tube flumes, each with three sets of funnels that send you coursing up one side and down the other with a sensational 'feel it in your tummy' weightlessness before final splash-down. **Big Surf Shores** wave pool offers big dynamic waves, while sister wave-pool **Cutback Cove** features gentler rolling surf. A huge sandy beach offers a large array of sun loungers and umbrellas, and private cabañas (from $49–125 in low season to the Ultimate Cabaña, including upgraded furniture, dining table and a second cabana with couch, coffee table and additional seating for up to eight, at $275–600 seasonally). Call 1888 800 5447 to book or go online.

As well as the gentle **Loggerhead Lane** (under 4ft/122cm must wear

Taumata Racer at Aquatica

life vest), you should try the dynamic **Roa's Rapids** (under 51in/129cm must wear a life vest), which provides a helter-skelter whirl along this river feature, with a series of fountains, jets and other watery boosts to keep you bobbing along with no effort.

Free life vests are on offer here and it is worth trying one for the feeling of floating along in high style!

Kids' features: The big success of the park, though, is its extensive features for children, from the youngest to young teens. **Kata's Kookaburra Cove** is an exclusive area for those under 4ft/1.2m tall, with a whole range of scaled-down slides, rides, pools and fountains to provide a gentler experience for the young 'uns. By contrast, **Walkabout Waters** is a vast and frenzied 60ft/18m-high water play structure with every kind of climb, slide and water eruptions and outpourings, including two giant buckets that fill and dump in spectacular fashion over those below. Small animal encounters are also designed to appeal to children, so watch out for these around the park (featuring macaws, leggy spoonbills, anteaters, tortoises and a kookaburra).

Shopping and dining: The imaginative **Kiwi Traders** is the biggest of the four shops, but both **Adaptations** and **Beachies** are worth a look. For dining, try **Waterstone Grill** (chicken tenders, burgers, salads, sandwiches, wraps), **Mango Market** (chicken tenders, sandwiches, salads, fries and desserts) or **Banana Beach Cookout** buffet (pizza, pasta, chicken, pork, hotdogs, salads, desserts, non-alcoholic drinks; all-day pass $20 adults, $15 ages 3–9; add refillable souvenir bottle for $6).

BRITTIP
Youngsters can learn to swim at Aquatica, with a week-long course of 45min lessons at $79/student. Book online or call 1888 800 5447.

Aquatica features unique elements Roa's Rapids and Kookaburra Cove. And, if you buy the two-visit ticket with SeaWorld, it's great value in summer, as you can spend the day in Aquatica and then go to the sister park for the evening.

That's the large-scale attractions, but let's explore some alternatives to the mass-market experience…

Walkabout Waters

8 Off the Beaten Track

or When You're All Theme-Parked Out

Orlando's main attractions are undoubtedly a lot of fun, but they can also be extremely tiring and you may well need a break from all the hectic theme park activity. Or you may be visiting again and looking for a different experience. If either is the case, this chapter is for you.

This chapter could easily be subtitled 'A Taste of the Real Florida', as it introduces the towns of Winter Park, Winter Garden, Celebration and Mount Dora, plus the natural delights of the area, including the state parks, day-trips, eco-tours and sports.

ORLANDO/Orange County

Winter Park: Foremost among the 'secret' hideaways is this elegant northern suburb, just about 20mins from the hurly-burly of I-Drive yet a world away from the relentless tourism. It offers museums and art galleries, boutique shopping, restaurants, walking tours, a delightful 50min boat ride around the lakes and, above all, a chance to slow down. Take exit 87 from I-4, Fairbanks Avenue; turn right on Fairbanks and go east for 2ml/3km and turn left at the junction with Park Avenue.

Morse Museum of American Art: A must for admirers of American art pottery, American and European glass, furniture and other decorative arts of the late 19th and early 20th centuries, as it includes one of the world's foremost collections of works by Louis Comfort Tiffany. The dazzling chapel restoration from the 1893 Chicago World Expo is on display in its original form for the first time since the late 19th century. It also has special Christmas exhibitions and periodic family programmes (9.30am–4pm Tues–Sat, 1–4pm Sun, also 4pm–8pm Fri only Nov–April; adults $6, Seniors $5, students $1, under-12s free; free 4–8pm each Fri Nov–April; **www.morsemuseum.org**).

Park Avenue: The heart of Winter Park is a classy street of restaurants, fine shops and a shaded park. At one end is Rollins College, housing the beautiful Cornell Fine Arts Museum, with the oldest collection of paintings, sculpture and decorative arts in Florida (10am–4pm Tues–Fri, 12am–5pm Sat and Sun, closed Mon and holidays; admission is free; **www.rollins.edu/cfam**).

Park Avenue Walking Tour: Free maps are provided for this tour by the Welcome Center (on W Lyman Ave; 8.30am–5pm Mon–Fri, 9am–2pm Sat; 407 644 8281). Park Avenue's classy shops are pricey but good for browsing the charming and friendly area.

For shops both unique and fun, look for **Simmons Jewellers**, **Ten Thousand Villages** (international arts and crafts),

Bebe's (children's clothes), the eclectic **Filthy Rich** (jewellery), **Tuni** (women's clothing) and **Williams-Sonoma** (kitchenware), plus **Peterbrooke Chocolatier**. Regular craft fairs and art festivals. Street parking allows 3hrs free, but there is a multi-storey car park on the corner of Comstock and Park Avenue, which is a better half-day option. Keep an eye out for the **Taste of Winter Park** in Apr and also for the **Autumn Art Festival** in Oct (**www.cityofwinterpark.org**).

Scenic Boat Tour: Started in 1938, this is located on East Morse Boulevard and offers a charming, 12ml/19km narrated tour, giving a fascinating glimpse of some stunning homes, (property prices start at around $1m and several top $10m!). Tours run every hour 10am–4pm daily (closed Christmas) at $14 adults and $7 2–11s, cash only (407 644 4056; **www.scenicboattours.com**).

Winter Park Playhouse: A charming non-profit theatre staging musical performances year-round and with an intimate style in their 123-seat venue on N. Orange Avenue. The offerings feature well-known comedies and revues from Broadway, Off-Broadway and regional theatres, with tickets from $20–40 (407 645 0145; winterparkplayhouse.org).

BRITBONUS

Buy one ticket for the **Winter Park Playhouse** and get the second at 50% off (subject to availability). Call 407 645 0145 and mention the *Brit Guide*.

Plant Street Market

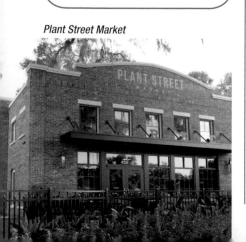

A dining delight

Winter Park boasts some of Orlando's finest dining. **Park Plaza Gardens** specialises in a modern mix of American and Continental cuisines, plus a wonderful Sunday brunch. **310 Park South** is the epitome of elegant, European café culture. We are also fans of pavement bistro **Briarpatch** (breakfast and lunch), the Italian style of **Pannullo's**, and the fabulous **Luma on Park**, a 'gastropub' featuring fresh, daily specials from simple burgers to gourmet offerings and a superb wine list (**www.lumaonpark.com**). The gorgeous **Ravenous Pig** on Orange Avenue has a wide-ranging pub choice, from its fine microbrewery to steaks and seafood (**www.theravenouspig. com**). Other choices are neighbourhood bar-kitchen-market **Boca** (**www.bocawinterpark. net**); **Scratch**, an imaginative tapas-style bistro (407 325 5165, **http://scratchtapas.com**); and **Cask & Larder**, a 'Southern public house' from the Ravenous Pig team (407 280 4200, **www.caskandlarder.com**). Next door to Cask & Larder is gourmet deli and sandwich shop **Swine & Sons** (**https://swineandsons.com**), while another must-try is **Hamilton's Kitchen** at the ritzy Alfond Inn hotel, where fresh food and creative cuisine make for a great lunch or dinner (**www.thealfondinn.com/dining/ hamiltons_kitchen**).

BRITBONUS

Show your *Brit Guide* and receive a FREE cocktail or appetiser with any entrée at the chic **Boca** neighbourhood bar in Winter Park. Offer limited to 1 per table.

Winter Garden: A taste of small-town America 18mls north of Disney, its historic district consists of 1 main street (Plant Street) for 5 blocks, with boutique shops, cafés, market and the superb Garden Theatre (**www.gardentheatre.org**). There are two small museums, an art centre, water fountains for children to play in and walking and cycling paths (part of the West Orange Trail). Farmers' market every Sat (9am–2pm). For dining, Urban Flats, Moon Cricket Grille,

Thai Blossom and the Chef's Table at The Edgewater are all good, while Plant Street Market boasts the fab Crooked Can Brewing Co. among fresh foods and crafts kiosks. See more at **www.cwgdn.com** and **www.plantstmarket.com**.

Lake Tibet-Butler Preserve: This small nature reserve is in south-west Orange County (just north of Disney) on SR535 (Winter Garden–Vineland Rd) and features 4ml/6.5km of trails and elevated boardwalks where the cypress swamps, freshwater marshes, scrub and pine flatwoods are home to gopher tortoises, turtles, armadillos and especially birds (it is on the Great Florida Birding Trail). (10am–5 or 6pm Wed–Sun).

MOUNT DORA/Lake County

To the west and north of Orlando is this large, rural county that is home to unspoiled Florida charms and small-scale attractions.

Mount Dora: This smallish town on beautiful Lake Dora is one of Florida's hidden gems. It is also renowned as a festival city, with 19 annual galas. Check your dates on **www.mountdora.com** (4 July and Christmas are notable, while the April Sail Boat Regatta is one of Florida's finest).

Mount Dora Trolley: Start with a 1hr narrated trundle around the streets from the Lakeside Inn, (11am, noon, 1 and 2pm Mon–Sat, $16 adults, $13 2–13s; 352 385 1023), a fascinating tour of what was a key stop on the now-defunct Florida railroad. Then stroll round the quaint shops, cafés and bars in the compact centre. Antique hunters are spoiled for choice but should visit **Village Antique Mall**, with more than 80 vendors, and **Pak Ratz**, plus **Uncle Al's Time Capsule**, for film and celebrity memorabilia, while other stores include **Papilio** (gifts), **Gold In Art** (jewellery) and **La Petite Maison** (aromatherapy gifts). The town even boasts the **Rocking Rabbit Brewery**, with live music on Fri and Sat 8–11pm (**www.mountdorabrewing.com**). Other stops of interest include **Mount Dora**

Historic Museum (the old town jail), which displays more (free) local history, and the **Museum of Speed**, a homage to high-powered American sports cars of yesteryear (plus other memorabilia such as vintage jukeboxes; 10am–5pm Mon–Fri; $15/person or $20 with tour, no under-14s, no credit/debit cards; 352 385 0049, **www.classicdreamcars.com**).

Guided Tours of Segway of Central Florida: One of the best ways to see Mount Dora is with these fully narrated tours using two-wheel Segways to take small groups downtown, on to the iconic **Mount Dora lighthouse** and around scenic **Palm Island Park**. They pass some of the city's many fine B&Bs (including the award-winning Magnolia Inn on East 3rd Avenue) and the genteel 125-year-old **Lakeside Inn**, on the National Register of Historic Places, where you can stop for a drink in Tremain's Lounge or dine in the Beauclaire Dining Room (great Sunday brunch – **www.lakeside-inn.com**). The Segway is easy to master (after a brief hands-on lesson) and ideal for the quiet streets. If you enjoy the 1hr tour, there is a second guided tour of nearby Dogwood Mountain. Each one costs $55/person and tours run daily 9.30am, 11.30am, and 1.30pm (reservations advised; 352 460 2039, **www.segwayofcentralflorida.com**; save $6 if booking online). Riders must be 14 and no more than 260lb/118kg.

Premier Boat Tours: You can see more via the *Captain Doolittle* from

Simon and Susan love Segway tours

the Lakeside Inn for a fascinating eco-tour of the lakes and Dora Canal. As well as gators, you may see raccoons, turtles, otters, birds of prey and other nesting birds along this beautiful waterway. There are narrated 2hr tours daily at 11am and 2pm ($27 adults, $15 children) and 1hr Sunset Tours daily ($17 and $12, bring your favourite beverages; reservations advised on 352 434 8040, **www.doracanaltour.com**). Pontoon rentals are also available.

CraigCat Tours: 2hr narrated guided tours along Lake Dora and the Dora Canal aboard CraigCat, motorised two-person watercraft. Bottled water and lifejackets provided. No experience necessary, drivers must be 21+ with valid driving licence, passengers must be 12+. Non-marking soft-soled shoes or sandals required ($99/person; 352 816 9339; **www.catboattours.com**; check website for periodic discounts).

Getting there: On US Highway 441 north-east of Orlando, take the (toll) Florida Turnpike to exit 267A for the (toll) Western Beltway (429), and the Beltway north to its junction with 441, from where Mount Dora is 10ml/16km further north. For more info, contact the excellent Mount Dora Chamber of Commerce on 352 383 2165 or **www.mountdora.com**. The visitor centre is at 341 Alexander Street.

◀■▶ **BRITBONUS**
$ Take a kayak tour with Central Florida Nature Adventures and, when you book for three, the fourth person paddles free! Just remember to quote the *Brit Guide* offer when you book and show your copy when you turn up.

Central Florida Nature Adventures: Head north from Mount Dora to Eustis, from where this company offer guided tours of the Dora Canal and the Lil' Amazon in Lake County, Rock Springs Run and the Wekiva River in Seminole County, Blackwater Lake in Marion County and the Silver River in Ocala; plus a winter Manatee tour and a kayak

Mount Dora dining

Try a leisurely lunch at the excellent **Copacabana Cuban Café** or **One Flight Up**. **Village Coffee Pot** is the place for coffee and the **Windsor Rose** is an English tea-room. For something stronger, there are notable pubs like **Tremain's Tavern** or **The Lost Parrot**. All also offer dinner, but our top two – especially if you arrive before sunset – are **Pisces Rising**, a lovely Key West-themed restaurant, with a grandstand view of sunsets over Lake Dora, plus fresh Florida seafood and steaks (352 385 2669, **www.piscesrisingdining.com**); and the charming **Goblin Market** bistro tucked away in a quiet corner of town (352 735 0059, **http://thegoblinmarketrestaurant.com/**). With a small patio dining area, a conservatory-style ground floor and clubby upper floor with bar, this renovated warehouse is ideal for a refined lunch or upmarket dinner (11am–3pm and 5pm–9pm, 10pm Fri and Sat; 11.30am–3.30pm only Sun; closed Mon).

and horse-riding combo. Their two chief guides are experienced kayakers but most of these scenic trips (2–7hrs) require no experience. Tours vary from $64–129 (352 589 7899, **www.kayakcentralflorida.com**).

Lake Louisa State Park: Another gem just off Highway 27 (at the west end of Highway 192), this offers beautiful countryside, with six lakes and rolling hills. There are over 20ml/32km of hiking trails, a picnic pavilion, swimming in Lake Louisa (with lifeguards late May– Aug), plus 20 cabins, sleeping up to six (8am–dusk daily, entry $5/car; 352 394 3969, **www. floridastateparks. org/park/Lake-Louisa**). Further up Highway 27 is the **Citrus Tower**, built in 1956, with panoramic views from its 22-storey glass observation deck (9am–5pm Mon–Sat, $6 adults $4 3–11s; 352 394 4061, **www.citrustower. com**); and **Lakeridge Winery**, a 127acre/51ha producing some award-winning wines with free tours and tastings (10am–5pm Mon– Sat, 11am–5pm Sun; 1800 768 9463, **www.lakeridgewinery.com**).

Revolution Off Road: Perfect for those families seeking attractions outside the major theme parks and looking to enjoy the real Florida, this British-run attraction is set in 240acres/97ha of countryside with a private lake. They offer self-drive guided ATVs (quad-bikes), Dune Buggies and an amphibious vehicle (the Mucky Duck). The purpose-built ATV trail features 2 x 40 min sessions of fab driving (must be 16 or older but no driving licence required). There's a short safety briefing to ensure riders are in control, then it's off over the sand-hills and grasslands on dirt trails and tracks groomed for off-road activity.

◄█► BRITTIP

If you're looking for a wedding venue with a difference, Revolution Offroad can now be used as a venue for a variety of outdoor occasions. Call them for details.

You WILL get dirty, so wear old clothes – and close-toed shoes or trainers. The dune buggies are open to all 18 years or older with a valid driving licence, under 280lb/127kg and under 1.9m/6ft 3in. Revolution has a specially designed 2ml/3.2km trail and you get to drive five laps. It is one of Florida's best off-road

Revolution Offroad ATV tour

© Revolution Offroad

drives – novel, enjoyable and highly addictive! The **Mucky Duck** tour is also self-drive in these four-passenger amphibious vehicles. The 75min experience includes training in the six and eight-wheel Argo UTVs, then the chance to drive around the trails and into the main lake. Drivers must be at least 18 and hold a full licence, but passengers can be as young as four (with safety vest provided). They also feature Target Archery on an Olympic range with level 2 coaches on staff to assist and teach, and have recently introduced Clay Shooting, which is available for all guests over 18. The privately owned lake has no public access and is stock managed to a high level. There is a catch-and-release policy but they do offer a 10lb club bonus if you hook a large trophy bass.

Booking is essential on 352 400 1322 or **www.revolutionoffroad.com**. ATV is $80/person; ATV & Dune Buggy or ATV & Duck $140; or all three for $190. Mucky Duck tour $80/driver, $40/passenger. Fishing is $250 for two guests for 4hrs with all equipment and licenses included. Target Archery is $45/person and Clay Shooting $75 for 30 clays and shots. To get there, take Highway 192 west to Highway 27; go north on 27 for 3 traffic lights; turn left on Highway 474 when it hits 33, then go right for 2ml/3km and it is on the right.

◄$► BRITBONUS

Get $5/person off any activity at Revolution Offroad by showing your copy of the *Brit Guide* or mentioning it when booking.

OSCEOLA COUNTY

You'll find some of Florida's most scenic natural attractions in the Kissimmee area – you just need to know where to look!

◄█► BRITTIP

Dresses are not advisable for balloon trips and hardwearing shoes for the set-up and landing areas are essential.

Orlando Balloon Rides

Balloon trips

Florida is popular for ballooning and you will often see them in Osceola County. The utterly smooth way in which you lift off is breathtaking, but the peace and quiet, and the stunning views, are awesome.

It's not cheap, but it is appealing to all but young children or those with a fear of heights. It can also be a highly personal ride, with basket capacity starting at just four people.

Orlando Balloon Rides: The main operator in central Florida flies every day, weather permitting, meeting at their smart new Reception Center on Highway 27 (near the junction with I-4) at 5.30–6.30am depending on season, as the best winds are nearly always early, then transferring in their vans to the take-off site. Here you can help the friendly crew set up their balloons (which take up to 20 passengers in comfort, one of which is also disabled-accessible).

Then you fly off for an hour, floating serenely or sinking to skim the treetops or one of the many lakes. After your flight, enjoy a champagne landing ceremony before returning to the Center, where there are free snacks and drinks. It lasts 3–4hrs and costs $195/adult, $99 ages 4–10 ($225 and $109 at weekends; no under-4s or expectant mothers).

Select hotel pick-ups are available at $15/person for the round trip, or for $30 you can be part of the chase crew and just enjoy the champagne landing. Balloonist Certificates can be downloaded from the website. Book well in advance on 407 894 5040 or **www.orlandoballoonrides.com**.

◀$▶ BRITBONUS
Mention the code BG2017 and show your copy of the *Brit Guide* with Orlando Balloon Rides for a 10% discount on all their flights.

Thompson Aire: Top local pilot Jeff Thompson, a veteran with more than 35 years' flying, also flies every day (weather permitting), meeting at the Maingate Lakeside Resort on Highway 192, and returning there for a hearty buffet breakfast. Fares are $185 ($105 10–15s; 1 child 5–9 can fly free with a paying adult; discounts for four or more adults travelling together). Chase package available for non-flyers. Call 407 421 9322 or visit **www.thompsonaire.com**. Hotel pick-ups can be arranged at $15/person.

Airboat rides

The thrill of airboat rides – like flying at ground level – can be experienced on many of Florida's waterways, but especially in Osceola County. You can explore areas otherwise inaccessible to boats, skimming over the marshes to give you an alternative, close-up view. Travelling at up to

50mph/80kph means it can be loud (you will be given ear protectors) and sunglasses are also a good idea to keep stray flies out of your eyes. It is NOT the trip for you, however, if you are spooked by crickets, dragonflies and similar insects that occasionally land in the boat! In summer, a good insect repellent is essential.

BRITTIP
Look out for some great discounts and special offers on Boggy Creek's website, **www.bcairboats.com**.

Boggy Creek Airboat Rides: Get out into rural Osceola County with this great operator, who sets out from peaceful **Southport Park**, all the way down Poinciana Boulevard, off Highway 192 between markers 10 and 11, and across Pleasant Hill Road into Southport Road – about a 35min drive. Boggy Creek's half-hour ride features the most modern 18-passenger airboats in Florida, skimming over the local wetlands for a close-up of the majestic cypress trees and wildlife including eagles, ospreys, snakes and turtles, as well as the ever-present gators. Southport Park feels a million miles away from the main tourist area and it is likely you'll see a variety of wildlife, especially in spring.

You don't need to book, just turn up, as boats go every 30mins (9am–5pm daily; $27.95 adults, $21.95 3–10s). Don't forget the sunscreen as you can really burn on the water. Boggy Creek also does a 1hr Sunset Tour ($52.95 adults, $48.95 3–10s, from 6.45pm late March–late Sept) or Night Tour ($52.59 adults, $48.95 3–10s, from 7.30pm Oct–Mar, 8:30pm March-Sept) for a completely different and exhilarating experience (gator eyes glow red in the dark!), but you must book in advance. Or go all out with the 45min Swamp Excursion, exploring remote areas beyond the regular tour ($57.95/person). Round-trip hotel transport is offered (call for pricing). Stay after your ride for a live alligator demonstration – and have the chance to hold a gator and have your picture taken! (book on 407 344 9550 or **www.bcairboats.com**).

BRITBONUS
Brit Guide readers qualify for 10% off any tour with Boggy Creek Airboats when showing the book at check-in or using code *BritGuide* when booking in advance.

Wild Florida: Set on tranquil Cypress Lake, this airboat ride and wildlife reserve features 30min, one-hour and night-time rides from their purpose-built dock (a great place for wildlife watching) with the chance to see gators, turtles, birdlife and even snakes from the safety of their six and 17-passenger airboats. It also features a self-contained 13acre/5.2ha **Wildlife Park** that is home to their growing collection of exotic animals such as emus, zebras, watusi cattle and sloths, plus plenty of Florida wildlife like raccoons, bobcats and a huge gator pond. There is also an aviary and a peaceful boardwalk cypress swamp walk. You can feed some of the animals (for a small fee) and there is an excellent gift shop (remember you can't bring alligator products back to the UK) and the excellent **Chomp House Grill**, for a snack or lunch (featuring burgers, chicken tenders and barbecue specialities – but we dare you to try the Swamp Sampler, with gator, catfish and frogs legs!) under their lovely covered pavilion. Their alligator handling and photo opportunities (single photos $15–20; percentage of all photos goes to Florida Panther Conservation Society) are good, too, and you won't see any sign of human habitation out on the Lake.

BRITTIP
Want an airboat ride but don't have a car? Taxis are seriously expensive but **Gray Line Orlando** feature a ride with Wild Florida plus round-trip transportation from $69 (see p264).

⚓ BRITTIP

Want a real Florida dining experience after visiting Wild Florida or the Lazy H Ranch (see right)? Head back on to Highway 192 in St Cloud for **The Catfish Place**, a real locals' hotspot serving up specialities like catfish, gator and turtle (as well as steaks, chicken and shellfish). It's as authentic as it gets – see http://thecatfishplacestcloud.com.

Booking is advisable but they do go out regularly from 9am–6pm Mon–Sat (closed Sun). The ½hr tour is $26.50 for adults and $23 for 3–11s; 1hr is $47.50 and $37; 1hr private tour and night-time tour $63/person (must pre-book). Also try their Ranch Buggy Tours ($25 and $20) for a gentle trundle around the 15,000-acre Doc Partin Ranch, hearing the story of one of the oldest cattle ranches in the state and seeing some of the abundant local wildlife, which can include deer, wild hogs, raccoons and bobcats. All tours include Wildlife Park, or $18 and $15 on its own (1866 532 7167, **http://wildfloridairboats.com/**). To get there, take Highway 192 east to St Cloud (about 20mls/32km), turn right on Vermont Ave (12mls/19km), which becomes Canoe Creek Rd, then right on to Lake Cypress Rd for the final 2mls/3.2km. From Orlando, you can take the (toll) Florida Turnpike to 192 at Exit 244, then continue east to Vermont and follow the other directions from there.

💲 BRITBONUS

Wild Florida offers $5 off all one-hour airboat tours, free kids-size ice cream cone with any Wildlife Park admission, and $3 off all ranch buggy tours when you use promo code WILDBRITS to redeem online, by phone or in person. Cannot be combined with any other offers.

Paddling, climbing and horse-riding

Kissimmee Paddling Center: Here's a great chance to get up close with the heart of Osceola County nature, with kayaks, canoes and paddleboards on offer at this new site ideally located on Highway 192. Shingle Creek forms the headwaters of the Everglades and is a haven of peace and quiet, perfect for a paddling adventure whether for 1hr or a half day. There are even 45min electric boat tours for those who just want to enjoy the scenery. You can just turn up and go but bookings are advisable. Open daily, 8am–5 or 6pm, rentals are from $13–18/hr while 2hr guided tours are $55/person and 4hr round-trip to Makinson Island is $99 (located in Shingle Creek Regional Park just past Medieval Times, plus a new launch dock at Marsh Landing in south Kissimmee; 407 344 0881, **http://paddlingcenter.com/**).

Orlando Tree Trek: Adventure-seekers will want to test out this challenging new aerial ropes course in a forested area of Kissimmee south of Disney. There are two kids' courses (ages 7–11; must be 4ft 7in/140cm) and three for ages 12 and up, from beginner to advanced in skill level, plus a dual giant zipline to finish. There is a full instruction session, then it is off into the treetops for a series of obstacles ranging from short ziplines to cargo nets, ladders, cable bridges, Tarzan swings and more. It is huge fun but the full four-course challenge will take at least 2hrs, and bottled water, stout shoes and older clothing are essential. Priced from $29.95– 49.95, it is open daily 8am–dusk (last tour 2hrs before dusk). Take Old Lake Wilson Rd south from Highway 192 to Sinclair Rd, turn right and it is on the right. Bookings advisable (407 390 9999, **www.orlandotreetrek.com**).

Lazy H Ranch: For a horse-back view of the Osceola County country-side, head to this wonderful family-owned ranch in rural Kissimmee. It can accommodate groups up to six, by reservation only, for trail rides of 1–1½hrs into the neighbouring Twin Oaks Conservation Area, bordering beautiful Lake Tohopekaliga. A former

A cause for Celebration

Dining in Celebration is a real highlight. Try **Market Street Café**, a 50s-style diner serving down-home favourites such as turkey dinners and meatloaf, plus milkshakes and desserts. Spanish-Cuban **Columbia** uses unique combinations of authentic ingredients (407 566 1505, **www.columbiarestaurant.com**); **Celebration Town Tavern**, a casual ambiance, specialising in New England seafood; **Ari Sushi**, is the place for sushi and hibachi dishes; and the **Imperium Food & Wine** is an excellent option for fine wines and cocktails, plus a tempting light bite menu, including soups, sandwiches, salads and flatbreads (407 566 9054, **www.imperiumfoodandwine. com**). You should also consider the **Bohemian Bar & Grill** at the Bohemian Hotel, a contemporary American steakhouse with old-world Florida charm, while **Kilwins** is great for chocolate and ice-cream treats.

370acre/1530ha cattle ranch, the scenery now includes grassland, live oak hammocks, wet prairies and marshes, and the birdlife is usually plentiful. You may even spot a gator or two lurking in the lake! It is a wonderfully refreshing escape from the theme park hubbub only 19mls from Disney and, while the trail-ride is designed for beginners, owner Abby Horner also offers full riding lessons and even a **Total Horse Experience**, with the chance for horse fans to spend 2hrs grooming, tacking and riding, as well as untacking and horse-bathing at the main horse barn ($90/person). The trail rides operate year-round (mornings-only in summer) and cost $45 and $60/person but must be booked in advance on 407 414 3113 or **http://lazyhranch.net/** (see website for age and weight restrictions).

BRITTIP

For Celebration, don't stop at the first set of shops and services you come to off Highway 192. Keep going until you find Market Street and the centrepiece lake that is the proper downtown area.

Celebration

In 1994, the Walt Disney Company set out to build a 'new urban' neighbourhood, a model community with a friendly, welcoming spirit and strong traditional values. The result was Celebration, where picture-perfect Victorian homes mingle with smart town-houses with an array of shopping, dining and entertainment options. Today, it is a self-sufficient, bustling town with a hospital, schools, cinema and two hotels. On Disney's southern border off Highway 192, enter at the landmark water tower via Celebration Ave, then follow signs to the Bohemian Hotel in the town centre.

Market Street shops: Feature delightful boutiques like **Market Street Gallery** (Disney collectables, Swarovski crystal, Lladro and gifts), **Confetti of Celebration** (speciality and customised gifts), **Once Upon A Time** (children's clothing) and **Soft as a Grape** (casual wear for the family). Other specialists include **Enchanted Boutique** and **Woof Gang Bakery** (pet needs). There are miles of bike and walking paths, with the pretty lakefront setting, children's play area and periodic festivals. A huge event is held on American Independence Day 4 July, with picnics, entertainment and face-painting (parking is at the town entrance, with a park-and-ride bus), while the Christmas period also sees festive events and nightly snowfall on Market Street (**http://celebrationtowncenter.com**). You can also take a 20min carriage ride

Lazy H Ranch

© Lazy H Ranch

(Fri–Sun, 6–10pm, weather permitting) at $45 for 1–4 people.

Segway Tours

An outstanding feature in Kissimmee/ Celebration is this super opportunity to try out the fab two-wheeled Segway transporter and get a guided audio tour of the area as well. Ideal for young and old alike (age 14 and up), they are easy to master, fun to ride and a breeze to enjoy as you trundle along Highway 192 and around the most scenic parts of Celebration in true eco-friendly style.

ZE Tours: Choose from three separate tours in the company of a personable guide (10am–4pm daily), heading out from their store in the Rock Church plaza on Highway 192 (by Marker 10; next to the Helicopter Tours) and rolling along for 70, 100 or 130mins to discover the heart of Celebration, its many lakes, paths and byways, plus lots of wildlife – from playful squirrels (which you can feed) to gators (which you can't!). There is a quick ride-around to get your 'Segway legs', then it is off in single-file, with the tranquil tour enabled by small walkie-talkies that clip on to your helmet. There are plenty of stops to ask questions and compare notes with your group, and your guide is a great source of knowledge about the town and the area (especially Disney). ZE Tours also offer bike rentals to tour Highway 192 at your leisure (and it's all completely flat). The Segway tours cost $60, $75 and $90/person (70, 100 and 130mins; 14–17-year-olds must be accompanied by a parent; minimum weight 100lb/45kg, max 250lb/113kg), or you can just try a ride on a Segway at $10 for 10min, $20 for 20mins, and $30 for 30 mins. Bike rental is from $5–25 (hourly or all day). Reservations are highly recommended for both on 321 250 1211 or online, **www.zetours.com**.

Forever Florida

For our money, this is one of the most outstanding non-theme-park attractions in Florida. Both a 4,700acre/1,900ha wilderness preserve and working ranch, it offers a close-up of the flora, fauna and conservation issues, plus a real taste of cracker-style life ('crackers' were 19th century Florida cowboys), as well as their own EcoPark, with six thrilling adventures.

Cypress Restaurant and Visitor Center: Start here with its essential 30min orientation programme into the preserve's creation. Beginning as a dream of gifted biologist and ecologist Allen Broussard, it was completed after his death (from complications of Hodgkin's disease) by his parents, Dr William and Margaret Broussard as a non-profit-making memorial to their son. The education element alone is awesome, and the two tours feature a strong conservation message. The two-hour **Coach Safari** is a tranquil trundle in a large-wheeled, open-sided buggy round much of the woods, swamp and prairie of the Crescent J Ranch and Conservancy. Your guide gives the lowdown on the history and environmental issues. A boardwalk along Bull Creek affords the chance to get up close with a typical cypress 'dome' and breathe the amazingly pure air. You are likely to see alligators, turtles, whitetail deer, armadillos and a host of bird life – including bald eagles and wild turkeys – as well as native cattle and horses, and you'll leave with a good understanding of the REAL Florida ($29 adults, $20 6–12s; 23 times a day, variously 10am and 1pm).

Horseback Safaris: For ages 10 and over; here's the chance to enjoy Western trail rides for 90min with a native cracker guide ($69.99/person, book at least 24 hours in advance on 407 957 9794).

BRITTIP

Long trousers and closed-toed shoes are essential for Forever Florida's Horse Safaris. Early morning rides are especially enjoyable.

EcoPark: THE must-not-miss attraction in Central Florida for serious thrill-seekers, featuring a zipline course, zipline roller-coaster, hair-raising straightaway zipline and free-fall attraction.

Zipline Safari: This 2½-hour adventure starts with a short scenic hike to the launch point, which provides a breathtaking aerial view of the preserve at up to 55ft/16.8m high. The course includes seven different ziplines, 10 observation platforms and three sky-bridges over three eco-systems. The longest run is 750ft/229m and riders reach top speeds of 25mph/40kph. The final zip brings you down to its wildlife interaction area, including a Florida panther, alligators and other animals. There is also a Starlight Safari or Moonlight Safari every Sat night, but you must book in advance ($79.99/ person, ages eight and up).

The Thrill Pack – The Rattlesnake, Peregrine Plunge & Panther Pounce: The Rattlesnake is 'next generation ziplining' at its best, a 1,000ft/205m long, 20mph/32kph diving and soaring 'roller-coaster' ride from the 65ft/20m high tower. Peregrine Plunge launches from a 71ft/22m tower with 1,300ft/396m of line – the longest single zipline in Florida, at up to 30mph/48kph – and not for the faint of heart. But do it once and you'll want to go again. Want to get to the ground quicker? Tethered to an overhead crane and fitted into a secure harness at Panther Pounce, step off the 68ft/21m tower and go straight into free-fall! The effect is mindboggling, with serious bragging rights when it's over. All the adventures are covered by The Thrill Pack, at $69.99/ages 8 and up (max weight 275lb/125kg; 265lb/120kg for Panther Pounce; min weight 70lb/32kg and age 10).

The **Horseback Safaris** can also be extended to two days ($199), staying in bunk-house accommodation. Forever Florida is a good 80min drive out of Orlando, 40ml/64km east on Highway 192, through St Cloud as far as Holopaw, then 7½ml/12km south on Highway 441, but is well worth the journey to experience the charm and tranquillity (407 957 9794, reservations recommended for all experiences, **www.foreverflorida.com**).

BRITBONUS Receive $5 off any adventure at Forever Florida when mentioning code RC. Reservations are required.

Osceola County History Center & Pioneer Village

Highway 192 (just by Marker 15) features the **Osceola County Welcome Center** and **History Museum**, a collaboration between the County and Historical Society, providing a small-scale but engaging look at the area's history and nature. There is a 'steamboat' entryway inside, then a tour of local history from 1867 to the present, through the four main 'habitats' (swamplands, pine flatwoods, oak hammocks and lakefront) with a series of tableaux and nature exhibits that depict the true rural and agricultural nature of central Florida, plus the original Indian tribes. Outside, you can wander alongside Shingle Creek, the headwaters of The Everglades (free admission daily 9am–5pm; 407 396 8644, **www.osceolahistory.org**). After seeing the museum, cross over Highway 192 to Shingle Creek Regional Park for a chance

Simon & Susan take the Lazy H Ranch tour

to wander the hiking trails and experience Osceola nature at first hand.

Next, head for the **Pioneer Village**, just off Highway 192 on Babb Road. This delightful discovery pays real-life homage to 19th-century Florida life, with a preserved 'cracker' homestead, blacksmith shop, Seminole Village and other buildings portraying how settlers lived in the 1880s. The charming outdoor museum traces more Osceola County history and includes an array of homes owned by historically-known Floridans, plus a citrus-packing operation from nearby Narcoossee, originally started by a family from the UK! The tours are self-guided, or volunteers can take you round, providing a fascinating view of life here more than 130 years ago (2491 Babb Road, just off Highway 192. Take Old Vineland Rd to Babb Rd and turn left; 10am–4pm daily; $7 adults, $3 6–12s, under-6s free).

Warbird Adventures and Kissimmee Air Museum

This is the most exhilarating ride in town, bar none – guaranteed. It's the only place we know of where, 20mins after walking in with no previous experience, you can actually be flying a 1945 T-6 Harvard fighter-trainer plane... and doing all manner of aerobatics. It's enhanced by in-flight video and wingtip camera to record every moment. Roller-coasters? They're for wimps! Mind you, this is not cheap – a 15min flight costs $290,

Stallion 51

30mins is $490, 45mins is $630 and an hour $780 (aerobatics on 30min flight $35 extra), while the DVD is $50 and photos $25. Nevertheless, the memory will last a lifetime and just the thought of it is thrilling. Max weight is 18st/115kg and minimum height is 4ft/122cm. Also on the same site at Kissimmee Gateway Airport is Kissimmee Air Museum, combination warplane showcase and restoration centre where you can get up close with 22 exhibits, which include a 1947 Hiller Raven helicopter, a 1928 Arrow Sport, a Boeing Stearman biplane, three T-6 Harvards and the amazing one-off Aerocar, plus small-scale offerings like a WWII rifle collection and Luftwaffe memorabilia. Other exhibits include Air Power and Pearl Harbor, with rare photos and artefacts behind the story. Other aircraft include a racing P-51 Mustang, a French Fouga Magister and a MiG 17. It can all be found just off Hoagland Boulevard, ½ml/800m south of Highway 192, on the left (Air Museum open 9am–5pm Mon–Sat; $10/person, ages 6–12 $5, under-5s free; 407 870 7366, **www.warbirdadventures.com**).

Stallion 51: If the T-6 Harvard isn't thrilling enough, how about a P-51 Mustang? Yes, seriously. This two-plane operation also flies out of Kissimmee and offers orientation flights in their special dual cockpit WWII fighters, from basic maneuvers to full aerobatics. It is a real connoisseur's experience, hence very pricey ($2,350 for a half-hour flight; $3,150 for 1hr), but just watching the planes in flight is a thrill, while being in the cockpit is truly mind-blowing (407 846 4400, **www.stallion51.com**).

POLK COUNTY

Head south from Kissimmee/Osceola County and you head into Polk territory, another of Florida's oldest-established and most authentic areas. It is home to the large-scale attractions of LEGOLAND Florida (p220) but also has its share of off-the-beaten-track experiences.

Bok Tower Gardens

For those wishing to experience the genuine peace, tranquillity and floral ambience of Florida, there is no better recommendation than this national monument and garden centre at Lake Wales, 50ml/80km to the south-west of Orlando (go west on I-4, then south on Highway 27). With one of the most unusual attractions in the state – a majestic 205ft/62.5m pink-and-grey marble Carillon Tower: Set in 50acres/101ha of parkland, this is a feast for the eyes and soul. Called the Singing Tower, the 1920s-built carillon is the centrepiece and concerts are given every day at 1 and 3pm. The Tower is wonderfully photogenic and quite stunning on a cloudless day.

Gardens: Around the Tower is a wide moat, a pond and semi-formal gardens. At one of the highest points on Florida's peninsula (all of 298ft/90m above sea level), the view is inspiring and uncluttered, and retains an inherent peace and solitude that persuaded the founder, philanthropist Edward Bok, to grant the estate to the community in 1929. The gardens also provide a wildlife observatory, nature trails, an endangered plant exhibit, butterfly and woodland gardens and pine forests. There is a kids' play area, plus brass rubbing and art classes.

Education and Visitor Center: The award-winning centre illustrates the story of Edward Bok (don't miss the film about his impact on US society) and his vision for Bok Tower Gardens. The Blue Palmetto Café adds a pleasant opportunity for a light lunch and snacks, while the Tower & Garden Gift Shop offers souvenir items.

Pinewood Estate: For an additional fee ($6 adults, $5 5–12s, noon–4pm Mon–Sat, 1pm–4pm Sun), you can tour a fine example of Mediterranean-style architecture in this 20-room mansion, built as a winter retreat for a Pennsylvania steel tycoon in the early 1930s and lovingly maintained to show a slice of period opulence.

Getting there: Off US Highway 27 on Burns Avenue; take I-4 west to exit 55, go south on US 27 for 25ml/40km, then left on Mountain Lake Cutoff Road (2 traffic lights past Eagle Ridge Mall) and follow the signs. Admission: $12 adults, $3 5–12s (under-5s free), apart from occasional ticketed events (mainly carillon festivals and recitals). Open 8am–6pm daily (last entry 5pm; Visitor Center 9am–5pm only; 863 676 1408, http://boktowergardens.org/).

BRITBONUS

$ Receive a $3 discount off regular adult combo admission tickets at Bok Tower Gardens by producing your copy of the *Brit Guide* (includes Gardens and Pinewood Estate.)

Lake Wales

Continue on to the Lake Wales area after Bok Tower Gardens and you encounter some other local gems.

Head into the quaint 1920s town of Lake Wales and you discover **Spook Hill** (where cars mysteriously roll uphill!), **Grove House Visitor Center** (home of Florida's Natural fruit juice products – as fresh as it gets; 10am–5pm Mon–Fri; 10am–2pm Sat, seasonally. Closed Memorial Day–end of Sept) and the quaint **Museum and Cultural Center** (set in a restored 1928 Atlantic Coast Line railroad station; 9am–5pm Mon–Fri, 10am–4pm Sat).

Westgate River Ranch: In rural Polk County is this superb ranch and activity centre that boasts great accommodations (including 'glamping' for those who like to camp in style, plus new Luxe Tepees) and the chance to try horse-riding, fishing, airboating, trap shooting and archery, as well as take in the exciting Saturday night Westgate Rodeo in the 1,200-seat arena. You can visit just for the day to try any of the activities or the weekly rodeo (followed by live music, line dancing and a family-friendly Street Party), but the accommodations are excellent and you can sample the River Ranch Saloon without having to drive afterwards – guaranteed family fun and a taste of Florida's cowboy country. See more at **www.westgatedestinations. com** and click on River Ranch, FL.

SEMINOLE COUNTY

You may have flown into the airport at the historic town of Sanford and there are plenty of diversions to get you well off the beaten track. If you want to finish your holiday with a day or so in the area, there are many good hotel choices (often significantly cheaper than their big-name rivals elsewhere) and you can catch your breath after all the hectic theme-parking!

Adventures in Florida: Get into the wilds with this specialist company that features kayaking adventures along the picturesque Econlockhatchee and Wekiva rivers, with expert guides and an in-depth understanding of the flora and fauna. They offer 2–3hr trips, all-day tours and even night-time paddles, as well as expeditions and lodge-based trips further afield. Along the Wekiva River you may encounter gators, manatees, turtles and all manner of birdlife, all in safety and with personable guides. Trips must be booked in advance and cost $40–100/person (407 924 3375; **www.adventuresinflorida.com**).

Central Florida Zoological Park: This private, non-profit organisation puts a natural accent on the zoo theme, set in a wooded 116acres/47ha of unspoilt countryside with boardwalks and trails around the attractions. These include over 100 species of animal, weekend feeding

Central Florida Zoo

demonstrations, educational programmes, a picnic area, pony rides and a butterfly garden, plus the Zoofari Outpost gift shop and Tropical Splash Ground water play area. It's good value at $19.50 adults, $15.95 seniors (60+) and $13.75 3–12s and is open 9am–5pm daily (not Thanksgiving Day or Christmas Day). Also try **ZOOm Air Adventures**, a separate series of eco-friendly rope bridges, ziplines, guide wires and other aerial challenges through the Zoo's treetops. The two courses can be taken separately or combined (4ft 6in/137cm to take part), plus there is a children's course (for 3–5ft/92–152cm). It costs $33.95 for the Upland course and $21.75 for the kids' version, while the combo Upland and Rainforest costs $54.95. ZOOm opens at 9am, last adventure 4pm (off exit 104 of I-4; 407 323 4450, **www.centralfloridazoo.org** and **www.zoomair.us/orlando**).

> ⚡ **BRITTIP**
>
> Visit Central Florida Zoo at the weekend and you will be offered a series of educational and enjoyable animal encounters (ranging from gators and snakes to hedgehogs).

St Johns River Eco-Tours: Drive through Seminole County to the Highbanks Marina & Camp in Debary (take I-4 east to exit 104, turn right and go north on SR600 for 4ml/6.5km, then turn left on W Highbanks Rd and follow it due west for 3ml/4.5km to the Marina) and you find this wonderful opportunity to immerse yourself in Florida nature on the beautiful St Johns River, with a two-hour pontoon boat ride in the company of naturalists Jeanne and Doug. You will gain expert insight into the magnificent local flora and fauna as well as seeing an array of birdlife, gators, turtles and even manatees. There is complimentary bottled water and a restroom on the boat. Tours leave Tues–Sun at 10am and 1.30pm, and there is a sunset tour seasonally, but booking is advisable ($25 adults, $12.50 under-13s; 386 626 9004, www.stjohnsriverecotours.com). You can also enjoy a pre or post-cruise lunch at the fun **Swamp House Riverfront Grill**, with an elevated view of the river and marina and the chance to sample catfish and gator nuggets (**www.swamphousegrill.com**).

Sanford: The heart of Seminole County, this quaint town on Lake Monroe boasts a historic centre full of brick-paved streets, antique shops and an artist colony regeneration project (Jeanine Taylor Folk Art). It's small-town America, having lost the growth battle with Orlando decades ago, but it makes a peaceful diversion with the lovely Riverwalk along the lakefront. Head first for the Historic Sanford Welcome Center (230 East 1st Street 10am–2.30pm Mon, 10am–5pm Tues–Fri, 11am–5pm Sat, noon–5pm Sun) and the **Sanford Museum** (520 East 1st Street) for an overview of city history, founded in 1877 by pioneering lawyer and diplomat Henry Sanford as a hub on the St John's River, the 'Nile of America.' The free museum (11am–4pm Tues–Fri, 1–4pm Sat) illustrates the life and times of the city's founder, its growth as the 'celery capital of the world' and recent life as a naval base. Part of that river-going heritage is now on display with the **St John's Rivership Co**, an authentic sternwheel paddle-boat that offers 3–4hr lunch cruises (and some Sat evenings). With good food, live music and dancing, it is a great way to get a close-up of the river and its wildlife aboard the five-deck *Barbara-Lee* that includes an open-air top deck, 60-seat dining room, dance floor and bar. It runs 11am–2 or 3pm Wed, Thurs and Sat, noon–3pm Sun and 7.30–10.30pm some Sats (book on 321 441 3030 or **www.stjohnsrivershipco.com**). In the evening, stop for a bite on First Street, with its many restored turn-of-the-century buildings. Try **The Corner Café** (fresh sandwiches, soups and salads) or the down home family cookin' of the **Colonial Room**. **Hollerbach's Willow Tree Café** is a German diner featuring traditional food, beers and live music Thurs–Sun evenings (11am–9pm Sun–Thurs, 10pm Fri and Sat; 407

321 2204, **www.willowtreecafe.com**). If you like the food, visit Magnolia Square Market, a lovely deli run by the Hollerbach family just round the corner. **The Imperial** at Washburn Imports (an antique store by day) is a fabulous evening bar, with cocktails and craft beers. For great burgers, fish and sandwiches, we also like **The Breezeway Restaurant & Bar** (11am–10pm Mon–Thurs, midnight Fri, Sat, 10pm Sun; 407 878 1284, **www.thebreezewayrestaurantandbar.com**).

The second Thurs in every month in Sanford features the **Alive After Five** street party 5–8pm on First Street, with music, street artists, restaurant samples and more. Admission is free, food and drink extra. Look up details at **www.sanfordinfo.com**.

State Parks: You could head for one of the splendid parks and follow the well-marked trails. **Wekiva Springs State Park** offers bike rentals, hiking, canoeing, swimming, picnic areas and shelters, and **Little Big Econ** state forest has 5,048acres/2,045ha of scenic woodlands and wetlands. **Spring Hammock Preserve** offers 1,500acres/607ha of wilderness and the Lake Proctor area has 6ml/10km of equestrian, hiking and biking adventures. There are more trails along the Econlockhatchee River at the **Econ River Wilderness Area**, while Chuluota has 625acres/253ha and the **Geneva Wilderness Area** 180acres/73ha, including Ed Yarborough Nature Center.

Where to stay: At Altamonte Springs, the refurbished **Hilton** is an upmarket choice without the price-tag, with large rooms, excellent amenities, a swish bar and versatile restaurant for breakfast, dinner and lunch (407 830 1985, **www.hilton.com**). At Lake Mary, the **Westin** offers ultra-comfy rooms, exceptional service and the bonus of Shula's 347 Grill, a stylish, casual eatery featuring exceptional Black Angus steaks, signature salads, speciality dishes and a full bar (407 531 3555; **www.westinlakemary.com**). As an alternative, **Danville B&B** is an amazing creation in rural Seminole county. Built with a totally false front, the building opens to reveal the 'village' of Danville, which is a superbly equipped guesthouse boasting its own pub and cinema! It is also a magnificent setting for the many weddings it hosts each year, so advance bookings here are essential (407 349 5742, **www.danvillebnb.com**).

More info: See **www.visitseminole.com** or go to one of the Visitor Centers at Orlando Sanford International Airport (in the Welcome Center as you exit the main building) or the office at the Heathrow junction of I-4 (exit 98, go west on Lake Mary Blvd, right on International Parkway and left at AAA Drive; 407 665 2900).

CITRUS COUNTY

If you want to travel a little further, the two state park delights of Citrus County, on the Gulf Coast north-west of Orlando, are worth seeking out.

Crystal River Preserve State Park: Just north of Homosassa Springs, the Crystal River is home to the endangered manatee and it is possible to go swimming with these wonderful creatures, either on a self-guided or an organised tour. Winter and spring are ideal times for manatee sightings, but the park offers year-round adventure, with hiking and biking trails, kayaking, canoeing and fishing – or just pack a picnic lunch and enjoy a relaxing afternoon amid the natural beauty. You can also catch a relaxing and educational ride with **Heritage Eco-Tours** aboard the 24-passenger *Monroe* for a unique 1½hr look at local history and wildlife (seasonally, Sept–May, Mon, Wed, Fri, 10.30am and 1.30pm weather permitting; $15 adults, $10 under 13s, cash only; call to confirm on 352 228 6028).

BRITTIP

Manatee are protected and there are heavy fines, strictly enforced, for disturbing them.

Getting there: Take the (toll) Florida Turnpike north to I-75, then, almost immediately, take SR44 west to

Crystal River. Admission: Free (8am–dusk; **www.floridastateparks.org/ crystalriverpreserve**).

Homosassa Springs Wildlife State Park: This park also showcases the manatee (via its underwater observatory), plus whooping cranes, deer, bobcats, black bear and even a hippopotamus among an active display of rehabilitating animals. There are daily programmes on its wildlife (every hour from 10.30am–3.30pm), notably snakes and birds of prey, plus a hands-on children's education centre. The park's 210acres/ 85ha take in some of the state's loveliest landscape as well as the headwaters of the Homosassa River and this is extremely popular in the spring.

Getting there: As for Crystal River, but turn left on to CR490 just after Lecanta on SR44. Admission: $13 adults, $5 6–12s (9am–5.30pm, last entry 4pm; 352 628 5343, **www.homosassasprings.org**).

Where to stay: The ideal place for a night or two in the heart of Citrus County's natural beauty is the **Plantation on Crystal River**, a mansion-esque resort in Kings Bay on the river itself. It features gorgeous rooms and villas, great dining, golf and its own manatee eco-tours, as well as lashings of old-fashioned Southern hospitality. If nothing else, you should definitely try lunch or dinner (or the fab Sunday Brunch) at the West 82° Bar & Grill (352 795 4211, **www.plantationoncrystalriver.com**).

More info: Look up **www.visitcitrus.com** or call 352 794 5506.

BREVARD COUNTY

Out on the Atlantic coast is Cocoa Beach's Thousand Islands. Tranquil canals wind past mangrove stands, wildlife flourishes in the still waters and the Indian River Lagoon Estuary is one of the most biodiverse eco-systems in the world.

Island Boat Lines: This family-owned enterprise offers eco-tours, fishing and the wonderful *Indian River Queen* dinner boat, recalling Mark

Twain's tales of paddleboats and peaceful gentility. A relaxing 2hr In Search of Wildlife eco-tour onboard Coast Guard-certified pontoon boats departs from the Sunset Waterfront Café on Highway 520 (W Cocoa Beach Causeway), passing some of the area's most impressive homes before heading into the Thousand Islands. Here you may spot bottlenose dolphins, manatees and coastal birds. Knowledgeable guides offer a wealth of info. Tours run at 10am and 2pm Mon–Sat, 2pm Sun ($28 adults, $26 seniors and military personnel, $23 2–12s; call to book on 1800 979 3370; **www.islandboatlines.com**)

Getting there: Take the Beachline Expressway (Highway 528) to Highway 1 south, then Merritt Island Causeway (Highway 520) east, approx. 2ml/3.2km with the café on the right.

BRITBONUS

Get $8 off the regular adult price with Island Boat Lines by showing your copy of the *Brit Guide*. Book in advance, though, on 321 454 7414.

Indian River Queen: Also used for private events, this beautifully appointed triple-deck paddlewheel riverboat is open to the public at weekends, with an elegant **Dinner & Party Cruise** every Fri featuring a red carpet reception, live music, themed dinner buffet and full bar. Captain Todd and owners Penny and John provide authentic Southern hospitality. Boarding begins at 6.30pm, sailing from 7–9.30pm ($40/ person, dinner $20). The **Scenic Historical Cruise** offers 2hr narrated tours with souvenir photo for $30/ person, select dates only (booking required on 321 454 7414 or **www.indianriverqueen.com**).

Getting there: To reach Cocoa Village Marina, take the Beachline (Highway 528) east to Highway 1, go south to Highway 520, make a slight left at Bee Line, continue to N Cocoa Blvd, turn left at King, then left at Delannoy.

Cocoa Beach Sportfishing: Board the fully equipped *Centerfold*, a 33ft/10m Tournament-rigged boat, and get ready for big game fishing! Troll for mahi-mahi, sailfish, wahoo, kingfish, grouper and more with a crew who boast plenty of experience in finding 'the big one.' Captains Tim and Beau share their passion for fishing with anglers of all experience levels (novice to pro), and do it with humour and professionalism. *Centerfold* offers 5, 7 and 9hr offshore trips at $600, $700 and $800; the 19ft custom in-shore fishing Flatsboat accommodates 1–3 passengers at $150–300 for 2–4hrs, $50 per extra hour; and the 26ft *Center Console* takes 1–4 anglers out for 4, 6 or 8hrs at $400, $500 or $600 (fishing licence, tackle, bait included; reservations on 321 848 2662, **www.cbsportfishing.com**). For more Cocoa Beach info, p277.

Plantation on Crystal River

Port Canaveral: This area immediately adjacent to the busy cruise port (right off Highway 528) is now well worth a visit as it boasts some great small-scale attractions as well as tempting places to eat, all with a great view of the port. Start at the **Exploration Tower**, a seven-storey museum and exhibition centre featuring the region's history and livelihood through a range of multimedia presentations and hands-on exhibits (like the Port Navigation simulator). There is also a wonderful top-floor open-air observation deck, plus a café and gift shop (daily 10am–5pm, 7pm Fri and Sat; adults $6.50, seniors $4, children $3.75; closed public holidays; 321 394 3408, **www.explorationtower.com**). **Space Coast Segway Tours** are a great way to have fun and see the whole area on these two-wheel vehicles, with a tour guide who takes you round and points out the key elements of the Port and its many facilities. Tours for four run five times a day, including a new evening tour, (not Tues and Thurs Sept–Feb) and can take anyone from 45–118kg/7–18st, following a short training session. An alternative tour features historic Cocoa Village. $75/person, cash only; reservations required (321 652 4169, **http://spacecoastsegwaytours. com**). Another real collector's item is **Parker Brothers Concepts**, who make all kinds of amazing vehicles for TV and films (notably the *Batman* series), with tours daily (Mon–Sat 10am–5pm **www.parkerbrothersconcepts.com**).

There is an excellent choice of restaurants along Glen Cheek Drive. Try any of Grills Seafood Deck & Tiki Bar, Rusty's Seafood & Oyster Bar, Fishlips Waterfront Bar & Grill, Seafood Atlantic, Baja Chowder &

Clarwater Marine Aquarium

© Gray Line Tours

Seafood and, our fave, **Milliken's Reef**, a fabulous inside/outside diner and bar with a great seafood-orientated menu, superb views, live music Fri and Sat evenings, Happy Hour 4–6pm daily, and even its own beach (321 783 0100, **www.millikensreef.com**).

Excursion operators
For those without a car (or wanting to put their feet up for a bit), there are tours and day trips visiting as far afield as the Everglades, Miami, Florida Keys and even the Bahamas. You can see a lot if you don't mind a long day (up to 16 hours). However, if the main attraction of a trip to the Everglades is the airboat ride, you are better off going to Boggy Creek Airboats or Wild Florida (p253).

BRITTIP

For more info on all tours, see our booking section online at **www. britguideorlando.net** and look up our *Brit Guide* partners for the full range of **Gray Line** excursions – with your exclusive 15% discount.

Gray Line Tours: Orlando's biggest excursion company and a *Brit Guide* partner, offering 15% off all tours, from transport-only trips to Kennedy Space Centre to all-day tours to the Everglades, plus limo pick-ups for Disney character dining. Air-conditioned coaches, knowledgeable guides. See website for full range.

Kennedy Space Center: Gray Line has an exclusive bonus with their KSC tour as guests are greeted and given a welcome briefing by a bona fide astronaut before they explore the Visitor Complex at their leisure for the day. The KSC can also be combined with an airboat ride, the Dine With An Astronaut experience, or the Ultimate Space Experience for maximum access to the Space Center ($59–169).

1-Day Miami: Get the best of Miami with this long day-trip to Florida's biggest city, taking in the Bayside Marketplace shopping centre, marvellous South Beach and the Island Queen sightseeing cruise.

Another option is to include an Everglades airboat ride, or just the Miami hop-on, hop-off bus tour around the city. It does require a whopping 16hr day, but you will see a *lot* ($95–135).

Wild Florida: This is another tour that can be combined in multiple ways, from the straightforward transport and airboat ride, to combos with shopping, Gatorland and a tour to a citrus farm ($49–75).

Western Ranch Adventure: Another Gray Line exclusive, this takes visitors to Westgate River Ranch in Polk County (see p259) for the Saturday Night Rodeo. As well as comfortable round-trip transport, it includes a barbecue dinner, hayride, live entertainment and line dancing, as well as the weekly rodeo ($89).

St Augustine: Florida's oldest city is well worth visiting, and makes for a great day-trip to tour the famous Castillo de San Marcos, the oldest schoolhouse in America and ride the hop-on, hop-off Trolley that travels around the main area. St Augustine is also offered with a special swim-with-the-dolphins experience ($67–279).

Clearwater Beach: Ready for a trip to the beach? This is one of the best

and, again, is a day-trip that can be combined with several different elements, such as the Clearwater Marine Aquarium (home of Winter the dolphin; p282); a dolphin cruise, Captain Memo's Pirate Cruise and the huge Sea Screamer powerboat ($75–110).

Swim with the Manatees: Head out to the Crystal River with your tour guide for the chance to experience this rare opportunity to swim and snorkel among the gentle manatees that frequently make the river their home ($109).

Orange Groves: Find out what made Florida tick before tourism on this 3hr journey into a major citrus farm, aboard a giant-wheeled open-air truck for a great all-round view ($55).

Other Gray Line highlights are the fishing and shopping tours ($45–130); Disney character breakfast with limo transport ($89–119); and a City Tour of Orlando, including Lake Eola and Winter Park ($69). Book all tours in advance, on 1800 472 9546 or **www.graylineorlando.com**.

Wild Florida Ranch Tours

BRITTIP

For something different and uplifting, book Gray Line's Gospel Brunch at Disney Springs' House of Blues, including round-trip transport, admission, buffet, show and a city tour. Sun, from $99.

Florida Dolphin Tours: This British-owed company offers 18 tours, notably swimming with dolphins, manatee adventure, Gatorland and airboats, beaches, sports events, and Christmas dinner. No. 1 is the **Florida Adventure Tour**: breakfast, a 2hr boat trip (with snorkel to check out the manatees), picnic lunch, then an airboat ride and trip to Homosassa State Wildlife Park to see the manatees being fed ($119 adults, $89 3–11s). Call freephone from the UK on 0808 189 1245 or visit **www.floridadolphintours.com**.

O-Town Tour: Experience the best of downtown Orlando with this 5hr city tour, featuring stops in Lake Eola, Leu Gardens and Winter Park. Learn about Orlando's history, take the Winter Park scenic boat tour, and indulge in boutique shopping and dining. Advanced booking required, limited availability per tour, and weather permitting. Prices start at $59/person; private O-Town Tour starts at $109; must call for pricing and booking (407 470 6939, **http://stonevips.com/o-town-tours**).

BRITBONUS

Mention promo Code otown11 when booking and receive a special *Brit Guide* reader discount of 10% on the O-Town Tour.

Brewlando Tours: Here's a great idea that springs from Orlando's growth in craft breweries, with the chance to try 1 of several tours that visit the best of the local beer-makers. Both afternoon and evening tours are available, as well as tailor-made private tours, all by comfortable 10-seater mini-bus. They meet at the World of Beer bar/restaurant in the Dr Phillips plaza and then set out for 4-5hrs of touring and tasting at 3 breweries (varying

seasonally). Orlando boasts almost a dozen distinctive brewers, including Orlando Brewing Co, Red Cypress Brewery and lively Ten10 Brewing, and your personable tour guides provide great insight into each one. It is up to you what you sample at each stop, but every brewery offers flights as well as pints, and the tour includes discounted pricing. Bottled water and pretzels are provided between each stop, and there is a free souvenir beer glass at the end. Tours are $30/person and must be booked in advance on 407 965 1387 or **https://brewlandotours.com/**.

Of course, you can also have a great day-trip by heading for the beaches in your hire car (see Chapter 9).

SPORT

In addition to virtually every form of entertainment known to man, central Florida is one of the world's biggest sporting playgrounds, with a huge range of opportunities to either watch or play your favourite sport.

Golf

The No.1 sport is golf, with almost 200 courses in central Florida. There are numerous packages for golfers of all abilities. With an 18-hole round, including cart hire and taxes, from as little as $25 (average around $65), it's an attractive proposition and quite different from British courses. If you go in for 36-hole days, it's possible to save up to $30 by replaying the same course, while it is cheaper to play Mon–Thurs, and there are often lower rates for afternoon tee-times in summer. Sculpted landscapes, manicured fairways, abundant water features and white-sand bunkers add up to memorable golf. Winter is the high season, hence more expensive, but many courses are busy year-round. Some courses pair golfers with little thought for age, handicap, etc, so if two of you turn up, you may be paired with two strangers.

BRITTIP

Golf balls are cheap so there's no need to bring them. Good-quality clubs are usually available for hire.

Virtually every course will offer a driving range to get you started, plus lockers, changing rooms and showers, while the use of golf carts is universal (including the GPS system, which gives the yardage for every shot). They feature comforts like iced-water stations and drink carts that circulate the course (don't forget to tip the trolley drivers). Some have swimming pools, and all offer a decent bar and restaurant. A good starting point is visiting one of the two **Edwin Watts** golf shops for a free copy of the Golfer's Guide and a handy introduction to most of the courses (and perhaps some new clubs at the Watts Clearance Center at 7024 International Drive; 407 352 2535 **www.edwinwatts.com**). **Tee-Times USA** (1800 374 8633, **www.teetimesusa.com**) offers excellent advice and a reservation service. Visit Florida has its own golf section at **www.visitflorida.com/golf**. Website **www.golfnow.com** is also a great source of tee times all over Central Florida, and usually at reduced rates. Then you can take your pick from the following representative selection:

Walt Disney World: Quick to attract the golf fanatic, Disney has 3 high-quality courses, including the 7,000yd/6,400m Palm, rated by Golf Digest in its top 25 (the 18th hole is reputedly one of the toughest in America), plus a nine-hole par-36 course, Oak Trail. Fees are $62–126 for Disney resort guests and $105–130 for visitors ($40 at Oak Trail) varying seasonally, with a third off Twilight Rate. Call 407 938 4653 for tee-times. Private and group lessons are available under PGA pro guidance, with video analysis and club rentals. Former Disney course Osprey Ridge is now part of the magnificent Four Seasons Resort as Tranquilo Golf Club.

BRITTIP
Some of the best tee-times at Walt Disney World golf courses are reserved for those staying at a Disney resort.

Champions Gate: Challenging and eye-catching, the two magnificent Greg Norman-designed courses to the south of Disney (exit 58 off I-4) are the International (a British-style links course) and the National (a more traditional style). The practice facilities, clubhouse, service and coaching (at the HQ of the renowned David Leadbetter Academy) are world class, and there are stay-and-play packages with the superb Omni Orlando Resort; $77–142 (407 787 4653, **www.championsgategolf.com**).

Dubsdread: The oldest public course in Orlando and the only municipal one, just east of the city centre, this offers a testing 18 holes ($38–50) featuring narrow fairways and 'postage stamp' greens. It offers a beautiful clubhouse, restaurant and pub, where the likes of Sam Snead and Ben Hogan rubbed shoulders in the past. They also have a free shuttle from some area hotels (407 246 2551, **www.historicaldubsdread.com**).

BRITTIP
Visit Dubsdread Golf Course and be sure to spend some time in The Tap Room, their speciality bar and restaurant, with a great setting for a memorable meal or just a beer and a burger.

Falcon's Fire: An outstanding course in Kissimmee, featuring the ProShot digital caddy system carts. Plenty of water around the course assures a testing 18 holes, but it is highly picturesque; $34–85 (407 239 5445, **www.falconsfire.com**).

Gospel Brunch at the House of Blues

© Gray Line Tours

Grande Lakes Orlando: This wonderful resort complex just off John Young Parkway is a Greg Norman masterpiece, offering 18 holes of Florida nature with a caddie-concierge service; $63–185 (407 393 4900, **www.grandelakes.com**).

Hawk's Landing: At the Orlando World Center Marriott, this beautiful course boasts extensive practice facilities, a superb shop, resort exclusivity and the world-class teaching of Bill Madonna's Golf Academy: $50–79 (407 238 8660, **www.marriottworldcenter.com**).

Hyatt Grand Cypress: A true luxury experience on Winter Garden-Vineland Road, with three elegant nine-hole courses and a superb 18-hole links-style offering, all designed by Jack Nicklaus, and a gorgeous clubhouse to enjoy afterwards; $99–150 (407 239 4700; **www.grandcypress.com/golf_club**).

Kissimmee Oaks: Some majestic moss-draped oaks as well as 18 holes of memorable lakeside golf, all just 3½ml/6km south of Highway 192 in the Oaks Community off John Young Parkway $35–45 (407 930 4710, **www.kissimmeeoaksgolf.com**).

Legends Golf & Country Club: Just 25mins from Disney on Highway 27 towards Clermont, this has a pleasant layout with unusually rolling hills in a peaceful location; $25–40 (352 243 1118, **www.legendsgolforlando.com**).

Mystic Dunes: Just off Highway 192 near the Disney entrance, this course winds through native oaks and is a real test. There's a wonderful menu at the clubhouse, plus the latest equipment; $35–55 (407 787 5678; **www.mysticdunesgolf.com**).

Orange Lake Country Club: Massive vacation resort 4ml/6km from Disney offers 2 18-hole, a 9-hole and a rare par-3 floodlit 9; $30–95 (407 239 0000; **www.orangelakegolf.com**).

Shingle Creek: Arguably the cream of the crop after a major Arnold Palmer re-design in 2016, this world-class facility at the five-star hotel is set among beautiful oaks and pines. It also boasts the Brad Brewer Golf Academy, which offers state-of-the-art technology for novices and pros; $40–150 (407 996 9933, **www.shinglecreekgolf.com** and **www.bradbrewer.com**).

Be sure to ask if fees are negotiable. There are often reductions for seniors but check the dress code, as they can vary. Typically, you need a collared shirt, Bermuda shorts and no denim.

Fans: For those just looking to see the stars in action, the big annual event is the Arnold Palmer Invitational at the Bay Hill Club off Apopka-Vineland Road in west Orlando each March. It is a major tournament on the US PGA tour, with Jason Day, Rory McIlroy and Justin Rose all regular visitors (**http://arnoldpalmerinvitational.com**). The Players Championship is also held at TPC Sawgrass in Ponte Vedra Beach each May, just 2hrs from Orlando (**www.tpc.com/tpc-sawgrass**).

Mini-golf

Not exactly a sport, but Orlando's many extravagant mini-golf centres are a big hit. Several attractions and parks offer mini-golf as an extra, but for the best try the self-contained centres.

Disney's Fantasia Gardens: Next to the Swan Hotel just off Buena Vista Drive is a two-course challenge over 36 holes. The style is taken from classic film *Fantasia*. Fantasia Fairways is a cunning putting course, complete with rough, water hazards and bunkers. 18 holes can take more than an hour ($14 adults, $12 children, 10am–11pm daily).

Winter-Summerland Mini-Golf: At the entrance to Blizzard Beach is a half beach and half snow-themed 36 holes. An adult round is $14 ($12 3–9s), a double round is half price (10am–11pm; Blizzard Beach admission not required).

Universal's Hollywood Drive-In Golf: This imaginative twin 18-hole set-up is at the entrance to Universal's CityWalk. The two sides are The Haunting of Ghostly Greens, a 1950s mock-horror themed selection that includes putting through a cemetery and a giant spider's lair, and Invaders

From The Planet Putt, 18 holes of best sci-fi humour that feature an alien spaceship and a 30ft/9m robot. There are also special effects, surprises (you may get a little wet!), atmospheric music and a riot of visual gags. And, while it looks good during the day it positively sparkles at night under its LED lighting system. It also stays open long after the theme parks have closed, hence is ideal for saving for late in the day. Open 9am–2am daily, it costs $15 for adults, $13 (3–9s) for 18 holes, or $28 and $24 for both courses (9am–2am; 407 802 4848, **www.hollywooddriveingolf.com**).

International Drive: Mini-golf is a staple of the scene here, with no fewer than five courses in the vicinity (and be sure to see their websites for valuable discount coupons).

Check out the 18-hole **Congo River** in front of the Four Points by Sheraton Orlando Studio City Hotel ($13 adults, $11 under-10; 10am–11pm Sun–Thurs, 10am–midnight Fri and Sat); **Hawaiian Rumble's** 36 holes by WonderWorks on I-Drive and in Lake Buena Vista on Apopka-Vineland Ave; (10am–10pm Sun–Thurs, 10am–11pm Fri and Sat; $9.95 for 18 holes, $12.95 for 36); **Pirates Cove** remains the original and most imaginative I-Drive set-up, with a whole Pirate 'village' at its entrance, while the eye catching courses include caves, waterfalls and rope bridges to test your skill over twin 18-hole challenges the Captain's Course and harder Blackbeard's Challenge; (9am–11.30pm daily; $13.50 adults, $11.95 4–12s, or $22.50 for all 36); There is another Pirates Cove set-up at Lake Buena Vista, at the back of the Crossroads shopping plaza ($11.45 and $10.45, 9am–11pm). The unique **Putting Edge** has indoor glow-in-the-dark mini-golf at Artegon Orlando (11am–9pm Mon–Thurs, 11am–11pm Fri–Sat, 11am–7pm Sun; $10.50 adults, $8.50 under-13s), finally the extensive **Gator Golf & Adventure Park** is just past Carrier Drive, next to Murphy's Arms Pub. With a variety of gator shows daily, you can sink your teeth into some challenging mini-golf (10am–10pm, admission to park $5;

golf $9.99 adults, $7.99 3–11s; gator photos, feeding and handling for additional fees).

Kissimmee: Here you'll find the scenic 36-hole **Congo River Golf & Exploration Co** on Highway 192 (by Marker 12; $12.49 adults, $10.49 under-10s; 10am–11pm Sun–Thurs, 10am–midnight, Fri–Sat); **Pirates Cove**, a 36-hole course next to Old Town (behind the Red Lobster, between markers 9 and 10; 10am–10pm; $12 adults, $9 4–12s, additional rounds $5); **Mighty Jungle Golf**, with two African-themed courses on Highway 192 by Formosa Gardens Blvd (10am–9pm Sun–Thurs, 10pm Fri & Sat; $10.50 adults, $9.50 under 12s; $4 extra for 2nd 18 holes); and **Pirates Island Adventure Golf**, off Highway 192 between markers 14 and 15 (10am–10pm Sun–Thurs, 11pm Fri and Sat; $12 adults, $9 4–12s, additional rounds $5).

FootGolf: This all-new activity is one of the world's fastest-growing sports and the most fun and challenging we have tried to date. A mixture of soccer and golf, it is played on a full golf course, but with a football and extra large holes. New courses are springing up all the time but the No.1 right now is **Sanctuary Ridge** in Clermont, overseen by Brit-born US international Steve Crane. It costs $15/adults and $10 for under 12s (plus $5 for ball hire, although you can bring your own), while golf cart hire is $5. The course is open to FootGolf after 1pm every day but tee-times must be booked in advance. It is a hilly course, hence quite a test. Golf attire is required (no denim or T-shirts), and you must wear trainers (no studs). Call 352 243 0411 or look up **www.centralfloridafootgolf.com**.

Freshwater fishing
Freshwater fishing attracts enthusiasts worldwide. The primary draw is the chance to catch giant Florida bass – which grow to record sizes in the area's grassy waters – and view some of the wildlife.

Florida Freshwater Fishing License: To fish here you need to get this from the Florida Fish and Wildlife Commission (**http://myfwc.com/license/ recreational/freshwater-fishing** with a credit card). You'll be issued with a temporary licence number within minutes, enabling you to fish right away. A permanent licence will be mailed within 48 hours. A three-day licence costs $17, seven-day $30. It's advisable to book at least two weeks in advance, especially at peak times.

AJ's Freelancer Bass Guide Service: This long-running company specialises in trophy bass fishing on Lake Toho in Kissimmee. Toho is rated the best big bass lake in the USA, and AJ's holds the record for largemouth bass – 16lb 10oz/7.5kg! Saltwater trips are also offered. All guides are experienced, full-time professionals and run trips of 4–8hrs. Rates start at $250 for a 4hr guided trip, max three clients per boat ($50 for 3rd person; 12 and under free). Visit the excellent website at **www.orlandobass.com** or call 407 288 9670.

Ultimate Guide Service: Another personal guide and fishing service with 36 years' experience and with trophy bass the principal aim, this is led by Captain Jim Passmore and is great for novices and even better for those seeking a real challenge. It makes for a superb day or half day and their attitude is notably one of low environmental impact. It costs $275 for 4 hours of fishing for one or two anglers, $325 for 6 hours or $375 for 8hrs (extra person $50), excluding fishing licence and lunch (407 572 5391, **www.fishcentralfla.com**).

Go bass fishing (catch-and-release) at Walt Disney World for $270–$455 for 2–4hrs for a boat with 2–5 people, all equipment and refreshments. Book 24hrs in advance on 407 939 7529. Also see, **www. experiencekissimmee. com**, Things To Do, Nature, Fishing & Charters.

Water sports

Florida is mad keen on water sports so, on any area of water bigger than your average pond, don't be surprised to find the locals indulging in many watery pursuits.

Buena Vista Watersports: This is the place for jet-skiing ($60/30 min, $105/hr; seats two adults and one child), water-skiing, wakeboard and tube rides ($55/15 min, $95/30min, $165/hour), plus rent pontoon boats, canoes, kayaks and stand-up paddle-boards ($25–300) on Little Lake Bryan by the Holiday Inn Sunspree on Highway 535 (407 239 6939, **www.bvwatersports.com**).

Orlando Watersports Complex: Just off the Beachline Expressway (528) near Orlando International Airport, this is an elaborate facility featuring wake-boarding and water-skiing, by boat and suspended cable, for novices and experts (407 251 3100, **www.aktionparks.com**).

Walt Disney World: Disney offers all manner of boats (from kayaks and canoes to sailboats and motorboats holding from 2–10) and activities like water-skiing and parasailing on Bay Lake, as well as the smaller Seven Seas Lagoon and Crescent Lake. **Sammy Duvall's Watersports** offers Parasailing (from Disney's Contemporary Resort – p60) in two price categories: a Regular flight, which goes to 450ft/137m for 8–10 mins, and a Deluxe flight to 600ft/183 for 10–12mins. It costs $95–130 solo or $170 tandem, while there is also tubing, wakeboarding and slalom skiing. Hugely popular are their Personal Watercraft rides, either as a morning tour or an hour's free riding. Each wave-runner-type PWC holds up to three (max 400lb) and costs $135/hr (bookings advisable, 407 939 0754; **www.sammyduvall.com**). Disney boat rentals vary from $6.50 per 30 mins for a kayak to $45/30mins for a pontoon boat) and can be found at 10 resorts. To book, call 407 939 0754.

Spectator events

American sport is well worth trying for a great entertainment event and there is a lot on offer. From the Orlando Predators of the Arena League (an indoor version of American football) to Spring Training baseball each March (at Disney's ESPN Wide World of Sports), all sports are represented.

Basketball: This is one of the two main sports in town, with the Orlando Magic of the National Basketball Association (NBA). The season runs Nov–May (with exhibition games in Oct), and the only drawback is the 18,500-seat Amway Center where the team plays (on W Church Street, exit 82B off I-4) can be sold out. Contact the Magic (407 896 2442, **www.orlandomagic.com**) to see if there are any tickets, but you'll have to call in person to buy them (from $15 in upper seats to over $1,500 courtside), or try StubHub (**www.stubhub.com** or 1866 788 2482).

◀▶ **BRITTIP**
You don't need to understand the game to experience some real Americana, just turn up and enjoy the excitement and fan friendly atmosphere. Sports are a family event here.

American football: For the real thing, the nearest teams in the National Football League (NFL) are Tampa Bay Buccaneers, 75ml/120km to the west, Miami Dolphins, 3 4hrs' drive south down the Florida Turnpike, or Jacksonville Jaguars up on the east coast past Daytona, a 3hr drive on I-4 and I-95. Ticket prices and availability from StubHub ($50–300) (Sept–Dec).

For the best baseball, head to St Petersburg where the **Tampa Bay Rays** play at indoor Tropicana Field (Apr–Sept). Tickets are nearly always available and the indoor stadium is superb (p281).

Orlando City Soccer Club: Soccer is firmly entrenched as Orlando's other big sport thanks to our Major League team, playing Mar–Oct at the new 26,000-seat stadium in downtown Orlando. They have built up a loyal following and games have a superb atmosphere, with tail-gating (a big car park party) and live music prior to kick-off. Ticket prices vary from $25–130 but may be hard to find in the first year of their new stadium (check StubHub). For the 2017 schedule, see **www.orlandocitysc.com**). The Church Street area is great for pre-game excitement, the weekly 'March to the Match,' and Watch Parties for away games. A soccer-themed bar and restaurant, the **Lion's Pride**, is due to open in the old Church Street Station later in 2016.

ESPN Wide World of Sports™

Disney's big sports development is an impressive 220acre/86ha state-of-the-art complex, featuring 30 sports. It boasts a 9,500-seat baseball stadium, softball quadraplex, 10-court tennis complex, 5,000-seat indoor facility, athletics and extensive sports fields.

The Ballpark: Top of the crop for a must-see visit, this is home for spring training of baseball's Atlanta Braves, where the crowds flock for 16 pre-season games late Feb–late Mar (advance tickets highly recommended; individual tickets from Ticketmaster or the box office only). This is a big deal for American sports fans and games do sell out.

The centre's extensive fields also cater for soccer, lacrosse, baseball and softball, and you can often see some keen sporting action just with college and school teams. Disney's Soccer Showcase (Sept–Jan) is a fine example of this, with some 400 skilful youth teams competing under the eye of various scouts. Standard admission is $17.50 adults, $12.50 3–9s, but it is also an option with Ultimate tickets (excluding special events like baseball). ESPN Wide World of Sports™ is off Osceola Parkway, on Victory Way (**www.espnwwos.com**).

Run Disney: Marathons, half-marathons and 10k and 5k fun-runs are now big business, with some great spectacles up to six times a year.

The 'Big One' will be the 24th running of the annual Marathon on 8 Jan 2017. Up to 55,000 runners take part – including some of the world's leading athletes – drawing huge crowds and taking in all four Disney theme parks. Be aware of serious disruption in the parks. The annual half-marathon takes place the day before (**www.rundisney.com**)

Cycling Tours

Elite Road Bike Rentals deliver bikes for rent (from 1–7 days) at all area hotels and offer guided tours, from high-energy workouts to 4hr scenic cycles around the likes of Winter Garden, Winter Park, Polk City and Davenport ($100–150). All equipment, food and drink is included with the tours and transport can be arranged to and from hotels. They have both Road Bikes and Hybrids, set up to your specification. Rates vary from $50–105 for a day, and from $200–375 for seven days (407 900 5783 or **www.eliteroadbikerentals.com**.

BRITBONUS

$ Elite Road Bike Rentals offer *Brit Guide* readers a 15% discount off rentals and tours when you mention the book. Call in advance or go online.

Rodeo

An all-American pursuit, the **Silver Spurs Rodeo** is staged twice a year at the 8,300-seat Silver Spurs Arena. The biggest event of its kind in the south-east, it is held in Feb and early June (check website for dates). It sells out fast so book in advance on 321 697 3495 (**www.silverspursrodeo.com**). The event features classic bronco and bull riding and attracts competitors from as far as Canada. The arena is part of Osceola Heritage Park, which includes Osceola County Stadium (for baseball) and the Kissimmee Valley Livestock Show and Fair Pavilion. The Arena is a state-of-the-art facility and there isn't a bad seat in the house. There is also a weekly Saturday Night Rodeo at **Westgate River Ranch** (p259).

Motor sport

The Richard Petty Driving Experience has closed at Walt Disney World but is still available at **Daytona International Speedway** (take I-4 east, then I-95 and Highway 92), where race fans will find some big-league thrills at this massive stadium. The renowned track hosts more than a dozen events a year, including motor-bike, stock car, sports car and go-karts. Highlights are the **Rolex 24** (a 24hr sports car event, late Jan), the famous **Daytona 500** (Feb), and **Coke Zero 400** (early July). The big events attract crowds of 200,000-plus and offer exhilarating sport. A $400m rebuild of the Speedway in 2016 made this a technological marvel as well as a sporting one, and provides some great daily tours. Choose from the basic 30min Speedway Tour, which provides an up-close look at the fiendishly banked track ($17 adults, $11 6–12s); a 1hr All Access Tour that explores the massive 2.5ml/4km tri-oval in more detail, including behind-the-scenes visits and a photo trip to Victory Lane ($24 and $18); and the 3hr VIP Tour, with visits to the Archive and Research Center and other off-limits areas to the general public ($52/person). A huge gift shop and a Café complete the set-up. The **Motorsports Hall of Fame** will also be here later in 2016 (**www.mshf.com**), and it is fascinating, guaranteed fun, even for non-race fans! (1800 748 7467, **www. daytonainternationalspeedway.com**). The **Richard Petty Driving Experience** is a great opportunity to sample the thrills of NASCAR racing first hand, either as passenger or driver, with a range of different on-track experiences. It costs $135/person for the high-speed, three-lap Ride-Along (age 14 and up, under 18 must be accompanied by an adult); $69 for Junior Ride Along (6–13s); $549 for 3hr Rookie Experience (tuition plus 8 laps of the Speedway); $1,299 for Kings Experience (tuition plus 16 laps); $2,199 for the Experience of a Lifetime (an intense 24-lap programme), and $3,200 for the full 50-lap Racing Experience. You must be 18 or over for all but the Ride-Along (1800 237 3889, **www.drivepetty.com**).

OK, that's the local area sorted out; now let's take you further afield…

9 The Twin Centre Option

or To Orlando – and Beyond!

While Orlando continues to get bigger and better, it is equally true there is a LOT more to see in the rest of Florida, with some magnificent twin-centre options. From St Augustine in the north-east to Key West in the extreme south (the 'Floribbean'), it's easy to find wonderful resorts, glorious beaches and more family attractions.

The beaches of the Gulf (west) coast, the Atlantic coast from Ormond Beach all the way to Miami, and the fabulous Florida Keys all feature some of the best seaside escapes in the world, while cities like West Palm Beach, Daytona, St Augustine, Fort Lauderdale, Tampa, Miami and Key West provide more Sunshine State fascination. Two-centre (or fly-drive) options are common with most tour operators, but it is also easy to arrange your own, for one or two weeks or just a night. A cruise-and-stay holiday is also a great choice, with the ports of Tampa, Port Canaveral, Fort Lauderdale and Miami within easy reach.

You can head out from Orlando in any direction in search of a great twin-centre experience. Go East to Cocoa Beach, New Smyrna Beach, Ormond Beach and Daytona Beach, all with terrific appeal and barely an hour's drive away; the sea is a degree or so cooler on the Atlantic side, and the surf and currents are more noticeable, hence this is good surfing territory, but beware possible undertows if you are travelling with children. To the north-east you have historic St Augustine about 2hrs away. To the north-west is the growing resort area of Panama City Beach. Go West for Tampa and miles of pristine sands, from Clearwater Beach south to Naples and lovely Marco Island; this is better for families with younger children, while the Clearwater-St Pete Beach area is a perfect combo with Orlando (about 1½–2hrs' drive). Go south-east and you hit Vero Beach, West Palm Beach, Fort Lauderdale and Miami (about a 3½hr drive). Continue south and there are the Keys, a superb 110ml/177km chain of islands linked by roads and bridges, culminating in eclectic Key West. So, heading north-east first, here's what you find.

⬛ BRITTIP
The Florida Turnpike (toll) is the main route south-east from Orlando, but it is a dull drive. If time is not a factor, take the Beachline Expressway (528) east and then I-95 or, better still, Highway 1, south for a more rewarding journey. Or go south on Highway 27 and take in the charming town of Sebring.

St Augustine
A 2hr drive up I-4 and I-95 brings you to America's oldest city. Founded by Spanish conquistadors in 1565, St Augustine is full of authentic buildings and signs of the original

settlement around the imposing Castillo de San Marcos. Much of the original walled city still remains and 'old' is a much-revered term here, as 18th and 19th-century Mediterranean influences are everywhere. Walk the narrow, uneven streets of the Restoration Area to discover colonial architectural treasures, now home to gift shops, restaurants, pubs, ice-cream parlours, antique shops, quaint B&Bs and other attractions.

BRITTIP

Spanish adventurer Ponce de Leon was searching for the Fountain of Youth when he arrived at the site of St Augustine in 1513. The modern day Archaeological Park tells the story of his arrival and discovery of the continent of America – and offers the chance to drink the famous waters. Visit **www.fountainofyouthflorida.com**.

Tours: To see as much as possible, hop on a horse-drawn carriage, the **St Augustine Sightseeing Train** or the **Old Town Trolley Tours** for a narrated tour. For a spookier experience, walk the streets with **Ghost Tours of St Augustine**, with your guide in period costume. Other tours reveal the architectural heritage (also the product of British and colonial American rule).

Other attractions: Florida railway mogul Henry Flagler was another big influence, building some magnificent hotels for his 'passengers to paradise'. The ornate **Lightner Museum**, formerly Flagler's Hotel Alcazar, is home to his turn-of-the-century treasures, including Tiffany and other glass works of art. There's a

Shores Resort, Daytona Beach

modern theatre, art galleries, **Potter's Wax Museum**, **Ripley's Believe It Or Not Museum** and **Whetstone Chocolates Factory**. St Augustine Distillery offers a chance to visit a working small-batch premium distillery and learn the history of the converted ice factory (free tours daily, 10am–6pm Mon–Sat, 11am Sun; **http://staugustinedistillery.com/**). Golf fans should visit nearby Ponte Vedra for the **World Golf Hall of Fame**.

Restaurants: These range from **Hot Shot Bakery** and the famous, family-owned **Columbia Restaurant**, to a modern microbrewery, **A1A Ale Works**.

Where to stay: The premier hotel is historic **Casa Monica** (904 827 1888, **www.casamonica.com**), while the boutique **St George Inn** (904 827 5740; **www.stgeorge-inn.com**) is also a good choice, but there are numerous B&Bs, plus chain hotels like Best Western and Hampton Inn.

BRITTIP

Festivals are an integral part of St Augustine, from monthly art walk nights to annual costumed torchlight re-enactments of British occupation and the City Birthday on 8 Sept.

More info: St Augustine Visitors & Convention Bureau (1800 653 2489 or **www.floridashistoriccoast.com**).

Daytona Beach/Volusia County

Travel south from St Augustine and you arrive in this famous beach area.

BRITTIP

Look out for Speeding Through Time, a series of memorials and plaques along Daytona Beach's Boardwalk, highlighting the world speed records set on the beaches, including those of Britons Sir Henry Segrave and Sir Malcolm Campbell.

Daytona Beach: 1hr from Orlando along I-4 east, this family-friendly area includes some chic hotels and restaurants. It is busiest mid-June to mid-Aug but there is something for everyone, especially after Easter when there are often good deals. The prime attraction is the good beaches (some of which you can drive on – for a $10 toll, speed limit 10mph/16kph). From there, you can go boating, parasailing, biking, jet-skiing and fishing. Stay in the Oceanfront area at the heart of all things beach-related, with the Pier – with the huge Sand Blaster rollercoaster – Bandshell, Boardwalk and the shops and restaurants of **Ocean Walk Village.**

Ocean Walk Village: Here you have **Paragon Ocean Walk 10 Cineplex**, the fun of the **Mai Tai Bar, Johnny Rockets Diner, Cold Stone Creamery, Starbucks, My Pi Custom Pizza, Sloppy Joe's** and unique shopping at **Maui Nix Surf Shop, Point Break** resort wear, **Best Gift Ideas Ever** and **Sunglass Hut.** When you're hungry, try the film-themed style of **Bubba Gump Shrimp Co** (based on the movie *Forrest Gump*). With fun decor, wonderfully casual vibe and an excellent menu, it is ideal for a quick lunch or leisurely dinner (**www. bubbagump.com** and **www.oceanwalkshoppes.com**).

BRITTIP

After a day on the beach, try some water park fun at Daytona Lagoon after 3pm, when admission is only $14.99.

Daytona Lagoon: Opposite Ocean Walk Village, this is a water park, go-kart track, mini-golf course, arcade and laser tag centre. The water park has a wave pool and lazy river, seven flumes and an area for toddlers (adults $29.99, children under 3ft 6in/108cm $20.99). The 18-hole mini-golf course ($7), single and double go-karts ($8–10), laser tag (must be above 3ft 6in/108cm, $7), Island Hopper kiddie ride ($3.49) and Rock Wall ($7) are separate items. **www.daytonalagoon.com.**

Historic Downtown Daytona Beach: The heart of the city is on Beach Street, with a museum of local history, restaurants, nightclubs, coffee bars

and Daytona Beach's only art-house cinema, Cinematique. **The Angell & Phelps Chocolate Factory** (with free tours, **www.angellandphelps.com**) is another curiosity. Head to the Riverfront in early evening when the street takes on a café society style.

There are plenty of good places to eat, but for something different try the lively **Caribbean Jack's** (on the river at Ballough Road) or chic **Chez Paul** (on N Beach St with a river view). Similar upscale choices are **Martini's Organic** (on S Ridgewood Ave), the fine Italian dining of **The Cellar** (on Magnolia Avenue), and the Latin American taste sensation of **Chucherias Hondurenas** (**www.chucheriashondurenas.com**).

Other highlights: The Manatee scenic river voyage out of Ponce Inlet is a leisurely 2hr tour year-round at 10am, 1 and 4pm, or there's a 7pm Sunset Cruise Jun–Sept (on Inlet Harbor Rd; $25 adults, $22 seniors, $16 children; reservations on 386 761 2027, or **www.manateecruise.com**). Go south on Atlantic Avenue for more choice of beaches and attractions, including **Sun Splash Beach, Frank Rendon Park** and **Lighthouse Point Park**, a 52acre/21ha stretch of nature trails, fishing, observation deck, swimming and picnicking (sunrise to sunset; $10/ car). The tide here can retreat up to 500ft/150m and the beaches, open to the public year-round, tend to be quieter, though there can be some serious rip-tides (watch out for the beach signs). At the southern end is the **Ponce de Leon Inlet Lighthouse**, with 203 spiralling steps, a re-creation of 19th-century Florida maritime life from the top of America's second tallest lighthouse, with a superb view (10am– 6pm, 9pm Jun–Aug; $6.95 adults, $1.95 under-12s; **http://ponceinlet.org/**). It also has a lovely gift shop, while Ponce Inlet boasts great deep-sea fishing – see **www.inletharbor.com.**

Marine Science Center: More family fun can be found round the corner from the lighthouse, showcasing mangrove, manatee and sea turtle exhibits, a seabird sanctuary and turtle rehab facility. It has a huge artificial reef aquarium, plus static and interactive educational displays. A boardwalk and nature trail extend through the Center, which also has a gift shop (10am–4pm Tues–Sat, noon–4pm Sun, closed Mon; $5 adults, $4 seniors, $2 under-13s; http://marinesciencecenter.com/).

⊞⊞ BRITTIP —————————

Try a meal at the Hidden Treasure Rum Bar & Grill at Ponce Inlet for an eclectic Floridian experience.

Daytona Speedway: This is one of the biggest draws (p272), with three great tours of this amazing facility that has undergone a $400m transformation.

Three Brothers Boards: This family-run business of handcrafted stand-up paddleboards offers tours and rentals on the beautiful Halifax River, with its plentiful wildlife. Choose from the 2hr Dolphin & Manatee Adventure or the Nature Tour through mangrove trails and bird sanctuaries. You may even be inspired to try paddleboard yoga! Call 386 310 4927 or visit http://threebrothersboards.com.

Where to stay: You'll find some terrific resorts and small inns in Daytona Beach (www.daytonbeach.com/hotels). The **Wyndham Ocean Walk Resort** is a huge complex on the beach at Ocean Walk Village, with one, two and three-bed condos (all with kitchens and fab views). Family-friendly, with three outdoor pools, waterslide and lazy river, kids' water play area, two indoor pools, indoor mini-golf, kids' programmes, spa, lounge and food court, (386 323 4800, www.wyndhamoceanwalk. com). The nearby **Hilton Daytona Beach Oceanfront Resort** is another large, recently renovated hotel with spacious rooms, beachfront cabañas and suites, plus terrific dining (notably Hyde Park Prime Steakhouse, two pools and a fitness centre (386 254 8200, www.daytonahilton.com). **The Shores Resort & Spa** is a great boutique choice on a quieter stretch of the beaches, (386 767 7350, www.shoresresort.com), with extra-large rooms, Spa, gracious service and dining. The 10-storey oceanfront **Hyatt Place** is also a chic choice with

spacious family rooms (386 944 2010, http://daytonabeach.place.hyatt.com).

Try **Flamingo Inn** for a great example of the Small Inns of Daytona Beach. With a tranquil oceanfront setting, heated free-form pool, tropical Key West styling and some rooms with kitchenettes (and all with fridges), it is a real boutique bargain here (386 451 5577, www.daytonaflamingoinn.com).

More info: 01737 643 764 in the UK, 386 255 0415 in the US or visit www.daytonabeach.com.

New Smyrna Beach: Continue south on Highway 1 to this 13ml/20km stretch of pristine white sands with great surfing, shell collecting and boating. Also a big festival destination, notably for the **Shrimp & Seafood Festival** each August and the **Beach Jazz Festival** in late Sept. Other highlights include the shopping and dining of historic and pedestrian-friendly Canal Street, with a Saturday farmers' market (7am–12.30pm, www.canalstreetnsb.com), more shops and galleries along Flagler Avenue (www.flaglerave.com), the kid- friendly **Marine Discovery Center** and the **Atlantic Center for the Arts**. For dining, don't miss **The Garlic**, with outdoor seating under huge oaks **More info**: http://nsbfla.com.

Ormond Beach: Immediately to the north is another happening area with more smart resorts and beaches, notably at **Bicentennial Park** (with a nature walk, playground and fishing dock) and **Birthplace of Speed Park** (honouring the first beach automobile race in 1903). Don't miss **The Casements**, the restored former **John D Rockefeller House and Gardens**, with free tours twice a day Mon–Sat (www.thecasements.net). And, for a different shopping experience, **Dunn's Attic & Auction House** is an unusual venue (www.dunnsattic.com). Try a meal at the fun **Lulu's Oceanside Grill** with a great seafood menu, cocktails and weekend brunch, (www.lulusoceansidegrill.com). Or sample the chic **Rose Villa** (www.rosevillarestaurant.com), eclectic **Grind Gastropub & Kona Tiki Bar** (www.grindgastropub.com) and new

Cook-it-yourself breakfast

Just north of DeLand in DeLeon Springs State Park is the unique **Old Spanish Sugar Mill** grill and griddle house famous for hearty cook-it-yourself breakfasts (9am–4pm; 8am at weekends), including pancakes, bacon, eggs, ham, sausage, home-made breads, French toast, sandwiches and salads. You'll struggle to pay more than $10/person and it's great fun, as well as a local institution. However, as it is inside the State Park, there is a $6/car entry fee (386 985 5644, **www.oldspanishsugarmill.com**). You can then try the park facilities, which include canoes, kayaks, hiking trails and boat tours (**www.floridastateparks.org**).

Speakeasy style of **31 Supper Club** (**http://31supperclub.com/**).

The Space Coast

Further south on the Atlantic seaboard is the 'Space Coast', home to the iconic Kennedy Space Center (p213).

BRITTIP
For good info on all Kennedy Space Center rocket launches, especially good public viewing locations, see **www. visitspacecoast.com/launch-schedule/**.

Cocoa Beach: Closest to Orlando, barely 50mins east (on the Beachline Expressway 528, then south on Highway A1A), this area has two excellent public beaches plus trademark shopping at Ron Jon's Surf Shop, a massive neon emporium of all things water related. As it's the Atlantic, the sea can be chilly Nov–Apr, but its resort style ensures good facilities (**www.cocoabeach.com**). If you haven't tried an airboat ride, you should definitely head for **Midway Airboats** on the nearby St John River (daily from 9am; 407 568 6790, **www.airboatridesatmidway.com/**), and don't forget **Island Boat Lines** (p263).

Cocoa Village: This little town in the intracoastal waterway just inland from Cocoa Beach offers a fun array of shopping and dining, with some original boutiques, the historic Cocoa Village Playhouse and two of our favourite restaurants on the coast (**http://visitcocoavillage.com/**). For casual dining, try **Murdock's Southern Bistro & Bar** (**www. murdocksincocoavillage.com/**) while **Crush Eleven** is a chic and stylish option with a creative cocktail list and menu (**www.crusheleven.com**).

Titusville: Head here for attractions like the US Space Walk of Fame (a river walk with displays of memorabilia, plaques and public art depicting America's history in space), **Merritt Island National Wildlife Refuge** (a 6ml/9km driving tour adjacent to the Kennedy Space Center) and the fascinating and rather moving **American Police Hall of Fame & Museum**, with all you ever wanted to know about the history of crime and law enforcement, and a tribute to police officers who have died in the line of duty (see **www. aphf.org** for $3 off coupon). **Dixie Crossroads** is a local institution for great Florida seafood (**www.dixiecrossroads.com**).

Aviation fans will enjoy the **Valiant Air Command Warbird Museum**, with dozens of vintage warplanes and fully guided tours through the exhibits and history of military aviation, as well as their dedicated restoration programme (**www.vacwarbirds.net**). Look out especially for the three-day **Warbird Air Show** here in Mar.

BRITTIP
For something truly unique, Valiant Air Command Warbird Museum now offers periodic flights on its beautifully restored vintage WWII C-47 paratroop transport plane for $175/person. Call 321 268 1941 or email **vacwarbirds@ bellsouth.net** for full details and availability.

Melbourne: Family-friendly **Brevard Zoo** is well worth a visit, with almost 500 animals in five themed areas, including the excellent Cheetah Complex in the Expedition Africa exhibit. Other highlights include Australasia, La Selva (South America),

Wild Florida and Paws On Play, where children can enjoy water play, and the new Meerkat Hamlet (9.30am–5pm; $18 adults, $17 seniors, $14 2–12s; 321 254 9453, **https://brevardzoo.org/**).

BRITTIP

For top value at Brevard Zoo, try an Explore! Package (admission, train ride, giraffe and lorikeet feeding at $24, $23 and $19) or Adventure! Package kayaking in Expedition Africa, giraffe and lorikeet feeding at $30, $29 and $25).

Where to stay: Try lively, surf-themed **Four Points by Sheraton Cocoa Beach** (321 783 8717, **www.fourpointscocoabeach.com**) or **International Palms Resort** (321 783 2271, **www.internationalpalms.com**).

More info: 321 433 4470 or **www.visitspacecoast.com.**

Panama City Beach

For one of Florida's hidden gems (albeit not during the pre-Easter Spring Break holiday when it is Party Central!), head north-west to the 'Panhandle' area where this charming nature-based stretch of coastline offers fabulous sightseeing, nature tours and downhome local style. It's a long drive from Orlando but you can fly there for a short-

Kayaking is a popular relaxation

break option and it is blissful from mid-Aug to late Oct. **St Andrews** and **Camp Helen State Parks** are natural wonderlands, and you can see it all via helicopter tours, sunset cruises, paddleboarding, kayaking, snorkelling and hiking.

Gulf World Marine Park is a local institution and the sea hereabouts is often full of dolphins, turtles, rays, tarpon and even the occasional shark. Dining is full of one-off opportunities, notably the fun beachfront vibe of **Barefoot Hide-A-Way Grill** (**http:// barefoothideawaygrill.com/**), the elegant chic of **Firefly** (**http://fireflypcb.com/**), and local seafood specialities of **Capt Anderson's** (**www.captanderson.com**).

Where to stay: The modern condo-style resorts of the **Tidewater Beach Resort**, with one, two and three-bed apartments (850 636 8000, **www. wyndhamvacationrentals.com**) and the superbly equipped **Edgewater Beach Resort** (855 874 8686, **www. edgewaterbeachresort.com**) are both worth trying. **More info:** 1800 7223224,**www.visitpanamacitybeach.com.**

Tampa

Going west from Orlando brings you down I-4 to the bright city of Tampa, right on a major sea bay and with some excellent attractions of its own (including Busch Gardens, p200).

Dinosaur World: Right on I-4 as you head to Tampa (and a nice stopping point by exit 17) is this family-run attraction ideal for 3–8s. With more than 200 life-sized dinosaurs in a lush, natural setting, plus walking trails, picnic area, playgrounds and gift shop, it makes a good diversion for several hours. There are no rides, but there are various life-size animatronic set-pieces – including a triceratops and pterodactyl – plus a Prehistoric Museum featuring authentic fossils from dinosaur eggs to raptor claws and mammoth teeth. The different trails then feature more dino models with explanatory signs, plus a cave-themed video theatre, while the Skeleton Garden features six replica skeletons. There are also two play areas, for under 7s and older children, and an expanded fossil dig with fossils you can take home. The park is totally laid back and a nice change of pace from the main parks. There is no café (just drinks machines), but it does have picnic facilities and there are fast-food locations nearby, including a pizza delivery service (9am–5pm; $16.95 adult, $14.95 seniors, $11.95 3–12s, under-3 free; 813 717 9865, **http://dinosaurworld.com/florida/**).

Florida Aquarium: In the heart of Tampa is this superb child-friendly draw in four main sections: Wetlands, Bays & Beaches (including Sea Turtle Corner), Coral Reef Gallery and Ocean Commotion (interactive touch-screens, videos and podcasts). The Explore a Shore water-play area adds squirt pools, fountains and pirate ship, plus Bar & Grill. There's a daily Penguin Promenade (meet-and-greet a penguin), and Shark Bay, where scuba-certified 15s and older can join the daily dive into the lagoon ($150/person, reservations required on 813 273 4015), a daily 20min non-scuba 'Swim with the fishes' reef swim ($75/person), a 2hr Shark Feeding programme every Sun, a daily 30min Behind The Scenes tour ($12) and Penguins Backstage Pass (a 30min penguin interaction at $30/person). There's also a twice-daily (weather permitting) Wild Dolphin Cruise on their 130-passenger catamaran, (9.30am–5pm daily, closed Thanksgiving, Christmas Day; parking $6; $25 adults, $23 seniors, $20 under-12s; with Dolphin Eco-Tour, $49.90, $44.90 and $40.90; 813 273 4000, **www.flaquarium.org**; also on Tampa CityPass, p281).

◀🇬🇧▶ **BRITTIP**
Book tickets online for the Florida Aquarium and save several dollars.

Lowry Park Zoo: Rated one of the top zoos in America, this lush 60acre/24ha spread showcases manatees, koalas, elephants, tigers, penguins, giraffes and orang-utan among its more than 1,000 animals. Kids will also enjoy the water-play areas, educational shows and even rides, like Gator Falls flume ride, African Guided Safari and Outback Bumper Boats. There are extensive natural animal habitats and the chance (for a few extra dollars) to interact with some of them, including giraffes and lorikeets (9.30am–5pm; $27.95 adults, $20.95 3–11s; **www.lowryparkzoo.com**; also on Tampa CityPass, p281). Animal lovers should also make a note of **Big Cat Rescue**, a non-profit park. It runs 90min tours and all proceeds go into the care and rehab of their 100-plus animals. Other options include Feeder, Keeper and Private tours (3pm Mon, Tues, Wed and Fri, 10am and 3pm Sat and Sun, $36/person, over 10s only; under-10s tour 9am Sat & Sun for $19; other tours $65–125; 813 920 4130, **http://bigcatrescue.org**).

Museum of Science and Industry: More family fun (especially for 4–12s) can be found at this entertaining science centre, with three floors of educational exhibits, activities and large-screen IMAX films. Highlights include the Kids In Charge science play area (under-13s), and The Amazing You (a tour of the human body). Permanent exhibits include Sky Trail Ropes Course (with two ziplines) and The Saunders Planetarium, while the IMAX® Dome Theatre offers a range of films daily and there are periodic travelling exhibits. Outside is the BioWorks Butterfly Garden and the Historic Tree Grove, providing more insight into natural Florida (10am–5pm Mon–Fri, 6pm Sat and Sun; $26.95 adults, $25.95 seniors, $20.95 2–12s, includes Kids in Charge, a standard IMAX film and Planetarium show; additional films $8.95, $7.95 and $6.95; combo SkyTrail Ropes and Zipline are $20 extra with admission; 813 987 6100, **www.mosi. org**; also on Tampa CityPass, p281).

Ybor City: Tampa's historic entertainment district can be found in the rejuvenated Cuban quarter of the city, where a fine mix of shops and restaurants provide a lively vibe both by day and at night. Top dining choices include **Hamburger Mary's** (tempting burgers and risqué cabaret!), **Carne Chophouse**

(fine steaks and seafood) and **Samurai Blue** (sushi and sake). The lively bar scene offers **Centro Cantina**, the **Brass Tap** (for craft beers and live music), **Mary's Pub** (next to Hamburger Mary's) and the excellent **Tampa Bay Brewing Co**, a British-run brewpub with a varied menu, great range of beers, multiple TV screens and pool table (brewery tours Sat 2–8pm, $10/person, **www. tampabaybrewingcompany.com**). Find more fun at **Game Time**, an upscale arcade of games and bars, the **Muvico** 20-screen cinema complex and the **Improv Comedy Theatre**, busiest on Fri and Sat but bustling most nights (**www.centroybor.com**). Start at the **Visitor Center & Museum**, which shows a fascinating film on the history of the city, and the well-presented **Ybor City Museum** on East 9th Avenue (9am–5pm; $4/person, under-6s free; **www.ybormuseum.org**).

You can also tour the area on the new **Electric Glide Segway** tours, a fabulous way to sight-see and have fun at the same time on these two-wheeled machines (Mon–Wed at 10am, 1 and 3.30pm; $65/person; 1800 975 3177, **http://electricglidetours.com/**).

TECO Line Streetcar: Much of downtown Tampa, including Ybor City and Channelside, is linked by replicas of authentic electric trams, with one-way fares of $2.50 (cash only; $1.25 for under 17s and seniors) or $5 for an all-day card. A Family All Day Ticket ($12.50, for up to five) is available from ticket machines.

⬛🇬🇧 BRITTIP

Visit the Columbia Restaurant in Ybor City. Opened in 1905, it incorporates a whole city block that was gradually absorbed into this Spanish/Cuban bar-diner. Ask at the host stand if they can give you a tour, with the story of the Gonzmart family (813 248 4961, www.columbiarestaurant.com).

Brewery Central: Tampa is fast becoming a major centre for breweries and craft beer, with one of the biggest real ale profiles in the US. There are more than 30 breweries in the greater Tampa area, the vast majority small-scale brewers producing high-quality ales, lagers, ciders and more. Many offer tours and the chance to sample their wares, while the brew-pub phenomenon (like Tampa Bay Brewing Co) is going gangbusters. You can also try guided tours like **The Brew Bus** (**www.brewbus usa.com/tours/ tampa-bay/**) and **Tampa Brew Tours**, travelling by stretch limo (**www.tampabrewtours.com**). For a good sample, try any of the following:

Yuengling Brewery: This modern facility near Busch Gardens (on 10th Street, parallel to McKinley Drive) brews up to nine beers (two seasonal), including a fab lager and porter. Free guided tours at 10am, 11.30am and 1pm Mon–Fri (10.30am and noon Sat; closed Sun), with a couple of samples! Gift Shop open 9am–3pm, 10am–2pm Sat (813 972 8529, **www.yuengling. com/ breweries/tampa/**). NB: Closed-toe shoes only, no sandals or flip-flops; children welcome. **Cigar City Brewing:** Celebrating Tampa's Cuban heritage, Cigar City features some wildly creative beers, like their Jai Alai and Café Con Leche Sweet Stout, and with tours on the hour ($8/person, 11am–3pm Weds and Thurs, 4pm Fri, 5pm Sat and Sun; **https:// cigarcitybrewing.com/**). **Coppertail Brewing**: This recent brewery features at least 8 beers, including a great IPA and Wheat Ale, with tours Thurs-Sun ($7/person, 5–8pm Thurs and Fri, 2–7pm Sat, 2–5pm Sun; **http:// coppertailbrewing.com/**). **Angry Chair Brewing:** Another hugely creative brewery with a great Tasting Room, in the trendy Seminole Heights area that also boasts several other brew-pubs, (Tues–Thurs 2–11pm, Fri and Sat noon-midnight, Sun noon–9pm, **http://angrychairbrewing.com/**).

Where to stay: Arguably the most distinctive place in town is the **Epicurean Hotel**, a fabulously stylish boutique property with a blissful Spa and superb dining. It features designer rooms and suites, the true gourmet food of restaurant Elevage and gorgeous rooftop bar Edge, with its hand-crafted cocktails (813 999 8700, **www.epicureanhotel.com**). Equally upmarket is **Le Meridien,**

a sumptuous conversion of the old Federal Court building into an ultra-chic modern hotel (813 221 9555, **www.lemeridientampa.com**). A more modest choice is the **Westin**, with great views over the intracoastal waterway (813 281 0000, **www.westintampabay.com**).

More info: Visitor Center 813 223 2752 or **www.visittampabay.com**.

St Pete/Clearwater

Continue west and you have the gorgeous Gulf Coast, a 2hr drive down I-4 and through Tampa on I-275 south to St Pete Beach (105ml/169km) or Clearwater Beach (110ml/177km), with a string of beautiful resorts in between, all featuring white-sand beaches, water sports and fewer crowds than you would think, plus the smart Beach Walk in Clearwater. The sea is a bit warmer and calmer on this side of Florida so is more suitable for small children. The 35ml/56km stretch from St Pete–Clearwater represents the heart of the Sunshine State beach experience and is one of the most popular two-centre options. It has a wonderful array of attractions and averages 361 days of sun a year.

St Petersburg: This city, just across the Howard Frankland Bridge from Tampa, is a wonderful mix of the old and the new, with a fast-developing Art District (eight museums, dozens of galleries and counting) and a real café society feel. Take time for the world-renowned **Dali Museum**

(10am 5.30pm, 8pm Thurs; $24 adults, $22 seniors, $17 13–18s and students, $10 6–12s; **www.thedali. org**), and the **Chihuly Collection** across the street from **Morean Arts Center**, a superb showcase of the American glass artist, with guided tours each hour. There's also a separate glass studio and hot shop nearby (10am–5pm Mon–Sat, noon–5pm Sun; $15 adults, $14 seniors, $11 students and children over 5; $9 $7, $5 for Hot Shop; combo ticket $20, $18, $13; 727 896 4527, **www.moreanartscenter. org**; also on Tampa CityPass, see left). Other highlights include the elegant **Museum of Fine Arts**, with its two interior gardens (**www.fine-arts. org**), the **St Petersburg Museum of History** (**www.spmoh.com**), and fascinating **Great Explorations Children's Museum** (**www.greatex. org**). Pedestrian-friendly streets provide plenty of interest, while the **Bay Walk** complex adds restaurants, shops and a **Muvico IMAX 20-screen cinema** (**www.yourbaywalk.com**). Also visit the fan-friendly **Tropicana Field**, which hosts the Tampa Bay Rays baseball team (Apr–Sept) for terrific local entertainment ($25–325; **http:// tampabay.rays.mlb.com**). And try the **All About Fun Tours** from the Museum of History on two-wheeled Segways. They are easy to master and provide a superb view of the city's miles of waterfront parks, beaches and residences with your knowledgeable guide. Ages 12 and over (max 275lb/125kg; Tues–Sat 10.30am and 2pm, Sun 12.30 and 2.30pm; 1hr tour $35, 90min $50; call for reservations on 727 896 3640, **www.gyroglides.com**).

Weedon Island Preserve: Enjoy the rich cultural history of this 3,700acre/1,500ha seaside nature park in St Petersburg. Start at the Natural History Center (the main entrance is at the back) and learn about the prehistoric and Native American settlements here (plus periodic exhibitions), then go up to the 3rd floor observation deck. There are several miles of boardwalks and trails around the tidal wetlands, which are home to wildlife like ospreys, turtles, spoonbills, turtles, mangrove crabs, raccoons and gopher tortoises, and guided hikes on Sats at 9am (call to register; Center open 9am–4pm Thurs–Sat, free entry; Preserve open 7am–dusk; 727 453 6500, **www.weedonislandpreserve.org**). The more energetic may want to try a paddle round the shallow waters with **Sweetwater Kayaks**. This close encounter with nature (stingrays, jumping mullet and the occasional manatee) is offered on an hourly or 4hr basis (9am–5pm daily; $40 for a 4hr single-kayak rental, $56 for double, or $17 and $25 hourly, $34 and $50 for 2hrs; stand-up paddleboards $20/$40/$50; booking advised on 727 570 4844 or **www.sweetwaterkayaks.com**).

◄╬► BRITTIP
Insect repellent is essential for any visit to Weedon Island Preserve as it is not sprayed for mosquitoes, and the little pests will feed on tourists!

Beaches: You are spoiled for choice, from the 1,100acre/445ha **Fort De Soto Park** in the south to stunning **Caladesi Island State Park** in the north (regularly voted in America's Top 10). There is plenty to do, too, with the likes of Treasure Island, Sand Key and St Pete Beach all receiving the Blue Wave Award for cleanliness and safety. **John's Pass Village** is an eclectic shopping district and marina full of art galleries and restaurants, plus the fun **Pirate Cruise** – a replica sailing ship offering a 2hr party cruise ($35 adults, $30 65 and over, $25 under-20s, $10 under-3s, inclusive of beer, wine and soft drinks; 11am, 2pm and sunset), and 90min **Dolphin Quest** tour at noon, 2, 4 and 6pm daily ($19.50 adults, $17.50 seniors, $15 under 20s; call for reservations on 727 350 1101, **http://boattoursjohnspass.com/**).

Parasailing, jet-skiing, fishing, boat rentals and tours are also popular (**www.johnspass.com**).

Dolphin Landings: A 'Don't miss' in St Pete Beach, with a pair of 51ft/15.5m yachts that sail on 2hr trips along the calm inland waterway (9.30am, noon and 2.15pm, Mon–Sat, noon and 2.15pm Sun; $35 adults, $25 children) for close-up dolphin-watch cruises and sunset sailings, plus a Sunset Sail, 4hr trip around beautiful Egmont Key and a 3½hr trip to Shell Key, with up to 2hrs on the beach ($40–45; 727 399 6849, **www.dolphinlandings.com**).

◄╬► BRITTIP
Most public beaches will have toilets, changing facilities and picnic tables, but there is usually a parking fee.

Suncoast Seabird Sanctuary: Further north at Indian Shores is America's largest wild bird hospital, caring for injured birds including birds of prey, pelicans, spoonbills and egrets. No charge but donations to visit this non-profit-making rehabilitation centre (9am–sunset, 727 391 6211, **www.seabirdsanctuary.com**).

Clearwater Beach: Continue north to acres of clean, white sands and the **Clearwater Marine Aquarium**, a wonderful non-profit organisation that rescues and rehabilitates injured dolphins, turtles, river otters and more (especially good for under-12s). There are 17 main exhibits, including Turtle Cove, Otter Oasis, Shark Pass and Shipwreck Alley but much of the focus is on the area's Hollywood 'star', Winter the tail-less dolphin (see Brit Tip) in the Winter Zone.

◄╬► BRITTIP
Don't leave without visiting the area's top attraction, a dolphin called Winter, the star of films *Dolphin Tale* and *Dolphin Tale 2* with Morgan Freeman. Rescued from a crab trap, her tail had to be amputated and she was not expected to survive. Happily, she not only lived but has learned to swim with a prosthetic tail!

There are dolphin presentations (into behaviour and care – not 'shows') three times a day and interactive animal encounters, plus a Trainer for a Day, at $325/person. Their behind-the-scenes tour, or 2hr Sea Life Safari (great for kids) that goes out on the coastal waterway. There are also another seven animal encounters, including dolphins, pelicans and sharks, and an Assistant Trainer with Winter opportunity ($5–449/ person).

The Dolphin Tale Adventure – with re-built scenes, film images, interactive kids area and mini-theater – in downtown Clearwater is also included if you buy tickets at the Aquarium, from where there is also a free trolley ride to the Adventure (Aquarium hours 9am–6pm daily, 10am–6pm for Dolphin Tale Adventure; $22 adults, $20 seniors, $17 3–12s; behind-the-scenes tour $17, $15 and $12; Sea Life Safari $26, $23, $17; Aquarium plus backstage tour $35, $32, $27; Aquarium plus Safari $41, $38, $30; or all 3 $54, $50, $40; 727 441 1790, **www.seewinter.com**; also on Tampa CityPass, p281).

The Beach Walk: The heart of the area is a winding beachside promenade of lush landscaping and artistic touches that links a ½ml/1km stretch of resorts, shops and restaurants (like the fun **Frenchy's** and **Crabby Bill's**) to Pier 60 where the daily sunset celebration (with craft stalls and music) is held.

Also here is the marina where you can catch the 2hr **Captain Memo's Pirate Cruise** (10am and 2pm daily; $36 adults, $33 seniors, $31 teens, $28 under-13s, $11 under 3s) or the **Sunset Champagne Cruise** (at 4.30, 5, 6 or 7pm, $39, $33, $31, $28, $11, online discounts available at **www.captainmemo.com**).

Sugar Sand Festival: While Clearwater Beach is fun at all times of the year, it is at its best for April's 10-day Pier 60 Sugar Sand Festival with sand-sculpting competitions, concerts, films and other special events (**www.sugarsandfestival.com**).

Suncoast Beach Trolley: For those not wanting to drive, this is the perfect option (6.10am–11.25pm daily) both along the beaches and into St Petersburg for $2.25 a ride, $5 for an all-day pass and $20 for a week pass (info line 727 540 1900, **www.psta.net**).

Restaurants: The area also boasts 2,000 restaurants, of which the Key West bistro style of the five **Frenchy's Cafes** (Original Café, Rockaway Grill, South Beach and Salt Water Café all in Clearwater Beach, plus **Frenchy's**

Outpost in Dunedin), the **Daiquiri Shak** (Madeira Beach), **Crabby Bill's Seafood** (in Clearwater Beach) and the **Moon Under Water** (St Petersburg) are all worth visiting. The chic **Parkshore Grill** in downtown St Pete is ideal for a relaxing lunch or elegant dinner (727 896 9463, **www.parkshoregrill.com**), as is **400 Beach Seafood & Tap House**, which also features a fabulous Sunday brunch (727 896 2400, **www.400beachseafood.com**).

Where to stay: A range of **Superior Small Lodgings** combine beachfront locations with small-scale service. Weekly rates can be from $800 for a three-room apartment (727 367 2791, **http://floridassl.com/**). Upscale hotels include family-friendly **Tradewinds Island Resorts** on St Pete Beach, a 743-room complex with great facilities and dining in a blissful location (1800 360 4016, **www.tradewindsresort.com**); the superb **Sandpearl Resort**, a four-star choice on Clearwater Beach, with a mix of stylish standard rooms and spacious suites. The pool, bar and grill are a beachfront sanctuary, and the modern Spa has a fab array of treatments. Caretta on the Gulf offers memorable dining with an inventive fusion cuisine (866 384 2995, **www.sandpearl.com**); and the **Hyatt Regency Clearwater Beach Resort & Spa**, an all-suite hotel at the heart of Beach Walk with fantastic pool facilities and picturesque Gulf views, plus the eco-friendly Sandova Spa, state-of-the-art gym and two good restaurants (727 373 1234, **www.clearwaterbeach.hyatt.com**). By contrast, the **Vinoy Resort** (in St Petersburg) is the area's oldest formal hotel, a 1920s treasure that is well worth a look just for its Spanish Revival style (727 894 1000, **www.marriott.com/hotels/travel/tpasr-the-vinoy-renaissance-st-petersburg-resort-and-golf-club**). Another personal favourite is the **Grand Plaza Hotel** right on St Pete Beach, where the ultra-friendly service and fresh style are ideal for a beach getaway, especially with the revolving restaurant and bar of Spinners on the 12th floor providing grandstand Gulf views (727 360 1811, www.grandplazaflorida.com). **Sunset Vistas Beachfront Suites** on Treasure Island, with one and two-bed suites and fully-equipped kitchens, is a top self-catering choice (727 726 4770, **www. providentresorts.com**). **More info:** 0208 651 4742 in the UK, 727 464 7200 in the US, or **www.visitstpeteclearwater. com**.

🔴 **BRITTIP**

Don't miss the chance to dine at the Hyatt Regency's SHOR Seafood Grill, with its dramatic show kitchen and superb local seafood dishes.

The south-west

Bradenton/Sarasota: Around 2hrs' drive from Orlando is this artsy area (take I-4 then I-75), which features the superb beachfronts of Anna Maria Island (charming and secluded beaches), Longboat Key and Venice ('the shark tooth capital of the world' and great for fossil hunters).

Sarasota is year-round home to the Ringling Circus, and there are many circus-influenced offerings here, including the unmissable **Ringling Estate and Museum of Art**, which includes the unique Circus Museum and Tibbals Learning Center (the world's largest scale model of a classic circus). The Museum of Art features a multi-million-dollar collection of Old Masters in a palatial setting while the former family home, the dazzling Ca d'Zan Mansion, grounds and gardens are also part of the entry fee (daily 10am–5pm, 8pm Thurs; closed Thanksgiving, Christmas, New Year's Day; $25 adults, $23 seniors, $5 6–17s and students; **www.ringling.org**). There is superb shopping at **St Armand's Circle** in Lido Key, and the **Mote Aquarium** is also worthy of note. In Bradenton, look out for the **Village of Arts**, and the sophisticated **South Florida Museum**, which includes the **Parker Manatee Aquarium** and **Bishop Planetarium**. The Aquarium is home to Bradenton's mascot, Snooty, the world's oldest living manatee (10am–5pm Mon–Sat, noon–5pm Sun; closed Mon in May,

Jun and Aug–Dec; $19 adults, $17 seniors, $14 4–11s; 941 746 4131, **www.southfloridamuseum.org**). Good food is always on the menu, and you should try another outlet of the excellent Spanish-Cuban **Columbia Restaurant** in St Armand's Circle (941 388 3987, **www.columbiarestaurant.com**), the al fresco dining of **Mattison's City Grille** in downtown Sarasota (941 330 0440, **www.mattisons.com**) and **Siesta Key Oyster Bar** in Siesta Key Village (941 346 5443, **www.skob.com**).

Where to stay: Anna Maria Island is full of small-scale B&Bs and cute beachfront inns. The **Hyatt Regency Sarasota** is one of the top resorts in the area (941 953 1234, **www.sarasota. hyatt.com**), while the **Ritz-Carlton** is a Gulf Coast landmark (941 309 2000, **www.ritzcarlton.com**). For a great self-catering option, try the **Beach Club at Siesta Key** (941 552 9810, **www. beachclubatsiestakey.com**).

More info: Sarasota, call 941 957 1877 or **www.visitsarasota.org**; **Bradenton and Anna Maria Island**, 941 729 9177 or **www.bradentongulfislands.com**.

Charlotte Harbor: Go further south (170ml/272km from Orlando) and you have the lower-key destinations of Punta Gorda, Port Charlotte, Englewood and Boca Grande. Port Charlotte is the place to be for some of the best shelling in Florida, while kayakers should try the 'tunnel of love' mangrove tunnels and other nature adventures with **Phoenix Rising Kayak Tours** (941 586 2836; **www.prkayak.com**). To immerse completely in nature, try an overnight stay on **Little Gasparilla Island**, where there are no roads, cars or shops, just miles of beaches and exceptional bird-watching and tarpon fishing. Eco-adventures can be found at **Babcock Wilderness Adventures**, with swamp buggy tours through the Telegraph Swamp (1800 500 5583; **www.babcockwilderness.com**). Downtown Punta Gorda has free bike rentals and a lovely walk along the Peace River where you'll feel miles off the usual tourist trail. If you are looking for 'small town America', this is it.

More info: 941 743 1900 or **www.charlotteharbortravel.com**.

Fort Myers/Sanibel: It's only a short drive to the mini tropical paradise of the Lee Island Coast, featuring history and nature-rich Fort Myers and funky Pine Island. Among the many highlights are bustling family-orientated Fort Myers Beach; Sanibel Island, centred around its shell-strewn beaches; the bird-watching Mecca at the **Darling National Wildlife Refuge**; the shops and restaurants in Captiva Island; and Bonita Beach. Sanibel is home to the unique **Bailey-Matthews Shell Museum**, plus a quaint **Historical Museum & Village**, several wildlife attractions, canoeing and nature tours.

Where to stay: There is a good mix of vacation homes and cottages in Fort Myers Beach and Sanibel, while the top hotels are **Lovers Key Resort** (239 765 1040, **www.loverskey.com**) and **Sanibel Harbor Marriott Resort & Spa** (239 466 4000, **http://www.marriott.com/hotels/travel/rswsb-sanibel-harbour-marriott-resort-and-spa**). **More info:** 239 338 3500 or **www.fortmyers-sanibel.com**.

Paradise Coast: Continue south to the magnificent 'Paradise Coast' of Naples and Marco Island. Naples is a fresh, modern city with plenty of attractions (notably the **Museum of Art, Naples Nature Center** and **Corkscrew Swamp Sanctuary**, plus ultra-chic shopping) and a top beach destination. Its art-tinged ambience is well-evidenced in its two main areas of 5th Avenue South, with boutique shops, sidewalk cafés and art festivals, and Third Street South, with more distinctive stores, galleries and café society atmosphere (try the **Old Naples Pub** for fine food in a relaxed ambience with an outdoor patio and live music Thurs–Sat). The beaches are mere steps away; at the municipal beach, Naples Pier juts into placid Gulf waters, while Lowdermilk Beach is family-friendly, with volleyball and other facilities. Marco Island is the largest of the Ten Thousand Islands, consisting of Marco, known for its wide beach, fine resorts and sea-fishing charters; and Goodland, with its fish restaurants, and Everglades fishing charters.

Where to stay: Pick from high-quality resorts like **Marco Island Marriott Beach Resort** (239 394 2511, **www.marcoislandmarriott.com**), **Marco Beach Ocean Resort** (239 393 1400, **www.marcoresort.com**) and **Naples Grande Beach Resort** (239 227 2182, **www.naplesgrande.com**). We also like the small-scale Caribbean-tinged **Lemon Tree Inn** in Naples (239 262 1414, **http://lemontreeinn.com/**).

More info: 001 239 225 1013 or **www.paradisecoast.com**.

BRITTIP
The Naples/Marco Island area is the perfect base from which to explore the amazing Florida Everglades, though you can also reach them from Fort Lauderdale.

Treasure Coast

Returning to the Atlantic Coast, heading south on Highway 1 brings you to an often-overlooked Florida jewel, Vero Beach. Nicknamed the Treasure Coast (for its history of shipwrecks), it boasts the intriguing **McLarty Treasure Museum** and the **Pelican Island National Wildlife Refuge**. Vero Beach itself is located on the barrier island of North Hutchinson but spreads to the mainland, with art galleries, smart shops, restaurants, small resorts and

Pelican Island National Wildlife Refuge

© Pelican Island National Wildlife Refuge

beach parks, including a boardwalk atop the dunes. Go south for another hour and you reach the **Palm Beaches** and the mainland city of West Palm Beach, foremost among Florida's chic cities. A playground of the rich and famous, the fabulous **Flagler Museum** (formerly the rail tycoon's 1902-built Whitehall mansion) is a highlight, while the many restaurants are places to go celebrity-watching and **Worth Avenue** is one of America's most iconic shopping streets. Don't miss dining at Italian style **Bice** (561 835 1600 **http://www.bice-palmbeach. com**), the ultra-chic **Meat Market** (561 354 9800, **www.meatmarket.net/palm_ beach/**), small-plate specialist **Buccan** (561 833 3450, **www.buccanpalmbeach. com**) and indulgent **HMF** at The Breakers, plus the celebrity bistro of **Ta-boo** (561 835 3500, **www. taboorestaurant.com**). This is also a great place to take a fishing charter or yacht hire, like **Palm Breeze Charters** (561 368 3566, **www.airandsea.com**), while, for something different, check out the **International Polo Club** (games from Jan–Apr; 561 204 5687, **www.internationalpoloclub.com**) and **National Croquet Center** (lessons every Sat, plus a great bar-restaurant; 561 478 2300, **www.croquetnational. com**). Also here is **Lion Country Safari**, with lions, elephants and giraffes (**www.lioncountrysafari.com**).

Where to stay: Disney's Vero Beach Resort doesn't always have availability (it is a Disney Vacation Club hotel), but is the ideal family resort on this coast (772 234 2000, **http://disneyvacationclub.disney.go.com**). The Palm Beaches boasts an array of 5-star hotels, notably the blissful **Eau Palm Beach** (561 533 6000; **www.eaupalmbeach.com**), the period style of **The Brazilian Court** (561 655 7740, **www.thebraziliancourt.com**), the gorgeous **Four Seasons** (561 582 2800, **www.fourseasons.com**) and the ultimate opulence and style of **The Breakers**, one of America's legendary resort destinations, with breathtaking décor and design (561 655 6611, **www.thebreakers.com**).

More info: 1800 554 7256 or **www.palmbeachfl.com**.

Seminole Central

Head west out of Fort Lauderdale to Big Cypress and you find the rewarding Ah-Tah-Thi-Ki Museum, home to the Seminole tribe of Florida. See the Living Village and walk the 1ml/1.6km Boardwalk over the Cypress Swamp. Then try the Billie Swamp Safari, a 2,200-acre/1.6ha Cypress Reservation featuring close-ups of the wildlife (including snakes and gators) via its giant-wheeled buggy, airboat rides and swamp critter shows. And you can even stay overnight in its Chickee huts (863 983 6101, **www.floridaseminoletourism.com**).

Miami and Fort Lauderdale

From Palm Beach, you reach increasingly built-up resort territory – Delray Beach, chic Boca Raton, Deerfield Beach, Pompano Beach and Fort Lauderdale, one of Florida's most upmarket destinations.

It also has a canal and waterway network that makes it the 'Venice of America', with water taxis being more plentiful than the wheeled variety.

Top things to see are the **Museum of Discovery & Science** (one of the state's finest), **Bonnet House Museum & Gardens**, **Old Fort Lauderdale Village & Museum** and **Las Olas Boulevard**, full of boutiques and restaurants. Shop at **Sawgrass Mills**, Florida's largest mall, which has more than 300 outlet-style stores from big-name designers. Fort Lauderdale is also a perfect stay for a few days before or after a cruise, as both Port Everglades and Miami are only a short distance away.

Where to stay: Look for their **Superior Small Lodgings** or the many high-class resorts now dotting the beachfront, like the fab **Margaritaville Beach Resort**, with an amazing array of amenities, great dining and superb rooms (954 874 4444, **www. margaritavillehollywoodbeachresort. com**) and the dramatic five-star **Ritz-Carlton** (954 465 2300, **www.ritzcarlton. com**). For more of a family self-catering touch, the **Beachwalk Resort** on Hallandale Beach has one, two and three-bed suites with full kitchens in an ideal location but still with plenty

Miami nice

If you see nothing else in Miami, do spend some time in South Beach (or SoBe as it is known) and über-cool Ocean Drive, full of open-air cafés, art galleries and pulsating nightclubs. Tranquil during the day, non-stop at night, this is where the beautiful people hang out, or just cruise in their Ferraris and Hummers. The restored Art Deco gems twinkle at night and will use up lots of capacity on your camera's memory card.

of amenities, including a great pool deck and restaurant (954 266 0147, **http://beachwalkresortfl.com/**).

More info: 954 765 4466 or **www.sunny.org**.

Miami: If you have taken the 3½hr drive south from Orlando, you will finally arrive in the state's biggest and most glamorous city, Miami. With superb high-rise resorts, miles of open, accessible beaches, the ultra-chic **South Beach** area (with its Art Deco District), fantastic shopping, sports, restaurants and nightlife you could easily spend a week here.

The city is actually 5ml/8km from the beach area, which runs north for almost 15ml/24km along the sprawling corridor of Collins Avenue, where you have most of the resorts and nightlife. High style is almost everywhere – a narrated boat tour (from the Bayside Marketplace) will show off the mansions of the rich and famous, while you should also tour Coral Gables and the older, neater Coconut Grove, with its **CocoWalk** shopping district and ornate **Vizcaya Museum**.

Other attractions include **Miami Seaquarium** on the island of Key Biscayne (**www.miamiseaquarium. com**), the amazing Venetian Pool at **Coral Gables** and the surprising and entertaining family attraction **Jungle Island**, a combination of zoo, animal shows and gardens with great up-close encounters (**www.jungleisland.com**). You are spoiled for choice for shopping, from fashion-conscious **Bal Harbor Shops**, to the massive **Aventura Mall** and funky **Lincoln Road** in

South Beach. Or try the **Village of Merrick Park** in Coral Gables, a Mediterranean-style outdoor mall with more designer style, including the iconic **Nordstrom** department store and superb dining, notably at fab Italian restaurant **Villagio** and gastropub **Yard House** (305 447 9273, **www.villageofmerrickpark.com**).

Miami Food Tours: Try this fascinating insight into the Art Deco district's architecture and eclectic dining. Sample 'neighbourhood specialities' at six South Beach restaurants and cafés along this fun walking tour, while learning about the area's culture, history and unique building style. (786 361 0991; **www.miamifoodtours.com**)

Dining: This is a strong feature of Miami these days. Consider the sumptuous Latin American cuisine of **Ola Miami** (305 695 9125; **www. olamiami.com**); fresh and authentic Northern Italian trattoria offerings at **Salumiera** 104 (305 424 9588; **www. salumeria104.com**); ultra-swanky **Casa Tua** (the place to see and be seen; 305 673 1010, **www.casatualifestyle.com/ miami**); and the casual comforts at eclectic **Soyka**, a train station turned car collector's warehouse turned restaurant, with live jazz each Fri (305 759 3117; **www.soykarestaurant.com**).

Where to stay: There are boutique hotels and dazzling resorts aplenty, but two we like a lot are **The Beacon** in the heart of bustling South Beach on Ocean Drive, and an iconic breakfast location (305 674 8200; **www. beaconsouthbeach.com**) and the **Miami Beach Edition**, a chic conversion of the 1950s Seville Hotel (786 257 4500, **www.editionhotels.com/miami-beach/**).

More info: 305 539 3000 or **www.miamiandbeaches.com**.

Miami city skyline

© Gray Line Tours

Florida Keys

Leaving Miami behind on Highway 1 brings you to the unique realm of the Keys, a loose archipelago of 1,700 islands that arc down into the Caribbean. If you thought mainland Florida was easy-going, just try the laid-back 'Conch Republic', where shorts and flip-flops are official wear and the mix of influences merges into a 'Floribbean' culture. Scuba divers enjoy some of the world's best coral reefs, with renowned **John Pennekamp Coral Reef State Park** the highlight of miles of National Marine Sanctuary. Or try Vandenberg Artificial Reef off Key West, an old US Navy ship sunk in 2009 to create a man-made reef. The first city you encounter is **Key Largo**, followed by **Islamorada**, where you should stop to see **Theater of the Sea**, with its dolphin and sea-lion programmes. For fishing, some of the best charters are at Islamorada, Marathon and Big Pine Key.

Marathon is the starting point of the **Seven Mile Bridge**, the unofficial eighth wonder of the world, which connects the biggest gap between the islands, while **Big Pine Key** is home to **Bahia Honda State Park**, one of Florida's finest beaches. Finally, the 375ml/600km drive from Orlando brings you to America's southernmost city. **Key West** is possibly the most eclectic city in the US, a mix of the laid-back and outrageous, with street performers, sidewalk artists, cafés and bars, plus the former home of Ernest Hemingway. You should also see **Key West Aquarium** and **Key West Shipwreck Museum**, and the wonderfull shops. You must be on the harbour front for the daily Sunset Celebration, when Key West's party spirit is in full force. The other great feature of Key West is its myriad ways to get around – you can try the **Conch Tour Train**, **Old Town Trolley Tours**, pedicabs and bicycles. Just don't expect your stay to be sedate!

Where to stay: Guest houses, inns and B&Bs are plentiful. Try **Old Customs House Inn** (305 294 8507, **www.oldcustomshouse.com**) in Key West's Old Town or charming **Banyan Resort** (305 296 7786, **www.thebanyanresort.com**).

More info: 1800 352 5397 or www.fla-keys.com.

Cruise-and-stay

Taking a cruise is increasingly popular with an Orlando stay and there are well-priced 3, 4, 5 and 7-day sailings out of Port Canaveral, Tampa, Fort Lauderdale and Miami. From here, you can visit the Bahamas, much of the Caribbean, Mexico and even Central America.

Select from **Disney Cruise Line** (from their own dedicated cruise terminal at Port Canaveral and Miami), with four fabulous ships and voyages from 3–7 days (0800 951 3532, **http:// disneycruise.disney.go.com**); party-style **Carnival** (from Port Canaveral, Miami and Tampa), 3–7 days (0843 374 2272 in the UK, **www.carnival. co.uk**); **Royal Caribbean**, with some of the biggest ships (from all four ports) for 3–14 days (0844 493 4005, **www.royalcaribbean.co.uk**), **Norwegian Cruise Line** (from Port Canaveral, Miami and Tampa) from 3–7 days (0333 241 2319 **www.ncl.co.uk**) and **Princess Cruises**, 7–14 days (from Fort Lauderdale; 1800 774 6237, **www.princess.com**).

Now we need to tell you about how to enjoy all the night-time entertainment…

Disney Cruise ship Fantasy

10 Orlando by Night

or Burning the Candle at Both Ends

If Orlando and the parks are hot during the day, they positively sizzle at night, with yet more diverse and thrilling entertainment, much of it family friendly. Disney and Universal lead the way, but there is much to enjoy throughout the area.

The full range runs from purpose built entertainment complexes and an amazing variety of dinner shows to a unique array of bars and nightclubs. The choice is widespread and almost always high quality. Downtown Orlando has some great offerings, while there is more being added to I-Drive all the time. What used to be called Downtown Disney – and which had already raised the bar for night-time fun – is now the all-new Disney Springs, with almost double the shopping and dining choice, while Disney's Boardwalk Resort is also a good evening option.

DISNEY SPRINGS

Disney's big shopping, dining and entertainment district has been transformed into a four-part adventure in the last few years. The original Marketplace and West Side were joined in 2015 by The Landing (the old Pleasure Island area), with the Town Center added in 2016, featuring iconic restaurants, bars and live entertainment (see also Dining, p307; Shopping, p330).

BRITTIP
Photo ID is essential for most bars and clubs, even if you happen to be the 'wrong' side of 30. No ID equals no alcohol, and there are no exceptions.

The Landing

Raglan Road: This pub features traditional live Irish music each night in its Grand Room 4pm–1am Mon–Fri, 12pm–1am Sat–Sun, plus hourly Irish dancing 4–9pm Mon–Sun. Enjoy its full bar, ample collection of genuine Irish whiskey, nine European beers, four beer flights, plus local brews, great bartenders and even better menu (p308) (407 938 0300, **www.raglanroad.com**).

Paradiso 37: This expansive, split-level bar-restaurant offers a fine array of food from the Americas (all 37 countries) plus a Tequila Bar featuring

Paradiso 37

over 50 varieties. Live music adds to its picturesque waterfront location (p308).

The Boathouse: This bar-restaurant venue offers live music nightly, 5pm–closing, but the real feature is the Amphicar rides. Each land-to-water car accommodates up to three guests and a Car Captain (driver), with 20min rides costing a whopping $125, but it's a great opportunity. Tickets can be purchased at The Boathouse. For the best spectator value, watch the Amphicars on the lake from the comfort of the waterside Boathouse bar. Tours run 10am–10pm, weather permitting.

◄╬► BRITTIP
For a special occasion, try The Boathouse's special water-taxi *The Venezia* for a guided tour of Disney Springs, complete with chocolate-covered strawberries, champagne and music ($75/person, $50/under 13s).

Jock Lindsey's Hangar Bar: Indiana Jones fans will love this wonderfully themed bar for the pilot of the Indy films. There is a boat-themed patio and aeroplane memorabilia, plus reminders of the former Adventurer's Club at Pleasure Island, as well as a range of craft beers, cocktails and a small-plate dining menu.

The Edison: This massive 1920s-themed 'Industrial Gothic' destination will open in early 2017, offering classic American food, cocktails and a range of cabaret-style shows, contortionists, palm readers, DJs and more. Eclectic? You bet! But it should add a more creative, individual touch that we haven't seen since the old Adventurers Club closed.

Paddlefish: The former Fulton's Crabhouse 'riverboat' restaurant is undergoing a complete rebuild as we write and is due to re-open as seafood-themed offering, including a rooftop lounge and bar, open until 2am with a view over Disney Springs.

STK Orlando: The latest outlet of this über-chic international steakhouse has a high-energy vibe that features an in-house DJ and a fabulous patio with great views over Disney Springs – ideal for cocktails and people-watching.

West Side

AMC® Dine-In Theaters Complex: With 24 screens and 6,000 seats plus a huge choice of snacks, drinks and even its own bar, this superb cinema multiplex shows first-run films in state-of-the-art surroundings, including the Enhanced Theatre Experience (a bigger screen, with 3D technology, 12-channel audio and digital projection) and a Dine-In option, with six of the auditoriums converted to serve meals and drinks while you watch. The menu includes starters like wings and sushi rolls, then salads, fish and chips, pasta, burgers, doughnuts and milkshakes, plus wine, beer and cocktails (tickets $8–18, prices vary by show; food and drink extra; call 1 888 262 4386 for show times; under 18s must be accompanied by an adult in Dine-In theatres; **www.amctheatres.com**).

Disabled accessible; assisted listening devices available at Guest Services.

◄╬► BRITTIP
Some films have added features, such as enhanced sound, larger screen, or 3-D that will increase your ticket price. However, you can save $2 on adult tickets at the AMC® cineplex by visiting before 3.55pm.

Bongos Cuban Café: The 'big pineapple' restaurant with Latin flair has salsa music and a live band nightly after 6pm. Sit on the balcony on a balmy evening and soak up the atmosphere (407 828 0999; **www.bongoscubancafe.com**).

House of Blues: Free live music every night at the Front Porch bar, with full concerts at the separately accessed music venue next to the restaurant. The main venue offers a mix of big-name headliners (recent visits from The Cult, Fall Out Boy, Evanescence and Sister Hazel), up-and-coming bands and local acts. Standing only. Tickets required, no discounts for children ($20–89 and up; 407 934 2583, **www.houseofblues.com**).

Cirque Du Soleil: The greatest show we've seen anywhere is Cirque du Soleil's *La Nouba*™. Twice a day, five times a week, the company's purpose-built, 1,671-seat theatre stages the most stupendous combination of dance, circus, acrobatics, comedy and live music in a 90min show by more than 60 performers. Unique styling, outrageous costumes and captivating sounds – this is a stunning multi-dimensional assault on the senses.

The show title comes from the French *faire la nouba*, to live it up, and this it does in grand style. It features trampolines, acrobatics, trapezes, juggling and even mountain bikes, woven with comedy, innovative dance, spellbinding music and brilliant staging. Some of the stunts are jaw-dropping, notably the Chinese diabolo acrobats, BMX cycling stunts and the high-energy final act, Power Track/Trampoline, which features a 3D building and performers flipping and twisting in and out of the structure in quick succession. It is not cheap, but we believe it is worth every cent and a highlight of any visit to Orlando. Booking is vital and can be done up to six months in advance on 407 939 7328 (or **www.cirquedusoleil.com**). Shows are at 6pm and 9pm Tues–Sat, but try to be early for some excellent pre-show fun. Admission: Golden Circle at $148/adults, $122/3–9s; Front & Center, $132, $108; Cat 1, $105, $85; Cat 2, $85, $68; Cat 3, $79, $63; and Cat 4, $62, $51 (but there is hardly a bad seat in the house).

Splitsville: An imaginative venue in which to 'dine, dance, drink – and bowl'. But with a difference. Built in best 1950s period style, this twin-level entertainment palace offers 30 lanes of bowling, multiple bars, billiard tables and a full-service restaurant, plus elegant indoor and outdoor seating, including a 1st-floor patio for a great view over Disney Springs. The upper floor also has more of a grown-up style in the evening, with DJs

adding a nightclub vibe. Walk-in rates are $15/person Mon–Fri 10am–4pm and $20 after 4pm; $20/person all day Sat and Sun, with Early Bird specials until 12:30pm. Book a lane in advance by calling or online (10.30–1am Mon–Fri; 10–2am Sat and Sun; 407 938 7467, **www.splitsvillelanes.com**).

Town Center

While this is primarily a shopping area, with a few smart dining outlets like D-Luxe Burger and Blaze Pizza, there are a couple of worthy candidates for evening fun.

Coca-Cola Store: Another iconic building, this is home to Coke products, gift items and memorabilia, and features a glamorous rooftop tasting bar.

Planet Hollywood Observatory: The new-look Planet Hollywood features a futuristic space observatory theme to go with its celebrity style. As well as the main restaurant, there's the Stargazers outdoor terrace and bar with live entertainment.

Marketplace

This area is again primarily about shopping and dining but there are still a couple of nice spots to stop for a drink, notably the **Lava Lounge** (behind the Rainforest Café and with a view over Crescent Lake), and **Dockside Margaritas**, an open-air terrace facing the water that also serves great cocktails.

Other entertainment: The evening sees a variety of live music performers throughout Disney Springs, from flamenco guitarists to classical quartets and more. Look for them in all four sections.

Cirque du Soleil

Disney Resorts

Disney's Boardwalk: Disney's other big evening entertainment offering is part of its impressive BoardWalk Resort, where the waterfront entertainment district contains several notable venues (not counting the excellent micro-brewery and restaurant of the **Big River Grille and Brewing Works**, the thrilling **ESPN Club** for sports fans and five-star **Flying Fish Café**). **Jellyroll**s is a variation on the duelling piano bar, with the pianists conjuring up a humorous and often raucous evening of audience participation (7pm–2am, music from 8pm; $12 cover charge; 21 and over only).

Atlantic Dance Club: Features mainly modern dance music with house and guest DJs, plus occasional live music, a huge dance floor and a great bar service and ambience. Video DJs feature on Tues, Wed and Sat, with 'duelling DJs' on Thurs and Fri, and it's especially popular on Fri and Sat nights (9pm–2am; closed Sun and Mon). It's strictly 21 and over, so bring your ID. The Boardwalk also features some amusing stalls and live entertainers, while the ESPN Club features regular celebrity (American) sports guests.

Coronado Springs Resort: A hidden gem here is the **Rix Lounge**. A bar-nightclub with a smooth ultra-lounge vibe, it features its own cocktail list, from martinis to shooters and tequila and margarita flights, plus a light-bite menu of appetisers and flatbreads. With a live DJ Thurs–Sat, it is a cool place just to go for an early-evening drink or a great full-on nightclub later on (6pm–midnight; www.rix-lounge.com).

Electrical Water Pageant: This is another nightly (and free!) alternative, a 'parade' that circles Bay Lake and the Seven Seas Lagoon. It lasts just 10mins, but it's almost a waterborne version of the Main Street Electrical Parade, with thousands of twinkling lights on a cavalcade of pontoons, all set to music. The usual schedule is 9pm at the Polynesian Resort, 9.15 at Grand Floridian Resort & Spa (get a grandstand view in Narcoosee's restaurant), 9.35 at Wilderness Lodge, 9.45 on the shores of Fort Wilderness Resort and 10.05 at Contemporary Resort. It can also be seen outside the Magic Kingdom at 10.20pm during extended hours.

UNIVERSAL'S CITYWALK

As part of the big Universal Orlando development, this 30acre/12ha

NBC Sports Grill and Brew

© Universal Orlando Resort

spread offers a bustling expanse of restaurants, snack bars, shops, open-air events and nightclubs. It offers a huge variety of cuisines, from fast food to fine dining, an unusual blend of speciality shops and an eclectic nightclub mix, from reggae and rock 'n' roll to salsa, jazz and high-energy disco, plus the superb **Blue Man Group** show and a karaoke theatre/bar. There's a $7 entry fee at the six clubs but you can buy a **CityWalk Party Pass** ($12) or **Party Pass with Movie** (one free film at the 20-screen Universal Cineplex; $15) for entry to all of them, while most multi-day tickets include a Party Pass. The area splits into the Main Plaza (shopping and dining), Lagoon Front (dining, live music and theatre) and the Promenade (dining and nightclubs). For dining, see p312.

Blue Man Group: The most entertaining element here offers a unique brand of comedy, music and multi-media theatrics, adding something novel to the Universal line-up. In the hands (or mouths!) of the Blue Men, mundane items like pipes, paintballs, cereal, GI-Pads, and even audience members become the instruments of wild creativity with sometimes stunning, occasionally slightly gross but always hilariously gratifying outcomes. There is a strong live music element and it can feel a bit like a rock concert. Their ability to drum up a tune on various bits and pieces is amazing. The wild finale, involving the whole theatre, is a real corker, and don't worry if you're seated in the 'poncho section'; the Blue Men will make sure you have adequate protection. An unforgettable evening of family entertainment, from $70/adults, $30/3–9s. Tickets are available at **www.universalorlando.com** or from the theatre box office (book online for a $10 discount).

BRITTIP

Park in Universal's multi-storey car park for all CityWalk venues – only $5 after 6pm (except during special evening events), free on weekdays after 10pm. For more info, call 407 363 8000.

Bob Marley – A Tribute to Freedom: A clever re-creation of Marley's Jamaica home is turned into a courtyard music venue and restaurant. The bands are excellent, the atmosphere authentic and the place comes alive at night (bar open until 2am, 21 and over only after 9pm; cover charge after 9pm).

The Groove: For club-minded visitors this is a high-tech dance venue designed like a Victorian theatre but with the latest in club music, lighting and special effects (9pm–2am; 21 and over only; attire casual chic, no hats, no tank-tops).

Hard Rock Live: A massive mock-Coliseum styled 2,500-seat theatre with high-tech staging and sound, big-name artists are on stage several times a week (Culture Club, Goo Goo Dolls and the fantastic Classic Albums Live all appeared in 2016) in this slightly retro rock 'n' roll venue (407 351 5483, **www.hardrock.com**).

Jimmy Buffet's Margaritaville: Live music and three bars (11.30am–2am). Band (and cover charge) starts at 10pm.

Red Coconut Club: Retro dance club with a trendy, tropical vibe. Live music, signature cocktails, tapas-style menu and eclectic South Seas décor make it a popular venue (7pm–2am Mon–Sat; 8pm–2am Sun; free admission for ladies on Thurs; 21 and over only). DJ daily, live music Thurs–Sat.

Rising Star Karaoke: It's karaoke taken to the next level and it's hugely entertaining, with a live band, back-up singers, a large selection of songs and a host who makes every volunteer singer feel like a star. There is a full bar with speciality cocktails and appetisers (8pm–2am nightly; 18 and over on Sun–Thurs; 21+ Fri–Sat). Tues–Sat live band, back-up singers and host; back-up singers and host only on Sun and Mon.

NBC Sports Grill & Brew: For a sports bar raised a level, this is perfect for live sporting events (or just a good meal or a drink at one of the two bars). The atmosphere is lively, its own brewery offers great beers and the multi HD TV screens feature multiple views of the action – as well as a giant video screen that covers the front of the building! The food is well above usual sports bar cuisine, though, and even non-sports fans should feel comfortable with the more sophisticated style. We especially like the Devilled Eggs, Cedar-Planked Salmon, Bang-Bang Chicken and succulent barbecue dishes (11am–2pm).

Toothsome Chocolate Emporium & Savory Feast Kitchen: This temple to all things sweet is a work of art, with its steampunk décor and built-in gadgetry, as well as actors playing the roles of Penny Toothsome and robot companion Jaques. The entertainment value is high but the range of milkshakes, sundaes and desserts is dazzling. Look out for the Chocolate x 5 (with five different kinds of chocolate ladled into a milkshake), the S'mores Sundae and their Key Lime Pie. The restaurant will also serve burgers, steak, pasta and seafood, but we're betting you're coming for the sweet stuff! There is also a gift shop (11am–midnight).

Not breathless yet? Well, there's still the 20-screen **Universal Cineplex** with a capacity of 5,000 and the latest in movie comfort. There's also a Meal & Movie Deal for a film and dinner at one of the eight restaurants for $21.95. And, of course, there's the Hollywood Drive-In Golf (p269).

Blue Man Group

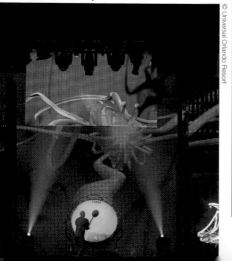

© Universal Orlando Resort

POINTE ORLANDO

This development on I-Drive, almost opposite the Convention Center, is a mix of shops, cinema, restaurants, live entertainment and the WonderWorks fun centre (with its magic-themed dinner show). The Pointe has day and night appeal.

Adobe Gila's: Popular with locals and packed at weekends, it stays open late and features live outdoor music and DJs several days a week. On Fri and Sat lively from 6.30pm on weekdays it's likely to be 8.30pm. (407 903 1477; **www.adobegilas.com**).

BB King's Blues Club: Live jazz and blues make this a fine choice for a meal or drinks and a show in this imaginative venue, featuring a two-storey concert hall and a variety of bars. Live music nightly from 7.30pm with one of its two excellent house bands, plus guests (407 370 4550, **www.bbkingclubs.com**).

Cuba Libre Restaurant and Rum Bar: Offers live Latin music on Fri and Sat nights (**www.cubalibrerestaurant.com**).

Minus 5° Ice Bar: Don a Minus 5° parka or faux fur and a pair of gloves and party until your nose turns blue! The entire bar is made of ice – and so are the glasses – in this deep-freeze setting with LED light show, music and themed ice rooms. (**www.minus5experience.com**).

Orlando Improv Comedy Club and Fat Fish Blue: The Improv pulls in top name comedians from across the US, with shows ranging from mildly risqué to downright raucous. The theatre is intimate, making it easy for entertainers to interact with guests (often with hilarious results) and it is a terrific change of pace for a grown-up night out. Seating is first-come, first-seated, full food and drinks menu available, all shows 21 and over, with two performances on Fri and Sat (no shows Mon and Tues). Connected to the Improv is the bistro-style Fat Fish Blue, featuring American fare with a New Orleans accent. Full bar, a good range of speciality beers, and live music five nights a week. All ages welcome (407 480 5233, **www.theimprovorlando.com**).

Taverna Opa: A lively Greek option, with belly-dancing, other live entertainment and a great ouzo bar! (407 351 8660, **www.opaorlando.com**).

Regal Cinema: A 21-screen movieplex (one an IMAX) that features state-of-the-art stadium seating and sound systems, where you can often see a new film before it arrives in the UK. Ticket office is now inside the cinema lobby. For more on Pointe Orlando, 407 248 9228 or **www.pointeorlando.com**. For more on the restaurant choices, see p320.

DOWNTOWN ORLANDO

Church Street is the epicentre of this nightlife hub, with a wide variety of dining choices (from the distinctive supper-club of **Kres Chophouse** and its elegant bar, the award-winning gastropub-style **Rusty Spoon** and the all-American burger bar frenzy of **Graffiti Junktion** to the full-on German vibe of **Schumann's Jager Haus**, with live entertainment Wed, Fri and Sat), high-energy bars (notably **Don Jefe's Tequila Parlor**, **Dubliner**, **Native Social Bar**, rooftop **Latitudes** and the **Church Street Tavern**), plus cabaret, theatre and live music, making it Party Central at weekends and fairly lively Wed and Thurs, too. The **Church Street Tavern** should appeal to sports fans, along with lively **Harry Buffalo**, while **Lion's Pride**, a soccer-themed pub, should be open later in 2016. Don't miss the eclectic **Mad Cow Theatre**, which presents major plays and theatrical events, including an annual Cabaret Festival (Apr–May; 407 297 8788, **www.madcowtheatre. com**) and the atmospheric **Ceviche** lounge, offering live flamenco dance shows, outstanding cocktails with a Mediterranean twist and an extensive wine list to go with the restaurant's high-end cuisine; (**http://ceviche. com**). **Hamburger Mary's** takes some beating, with its outrageous drag acts and live comedy (distinctly X-rated but lots of fun), to complement its great burgers, sandwiches, decadent desserts and cocktails. They feature Twisted Sisters Bingo on Tues, Trivia with Doug on Weds, the Facebook Friday Show ('an interactive drag show'), Leigh Shannon's Cabaret on

Sat and a Broadway Brunch on Sun (shows variously 6.30–8pm, booking highly advised; 321 319 0600, **http:// hamburgermarys.com/orlando**). Nearby, **Wall Street Plaza**, between Orange Ave and N Court Ave, is equally lively Thurs–Sat as the locals bar-hop the seven bar venues – including live music at Sideshow! (**http://wallstplaza.net**). More downtown entertainment can be had at **The Social**, an indie club staging eclectic bands most nights, plus a busy bar; the **Bosendorfer Lounge**, for great live jazz inside The Grand Bohemian Hotel; and **The Beacham**, a nightclub and concert venue next to The Social. The Speakeasy phenomenon can also be found here, with the 1920s 'hidden bar' style well evidenced by **Hanson's Shoe Repair** (call in advance on 407 476 9446 and they will contact you with the nightly password!) and **The Treehouse** (407 205 2062, **http:// thetreehouseorlando.com**).

Due to open later in 2016 was the first US outlet of the famous British transport café and motorbike centre, the **Ace Café**. Orlando's version, on W Livingston St, will be a large-scale venue featuring live music nightly, multiple bars, special events and gastropub food. Show cars and vintage motorcycle gatherings will be weekly events, with something different each night and concerts on Fri and Sat in The Barn. There will be a huge shop, while the café will feature two kitchens, three bars, a coffee and tea bar and the famous Ace communal counter experience. Food will run the gamut from British classics to American diner dishes. For hours, events and more detail, see **www.acecafeusa.com**.

DINNER SHOWS

Dinner shows are an Orlando phenomenon: live entertainment coupled with dinner and free soft drinks in a fantasy environment, where even the waiters and waitresses are in costume. They have strong family appeal and you are usually seated at large tables where you get to know other people, but at $40–76, they are not cheap (especially with taxes and tips). Be aware, too, of the attempts to extract more from you with photos, souvenirs and upgrades.

BRITTIP
American cinema popcorn is invariably SALTED. Sweet popcorn in the US is usually called Kettle Corn.

Disney shows

Visitors often overlook Walt Disney World's offerings unless they are staying at one of the hotel resorts, but they are worth considering.

Disney's Spirit of Aloha: For an excellent night of South Seas entertainment, go to Luau Cove at Disney's Polynesian Resort. It's a bit expensive at $76 /adults (Category 1 main floor centre seating) and $45/ under-10s; or Cat 2 upper floor and sides $72 and $43; Cat 3 extreme sides or extreme upper level $64 and $38 – but good value as the 2hr show features some splendid entertainment, such as Hawaiian singers and dancers, and an amazing Samoan fire juggler. Tax and gratuity are included. The food is plentiful, with salad, barbecue ribs, roast chicken, pulled pork, vegetables, pineapple and rice, plus a pineapple bread pudding (limited kid-friendly menu). Beer, wine and soft drinks are included, and shows are at 5.15 and 8pm Tues–Sat. Make reservations up to 180 days in advance, with full payment when booking.

Hoop-Dee-Doo Musical Revue: At Disney's Fort Wilderness Resort & Campground, this is a popular nightly dinner show that maintains the resort's Western theme, and has great food (all-you-can-eat ribs, fried chicken, seasonal vegetable, baked beans, corn bread and strawberry

Spirit of Aloha

© Disney

shortcake, plus unlimited beer, wine, sangria and soft drinks). Especially popular with children, it features the amusing song and dance of the Pioneer Hall Players in a merry American hoedown. We're slightly biased but we love this show as it's been running since 1974 and remains a Disney tradition, full of genuine wit and humour, plus a hugely energetic cast that keep things fresh every night. The Revue plays at 5, 7.15 and 9.30pm at the authentic Pioneer Hall, Category 1 seating (main floor centre) is $72/ adults, $43/under-10s; Cat 2 (back and balcony) $67 and $39; Cat 3 (side balconies) $64 and $38 (under-3s free; prices include tax and gratuity) and the show lasts almost two hours. Reservations are ALWAYS necessary and can be made up to 180 days in advance (full payment at booking).

Mickey's Backyard Barbecue: If you can't get enough of the Disney characters, try this dinner show (select dates, Mar–Dec at 6.30pm, at Disney's Fort Wilderness Resort). It features Mickey and the gang in a country buffet-style dinner at picnic tables under an open-air pavilion with live music, line dancing, rope tricks and other entertainment, and plenty of character interaction (great for younger children). The all-you-can-eat buffet offers barbecued pork ribs, baked chicken, hot dogs, hamburgers, macaroni and cheese, ice-cream and more. Like all Disney dining, this is a no-smoking environment. The show may be cancelled if bad weather threatens ($62/adults, $38/3–9s). To book a Disney show, call 407 939 3463.

BRITTIP
Most dinner shows can be quite chilly, especially those with animals, like Medieval Times, so bring a jacket or sweater to beat the air-conditioning.

Medieval Times

Spain in the 11th century is the entertaining setting for this two-hour extravaganza of medieval pageantry, falconry and robust horseback jousts

Pirate's Dinner Adventure

that culminate in furious hand-to-hand combat among six knights. It's worth arriving early to appreciate the clever mock castle design and the staff's costumes as you are ushered into the pre-show hall before being taken into the arena. The show features jousting, sword-fighting and other well-scripted hand-to-hand combats, along with some superb horsemanship, with the basic idea of cheering on one of the Knights of the Realm in the six colour-coded sections. The show also includes a dramatic musical score by award-winning film composer Daniel May, the weapons are all real and used with great skill, and there are some neat special effects. You need to be in full audience participation mode as you cheer on your knight in the traditional good-v-evil scenario, but kids (and many adults) get a huge kick out of it and they'll also love eating without cutlery (the soup bowls do have handles, though!). Soft drinks are included, but alcohol is cash bar only. The elaborate staging is backed up by a succulent chicken, soup, corn and potato dinner (vegetarian meal available) and the serfs and wenches who serve you make it a fun experience. Prices, which include the Medieval Life exhibit, are $62.95/adults and $36.95/3–12s. A basic Royalty Package upgrade for $12/person includes preferred seating, knight's cheering banner, commemorative programme and behind-the-scenes souvenir DVD. The King's Royalty Package adds VIP first-row seating all sections or second row in the centre seating area, plus a framed group photo ($22); and the birthday Celebration Package

adds a group photo per person, VIP seating, programme, banner, DVD, personalised announcement during the show and a slice of cake ($18 more). Doors open 90mins prior to show time. Times vary seasonally, so call 407 396 2900 or visit **www.medievaltimes.com** for reservations and details. The Castle is on Highway 192, 5ml/8km east of the junction with I-4.

If you have 45mins to spare before the show, visit the interesting Medieval Life exhibition. This mock village portrays how they lived 900 years ago (with some gruesome dungeon and torture chamber scenes not for young 'uns!). Stay on after the show (2nd show only on busy nights) for a meet-and-greet with the Knights.

Pirates' Dinner Adventure

This show, sub-titled Rise of the Sea Dragon, features one of the most spectacular settings, with a life-size pirate ship 'anchored' in a huge indoor lagoon – and a giant animatronic dragon! It delivers good value with its pre-show elements, plentiful food, soft drinks and beer

Hoop-Dee-Doo Musical Revue

(with the main show, plus a cash bar during the pre-show). A kids' meal choice (chicken fingers or mac and cheese) is available if the hearty main meal of pot roast or chicken with mash and seasonal vegetables, or vegetarian pasta doesn't appeal. The story starts in period style at the Seaport Village where the Governor's annual gala is taking place, with entertainment provided by the magic and stories of Raddu the gypsy king before guests are spirited off to the pirates' realm. Here, Captain Sebastian the Black is preparing to raid Treasure Bay for the booty that awaits him if he can get past the fearsome sea serpent that guards the way. The evil captain thinks he can win the day with a royal sacrifice, but the kind-hearted Benjamin Blue is ready to save the imperilled princess, even if it means fighting off the whole band of scurvy pirates. That's the cue for all manner of songs, duels, acrobatics, fights and trapeze acts with plenty of audience participation and cheering. Highly family friendly and a big hit with kids ($67.95/adults, $41.45/3–11s, includes one round of beer or two of soft drinks during the show; see website for savings).

There is a Treasure Experience upgrade that adds 2nd-row seating, guaranteed pirate interaction, unlimited soda and beer during the show, and gift shop discount ($25 extra); a Governor's VIP Upgrade ($30) adds exclusive pre-show lounge, restroom and cash bar, front-row seating, special appetiser buffet, and champagne toast; or a Captain's Upgrade ($15) with third row seating, and discounts at the gift shop. It is located on Carrier Drive between I-Drive and Universal Boulevard, and runs at 7.30pm or 8.30pm, with appetisers served for 45mins prior to seating (407 206 5102, **www.piratesdinneradventure.com**). There is a fee for parking but also a special Pirates Christmas Dinner Adventure show, which adds festive themes.

Sleuth's Mystery Dinner Shows

This is a live version of Cluedo acted out before your eyes in hilarious fashion while you enjoy a substantial meal with a main course choice of honey-glazed poussin (Cornish hen), lasagne with or without meatballs (or, for $6 extra, prime rib) and unlimited beer, wine and soft drinks. You can choose between three theatres and 12 different plot situations (several of which have amusing British settings), including Squires Inns, Roast 'Em & Toast 'Em and Lord Mansfield's Fox Hunt Banquet (mayhem at an English banquet), that add up to some elaborate murder mysteries. The action takes place all around you and members of the audience can take some cameo roles. The quick-witted cast keep things moving and keep you guessing during the theatrical part of the 2½-hour show, then during the main part of dinner you think up questions for interrogation (but the real murderer is allowed to lie!). Solve the crime and you win a prize, but that is pretty secondary to the overall enjoyment and this is a show we enjoy a lot, plus it's a terrific choice with teens ($61.95/adults, $28.95/3–11s; times vary; 407 363 1985, **www.sleuths.com**). Also check out their periodic Stand Up Comedy Spotlight (see website for dates, times, and comedians). Sleuth's is in the plaza just past Ripley's Believe It Or Not on I-Drive, with three theatres, a smart pre-dinner bar area and gift shop.

WonderWorks: Outta Control Magic Comedy

This smaller-scale dinner show is at WonderWorks on I-Drive (at Pointe Orlando). A novel mixture of improvised comedy and magic, with all-you-can-eat pizza, salad, popcorn and dessert, plus beer, wine and Coke. Set in the intimate Shazam Theater, it features live music, special lighting from illusionist (and funny guy) Tony

Brent served up with style and plenty of audience participation, especially if you sit close to the stage. Twice nightly at 6pm and 8pm, it costs a good-value $29.99/adults, $19.99/4–12s and seniors. A Magic Combo ticket for the show and access to WonderWorks (open until midnight, p236) is $49/$38 (407 351 8800, **www.wonderworksonline.com**).

Capone's Dinner & Show

This 1930s gangland version of *Chicago* is home to Al himself and a 'family gathering' that goes hopelessly wrong. Try to keep track of local gangster Fingers Salvatorio and his ditzy wife, Bunny-June, as they look to provide for Fingers Jnr, aka Little Pinky, and fail miserably, causing all manner of mayhem for the hapless parents, Bunny-June's sisters Babs and Bubbles, and a vengeful – if slightly dim – beat cop, ex-detective Marvel. The audience can often be at the centre of the action and there is a hilarious 'shoot-out' finale. A huge Italian-American buffet offers pasta, meatballs, pizza, salad bar, a carvery and side dishes. Unlimited Bud Light, a selection of wines and cocktails, plus soft drinks, juice, Kiddie Cocktails and Mama Capone's 'dessert surprise' round out the all-you-can-eat-and-drink menu ($66/ adults, $44/4–12s, 3 and under free; 407 397 2378, **www.alcapones.com**).

BRITBONUS

Mention your **Brit Guide** and receive 50% off the General Admission for Capone's Dinner Show, plus $1 off per paid ticket. Not valid for New Year's Eve Gala.

Live music

Orlando's live music scene is lively and always changing but several venues can be relied on for quality entertainment. As already noted, the House of Blues and Hard Rock Live provide regular big-name concerts, while international acts appear at the state-of-the-art **Amway Center** in downtown (as well as the Orlando Magic, Orlando Predators and Orlando Solar Bears sports teams), including Selena Gomez and Def Leppard in 2016 (**www.amwaycenter.com**).

The new **Dr Phillips Performing Arts Center** also features big-name concert performers as well as touring Broadway performances and the Orlando Ballet company (1844 513 2014, **www.drphillipscenter.org**).

Sports bars

The sports bar is an American invention and if you'd like to sample the way the locals follow their sport (American football is usually the biggest at weekends Sept–Jan, but basketball is also popular along with baseball and ice-hockey) try these locations.

Orlando Ale House Group: Among the multitude of sports bars, one of our favourites has fine examples on Kirkman Road, opposite Universal Studios (407 248 0000) at Lake Buena Vista on Highway 535 near Disney Springs (407 239 1800), on I-Drive (407 370 6688) and the Kissimmee location on Highway 192 (407 238 4499). The Ale Houses feature more than 30 TVs (each!), classic American bar food, including their signature spicy 'chicken zingers' and an above-average range of beers (**www.millersalehouse.com**).

Buffalo Wild Wings: Another chain worth noting has five Orlando locations (notably on I-Drive, 407 351 6200; Lake Buena Vista near Disney Springs, 407 827 0444; and I-Drive 360, 407 413 5115), where

Sleuth's Mystery Dinner Show

masses of chicken-orientated dishes (watch out for the Blazin' sauce – it's seriously hot!) are served up in a casual, lively atmosphere, highlighted by its Buzztime Trivia System at each table and multiple big-screen TVs (**www.buffalowildwings.com**).

Other options: Also look out for the revamped **Uno Chicago** chain (**www. unos.com**) or any **TGI Fridays**, **Graffiti Junktion** or **BJ's Brewhouse** outlet. Then there are **The Pub** and **Marlow's Tavern**, both at Pointe Orlando (p319). In the Dellagio complex on Sand Lake Road, **Miller's Field House** is the place to visit.

Disney boasts the excellent **ESPN Club** at Disney's BoardWalk Resort, a full-service restaurant with sports broadcast facilities, video games, more than 70 TV monitors, giant scoreboards and even a Little League menu for kids.

Universal CityWalk boasts **NBC Sports Grill & Brew**, with more big-screen TV style and exceptional food in an elegant and comfortable atmosphere even non-sports fans will enjoy. By Mall at Millennia, give **Duffy's Sports Grill** a try or, for possibly the most impressive TV screen, **Wreckers Sports Bar** at the grand Gaylord Palms resort takes some beating (as does its food). For something different, **Dewey's Indoor Golf & Sports Grill** has terrific appeal with its golf simulators, as well as plenty of TVs and good food. The various British-style pubs also offer sports-bar style. Try the **Orlando George & Dragon** on I-Drive (**www.orlandogeorgeanddragon. com**) and **Frankie Farrell's Irish Pub** at Lake Buena Vista Resort & Spa (next to the Factory Stores).

Something different

Icebar: Spend 45mins surrounded by 50 tons of carved ice while sipping a chilled vodka beverage, then warm up in the Nordic-inspired Fire Lounge, at this fun venue on I-Drive just north of WonderWorks. Coats and gloves are provided or you can upgrade to a glam mock fur coat for

$10, and entry fee is $19.95 (drinks not included; save 25% by booking online). Open 5pm–12am Sun–Wed, 5pm–1am Thurs, 5pm–2am Fri–Sat, with the first ICEBAR entry time at 5.15pm; ages eight and up allowed 5pm–9pm only. No cover charge for Fire Lounge (which also features DJs), but no children. Happy Hour 7–9pm Sat–Thurs, and Expedition Package at $29.95, including one premium drink in ICEBAR and one in Fire Lounge (407 426 0361 or **www.icebarorlando.com**).

$ BRITBONUS
Pay for entry to the Icebar and receive a FREE pint in the Fire Lounge afterwards. Just show your copy of the *Brit Guide* for the free drink.

Howl at the Moon: If you're looking for a serious party, try Howl at the Moon on I-Drive, where the live music doesn't stop until the wee hours! An energetic piano-playing duo pound out a rockin' good time, highlighted by 'Showtime', when the whole bar joins in a choreographed dance-fest. Cocktails are available by the glass or the bucket(!), with drink specials nightly (21 and over only; 7pm–2am Sun–Thurs and Sat, 6pm–2am Fri; cover charge $5 Mon–Wed, $7 Thurs, $10 Fri and Sat, $7 Sun; 407 354 5999, **www.howlatthemoon.com**).

Now you'll want to know a lot more about where, when and how to tackle that other holiday dilemma – where to eat. Read on…

Icebar

11 Dining Out

or Eat, Drink and Eat Again!

Orlando dazzles with its attractions, delights with its quality and bewilders with its quantity and variety. And that is also true when it comes to dining. There has never been more choice, in more ways and more alternatives than ever before. Hold on to your waistbands, we're going in....

Variety

The diversity of food on offer, from fast-food counters to five-star gourmet experiences, is now Orlando's speciality.

Chain restaurants are seemingly everywhere, and you need to know your Applebees from your Sweet Tomatoes. But, at the same time, there are a range of one-off restaurants of all kinds that maintain the local tradition for convenience, value and superiority.

As a rule, food is plentiful, relatively cheap, available 24 hours a day, and nearly always appetising and filling. You will find an increasing number of fine-dining possibilities, but the basic emphasis is on value, so unless we have marked somewhere as 'pricey', you'll find prices are fairly consistent. Portions are large, service is efficient and friendly, and it's hard to come by a bad meal. The one real exception is if you dine mainly at fast-food places and the likes of Dennys and Co, you won't find much fresh veg. But if you look up the vegetarian options, visit outlets like Sweet Tomatoes or ask for the vegetable option instead of fries or potatoes at other restaurants, you will find a balanced choice. Plus, salads are almost always on the menu.

Exceptional deals

Most restaurants tend towards the informal (T-shirts and shorts are nearly always acceptable) and cater readily for families; you will always find a kids' menu, and many have activity packs. Many hotels and restaurants offer Kids-eat-free deals (from under-10 to under-14), provided parents are also dining. The age limits vary. The all-you-can-eat buffet is another common feature, where you can probably eat enough at breakfast to keep you going to dinner! Some places offer early-bird specials for dining before 5.30pm as 5.30–7.30pm is peak time for most restaurants. You may have a wait if you arrive between 6 and 8pm.

BRITTIP

Portions are often so large, you can save money by sharing a main course. Your waiter or waitress should be happy to oblige (but keep their tip up to the full rate).

Don't be afraid to ask for the leftovers 'to go' and don't hesitate to say if something isn't right; the locals will readily complain (politely) if they are not happy, so restaurants are keen to ensure everything is to their diners' satisfaction. And, please, don't forget to tip; the basic wage for waiters and waitresses is low, so they rely heavily on tips as part of their income and are taxed on an assumed level of tips. Unless service really is shoddy (in which case mention it), the usual tip rate is 10% of your bill at buffet-style restaurants and 15–20% at full-service restaurants. Check if service is already added to your bill, though this isn't common.

You will encounter a huge range of food types. Florida is renowned for its seafood, which comes much cheaper than in the Mediterranean: crab, lobster, shrimp (what we call king prawns), scallops and oysters, as well as several dozen varieties of fish, many unusual (like mahi mahi and grouper). Latin-style cuisines, notably Cuban and Mexican, are common, and the South American influences mean the delicious citrus-marinated seafood called ceviche is often featured. There is also plenty of Asian fare, from Chinese and Indian to Japanese, Thai and Vietnamese.

The big shopping malls all offer good-value food courts. 'Cracker' cooking is original Floridian fare, and the speciality is alligator, either stewed, barbecued, smoked, sautéed or braised. Fried gator tail 'nuggets' are a local favourite, as are catfish and frogs' legs. And do try key lime pie!

◄ BRITTIP

An excellent section of the All Ears website run by Deb Wills lists places that cater for special diets, including veggie, at **www.allearsnet.com/din/special.htm**. Many restaurants now offer gluten-free options, too.

Vegetarian options

In a country where beef is king, vegetarians often find themselves hard done by. However, there are some bright spots. Most good-quality restaurants should provide a veggie option and are usually happy to provide something even if it's not on the menu. All Disney's full-service restaurants will be able to oblige, and most at Universal, too. There are also several vegetarian restaurants, including the Indian cuisine of **Woodlands** on S Orange Blossom Trail (407 854 3330, **www.woodlandsusa. com**; closed Mon); **Ethos Vegan Kitchen** (407 228 3898, **www.ethosvegankitchen.com**); and **Daya** (407 636 9461, **www.dayarestaurant.com**) both in Winter Park; **Sanctum** in the trendy Mills 50 district east of downtown (407 757 0346, **http://thesanctumcafe.com/**); and the bohemian **Market On South**, in Orlando's Milk District (407 613 5968, **www.marketonsouth.com**).

More mainstream is **Sweet Tomatoes,** with six outlets in the main tourist areas, notably on I-Drive by Kirkman Road; in the Crossroads Plaza at Lake Buena Vista; and just off West Highway 192 in Kissimmee on Rolling Oaks Blvd. It is a buffet restaurant and is not totally vegetarian, but most of its fare – salads, soups, pastas, breads and desserts – are either veggie or vegan, and all is clearly labelled.

◄ BRITTIP

Sweet Tomatoes is a restaurant chain we recommend highly, and you can benefit from its enhanced dinner menu by arriving a little before 4pm but still paying only the lunch buffet price.

The all-you-can-eat lunch is $9.99, dinner (after 4pm) is $11.99, and both include the vast salad counter, freshly made soups, pizza, pasta, bread and pastries, plus fruit and frozen yoghurt. Drinks are $2.99 (refills free) and kids' meals are $4.29 3–6s and $6.29 7–12s. Some locations now serve breakfast 8–11am Sat-Sun, $8–10/person (11am–9pm Sun–Thurs, 11am– 10pm Fri–Sat; **www.souplantation.com**).

The **Panera Bread** chain also offers some decent veg options (and free wi-fi).

Drinking

Looking for a good beer or cocktail? Orlando definitely has you covered. You can run a tab in the majority of bars and pay when you leave. But be aware US licensing laws are stricter

Belly up to the bar!

If you'd like just a snack or sample of a restaurant's fare, many places offer a bar or appetiser menu, including Bar Louie, Big Fin Seafood, Bongos Cuban Café, Bravo, Bonefish Grill, Capital Grille, Carrabba's, Cask and Larder, Eddie V's, Emeril's Tchoup Chop, Fishbones, Fleming's, Hillstone, House of Blues, Kres Chophouse, Luma on Park, Moonfish, Morton's, The Oceanaire, Old Hickory, Paddlefish, Portobello, Rainforest Café, Ravenous Pig, Roy's, Seasons 52, Texas de Brazil, Tommy Bahama Café and T-Rex Café, plus Brio Tuscan Grille (weekdays only, in the bar), Landry's Seafood House (3–6pm Mon–Thurs) and The Palm (5–7pm Sun–Fri).

than ours and you MUST be 21 to drink alcohol in a bar or lounge. You'll often be asked for proof of age before you are served (or allowed into a club), so take your passport or photo driving licence. No arguing: no photo ID, no beer!

Ice: Drinks usually come with a LOT of ice. If you want your whisky (or vodka, etc) without ice, ask for it 'straight up'. If you prefer soft drinks without the usual iceberg, ask for 'no ice' or 'light ice'.

Spirits: Called 'liquor' in the US, these come in a large selection, but beware of ordering just 'whisky' as you'll get bourbon. Specify if you want Scotch or Irish whiskey.

Cocktails: There is a massive choice of cocktails and most bars and restaurants have lengthy happy hours with good prices.

BRITTIP
Possibly the best Happy Hour deal is at swish **Seasons 52**, which offers a small-plate menu at $5/item 4–6.30pm Mon–Fri, plus select wines at $6/glass and cocktails $6–8.

Wines: Good-quality Californian wines are better value than European.

Soft drinks: If you stick to 'sodas' or coffee, most bars and restaurants give free refills.

Dollar Off Drinks Card: This new programme does exactly what it says – provides a dollar off drinks (beer, wine, cocktails, sodas, tea and coffee) at more than 60 bars and restaurants around Orlando. It costs $15 for a month's use per person ($25 for six months, $40 for a year), valid on all full-priced drinks (not happy hour or other specials), and can be used with *every* drinks order, so you could save $41 if you used it just four times a day for two weeks (potentially a lot more with greater use or a longer visit). Look up more at **www.dollaroffdrinks.com.**

BRITBONUS
Order one **Dollar Off Drinks** card and get a second FREE with your *Brit Guide*. Just use the code BRITS17 in the 'Apply Coupon' box when ordering online.

Breweries

There's a rapidly growing craft beer scene, with new breweries seemingly popping up all the time. American big-label beers (Budweiser, Coors and Miller Lite) leave a lot to be desired in taste terms, hence there has been big growth in alternatives both large and small. National brands like Sam Adams, Leinenkugel's, Yuengling, Goose Island, Blue Moon, Shock Top and Kona are all well worth trying but, for the aficionado, there is now a great local source of beer enjoyment, with both brew-pubs and full-on breweries open to the public. There are even tours (see Brewlando Tours, p266) to showcase the best of Central Florida's brewers. To sample a great range of craft beers (and most places offer flights as well as pints), try any of the following.

Bowigens Beer Company: This Casselberry brewery and taproom offers 10 drafts and more than 20 bottled beers at any one time, including their staples like a Citrus Pale Ale, 7 Layer Stout and Peanut Butter Hefeweizen (yes, really!). Open daily, you are welcome to bring in food from their six neighbour breweries (5–10pm Mon–Thurs, 3pm–midnight Fri, noon–midnight Sat, 3–10pm Sun; 407 960 7816, **www.bowigens.com**).

Crooked Can: In the new Plant Street Market in Winter Garden is this boutique brewery that produces a wide range, including a Belgian Golden Ale, Chocolate Stout and tasty Cider. Their onsite tap and tasting room is open 11am–11pm Sun–Thurs and 11am–2am Fri and Sat, with food available from any of the neighbouring market stalls, and tours each Sun noon–4pm ($10/person, including one 9oz/250ml pour and a souvenir glass; 407 395 9520, **www.crookedcan.com**).

The Hourglass Brewery: Established in 2012 in the suburb of Longwood, this brewer has a reputation for unique beers – notably a barrel-aged selection – as well as flagship, year-round ales like the Belgian Saison and Frankie Rock hefeweizen (11am–midnight Mon–Thurs, 11am–2am Fri and Sat, 11am–midnight Sun; 407 262 0056, **http://thehourglassbrewery.com/**).

Ocean Sun: New in 2016 was this brewery and taproom with another imaginative range, including a great Porter, Kolsch and Westende, a fusion of Belgian Trippel ale and pale ale styles (3–11pm Mon and Tues, noon–11pm Wed and Thurs, noon–1am Fri and Sat, noon–11pm Sun, 407 745 5551, **www.oceansunbrewing.com**).

Orlando Brewing Co: The oldest and biggest, and an organic brewer to boot, they feature a huge range of annual and seasonal beers, from pale ales to stouts and porters, with more than 20 at any time. Just south of downtown (in an awkward location, but worth finding), they offer an excellent taproom (3–10pm Mon–Thurs, 1pm–midnight Fri and Sat, 1–9pm Sun) and free tours Mon–Sat at 6pm (407 872 1117, **www.orlandobrewing.com**).

Red Cypress Brewery: A relative newcomer in Winter Springs, this uses a lot of local ingredients in beers like its Devil's Chair IPA and Spook Hill Pale Ale (2–11pm Mon–Thurs, 2pm–midnight Fri, noon–midnight Sat, noon–9pm Sun; 407 542 0341, **http://redcypressbrewery.com/**).

Redlight Redlight: Celebrating its 11th anniversary in 2016 is this Winter Park success story, with a regularly changing array of craft beers, lagers, cider and even barley wine, though they specialise in sour and wild beers. The taproom also features beers from other US brewers (5pm–2am daily, 407 893 9832, **www. redlightredlightbeerparlour.com**).

Ten10 Brewing: This lively brewer is in the heart of the Mills 50 district, hence popular with the locals for its tempting range, including a tasty Plum Fennel Farmhouse Ale and superbly sweet Sundae Best Brown. Their small-plate menu is good, too (4.30pm–midnight Mon–Thurs, 4.30pm–1am Fri, 11.30am–1am Sat, 11.30am–10pm Sun; 407 930 8993, **www.ten10brewingcompany.com**).

BRITTIP

If there are several of you drinking beer, ordering a pitcher will work out cheaper than buying it by the glass.

Brew-pubs

These are also extremely popular and can be found in growing numbers, offering their own craft beers and surprisingly good food. The pick of the bunch include the superb **Cask & Larder** in Winter Park; **Big River Grille & Brewing Works** at Disney's Boardwalk Resort; **NBC Sports Grill & Brew** at Universal's CityWalk; **BJ's Restaurant & Brewhouse** in five Central Florida locations (**www.bjs restaurants.com**); **Seadog Brewing Company** in Lake Buena Vista; **The Yardhouse** at I-Drive 360; and the chic **Whisper Creek Farm: The Kitchen** at the smart JW Marriott hotel at the Grande Lakes Resort.

Magical Dining Month

Orlando has become a foodie's paradise in recent years and, to celebrate, each Sept is dedicated as **Magical Dining Month**, with an array of special events and a selection of top restaurants offering a three-course prix fixe menu at $33/head, a great saving on regular prices. These have included A Land Remembered (Rosen Shingle Creek), Seasons 52, and Emeril's Tchoup Chop. Check out more at **www.visitorlando.com/ magicaldining**.

Who's who

Despite the emerging foodie culture, most restaurants you encounter in the main tourist areas will still be the big chains, so here is a run-down of who they are (apart from the obvious fast-food places like McDonalds, KFC, Subway, Wendy's, etc).

Fast food: A few notable US additions to the burger scene, with a more distinctive touch, include BurgerFi, Five Guys Burgers & Fries, Fuddruckers, Steak 'n Shake and the fun drive-in option of Sonic.

Breakfast-style: Serving throughout the day but with a speciality for breakfast, and none of them serving alcohol: Bob Evans, Cracker Barrel, Dennys, First Watch, Friendly's, IHOP, Keke's Breakfast Café, Panera Bread, Perkins, Village Inn, Waffle House.

BRITTIP

American bacon is always streaky and crisp fried, and sausages are chipolata-like and slightly spicy. Very different from the British versions.

Buffet style: The all-you-can-eat options; cheap and cheerful: CiCi's Pizza, Golden Corral, Ponderosa, Shoney's and the excellent Sweet Tomatoes.

Bar-restaurant style: The full American dining experience, with typical bar food and drinks: Applebee's; Bahama Breeze (with a Caribbean twist); BJ's Brewhouse (wide-ranging menu and craft beers); Buffalo Wild Wings and Orlando/ Miller's Ale House (both in sports bar territory); Cheesecake Factory (a huge menu, and decadent desserts); Chevys, Chilis and Chuys (all with Tex-Mex flavours); Hooters (with their 'Hooter Girl' waitresses); Manny's Chophouse (a local favourite); Red Robin (for some of the best burgers in town); Shake Shack (a lot more than just great milkshakes!); TGI Friday's (eclectic American style); Uno Pizzeria & Grill (with a more upmarket touch).

Steakhouse style: Where you'll get a really good steak, but also fish, chicken and salads: Capital Grille (the fancy touch); Charley's Steakhouse (also with a deluxe ambience); Logan's Roadhouse; Lone Star Steakhouse; Longhorn Steakhouse; Morton's Steakhouse (the sophisticated touch); Outback Steakhouse (Brit-popular and consistently good value); Ruth's Chris Steakhouse (another superb upmarket choice); Sonny's Real Pit Bar-B-Q (with the accent on barbecue everything); and Tony Roma's (especially good for ribs).

Italian flavours: With classic Italian menus: Brio Tuscan Grille (one of the best); Carrabba's; Macaroni Grill; Maggiano's; Little Italy; Olive Garden.

Seafood specials: Where you can indulge in the full range of Floridian specialities like grouper and stone crabs: Bonefish Grill (with an upmarket touch); Boston Lobster Feast (pile 'em high!); Joe's Crab Shack (family-friendly style); Red Lobster.

Where to eat

That gives you the inside track on HOW to eat and drink like the locals. Now you need to know WHERE. There are 4,000-plus restaurants in the area, so the following selection covers the main ones, grouped by area.

As with most things Orlando, we start with Walt Disney World.

DISNEY DINING

Having said how Orlando is dominated by chain restaurants, you'll find little evidence of that in Walt Disney World, apart from one McDonalds near the All Star resorts; Earl of Sandwich, Starbucks, Planet Hollywood and

Disney's California Grill

© Disney

House of Blues at Disney Springs; and niche upmarket names like Morimoto, Wolfgang Puck, Todd English and Shula's Steakhouse. Some of the most distinctive dining is from Disney's own creative team around the resorts, and we strongly recommend trying at least one of them.

Animal Kingdom Lodge: Jiko is one of Disney's finest dining choices, with a creative new world fusion cuisine boasting hints of Africa, India and the Mediterranean, as well as a superb South African wine list. **Sanaa** has similar African-Asian influences, but with more accent on Indian food and a couple of great curry dishes, all with a view over the animal savannah. For families, **Boma** is the ideal buffet choice, with a fabulous array of different dishes, both exotic and more familiar, and it's a great opportunity to sample more unusual offerings – as well as tasty desserts, like Boma's signature Zebra Domes (an Amarula mousse dome covered with a chocolate ganache and striped like a zebra).

Contemporary Resort: The **California Grill** is the classic rooftop dining experience, with spectacular Pacific-coast flavours, including superb sushi and an amazing Sunday Brunch (with the price tag to match); **The Wave** offers another take on

Jiko

© Disney

modern American cuisine in stylish surroundings, with a great cocktail bar, and not quite so much of the expense.

Disney's Boardwalk Inn: There is more wonderful seafood on offer at the **Flying Fish** (heavily remodelled in 2016 with eye-catching décor and cocktail lounge), where the culinary team serve up some of the best seafood in Orlando.

Trattoria al Forno; Features classic Italian cuisine with regional specialities like Venetian mussels and Milanese osso buco, as well as excellent desserts and an all-Italian wine list.

Grand Floridian: First-class seafood is on offer at gorgeous waterfront restaurant **Narcoossee's**, which is a great special-occasion choice, if a touch pricey; **Citricos** offers fine dining with a Mediterranean-infused twist; and **Victoria & Albert's** is Disney's crème-de-la-crème, a superb gourmet experience with white-glove service and New American cuisine.

Polynesian Village Resort: The full South Seas dining experience is on display at **'Ohana**, where food is served family-style, with large plates of food for the whole table, and as much as you can eat; **Kona Café** also offers a Polynesian and Asian-tinged menu but with a more sophisticated ambience.

Swan and Dolphin: The choice here is dazzling, from the elegant supper-club style of **Shula's Steakhouse** to the classic Italian of **Il Mulino**, an upmarket New York trattoria with lashings of style. Japanese cuisine and excellent sushi is on offer at **Kimonos**, where the Kobe beef and duck satay are outstanding, and there is also karaoke nightly. Todd English's **bluezoo** is another sumptuous seafood choice, both for the décor and the cuisine, as well as another wonderful bar area and wine list.

Wilderness Lodge: A great fine-dining experience is on offer at **Artist Point,** where steaks and seafood are superbly cooked and presented in elegant surroundings with a Pacific North-West culinary touch; **Whispering Canyon Café** is a rowdy, family-style

Our Disney Hotel Top 10

For a special evening, try dinner at any of these fabulous venues:

1 Jiko
2 Bluezoo
3 Victoria & Albert's
4 California Grill
5 Shula's Steakhouse
6 Narcoossee's
7 Artist Point
8 Yachtsman Steakhouse
9 Sanaa
10 Flying Fish

restaurant, where the food has an Old West style and is served family-style to ensure no-one goes hungry.

Yacht & Beach Club: Fine dining is on offer at the **Yachtsman Steakhouse**, where succulent steaks are the order of the day, as well as fine seafood and gracious service. It's not a cheap option but the quality is unarguable. **Cape May Café** is themed like a New England beachfront, with the seafood to match, served buffet style and with the kind of quality you expect.

That is the full range of signature dining at Disney resorts, but there are a handful of smaller gems worth noting. The Caribbean Beach Resort has **Shutters**, where American favourites are given a Caribbean twist and the quality is well above average (try the seared sea scallops or island pasta) while, at Coronado Springs, **Maya Grill** has a Latin-infused menu that excites the tastebuds and elevates dining beyond the norm. Finally, the eye-catching **Boatwrights** at Port Orleans serves up tastes of Louisiana in its heavily themed interior, including fabulous jambalaya and catfish.

Disney Springs

With all the new development in this area, the dining choice now is immense. Going through all four areas by turn, here's your choice.

Just remember you're paying for the scenery and ambience as well as the food.

The Landing

The Boathouse: New in 2015, this is nautically themed, with the obvious focus on great seafood, but also excellent chicken, chops, salads, raw bar and some of the best steaks in Florida. A well-presented kids' menu is also available, and the presentation is stylish. There are three bars, outdoor dining, live music, gift shop, boat rides and a water view from each dining room, which makes for memorable dining, but with the price tag to match (11am–11pm, 407 939 2628).

BRITTIP
The signature dessert at The Boathouse is the eye-popping S'Mores Baked Alaska. It costs $40 but it will easily feed a family of four – or more!

The Edison: This imposing new nightclub/restaurant (set to open in early 2017) will be a big draw for its cabaret and live music, but it also promises memorable cuisine, with a range of artisanal snacks, small plates, flatbreads, sandwiches and charcuterie to go with their immense range of cocktails. The style should be upmarket and lively, with a 1930s vibe and wildly imaginative design and décor.

Homecoming – Florida Kitchen & Shine Bar: Celebrity chef Art Smith brings true Florida cooking to Disney in this elaborately rustic setting, with a glass-walled show kitchen. Smith specialises in genuine old-time 'Cracker' fare, with a modern twist and all fresh local ingredients.

The Boathouse

Treat yourself to his cheese-laced drop biscuits, fried chicken, and shrimp and grits, plus the signature cakes and fresh fruit cobblers for dessert. The adjacent Shine Bar offers wonderful coolers, cocktails and punches, many based on varieties of moonshine (11am–11pm daily).

Jock Lindsey's Hangar Bar: This Indiana Jones-themed lounge bar is packed with eye-catching novelties, as well as great cocktails, but it also serves up some excellent small-plate meals, like the Rolling Boulder Sliders and Lao Che's Revenge – superbly spicy chicken wings; (11.30am–midnight Sun–Thurs, midnight Fri and Sat).

Morimoto Asia: Another newcomer in 2015 was the Pan-Asian style of Chef Masaharu Morimoto (of TV's *Iron Chef* fame), which puts the emphasis on Japanese cuisine, seafood and elaborate sushi offerings in a sleek two-storey setting. Exhibition kitchens, a contemporary cocktail lounge and patio dining add to the ambiance, while the menu features classics such as Peking Duck and Dim Sum, plus plenty of contemporary twists. Definitely a special-occasion night out. A 'Street Foods' patio window also serves small-scale tastes of many main dishes (11.30am–midnight Mon–Thurs, 1am Fri–Sun; 407 939 2628; **www.patinagroup.com/morimoto-asia**).

BRITTIP
Even if you only sample them from the Street Foods window, make sure you taste Morimoto's Spare Ribs, deep-fried with a hoisin sweet chilli glaze –out-of-this-world and perfect for sharing, either as a half-rack starter or full-rack main course.

Paddlefish: The former Fulton's Crabhouse (and Empress Lilly before that) has been re-imagined with a stern-to-bow makeover that gives it a smart new look to go with its excellent seafood menu. A fun addition is lobster guacamole made tableside with Maine Lobster, chillies, coriander and lime, while the Sunday Brunch is also excellent. It's not cheap but the rooftop lounge is worth checking out just for a drink.

Paradiso 37: This 'Taste of the Americas' offers a wide variety of foods, much with a Latin-tinged flavour, and live music nightly. A tempting menu includes Argentinean skirt steak, Chilean salmon, Mexican fare, plus cocktails and tequila. The lively style, split-level restaurant, chic bar area (inside and out) and lakeside setting mark this out for a relaxing lunch or upbeat dinner, or just somewhere to kick back with a drink or speciality coffee (11am–11pm Sun–Thurs, midnight Fri and Sat, bar until 2am; 407 934 3700, **www.paradiso37.com**).

Portobello: Don't overlook this Tuscan trattoria for a great dining experience. From the fresh bread with oven-baked garlic to the family-style menu and full wine list, there's everything from pizza to zucchini ribbons in a tomato seafood broth. We are big fans of their insistence on locally sourced fresh produce, and it really shines through in the great taste of things like the Rigatoni and Black Linguini with Florida Rock Shrimp (11.30am–11pm; 407 934 8888, **www.portobellorestaurant.com**).

BRITTIP
For a great light lunch at Portobello, try the antipasti platter ($21), which serves two. Their Cafe Shakerato (Italian iced coffee) is also a real treat.

Raglan Road: This Irish-themed pub, with lively music, food to match and a genuine Emerald Isle style, is where you really can enjoy the craic. Much of the restaurant's interior was shipped over from Ireland (including four reclaimed 130-year-old bars), establishing an authentic backdrop to an original menu created by celebrity master chef Kevin Dundon. Fresh, simple ingredients with an imaginative twist: shepherd's pie, mussels, beef stew, Irish sausages, plus excellent curries, a range of original sandwiches at lunchtime and a Portobello mushroom vegetarian entrée. They also feature a great weekend brunch and special dining events, and it's not too taxing on the wallet (11am–11pm, bar menu to 1am, 407 938 0300, **www.raglanroad.com**).

STK Orlando: This fabulous take on steakhouse chic opened in summer 2016, with the STK group bringing vibrant, edgy style to a traditional area, combining restaurant and lounge (with great cocktails). Instead of dark, brooding and formal, STK goes for bright, playful and innovative (including a live DJ), with a creative touch to the décor and a decadent depth to their flavours. Rooftop dining – perfect for warm Floridian evenings – is another feature, along with trendy menu items that include grilled octopus, spiced duck breast and seared foie gras, along with large, medium and small steaks, plus some sizzling signature cocktails (11.30am–11pm Sun–Thurs, midnight Fri, Sat; 407 917 7440, **http://togrp.com/restaurant/stk-orlando/**).

Other choices: To one side of Raglan Road is **Cookes of Dublin**, a chippie serving up real chips, beer-battered fish, gourmet battered sausages and 'Do bars' (deep-fried Snickers bars!). Chocolate lovers will want to make a bee-line for **The Ganachery** for some superb confectionery, including Disney character themed chocolate lollipops! Fabulous Italian-style ice cream is on offer at **Vivoli Il Gelato** (direct from Florence) or head to **Tea Trader's Café by Joffreys** for a really good cuppa.

BRITTIP
For reservations at any Disney restaurant, call 407 939 3463 (407 WDW DINE), or book online at **www.disneyworld.co.uk**.

The Marketplace
While The Marketplace is largely a shopping area (p328), it also offers tempting dining.

Rainforest Café: With its safari-style 'adventures' under a spectacular volcano-topped exterior (that belches fire and smoke!), this is the place to entertain the family while they fill up on huge platefuls of chicken, pasta, steak, seafood and burgers, surrounded by audio-animatronic animals and periodic 'rainstorms', with an excellent kids menu. The Lava Lounge features small-plate appetisers from the main menu, great cocktails and other drink specials in a lakeside setting (11am–10.30pm Sun–Thurs, 11.30pm Fri–Sat; 407 827 8500, **www.rainforestcafe.com**).

T-Rex Café: Enter an audio-animatronic prehistoric world, with a vast series of themed areas like the Ice Cave and Jurassic Forest, which are home to all manner of roaring dinos, with meteor strikes and thunderstorms for good measure! The food is straightforward (albeit with fancy names like Woolly Mammoth Chicken and Boneyard Buffet) but portions are large and it is also somewhere you can pop into just for a drink (11am–11pm, midnight Fri and Sat, 407 828 8739. See more at **www.trexcafe.com**).

Other choices: **Ghirardelli Ice Cream & Chocolate Shop** is a great option for dessert or a milkshake. **The Earl of Sandwich** serves great sandwiches and lighter meals, and **Wolfgang Puck Express** has quick-service Californian cuisine, while there are new quick-bite counter service offerings at **Aristocrêpes** (both savoury and sweet), **The Daily Poutine** (Canadian-style French fries with different toppings), and **BB Wolf's Sausage Co** (tempting artisan sausages with a variety of toppings).

BRITTIP
We think the best value at Disney Springs is the excellent Earl of Sandwich, where one of their hot sandwiches is often enough for two.

Jock Lindsey's Hangar Bar

© Disney

West Side

Back in the more hip night-time district of Disney Springs are another four options.

Bongos Cuban Café: Co-owned by Gloria and Emilio Estefan, the sounds and tastes of Old Havana enliven this imaginative setting, with red-hot Latin music (after 6pm) and excellent Cuban fare. You'll struggle to get a tastier – or more eye-catching – platter than their speciality seafood skillet while the Skirt Steak and Roasted Chicken are equally flavour-packed (11am–11pm, Sun–Thurs, 11.30pm Fri and Sat; 407 828 0999, **www.bongoscubancafe.com**).

House of Blues®: This restaurant in 'backwoods Mississippi' is a must for those who like a little rock 'n' roll with lunch or dinner. The trademark Gospel Brunch on Sun serves up some fab food with a full gospel show (10.30am and 1pm; $41.50 adults, $23.25 3–9s), while the main restaurant offers some fine fare, including seafood jambalaya, fresh fish and a host of Cajun delicacies, with live music Thurs–Sat (11.30am–11pm Sun–Thurs, 1am Fri–Sat; 407 934 2583, **www.houseofblues.com**).

Splitsville: OK, so it's a bowling alley, but the food and drink are good, so

Morimoto Asia

© Disney

you might want to consider this as a dining option on its own. Fresh sushi is their speciality, but the menu also offers gourmet burgers, sandwiches, pizza, entrée salads and main-course dishes like pulled pork, fish 'n' chips, chicken parmesan and Steak Alfredo. They feature sundaes for dessert and the cocktail menu is extremely tempting. (10.30–midnight Mon–Fri, 10–1am Sat–Sun; 407 938 7467, **www.splitsvillelanes.com**).

Wolfgang Puck® Café: A 4-part experience from the top Californian chef with the Café, gourmet food in a casual setting; Wolfgang Puck Express, the fast-food version; the Sushi Bar for seafood and pizza; and the Dining Room, an upmarket restaurant featuring top international cuisine. It caters for just about every taste (the sushi is excellent) and is highly family friendly (11.30am–11pm, 6–10pm in Dining Room; 407 938 9653, **www.wolfgangpuckcafeorlando.com**).

Other choices: Grab a snack at **Wetzel's Pretzels**, with the choice of pretzels, hot dogs and lemonade; try **Haagen-Dazs** ice-cream, or coffee at the inevitable **Starbucks**; or sample more fun offerings at the **Food Truck Park,** with the four trucks each geared to one of the main theme parks, food-wise. You can also try flavoured shaved ice at **Italian Ice** and unique frozen sakes and street food offerings at new **YeSake** kiosk.

Town Center

The newest part of Disney Springs is focused firmly on shopping, but there are still several tempting food offerings, and the return of an 'old favourite.'

Blaze Fast-Fire'd Pizza: For counter-service artisan-style pizza (from a set selection or build-yourself), plus salads and desserts, this new offering is another fresh choice (and at a lower price than many hereabouts). Everything is flash-cooked in their "blazing hot" ovens, so beware biting too soon! This is also a growing national chain, but you'd never know from the distinctive style (11am–11pm).

Our Disney Springs Top 10

You'll definitely be in for a treat at this selection of fine-dining choices:

1 Morimoto Asia
2 The Boathouse
3 Raglan Road
4 STK Orlando
5 Portobello
6 Homecoming – Kitchen & Shine Bar
7 Wolfgang Puck Dining Room
8 House of Blues
9 Bongos
10 Jock Lindsey's Hangar Bar

D-Luxe Burger: You'll need both hands for these huge gourmet burgers, each prepared to order from a relatively simple (but delicious) selection. Fries are separate and come with four dipping sauces, and there are magnificent milkshakes, soda floats and a Red Velvet Burger Macaron for dessert (11am–11pm).

◀🇬🇧▶ BRITTIP

For a drink with a kick, try the alcoholic shakes at **D-Luxe Burger**, including a Godiva Raspberry, Smoked Bourbon and Beer Gelato. A cocktail and dessert in one!

Frontera Cucina: Here's more celebrity chef style, with TV's Rick Bayless presenting his modern version of traditional Mexican cuisine in another imaginative setting. As well as tacos and his famous tortas (sandwiches), there are luscious chicken and shrimp dishes, plus a heavenly Carne Asada – red chilli-marinated Black Angus steak. For smaller tastes, there is a grab-and-go window (11am–11pm).

Planet Hollywood Observatory: The largest and busiest of this worldwide chain was undergoing a major transformation in 2016, from its brash film style to a sleek, sophisticated look more befitting the Disney Springs vibe. Instead of the 'Planet' motif, it becomes an Observatory, with an outside bar and patio. The full-on movie theming inside will also give way to a similar vibe, albeit with plenty of displays for their film memorabilia and TV screens. The food will also get an upgrade, but will still lean heavily on its fairly standard burger-and-steak orientated menu, plus wonderful cocktails (11am–12am; 407 827 7827, **www.planethollywood.com**).

Sprinkles: All the cupcakes (and cookies and ice-cream sundaes) you could imagine, in regular and mini sizes, served up with immense style in this modern bakery (but, again, with the price to match – watch your wallet here! 10am–midnight).

UNIVERSAL ORLANDO

As with Disney, Universal has a terrific array of dining in its hotels many of which are worth trying even if you're not staying there.

Hard Rock Hotel: The Palm is a signature New York steak-and-lobster supper club restaurant, hence slightly more formal by Florida standards. The celebrity cartoon caricatures on the walls pay tribute to the original restaurant's roots in the newspaper district of Manhattan, while the food features Nova Scotia lobster, prime cuts of meat and Italian specialities. **The Kitchen** epitomises more of the hotel's rock star style with a livelier atmosphere and imaginative menu that features flatbreads, burgers, pasta, excellent fish dishes and comfort foods with a modern twist, like bacon-wrapped meatloaf and gourmet mac and cheese.

Portofino Bay Hotel: The jewel in the crown here is **Bice**, a wonderful Italian-themed and superbly presented formal restaurant with genuine Italian flair and tastes. For a special night out it takes some beating, and their Antipasto, Truffle-flavoured lamb chops and grilled swordfish are divine. **Mama Della's Ristorante** is more Italian style, but with a more traditional touch in the fish and pasta dishes (still not cheap, though). **Trattoria del Porto** is more brasserie style, with salads, sandwiches and a great pasta selection.

Royal Pacific Resort: Tucked away here is one of Orlando's finest restaurants, the unique **Tchoup-Chop** (pronounced chop-chop). From the gourmet stable of New Orleans master chef Emeril Lagasse, it offers Asian-Pacific fusion cuisine in the most eye-catching setting. Blending aromatic and flavoursome elements of Thai, Chinese, Japanese, South Seas and other Pacific cuisines, Lagasse has conjured up a delectable array of dishes. We're big fans of the Iron Skillet Seared Edamame and Smoked Pork Ribs, followed by Korean Fried Chicken or a selection of Maki and Sashimi. The desserts are equally delicious and the whole experience is a five-star treat. The **Islands Dining Room** is also a good choice for dinner, with Wok specials and other Asian-influenced dishes, like Lemongrass Braised Beef.

Sapphire Falls Resort: this new hotel has just one main restaurant but it's also a highlight, with **Amatista Cookhouse** featuring a Caribbean-inspired menu to go with its show kitchen and views over the central lagoon, plus the lure of the adjacent **Strong Water Tavern** with its rum-based cocktail creations and tapas menu.

BRITTIP

Can't get in to Tchoup-Chop for dinner? Try their lunch-time offerings instead as they are rarely over-booked (11.30am–2.30pm).

Universal CityWalk

Citywalk provides the other great concentration of dining opportunities, especially since a big 2014/15 revamp that added several new restaurants.

Antojitos Authentic Mexican Food: This cavernous party restaurant offers bags of Mexican style and atmosphere, from their own Mariachi band to fabulous cocktails. The menu is equally good, running the culinary gambit from street food (tacos, enchiladas, fajitas) to refined twists on traditional dishes such as Orange Salmon and Churrasco Steak, along with

203 authentic tequilas (4–11pm Sun–Thurs, midnight Fri–Sat; 407 224 3663).

Bob Marley: Jamaican cuisine in a funky setting, featuring entrées such as curry, oxtail stew and Jamaican Jerk Chicken (4–10pm Sun–Thurs, 11pm Fri–Sat and Sun; 21 and up after 9pm; 407 224 3663).

Bubba Gump's Shrimp Co: This has the full *Forrest Gump* theme, and is heavy on seafood but also includes chicken, sandwiches, ribs, salads and more, with catchy names like Bubba's After the Storm 'Bucket of Boat Trash' (gluten-free menu available; 11am–midnight; 407 903 0044, **www.bubbagump.com**).

BRITTIP

Mention you are celebrating a birthday at Bubba Gump's and you'll find you quickly become the centre of attention!

The Cowfish: Fresh and innovative, this claims to be the world's first restaurant to feature great sushi AND burgers (hence their trademark 'Burgushi'), with a wide variety of both in an eclectic, lively setting. Spiked milkshakes, premium sakes, craft beers, wine and exotic martinis add to the temptations here, along with a great pure sushi bar (11am–11pm Sun–Thurs, midnight Fri–Sat; 407 224 3663, **www.thecowfish.com**).

Emeril's: This is a sophisticated five-star journey into the cuisine of New Orleans with master chef Emeril Lagasse. Fine wines and a cigar bar enhance Emeril's Creole-based gourmet creations, and, if you don't try his version of Shrimp and Grits, you'll have missed a real treat (lunch 11.30am–3pm; dinner 5–10pm Sun–Thurs, 5–10.30pm Fri and Sat; 407 224 2424, **www.emerils.com**).

BRITTIP

If Emeril's is full for dinner, consider lunch there instead, which rarely books up. Or try its daily Happy Hour (4–8pm) with reduced prices and special small-plate dishes at the bar.

Our Universal Top 10

For a memorable meal, choose any of our Universal faves:

1   Tchoup Chop
2   Bice
3   Vivo Italian Kitchen
4   The Palm
5   NBC Sports Grill & Brew
6   Antojitos
7   Emeril's
8   The Cowfish
9   Amatista Cookhouse
10 The Kitchen

Hard Rock Café: The largest example of this worldwide chain, with its collection of rock 'n' roll memorabilia (including a pink 1959 Cadillac) and full concert venue, is hugely popular, so try to get in early for lunch or dinner, with their signature burgers, steaks, fajitas, ribs and sandwiches, or try their new breakfasts until 11am (8.30am–midnight, Rock Bar until 1.30am; 407 351 7625, **www.hardrock. com/cafes/orlando/**).

◄▋▌► BRITTIP

After dining at the Hard Rock Café, ask for one of their VIBE Tours with a special 'rock guide'. You'll get an insight into much of their unique memorabilia, the history of the Café (which began in London), a look inside the John Lennon-themed VIP room and a tour of the music venue's back-stage areas. An amazing – and free – treat, available 1–9pm most days.

Hot Dog Hall of Fame: All manner of hot-dog styles, frankfurters and stuffed dumplings from around the USA, allied to hundreds of condiment variations make this a fun offering (11am–10pm Sun–Thurs, 1am Fri-Sat, **www.hotdoghalloffame.com**).

Jimmy Buffet's Margaritaville: An island homage to Florida's laid-back musical hero, with 'Floribbean' cuisine (a mix of Key West and Caribbean), with the Volcano Bar, which 'erupts'

margaritas periodically (11.30-2am, live music until midnight; 407 224 2155, **www.margaritavilleorlando.com**)

NBC Sports Grill & Brew: New in 2016, this sports bar brings a sophisticated – and large scale – vibe to the genre, with more than 100 TV screens and an excellent menu. It has its own range of beers, features two bars, and most of the food comes from huge custom-made gas grills in the main show kitchen. The outdoor stadium-style screen sets the scene and there are a lot of smart touches inside, not least with the menu that includes Cedar-Planked Salmon, a gorgeous chicken curry (Bang-Bang Chicken), Caribbean grouper and succulent barbecue ribs, brisket and pulled pork, as well as standards like burgers, sandwiches and wings (11–1.30am).

Pat O'Brien's: This is a reproduction of the famous New Orleans bar and restaurant with its Flaming Fountain courtyard, main bar and duelling piano bar. Excellent Cajun food and world-famous Hurricane cocktails. (4pm–2am; 5pm–2am for the piano bar, with a $7 cover charge after 9pm; 21 and over only; 407 224 3663, **www. patobriens.com/patobriens/orlando/**).

Red Oven Pizza Bakery: Authentic artisan pizza – five varieties of white and red Neapolitan style – are on offer at this chic new restaurant, with some imaginative flavours all baked in their signature 900° Red Oven (11am–2am).

Vivo Italian Kitchen: Fine Tuscan dining gets a full workout here, with fresh ingredients served from an open kitchen that offers a customisable menu for its pasta and other featured dishes. Everything is made from scratch and the details include freshly pulled mozzarella, house-cured meats and slow-cooked ragu. Excellent wine and cocktail list (5–11pm; 407 224 3663).

Other choices: Try **Menchie's** for fab frozen yoghurt, **Breadbox** for great sandwiches, **Cinnabon** for cinnamon rolls and other pastries, **Cold Stone Creamery** for indulgent ice-cream creations and the inevitable **Starbucks** coffee house.

The Top of the Walk food court also features the **Burger King Whopper Bar**, **Panda Express**, **Moe's Southwest Grill** and **Fusion Bistro Sushi & Sake Bar**. Look up more details at **www.universalorlando.com/Restaurants/CityWalk-Restaurants.aspx**.

BRITTIP

Can't get in any of the CityWalk restaurants? Jump on one of the boats to the Hard Rock Hotel or Portofino Bay Hotel and you can usually dine without a wait at The Kitchen (Hard Rock), Trattoria del Porto or Mama Della's (Portofino Bay).

INTERNATIONAL DRIVE

Going out into the main tourist areas, here's the best of the dining in this long street. We divide it into I-Drive North, Sand Lake Road (the 'Restaurant Row' district west of the junction with I-Drive), I-Drive South, The Pointe and I-Drive 360.

I-Drive North

The section north of Sand Lake Road is largely fast-food and buffet restaurant territory, but with some notable exceptions.

Tchoup Chop

© Universal Orlando Resort

BRITTIP
A buffet breakfast at one of Golden Corral, Ponderosa or Shoney's should keep you going until tea-time and is a good way to start a theme-park day.

Fast food: Burger King, Dairy Queen, Del Taco, Dunkin' Donuts, Fuddruckers, KFC, McDonalds, Panda Express (Chinese), Pizza Hut, Popeye's (fried chicken), Starbucks (Orlando Premium Outlets), Sonic, Subway, Taco Bell, and Five Guys (Orlando Premium Outlets).

Breakfast style: Denny's, IHOP, Perkins, Ponderosa.

Buffet style: CiCi's Pizza, Sweet Tomatoes.

Bar-restaurant style: Applebee's, Buffalo Wild Wings, Chili's, TGI Friday's.

Steakhouse style: Black Angus.

Seafood specials: Fishbones, Red Lobster.

Individuals: Look for the home-from-home pub style of the **Orlando George & Dragon**, with good food, a decent pint and live entertainment (9am–11pm; 7.30am for live football; **www.orlando georgeanddragon.com**); **Hash House A Go-Go**, for an inspired, fresh take on classic dishes like burgers, salads, meatloaf, chicken and waffles, and *huge* portions (8am–10pm, 11pm Sat; **www.hash houseagogo.com**); and the spectacular upmarket Brazilian steakhouse **Texas de Brazil**, which features an all-you-can eat menu for a set price, with a huge salad bar and fresh-cut meats. Pricey but worth it (5–10pm Mon–Thurs, 10.30pm Fri, 4–10.30pm Sat, 4–9.30pm Sun; **www.texasdebrazil.com**).

Sand Lake Road

This is an area that has more notable one-off restaurants than almost anywhere in town.

Fast food: Chick-fil-A, Chipotle (more Mexican), Jimmy John's (sandwiches), McDonalds, Starbucks, Tijuana Flats (fresh Mexican style).

Breakfast style: First Watch, Panera Bread.

Steakhouse style: Ruth's Chris.

Seafood specials: Bonefish Grill, the beautifully upmarket **Ocean Prime** for a special dinner occasion, and the inventive **Moonfish**, with superb sushi, and more.

Amura: Some of Orlando's best sushi can be found in this eye-catching Japanese restaurant that also features Asian table barbecue, plus flavourful beef and chicken dishes and first-class seafood. 'Fresh, healthy and delicious,' they promise, and we agree (407 370 0007; 11.30am–3pm, 5–10.30pm Mon–Fri, 5–11pm Sat, noon–10pm Sun; **http://amura.com/**).

Bar Louie: Another smart bar-restaurant chain with a wide-ranging menu (burgers and salads to flatbreads and fab chicken dishes), great wine and cocktails, DJ nights Thurs–Sat and a tempting happy hour 4–7pm Mon–Fri (11am–2am; 407 608 5190; **www.barlouie.com**).

Cedar's: Lebanese cuisine here, and it's some of the best chicken and lamb in town. A family-run Middle Eastern delight, it offers the full range of kebabs, falafel and hummus as well as specialities like fish tagine, grilled quail and baked kibbeh. A really different alternative and an aromatic treat, with the bonus of live music and belly dancing Fri and Sat (11.30am–10.30pm Mon–Thurs, 11.30–12.30am Fri, noon–12.30am Sat, noon–9.30pm Sun; 407 351 6000; **www.orlandocedars.com**).

Eddie V's: Supper-club style venue featuring succulent seafood with live jazz most evenings. A stylish option but with a more informal V Lounge that is first-come, first-served. The menu is a mouth-watering collection of fresh fish and shellfish, as well as fine steaks, backed by a superb wine list and signature cocktails (4–11pm Sun–Thurs, midnight Fri and Sat; 407 355 3011, **www.eddiev.com**).

The Melting Pot: Every night is fondue night at this smart dining experience, which features seasoned vegetables, fresh-cut meats and artisan cheeses.

A great choice (5–10pm Mon–Thurs, 5–11pm Fri, 4–11pm Sat, 4–10pm Sun; 407 903 1100, **www.meltingpot.com/ orlando-fl/**).

Rocco's Tacos: Wildly eclectic but quality-conscious Mexican offering, great for a fun lunch or lively evening out. Start with their table-side guacamole, then consider one of the signature Molcajete dishes – a sizzling fajita choice served in a lava rock bowl with fresh flour tortillas. Their taco choice is equally tempting, as is the array of margaritas and speciality drinks from their Tequila Bar, where it is party night every night! (11.30am–2am; 407 226 0550, **www.roccostacos.com**).

Roy's: Go upmarket Hawaii style at this grand choice, where the Asia–Pacific fusion cuisine is as spectacular as the decor and service. Creator and celebrity chef Roy Yamaguchi displays his style in every dish and the specialities include Macadamia-Nut Crusted Mahi-Mahi, Blackened Island Ahi and Braised Short Ribs, as well as fabulous cocktails and an 'Aloha Hour' bar menu (4.30–6.30pm), with $7 appetisers, wines and cocktails (5–10pm, 11pm Fri and Sat, 9pm Sun; **www.roysrestaurant.com**).

Saffron: Smart and stylish Indian choice, with fab-value lunch deals, weekend champagne brunch buffet and classic fine-dining dinner menu. All dishes can be prepared to individual levels of spiciness and the Chicken Xacutti and Jhinga Malabaru (a shrimp dish in a coconut-based sauce) are worth coming in for alone (407 674 8899; 11.30am–2.30pm, 5.30–10pm Sun–Thurs, 10.30pm Fri–Sat; **www.saffronorlando.com**).

Seasons 52: A trendy national chain, with 10 outlets in Florida, we think

this offers some of the best dining in the area, with a creative, seasonal, health-conscious menu. All appetisers, salads and soups range from 100–250 calories, and all mains are less than 475 calories. Seafood is the highlight but lamb, chicken, steaks and veggie options are equally tempting. The 'mini indulgence' desserts are ideal to finish a meal in style. The bar area, with its live piano music, and outdoor terrace are equally stylish, ideal for a romantic occasion, and great value for happy hour 4–6.30pm Mon–Fri (11.30am–10pm Sun–Thurs, 11pm Fri–Sat; 407 354 5212; **www.seasons52.com**). PS: This is where you will often find us at the end of a long week!

Vine's Grille & Wine Bar: This upmarket restaurant and wine shop features live jazz to go with a tempting menu that runs from grilled octopus and oysters to excellent salads, fine steaks (including a 28oz Tomahawk bone-in rib steak) and fresh seafood. Another special occasion night out that's worth the price (407 351 1227; 4pm–1am Mon–Thurs, 1.30am Sat, 11.30 Sun; **www.vinesgrill.com**).

The Whiskey: Great burgers, killer cocktails and almost 150 whiskies, ryes, bourbons and scotches are on offer at this surprisingly chic bistro-pub, offering a friendly welcome, keen service – and memorable drinks! Some excellent small-plate choices alongside their range of succulent burgers, chops, salmon and salads (11am–2am; 407 930 6511, **http://downatthewhiskey.com/**).

Sand Lake Road – Dr Phillips Plaza,

Staying on Sand Lake Rd but moving into the Dr Phillips Plaza, there are:

Fast food: Chipotle, Pizza Hut, Starbucks, Subway, Toojay's Deli (excellent sandwich choice).

Breakfast style: Keke's.

Steakhouse style: Morton's.

Bosphorous: Turkish flavours with a delicious range of authentic breads, hot and cold appetisers, salads, soups, pides (Turkish pizzas), kebabs and specialities like moussaka and

Big Fin Seafood

baklava. You can dine royally without breaking the bank. Try babaganoush (char-grilled aubergine with fresh herbs and spices), tabbuli, lamb kofte or chicken adana (11am–10pm Sun–Thurs, 11pm Fri and Sat; 407 352 6766, **www.bosphorousrestaurant.com**).

Christinis: a wonderfully upmarket and formal Italian restaurant that has been around almost 50 years and remains stylish and traditional, with a classic menu. Reservations nearly always required (6–11pm; 407 583 4472; **www.christinis.com**).

Mama Louise: More Italian, but more family-style and relaxed, with traditional, home-inspired dishes from chef Joe Esposito. Choose from pizzas, pastas and classics like chicken parmigiana and lasagna, as well as an excellent kids' menu (11.30am–10pm Mon–Thurs, 11pm Fri-Sat, 9pm Sun; **www.mamalouiserestaurant.com**).

Pincho Factory: imaginative Cuban counter-service food, combining wraps, bowls and salads with chicken, steak and shrimp, plus some hugely tasty burgers and local beers (11am–10pm Sun–Thurs, midnight Fri–Sat; 407 745 4462; **http://pinchofactory.com/**).

World of Beer: A classic American bar that specialises in a mind-boggling selection of beers, both national and international, with a tavern-style menu and different themes each night, like Trivia Wednesdays (11–2am; 407 355 3315; **https://worldofbeer.com/**).

Sand Lake Road – Dellagio complex

Moving on to the final part of Sand Lake Road is the **Dellagio** complex, with eight more worthy options.

Big Fin Seafood: One of Orlando's most imaginative seafood options, Big Fin is refined but relaxed, a big-scale experience that offers special-occasion atmosphere. The main dining room features a grand salon style but two smaller rooms are more intimate, while the Trophy Bar is ideal for a pre-dinner drink. The menu features sushi, sashimi, oysters and ceviche; classic salads and chowders; steak, chops and chicken; crab and lobster dishes; fresh fish; and tempting pastas. You can push the boat out with the $79 Shells and Tails platter or opt for their Famous Fish & Chips at $22. Notable are the succulent signature Swordfish Filet Mignon, lobster mac-n-cheese, crab cakes and the Shrimp or Scallop Orleans. Happy Hour is 5–7pm Mon–Sat, 5-9pm Sun, at the Bar with $7 drink specials and a reduced-price menu (407 615 8888; 5–10pm Sun–Thurs, 11pm Fri & Sat; **www.bigfinseafood.com**).

BRITBONUS

Show your copy of the *Brit Guide* upon arrival at Big Fin Seafood Kitchen to receive a Chef's Tasting for each guest at the table. Not valid with any other offers/specials.

Bravo Cucina Italiana: This fresh twist on classic Italian fare features home-made pasta, pizza, flatbreads, steaks, chops and seafood in an inviting 'Roman-ruin' decor. Casual and chic, and fun for the grown-up crowd (11am–10pm, to 11pm Fri and Sat; 407 351 5880; **www.bravoitalian.com**).

Dragonfly: Get ready for a Japanese taste sensation from the super-hot *Robata* grill that produces delicious fish, beef, chicken, shrimp and pork. Dragonfly also specialises in fresh sushi and sashimi, as well as its own cocktails and sake for an authentic dining experience (407 370 3559; 5–10pm Sun–Thurs, 11pm Fri–Sat; **www.dragonflyrestaurants.com**).

Fleming's: Award-winning steakhouse that serves up succulent cuts of the best meats, fish and chicken, including a heavenly 14oz Wagyu New York Strip Steak. All can be enhanced with rubs, toppings and sauces for the ultimate steak aficionado, but this is a premium experience, with all side dishes extra (407 352 5706; 5–10pm Sun–Thurs, 11pm Fri–Sat; **www.flemingssteakhouse.com**).

Miller's Field House: Great sports-bar territory, with more than 70 TVs showing all the action and an 'Owner's Box' for high rollers. The menu is sophisticated, with steaks and tacos as well as the usual burgers and wings, plus daily drink specials (407 248 3474; 11.30am–2am; **www.fieldhouseorlando.com**).

The Pharmacy: Try the Speakeasy style here, behind fake elevator doors but ensuring you know the password (issued online) in advance! Great cocktails, a varied, high-quality menu and a lively atmosphere make for a fun night out (5–10pm Mon–Thurs, midnight Fri, 11am–2pm, 5–midnight Sat, 11am-2pm Sun; 407 985 2972; **http://thepharmacyorlando.com**).

Slate: A smart new upmarket restaurant at the far end of the Dellagio complex (just past Trader Joe's), featuring wood-grilled cuisine, with indoor and open-air dining. Imaginative menu offers pizza, pasta, salads, seafood and steaks with a lighter touch, plus a fab weekend brunch (407 500 7528; 11am–3pm and 5–10pm Mon–Thurs, 11–3 and 5–11 Fri, 10.30–3 and 5–11 Sat, 10.30–3 and 5–10 Sun; **www.slateorlando.com**).

Urbain 40: Gorgeous 1940s style, from the décor to the music (but with a contemporary menu) is the key here, with a gracious, more formal style that includes live jazz most evenings. Billed as 'An American brasserie and lounge', its sumptuous main dining room is the place to be for a special night out, while the lounge is more casual and lively. The food is exquisite, from salads and pastas to seafood and steaks, as are the cocktails and even a craft beer selection (407 872 2640; 11am–3pm, 5–10pm Sun–Thurs, 11pm Fri–Sat; **http://urbain40.com/**).

Naru Sushi

BRITTIP

For a taste of Urbain 40 without the full price, try their Happy Hour in the Lounge 5–7pm, Sun–Thurs, and soak up the wonderful ambience.

International Drive South

Heading back to I-Drive south of Sand Lake Road, you'll find a dazzling range of choice.

Fast food: Checkers, Domino's Pizza, Dunkin' Donuts, Firehouse Subs, McDonalds, Starbucks, Subway.

Breakfast style: Friendly's, Denny's, Panera Bread.

Buffet style: CiCi's Pizza, Golden Corral, Ponderosa.

Bar-restaurant style: BJ's Brewhouse, Bahama Breeze, Brick House Tavern & Tap (good sports style), Buffalo Wild Wings.Chuys, Hooters, Red Robin, Miller's Ale House, TGI Friday's, Uno Pizzeria & Grill, Houlihans (classic bar-restaurant),

Steakhouse style: Charley's Steakhouse, Longhorn Steakhouse, Tony Roma's, Vito's Chophouse.

Italian flavours: Olive Garden.

Seafood specials: Boston Lobster Feast, Joe's Crab Shack, Red Lobster.

Café Tu Tu Tango: A wonderful tapas-style menu is boosted by live music and local artists at work in this Bohemian-style cafe. Vegetarians are well catered for, and you can try succulent pizzas, seafood, salads and soups, plus imaginative Mexican dishes and a thoughtful kids' menu (11am–midnight, Mon–Thurs, 1am Fri–Sat, 10am–11pm Sun; **www.cafetututango.com**).

Cooper's Hawk: Wine lovers are spoiled for choice here, with a massive range in their Tasting Room to complement an excellent wide-ranging menu that runs the gamut from burgers and flatbreads to seafood and prime steaks (407 954 3400; 11am–10pm Sun–Thurs, 10.30 Fri–Sat, 11.30 in the bar; **www.coopershawkwinery.com**).

Del Frisco's Double Eagle: I-Drive's new standard for fine steaks and stylish dining, with an amazing array of fresh-cut meats, plus seafood, chicken and great cocktails, but with the price to match. There are two gorgeous bars and a picturesque patio (407 351 5074; 5–11pm Mon–Fri, 4–11pm Sat, 4–10pm Sun; https://delfriscos.com/).

Don Pablo's: An elaborate Mexican offering with clever theming, a fun, lively atmosphere (especially round the Cantina bar) and classic, well-explained menus (407 354 1345; 11am–10pm Sun–Thurs, 11pm Fri–Sat; www.donpablos.com).

Everglades: Tucked away inside the Rosen Centre Hotel is this beautiful Florida speciality restaurant, specialising in great steaks and fine seafood. Don't miss the Broiled Florida Grouper and melt-in-the- mouth Filet Key Largo (5.30–10.30pm; 407 996 2385; www.evergladesrestaurant.com).

◀▣▶ BRITTIP

For a great lunch or dinner alternative, visit Fogo de Chao and just sample their 30-item Salad Buffet at $15 (lunch) or $27 (dinner). It is WAY more than just salad, with the likes of aged Parmesan, Italian salami and smoked salmon, and is wonderfully fresh and appetising.

Fogo De Chao: This Brazilian churrascaria is superbly authentic and flavourful, with an enchanting mix of elaborate serving style and succulent cuts of meat, all cooked on the traditional 'churrasco' skewer grill. It is a set-fee lunch or dinner, including a huge Salad Buffet, with 14 different meats, from filet mignon to linguica (Brazilian sausages), along with a selection of side dishes like crispy polenta, caramelised plantains, rice, beans and heavenly garlic mashed potato. The bacon-wrapped filet is worth coming in for on its own while the lamb chops are outrageously delicious. The weekday set lunch is a bargain $33.95 for the full churrascaria experience, while dinner is $50.95 (noon–2.30pm and 5–10pm Mon–Thurs, noon–3pm,

5.30–10.30pm Fri, noon–3pm, 5–10.30pm Sat, 5.30–10pm Sun; 407 370 0711, www.fogodechao.com).

Spencer's: The Hilton by the Convention Center is home to this beautiful restaurant that features magnificent steak, chops and seafood. Side dishes (all organic, local produce) are extra, but the natural steaks are all pasture-raised without hormones or antibiotics, aged for 21 days and cooked in a custom-made grill (5.30–10.30pm Tues–Sat; 407 313 4300; www.thehiltonorlando.com).

I-Drive 360

This extensive entertainment complex is now a restaurant destination in its own right.

Fast food: Ben & Jerry's (ice cream), iCafe de Paris, Pretzelmaker.

Bar-restaurant style: Buffalo Wild Wings, Shake Shack.

Steakhouse style: Outback Steakhouse.

Italian flavours: Carrabba's.

Cowgirls Rock Bar: Another country style offering with an emphasis on Hooter's style "cowgirl" servers, this one may not be appropriate for some families. The limited menu features burgers, hot dogs, soups, salads, and sandwiches, but you're there for the 'sassy banter,' drinks and music more than the food (4pm–2am Mon–Fri, 11–2am Sat–Sun; 407 930 3654; www.cowgirlsorlando.com).

Naru Sushi: Japanese cuisine with an innovative, Brazilian touch. The highlights are their sushi offerings, which can be custom ordered for those with allergies or 'particular' tastes, as well as a grand Table Gourmet sampler offering (407 801 0005; 5–10pm Mon-Thurs, 11.30am–11pm Fri-Sat, 11.30am–10pm Sun; www.narusushibar.com).

◀▣▶ BRITTIP

Naru Sushi is another to offer an excellent Happy Hour, 4–7.30pm Mon-Fri, with drink specials and $5 'quick bites'.

Paramount Fine Foods: This Middle Eastern speciality is a terrific choice for vegetarians, though meat-lovers are also well catered for. Delicious Shawarma, crisp salads, and all the expected, aromatic favourites highlight a fresh-as-it-comes menu. Family Platters are available and watch for Weekend Specials (407 930 8645; 11am–midnight Sun–Thurs, 1am Fri–Sat **www.paramountfinefoodsusa.com**).

Sugar Factory: An 'American brasserie catering to those of a sweet-toothed persuasion, it still serves crêpes, burgers, salads, flatbreads and sandwiches, but really dazzles with its ice-cream-based desserts, milkshakes and candy-inspired cocktails. Don't miss the wonderful gift shop, while there is also a coffee and milkshake window (11am–11pm Sun–Thurs, 1am Fri–Sat; 407 270 8072; **http://sugarfactory.com/orlando**).

◄❚❚► BRITTIP

Want a 'Tourist v Food' challenge? Go for The **Sugar Factory's** mammoth 24-scoop King Kong Sundae with ALL the toppings. At $99, it feeds 12!

Tapa Toro: Classic and contemporary Spanish specialties with a focus on tapas and paella, plus live music and tableside flamenco dancers in this elegant and multi-faceted restaurant (11am–midnight Sun–Thurs, 2am Fri–Sat; 407 226 2929; **http://tapatoro.restaurant**)

Tin Roof: Country music fans will love the live entertainment here, with a smattering of rock, soul, Americana and pop. The menu features Tex-Mex favourites, and specialties include O-Eye Mac and Cheese, Shrimp

Marlow's Tavern

and Grits, and succulent Baby Back Ribs. Full bar, funky style, and a somewhat raucous atmosphere after 10pm (11am–2am; 407 270 7926; **www.tinrooforlando.com**).

Yard House: With a huge selection of beers on tap and a wonderfully inventive menu, this isn't your typical bar. Its air of comfortable refinement is also family-friendly, and the menu is several steps above the norm, featuring twists on bar favourites, such as Korean Pork Belly Tacos, Black Truffle Burger and Vodka Shrimp Pasta, plus other gourmet offerings. There is a good selection of healthy/vegetarian dishes, along with steaks, pizza, seafood, pasta and a good kids menu (11–12.30am Sun–Thurs, 1.20am Fri–Sat; 407 351 8220; **www.yardhouse.com**).

Pointe Orlando

Head to this other I-Drive entertainment complex, and you'll find more great dining options.

Fast food: Ben & Jerry's.

Bar-restaurant style: Johnny Rockets (classic diner), Marlow's Tavern (above-average menu and live music).

Steakhouse style: Capital Grille.

Italian flavours: Maggiano's Little Italy.

◄❚❚► BRITTIP

Looking for a great burger? Look no further than the **Capital Grille** (at Pointe Orlando and Mall at Millenia). Although it's an upmarket steakhouse, their lunch menu features a Kona-Crusted Wagyu Burger at $17 that is truly heavenly.

Adobe Gila's: This lively bar and Mexican cantina style features dozens of tequilas, plus south-of-the-border dining delicacies like the Carnitas Platter and Paella Skillet. Feeling brave? Tackle the signature 64oz Margarita – if you dare! (11am–2am; 407 903 1477; **www.adobegilas.com**).

BB King's Blues Club: Live jazz and blues (see p294) with a Southern comfort-food menu, such as Fried Shrimp Po Boy and Southern Fried Catfish, and a full bar (4pm–midnight

Sun–Fri, 11am–1am Sat; 407 370 4550, **http://bbkings.com/orlando/**).

Blue Martini: Upmarket bar with 42 signature martinis, plus beer, wine and cocktails. Light fare, flatbreads and signature dishes such as Lollipop Lambchops and Main Lobster Salad. Live music nightly, plus a good happy hour 4–8pm each day (407 447 2583; 4pm–2am Mon–Fri, 3pm Sat–Sun; **www.bluemartinilounge.com**).

Copper Canyon Grill: This appeals to hearty appetites with its wood-fired rotisserie chicken, hearty chicken pot pie, steaks and barbecued ribs (11.30am–10.05pm Sun–Thurs, 11.05pm Fri–Sat; 407 363 3933; **https://ccgrlll.com/**).

Cuba Libre: This bar/restaurant adds a touch of 1940s Havana, featuring Latin-inspired cuisine with an exciting twist, from tasty tapas and ceviche to honey-mango glazed salmon – and wicked cocktails! (5pm–10pm daily, bar and nightlife 10pm-2am Fri–Sat; 407 226 1600, **www.cubalibrerestaurant.com**).

Funky Monkey: Eclectic restaurant/ wine bar that features an imaginative Asian–American fusion menu of tapas-like appetisers, burgers, seafood and hand-rolled sushi. Be aware the hilarious Las Vegas Divas drag show appears in the dining room Fri and Sat nights, with a $10/person fee (407 418 9463, noon–11pm Mon– Thurs, midnight Fri-Sat, 5–11pm Sun, **www.funkymonkeywine.com**).

Itta Bena: A New Orleans-inspired piano bar, with contemporary Southern cuisine to go with the live music. Try their signature 16oz bone-in Ribeye Steak or the Surf and Turf (an 8oz filet topped with 5oz of lobster tail), or just chill out with a cocktail in the bar (407 757 2910; 5–11pm; **http://ittabena.com/orlando/**).

The Oceanaire: Step back in time at this relaxed and stylish seafood room. The decor, reminiscent of a classic 1930s ocean liner, and mood music lead you into a fish and shellfish wonderland, complete with a superb oyster bar. Shrimp, crab, scallops, clams, lobster and as many as 15 types of fish all jostle for attention on a sumptuous menu that also offers great salads, steaks and chicken. The selection varies daily with the latest catch, but examples include Swordfish 'Black & Bleu', Flounder Florentine, Pan-seared Grouper and stuffed Atlantic lobster, as well as a surf and turf option and a dozen types of oyster. Its chilled shellfish platter (at $48/person) is an extravaganza of shrimp, crab, lobster and oysters and it has an impressive wine list. Service is top-notch (5–10pm Sun–Thurs, 11pm Fri–Sat; 407 363 4801; **www.theoceanaire.com**).

RA Sushi Bar: Japanese fusion cuisine and sushi bar with a varied menu, including Bento Boxes, Sushi and Sashimi selections, Tempura, Teriyaki and some creative twists on traditional favourites, plus Happy Hour specials (11am–midnight Sun–Thurs, 1am Fri–Sat; 407 454 5600, **www.rasushi.com**).

The Pub: This huge pub-style offering features a wide variety of cosy seating nooks, a fantastic mix of UK and US beers (including the Orlando

Cuba Libre

Brewing Co), a sharp menu and multiple TV screens for sports fans. The unique 'Pour Your Own Beer Walls' are a fun feature, as is Happy Hour Mon–Fri 3–7pm, and Wine Down Wednesdays (half-price select bottles; 407 352 2305; 11am–2am; **www.experiencethepub.com/orlando**).

Taverna Opa: Lively Greek option, with an appetising menu, from hot and cold meze to moussaka, souvlaki, kebabs and signature lamb chops, but much more besides, like fine steaks, fresh seafood and a great ouzo bar. Watch for table dancing and napkin throwing! (noon–11pm Sun–Thurs, 2am Fri–Sat; 407 351 8660, **www.opaorlando.com**).

Tommy Bahama's Tropical Café: Inspired dining in a laid-back, tropical setting. The menu is refreshing for lunch or dinner, with highlights being its coconut shrimp and tuna appetisers and seafood entrées, plus sandwiches, chicken, steaks and fab salads. Bar drinks are equally tempting (11.30am–10pm Mon–Thurs, 11pm Fri–Sat, 9pm Sun; 321 281 5886, **www.tommybahama.com/restaurants/orlando**).

◀🇬🇧▶ BRITTIP

There is free valet parking at Pointe Orlando if you're dining at Tommy Bahama, Cuba Libre, Capital Grille and The Oceanaire. Just pull in at the drop-off point next to Capital Grille (but don't forget to tip the valet when you pick up your car).

LAKE BUENA VISTA

At the junction of I-4 and Highway 535 (Apopka-Vineland Rd) is this busy area of hotels, shops and restaurants – lots of restaurants. It falls into two sections, south of I-4 and north of the motorway.

Lake Buena Vista South

Fast food: Chick-fil-A, Dunkin' Donuts, Starbucks, Subway, Wendy's.

Breakfast style: Panera Bread.

Buffet style: CiCi's Pizza, Golden Corral.

Bar-restaurant style: Applebee's, Bahama Breeze, BJ's Brewhouse.

Steakhouse style: Longhorn Steakhouse, Outback Steakhouse (opposite Orlando Premium Outlets).

Italian flavours: Carrabba's.

Hurricane Grill & Wings: A smart new bar-restaurant (also on south I-Drive, on Highway 27 in Clermont and in Winter Haven), with a laid-back Key West theme, this serves up salads, burgers, seafood and steak, with 35 flavours to go with their chicken wings! (407 938 9090; 11–2am; **www.hurricanewings.com**)

Frankie Farrell's: Inside the Lake Buena Vista Resort Village & Spa is this smart pub-style restaurant and bar with an imaginative menu, good range of beers and live entertainment

Hyatt Recency Grand Cypress

Join The (Curry) Club!

While Orlando has a handful of reliable Indian restaurants, few match up to the consistency and flavours of a British curry-house – until now. Step forward the **Viceroy Chipshop Curry Club**, a new venture taking typical flavours into existing restaurants for a special Curry Night several times a month. It costs $22/person and provides a set meal with a choice of entrée, with rice, naan bread, onion bhaji, samosa and vegetables. It is the brainchild of a British couple who have run several successful dining ventures in Orlando, but it can only be booked via their Facebook page under The Viceroy Chipshop's Curry Club, and you must order in advance. One of their regular locations is El Patron in Lake Buena Vista, and we are keen customers!

(10.30–1am Mon-Fri, 8-1am Sat-Sun; 407 238 1003; **www.frankiefarrells.com**).

Landry's Seafood: This big-name company boasts a genuinely elegant touch, featuring a fresh fish of the day, magnificent seafood platters and excellent salad bowl with each dish, while the service and wine list are top notch. For a special occasion, the Stuffed Flounder and Seafood Feast for two are ideal. Happy Hour 3pm–6pm Mon-Fri, noon–4pm Sat-Sun, with drinks specials and appetisers (3–10pm Mon-Thurs, 11pm Fri, 11.30am–11pm Sat 10pm Sun; **www.landryseafood.com**).

BRITTIP

Landry's Seafood features an excellent Sunset Dining menu, 3–5pm daily, with a three-course dinner for $20/person.

Lake Buena Vista North

Fast food: Burger King, Domino's Pizza, Dunkin' Donuts, Firehouse Subs, Flippers Pizzeria, Fuddruckers, McDonalds, Pizza Hut, Steak 'n Shake, Taco Bell.

Breakfast style: Denny's, IHOP, Perkins, Waffle House.

Buffet style: CiCi's Pizza, Shoney's, Sweet Tomatoes.

Bar-restaurant style: Buffalo Wild Wings, Chevys, Chili's, Hooter's, Orlando Ale House, Seadog Brew Pub, TGI Friday's.

Steakhouse style: Black Angus Steakhouse, Black Fire Brazilian Steakhouse.

Italian flavours: Macaroni Grill, Olive Garden.

Seafood specials: Joe's Crab Shack, Red Lobster.

El Patron: Reliable and great value-for-money Mexican choice, with good traditional dishes given a contemporary twist, like the stuffed chicken breast and slow-braised pork, plus great artisan tacos and a signature lunch buffet daily 11.30–2.30 (407 238 5300; 11.30am–10pm; **www.elpatronorlando.com**).

Hemingway's: Worth finding inside the Hyatt Grand Cypress Resort is this gorgeous formal dining room that features superb seafood, steaks and more in a Key West ambience. Specialities include the Crab Cakes and Seafood Paella, but all the seafood is superb (6–10pm, 407 239 3854).

Johnnie's Hideaway: Stylish lakefront supper club in the Crossroads plaza, serving a rich mix of salads, premium seafood, stone crabs, veal and succulent, dry-aged steaks. The menu is colossal, and there is also a raw bar and some of the biggest desserts we've seen, along with a charming bar area, outdoor terrace and Happy Hour 4.30–6.30pm (5–10.30pm Sun–Thurs, 11pm Fri–Sat; 407 827 1111; **www.johnnieshideaway.com**).

Sofrito Latin Café: Simon's favourite new place for a quick lunch or dinner, serving traditional authentic South and Central American dishes. You order at the counter then wait at your table for the fresh-cooked meal, with tapas-style plates and main courses from Venezuela, Colombia, Argentina and Cuba. No recommendations – just try anything! They also have local craft beers and wine, and a breakfast menu 11am–noon (11am–9pm; 407 778 4205, **www.sofritocafe.com**).

KISSIMMEE

Heading out into the long tourist corridor of Highway 192, you are largely in fast food territory, but there are some notable individuals. We divide it East and West of T-4.

Highway 192 East

Fast food: Arby's, Burger King, Checkers, Chick-Fil-A, Chipotle, Domino's Pizza, Dunkin' Donuts, Five Guys, Jimmy John's, KFC, McDonalds, Panda Express, Pizza Hut, Starbucks, Steak 'n Shake, Subway, Taco Bell, Wendy's.

Breakfast style: Cracker Barrel, Denny's, IHOP, Panera Bread, Perkins, Waffle House.

Buffet style: CiCi's Pizza, Golden Corral, Ponderosa.

Bar-restaurant style: Applebee's, Chili's, TGI Friday's, Uno Pizzeria & Grill.

Steakhouse style: Black Angus, Charley's Steakhouse, Longhorn Steakhouse, Logan's Roadhouse, Sonny's BBQ.

Italian flavours: Carrabba's, Macaroni Grill, Olive Garden.

Seafood specials: Joe's Crab Shack, Red Lobster.

Smokey Bones: With a rustic, log-cabin touch and succulent, deep-smoked BBQ, this eye-catching venue serves up fire-grilled steaks, salmon, chicken, burgers and salads. Try the BBQ platters and rib combos especially. Sports fans can also enjoy

Brio Tuscan Grille

a huge array of TVs (11am–2am; 407 397 7102; **www.smokeybones.com**).

Old Hickory Steakhouse: In the Gaylord Palms Resort is this five-star beacon of steakhouse style, set amid elaborate Everglades theming. Their steak needs no gimmicks as the house speciality of certified prime-aged beef is cooked to perfection. There are a handful of alternatives, including fish, chicken and an excellent vegetarian dish, but all side dishes are extra and this is a pricey experience, albeit memorable (5pm–10pm; 407 586 1600).

Pacino's: A Highway 192 feature in Kissimmee for more than 20 years, this 'taste of Sicily' features a signature open-flame oven that delivers great pizza, seafood and steaks, as well as an authentic range of pasta dishes. Couples can also take advantage of their Wine Cellar setting for a romantic evening out (4–11pm; 407 396 8022, **www.pacinos.com**).

Highway 192 West

Fast food: Burger King, Chick-Fil-A, Domino's Pizza, Dunkin' Donuts, McDonalds, Pizza Hut, Starbucks, Subway, Taco Bell, Wendy's.

Breakfast style: Bob Evans, Cracker Barrel, Denny's, IHOP, Panera Bread, Perkins.

Buffet style: CiCi's Pizza, Golden Corral, Ponderosa, Sweet Tomatoes.

Bar-restaurant style: Applebee's, Bahama Breeze, Buffalo Wild Wings, Chuys, Miller's Ale House, TGI Friday's.

Steakhouse style: Logan's Roadhouse, Longhorn Steakhouse, Outback Steakhouse, Texas Roadhouse.

Italian flavours: Carrabba's, Olive Garden.

Seafood specials: Bonefish Grill, Joe's Crabshack, Red Lobster.

Manny's Chophouse: This growing local chain that is popular on Highway 27 in Haines now has a new outlet in Kissimmee that brings its great value bar-restaurant-steakhouse style closer to mainstream tourist territory. Great value and great fun, it features a steak-orientated menu with bags of local style and original décor, as well as a 2-for-1 Happy Hour daily from 4–7pm. It is often packed by 6pm as locals and tourists alike flock here for the lively style and well-priced food (all steaks under $25, and many just $15–20), which also includes fab burgers, ribs, fajitas, seafood and chicken. They don't take reservations but do have Call-Ahead seating, which puts you on the waiting list in advance (4–10.30pm Mon–Thurs, 11pm Fri–Sat, noon–10.30pm Sun; 407 396 9990; **www.mannyschophouse.com**).

Wildside Bar & Grill: Great barbecue here, with the first Kissimmee outlet of the Thornton Park-based restaurant It serves up signature steaks and seafood, as well as burgers and sandwiches, but the real speciality is their delicious home-smoked pulled chicken and pork, smoked sausage, Angus brisket, smoked turkey, St Louis ribs and baby back ribs (4–11pm Sun–Thurs, 2–11pm Fri–Sat; 407 396 1166; **www.wildsiderestaurant.com**).

Mall at Millenia
In and around the upmarket Mall at Millenia you will find another tempting choice of restaurants.

Fast food: Burger 21, Jimmy John's, McDonalds, Panda Express, Wendy's.

Breakfast style: Keke's.

Bar-restaurant style: BJ's Brewhouse, Cheesecake Factory, Johnny Rockets, TGI Friday's.

Steakhouse style: Capital Grille.

Italian flavours: Olive Garden.

Brio Tuscan Grille: Also inside the Mall (and at Winter Park Village), this stylish Italian offering makes for a superb casual lunch or romantic dinner, with delicious flatbreads, luscious salads, superb steaks and surf and turf, creative pastas and regional specialities like chicken limone and grilled pork chops, plus daily fish specials. The Tuscan country-style ambience and fresh kids' menu all add up to memorable dining. Great weekend brunch, too (407 351 8909; 11am–10pm Mon–Thurs, 11pm Fri and Sat, 10am–10pm Sun; **www.brioitalian.com**).

BRITTIP
At Brio Tuscan Grille, don't miss the melt-in-the-mouth beef carpaccio starter, the bistecca insalata and Shrimp Mediterranean as a fab dinner combo.

Duffy's Sports Grill: Sports bar and restaurant that features an extensive menu, great beers and cocktails, and a vast array of TVs for live sporting action (11am–11pm; 407 930 2960; **www.duffysmvp.com**).

PF Chang's China Bistro: Inside the Mall, this mixes classic Chinese fare with American bistro style that makes fans of virtually all who sample it. Try the Black Bean Chicken, Hong Kong Style Sea Bass and fiery Beef à la Sichuan. There is also a good veggie selection (407 345 2888; 11am–11pm, midnight Fri–Sat, 10pm Sun; **www.pfchangs.com**).

Eat Like a Local
OK, so we live here and we don't necessarily head to the tourist areas for lunch or dinner (although there is a great choice). Instead, we stay in the more residential areas and sample off-the-beaten track choices that we're happy to flag up for readers who don't mind a drive.

4 Rivers SmokeHouse: Annually rated the best barbecue in Central Florida, this Winter Park diner draws long queues at peak times, but it's worth the wait for their succulent pulled pork, brisket, ribs and chicken (11am–8pm Mon–Thurs, 9pm Fri–Sat; 1844 474 8377; **https://4rsmokehouse.com/**).

Crafted Block & Brew: For a neat twist on the gastro-pub theme, we enjoy the style here in the Metro West area, either in the evening or for Sunday brunch. They take the same artisan approach to the excellent variety of food and the craft beers, which means you'll find something really different, as well as great burgers and comfort food (11.30am–12.30am Mon, 2am Tues–Fri, 10am–2pm Sat, 9am–12.30am Sun; 407 601 6887; **www.craftedorlando.com**)

Dixie Cream Café: When we want a home-cooked breakfast or lunch, we head to this charming café/bakery/coffee shop in the heart of the ritzy suburb of Windermere and enjoy a variety of Southern comfort food, burgers, sandwiches and salads (407 217 5047; 8am-2.30pm Tues–Sun; **www.dixiecreamcafe.com**).

Hagan O'Reilley's: When we've finished shopping in Winter Garden, we will sometimes head over to the Irish pub style at Hagan's (about 20 minutes north of Disney), boasting good beers, classic fare and live entertainment most nights. With 15 beers on tap and Happy Hour from 11am–7pm, you could easily be in the Emerald isle, although the beer garden is pure Florida! (11am–2am; 407 905 4782; **www.haganoreillys.com**).

Hamilton's Kitchen: For a stylish lunch or when we're feeling fancy, we head to Winter Park and enjoy the chic and artsy feel of the Alfond Inn, where this signature restaurant is a treat and the food wonderfully fresh and inventive. You might bump into a few local celebrities, too (7am–10pm; 407 998 8090; **www.thealfondinn.com/dining/hamiltons_kitchen**).

> ◀◖▶ **BRITTIP**
>
> For something special, try **Hamilton's Kitchen's** 'Pickled' Saturday Brunch (7am–2pm), with live acoustic music, cocktails from the Bloody Mary and Mimosa bars, and local menu highlights.

Kres Chopchouse: For an elegant night-on-the-town, this is a great go-to choice in downtown Orlando, in the heart of the busy Church Street area. Ideal for a pre-dinner drink, cocktails, a late-night nightcap or a full, elegant dinner, Kres features signature steaks, chops and seafood, plus a grown-up supper-club style that is genuinely classy (11.30am-midnight Mon-Fri, 5pm-midnight Sat; 407 447 7950; **www.kresrestaurant.com**).

Spice Modern: After enjoying a Sunday stroll around Lake Eola or the weekly farmers' market, we often retreat to the patio here for a great view over the lake, great cocktails and either brunch (10am–3pm) or the classic lunch, with tasty salads, burgers and sandwiches (11am–10pm Mon, 11pm Tues-Thurs, midnight Fri–Sat, 10am–10pm Sun; 407 581 9533; **http://spicesteakhouse.com/**).

The Taproom at Dubsdread: Yes, Dubsdread is a golf course (just west of downtown Orlando, a mile off I-4), but it also boasts the 'secret' of a great clubhouse restaurant with some of the best burgers in town. You can go seriously upmarket with great steaks and seafood, and their desserts are truly decadent (11am–10pm Mon–Thurs, 11pm Fri–Sat, 9pm Sun; 407 650 0100; **www.taproomatdubsdread.com**).

Urban Flats: After a day shopping in the delightful Winter Garden (just north of Disney), we will often pop in to this great bar-restaurant for their flatbreads and cocktails. Very much a locals' hangout with a classy touch, it is ideal for dinner before going to the Garden Theater (11am–10pm; 407 614 2765).

Capa

Our Orlando Top 10

Here's our annual 'Best Of' list for the Orlando area in general.

1   Urbain 40
2   A Land Remembered
3   Capa (Four Seasons)
4   Seasons 52
5   The Oceanaire
6   Hamilton's Kitchen
7   The Ravenous Pig
8   Cask & Larder
9   Highball & Harvest
10 Yellow Dog Eats

Yellow Dog Eats: Just past Windermere in rural Gotha is this eclectic deli-restaurant-country store with a hugely appealing mix of salads, sandwiches, tacos, nachos and veggie offerings, plus their succulent barbecue specialities. There is also a good beer and wine selection, plus Happy Hour 2–6pm, live music Thurs–Sat and trivia nights on Tues (11am–9pm; 407 296 0609; http://yellowdogeats.com/).

Zen: For great Asian dining, we head to the Omni Orlando Resort at Champions Gate (south of Disney), where this stylish restaurant features a sake and sushi bar to go with its full Oriental style. An oasis of relaxed charm, highlights include the Szechwan-style Beef Tenderloin and Sautéed Shrimp in Black Pepper Sauce and Spinach. Or try the superb Zen Experience – a multi-course feast (6–10pm; 407 390 6664; www.omnihotels.com).

DELUXE DINING

As if we haven't given you enough high-quality food for thought (ho ho), we have a final selection where you can really go to town for a special couple's night out or if you have something to celebrate.

Boca: New in Winter Park, this 'neighbourhood bar-kitchen-market' features fresh seasonal ingredients from local growers, with a cosy, European ambience that encourages visitors to slow down and join in the chat. Salads, flatbreads, sandwiches, seafood and daily specials are their stock in trade, but there is plenty of imagination (and organic produce) incorporated into dishes like braised short ribs, meatloaf and their cured-meat flatbread (11am–11pm; 407 636 7022; www.bocawinterpark.net).

BRITBONUS
Show your *Brit Guide* and receive one free cocktail or appetiser at the chic **Boca** in Winter Park (limit one per table).

Cala Bella: A proven winner at the stylish Rosen Shingle Creek Resort, this superb Italian-influenced restaurant is heavy on pasta and seafood, but also offers signature dishes like its sensational Cala Bella Lamb, Veal Marsala and Seafood Pescatore. Save room for dessert – the pastry chefs are among the best in America (5.30–10pm; 407 996 3663; www.calabellarestaurant.com).

Capa: The signature 17th floor rooftop restaurant at the Four Seasons hotel in Walt Disney World is superb for style, elegance and the nightly views of the Magic Kingdom fireworks. Even better is its contemporary Spanish steakhouse cuisine, with dishes from delightful small plates, freshly shucked oysters and fine Florida seafood to succulent steaks from the wood-burning grill in the show kitchen (6–10pm; 407 313 7777; www.fourseasons.com/orlando/dining/ restaurants/capa/).

Highball and Harvest: This exquisite choice in the Ritz-Carlton resort at Grande Lakes features Southern cuisine with an upmarket twist. Lightened-up favourites include Shrimp and Grits, Chicken Picnic, and Blackened Grouper, plus an artisanal cheese plate and the signature Pig-n-Potatoes (pork belly with Yukon hash, an egg, Hollandaise and the in-house hot sauce) for a menu that offers inspired dining amid relaxed elegance. Belly up to the

Highball & Harvest

bar for a funky handcrafted cocktail (11am–11pm), drop by for lunch, and don't miss the Red Velvet Cake for dessert! (6.30am–10pm, 407 393 4422; **http://www.ritzcarlton.com/en/hotels/florida/orlando/dining/highball-and-harvest**.

Hillstone: This lakeside location in Winter Park provides a relaxed but upmarket choice for a casual lunch, evening drink or full-scale dinner. Where the locals go for a 'power lunch,' it is also an evening oasis of calm and gracious service, with the chance to enjoy a drink on their pier or grab a window or patio table with a wonderful view of Lake Killarney. The menu varies from simple burgers and salads to epic fresh fish dishes, rotisserie chicken and succulent steaks. A good wine list, daily soup specials and signature desserts round out a superb offering – this really is *the* place to be when the sun goes down! (11.30am–10pm Sun–Thurs, 10.30pm Fri–Sat; 407 740 4005, **www.hillstone.com**).

A Land Remembered: For our money, this is the best steakhouse we've visited. Inside the golf clubhouse of the Rosen Shingle Creek Resort (but open to non-residents), it is a superbly refined venue boasting exquisite service and an outstanding wine list. The menu oozes class and even features local specialities like frogs' legs, gator stew, and a fresh fish selection. But, while the lamb, chicken and short ribs are outstanding, the steak choice is out of this world (featuring all-natural prime black Angus beef from the Harris Ranch in California). Various cuts of steak and a surf and turf (with lobster) are among the most succulent meat dishes you will find and, while

it is pricey, we believe it is worth every cent (5.30–10pm; 407 996 1956; **www.landrememberedrestaurant.com**).

Luma on Park: Also in Winter Park, this trendy gastropub can offer cuisine as simple as a well-cooked burger or pizza or a fabulous filet mignon. The mix of outdoor patio, lounge bar and restaurant makes it chic and lively, with fresh contemporary cuisine. Fine fish, steaks and chicken are among the highlights, with a great wine cellar. It also features a $35 three-course prix fixe Sun–Tues, and a special Chef's Table that should be booked in advance (4–11.30pm Mon–Thurs, 11.30am Fri- Sat; dining room, lunch 11.30am–3pm Fri–Sun, dinner 5.30–10.30pm daily; 407 599 4111; **www.lumaonpark.com**).

◀▓▶ BRITTIP

Need expert local advice on dining? Check out our good friend, restaurant critic and keen foodie Scott Joseph for up-to-date news, views and insight at **www.scottjosephorlando.com**. Not only is his 'Flog' (a Food Blog) essential reading, he also offers periodic special deals for ½-price coupons at a great range of restaurants. His Orlando Restaurant Guide is great reading and has a free app for iPhone, iPod and iPad at the iTunes store. Just look up Scott Joseph Orlando.

Ravenous Pig: Staying in Winter Park, local restaurateurs James and Julie Petrakis have crafted the British gastropub idea into a cosy hideaway that oozes style, with a menu that is superbly simple or simply superb, depending on if you just want great pub food or the full gourmet experience. Creative salads jostle with fresh pastas, fish dishes and a house-made charcuterie and cheese platter, as well as standards like a Pub Burger, Tacos and Steak Frites. Bookings are highly advisable though, as its popularity is widespread (5–10pm Tues–Sat, happy hour 4–6pm; 407 628 2333; **www.theravenouspig.com**).

OK, that's enough eating for now – on to another of our favourite topics – shopping…

12 Shopping

or

How to Send Your Credit Card into Meltdown

As well as being a theme park wonderland, this vast area of Florida is a shopper's paradise, with a dazzling array of specialist outlets, malls, flea markets and discount retailers. New centres spring up all the time, from smart malls to cheap gift shops – and you can't go a few paces in the tourist areas without a shop insisting it has the 'best bargains' of one sort or another.

With so much good shopping to be had for UK visitors, there's a danger of exceeding your baggage allowance for the flight home – or your duty-free allowance. American stores are genuinely fun just to browse, let alone splash out in, and you can expect to pay roughly the same in dollars as you do in pounds for items like clothes, books and jewellery, and real bargains are to be had in jeans, trainers, sports equipment and cosmetics. Almost everywhere offers free, convenient parking, while shop assistants are polite and helpful.

Sales tax: Be aware of the hidden extra costs of shopping. Unlike our VAT, Florida sales tax is NOT part of the displayed purchase price, so you must add on 6% or 7% (it varies by county) for the final price. Also, some shops will ask for photo ID with credit card purchases, so have a photo driving licence or photo ID with you.

Allowances: Your limit in the catch-all duty category of 'gifts and souvenirs' is only £390 per person. If you exceed that, you need to keep your receipts and go through the 'goods to declare' channel (though paying the duty and VAT can still be cheaper than buying the same items at home). Some items, such as clothing and footwear for children, do not incur a VAT rate. However, restrictions apply to all reduced-rate VAT items, so be sure to check details with HM Revenue & Customs. Your ordinary duty-free allowances from America include 200 cigarettes and 1 litre of spirits or 2 litres of fortified wine or sparkling wine and 4 litres of still wine.

BRITTIP

Don't buy electrical goods in the US – they won't work in the UK without a converter. Most games systems (notably X Box, Wii and PS4) are also NOT compatible with UK players. Hand-held games are fine.

Disney Springs

© Disney

Customs duty: You pay duty (which varies depending on the item) on the total purchase price (i.e. inclusive of Florida sales tax) once you have exceeded £390, plus VAT at 20%. You CANNOT pool your allowances to cover one item that exceeds a single allowance. Hence, if you buy a digital camera that costs £400, you have to pay the duty (at 4.9%) on the full £400, taking the total to £419.60 and then VAT on that figure. However, if you have several items that add up to £390, and then another that exceeds that, you pay the duty and VAT only on the excess item (and customs officers usually give you the benefit of the lowest rate on what you pay for). Duty rates are updated regularly and vary from 2.2% (e.g. video games) to 14% (e.g. a computer monitor) keeping in mind VAT rates change. For more info, contact the Customs and Excise National Advice Service on 0845 010 9000, **www.hmrc.gov.uk**.

Alligator products constitute those of an endangered species (to UK authorities) so require an import licence. Consult the Global Wildlife Licensing and Registration Service for more info.

◄┃▶ **BRITTIP**
Pick up the *Orlando Sentinel* newspaper on Sunday and you will get the full local lowdown on all the great sales for the coming week.

Disney Springs

In many ways, the heart of Walt Disney World is its new-look Disney Springs district (10am–midnight), split into four linked sections: Marketplace, The Landing, Town Center and West Side. This is typical Disney, a beautiful location, imaginative architecture and a host of one-off elements that make shopping a pleasure, with almost 100 shops, plus dozens of dining options. A handy (free) water-taxi also links each end, as well as Disney's Old Key West and Port Orleans Resorts.

Disney Springs can be found off exits 67 and 68 of I-4 and is well signposted

Up, up and away!

In Disney Springs West Side, across the bridge from The Landing, is Characters in Flight, a wonderful tethered balloon ride that gently soars up to 400ft/122m high carrying up to 30 at a time in a 19ft/5.7m gondola on 6min rides. It provides a fab panorama of much of the huge extent of Walt Disney World and is a great photo opportunity by day or night (8.30am–midnight). It costs $18/adult and $12/3–9s. In certain weather conditions the number of passengers is limited, while it is grounded in high winds or heavy rain.

(exit 68 can be congested at peak periods). Parking has been boosted by two new multi-storey car parks that feature clever technology to indicate every empty space on each floor (look for the green lights).

Marketplace: Don't miss the **World of Disney** store, the largest of its kind, with a mind-boggling array of Disney merchandise, from clothing and jewellery to toys and home goods. Equally impressive are the **LEGO Imagination Center** (an interactive playground and shop), the amazing **Art of Disney** and the **Marketplace Co-Op** (a number of small shops under one roof). **Once Upon a Toy** is a gigantic toy emporium complete with a host of classic games, many with a Disney theme, for kids to try. Here you will also find the new home of the **Bibbidi Bobbidi Boutique**, where young girls can have hair, make-up and nails done in true Princess style (and with the price to match!). Other worthwhile one-offs are the blissful **Basin** (for toiletries) and **Disney's Wonderful World of Memories** (for all scrapbook fans).

◄┃▶ **BRITTIP**
Parents beware! The Bibbidi Bobbidi Boutique hair and make-up shop is hideously expensive. Packages range from $64–$207, so you may want to steer your Princess gently away!

Princess Parade: Young girls in the princess mood may want to take part in the daily parade from the Bibbidi Bobbidi Boutique at 1–2pm (weather permitting). It marches in full pomp around the Marketplace, finishing at the Carousel, where all children get a free ride. Girls can dress up (or not) as they wish, and there is NO fee to take part.

Arribas Brothers: A big, attractive gift store, those keen on pin-trading should check out **Pin Traders**. Then there's **Disney Design-A-Tee**, **Tren-D**, a cutting edge Disney fashion store for women, **Little Miss Matched** for fun and funky socks, bedding and more (popular with young girls), and **Disney's Days of Christmas**.

For bargain-hunters, a section by **Goofy's Candy Company** offers **Marketplace Fun Finds** – everything at reduced prices. Dancing fountains and squirt pools (where kids tend to get seriously wet) and the lakeside setting all add to the appeal. **Build-A-Dino** and **Dino Store** can be found inside T-Rex Café.

The Landing: Take your pick from a variety of imaginative shops, including **Art of Shaving** (upmarket shaving products), **Sanuk** (footwear), **Sound Lion** (headphones, music players), **Apex by Sunglass Hut**, **Erwin Pearl** jewellery, **Chapel Hats** (funky/vintage hats), **Havaianas** (flip-flops), **Erin McKenna's bakery NYC** (vegan/gluten-free baked goods), and **The Ganachery** (delicious handmade chocolates). They all opened in 2015 and 2016, along with several new restaurants (see dining chapter, p307). **Raglan Road** also has its own Irish-themed gift shop here.

West Side: Continuing into West Side gives you the superb **AMC 24** cinema complex (p290), plus another 27 retail and dining outlets, notably the big **Harley-Davidson** store. **D Street** features Vinylmation figurines and collectables while **Pop Gallery** is also original for collectable artwork. **Goofy's Candy Cauldron** is a big hit with kids, as is **Star Wars Galactic Outpost**, but other shops, including **Something Silver** (contemporary jewellery), **Curl by Sammy Duvall**

(water sports), **Sosa Family Cigars**, **Sunglass Icon** and **Fit2Run** are all places you could find in the average mall and are rather dull. There are gift shops for **House of Blues**, **Bongos Cuban Café**, **Cirque du Soleil**, and **Splitsville**, though. This is also where you'll find the **Food Truck Park**.

Town Center: The final addition to Disney Springs opened in stages through 2016, adding even more shopping and dining. In fact, this looks more like an upmarket mall than anything else, but there are still some nice touches in the architecture and with the story of Disney Springs itself. The central water features are extremely eye-catching and there are great family back-stories at **D-Luxe Burger** and **Amorette's Patisserie** in particular (the latter of which serves up some decadent cakes and pastries). Be sure to ask the Cast Members about them. The shops themselves are nothing you won't find in most good shopping centres (and at a premium price here), but take your pick from the likes of **Everything But Water**, **Kipling**, **Lucky Brand**, **Tommy Bahama**, **American Threads**, **Kate Spade**, **Under Armour**, **Columbia** and **Lacoste** for the latest fashions, apparel and sportswear. There are 6 jewellery shops, including **Vera Bradley**, **Alex and Ani** and **Pandora**, another five for footwear, including **UGG**, **Sperry** and **Trophy Room**, and four for comestics, notably **Sephora** and **L'Occitane**. For true one-offs, sample **Sprinkles** for

Disney Springs

© Disney

wonderful cupcakes, ice cream and shakes; **Sugarbee** for arts and crafts; and the **Coca-Cola Store**, with its amazing array of products.

The shops of Disney Springs are open 10am–11pm daily. For more details, see **www.disneysprings.com.**

International Drive

This core tourist area is awash with shopping of all kinds, from the cheapest and tackiest plazas full of tourist gift shops, to four purpose-built centres. Some of the shops just north of the Sand Lake Road junction are best avoided, while the northern end of I-Drive has undergone a major redevelopment. This area is also renowned for discount outlet shopping – a local speciality – offering name brands at heavily reduced prices.

Universal CityWalk: Among the most original of the 12 shops are **Quiet Flight**, for radical surf and beachwear; the retro-American decor of **Fossil** for leather goods, watches and sunglasses; **Fresh Produce** for swimwear, casual clothing and accessories; **P!Q** toys and household; the large **Island Clothing Company** for Tommy Bahama clothing and merchandise; **Hart & Huntington Orlando Tattoo Shop** with an array of permanent tattoos, as well as clothing and accessories; and the skate-boarding chic of **Element**. Again, none of these is anything special but the huge **Universal Studios Store**

Universal CityWalk

offers a wide range of park souvenirs and merchandise.

Artegon Marketplace: Formerly Festival Bay, this large development at the top of In-Drive is undergoing a two-stage makeover to change it into an artisan market, shopping, dining and entertainment complex. Anchor stores are **Bass Pro Shops**, **Ron Jon Surf Shop**, **Boot Barn** (for Western wear and jeans) and the **Cinemark** cinema, plus iconic **Gods and Monsters**, a comic, collectibles and pop culture mega-shop. Then there are the **Artegon Sky Trail** ropes course and **Sky Zone** trampoline park, as well as **Putting Edge** indoor glow-in-the-dark mini-golf and a variety of dining choices, notably fab burgers at **Fuddruckers, Sugar Daddy's** bakery and **Pizza @ Artegon**. The main area, The Marketplace, features a collection of 165 arts and crafts stalls, from the way out to the remarkable, as well as the wonderful **International Hot Glass** glass-blowing studio and a array of gifts and artwork. Live entertainment and special events feature at most weekends (407 351 7718, **www.artegonmarketplace.com**).

Orlando Premium Outlets I-Drive: At the top of I-Drive, this attractive 175-shop 'lifestyle centre' has gone all out for the big, semi-open-air style that encourages people to wander the long promenades full of shop fronts and big-name brands. Boasting a landscaped canal running through the centre, outdoor seating, cafés, a Market Place food court and a Guest Services centre, it provides a luxury touch. Major brands include the **Neiman Marcus Last Call Clearance Center**, which will attract the fashion-conscious, as will the **Kate Spade New York, Calvin Klein, Lacoste** and **Jones New York Outlet**. Other familiar names include **Nike Factory Store, Tommy Hilfiger, Crabtree & Evelyn, Banana Republic, Bath & Body Works, Aeropostale, Coach** and **Brooks Brothers**, plus, inevitably, a Starbucks. New in 2015 were **Basler Outlet** (designer fashions), **Diesel** (clothing), **American Eagle, Vera Bradley** and **DC Shoes**. With its

A Kissimmee tradition

Old Town is home to some weekly events that appeal to both locals and tourists alike. **The Saturday Nite Cruise** at 8.30pm is a trademark drive-past of 300-plus vintage and collector cars (the biggest in America; viewing starts at 1pm). A **Friday Nite All American Muscle Car Cruise** features cars built between 1964 and today (viewing starts at 4pm, cruise starts at 8.30pm), **Sunday Show 'n' Shine** (4pm) features trucks, Jeeps, and SUVs, while Wed night's 5pm **Little Darlin' Street Party and Cruise In** brings out the pre-1988 cars. There is live music, fairground stalls and prizes, and it can get fairly raucous later on, with plenty of alcoholic libations (witness the Sun on the Beach bar!).

attractive food court, including the popular Five Guys Burgers, Panera, plus Jack's Steakery restaurant and the smart Italian-styled Vinito, you have one of the area's brightest shopping centres that is also at the top of the I-Ride Trolley route (10am–11pm Mon–Sat, 10am–9pm Sun; www.premiumoutlets.com/orlando).

Pointe Orlando: Easily accessible from I-Drive, this is a good choice for an evening out with a bit of retail therapy. With 16 smart stores, you can indulge your passion for fashion at **Victoria's Secret**, **Armani Exchange** and **Hollister** or stock up on gifts and souvenirs at **Tommy Bahama**, **Charming Charlie**, **Design By You**, **Brighton Collectible**, **Flow** and the excellent **Tharoo & Co** jewellery.

For the full rundown on all 18 places to eat at Pointe Orlando, see p320.

Parking is at The Pointe's multi-storey car park, but some stores and restaurants will redeem your parking ticket if you shop there. It's open noon–10pm Mon–Sat, noon–8pm Sun Oct–May; noon–9pm Fri–Sat, noon–8pm Sun–Thurs June–Sept; later at the bars and restaurants (407 248 2838, www.pointeorlando.com).

I-Drive 360: Orlando's newest entertainment and dining complex (see p230) has a selection of shops, including the big chemist and general store **Walgreens**, **Tervis** (durable drinkware), **Expo Electronics**, **360 Gifts** (I-Drive 360 souvenirs), and the **Flip Flop Shop**. Nearby are the I-Shops, which include another **Walgreens**, **O'Neill** (swimwear), **US Gift Factory** (souvenirs), a jewellery store and **World of Electronics** (discount electronics).

Kissimmee

Along the tourist territory of Highway 192, you will again find a complete mix of outlets, with a profusion of the cheap and cheerful, but also several highly enticing possibilities.

BRITBONUS

Brit Guide readers receive a FREE Florida Mall discount booklet with the cut-out ad on the back flap of this book. Take advantage of this exclusive opportunity for added savings on your holiday shopping.

Old Town: This is Kissimmee's version of the purpose-built tourist shopping centre, an antique-style offering with an eclectic mix of shops, restaurants, bars and fairground attractions set out along brick-lined streets that have recently been renovated and refreshed. The shops range from standard souvenirs and novel T-shirt outlets to sportswear, and collectibles (check out the **Old Town General Store** for a step back in time, or the **Old Town Portrait Gallery** for period-style photos). The individual style of **Out of This World Embroidery** offers a 'you name it, we'll stitch it' service, while, **Filthy Rich** jewellery, **Wild Billie's Gifts** and **Lucky Mouse** are all great for gifts. There are also 18 restaurants or snack bars. For lunch or dinner, try **Tex Mex Express** cuisine or **Blue Max Tavern**, another fun alternative. **Flippers Pizzeria** and **Bamboo Court** are also worth trying, while there are other snack outlets, with offerings from popcorn to candy and the wonderful **Sweet Dreams Ice Cream Café**. **Sun on the Beach** is a good nightclub in evenings (until 2am, like Blue Max).

Parking is free (10am–11pm daily; ride hours vary monthly; 407 396 4888; www.myoldtownusa.com).

Downtown Kissimmee: This offers the more local, authentic face of shopping in Florida, with the charming Main Street area featuring antique shops, one-off boutiques, cafés and restaurants. Much attention has been paid to the historic district in recent years, and it is now a relaxing place for a wander and a meal. **The Welcome Station** on Main Street (formerly an old-fashioned petrol station) is a great place to start, and even has local crafts, keepsakes, and books focusing on Floridian history (9am–5pm Mon–Fri). Then look into the likes of local landmarks **Lanier's**, **Makinson Hardware** (the oldest hardware store in Florida), and **Gallery One Artists**. The authentic Mexican family style of **Azteca's** is worth trying, along with the casual sports-bar style of **Broadway Pizza**, while we're fans of the smart **3 Sisters Speakeasy** wine bar and café, which has **Trivia Night Tuesdays**, an **Antique Car Show** on the first Fri every month and live music Wed–Sat from 9pm–midnight (407 201 3270, **www.3sistersspeakeasy. com**). Every Tues you can also sample Kissimmee Valley Farmers' Market in the Kissimmee Civic

Abracadabra Ice Cream

Center (3–7pm; hours may change without notice, so be sure to check **www.experiencekissimmee.com**).

⬛ BRITTIP

For something different, don't miss Abracadabra Ice Cream Factory, just outside Kissimmee town centre (on North Main Street). Here, they mix fantastic creamy creations using a wonderful variety of ingredients – and flash freeze it all with liquid nitrogen for a true taste sensation! It's open 11am–10pm daily.

The Loop and The Loop West: Apart from Old Town and Downtown, the Kissimmee area is largely short of quality shopping, but head to the Osceola Parkway (at the junction with John Young Parkway), running parallel to Highway 192, to find these extensive developments. They offer a mix of 75 shopping and dining outlets plus a 16-screen Regal Cinema in a pedestrian-friendly setting, with the shops grouped around two large car parks. Many of the shops may be unfamiliar but are worth visiting.

Of note at The Loop are **Ross** (a huge discount warehouse of clothes, shoes, linens, cosmetics and more), **Kohl's** (a well-priced department store), **Bed, Bath & Beyond** (household), **Old Navy** (clothing), **Michaels** (arts and crafts), **Famous Footwear** (discounted shoes) and a hairdresser, nail salon and chemist (**CVS**).

At The Loop West, look for the big department stores of **JC Penney** (clothing and housewares) and **Kirkland** (homeware), plus **Ulta** (cosmetics), **TJ Maxx** (clothing) and **DSW** (shoes), plus 16 other shops.

The extensive dining choice includes classic 1950s diner **Johnny Rockets**, **Ben & Jerry's** ice cream, the counter-service of **Pei Wei Asian Diner**, Mexican choice **Abuelo's**, **Tropical Smoothie Café** and the big-name chains of **Chick-Fil-A**, **Chili's** (p311), **Panera Bread** (p310), **Bonefish Grill** (p318) and the distinctive **BJ's Brewhouse** (p311) offering great burgers, sandwiches, salads and steaks, plus an impressive beer

A must for Disney collectors

Theme Park Connection is an amazing repository of past merchandise, collectors' items, cast-offs, old park signs, artwork, books and MUCH more. It is a touch pricey as most of its stock is rare or discontinued, and it can take *hours* to search through its warehouse-sized quarters, but you are bound to turn up a real treasure or two and revel in the astounding collection of Disney material. It is tucked away on a small industrial estate at 2160 Premier Row in Orlando, hence you should check its exact location on its website (**www.themeparkconnection.com**) or call 407 284 1934. Open 10am–5pm Mon–Fri, 10am–3pm Sat; closed Sun.

choice; 407 932 5245, **www.bjsbrewhouse.com**). The shops are open 10am–9.30pm Mon–Sat, 11am– 6pm Sun, later at the restaurants and cinemas (407 343 9223; **www.experiencetheloop.com**).

Lake Buena Vista

The Lake Buena Vista area offers two of the best discount outlet centres, with great range and prices.

Orlando Premium Outlets Vineland Ave: High on your 'must visit' list, this is a huge hit with UK visitors. With a fresh look and style, and a legion of big-name designers, it can be found on Vineland Avenue between I-Drive and I-4 (just south of SeaWorld; or exit 68 off I-4).

 BRITTIP

Don't try to battle with the crowds in the main open-air car park at Orlando Premium Outlets Vineland Ave. Instead, head towards the back of the centre where you will find the 1,600-car multi-storey car park.

In all, it offers more than 170 stores of well-known brand names (like **Diesel**, **Armani Exchange**, **Kenneth Cole**, **Banana Republic**, **Prada**, **Coach**, **Kate Spade** and **Calvin Klein**) in a semi-covered pedestrian plaza, with free parking and the convenience of being at the south end of the I-Ride Trolley (main line). Other signature shops are **Samsonite Company Store**, **Ecko Unltd** (jeans and sportswear), **UGG Australia** (Ugg boots), **OshKosh B'Gosh** (baby/toddler clothes), **Famous Footwear** (a mini-warehouse of footwear fashion) and **Perfumania**.

Watch out also for big Disney bargains at the **Disney Outlet**, which offers the previous season's items. The adjoining expansion of The Promenade adds 12 more stores, including a two-storey **Sak's Fifth Avenue Off 5th**, **Tommy Bahama** and **Forever 21**, plus the eclectic (and distinctly lively) bar/ restaurant style of **Dick's Last Resort** (**www.dickslastresort.com**).

 BRITTIP

Brit Guide Touring Plan clients will receive Orlando Premium Outlets' special Premier Platinum VIP Passport voucher, for significant extra savings at many shops (p39).

The food court is quite tempting, too, with 15 outlets, from **Villa Fresh Italian Kitchen** and **Maki of Japan** to **Starbucks**, **Taco Bell** and **Subway**. There is even a beer and wine café.

Orlando Premium Outlets

The Lynx bus service also stops here (407 841 2279), while **Mears Transport** has on-site taxi stands (407 422 2222). Premium Outlets is open daily 10am–11pm (9pm Sun; 407 238 7787; **www.premiumoutlets.com/orlando**).

BRITTIP
Want to see a REAL shopping frenzy? Visit either Orlando Premium Outlets centre for Midnight Madness on the Fri after Thanksgiving when they open at midnight and stay open for 24 hours – and thousands pour in to shop!

Lake Buena Vista Factory Stores: Get ready for more big-name products at discount prices here, from **Fossil, Converse, Reebok, Tommy Hilfiger, OshKosh B'Gosh** superstore and (the better-priced) **Carter's For Kids**. It is another open-air plaza, with 44 stores spread over 6acres/2.5ha and with plentiful parking. It's slightly off the beaten track and therefore not quite as busy as some of the others.

Another option is **Theme Park Outlet**, which replaced the Disney Character Outlet. There is also a decent food court with a pleasant outdoor deck, and a kids' playground. Some of the stores and brand names may not be well known to us, but the likes of **Old Navy** (excellent-value casual clothing),

Florida Mall

© Gray Line Tours

Easy Spirit (super-comfortable shoes), **SAS Shoes** (think Hush Puppies, only cheaper!), **Travelpro** (luggage and travel accessories) and **Rack Room Shoes** (big names at serious savings) are worth discovering. **World of Coffee** is both an internet café and one of the best places you could find to sip a latte and enjoy a cake or pastry, with its outdoor terrace and bird cages (plus some British snacks and chocs!). Worth noting at the neighbouring Lake Buena Vista Resort Village and Spa are the luxurious **Reflections Spa** for a bit of pampering after your day of shopping, and **Frankie Farrells Irish Pub** (p322).

The Factory Stores are on SR 535 (2ml/3km south off exit 68 on I-4) and are open daily 10am–9pm (to 7pm Sun). Their shuttle service picks up at 60 participating hotels and condos in a 10ml/16km radius (407 238 9301, **www.lbvfs.com**).

BRITTIP
Don't miss the Lake Buena Vista Factory Stores website for valuable weekly coupons and do 'friend' their Facebook page for even more special offers and discounts. Or just visit Travelpro store for a coupon booklet.

Malls
Head out slightly beyond the main tourist territory and you will discover the further choice and style of the area's many malls. They contain a huge range of shops and, if you take advantage of their periodic sales, you will be firmly back on the bargain trail. The top two locally are the Florida Mall and the Mall at Millenia, and both offer a contrasting experience.

BRITTIP
For a good book, head for one of the two big **Barnes & Noble** shops, either on West Sand Lake Road in the Venezia Plaza, or on the South Orange Blossom Trail opposite the Florida Mall. Both have great coffee shops, too.

Florida Mall: The largest in central Florida, this features more than 260 shops, with five large department

Our shopping tips

As we live locally, shopping is close to our hearts and we recommend the following.

Bookshop: Barnes & Noble

Chemist: Walgreens

Clothing: Marshall's and Ross stores

Disney store: Theme Park Connection

Electronics: Best Buy

Home goods: Home Goods

Mall: Mall at Millenia

Open-air centre: Winter Garden Village

Outlet shopping: Orlando Premium Outlets

Specialist store: Boot Barn (Artegon)

Supermarket: Whole Foods Market

stores and a 24-counter food court, plus a children's play area, the popular fresh offerings of **Nature's Table** and hearty **Buca di Beppo**. Located on the South Orange Blossom Trail, on the corner of Sand Lake Road, this spacious and smart mall is open 10am–10pm Mon–Sat, noon–8pm Sun. Highlights are the department stores, led by the upmarket **Macy's**, plus **JC Penney**, **Sears** and **Dillard's**. Other shops worth looking out for are **Bath & Body Works**, **Gap**, **PacSun** (beachwear and more) and the **Build-a-Bear Workshop**, **Game Stop** and the fun **M&M's World** store. New in 2016 were **Bellagio Jewelry**, **Pagoda Piercings** and **Soho** hair extensions. Also here is the massive **Crayola Experience** (interactive fun and design for kids; **www.crayolaexperience.com/orlando**). Guest services offers a discount booklet with a handy international size chart to help with American sizing, while there is also free wi-fi throughout the mall, free wheelchair use, pushchair rental and foreign currency exchange. There are even spa and beauty treatments in the Lancôme Institut de Beauté in **Dillard's**, and the **JC Penney** styling salon (407 851 7234; **www.simon.com**). The Mall also benefits

from the integral **Florida Hotel**, with **Cricket's Bar**.

BRITTIP

With 25 hands-on attractions – from melting, moulding, spinning, and painting to drawing, doodling, and digital design – Crayola Experience is a good distraction when it's too hot or wet for the parks. There is even a Crayola Café for lunch or a snack. Admission is $19pp, under-3s free.

Mall at Millenia: If the Florida Mall is the biggest shopping venue, this is the smartest. Just off I-4 to the north of Universal Orlando (exit 78), it is the most upmarket, dramatic and technologically advanced shopping complex in Florida, with New York's most famous department stores – **Bloomingdale's**, **Neiman Marcus** and **Macy's** – among a select number of other top-name boutiques such as **Louis Vuitton**. The entrance features a 60ft/18m glass rotunda with a flowing water garden theme and a concièrge desk (valet parking is available). Then you can head in one of four directions over the marble and terrazzo floors or go upstairs to the high-quality 12-outlet food court. Try any of **Bistro Europa** (salads, soups, wraps), **Firehouse Subs**, **Haagen-Dazs** (decadent ice cream), the authentic Mandarin-style of **Chinatown**, the fresh **Chipotle Mexican Grill** (salads, tacos and burritos) and **Southwest Grill** (succulent chicken, barbecue beef and salads), plus **Tony's & Bruno's** for Italian specialities (pasta, pizza, salads and cheesecake).

BRITTIP

Visit the Mall at Millenia Concièrge, located inside the main entrance on level 1, and show this book to receive a complimentary savings book.

The grand architecture is also focused on five separate courts along a flattened, serpentine S-shape, topped by an arched glass roof like a gigantic conservatory. On two airy levels (three in Bloomingdale's and Macy's) and with eight Juliet balconies connecting the two sides, the mall consists of a colossal amount of glass, plus a stunning Grand Court, featuring a dozen 20ft/6m columns capped by curved plasma video screens. And, while around 20% of the 150 stores are upmarket (**Cartier**, **Chanel**, **Jimmy Choo**, **Burberry** and **Gucci**), there are many unexpected options, such as **Urban Outfitters**, **Apple**, **MAC Cosmetics** and **Anthropologie**. You will also find plenty of mainstream names like **Abercrombie & Fitch**, **Hollister**, **Gap**, **Banana Republic** and **Victoria's Secret**. The five main restaurants are also first class: the heavenly **Cheesecake Factory**, **Earl's Kitchen + Bar**, **PF Chang's China Bistro**, the stylish Italian of **Brio Tuscan Grille**, and the swanky **Capital Grille** (for that special evening out). On top of that there is the excellent fresh sandwich style of **Panera Bread**, the **California Pizza Kitchen** and a **Johnny Rockets** diner. This is also the only mall with a US post office inside (NB: Standard postcards to the UK cost $1.15). A currency exchange is available, as are international phone cards. All in all, this takes the Florida shopping experience to a new level, and there is even a new Personal Shopper service to provide individual guidance to the stores and their latest collections, and help when trying on the latest styles (10am–9pm Mon–Sat,

11am–7pm Sun; 407 363 3555; **www.mallatmillenia.com**).

Other malls: There are three alternatives to these popular and busy malls. The **Altamonte Mall** is on Altamonte Avenue in the suburb of Altamonte Springs (take exit 92 off I-4 and head east for ½ml/800m on Route 436, then turn left); **Seminole Towne Center**, just off I-4 to the north of Orlando on the outskirts of Sanford (exit 101C off I-4); and **Oviedo Marketplace**, to the east of Orlando (right off exit 41 of Central Florida Greeneway, 417). The Altamonte Mall is the best of the bunch and well off the beaten tourist track, featuring 94 speciality shops, four major department stores – **Macy's**, **Dillard's**, **JC Penney** and **Sears** – and 24 eateries, including the fun **Bahama Breeze** (p305), **ispice** Indian cuisine, and pub-style **Orlando Ale House** (p305). An 18-screen cinema and children's soft-play area round out the offerings. Open 10am–9pm Mon–Sat, noon–6pm Sun, the Customer Service Centre offers a VIP savings book to visitors (**www. altamontemall.com**). Shop during the week and you'll feel as if you have the place to yourself!

Winter Garden Village: A final recommendation, 10ml/16km north of Walt Disney World on Highway 535 at the junction with toll road 429, which is primarily a locals' centre but still has visitor appeal. The expansive open-plan design, set around key stores like **Super Target**, **Best Buy**, **Ross**, **Marshall's**, **Home Goods** and **Beall's**, features a mix of the big names and smaller boutiques, as well as an array of 21 cafes and restaurants. Look for the upmarket seafood choice of **Bonefish Grill**, the elegant **Longhorn Steakhouse**, family-style **Chili's**, **Cracker Barrel**, **UNO Chicago Grill** and **Village Inn**, or the counter-service options like **Five Guys Burgers**, **Panda Express**, **Coldstone Creamery** and **Chick-Fil-A**, and the first Orlando outlet of our favourite burger restaurant, **Red Robin** (**www.facebook.com/wintergardenvillage**).

Winter Garden Village

© TCA Project

Specialist shops

Wal-Mart: High on many people's lists, this warehouse-like store sells just about everything. There are 21 Wal-Marts in central Florida, 16 of which are 24hr Supercenters. The main tourist area stores are on Highway 27 (just north of 192); Highway 192 by Medieval Times (between markers 14 and 15); Osceola Parkway (at Buenaventura Lakes); John Young Parkway (at Sand Lake Road); on Kirkman Road (north of Universal Boulevard); by Highway 535 and Osceola Parkway; and on Turkey Lake Road.

Other supermarkets: There are plenty of other supermarkets and you will find rather better quality at the likes of **Publix** (throughout the main tourist areas, notably on Highway 192 and 27) and **Winn-Dixie** (a major south-east US chain). But the real Rolls-Royce of food stores, **Whole Foods Market,** has an Orlando branch on Turkey Lake Road, with its signature superb fresh produce emporium and plenty of chances to sample, plus a magnificent hot-food counter to grab a meal (**www.wholefoodsmarket.com**).

BRITTIP

Whole Foods Market has a small, funky beer and wine bar, which also serves food and offers fresh daily specials. A great choice for a sophisticated bite when you're stocking up on groceries.

For clothes, DIY, home furnishings, electrical goods, household items, gifts, toys and groceries, visit **Target** (its superstores on Highway 192 just west of Highway 535, near Mall at Millenia and Winter Garden Village are fine examples). The big chemists ('drug stores') of **Walgreens** and **CVS** also carry a surprisingly wide range of goods that make them mini supermarkets.

BRITTIP

Wal-Mart offers 1hr photo printing at great savings on UK prices, as do branches of Walgreens.

Individual outlets: Keen shoppers will want to check out other unfamiliar options. **Ross** (10 in Orlando, see **www.rossstores.com**) carries a huge range of discounted brand-name clothes, shoes, linens, towels, etc (hours vary by store, roughly 9.30am–9.30pm), while **Marshalls** (five in Orlando, **www.marshallsonline.com**) and **TJ Maxx** (also five, **www.tjmaxx.com**) are similar. For American sports gear visit **Academy Sports** stores (**www.academy.com**), while golfers should visit the **Edwin Watts Golf** stores (including the I-Drive clearance centre; **www.edwinwatts. com**), or any of the **Special Tee Golf & Tennis** shops. You can pick up some great deals on golf clubs in particular. By the same token, anglers can stock up on the latest gear at bargain prices at **Bass Pro Shops** (at the Artegon Marketplace; **www.basspro.com**).

But now the shopping is done, it's time to think about the journey home…

The Mall at Millenia

© Gray Line Tours

13 Going Home

or Where Did the Last Two Weeks Go?

And so, dog-tired, lighter in the wallet but (hopefully) blissfully happy and with a wealth of lovely memories, it's time to deal with that bane of all holidays – the journey home.

Now you have come through the last two weeks relatively unscathed, here's how to avoid any last-minute pitfalls.

The car

Returning the hire car can take time if you used an off-airport car depot, so allow an extra half hour; the process is much slicker with firms that operate directly from the airports, as nearly all now do. Most airlines require you to arrive 3hrs before an international flight, so don't be tempted to leave your check-in until the last minute. The off-airport check-in facility for Virgin Holidays (at Disney Springs by Cirque du Soleil®) is a major bonus in making this process smoother.

Now you'll have time to kill, so here is a guide to the two main Orlando airports.

Orlando International

Timing: Orlando's biggest airport is 46ml/74km from Cocoa Beach and 54ml/87km from Daytona Beach on the east coast, 84ml/135km from Tampa and 110ml/177km from Clearwater and St Petersburg to the west, 25ml/40km from Walt Disney World and 10ml/16km from Universal Orlando, so always allow plenty of time for the return journey, check-in and security procedure. The Beachline Expressway (528) can get congested in late afternoon, for example, and the Central Florida Greeneway (417) is often better.

Should you have more than 3hrs to spare, it's worth taking the 15min taxi ride to the Florida Mall.

The car: A convenient 'quick turnaround' area for hire cars allows most of the big hire companies to have onsite locations, a huge boon especially when returning the car.

Facilities: One of America's biggest and rated top for passenger satisfaction, this modern airport handles 40 million passengers a year, which is more than Gatwick and San Francisco. It can get busy at peak times, but its 1,000acre/405ha complex usually handles crowds with ease, and this is one of the most comfortable airports you could find. It boasts great facilities and its wide, airy concourses make it feel more like an elegant hotel (one end is actually the airport-owned Hyatt Hotel). Be aware the airport is now engaged in a $3b expansion to increase capacity over the next five years, mainly with a new South Terminal but also with enlarging the current check-in areas. This should have minimal effect on arrivals but could affect departures – another reason not to cut it fine with check-in.

The airport always aims to stay a step ahead, with environmentally friendly enhancements, smart restrooms and a wide selection of food and drink outlets. It boasts a major food court, multiple restaurant options, good shops and plenty of seating.

Facilities for the disabled: Ramps, restrooms, wide lifts and large open areas ensure easy wheelchair access, and there are features like TDD and amplified telephones, wheelchair-height drinking fountains, Braille lift controls and companion-care restrooms to assist any travellers with disabilities.

◀▶ **BRITTIP**

You are advised to leave all luggage unlocked (no combination locks or padlocks) when you check in for your flight, as the TSA security staff open a LOT of bags during screening and have the right to access any case, locked or not. TSA approved locks are suggested, if you prefer to lock your cases.

Landside

As with all international airports, there is a division between LANDSIDE (for visitors) and AIRSIDE (where you must have a ticket). There are three levels to Orlando's Landside.

- Level 1 is for ground transportation, tour operator desks, parking, buses and car rental agencies, plus the Virgin Atlantic baggage claim.

- Level 2 is for main Baggage Claim and private vehicles meeting passengers.

- Level 3 is where you enter on your return journey, as it holds the check-in desks, shops and restaurants.

The main area of Level 3 is then further divided into interconnected sections:

Landside A: This houses the check-in for Gates 1–29 and 100–129. Here you'll find Aer Lingus, Southwest, JetBlue, Norwegian, Virgin America and Virgin Atlantic (though Virgin Atlantic departs from Gates 70-99).

Landside B: Check-in here for Gates 30–99 and American Airlines, Air Canada, BA, Delta, Icelandair,

Lufthansa, United, Spirit, and Thomas Cook.

Shopping: Once you've checked in, you can explore the East and West Halls of the Level 3 concourse. These house a good mix of shops and restaurants, plus currency exchange, information desks and ATMs, while the Hyatt Hotel is in the East Hall. The East and West Halls are linked by the restaurants, shops and services of the North and South Walks. In total, there are 109 places to shop and eat, including the food court, and it's almost like being in a smart shopping mall.

Many shops feature outstanding design and even photo opportunities: see the two **Disney** stores, **Harley-Davidson, Universal, SeaWorld/Busch Gardens** and **Kennedy Space Center**. Other notable shops are **Lush** bath products, **Brookstone, Ron Jon Surf Shop, Lids** (sports hats and clothes) and **Hudson Booksellers**.

Dining: Another pleasure here, the eight-counter food court features **Carvel** ice-cream, **Sbarro** pizza, **Quiznos** subs, **McDonalds** and **Panda Express**, plus the slightly healthier option of **Chick-Fil-A. Macaroni Grill** is a tasty full-service Italian restaurant option, while **Home Team Sports** adds a multi-screen TV set-up plus counter and table service. Upstairs at the West Hall is **Chili's Too**.

The East Hall is quieter and more picturesque as it is dominated by the eight-storey Hyatt Hotel atrium. Up the escalator is the main entrance, and, to see out your visit in style, **McCoy's Bar & Grill** (up and turn right) is a smart bar-restaurant with a superb airport view and a menu that includes a **Sushi Bar** and fresh salads, sandwiches, flatbreads and small plates ideal for sharing or lighter appetites (11am–12:30am, Sushi Bar 4–11pm; 407 825 1234, www.orlandoairport.hyatt.com).

To go really upmarket, take the lift to the 9th-floor **Hemisphere** steakhouse (breakfast and dinner only). You'll have an even more impressive view, and its five-star cuisine offers some of the best fare in the city, but it's pricey (5.30–10pm Mon–Fri).

ORLANDO INTERNATIONAL AIRPORT

Airside

Once it's time to move to your departure gate, be aware of the four satellite 'arms' that make up Airside. This is where you will probably need to queue as the security screening takes time, and you should allow AT LEAST 30mins. The arms are divided into Gates 1–29 and 30–59 at the West end, and 70–99 (UK international departures) and 100–129 (all American domestic flights) at the East. All the departure gates are here, plus duty-free shops and more cafés.

The four satellites are each connected to the main building by an automated tram, so you need to be alert when it comes to finding your departure gate. There are no Tannoy announcements for flights, so check your departure gate and time when you check in. However, there are large monitors in the terminal with all departure info. The usual gates are:

- **1–29:** Icelandair, Aer Lingus, Norwegian and JetBlue.
- **30–59:** American, Spirit, Bahamasair and United.
- **70–99:** Air Canada, British Airways, Delta, Lufthansa, Thomas Cook and Virgin Atlantic.
- **100–129:** Southwest and Virgin America.

Airside is clean and efficient. There's less choice than the main terminal but there are two duty-free shops (your purchases are delivered to the departure gate for you to collect as you board). Both stores include designer sunglasses, jewellery, handbags, fashion watches, new perfumes and a selection of travel retail exclusives.

Gates 1–29: Here you'll find the first duty-free shop, **Hudson News** (newsagent), **Za-Za's Cuban Café**, **On the Border Mexican Cantina**, and a mini food court with **Starbucks, Burger King, Cold Stone Creamery, Brioche Doree, Famous Famiglia, Urban Crave** street food and **Le Grand Comptoire** bar.

Gates 30–59: These have **Qdoba Mexican Grill, Manchu Wok, Nature's Table, Wendy's, Freshens Treats, Za-Za's Cuban Coffee,** full-service **Ruby Tuesday,** the fresh grab-and-go or bar style of **Camden Food Co, Hudson News** and **Hudson Gallerie** (clothing and gifts).

Gates 70–99: The main satellite for UK flights offers a good duty-free shop, currency exchange, **Stellar News & Gifts,** the speciality **Zoom System** shop, **CNN Kiosk** and **XpressSpa.** A food court contains **Burger King, Nathan's Hot Dogs, Carvel, Starbucks, Fresh Attractions** deli and **Pinkberry,** the excellent table-service **Outback Steakhouse** and bar, and a small **Cibo Express** grab-and-go and bar.

Gates 100–129: This revamped satellite offers a food court with **Asian Chao, Green Leaf's & Bananas** (salads, smoothies and frozen yoghurt), **Jersey Mike's Subs, Chipotle, McDonalds, Villa Italian Kitchen** and the grab-and-go **The Market by Villa.** Even better is a full restaurant from **Cask & Larder,** one of Orlando best gastropubs, plus eight shops and the **Terminal Getaway Spa.**

More info: See **www.orlandoairports.net**, with live flight departure and arrival details.

Orlando Sanford

Returning to the gateway for some British charter flights should be relatively simple, providing you retrace your route on the Central Florida Greeneway (following signs for Orlando Sanford Airport, NOT Orlando International) and come off at exit 49. Turn first right at the lights, then first right again on to Lake Mary Boulevard and follow it to the airport. The efficiency of Alamo and Dollar's car return adds to the simplicity.

◀🇬🇧▶ BRITTIP

The airport turn-off sign is right after the toll plaza before exit 49 and is easy to miss; once you go through that toll plaza, take the very next turn-off.

Orlando Sanford was created as a full international airport in 1996, as an initiative between the airport authorities and British tour operators. Thomson and various US domestic airlines all use this simpler option, as well as Belgian and Dutch charter flights. You are further north, so your journey time is 35mins longer with an extra $4–5 in tolls compared with the journey to and from Orlando International, but providing you follow the simple directions, you should have no problem retracing your steps here.

And, while this charter gateway is smaller than Orlando International, it boasts a spacious check-in area and works hard to make the departure as painless as the arrival, especially with its **Royal Palm Lounge** facility. Thomson and any other charters check in at Terminal A, with the departure lounge upstairs. Terminal B is the increasingly busy side for domestic flights only.

There are no food or beverage outlets at the check-in level at Terminal A, but you can walk across to Terminal B where there is a **Café Ritazza** and a food court. Once checked in, you need to pass through security (allow at least 30mins) to reach the International Departure Lounge. Here you have the **Budweiser Tap Room,** which serves a good selection of international beers, and the handy food court. The four-part outlet offers **American Grill, C, Sweet Endings** and **Grab-N-Go** (soft drinks, bottled water and snacks).

There is then an extensive duty-free store (also with an increased range of merchandise), **Hudson News** for sundries, **KidWorks** for educational games, books, and toys, plus **Indulgences.** There is also an information and currency exchange kiosk. There is an extensive outdoor deck for smokers.

Your chance to give something back

After a wonderful trip, you might be interested in two charities that help children with serious illnesses to have an equally memorable holiday.

Give Kids the World Village is an amazing organisation in Kissimmee, working with wish-granting foundations worldwide to provide an unforgettable week's holiday for children with life-threatening illnesses and their families. It is set up as a resort and includes meals, accommodation, transport, themed venues, donated park tickets and other thoughtful touches in a magical setting. It's a charity we support ourselves and we hope you will, too. You can donate via its website, **www.gktw.org**.

DREAMFLIGHT takes seriously ill and disabled children from the UK on a 'Holiday of a Lifetime' to the theme parks of Orlando. bringing fun and joy into the lives of children whose illnesses and treatments have brought pain, distress and disruption to their lives.

Each October Dreamflight takes 192 children aged 8–14 from all over the UK. For many, it will be their first time away and most will require medical treatment or supervision. One adult accompanies every two children, a high proportion from the medical professions. Helpers in Orlando accompany each child in the parks on a one-to-one basis.

Since 1987, more than 5,000 children have enjoyed what in many cases is a life-changing experience. Priority is given to children who would not otherwise be able to have such an opportunity. They meet others with similar experiences, form many long-term friendships and return with increased confidence and self-esteem.

For further information or to make a donation please see **www.dreamflight.org**.

Thanks in advance for any contributions to these worthwhile organisations.

Royal Palm Lounge: The big extra here, this premium space is available to all passengers for a modest fee. It's in a separate annexe from the main lounge and is an oasis of comfort and quiet, perfect for relaxing for the last few hours of your holiday (the only things it doesn't have are beds and shower facilities!). It boasts a pleasant café bar, where you can enjoy unlimited tea, coffee, soft drinks and snacks (with two glasses of beer or wine per over-21), plus two home theatre lounges, with widescreen TV and surround-sound, for recently released films; a quiet reading room; computer terminals for email and internet access; a youth entertainment centre with Sony PlayStation consoles; a separate toddlers' playroom with soft toys and games; a smoking lounge; and a left-luggage area. The Royal Palm is billed as an airport lounge with the comforts of home and is well worth the extra cost ($30/adult, $20/4–20s, under-4s free) if you're likely to be here more than an hour. Most tour operators offer it in advance at a discount, or you can book on arrival or through your resort reps. With its extra capacity and facilities, this is a very satisfying way to end a holiday. See the Royal Palm Lounge and more about the airport at **www.orlandosanfordairport.com** or email **royal.palm@tbiusinc.aero**.

Whether you are using Orlando International or Orlando Sanford, you can also expect the return flight to be about 1hr shorter than the journey out, thanks to the Atlantic jetstreams. Nevertheless, you'll land back home rather more jetlagged than on the trip out because the time difference is more noticeable on eastward flights, and it may take a day or so to get your body clock back on local time. It is important not to indulge in alcohol on the flight if you will be driving when you land. By far the best way to beat Florida jetlag is to enjoy the memories from this trip – then start planning your next Orlando holiday!

Believe us, the lure of this theme park wonderland is hard to resist – you WILL be back!

Example: 2 weeks with Disney's 14-Day Ultimate, Universal 2-Park Bonus & SeaWorld 3-Park Tickets

(Disney's Ultimate Tickets give 7, 14 or 21 days of unlimited admission at their 4 main theme parks, plus visits to Blizzard Beach, Typhoon Lagoon and ESPN World Of Sports™, valid for 7/14/21 days from first use. Universal 2-Park Bonus is valid for both theme parks and CityWalk for 14 days from first use. SeaWorld 3-Park ticket includes SeaWorld, Busch Gardens and Aquatica for 14 consecutive days).

Day	Our Example	Your Planner
1 (Mon)	Arrive 2.40pm local time, Orlando Sanford airport; transfer to resort – check out local shops and restaurants	
2 (Tues)	Attend tour operator Welcome Meeting; rest of day at MAGIC KINGDOM	
3 (Wed)	All day at UNIVERSAL STUDIOS for the Wizarding World of Harry Potter	
4 (Thurs)	Chill out day at Disney's Blizzard Beach water park	
5 (Fri)	All day at BUSCH GARDENS	
6 (Sat)	DISNEY'S ANIMAL KINGDOM Park. Eve: Rivers of Light Show (9pm)	
7 (Sun)	Shopping at Orlando Premium Outlets and Lake Buena Vista Factory Stores Eve: Medieval Times Dinner Show (7.15pm)	
8 (Mon)	ISLANDS OF ADVENTURE Eve: City Walk and dinner at Hard Rock	
9 (Tues)	All day at DISNEY'S HOLLYWOOD STUDIOS (Fantasmic! show at 8.30pm)	
10 (Wed)	Kennedy Space Center Eve: International Drive	
11 (Thurs)	All day at SEAWORLD (One Ocean at 3pm)	
12 (Fri)	Enjoy a UNIVERSAL ORLANDO highlights day; or chill out at Aquatica water park	
13 (Sat)	All day at EPCOT Park (IllumiNations at 9pm)	
14 (Sun)	Have a lie-in, then head for MAGIC KINGDOM Park (Wishes fireworks at 9pm)	
15 (Mon)	Gatorland/Back to airport; return flight at 5.30pm	

Busy Day Guide

NB: This is a *general* guide only as the parks do change their hours frequently and often without notice. However, this guide will still be accurate for the busiest times of the year.

Day	Busiest	Average	Lightest
Mon	Magic Kingdom, Animal Kingdom, Universal Studios	Disney's Hollywood Studios	Epcot, Islands of Adventure, SeaWorld, Busch Gardens; Kennedy Space Center, water parks
Tues	Epcot, Universal Studios	Disney's Hollywood Studios, Kennedy Space Center	Magic Kingdom, Animal Kingdom, Islands of Adventure, SeaWorld, Busch Gardens, water parks
Wed	Animal Kingdom	Magic Kingdom, Disney's Hollywood Studios, Islands of Adventure, SeaWorld	Epcot, Universal Studios, Busch Gardens, Kennedy Space Center, water parks
Thurs	Magic Kingdom	Epcot, Islands of Adventure, Kennedy Space Center, SeaWorld	Disney's Hollywood Studios, Animal Kingdom, Universal Studios, Busch Gardens, water parks
Fri	Islands of Adventure	Disney's Hollywood Studios, Animal Kingdom, Universal Studios, Kennedy Space Center, Busch Gardens, water parks	Magic Kingdom, Epcot, SeaWorld
Sat	Disney's Hollywood Studios, Universal Studios, Islands of Adventure, SeaWorld, Busch Gardens, Kennedy Space Center, water parks	Magic Kingdom, Epcot	Animal Kingdom
Sun	Epcot, Universal Studios, Islands of Adventure, SeaWorld, water parks	Magic Kingdom, Animal Kingdom, Busch Gardens Kennedy Space Center	Disney's Hollywood Studios

Only here for a week? Here's our suggestion for an action-packed 7 nights in Orlando:

Day 1: Arrive; visit Epcot in evening for IllumiNations

Day 2: Up early for Magic Kingdom

Day 3: All day at Universal and Islands of Adventure

Day 4: Epcot for the day; Disney's Hollywood Studios for evening

Day 5: Disney's Animal Kingdom for the day; Magic Kingdom evening

Day 6: SeaWorld with mid-day break at Aquatica

Day 7: Hollywood Studios for the day, Epcot evening

Day 8: Shopping and return flight

Index

Acknowledgements

The authors wish to acknowledge the help of the following in the production of this book: Visit Orlando, Experience Kissimmee, Walt Disney Attractions Inc., Universal Orlando, SeaWorld Parks & Entertainment, Visit Florida, St Petersburg/Clearwater Area Convention and Visitors Bureau, Seminole County Convention & Visitors Bureau, Visit Tampa Bay, Space Coast Office of Tourism, Mount Dora Chamber of Commerce, Greater Orlando Aviation Authority, Orlando Sanford International Airport and Alamo Rent A Car. In person: Amy Rodenbrock (Visit Orlando), Larry White, Rochelle Siegel (Experience Kissimmee), Danny Trosset, Stephanie Hunicke, (Seminole County), Patrick Harrison (Visit Tampa Bay), Duncan Wardle, Todd Heiden, Dave Coombs (Walt Disney), Kalina Subido-Person, Damian O'Grady (Space Coast), Lindsey Towers (Alamo Rent A Car), Fiona Duncan, Kevin Gibson, Ali Beemer (Universal), Andrea Farmer, Angelica Deluccia Morrisey (Kennedy Space Center), Brittany Williams (LEGOLAND Florida), Carolyn Fennell, Rod Johnspn (Orlando Aviation Authority), Sandy Sweatt (Forever Florida), Lorraine Ellis (Get Married In Florida), Tori Sullivan (Gray Line Orlando), Emily Kruszewski, Stephanie Fred, Lucy Dalton, Natalie Eales (SeaWorld Parks & Entertainment), Rose Vignetti-Garlick (Downtown Orlando), Debra Ray (Ace Cafe), Sam Haught (Wild Florida), Dana Gonzalez, Matt Tuchman (Medieval Times), Dana Berry (Four Seasons Orlando), John Stine, Dipika Joshi (I-Drive 360), Sandy Wade (StaySky Resort Management), Laura Richeson (Richeson Communications), Scott Joseph (ScottJosephOrlando.com), Michael Caires (Orlando Sanford International Airport), Allan Oakley (Alexander Homes & Associates), Nigel Worrall (Florida Leisure), Donna Ernbro (Sleuths), Gene Columbus (The Orlando Rep), Mary Deatrick (Deatrick PR for Rosen Hotels), Michelle Peters (Boggy Creek Airboats), Lorraine Gorham (Raglan Road), Lorena Garcia (Orlando Premium Outlets), Terry Lynn Morris, Jennifer Bisbee (Lake Buena Vista Factory Stores), Steve Sless (Paragon Outlets), Judy Perry (Dreamflight), plus all our ATD friends! Reader feedback via email: Mr D Ferguson, Jeanette Hatton, Jenny Dawson, Rebecca O'Neill, Moira Murphy, Roger Low, Kirsty Page, Angela Coulter, Kath Difiori, Darren Fewell, Chris Smeaton, and Simon and Jane Arnett. Check out *Orlando Attractions Magazine* for information and features on this great destination, **www.attractionsmagazine.com,** and don't forget to join us on the discussion forums at **www.attraction-tickets-direct.co.uk.** Got a red-hot Brit Tip to pass on? We want to hear from YOU to keep improving the guide each year. Drop us a line at: Brit's Guide (Orlando), W. Foulsham & Co. Ltd, The Old Barrel Store, Drayman's Lane, Marlow, Bucks SL7 2FF. Or e-mail **britsguide@yahoo.com.**

Photograph acknowledgements

With thanks to everyone for their help in supplying photographs for this edition.